The **ULTIMATE** Book of **SPORTS LISTS**

The
ULTIMATE
Book of
SPORTS
LISTS

● ● ● ● ● ● ● ● ● ● ●

Andrew Postman
and **Larry Stone**

BLACK DOG
& LEVENTHAL
PUBLISHERS
NEW YORK

Library of Congress Cataloging-in-Publication Data

Postman, Andrew.

The ultimate book of sports lists : "the greatest, the worst, the biggest, the strangest, the funniest, the most—" / Andrew Postman and Larry Stone.

    p.   cm.

Includes index.

ISBN 1-57912-277-9

1. Sports—Miscellanea. I. Stone, Larry. II. Title.

GV707 .P67 2003

796'.02—dc21

                                  2002152834

Cover and interior design: Martin Lubin Graphic Design

Manufactured in the U.S.A.

Published by

Black Dog & Leventhal Publishers, Inc.
151 West 19th Street
New York, New York 10011

Distributed by

Workman Publishing Company
708 Broadway
New York, New York 10003

g f e d c b a

ACKNOWLEDGMENTS

● ●

We wish to thank Laura Ross, our editor, for her tremendous insight, enthusiasm, and general brains. We would also like to thank Elaine Markson, our agent, for her support and unusual kindness; Shelley Postman and Lisa Stone for their great help; and Alex Postman for her contributions and patience. Bill McGee, Peter Wilhelm, and Peter Klein were gracious and knowledgeable contributors. We appreciate the contributions—is there another word besides "contribution"? Roget, a little help?—of Leslie Ben-Zvi, Jay Rosen, and David Holtz.

Finally, we wish to acknowledge our gratitude for several especially useful sources: the members of the Society for American Baseball Research (S.A.B.R.) and the fine articles included in their yearly *Baseball Research Journals; The Hockey Encyclopedia* by Stan Fischler and Shirley Walton Fischler; *The Kentucky Derby: The First 100 Years* by Peter Chew; and David Wallechinsky's *The Complete Book of the Olympics*, an enormously comprehensive and compelling history of the Olympic Games.

CONTENTS

● ●

5 NAMES

6 POLITICS

7 TEAMS AND RIVALRIES

8 SEX AND DEATH

9 OFF THE FIELD, AND EXTRACURRICULAR ACTIVITY

10 EXTREMES

11 THE GAME AND THE PLAYERS

12 FAMILY

13 HISTORY

14 GREATS

15 CURIOSITIES

16 THE ENDS

INTRODUCTION

• •

German Silva, winner of the 1994 and 1995 New York City Marathons and a native of the tiny, impoverished Mexican village of Tecomate, used his celebrity to convince the governor of his province to provide his hometown with electricity.

Legendary Russian pole vaulter Sergei Bubka not only broke the world record in his event, and re-broke it, and re-broke it, but also holds perhaps the most charming world record we've ever heard of: the world record for the most world records (35) in one event.

Seven years after retiring from competitive swimming, Dara Torres, now 32, an age at which swimmers simply don't compete at a world-class level, decided to see if she could match her old form. She did not: She *surpassed* it, became the oldest athlete ever to set an American swimming record, and came home from the 2000 Sydney Olympic Games with two gold and three bronze medals.

The Anaheim Mighty Ducks of the National Hockey League are the only major sports franchise (at least that we know of) that's been spawned by a movie.

A story is a story only when facts mean more than mere facts, when they're seen in relation to something else. And in sports—an endeavor that inspires scrupulous record-keeping, daily skill- and success-measuring, obscure connection-making, and endless comparing and contrasting—everything's a story. Every athlete, every game, every season, every career. Sure: If one wants to make sports just about numbers and results—statistics, the final score, wins and losses—one certainly can. But that's boring—or, rather, that's counting points while missing the point. When we remember a game, a season, a player, a moment, it's usually because of an unfolding storyline, or a mood that was evoked. Reggie Jackson is not a living baseball legend because he hit home runs, or hit them in the World Series, or even hit three of them in a single World Series game; Reggie's Reggie in large part because with each of the last four swings he took in the 1977 baseball season, the ball landed in the stands, in fair territory. What a story; what a feeling. *That's* special.

When we marvel at Mario Lemieux, we don't do so just because of his stick-handling, the rare coupling of power and finesse, the uncanny nose for the goal; we marvel that Super Mario still does all this *after* cancer, after multiple back surgeries, after his team declares bankruptcy, after he's been retired for years, after the drive should have died. What a tale; what an inspiration. *That's* special.

It's not just athletes who come with context and stories; it's dates, numbers, places. '1994' means disgust for fans of baseball (no World

Series for the first time in 90 years) and sadness for fans of the Chicago Bulls and great basketball (no Michael Jordan in the post-season for the first time in many years). The number 4 (to take one example) could suggest a host of evocative things: the great "Four Horsemen" of Notre Dame football; the four majors that make up the tennis and golf Grand Slam, one of the most elusive achievements in all of sports; Lou Gehrig's uniform number, the first ever retired in major-league baseball; the four-minute mile, a threshold once believed to be humanly impossible to break, until Roger Bannister did so in 1954 and suddenly every one could (within three years, 16 other runners had broken the four-minute mile).

Mary Lou Retton is a smile and a fire, as is Magic Johnson. Sara Hughes is a shocking upset and a performance of a lifetime, and so is Princeton beating defending national basketball champions UCLA in the first round of the 1996 NCAA tournament. Joe Namath is cockiness and talent, and so is Muhammad Ali. It's not that these athletes and teams are only one thing: Ali, to take perhaps the best example, evokes a hundred moods, and summons a thousand stories. But everything that's good and memorable about sports, as well as much that's bad and memorable, stays with us because it's part of a larger whole. (Indeed, the reason we as fans are at once thrilled and also disconcerted by the emergence of the very greatest athletes—a Gretzky, a Chamberlain, a Jim Brown, a Koufax, a Tiger Woods—is that, while they're the best among a group of excellent practitioners, they're also unlike anyone who has come before, and their uniqueness—their disconnectedness—jars us.)

This book is all about the connections. It's about finding a place to put the memories of our lives as fans, so that the memories don't feel so isolated, and neither do we.

Because there's so much inside, we'll shut up right here with the highfalutin theorizing. We do recommend, however, that you always keep your eye on the ball. Choke up. Watch your footwork. Don't drink and drive.

Hey: New connections. The beginning of another list. Advice Worth Following.

Enjoy.

ANDREW POSTMAN & LARRY STONE

October 2002

DEDICATION

● ●

for my girl, Alex, and my boys, Sam and Charlie

A. P.

to the "Babe Ruth of Families," Mom, Dad, Esther, and Judy;
and to my new "Family of the Century," Lisa, Jessica, Meredith,
and Jordan

L. S.

● ●

If all I'm remembered for is being a good basketball player, then I've done a bad job with the rest of my life.

Isiah Thomas

1

PERSONALITY AND STYLE

●●●●●●●●●●●●●●●●

The 20 Strongest Reactions in Sports History

▶ Elizabeth Ryan, holder of a then-record 19 Wimbledon titles, had said that she did not want to live to see her record broken. The day before Billie Jean King had a chance to break the record, Ryan collapsed on the grounds of Wimbledon and died that night. The next day, King won the women's doubles title and broke Ryan's record.

▶ Joseph Guillemot of France vomited on Finland's Paavo Nurmi as they crossed the finish line in the Olympic 10,000m race in 1920.

▶ *Washington Post* sportswriter Tony Kornheiser wrote an article parodying the trouble that Bolivia was having raising money to send a contingent to the 1984 Los Angeles Olympics. A Bolivian national spokesman said that the country took offense at the article, and that the article played a part in Bolivia's decision ultimately to not attend the Games.

▶ Much—too much—fan and media attention were directed at the showdown between New York Yankees pitcher Roger Clemens, a future Hall of Famer and notoriously hyper in big games, and future Hall of Fame catcher and slugger Mike Piazza of the New York Mets, in Game 2 of the 2000 "Subway" World Series. It was the first face-to-face encounter for the two since an interleague game earlier that season when Piazza, who'd hit Clemens extremely well, was beaned by the pitcher into near-unconsciousness—the intentionality of which was hotly debated. In fouling off a Clemens pitch in the top of the first inning, Piazza broke his bat, sending the top part toward the mound; Clemens, in a fit of almost pathological intensity, picked up the wood, and flung it disgustedly in the direction of Piazza, who, not knowing where the ball was, had taken a few steps toward first base. When Clemens, who would later be fined $50,000 for his action, was asked to explain why he did what he did, he proclaimed that he'd thought the broken bat was the ball—an explanation that makes sense only if he'd also thought, at the moment, that he was suddenly playing dodge ball.

▶ In July 1950, eight Uruguayans reportedly died of heart attacks as a result of their country's unexpected World Cup victory over Brazil.

▶ During the McCarthy era and the "Red Scare," baseball's Cincinnati Reds changed their name to the Redlegs. The team changed its name back to the Reds in 1960.

▶ When the distance of Bob Beamon's world-record long jump was announced at the 1968 Olympics, he sank to the ground with what doctors described as a cataplectic seizure, caused by emotional excitement.

▶ Boxer Alexis Arguello punched Cornelius Boza-Edwards with such force that Boza-Edwards lost control of his bodily functions and soiled his trunks.

▶ While flying in a small plane that he'd chartered from Detroit to Buffalo on September 17, 1935, outfielder Len Koenecke, recently released by the Brooklyn Dodgers, went berserk and tried to wrest control of the plane from the pilot. Koenecke was clubbed to death with a fire extinguisher by the pilot. Koenecke was reported to have been despondent over his release.

▶ At the 1964 Olympics, Elvira Ozolina of the Soviet Union was so anguished about finishing fifth in the javelin—she was the defending champion and world-record holder—that she punished herself by getting her head shaved. All the members of the Japanese wrestling team had their heads shaved after performing poorly at the 1960 Olympics.

▶ Basketball star Spencer Haywood admitted in a *People* magazine article on June 13, 1988, that he had plotted to kill Los Angeles Lakers coach Paul Westhead after Westhead had suspended him during the 1979–80 NBA Finals. Haywood said that he and two friends had planned to sabotage Westhead's car. Haywood's mother eventually talked her son out of it.

▶ San Diego Chargers football coach Harland Svare was so convinced that Oakland Raiders owner Al Davis had bugged the visitors' locker room at Oakland Coliseum that Svare started screaming at a light bulb.

▶ In the modern pentathlon at the 1968 Olympics, Hans-Jurgen Todt of West Germany attacked his horse after it had balked three times at one obstacle.

▶ CBS anchorman Dan Rather, upset that the broadcast of the U.S. Open tennis tournament had overrun into his news telecast, walked off the set on September 11, 1987. The CBS screen was blank for six minutes.

▶ When P. J. Brown of the Miami Heat and Charlie Ward of the New York Knicks got into a fight in the closing moments of an obvious Heat win in Game 5 of the second round of the 1997 NBA playoffs, several members of the Knicks—including most of the starters, who'd been benched after the outcome had become clear—stood and took several steps away from the bench area in the direction of the on-court fight, which Heat coach Pat Riley and Knicks coach Jeff Van Gundy were trying to contain. After the game, in an attempt to bring calm to what was fast developing into the most intense rivalry in the NBA (fueled in no small part by Riley's defection as coach of the Knicks), league commissioner David Stern inflamed passions when he applied the letter (if not the spirit) of a rule that calls for suspension of players for "leaving the bench area" during a fight. Stern suspended Knicks Patrick Ewing, Allan Houston, John Starks, Larry Johnson, and Charlie Ward, the only one of the five actually involved in the fight. So many Knicks players were suspended, in fact, that Stern had to divide the suspensions across Games 6 and 7 so that the Knicks could dress the required number of players. Except for Ward, the other four Knicks, along with the NBA Players Association, filed a request on May 16th with a federal court to have a temporary restraining order prevent Stern and the league from suspending the players until their case was heard by an arbitrator; their request was denied. Other fights in NBA playoff games were not so scrupulously adjudicated, and the Heat (which won the series in seven games) and the Knicks would grow to hate each other—and continue to fight—in ensuing years.

▶ In October 1977, in a Colombian second-division soccer match, Santa Rosa de Cabal leftwinger Libardo Zuniga replaced an injured goalie in an important league game and made several spectacular saves. Near the end of the game, an opposing striker, enraged by Zuniga's success in goal, ran up and kicked him full force in the groin. Zuniga died within moments, and the striker was arrested and charged with murder.

▶ On May 29, 1882, National League umpire James L. Hickey called out Cleveland outfielder John Richmond for going outside the baseline while running to first base *on a walk.*

▶ In a double dose of intense reaction, heavyweight Bob Fitzsimmons protested violently when he was disqualified in his 1896 non-title fight with Tom Sharkey. Finally, referee Wyatt Earp—of "O.K. Corral" fame—drew his gun on Fitzsimmons.

▶ On July 5, 2000, at the Burbank Ice Arena in suburban Boston, Thomas Junta beat Michael Costin to death after Costin, who was supervising a hockey practice involving their respective pre-teenaged sons and others, did not do enough—in Junta's mind—to stop the rough play. Junta, who outweighed Costin by over 100 pounds, was convicted of involuntary manslaughter.

▶ "Gorgeous Gussie" Moran caused a sensation at Wimbledon in 1949 by wearing lace panties designed by Ted Tinling. The All-England Club committee ruled that the panties were "unnecessarily attracting the eye to the sexual area," and terminated Tinling's services as an umpire for the next 20 years.

Hello in There? Is Anybody Home?: 11 Tales of People Without a Clue

▶ The Russian contingent showed up late for the military rifle team competition at the 1908 Olympics because they were operating on the Julian calendar rather than the customary Gregorian calendar. Twelve days separated the two calendars.

▶ Boston Celtics announcer Johnny Most visited team doctor Thomas Silva to complain of deafness in 1987. Silva extracted a TV earplug which had been lodged in Most's ear for a year and a half.

▶ At the 1896 Olympics, many fencing judges, unschooled in the sport, thought that a fencer earned points if he *received* a hit.

▶ On the 15th hole of the third round of the 1983 Canadian Open, golfer Andy Bean used the grip of his putter to knock in a two-inch putt. He was penalized two strokes. He finished the tournament two strokes behind the winner.

▶ One more installment from the let's-see-how-hard-we-can-make-it-on-ourselves school: 1988 Tour de France champion Pedro Delgado of Spain began defense of his title by showing up 2 minutes and 40 seconds late to the starting line of the 1989 Tour. He finished the opening prologue 2:54 behind the leader. After 33 days, he ended up in third place, 3:34 behind the winner.

▶ In a 1917 World Series game, Chicago White Sox pitcher Red Faber attempted to steal third base while a teammate was already occupying it.

▶ At the 1948 Olympics, one judge awarded a gymnast a score of 13.1.

▶ Miles Byrne, caddying for Ian Woosnam at the 2001 British Open, failed to remove from Woosnam's bag an extra driver that the golfer had used earlier on the practice range, meaning that Woosnam's bag contained excess clubs—15, or one over the limit, an infraction punishable by a two-stroke penalty. When Byrne noticed his gaffe at the second tee and announced it to Woosnam—steeling the golfer for the bad news by telling him he was "going to go ballistic"—it meant that Woosnam's energizing birdie on the first hole was now, in essence, a bogey. Woosnam finished the tournament in a third-place tie.

Two weeks later, Byrne, given another chance by the forgiving Woosnam, overslept on the final day of the Scandinavian Open and missed the tee time, forcing Woosnam not only to find a local caddie at the last minute, but also to get club officials to help him break into the locker room for his shoes, since Byrne had the key.

Woosnam tipped the local caddie well. He fired Byrne.

▶ American Emerson Spencer, the world-record holder in the 400m run (47.0 seconds) in 1928, only made the Olympic relay team. At the U.S. Olympic trials for the individual 400m, Spencer thought he was in a heat race and did not run at full speed. It was actually the final, and he did not qualify.

▶ On the fifth hole of the final round of the 1970 British Open, Lee Trevino shot for the wrong flag. Trevino, who started the day with a three-stroke lead, bogeyed the hole and finished tied for third.

▶ After losing money gambling, Cuban Felix Carvajal had to hitchhike to St. Louis for the 1904 Olympics. He arrived at the starting line for the marathon wearing heavy street shoes, long trousers, a long-sleeved shirt, and a beret.

The UNLV Basketball Team and
10 Other Athletes Who Would Know
How to Throw a Great Party

Some athletes sense that extraordinary times—on the field or off—call for extraordinary measures, and the way to publicly celebrate something special is to raise their game, get a hit, perform with authority. Outfielder Jimmy Piersall had the idea—sort of—when, on the occasion of his 100th career home run, he ran around the bases backward (not in reverse order, mind you, but backward, facing home plate as he headed to first base).

The following athletes did not do anything as radical as that; indeed, they stayed fully engaged in the game, perhaps even moreso than usual. And maybe that's precisely what enabled them to perform in a way that punctuated an already special occasion.

▶ On April 22, 1970, before a game against the San Diego Padres at Shea Stadium, New York Mets pitcher Tom Seaver was presented with his first Cy Young Award, for the 1969 season. To mark the occasion, he took the mound and tied one (then) major-league record by striking out 19 batters, and set another record by striking out 10 batters in a row—the last 10 he faced. He won the game, 2-1.

▶ On September 10, 1963, Stan Musial, in his first at-bat after becoming a grandfather, hit a home run off of Glen Hobbie.

▶ In an October 18, 1924, game against Michigan to dedicate the University of Illinois's new Memorial Stadium, Illini running back Red Grange had one of the greatest days in college football history. He returned the opening kickoff for a 95-yard touchdown, then scored on runs of 67, 56, and 44 yards—all in the first 11 minutes of the game. He later scored a fifth touchdown, threw for a sixth, and accounted for 402 total yards.

▶ American Pete Herman got married the morning of his 1917 world bantamweight title bout with Frankie Burns. That night, Herman won the fight.

▶ Cincinnati Red Johnny Vander Meer pitched the second of his consecutive no-hitters—a feat unmatched in major-league history—in the first night game in Ebbets Field history, June 15, 1938.

▶ Mike Scott pitched a no-hitter to clinch the 1986 National League West title for the Houston Astros.

▶ Philadelphia Phillies pitcher Jim Bunning was the father of six children when he took the mound against the New York Mets on June 21, Father's Day, 1964. He pitched a perfect game.

▶ Numerous athletes have done memorably well within hours of new (or repeat) parenthood. Kansas City Royals pitcher Bret Saberhagen shut out the St. Louis Cardinals, 11-0, in Game 7 of the 1985 World Series and won the Series MVP Award the night after he became a father.

In the summer of 2002, a day after returning to the lineup following the birth of his second child, New York Yankees catcher Jorge Posada hit a ninth-inning, game-winning single to beat the Detroit Tigers.

In pre-celebration for the great and blessed event, New York Knicks guard Allan Houston flourished in the most important game of his career—scoring a game-high 32 points to help the injury-depleted Knicks clinch the 1999 Eastern Conference Finals over the Indiana Pacers at Madison Square Garden—just hours before his wife gave birth to their first child.

▶ For University of Nevada–Las Vegas coach Jerry Tarkanian's 600th coaching victory on January 2, 1985, his team defeated Utah, 142-140, in triple overtime, the highest-scoring game to that time in the history of major-college basketball.

5 Instances of Low Self-Esteem from the Annals of Sport

▶ In 1980, Oakland Athletics owner Charlie Finley submitted a salary arbitration offer of $58,000 for infielder Mike Edwards. Edwards submitted a salary demand of $50,000.

▶ New York Yankees star Lou Gehrig, doing a live radio endorsement for a cereal called "Huskies," was asked, "To what do you owe your strength and conditioning?" By accident—and instinct—Gehrig replied, "Wheaties." Gehrig was apologetic afterward and tried to refuse compensation, but the "Huskies" people insisted on paying him.

▶ The Gaelic Athletic Association, the ruling body of the not very widely played sport of hurling, has stated among its laws that those who play and officiate hurling are prohibited to play, watch, or encourage soccer, rugby, cricket, or hockey.

▶ San Francisco Giants shortstop Johnnie LeMaster was booed so often that he once wore "Boo" on his jersey instead of his name.

▶ For the countries that boycotted the 1984 Los Angeles Games, Berlin held the "Alternative Olympics."

▷ Honorable mention: Former Chicago Bears running back Gale Sayers, whose autobiography is entitled *I Am Third*.

Some Unorthodox Techniques That Worked

Unorthodox—screw "unorthodox"; *weird*—techniques that have been employed by recent sports figures, notably from baseball, include Arizona Diamondback Craig Counsell's stiff, awkward, almost-painful-to-look-at batting stance; Los Angeles Dodger Hideo Nomo's looping, did-I-accidentally-hit-the-pause-button? of a pitching motion; and even Atlanta Braves pitching coach Leo Mazzone's hypnotic rocking action to (apparently) keep him calm (though it may unsettle his bench companion, Braves manager Bobby Cox, and the rest of us).

Here, from a variety of sports, are some other strange birds, who happen also to have been incredibly successful.

▶ Rick Barry shot free throws underhanded. At 90%, he is the second-most accurate free-throw shooter in NBA history. (The technique alone does not guarantee success: Wilt Chamberlain shot free throws underhanded, too, and was a career 51% shooter.)

▶ Harold Connolly wore ballet shoes for better footing in the finals of the 1956 Olympic hammer-throw competition, which he won.

▶ Washington Redskins placekicker Mark Moseley, who once made a record 23 consecutive field goals, wore five pairs of socks on his kicking foot.

▶ In the 1930s, golfer Leo Diegel used a putting style in which his left hand was inverted and his elbows were held out. Sam Snead putted croquet-style, a method that was later banned.

▶ 5,000m former world-record holder Zola Budd, American pole vaulter Desha McNeal Beamer, placekickers Tony Franklin and Rich Karlis, and India's national field hockey team all competed barefoot.

▶ Giants outfielder Willie Mays popularized the basket catch, and his teammate, pitcher Juan Marichal, the high leg kick.

▶ Rather than clear the hurdles in the steeplechase in traditional fashion, 1968 Olympic gold medalist Amos Biwott of Kenya hopped over them.

▶ The arc of Jamaal Wilkes's jump shot began over his shoulder and almost behind his head. He was a career 50% shooter from the field.

▶ New York Giant Mel Ott high-stepped into his swing, as did Japanese baseball great Sadaharu Oh. Ott hit 511 home runs, Oh 868.

▶ To keep loose, Canadian Earl Thomson, gold medalist in the 1920 Olympic 110m hurdles, tied his legs to the bed before going to sleep so that he could not curl up and cramp.

14 Scenes of Humiliation

▶ In Lewiston, Maine, on May 25, 1965, singer Robert Goulet, American-born son of French-Canadians, forgot the words to the National Anthem at the second Muhammad Ali-Sonny Liston fight.

▶ Oakland Athletics utility infielder Mike Andrews was "fired" by team owner Charlie Finley during the 1973 World Series after Andrews made two costly errors against the New York Mets in the 12th inning of Game 2. Finley announced that he was de-activating Andrews and tried to place him on the disabled list with a shoulder injury, and even got Andrews to sign a statement saying that he was hurt. Baseball commissioner Bowie Kuhn stepped in and ordered Andrews reinstated.

▶ In 1960, half-miler Wym Essajas became the first person ever to represent Surinam in the Olympics. He was given the wrong starting time for his heat and was resting when he should have been running. He went home without competing.

▶ Bernice Gera umpired a game between Geneva and Auburn in the New York–Penn League on June 24, 1972, but after making a controversial call and ejecting a manager, she resigned in tears before the second game of the doubleheader.

▶ Marv Albert, one of the most talented play-by-play announcers of his generation, pleaded guilty to misdemeanor assault and battery in a sex scandal that led to his then-dismissal by longtime employers NBC and MSG Networks. Lurid details of the scandal—including allegations of biting and of Albert's wearing women's lingerie—were trumpeted repeatedly by the media, especially in New York, where Albert had been the longtime voice of the basketball Knicks and hockey Rangers.

▶ Greek Spiridon Belokas took third place in the 1896 Olympic marathon in Athens but fourth-place finisher Gyula Kellner of Hungary protested that Belokas had ridden part of the way in a carriage. Belokas confessed to the charge. In punishment, he was stripped of both his medal and his shirt.

▶ During her second-round match against Billie Jean King at Wimbledon in 1979, the breasts of 18-year-old American Linda Siegel popped out of her low-cut tennis dress. The picture made the British tabloids.

▶ A fly ball, hit by Carlos Martinez of the Cleveland Indians on May 26, 1993, hit Texas Rangers outfielder Jose Canseco on the head, and bounced over the fence for a home run.

▶ The United States Olympic men's hockey team, loaded with NHL stars, not only underperformed at the 1998 Nagano Games—losing two of three games and not advancing to the medal round—but disgraced itself more significantly when several team members trashed their dorm rooms, causing several thousand dollars in damage.

The women's team behaved impeccably, and won their gold medal.

▶ After getting swept 8-0, 8-0, and 9-2 in their season-opening series in Los Angeles, the 1974 San Diego Padres were trailing the Houston Astros, 9-2, in the middle of the 8th inning of their fourth game—their home opener—when Padres owner Ray Kroc publicly dressed them down. Kroc grabbed the public-address microphone and announced to the fans, "I've never seen such stupid ballplaying in my life."

▶ At the 1988 U.S. Olympic trials, David Patrick finished the 400m hurdle race and took off on a joyful victory lap after a TV cameraman handed him a flag and congratulated him for finishing third. In fact, Patrick had finished fourth, and thus just missed earning a spot on the Olympic team. "I don't know who gave me the flag," Patrick said afterward, "but I'm going to look for him."

▶ Ewa Klobukowska of Poland, the 100m bronze medalist in 1964, was barred from international competition on September 15, 1967, when she failed a sex chromosome test.

▶ In June 1940, the Cleveland Indian players petitioned the team owner to fire manager Ossie Vitt. They later withdrew their demand but Vitt was let go at the end of the season.

▶ Australian tennis star Margaret Court was embarrassed in front of millions on television on Mother's Day, 1973, when aging hustler and former tennis great Bobby Riggs beat her in straight sets.

Triumph over Pain and Adversity: The Most Courageous and Inspiring Athletes

Images of athletes who have gone beyond pain, fatigue, "handicap," and anguish to perform—and perform extraordinarily—are among the most vivid in sports. For many, the most excruciating of such images may be that of Shun Fujimoto, the Japanese gymnast in the 1976 Olympics who dismounted from the rings with a broken leg that he had told no one about. He scored an astonishing 9.7 on the exercise, dislocated his knee on the dismount, and finally received medical attention and withdrew. Had Fujimoto withdrawn earlier, the Japanese team would have been out of the running for a team medal; with his help, they won the gold. For anyone who saw him land on his dismount—wobbly at first, then wincing to steady himself—the image is ineradicable.

Other images of athletes rising above their pain to perform in big games, or memories of them returning to their sports after debilitating injuries, compel us. There is Ken Venturi playing 36 holes in 100-degree heat, despite near-exhaustion that required medical treatment, to win the 1964 U.S. Open in what some have called "the most courageous round of golf ever played." There is New York Knicks center Willis Reed, on horribly battered knees, hobbling out to the Madison Square Garden floor to take his place as starter in Game 7 of the 1970 NBA Finals against the Los Angeles Lakers, and leading the team to the title more by inspiration than by any more tangible contribution (he scored only two baskets, in the opening moments of the game). There is Gabriele Andersen-Scheiss, the Swiss runner, suffering heat prostration at the end of the 1984 Olympic marathon, waving off medical assistance and, while staggering and weaving, finishing the final quarter-mile lap in 5 minutes and 44 seconds, good for 37th place. There is Jim Abbott, born with only one hand, blossoming into a formidable starting pitcher for the California Angels without a day of minor-league experience, and later throwing a no-hitter for the New York Yankees. There is Michael Chang, who, despite severe leg cramps that eventually forced him to serve underhand, upset Ivan Lendl in the 1989 French Open semifinals, on his way to becoming the first American in 34 years to win that tournament's men's title. Of more recent vintage, there is the hobbling but game gymnast Kerri Strug, landing her final vault at the 1996 Olympic Games to help the American women win the team gold, despite a seriously injured ankle; and a flu-weakened Michael Jordan still managing his usual Superman-like performance (38 points, including the tie-breaking three-pointer with 25 seconds to go) in Game 5 of the 1997 NBA Finals against the Utah Jazz, after which he would collapse into the arms of teammate Scottie Pippen.

Some of the most memorable examples of athletes overcoming adversity:

▶ Karoly Varga of Hungary won an Olympic gold medal in shooting in 1980 despite breaking his shooting hand two days before the competition.

▶ Six-time Olympic gold medalist swimmer Amy Van Dyken began swimming when her doctor suggested it might relieve the asthma she was born with. She has about 65% normal lung capacity.

▶ The leg of champion distance runner Glenn Cunningham was severely burned in a fire when he was eight years old.

▶ Tim Tam finished second in the Belmont in 1958 after fracturing the sesamoid bone in his right leg while passing the quarter pole.

▶ In 1989, soccer player Simon Keith was the first player chosen overall in the Major Indoor Soccer League draft, by the Cleveland Crunch, three years and a day after undergoing a heart transplant.

▶ Mario Lemieux, one of hockey's greatest-ever players, came back from career-jeopardizing health troubles not once, not twice, not three times, not four times...

In 1990, he had back surgery, and returned.

In 1991, he was diagnosed with a rare bone disease, and returned.

In January of 1993, he was diagnosed with a nodular lymphocytic form of Hodgkin's disease, and returned.

In the summer of 1993, he had another back surgery, and returned.

He sat out the 1994–95 season with fatigue from the after-effects of his radiation treatments for cancer, and returned the following season.

He retired after the 1995–96 season... then returned in 2000, in better health than he'd enjoyed in many years.

▶ Lemeiux's coach, Bob Johnson, helped (with some contributions from Mario) to lead the Pittsburgh Penguins to the Stanley Cup, in 1991, despite suffering from, and ultimately succumbing to, brain cancer.

▶ When he was seven, future Hall of Fame pitcher Mordecai "Three Finger" Brown caught his right hand in a corn grinder, lost most of his forefinger, and crushed his middle finger. He was a third baseman until he found that his mangled hand helped his curveball.

▶ In 1953, 3½ months after undergoing an emergency colostomy for cancer, Babe Didrickson Zaharias was back on the women's golf tour, finishing third in a tournament. The next year, she won the U.S. Open by 12 strokes. (The cancer eventually returned and she died September 17, 1956, at age 42.)

▶ Olympic equestrian competitor Konrad Freiherr von Wangenheim of Germany suffered a broken collarbone when he was thrown from his horse during the steeplechase portion of the two-day team event in 1936, but to keep the German team from being disqualified, he re-mounted and finished the remaining 32 obstacles without a fault. The next day, he arrived in a sling, which he removed for the jumping competition. Again, he was thrown from his horse, got back on, and again finished without a fault, helping Germany to win the gold.

▶ Defenseman Bryan Berard, 1997 NHL Rookie of the Year for the NY Islanders and the Toronto Maple Leafs, required emergency eye surgery after he was accidentally hit by the stickblade of Ottawa Senator Marian Hossa, on March 11, 2000, and suffered a cut cornea, detached retina, and fractured orbital bone. (The image of Berard on the ice, blood pooling around his head, will not be soon forgotten by those who saw it.) Doctors believed that the chance Berard would again see with his right eye was slim—he required further surgery to suck blood from the inside of his eye —and the chance for a return to pro hockey far more unlikely, since the league requires that players have a minimum of 20/400 vision in each eye.

In 2001, to returned to play, and play well, with the New York Rangers.

▶ Jockey Ricky Frazier broke his neck, fractured his skull, and was partly paralyzed when his horse fell during a 1984 race. Frazier came back to be a top rider.

▶ Swimmer Steven Genter was second to Mark Spitz in the Olympic 200m freestyle in 1972 despite surgery for a partially collapsed lung while in Munich. He was released from the hospital a day before the race.

▶ Hugh "One Arm" Daily pitched for six years in the majors (1882–87) despite having lost his arm below his elbow in a fireworks accident. One-armed Pete Gray, an outfielder, was the 1944 MVP for Memphis of the Southern Association, batting .333 with five home runs, and played in 77 games for the St. Louis Browns in 1945.

▶ Suffering from a severe gallbladder infection during the 1968 Olympics, Kenya's Kipehoge Keino still entered the 1,500m, the 5,000m, and the 10,000m competitions. During the 10,000m, he was leading with two laps to go when he collapsed. A stretcher was brought out but Keino got up and finished the race. Four days later, he ran in the 5,000m and took second place. In his final race, the 1,500m, he took gold in Olympic-record time.

▶ Kenny Walker's father died just before the 1989 NBA All-Star Game, to which the New York Knick had been invited to compete in the Slam Dunk competition. Walker wanted to withdraw from the competition but his mother told him to go and do well for his father. In an upset, Walker won the event.

▶ As Hank Aaron approached Babe Ruth's career home-run record, he was deluged with racist hate mail, and threats that he'd be killed and his children kidnapped. When he entered the 1974 season with 713 home runs, one behind Ruth, Aaron was assigned a bodyguard to protect him. Under enormous scrutiny from an army of reporters, Aaron, recently turned 40, hit his 714th home run on Opening Day in Cincinnati to tie Ruth, and four days later (on Hank Aaron Night at Fulton County Stadium) hit No. 715 off of Los Angeles Dodger Al Downing.

▶ Hubert Green won the 1977 U.S. Open despite a death threat. The threat was relayed to him during the final round but he decided to continue playing. He made a three-foot putt on the 18th hole to beat Lou Graham.

▶ New Zealand's Neroli Fairhall was the first paraplegic Olympian. She competed in the 1984 archery competition seated in a wheelchair and finished 35th. Fairhall was paralyzed from the waist down in a motorcycle accident.

▶ Dawn Fraser of Australia, who in 1962 became the first woman to swim the 100m freestyle competition in under a minute, was in a March 1964 car accident that killed her mother, knocked her sister unconscious, and chipped Dawn's vertebrae. Her neck was in a plaster cast for six weeks. She went on to win her third consecutive gold medal in the 100m freestyle seven months later.

▶ Of all the marathoners who inspire spectators, none surpasses the "runner" who owns the distinction of finishing last in virtually every New York City Marathon since 1988. Zoe Koplowitz, a New Yorker who suffers from multiple sclerosis, uses crutches and happily refers to herself as "The World's Slowest Runner," often taking 24 hours or more to complete the 5-borough, 26-mile, 385-yard course, well after all the other runners have finished, spectators have gone home, and traffic barriers have been removed; at times, Koplowitz has been escorted in the middle of the night by the crime-watch group, the Guardian Angels. In 1993, nine-time NYC Marathon winner and racing legend Grete Waitz stood at the finish line to meet Koplowitz at 6:30 in the morning, a full day after Koplowitz had started the race. No one had a medal for Koplowitz, so Waitz rushed back to her hotel room and grabbed the medal her husband had received for completing the race.

As of 2001, Koplowitz—author, businesswoman, lecturer—had completed 18 marathons, including Boston and London.

▶ Jeff Blatnick, who was diagnosed with Hodgkin's disease in 1980, won a 1984 Olympic wrestling gold.

▶ Alice Marble fainted on court at the 1933 French championships, was rushed to the hospital, and was diagnosed with tuberculosis. She came back to win the U.S. Championships four times.

▶ On the day that the Czechoslovakian gymnastics team began competition at the 1948 Olympics, teammate Eliska Misakova died of infantile paralysis. The Czechs went on to win the gold. (The flag raised for the medal ceremony was bordered with black ribbon.)

▶ Ben Hogan nearly died on February 2, 1949, in a Texas car accident that caused him multiple injuries and hospitalized him for a month. Hobbling badly, he captained the U.S.'s victorious Ryder Cup team in England later that year and in January 1950 entered the Los Angeles Open and tied for first with Sam Snead. A month later, Hogan won the U.S. Open in a playoff. Hogan won five majors after his accident.

▶ Weightlifter Tommy Kono, who set 21 world records in four different weight classes and won two Olympic gold medals, spent part of his youth in the Tule Lake detention camp for Japanese-Americans.

▶ Doug Herland, coxswain for the U.S. bronze medal pair-oared shell crew in 1984, suffered from osteogenesis imperfecta (brittle-bone disease). He was 4'9", 103 pounds, and had been born with broken hips, broken ribs, and a broken collarbone.

▶ With a broken foot, American diver Laura Wilkinson competed in the 10-meter platform event at the 2000 Olympics, and won the gold.

▶ Assault won the 1946 Triple Crown despite a permanently deformed foot.

▶ Jim Morris's professional baseball career flamed out in the low minor leagues in the early 1980s because of arm problems—or so it seemed. Morris married, began raising a family, and eventually became a high school teacher and baseball coach in Big Lake, Texas. What happened next, in 1999, would make a good movie—and in fact it did: The *Rookie*, with Dennis Quaid playing Morris. Pitching batting practice to his team, the left-handed Morris noticed his arm no longer hurt and he could throw hard again. Egged on by the players, he promised them he would try out for the pros if they made it to the state playoffs for the first time in school history. They did, and he did. After registering 98 mph on the radar gun at a Tampa Bay Devil Rays open tryout, Morris—by now age 35—was signed to a minor-league contract by the Devil Rays. In September, he was promoted to the majors and struck out the first batter he faced, Royce Clayton of the Chicago White Sox, on four pitches. Morris appeared in five games for the Devil Rays that year, and 16 the following season. But the Devil Rays released him after the 2000 season. Morris signed with the Los Angeles Dodgers, but after a flare-up of his old arm problems, he retired—for good, one presumes—in 2001.

▶ Ildiko Ujlaki-Rejto, gold medalist in the 1964 women's foil competition, was born deaf. Her coaches gave her instructions written on pieces of paper.

▶ George Eyser, gold medalist in the parallel bars and vault in 1904, had a wooden leg. He won two silvers in the pommel horse and combined, and a bronze in the horizontal bar.

▶ Paul Azinger returned to the PGA Tour less than a year after a 1993 diagnosis of lymphoma cancer in his shoulder blade. After enduring chemotherapy and radiation, he came back; in 2000, he finally won his first tournament in 121 tries, dating back to his play before the diagnosis, when he'd won a major and been one of the world's ten best players.

▶ Pitcher Lou Brissie lost his leg in World War II, and wore an artificial leg from his knee down. He returned to the major leagues and posted marks of 14-10 in 1948, and 16-11 in 1949, and played until 1953.

▶ Harry Greb, world middleweight champion, was blind in one eye.

19 Examples of Extraordinary Lack of Insight

▶ In 1950, Boston Celtics coach Red Auerbach passed up choosing Holy Cross star Bob Cousy, calling him a "local yokel." Celtics owner Walter Brown later picked Cousy's name out of a hat in a special dispersal draft, and Auerbach was "stuck" with Cousy. Cousy became the starting point guard and, along with Bill Russell, helped to create an NBA dynasty.

▶ Buddy Parker quit as the Detroit Lions coach during the 1957 training camp because he was not hopeful about his team's chances for success. Four months later, the Lions, now coached by George Wilson, routed the Cleveland Browns, 59-14, for the NFL title.

▶ In 1935, Chicago Cubs owner Philip Wrigley called night baseball "just a fad, a passing fancy."

▶ In 1875, when Matthew Webb, the first person to swim the English Channel, was honored by the city of Dover, the mayor proclaimed, "In the future history of the world, I don't believe that any such feat will be performed by anyone else." Swimmers have successfully crossed the English Channel over 800 times since.

▶ Baseball lore is filled with stories of spectacularly near-sighted trades. Babe Ruth had led the Boston Red Sox to three pennants in five-plus years when Harry Frazee, the Sox owner, sold him to the New York Yankees for $125,000 and a $300,000 loan to Frazee. The next year, 1920, Babe hit 54 home runs; the Sox as a team hit 22. Ruth would lead the Yankees to seven pennants. Boston would not win another one until 1946.

The Cincinnati Reds shipped Frank Robinson to the Baltimore Orioles before the 1966 season, writing him off as "an old thirty." In his first year with the Orioles, he won the American League Triple Crown, led his team to the pennant and victory in the World Series, and was named American League MVP. The best player that the Reds received in return for Robinson was pitcher Milt Pappas.

After 2½ years, the Chicago Cubs had seen enough of outfielder Lou Brock to trade him to the St. Louis Cardinals in June of 1964. Brock batted .348 the rest of the year, played 15 more seasons after that, helped the Cardinals to win three pennants and two World Series, and stole a then-record 938 bases. He entered the Hall of Fame in 1985.

▶ When the AAFC champion Cleveland Browns were absorbed into the NFL in 1950, most around the NFL believed that the competition in the other league was far inferior and were certain that the Browns would be humiliated. The Browns won the NFL title in their first year, and made the title game in each of their first six.

▶ Jim Brown was chosen sixth in the NFL draft, after having been fifth in the Heisman Trophy voting.

▶ In the late 1940s, University of Kentucky basketball coach Adolph Rupp, commenting on the wave of point-shaving and other scandals in the college game, said, "They couldn't touch my boys with a ten-foot pole." Soon after, it was discovered that some Wildcat players had been involved in game-fixing.

▶ In 1956, Bart Starr was not drafted until the 17th round, by the Green Bay Packers. He went on to win more championships than any NFL quarterback before or since, and was elected to the Hall of Fame.

Perennial All-Star Mike Piazza, arguably the best-hitting catcher in major-league history, was selected in the 62nd round of the amateur draft.

In the 1984 NHL entry draft, Brett Hull wasn't selected until the 117th pick, by the Calgary Flames.

The sports-scouting community showed a similar lack of insight about future All-Star first baseman Don Mattingly, who wasn't picked until the 19th round of the 1979 amateur baseball draft, and San Francisco 49ers quarterback Joe Montana, owner of four Super Bowl rings and the second-highest passing efficiency rating of any quarterback in NFL history, who was the 82nd pick (third round) in the 1979 draft.

▶ Steve Largent, the eventual all-time leader in pass receptions (since eclipsed), was cut by the Houston Oilers.

▶ Italy's Giovanni Benvenuti won the Val Barker Trophy for the most stylish boxer at the 1960 Games, the same Olympics in which a young fighter named Cassius Clay fought and won a gold medal.

▶ In a model example of teammates watching and learning from each other's mistakes, Toronto Blue Jay Barry Bonnell was picked off first base by Baltimore Orioles pitcher Tippy Martinez in a game on August 24, 1983. Blue Jay Dave Collins was walked and Martinez picked him off first base. Blue Jay Willie Upshaw got an infield hit and Martinez picked him off first base.

▶ Before the 1973 Kentucky Derby, alleged betting expert Jimmy "The Greek" Snyder said, "I don't know why, but I don't like Secretariat."

Quick Studies: 8 Athletes or Teams Who Learned Fast

This list is dedicated to Dave Stapleton, an infielder for the Boston Red Sox in the 1980s who was decidedly *not* a quick study. Stapleton spent seven years in the major leagues, and every year his batting average declined: .321, .285, .264, .247, .231, .227, and .128.

▶ American Elizabeth Ryan and Frenchwoman Suzanne Lenglen lost their first doubles match together, and then never again. They won six Wimbledon titles together.

▶ Lenglen was apparently a slightly quicker learner than Ryan: The first time the two faced each other in singles, Ryan beat Lenglen, and then never again. Lenglen won their next 36 singles matches.

▶ In 1996, just the second season for each in the NFL, the Jacksonville Jaguars and the Carolina Panthers, the most recent additions to the league, came within one game of meeting each other in Super Bowl XXXI. The Jaguars were particularly precocious: In the first two playoff games, they won *at* Buffalo, then *at* Denver, two notoriously difficult places for opponents to win—especially in winter, for a team from warm-weather Florida.

▶ On April 23, 1944, Boston Braves pitcher Jim Tobin pitched a one-hitter. Four days later, against the Brooklyn Dodgers, he pitched a no-hitter.

▶ In Secretariat's record-breaking Kentucky Derby (1:59.4) in 1973, each of his quarter-mile splits was faster than the preceding one.

▶ In just the second marathon of her life, Joan Benoit won the 1979 Boston Marathon, setting a then-American record (2:35:15) in doing so.

▶ At St. Andrews in 1921, in the third round of Bobby Jones's first appearance at the British Open, Jones picked up his ball in frustration and tore up his card. In each of his other three appearances in the tourney, he won the title.

What Do I Have to Do To Get a Menu Around Here?: Respectable Achievements Treated Without Much Respect

▶ In 1935, when Jesse Owens set or tied six world records, the Sullivan Award, given by the AAU to the best amateur American athlete, was won by golfer Lawson Little. In 1936, when Owens won four Olympic gold medals, the award was won by Glenn Morris, the Olympic decathlon champion. President Franklin Roosevelt did not invite Owens to the White House or send him a letter of congratulations after his Olympic performance.

▶ Doug Flutie won the 1984 Heisman Trophy, became the all-time passing leader in college football history, and led his Boston College team to a resounding victory in the Cotton Bowl and a final #5 national ranking. Because of his diminutive (5'10", 180 lbs.) stature, however, he wasn't drafted by the NFL until the 11th round (285th overall), and, after a stint in the USFL, decided to go to the Canadian Football League to establish himself as a professional quarterback. While there, he was named league MVP an incredible (and unmatched) six times, led his teams to three Grey Cups (the CFL Super Bowl) while being named Grey Cup MVP three times, and became the first CFL player to throw for 6,000 yards in a season… yet after returning to the NFL, Flutie was *still* labelled as too small, and not having a strong enough arm to play with the big boys. Wherever he went—the Chicago Bears, the New England Patriots, the Buffalo Bills, the San Diego Chargers—he struggled to win the starting position.

Through the 2001 season, Doug Flutie's record as an NFL starter—often with average teams—is 35-25; in home games, it is 21-7.

▶ In 1953, Kurt Nielson was unseeded when he made his mark on the tennis world by earning a spot in the Wimbledon finals. Two years later, in 1955, he again made the finals and again he had to do so as an unseeded player.

▶ In 1941, the season in which he hit .406, Ted Williams did not win the American League MVP. This is explainable in part by the fact that the player who beat him out, Joe DiMaggio, enjoyed a 56-game hitting streak that season. In 1942, Williams came back to win the Triple Crown—and this time the MVP Award went to New York Yankees second baseman Joe Gordon, who batted .322 with 18 home runs, and led the league in striking out, while Williams had twice as many homers as Gordon, 34 more RBIs, and batted .356. In 1947, Williams *again* won the Triple Crown, becoming only the second player in history to do it twice. The MVP Award that year went to Joe DiMaggio.

▶ The only man besides Ted Williams to win two Triple Crowns, Rogers Hornsby, fared no better. He was traded to the New York Giants following the 1926 season, in which he played and managed the St. Louis Cardinals to victory in the World Series.

▶ The WBC took away Marvin Hagler's world middleweight title after he outpointed Roberto Duran in their thrilling 1983 fight because the contest had been 15 rounds and not the WBC's new required distance of 12 rounds.

▶ Following David Wells's 1998 season, in which he compiled an 18-4 record for the New York Yankees, pitched a perfect game, and helped the team to the most wins in a season in their storied history, as well as a world championship—and proving to be perhaps their most clutch starting pitcher—he was traded (along with others) to the Toronto Blue Jays for Roger Clemens. (The Yankees would re-sign Wells for the 2002 season.)

▶ Rooting in great number and volume, fans of the Florida Marlins cheered their team to the 1997 World Championship. Almost immediately after the Marlins' thrilling, extra-inning, Game 7 victory over the Cleveland Indians, team owner Wayne Huizenga showed his regard for such loyalty: In a cost-cutting move, he rid himself of virtually every productive member of the team. By spring of 1999, only four champion Marlins remained.

▶ In a 2002 NFL pre-season game against the Seattle Seahawks, Denver Broncos kicker Ola Kimrin booted a 65-yard field goal, the longest in NFL history—including preseason, regular season, and postseason. (Because it was a preseason kick, it is not considered to be official.)

Kimrin was cut as soon as Broncos Pro Bowl kicker Jason Elam signed his contract.

▶ Bill Madlock, four-time batting title winner, never started in an All-Star Game and was traded by the Chicago Cubs to the San Francisco Giants in 1976 after winning his second consecutive batting championship.

▶ In 1998, Greg Vaughan hit a team-record 50 home runs for the San Diego Padres and helped them to their first National League pennant in 14 years. In the off-season, he was traded to the Cincinnati Reds.

▶ In 1989, four days after Dan Simrell became the winningest coach in University of Toledo football history, he was fired.

Wait Up—So Then You Guys *Are* Role Models? Or Not? Which Is It?

"I don't believe professional athletes should be role models," said, basketball star-turned-sage Charles Barkley not long ago. And while he may be right—his redeeming point was that *parents* ought to be role models—there are quite a few kids out there who revere athletes, watch how they act, then emulate their actions. Granted, maybe athletes shouldn't be role models. But whether they like it or not, they are.

So start acting like it.

▶ In 1999, after Liverpool soccer player Robbie Fowler scored a goal against rival Everton, he celebrated by dropping to his knees, lowering his face to the painted white line along the penalty area, then running his nose along the line, as if snorting cocaine.

▶ New York Yankees outfielder Paul O'Neill, an undeniably fine hitter who won a batting title and finished with 2,105 career hits—and seemingly a modest citizen off the field—was also the John McEnroe of baseball. Rarely was there a called third strike (or even a called first or second strike) by the umpire that went unchallenged, or an out he made that wasn't followed by some sort of tantrum—flung bat, destroyed water cooler, slammed helmet. In 1999, *Sports Illustrated* magazine polled players, managers, and coaches and determined that O'Neill was the #1 whiner/complainer/tantrum-thrower in the big leagues, and it wasn't close.

▶ In 1990, George Brett of the Kansas City Royals became the first player in major-league history to win batting titles in three different decades, but he was criticized by runner-up Rickey Henderson—and others in baseball—for sitting out three of the Royals' final five games to preserve his lead. Brett entered the season's final game as a pinch-hitter in the fifth inning and hit a sacrifice fly, then singled to raise his average one point to .329. Henderson finished at .325. "I came so far after hitting .200 in May and .250 in July and winning it meant so much to everybody that I thought it would be silly to risk giving it back," Brett said, defending his strategy.

▶ Giving us all a model of how to treat one's fellow competitor with respect, John L. Sullivan, the legendary heavyweight champion, refused to fight Peter Jackson, a black Australian and leading challenger, because he was "a member of the colored race."

▶ Tom Osborne, long-time football coach at the University of Nebraska, was known as "St. Tom" for his insistence upon running a clean program, unsullied by the sorts of scandals that rocked other colleges. But he was also known as a coach who couldn't win the big one; in one stretch, from 1988–94, Osborne lost seven straight bowl games. In the last five seasons of his 25-year career, however, the Cornhuskers began winning at an awesome rate, compiling a 60-3 record that included three national championships in four years, including a 12-0 record in 1997, when he resigned after a rout of Tennessee in the Orange Bowl.

It was also about that time—more than a coincidence?—that Nebraska's program was increasingly beset by ugly off-the-field incidents involving their players—incidents that were met with seeming leniency by St. Tom. Their national championship teams of 1994 and '95 featured Lawrence Phillips, convicted of misdemeanor assault for beating up his ex-girlfriend (drawing a six-game suspension, which many viewed as a mere slap on the wrist); Christian Peters, who had been convicted of third-degree sexual assault; Tyrone Williams, charged with firing a gun into an occupied car; and Riley Washington, charged with attempted murder. Six players on the 1995 Nebraska team were arrested.

▶ In 1996, Ken Caminiti of the San Diego Padres had a career year while becoming the National League's Most Valuable Player, hitting .326 with 40 homers and 130 runs batted in—11 more homers and 36 more RBI than he would produce in any other of his 15 major-league seasons. Caminiti later revealed the probable cause of his improvement, telling *Sports Illustrated* in 2002 that he used steroids that season, while claiming that at least 50% of major leaguers also used the drug. (In the resulting furor, Caminiti maintained his comments were misconstrued by *SI* and said, "Baseball's a pretty clean sport.") But even Caminiti's original claim paled compared to that of another former MVP, Jose Canseco, who said upon his retirement in 2002 that 85% of major leaguers took steroids. Canseco also said he would name names in a tell-all book, and his literary agent told the *Wall Street Journal* that Canseco would admit in the book that he used steroids and also helped other players to obtain them.

▶ In 1990, baseball great Pete Rose went to jail for filing false income tax returns. He was sentenced to five months in prison, three more in a treatment center, a $50,000 fine, and 1,000 hours of community service. "Charlie Hustle" served his sentence at a federal work camp in Marion, Illinois.

Ambidexterity

▶ At one Olympics only, the 1912 Stockholm Games, shot putters, discus throwers, and javelin throwers made one throw with the left hand, one with the right, and the greatest aggregate total won. (The standard one-handed competition in each event was also held that year.)

▶ Beverly Baker Fleitz, a 1955 Wimbledon finalist, switched her racket from one hand to the other so that her only groundstroke was a forehand.

▶ Natural right-hander Elton "Icebox" Chamberlain became a southpaw for two innings in an 18-6 victory for Louisville of the American Association, on May 10, 1888. He pitched the last two innings left-handed, giving up four hits and no runs.

In a July 18, 1882, American Association game against Baltimore, Louisville pitcher Tony Mullane, a right-hander, pitched left-handed in the fourth inning to Baltimore's left-handed hitters, retiring them all. Mullane's entry in *The Baseball Encyclopedia* reads: "BB TB" ("Bats Both, Throws Both").

A third ambidextrous pitcher of the 19th century was Larry Corcoran of Chicago, who was forced by a blister on his right index finger to throw left-handed on June 16, 1884. He had less success than Chamberlain and Mullane. Chicago lost, 20-9.

▶ Philadelphia Warrior Joe Fulks, who scored 63 points in one 1949 basketball game—especially impressive for that low-scoring era—took jump shots with either hand.

▶ In his day, Gordie Howe was the only ambidextrous player in the NHL.

▶ 1955 Grand Slammer Maureen "Mo" Connolly, a natural lefty, became a righthanded tennis player after her coach, Eleanor "Teach" Tennant, informed her that no lefthander in the 20th century had won a top women's singles championship. (Since then, Martina Navratilova and Monica Seles did their part to undo the right-handers' monopoly.)

The Most Efficient and Resourceful Athletes and Teams of All Time

▶ In the seventh inning of an April 22, 1959, game against the Kansas City Athletics, the Chicago White Sox scored 11 runs on just one base hit. The Sox were the beneficiaries of 10 walks, three errors, and one hit batter.

▶ In their 49-0 win over Stanford in the 1902 Rose Bowl, Michigan played the same 11 men the whole game.

▶ Dean Stone was the winning pitcher in the 1954 All-Star Game without retiring a batter. He entered the game in the eighth inning and threw out Red Schoendienst trying to steal home. The American League then scored three times in the bottom of the inning—the pinch hitter for Stone, Larry Doby, hit a home run—and a reliever pitched the ninth to preserve Stone's victory.

On May 21, 1998, Texas Rangers pitcher Scott Bailes came in with two outs in the top of the ninth inning, on the short end of an 8-6 game with the Seattle Mariners. He threw two pitches to Rob Ducey, then picked Russ Davis off of first base for the third out. When the Rangers scored three runs in the bottom of the inning, Bailes got the win.

▶ After winning the 10,000m walk at the 1912 Olympics, Canadian George Goulding sent a telegram to his wife that read, "Won—George."

▶ In the 1920–21 seasons, Larry Gardner of the Cleveland Indians knocked in 233 runs with just six home runs. In 1928, Pie Traynor of the Pittsburgh Pirates had 124 RBIs and only three homers.

▶ In 1999, Mark McGwire became the first player to knock in more runs (147) than he had hits (145) in a season.

▶ "Cactus" Gavvy Cravath won the 1919 home run title with only 214 at-bats.

▶ Detroit Lions wide receiver Mark Nichols co-owned a limousine service that carried his teammates to and from home games.

▶ Only nine Cincinnati Reds batted in the 1976 World Series, which they swept from the New York Yankees.

▶ After his first six completions against the University of New Mexico on October 27, 1967, UTEP quarterback Brooks Dawson had thrown six touchdowns.

▶ John Russell, the Philadelphia Phillies part-time outfielder in the 1980s, married Gail Clements, the left-field ballgirl.

▶ For the 1946 British Open, German prisoners of war were used to clear the rough before the tournament.

▶ In the 1963 World Series, the Los Angeles Dodgers used only four pitchers. In the 1928 Series, the New York Yankees used just three pitchers. In the 1910 Series, the Philadelphia Athletics used two pitchers. Each of those three teams won the Series.

▶ In Game 6 of the 1977 World Series, New York Yankees star Reggie Jackson took only three swings. He homered each time. (The last swing he took in Game 5 also produced a homer.)

The Most Efficient Baseball Player of All Time— And We Mean That in a Bad Way

▶ In his last two at-bats in Game 5 of the 1920 World Series, Brooklyn Dodgers pitcher Clarence Mitchell accounted for five outs by hitting into a triple play and a double play.

22 Prominent Bespectacled Sports Figures

1. George Mikan, Minneapolis Laker center
2. Billie Jean King, tennis player
3. Chick Hafey, the first bespectacled player to make it to the Baseball Hall of Fame
4. Reggie Jackson, the second bespectacled Baseball Hall of Famer
5. Chuck Muncie, football running back
6. Hale Irwin, three-time U.S. Open-winning golfer

7. Martina Navratilova, tennis player (who eventually switched to contact lenses)
8. Ryne Duren, pitcher
9. Jaroslav Drobny, tennis player
10. Bob Griese, Miami Dolphin quarterback
11. Richie "Dick" Allen, baseball slugger and 1972 A.L. MVP
12. Matti Jarvinen, 1932 javelin gold medalist
13. Kurt Rambis (nicknamed "Clark Kent"), basketball forward
14. Dom DiMaggio, Red Sox outfielder
15. Laurent Fignon, two-time Tour de France winner
16. Clint Courtney, first bespectacled catcher, 1951
17. Livio Berruti, 1960 Olympic 200m champion
18. Kent Tekulve, relief pitcher
19. Ingrid Kristiansen, Norwegian world champion distance runner
20. Eddie Rommel, first bespectacled umpire, 1956
21. Jay Bell, infielder
22. Eric Gagne, Los Angeles Dodger closer

Bobby Knight Wants You to Know He's Misunderstood— That, or You Can Kiss His Ass

He's obviously a winner: He played on the 1960 Ohio State NCAA championship team, coached Indiana University to the NCAA basketball titles in 1976, 1981, and 1987, the NIT title in 1979, and coached the U.S. Olympic team to gold in 1984. He has coached his teams (through the 2001–02 college basketball season) to 786 Division I victories, placing him 4th all-time.

He was for years a full professor of health, physical education, and recreation at IU, helped raise millions of dollars for the university's library, and boasted a superior graduation rate for his players. He experienced zero recruiting violations in almost 30 years at IU. His players, despite what one might guess, transferred out of the school at a rate about average for Division I programs.

We're told he's not so much "coach" as he is "teacher"; that he's a man of rare integrity in the modern college coaching ranks; that he's proof that substance ought to triumph over style, commitment and quality over laziness and mediocrity; that this military history buff treats his players the way he does to mold them into men.

Never mind that those who tell us this are usually either named Bobby Knight or belong to his tight circle of apologists.

We won't even waste your time with the famous chair-throwing incident of 1985. The player-kicking incident of 1993. The probably accidental head-butting-of-a-player incident of 1994. The profanity-laced dissing of former star player and now-coach of the University of Iowa Hawkeyes, Steve Alford. The reprimanding and $30,000 NCAA fine for another profane outburst at a post-game news conference at the NCAA tournament. The $10,000 Big Ten fine for berating a referee. The suspension for a sideline tirade in a home victory against Notre Dame. The obscenities he's displayed to crowds. The conviction in absentia (including a sentence of six months in jail) for hitting a Puerto Rican policeman during the Pan Am Games. The screaming at player Pat Knight, his own son, then seeming to kick him in the leg...

We wish to be more judicious than that.

Make up your own mind.

▶ To show his young players what he thought of their play, Knight came out of the locker room bathroom with his pants around his ankles, "wiped his ass," and "stuck his hand out with that toilet paper after he had wiped and kind of showed everyone and then walked back into the stall." The incident is corroborated by at least two IU players—Richard Mandeville and Neil Reed. "That's coach Knight," said a third player, Charlie Miller, about the incident.

▶ Reed (see above) would be excoriated not just by Knight but by legions of Hoosier fans whose obsession with winning college basketball games and titles may have influenced their view of right and wrong. What sin had Reed committed? He claimed that at a 1997 practice during his junior year, Knight criticized him for not yelling out the name of a teammate after Reed had passed the ball to him. Reed disagreed with Knight, insisting that he *had* yelled out Larry Richardson's name. When Richardson confirmed Reed's contention, Knight, according to Reed, attacked Reed. "He came at me with two hands but grabbed me with one hand," Reed told *CNN/Sports Illustrated* in the fall of 2000. "People came in and separated us like we were in a school yard fight, and I actually have respect for adults and I certainly have respect for coaches and that wasn't the case.... He had me by the throat for...about 5 seconds. I grabbed his wrist and started walking back and by this time people, coaches Dan Dakich [and Ron] Felling grabbed coach Knight and pulled him away."

Although former IU players and coaches, as well as some current players, rushed to Knight's media defense soon after Reed made the charges, *CNN/Sports Illustrated* corroborated Reed's account of the choking incident with three others at practice that day. According to *CNN/SI*, "[The other three] declined to go on camera and asked that their names not be used, because they were afraid that speaking out against Bob Knight could damage their careers. In describing the choking incident one said, 'If he touched me like that it would have been all over the news, there would have been a fight. I would have ended up with a black eye and he would have ended up in the hospital.'"

▶ Ricky Calloway, who started as a sophomore for Knight on IU's national championship team in 1987 (then transferred to Kansas for his senior year), told the *Houston Chronicle* he once saw Knight punch star guard Steve Alford and slap forward Daryl Thomas during practices. "We were all standing in a circle one day and he [Knight] just turned around and punched Steve right in the stomach, and for a minute-and-a-half Steve couldn't breathe," said Calloway. "I was shocked. I wasn't really surprised he hit someone, but I never expected him to hit Steve, his golden child. But Steve put up with a lot." Calloway also told the *Chronicle* that, when angry, Knight abused only those players he knew wouldn't fight back. "Coach knew the guys he could hit or really get into, and those he couldn't," said Calloway. "Daryl was a big guy (6'7", 240 pounds), but coach knew what type of personality Daryl had. He [Knight] was mad at him, and Daryl was sitting in his chair, and he [Knight] just came up and slapped him, and it was hard. Then he realized what he did and said, 'Go ahead and hit me back.'... [H]e realized what he did was all wrong, so he knew he had to try and correct it by telling Daryl to hit him back. But Daryl hit him real soft, and I remember when we got back to the dorm room we were like, 'Man, you should have hit him hard.'"

Alford later denied Calloway's contention that Knight had punched Alford.

Calloway said he chose to speak out about Knight after a 12-year silence because he was troubled by how Neil Reed (see earlier) had been vilified after Reed's *CNN/Sports Illustrated* interview. "Everybody says he's lying about all the abuse at Indiana, but he's not," Calloway said about Reed. "It took a lot of courage for him to come forward like he did."

▶ In 1988, responding to a question from then-NBC newscaster Connie Chung on how he handled stress, Knight said, "I think if rape is inevitable, relax and enjoy it."

▶ Knight once put a tampon in a player's locker to let him know he was playing "soft."

▶ When Luke Recker—a former Mr. Indiana high school star—told Knight at the end of his freshman season that he wanted to transfer out of IU, Knight—according to three sources, as verified by *CNN/Sports Illustrated*—"blew up, threatened to resign, told his coaching staff to find new jobs, and told Recker it was all his fault." Former player Richard Mandeville said: "After [Recker] talked to coach Knight he came to my house and was just a mess.... Oh my god, he felt like he was going to ruin all the assistant coaches' lives, the program, the state of Indiana. He thought if he left, he would probably never be welcomed back to Indiana, the state or anything."

▶ Transcript from an audiotape of a portion of a Knight-led practice in 1991: " ... then I'm leaving and you fucking guys will run until you can't eat supper. Now I am tired of this shit. I'm sick and fucking tired of an 8-10 record. I'm fucking tired of losing to Purdue. I'm not here to fuck around this week. Now you may be, but I'm not. Now I am gonna fucking guarantee you, that if we don't play up there Monday night, you aren't gonna believe the next four fucking days. Now I am not here to get my ass beat on Monday. Now you better understand that right now. This is absolute fucking bullshit. Now I'll fucking run your ass right into the ground. I mean I'll fucking run you, you'll think last night was a fucking picnic. I had to sit around for a fucking year with an 8-10 record in this fucking league and I mean you will not put me in that fucking position again, or you will god damn pay for it like you can't fucking believe..."

Said former player Mandeville: "I wish everyone...could hear, so they could really understand what it is like playing [for Knight] or when things are going bad there that take away from the enjoyment of the game where you hear something like that, you get to the point where you are like screw this, it just turns you off."

▶ Knight, notoriously antagonistic toward sportswriters (as well as other members of the media), once said, "All of us learn to write in the second grade. Most of us go on to greater things."

Apparently, Knight regressed: In March of 2002, Dunne Books published *Knight: My Story*, co-written by Bobby Knight.

▶ Knight agreed to settle a lawsuit filed by former assistant Ron Felling, who claimed he was shoved angrily by Knight when the two were coaching at Indiana University. Knight settled after the suit, originally for $1 million, was dropped to $25,000. Felling, who was fired in 1999, claimed that Knight struck him in the chest with two closed fists during a fight at Assembly Hall.

▶ Jeanette Hartgraves, a secretary at IU, said that Knight threw a vase that shattered near her, and that in 1998 he cursed at her and had to be restrained by athletic director Clarence Doninger.

▶ According to Neil Reed, Knight threw IU President Myles Brand out of his own team's practice. "Coach Knight could hear him and just stopped practice and [said] god dammit quit that talking," said Reed. "I don't come into your office and talk while you are working, get the hell out of here. And the president kind of looked, grabbed his stuff, and walked out." Former player Mandeville said, "[Knight] kicked [President Brand] out, I know that...he [didn't kick just] him out, he's kicked people out of practice...if he is pissed off or things aren't going well." Through a spokesman, Brand denied having been thrown out of practice by Knight.

▶ After 1987 and the appearance of *A Season on the Brink*, John Feinstein's bestseller about a season of IU basketball and Knight's coaching methods, philosophy, and style, IU's faculty council adopted a statement of student-athlete rights, which says "athletes shall not be subjected to physically or verbally abusive, intimidating, coercive, humiliating, or degrading behavior..." and that "athletes shall also be encouraged to report any violations of these policies to the appropriate university authorities."

Years later, Neil Reed was moved to say, "I am not out to get anyone and it seems so strange that the only weapon I have to fight this battle with is the truth and it seems like such a small weapon, you would think the truth is what everyone wants to know and everyone wants to hear. But it's not what everyone wants to know."

▶ After being let go by Indiana University, the school that he'd taught and coached at for 29 years, and which had tolerated his abusive behavior toward all kinds of people time after time after time, Knight gave a farewell speech to many gathered students and supporters (among others) in which, once again, he demonstrated his rare class. "When my time on earth is done, and my activities here are past," he said, " I want them to bury me upside down, and my critics can kiss my ass."

24 of the Best Moments of Integrity, Humanity, and Class

▶ After hockey's Lady Byng Trophy—the award given annually for gentlemanly play—had been won in 1935 by New York Rangers center Frank Boucher for the seventh time in eight years, he was given the trophy to keep, and Lady Byng had another one struck.

▶ Bobby Joe Morrow, a devout Christian who won the 100m in the 1956 Olympics, would not try to anticipate the starter's pistol with a "rolling start" because he felt it was unsportsmanlike.

▶ During the 2002 NBA off-season, Utah Jazz center Greg Ostertag donated a kidney to his sister, Amy Hall, a diabetic whose kidneys were failing.

▶ While dining in Texas following a July 1991 baseball game, American League umpire Steve Palermo heard that two waitresses were being mugged in the restaurant parking lot. While intervening, he was shot in the spinal cord and paralyzed in the lower extremities. He has since begun walking again, and started a foundation that funds research into spinal cord injuries.

▶ In the 1953 Walker Cup competition between the United States and Great Britain, American James Jackson was found to have 16 clubs, which called for immediate disqualification. The British, captained by Tony Duncan, refused to accept such a victory, and modified the penalty to a loss of two holes. (America went on to win the competition.)

▶ When it was discovered that 1932 U.S. Olympic sprinter Ralph Metcalfe, who had finished a disappointing third in the 200m, had dug his starting holes a few feet behind the other runners—through no fault of his own—he was offered a rerun. Metcalfe probably could have moved up to at least the silver medal but he declined, not wishing to jeopardize the American sweep in the event.

▶ New York Yankees manager Dick Howser was pressured by owner George Steinbrenner to fire his friend and third-base coach Mike

Ferraro, after Ferraro waved Yankees second baseman Willie Randolph home in Game 2 of the 1980 American League playoffs and Randolph was thrown out. Howser refused to carry out Steinbrenner's wish, and was eventually forced out with Ferraro. (A poignant footnote: When Howser stepped down as the Kansas City Royals manager six years later to have a brain tumor removed, Ferraro took over for him as interim manager.)

▶ Several members of the 1919 Chicago White Sox—who are known more familiarly and infamously as the Black Sox—were not on the take, and performed admirably in the World Series against the Cincinnati Reds, despite less-than-sterling support from the rest of the team. Pitcher Dickie Kerr won two games—a three-hit, 3-0 shutout and a 10-inning, 5-4 win—and compiled a 1.42 ERA in 19 innings. Other "clean" members of the team included Manager Kid Gleason, Eddie Collins, Red Faber, and Ray Schalk. (It should be noted that the great "Shoeless" Joe Jackson, whose actions before, during, and after the Series were scrutinized more than that of any player—and who was thereafter, and very likely unjustly, banished from baseball—hit .375, with 12 hits, over the eight games.)

▶ The University of Nebraska football team could have kicked an extra point for the tie in the final moments of the 1984 Orange Bowl with the University of Miami and thus preserved its #1 ranking and the national championship, but the Cornhuskers elected to prove that they were the best by going for a two-point conversion. (The conversion failed, and Miami won the game, 31-30, and the national title.)

▶ Mario Lemieux was credited with a goal and six assists in the Pittsburgh Penguins' 7-5 win over the Los Angeles Kings on February 13, 1988. A seven-point game would have been a Penguins team record, but Lemieux told officials that he did not deserve the final assist. A review showed that he was right, and the assist was credited to Doug Bodger.

▶ Swede Hugo Weislander and Norwegian Ferdinand Bie, runners-up to Jim Thorpe in the 1912 decathlon and pentathlon, respectively, were offered his first-place medals after Thorpe was stripped of them for having earned $25 a week playing minor-league baseball in 1909 and 1910. Weislander and Bie both refused to accept the gold medals.

▶ Race car driver Whitey Gerken stopped his vehicle during a 1970 race at the Indianapolis Fairgrounds to pull an unconscious opponent, Jack Bowsher, from his overturned car. "Why not?" Gerkin said. "I wasn't running well, anyway."

▶ During a barrage (fence-off) in the 1932 Olympics, Heather Guinness of Great Britain informed officials of two touches against her that they had missed, which turned out to be the margin of victory for the gold medal by Ellen Preis of Austria.

▶ In a 100-km Olympic cycling race in 1896, Leon Flameng of France stopped and waited while the bike of his opponent, G. Kolettis of Greece, was repaired.

▶ In the midst of trying to qualify for the 1988 LPGA Tucson Open, Mary Bea Porter jumped a fence to give CPR to a three-year-old boy who had been pulled out of a swimming pool, where he had been found facedown. Porter revived him. She returned to the golf course, bogeyed two of the next three holes, and missed the cut, but LPGA members signed a petition to include Porter in the tournament.

▶ India had a chance to win its first-ever Davis Cup in 1974 but defaulted to its opponents in the finals, South Africa, to protest apartheid.

▶ Russian Viktor Tsibulenko lent his steel javelin to Egil Danielson of Norway in 1956, and Danielson got off a world-record throw to win the Olympic gold. Tsibulenko took third.

▶ It's not true that nice guys finish last. The 1971–72 and 1984–85 Los Angeles Lakers, both of whom won NBA titles, had only seven players foul out of games all season, the second-lowest total in NBA history.

▶ In 1968, the Cuban team that finished second in the 4x100m relay mailed their silver medals to Stokely Carmichael in support of the cause of U.S. blacks.

▶ In Havana, Cuba, on April 5, 1915, heavyweight champion Jack Johnson, losing badly to challenger Jess Willard, motioned his wife over to the ring before the 26th round and told her to leave the arena so that she would not have to see him get knocked out.

▶ While in first place by a stroke, Greg Norman disqualified himself from the $625,000 Daikyo Palm Meadows Cup in Brisbane, Australia, in January 1990. Norman said that he had inadvertently taken illegal relief—moving his ball when he wasn't allowed—on a drive into the water in the first round and only later overheard that such a gesture was outside the rules. Norman had shot 66 in the first round and a course-record 63 in the second round before withdrawing.

▶ Lucien Duquesne of France pulled out Paavo Nurmi when he fell into the first water jump in a steeplechase heat in the 1928 Olympics. Nurmi reciprocated by pacing Duquesne the rest of the way.

▶ In 1987, Oakland Athletics rookie Mark McGwire, with 49 home runs, passed up the final game of the season—and the chance to become the first major-league rookie ever to hit 50 home runs in a season—so that he could witness the birth of his son, Matthew.

▶ Before their second run on the two-man bobsled in 1964, British pair Anthony Nash and Robin Dixon discovered that an axle bolt had broken off of their sled. Eight-time world champion Eugenio Monti removed a bolt from his own sled and gave it to them, helping Nash and Dixon to win the gold. Monti's Italian team took the bronze.

It's Just a Game, People

Every sports columnist in America has devoted too much ink decrying the fact that sport is no longer sport but a business, cold as any other. And they're right. There's too much lucre involved. Sadly, with the tremendous pressure to win on players, coaches, and owners, one of the basic satisfactions of sport—simply having fun—seems too often to get lost. Just listen to the hardened talk of any holdout-threatening phenom two weeks before training camp. Money must mean a great deal to anyone who, at the peak of his physical powers, threatens to sit out a year and wait to be paid uninsultingly enormous sums of cash, rather than play and receive simply very, very large sums of it.

Pitcher Lefty Gomez once called timeout while he was on the mound during a game to watch a plane fly overhead. We like that story.

Here are some others who have understood that it is, after all, just a game.

▶ Frenchman Jules Goux, winner of the 1913 Indianapolis 500, drank chilled champagne during pit stops.

▶ In September of 1989, Jamaican sprinter Linford Christie won a 100m race in London wearing a running suit designed to look like a James Bond-style dinner jacket with bow tie.

▶ On the last day of the 1952 season, St. Louis Cardinals outfielder Stan Musial and Chicago Cubs outfielder Frankie Baumholtz, one and two in the National League batting race, faced each other—literally. Musial came in from center field to pitch once to Baumholtz. Baumholtz, a lefty, batted right-handed against Musial, who had been a pitcher in the minor leagues. Baumholtz grounded to the third baseman, who made an error on the play. Musial then returned to the outfield. (Musial won the batting title.)

▶ In a 1985 game against the San Antonio Spurs, Quintin Dailey of the Chicago Bulls had the ballboy order a pizza during the game. Dailey ate it on the bench at the end of the third quarter.

▶ In 1950, the St. Louis Browns held a champagne celebration after their 55th win, because it meant that they could not lose 100 games that year. (The season then was 154 games long.)

▶ During long matches, Jack Crawford, a tennis star of the 1930s, liked to have a pot of tea, with milk and sugar, at the umpire's bench. He would relax with a cigarette during the interval after the third set.

The Dozen Gentlest College Mascots

The team mascots of most schools are robust or snarling or generally excitable creatures: Lions, Gators, Buffalo, a Wolfpack here and there. Presumably, such nicknames inspire the school's athletic teams—in other words, its football team—collectively to take on the personality of a junkyard dog. (We don't know if there's a school out there called the Junkyard Dogs.) If the school doesn't go in for animals, you'd probably be right to guess that its mascot name was something that sounded angry or destructive—Boilermakers, Fighting Irish, Hurricanes.

Other teams—some might say more self-motivated ones—don't require the yoke of an aggressive nickname to carry out their duties on the field, and in fact may perform more adeptly using a gentle nickname, the better to lull their opponents into a sense of complacency. The Saltillo Serape Makers of the Mexican Baseball League is such a team. The Chattanooga Choo Choos of baseball's Negro League was another.

More follow, from the college ranks.

▶ New York University Violets

▶ Whittier (California) Poets

▶ Centenary (Louisiana) Gentlemen

▶ St. Joseph's (Maine) Monks

▶ Heidelberg (Ohio) Student Princes

▶ St. Mary of the Woods (Indiana) Woodsies

▶ University of Pennsylvania Quakers

▶ St. Bonaventure (New York) Bonnies

▶ Whitman (Washington) Missionaries

▶ University of New England (Maine) Pilgrims

▶ Thomas Jefferson (Pennsylvania) Medics

▶ Boston University Terriers

6 Instances of Persons Who Took Baseball or Soccer Too Seriously

▶ On May 31, 1949, Charley Lupica, a fan of the seventh-place Cleveland Indians, held a vigil on the platform of a flagpole, vowing not to relinquish his perch until the team took over first place. They did not, rising only to fourth place, and Lupica was finally persuaded to come down after 117 days.

▶ Donnie Moore, closer for the California Angels, was a pitch away from sending his team—up three games to one over the Boston Red Sox —to their first-ever World Series appearance, when he gave up a two-run, game-extending homer to Dave Henderson. In extra innings, Henderson helped the Red Sox to win the game, on their way to winning the series, and by most accounts the result (and implications) of that single ninth-inning pitch to Henderson devastated Moore. He would float around baseball for another two years, beset by injuries and personal problems, and finally got released by the Omaha minor-league team. On July 18, 1989, at age 35, he shot and critically wounded his estranged wife, then killed himself.

(It should be noted that the burden Moore felt—or felt he should feel —may say as much about how *fans*, and not just Donnie Moore, take baseball too seriously.)

▶ For the 1982 World Cup, the Kuwait team president offered $200,000 per man for a victory over the French. (The French won, 4-1.)

▶ In 1889, M. H. Davidson, the owner-manager of the Louisville club in the American Association, fined one player $25 for a bobble and a wild throw, another one $25 for stupid baserunning, and then told the team that everyone would be fined $25 each if they did not win the next day. (The two fined players and four others went on strike, and the replace-ment players helped Louisville establish a major-league record of 26 consecutive losses.)

▶ During a pre-Olympic soccer match between Peru and Argentina on May 24, 1964, a riot broke out in which 328 people were killed and over 500 were injured.

▶ On the bottom of one tombstone in a Chicago-area Jewish cemetery is written, in Yiddish, "The Cubs Stink."

It's All About You, Right?

It's often said that there's no "i" in "team."
 There is, however, an "i" in "i."
 I, I, I, I, I.

▶ With 1.8 seconds left in a tied Game 3 of the 1994 NBA Eastern Conference finals against their fierce rivals, the New York Knicks, Chicago Bulls coach Phil Jackson called timeout to set up a final play. When Bulls forward Scottie Pippen, in his first season as putative team leader of the now Michael Jordan-less Bulls, saw that the first option being drawn up for the final shot was for fellow forward Toni Kukoc— an object of Pippen's resentment in part because he was being paid more—Pippen took a seat on the bench and sulked, refusing to go back in, as Jackson and Pippen's teammates looked on in disbelief. The Bulls, (with a replacement for Pippen), returned to the floor, and Kukoc hit a difficult buzzer-beater for the win.

▶ Before Joe Theismann's junior year at Notre Dame, the school's sports information director suggested that the quarterback change the pro-nunciation of Theismann—"THEEZ-man"—to "THIGHS-man," to rhyme with Heisman, as in Trophy. Theismann did so, but ended up second in the voting for the award in 1970 to Stanford's Jim Plunkett.

▶ After Venus Williams won her first Grand Slam singles champi-onship—the 2000 Wimbledon title—her father and coach, Richard Williams, who delivered periodic and bitter diatribes about (among other things) what he and his daughters had to overcome to succeed in the (in his view) racist tournament tennis ranks, stood up in his

Wimbledon box and held up a large, hand-made sign—making sure to turn it to the cameras so everyone at home could see—that declared, "IT'S VENUS'S PARTY AND NO ONE WAS INVITED!"

▶ In a 1995 game at the Montreal Forum, the Detroit Red Wings scored nine goals against future Hall of Fame goalie Patrick Roy, who was left in past the point that he felt his coach, Mario Tremblay, should have relieved him. When he was finally pulled, Roy screamed at Tremblay and Canadiens team president Ronald Corey as he got to the bench, vowed never again to play for Montreal, and stormed out of the Forum. (Four days later, Roy was traded to the Colorado Avalanche.)

▶ Rickey Henderson was *trying* to be gracious—we think—when he surpassed Lou Brock's career stolen base mark in 1991, hoisted the bag, and uttered, gracelessly, "Lou Brock was the symbol of great base stealing. But today, I'm the greatest of all time." (Actually, Rickey wasn't even the greatest of that *day*: Nolan Ryan would hurl his record seventh no-hitter for the Texas Rangers.)

Piling On

Yankee haters—and, increasingly, just average fans—view the most storied franchise in baseball as more than just the team to beat, but as bullies, too. The Bronx Bombers not only have the richest tradition, have won the most championships (by far), have the biggest budget, and can attract the top talent, but, ever unsatisfied (part of the reason for their success), they look for still more advantages to push the faces of their runty opponents into the ground. Indeed, New York has been known often to sign players they hardly needed (Jose Canseco and Jeff Weaver come to mind) just so their closest rivals couldn't have them. (While that strategy is followed by other teams, too, the Yankees have made it a habit.)

In hockey, the great Detroit Red Wings may be approaching Yankee-bully status: For the 2001–02 NHL season, with an already loaded team, and with a couple Stanley Cups won in the last six years, they felt it important to add to their roster of greats the top goal-scorer of his generation (Brett Hull) and the top goaltender (Dominik Hasek). At minimum, the 2002 Red Wings sported a staggering *nine* potential future Hall of Famers—ten, if you count their recently retired coach, Scotty Bowman—and three of the top five active goal scorers, and did what they should have done: won the 2002 Stanley Cup. (The Hall of Famers-to-be: Hull, Hasek, Steve Yzerman, Brendan Shanahan, Sergei Federov, Luc Robitaille, Chris Chelios, Niklas Lidstrom, and Igor Larianov.)

Some other examples of those who've piled on, and occasions when life itself seemed to be piling on:

▶ Before the institution of the NHL player draft, the league's premier team, the Montreal Canadiens, had the rights to sign any French-speaking player before any other team.

▶ Brett Jennings of Lingleville, Texas, so overpowered the Santo High School baseball team on April 28, 1986, that in only seven innings he struck out 24 batters. Three strikeout victims reached first base on dropped third strikes.

▶ Toward the end of the worst rout in NFL history—the Chicago Bears' 73-0 destruction of the Washington Redskins in the 1940 title game—officials asked the Bears not to kick extra points after touchdowns but to run or pass for them, because so many balls had already been lost in the stands.

▶ On April 12, 1988, Cal Ripken, Sr., had just returned from the courthouse, where he had pleaded guilty to a charge of driving while intoxicated, when he received the news that he had been fired as manager of the Baltimore Orioles.

▶ The California Golden Bears not only embarrassed Stanford in 1982 with perhaps the most dramatic game-ending play in the history of football—the famous five-lateral kickoff return for the winning touchdown that came to be known simply as "The Play"—but they did so with only 10 men on the field.

▶ The Dallas Cowboys also had only 10 men on the field in a 1983 game when running back Tony Dorsett set an NFL record with a 99-yard run from scrimmage against the Minnesota Vikings.

▶ At a gambling trial in Mississippi, outfielder Lenny Dykstra of the Philadelphia Phillies admitted that he'd lost $78,000 playing poker in two previous off-seasons. To top off his losses, baseball put him on one-year probation.

▶ Pete Rose was released from prison, for tax evasion, on January 1st, 1991. Nine days later, a special panel recommended that eligibility rules for the Baseball Hall of Fame be changed to bar anyone who was permanently ineligible for baseball. On February 4th, the Hall of Fame board voted unanimously that Rose was ineligible while banned from baseball.

▶ In the 1926 PGA, Leo Diegel lost to Walter Hagen in the match-play final by five and three strokes. On one hole, Diegel's ball finished under Hagen's parked car.

▶ Not long after invading Afghanistan, the Soviet Union beat them in team handball at the "Friendly Army Tournament" in Miskolc, Hungary, by a margin of 86-2, the highest score ever in an international handball match.

▶ Not only did Australian cyclist Phil Anderson lap several competitors in the final portion of a 1986 race in New York City, but he then drafted behind them to improve his time. (Anderson ignored repeated warnings to break from the pack, and was fined $5,000 by the U.S. Pro Cycling Federation.)

The Ultimate Athlete, from Head to Toe

If someone were to create a monster made up of sports history's most renowned body parts—not always the best parts, mind you, but the most renowned—the blueprint might look something like this:

▶ the brown SKIN of Brooklyn Dodger Jackie Robinson, who broke baseball's color barrier

▶ the electrified HAIR of boxing promoter Don King, the tenuously anchored HAIRPIECE of sportscaster Howard Cosell, or the over-gelled LOCKS of NBA coach Pat Riley

▶ the considerable BRAINS of UCLA basketball coach John Wooden, "The Wizard of Westwood"

▶ the historically intense BROW of Tampa Bay Buccaneers coach Jon Gruden

▶ the watchful EYES of hockey legend Wayne Gretzky, whose peripheral vision tested 30% better than average

▶ the partial EAR of Mike Tyson-bitten heavyweight champion Evander Holyfield

▶ the immediately apparent NOSE of American League slugger Ken "Hawk" Harrelson

▶ the handlebar MUSTACHE of many of the 1970s Oakland Athletics, "The Mustache Gang"—especially that of reliever Rollie Fingers

▶ the ever-moving MOUTH of major-league manager Leo "The Lip" Durocher

▶ the gapped TEETH of New York Giants linebacker Michael Strahan

▶ the searching TONGUE of basketball legend Michael Jordan

▶ the rock-firm CHIN of University of Tennessee women's basketball coaching legend Pat Summit

▶ the non-existent NECK of 5'6", 165-pound major leaguer Walt "No-Neck" Williams

▶ the sculpted SHOULDERS of San Antonio Spurs center David Robinson

▶ the chiseled CHEST of light-heavyweight boxer Roy Jones, Jr.

▶ the six-pack ABDOMINAL MUSCLES of U.S. World Cup soccer star Brandi Chastain

▶ the massive ARMS of Cincinnati Reds slugger Ted Kluszewski

▶ the sharp ELBOWS of Detroit Piston "Bad Boys" Rick Mahorn and Bill Laimbeer

▶ the powerful WRISTS of home run champion Hank Aaron

▶ the notoriously sticky HANDS of Oakland Raiders defensive back Lester Hayes

▶ the scarce FINGERS of Hall of Fame pitcher Mordecai "Three Finger" Brown

▶ the preternaturally attuned FINGERTIPS of Lynn Hill, the first person to climb the famous Nose route of Yosemite's El Capitan "free"—using no gear

▶ the flamboyantly painted FINGERNAILS of sprinter Florence Griffith Joyner

▶ the ample GLUTEUS MAXIMUS of Soviet weightlifter Vassily Alexeyev

▶ the elegant PELVIS of lithe Romanian gymnast Nadia Comaneci

▶ the muscular THIGHS of speedskater Eric Heiden

▶ the ravaged KNEES of Chicago Bears defensive lineman Dan Hampton, who underwent no fewer than 11 operations on them

▶ the stupendous FEET of basketball center Bob Lanier, who needs size-22 shoes to cover them, and featuring the precarious, arthritic BIG TOE of Los Angeles Lakers center Shaquille O'Neal

The Ultimate Getup, from Hat to Sole

…and the only thing more unnerving than watching this monster rise from the table would be to take it shopping. And as long as it's going shopping, it might as well wear the most renowned clothes, and use the most renowned accessories, from the sports world, including the following:

▶ the baseball CAP of hitting star Harry "The Hat" Walker, who took it off and put it back on after each pitch

▶ the cotton HEADBAND of tennis great Bjorn Borg or the scalp-hugging DOO-RAG of NFL running back Ricky Watters

▶ the outer-space GOGGLES of basketball legend Kareem Abdul-Jabbar or running back Eric Dickerson

▶ the glittering EARRING of brilliant cornerback (and less brilliant baseball player) Deion Sanders

▶ the shockingly loud SPORT JACKET of broadcaster Lindsey Nelson or the full-length black MINK COAT of New York Jets quarterback / Big Apple stud Joe Namath, which would cover the…

▶ …even louder, lucky SWEATER of St. John's University basketball coach, Lou Carnesecca

▶ the sleeveless SHIRT of Ted Kluszewski, the only shirt that will cover those massive arms (refer to monster's blueprint)

▶ the University of North Carolina SHORTS that Michael Jordan always wore under his Chicago Bulls shorts, for good luck

▶ the gold SHOES of Olympic sprinter gold medalist Michael Johnson or the white SPATS of home-run king Barry Bonds

Walking down the street toward the arena, the monster—with the HEART of four-time Tour de France cyclist and cancer survivor Lance

Armstrong (whose average resting heart rate is 32 beats per minute), and with the unswerving NERVE of San Francisco 49ers quarterback Joe Montana—would dab its brow with the white TOWEL of college basketball coach Jerry Tarkanian (and perhaps chew on it), puff on the CIGAR of basketball whiz Red Auerbach, and maybe, only then, pleased with its outfit, would flash the I-could-light-a-city SMILE of Los Angeles Laker Magic Johnson or American gymnast Mary Lou Retton.

Steady As They Go: Consistency

To call an athlete consistent is usually to compliment him or her—he or she puts out the same, presumably full, effort every game, and the level of performance doesn't waver all that much one day to the next. The athlete may do the usual great things each time out—score in double figures, pitch at least seven good innings, carry the ball 20 times for 100 yards. Or maybe the athlete just gives you a workmanlike effort—four or five rebounds in limited minutes, a couple of first downs on third-and-inches.

Ultimately, to call an athlete consistent is to know what to expect of him or her. Some of the best examples:

▶ Golfer Densmore Shute won the 1933 British Open with rounds of 73, 73, 73, and 73.

▶ In 1983, New York Mets outfielder Mookie Wilson hit .276. In 1984, he hit .276. In 1985, he hit .276. (Wilson was highly erratic before that: in 1981, he hit .271 and in 1982, .279.)

▶ From the 1950–51 through the 1954–55 seasons, Hall of Fame goaltender Terry Sawchuck had a goals-against average of between 1.90 and 1.99.

▶ Jimmie Foxx and Lou Gehrig both drove in 100 or more runs for 13 consecutive years.

▶ In 1968, the steady and unspectacular Jan Jansen of Holland became the first cyclist to win the Tour de France without having worn the yellow (leader's) jersey during the race.

▶ In 1993, their first year in the major leagues, the Florida Marlins finished in sixth place. The following year, they finished in fifth; the year after that, fourth; the year after that, third; and the year after that, second, when they won the wild card and World Series. (The following year, after being dismantled, they were in last place again.)

▶ After scoring only eight points in a game against the Cleveland Cavaliers on March 22, 1986, Chicago Bull Michael Jordan proceeded to score in double figures in his next 866 regular-season games. (His streak was stopped in late 2001, when the Indiana Pacers held him to six points.)

▶ Since 1900, two major-league teams have scored at least one run in every frame of a nine-inning game: the New York Giants, on June 1, 1923, and the St. Louis Cardinals, on September 13, 1964.

▶ Warren Spahn won 20 games a season a record 13 times, and never won more than 23.

▶ For the six seasons from 1944–45 to 1949–50, NHL defenseman Bill Quackenbush had the following assist totals: 21, 21, 22, 22, 23, and 25.

▶ In the 1971–72 season, the Los Angeles Lakers committed 1,636 fouls. The following season, they again committed 1,636 fouls.

▶ Where the following major leaguers played had no effect on their power. They each hit exactly the same number of career home runs at home as they did on the road:

▷ Wally Berger, 121 at home (mostly Braves Field), 121 away;

▷ Willie Jones, 95 at home (mostly Connie Mack Stadium), 95 away;

▷ Charles Gehringer, 92 at home (mostly Briggs Stadium), 92 away.

▶ In his first seven seasons in the major leagues, first baseman Jason Giambi's batting average improved each year—.256, .291, .293, .295, .315, .333, .342.

▶ In the 19 seasons from 1983–84 through 2001–02, Duke's men's basketball team made the final 32 of the NCAA tournament 17 times and the Sweet Sixteen 13 times (and won the championship three times).

▶ Don Sutton struck out at least 100 batters for 21 consecutive seasons.

▶ From 1962 to 1981, Jack Nicklaus played all 80 majors and made the top 10 in 60 of them. In 42 of them, he was in the top three.

▶ NHL goalie Eddie Giacomin's regular season goals-against average was 2.82. His playoff goals-against average was 2.82.

The 52 Most Exciting Athletes

You don't have to root for them, or even like them. But all these athletes share something: They are (or were, in their prime) mesmerizing to watch, either because they ooze so much talent or so much style, or both. It isn't just what they do, but how they do it. Some are modest, some arrogant; some display classic technique, some odd. The common thread: Taking your eyes off of them is not an option.

We admit it: You're quite capable of naming 52* we overlooked. Oh, well.

▶ Brett Favre

▶ Boris Becker

▶ Tony Hawk

▶ Mike Tyson

▶ Dominik Hasek

▶ Mark McGwire

▶ Olga Korbut

▶ Allen Iverson

▶ Jackie Stiles

▶ Wayne Gretzky

▶ Mickey Mantle

▶ Picabo Street

▶ Bob Hayes

▶ Arnold Palmer

- Ilie Nastase
- Ichiro Suzuki
- Fran Tarkenton
- Babe Didrickson
- Martina Navratilova
- Larry Bird
- John McEnroe
- Kirby Puckett
- Lee Trevino
- Thomas Hearns
- Paul Warfield
- Jimmy Connors
- Greg Louganis
- Willie Mays
- Peggy Fleming
- Sandy Koufax
- Guillermo Vilas
- Jake LaMotta
- David Beckham

- Michael Jordan
- Muhammad Ali
- Oksana Bayul
- Pelé
- Babe Ruth
- Gale Sayers
- Michael Johnson
- Jackie Robinson
- Andre Agassi
- Joe Namath
- Dick Butkus
- Nadia Comaneci
- Julius Erving
- Lawrence Taylor
- Maradona
- Franz Klammer
- Pete Rose
- Tiger Woods
- Earl Monroe

*Why 52? One for each week of the year. We're hoping this'll inspire someone out there to make a calendar.

2

NUMBERS AND STATISTICS

The Most Startling Positive Aberrations

For one game or season, the following athletes performed strangely better than they did the rest of their careers.

▶ Baltimore Oriole Brady Anderson hit 50 home runs in 1996. He never hit more than 24 in any other year.

Jay Bell of the Arizona Diamondbacks hit 38 home runs in 1999, 17 more than his next-best total.

Atlanta Brave Davey Johnson hit 43 homers in 1973. In his other 12 years, the most he could muster in a single season was 18.

In the 2002 regular season, Adam Kennedy of the Anaheim Angels hit all of seven home runs, averaging one every 68 at-bats. Batting ninth in the clinching Game 5 of the American League Championship Series that sent the Angels to their first-ever World Series, Kennedy hit three homers, becoming only the fifth player to go deep three times in a postseason game (joining the likes of Babe Ruth and Reggie Jackson).

▶ Running back Charles White rushed for an NFL-leading 1,374 yards in 1987, four yards fewer than his combined total for the seven previous seasons.

Although Atlanta Falcons running back Jamal Anderson has, on four occasions, amassed thousand-plus yard seasons, the second-best of those was 1,055 yards. The best? A staggering 1,846 yards—the ninth-best single-season total ever (through 2001)—when he helped take the 1998 Falcons to the Super Bowl.

▶ Broker's Tip won the 1933 Kentucky Derby. He had never won a race before and would never win one again.

▶ Wilt Chamberlain, a 51% career free-throw shooter, made 28 of 32 free throws—88% percent—and set the record for most free throws made in a game on the night that he scored 100 points.

▶ In 1912, Pittsburgh Pirate Owen Wilson set the major-league record of 36 triples. He had no more than 14 in any other year.

▶ Ali Haji-Sheikh set an NFL record with 35 field goals as a New York Giants rookie in 1983, then never kicked more than 17 in any other season.

▶ Bumpus Jones (career 2-4 record) pitched a no-hitter, as did George Davis (7-10) and Mike Warren (9-13).

▶ In 2001, Seattle Mariners second baseman Bret Boone led the American League with 141 runs batted in. In seven full or almost full seasons before that, his best total was 95 RBIs. (In 2002, he had his second-best season ever, but his not-too-shabby 107 RBIs were still a 24% drop from his best.)

In 1998, middling third baseman Scott Brosius of the Oakland As was brought onto the formidable Yankees mostly for his glove and perhaps a little pop in his bat. He outdid all expectations by winning the starting job; from the 9th spot in the order, he drove in 98 runs, almost 30 better than his previous (or ensuing) best; then drove in 6 more runs in the World Series, en route to winning the World Series MVP.

▶ Boone's (see above) team, the Seattle Mariners, tied the all-time record for most wins in a regular season, with 116 in 2001. Like Boone, their next highest total was the following season, when they won 93 games—a reputable number but still a significant dropoff from their historic 2001 season.

▶ Lee Fogolin, an NHL defenseman for 13 years, scored 13 goals in 1980–81, and no more than five in any other season.

▶ On July 18, 1948, Pat Seerey became one of the rare major leaguers to hit four home runs in one game—but he hit just eight more after that, and had only 86 in his career.

▶ Unknown Paul Pilgrim won the 400m and 800m in the 1906 Interim Olympic Games. He never again won a major race.

▶ In 1942, Johnny Beazley won 21 games. In his whole major-league career, he won 31 games.

▶ Oakland Athletics catcher Gene Tenace was a .251 career hitter, then batted .348 with four home runs and nine runs batted in in the 1972 World Series, then returned to being a .239 hitter for the rest of his career.

▶ Before 1989, when they lost their first-round NCAA tournament game to Siena, the Stanford University men's basketball team had made only one NCAA tournament appearance, in 1942. They won the national title that year.

▶ Detroit Tiger Norm Cash hit .361 to win the 1961 American League batting title. In his other 16 years in the league, he never hit more than .286.

Tito Francona, a lifetime .272 hitter, hit .363 in 1959.

▶ Don Woods rushed for 1,162 yards as a San Diego Charger rookie in 1974. The next-best season total for his seven-year career was 514 yards.

▶ Detroit Tigers pitcher Dave Wickersham won 19 games in 1964 but never more than 12 in any other year.

Pitcher Monte Weaver won 22 games for the 1932 Washington Senators, the only time he won more than 12 in a season.

▶ Fred Odwell hit one home run in 1904, then nine in 1905 to win the National League homer title, then no more.

▶ To win the only professional tennis tournament of his career, the 1981 Seiko Classic in Tokyo, Vince van Patten beat John McEnroe, Vitas Gerulaitis, Jose-Luis Clerc, and, in the final, Mark Edmondson. Van Patten's next-best success was reaching the quarterfinals of a tournament in Tel Aviv.

And a Few More Startling *Negative* Aberrations

▶ Joe Sewell of the Cleveland Indians struck out twice against Chicago White Sox pitcher Pat Caraway in one game on May 26, 1930. That may not seem like a lot for most players but it was for Sewell, the hardest man to strike out in the history of baseball. He did not strike out again for the rest of that season, and in his 14-year career, he fanned once every 63 at-bats (114 strikeouts in 7,132 at-bats).

▶ On April 26, 1931, New York Yankee Lou Gehrig, one of the most alert baseball players ever, passed a teammate on the basepaths and lost credit for the home run he had hit. That year, Gehrig and teammate Babe Ruth tied for the home run crown with 46.

▶ In 1999, Chicago White Sox slugger Frank Thomas, coming off eight consecutive 100+ RBI seasons in his first eight full years in the league, had 77 RBIs (he did miss a few more games than usual). While such a dropoff is not uncommon for a player who suddenly feels age creeping up, such was not the case with Thomas: The following season, he returned to his old habits—bettered them, in fact—when he drove in a career-best 143 runs, and slugged a career-best 43 homers.

▶ Nap Lajoie, one of the greatest players and fielders of all time, was once charged with five errors in a game. Brooks Robinson, the most brilliant third baseman of his era, made three errors in a game against the Oakland Athletics. It was the only time that happened in his career. And the record for most errors in a World Series, six, used to be held by baseball legend Honus Wagner.

The Tidiest Statistics in Sports

Something about the statistician—or the accountant—in all of us loves numbers ending in zero. There's something precise about it, something clean. In 1927, heavyweight Gene Tunney earned $990,445 for beating Jack Dempsey, but Tunney was paid with a $1 million check and then wrote his own check to make up the difference.

The following people did not fudge their numbers to look neat. It just happened that way.

▶ Joe Gordon played 1,000 games with the New York Yankees and had 1,000 hits.

▶ In his NBA career, basketball star Elvin Hayes played exactly 50,000 minutes.

▶ The career of Pittsburgh Pirate Roberto Clemente was cut short by a plane crash. He died with exactly 3,000 hits.

▶ NBA great Kareem Abdul-Jabbar scored in double figures in 787 consecutive games. The streak started on December 4, 1977. It stopped on December 4, 1987, exactly one decade later.

▶ Hall of Famer Lefty Grove won exactly 300 games.

▶ Gregg Pruitt rushed for exactly 1,000 yards for the Cleveland Browns in 1976, as did the Los Angeles Rams' Willie Ellison in 1971, and the Miami Dolphins' Mercury Morris in 1972. (Morris had 991 yards at season's end but in reviewing game film, NFL commissioner Pete Rozelle found a nine-yard error, bringing Morris up to exactly 1,000 yards.)

▶ Billy Goodman and Enos Slaughter each had a career batting average of .300.

▶ In 1964, Northern Dancer ran the Kentucky Derby in precisely 2:00.0, the only time that has ever happened in the Derby.

▶ Richard Petty won his 200th NASCAR race on July 4, 1984, in the Pepsi Firecracker 400 in Daytona Beach. He would never win a 201st.

The Most Memorable Uniform Numbers

An athlete's uniform number may signify many things: He plays a certain position, such as lineman, and thus can wear a number only within a narrow range; it's the number he's worn since Pee Wee League; it was the last clean jersey in the locker room when he joined the team.

This is about uniform numbers that carried a more compelling significance than that, and who wore them.

▶ *100*, by University of Kansas senior placekicker Bill Bell. Bell wore #12 in his sophomore and junior seasons, during which he scored exactly 100 points. Kansas coach Pepper Rodgers received NCAA permission for Bell to exceed the two-digit uniform number limit in his final year, 1969, which was also college football's 100th anniversary.

▶ *100*, by West Virginia University placekicker Chuck Kinder in 1963, to commemorate the Mountain State's centennial.

▶ *99*, by Willie Crawford of the Oakland Athletics in 1977. It is the highest number ever worn in baseball.

▶ *96*, by major-league pitcher Bill Voiselle, whose hometown was Ninety-Six, South Carolina.

▶ *85*, by NHL forward Petr Klima to commemorate 1985, the year he defected from Czechoslovakia.

▶ *72*, by Carlton Fisk of the Chicago White Sox, to represent the turnaround in his career—hence, the reverse of the #27 he wore with the Boston Red Sox.

▶ *50*, by New York Mets pitcher Sid Fernandez, in honor of his native Hawaii, the 50th state in the Union.

▶ *42*, by Dave Henderson of the Oakland Athletics, because it was the number worn by Jackie Robinson, whose strength of character opened the way for black players in the major leagues.

▶ *31*, by no Buffalo Bill ever. The Bills have never issued #31 because it was the number worn by the Buffalo player on the club's letterhead from the 1960s, when the Bills were in the AFL.

▶ *25*, by Miami Dolphin Louis Oliver, to remind him of the disappointing position he was selected in the first round of the 1989 NFL draft, after unsubstantiated drug rumors about Oliver, the country's top collegiate safety, circulated on draft day.

▶ *17*, by Carlos May, who was born on May 17, and thus is the only known major leaguer whose uniform displayed his birthdate.

▶ *17*, by Andy Messersmith of the Atlanta Braves, because Braves owner Ted Turner saw a chance to promote simultaneously his star pitcher and his station, WTBS, Channel 17.

▶ *Γ* (a backward 7), worn by John Neves, a minor-league baseball player whose name spelled backward is "seven."

▶ *4*, worn by Houston Rocket Rick Barry for road games.

▶ *2*, worn by Houston Rocket Rick Barry for home games.

▶ *⅛*, by Eddie Gaedel, the 3'7" midget hired by St. Louis Browns owner Bill Veeck to take one major-league at-bat. (Gaedel walked on four pitches.)

▶ *0*, by Al Oliver, in 1978, when he was with the Texas Rangers. It is the lowest uniform number ever worn in baseball. 0, as well as 00, has been worn by others, including Oddibe McDowell and Jeffrey Leonard.

▶ *00*, by Oakland Raider center Jim Otto, to commemorate the beginning and end of his last name.

▶ *?*, by Max Patkin, veteran entertainer and clown at minor-league baseball games (seen in the movie *Bull Durham*).

▷ Honorable Mention: *He Hate Me*, the name on the back of the jersey of Las Vegas Outlaw running back Rod Smart of the XFL, the half-football, half-wrestling league concocted by Vince McMahon, chairman of World Wrestling Federation Entertainment, to wrest(le) viewers away from the NFL. Because the league allowed players to put on their jersey virtually any name or word they wanted, Smart opted for a catchy phrase, and succeeded: "He Hate Me" is nearly the only thing anyone remembers about the league, which folded after one year. (In 2001, Rod "He Hate Me" Smart made the roster of the Philadelphia Eagles; in 2002, he was on the Carolina Panthers.)

Misleading Tallies: The Stories behind 6 Scores

Given little more than the final score, a fan can often tell a great deal about a game—how it progressed, whether it was exciting (no matter how you cut it, no 6-0, 6-0, 6-0 tennis match is exciting), maybe even make an educated stab at who did what. For example, if you hear that your team was involved in a high-scoring affair at Wrigley and you know the wind was blowing out, you can't help but instinctively add a homer or two to your favorite slugger's total before you even bother with the box score.

If you imagined a pat scenario for any of the following scores, you'd be wrong.

▶ On September 24, 1967, the St. Louis Cardinals beat the Pittsburgh Steelers, 28-14. However, the Cardinals did not score four touchdowns; 21 of their points were the result of a record seven field goals by kicker Jim Bakken.

▶ In the first round of the Ginny women's tennis tournament in Richmond, Virginia, on September 25, 1984, Vicki Nelson defeated Jean Hepner, 6-4, 7-6. It was a simple, straight-set affair. Right? Wrong. It was the longest match in duration ever played, lasting 6 hours and 31 minutes, not counting intermissions and interruptions. The match included one rally of 643 shots, and the final tiebreaker game lasted *one hour and 47 minutes*.

▶ In the 1964 NFL title game, the Cleveland Browns clobbered the Baltimore Colts, 27-0. But it was a much closer game than that; the halftime score, in fact, was 0-0.

▶ On August 23, 1961, a baseball version of that NFL title game occurred. The San Francisco Giants destroyed the Cincinnati Reds, 14-0. After eight innings, however, the Giants were leading only 2-0.

▶ In a 1970 game against Florence State University, Russell Thompson of Birmingham Southern State College scored 25 points. Oddly, however, Thompson did not make a single field goal. He was 25 for 27 from the foul line.

▶ In the 1929 World Series, the Chicago Cubs lost Game 4 in a thriller, 10-8. Sadly for Cub fans, their team had been running away with the game all along, leading 8-0 in the seventh inning.

Soft Accomplishments

Some feats are remarkable on the face of them, and then seem even more so if you know the surrounding circumstances. Roger Bannister's breaking of the four-minute mile was one of the great athletic achievements of the 20th century, yet it's more impressive still when you consider that Bannister had to contend with, according to reports in the *New York Times*, "a 15mph crosswind during the race and gusts [that] reached 25mph just before the event began." Al Geiberger's PGA record score of 59 for 18 holes (since tied) was accomplished in 1977, on the 7,249-yard Colonial Country Club Course in Memphis, the longest course played on the U.S. tour that year.

This is not about especially impressive records. The listed feats of the following athletes are commendable at first glance. But once we consider the competition against whom the feat was registered, or the fortunate circumstances that made it possible, or what the athlete's peers have achieved—or could achieve—when trying to accomplish the same thing under different conditions, we see that these accomplishments were really not so spectacular.

▶ Czechoslovakia's Jan Kodes won the 1973 Wimbledon title after 79 members of the Association of Tennis Professionals, including 13 of the 16 seeded players, boycotted the tournament to protest the suspension of Yugoslav Nikki Pilic for not playing Davis Cup.

▶ In 1983, Montreal Expos pitcher David Palmer threw a rain-shortened five-inning perfect game against the St. Louis Cardinals. (Major League Baseball considers the game official, but not as a perfect game.)

▶ Soviet Anatoly Parfenov won the 1956 Olympic Greco-Roman super heavyweight wrestling gold medal in rousing fashion: He lost his opening match, but a Soviet protest was upheld; he lost his second-round match; he won by forfeit in the third round; and he received a bye in the fourth. In the fifth round, he had his only undisputed win, a decision.

▶ The St. Louis Browns won their only pennant in 1944, a year when the major leagues were depleted by the war.

▶ Because of the 1982 NFL strike and the revised playoff format, the Cleveland Browns and Detroit Lions both made the playoffs with 4-5 records.

▶ In 1980, Max Schmeling became the first boxer to win the heavyweight title on a foul (over Jack Sharkey).

▶ Oliver Kirk won Olympic gold medals in both the featherweight and bantamweight divisions in 1904 though he had only one bout in each.

▶ Through 1921, the defending Wimbledon champion automatically advanced to the final to face the winner of a challenge round.

▶ Because of the disqualification of one American quarter-miler from the 1908 Olympic 400m competition, and the ensuing protests of two others, Britain's Wyndham Halswelle won the gold medal by running alone in the final.

▶ Steven Bradbury, Australian short-track speedskater, was in last-place in the 1000m event at the 2002 Winter Olympics when a spectacular fall among the leaders, on the last lap, left Bradbury alone to cross the finish line and win the gold.

▶ There are saves and there are saves. In the past, a closer entered a tightening game in the eighth inning, if not the seventh, and not at the beginning of an unblemished ninth; there were usually a couple of runners on, not many outs, and all kinds of potential disaster brewing. Now? Closers rarely "inherit" runners. The bloated save totals accumulated by major-league closers in recent years are due partly to the added emphasis on specialty relief, but also on generous, often illogical accounting. Today, if you come into the ninth inning with a three-run lead and give up two runs and five hits but manage to get three outs? You get the save. In the 2000 season, Florida Marlins closer Antonio Alfonseca, *Sporting News's* National League "Fireman of the Year" award—given to the "best" reliever, by their calculation—pitched in 68 games and registered 45 saves. But Alfonseca had a grand total of zero "tough saves"—a new stat, meaning that the pitcher faces at least the tying run. In short, arguably the best closer in the league that year did not once face the tying run the entire season (*and* record the save). To give another example: On June 14, 2002, Texas Rangers reliever Randy Flores entered a game in which his team led the Houston Astros, 9-6, in the ninth inning, with two outs and a runner on first. Flores threw one pitch, a ball... and catcher Pudge Rodriguez picked the runner off first base to end the game; Flores got the save. Similarly, in 2002, Atlanta Braves closer John Smoltz, who set the National League record for most saves in a season, recorded some of them without even facing the tying run in the on-deck circle.

▶ Although longtime NBA coach Gene Shue is 11th in all-time wins with 814, that honor seems largely a tribute to longevity, and little else. His career winning percentage is an unimpressive .477; his playoff winning percentage, a truly underwhelming .390.

▶ We're not suggesting that bowling a perfect game (12 strikes from start to finish, for a 300 score) is a soft accomplishment—but it has gotten softer. The number of perfect games recorded nationwide, each year, has increased from under 1,000 a generation ago to 43,431 in 2000–01—and this even as the number of league bowlers has *decreased* by roughly half. The greater ease is attributed largely, if not exclusively, to two developments: bowling proprietors who oil the lanes to guide the ball to the pocket, and improvements in equipment, especially the ball.

▶ Anthony Allen set a Washington Redskins team record with 255 receiving yards in a 1987 strike game.

▶ While Chilean Marcelo Rios is a tremendously talented tennis player —especially in 1998—he has never won a Grand Slam singles title and has made it to only one such final (the Australian Open in '98)... yet he was ranked #1 in the world for six weeks in 1998 (ending Pete Sampras's 102-week reign). Rios benefited, in part, from the byzantine pro tennis ranking system.

▶ In 1922, Mike Collins, a fight manager who was also publisher of a weekly called *The Boxing Blade*, invented a new division, the light welterweights, and held a competition among his readers to determine who should be the division's first champion. Not surprisingly, the winner of the poll was one of Collins's own fighters, Myron "Pinkie" Mitchell. Mitchell kept the title for four years without defending it. When he finally did defend it, on September 21, 1926, he lost a 10-round decision to Mushy Callahan.

▶ Because of the liberal NHL playoff system and the traditionally weak competition in the then-Norris Division, the Toronto Maple Leafs made the playoffs in each of the three seasons from 1985–86 to 1987–88. Their cumulative record over that span was 78-139-23.

▶ Many hitters are more than glad to go to Colorado for a few seasons where, thanks to Denver's thin air, they can inflate personal stats that are unreproducible elsewhere. Counting full seasons, the worst batting average that Dante Bichette (to take one example) registered in his seven seasons as a Colorado Rockie is still better than the best average he registered in five seasons—three before, two after—elsewhere (California, Milwaukee, Cincinnati, Boston). Colorado hitting star Larry Walker, on the other hand, is not such an example: The perennial All-Star and all-around player regularly hits about as well on the road as he does at Coors Field.

▶ In an NBA game on November 22, 1950, John Oldham of Fort Wayne won top scoring honors. He had five points.

▶ In 1984, Brigham Young University finished 13-0 and won the national championship. However, none of their wins, including a Holiday Bowl victory over Michigan, came against teams that finished in the final Top 20.

Beamonesque Achievements

The word "Beamonesque" has entered the vocabulary of sports historians to mean a feat so dramatically superior to its predecessors that it cannot be sufficiently appreciated except to be called, well, Beamonesque.

American Bob Beamon astounded the world when he won the long jump at the 1968 Olympics with his record 29'2½" leap, a standard that stood for 23 years (when it was finally bettered by Mike Powell). It is not that Beamon wasn't a world-class jumper before that day; he was. It is not that a world-record jump at those Games couldn't have been anticipated; it was, given the thin air of high-altitude Mexico City. What was astounding about the jump was that Beamon became not only the first human to clear 29 feet but also the first to clear 28 feet. In fact, the first long jump within the 28 foot range would not occur *for 12 more years*, until the 1980 Olympics, when Lutz Dombrowski did it. To put Beamon's feat further into perspective? His jump increased the world record by 21¾ inches, while in the 33 years before that, since Jesse Owens's jump of 26'8½" in 1935, the record had increased by a puny 8½ inches.

The following achievements reveal a level of proficiency that only one person or team has achieved, for a brief period or over a career. Because these feats may not be as "pure" as those in track and field, circumstances might have facilitated the achievement—for example, a team played a weak schedule, or the prevailing rules favored a player's style. Nonetheless, we believe they still deserve the high distinction of Beamonesqueness.

▶ American Mary T. Meagher was swimming's Bob Beamon; indeed, on the rare occasion when a swimmer utterly blows away the competition like Meagher did, the term "Meagheresque" is likely to be trotted out. On August 13, 1981, at age 16, she swam the 100-meter butterfly in 57.93 seconds. She broke the world record (her own) by a whopping 1½ seconds, and the record stood for an unfathomable 18 years, when Jenny Thompson broke it.

In the 200-meter butterfly, Meagher—known as "Madame Butterfly" —set the world record of 2:05.96 on August 16, 1981; at one point she owned all 10 of the fastest times in the event. Australian Olympian Susie O'Neill finally broke the 200m record after 19 years.

Her 100m and 200m times were the longest-standing records in swimming. The next-longest record had held for not quite 11 years.

▶ In 1984, Miami Dolphins quarterback Dan Marino passed for 48 touchdowns, eviscerating the old mark of 36 held by Y. A. Tittle and George Blanda.

▶ LSU basketball star Pete Maravich holds the Division I scoring average record of 44.2 points per game (1968–70). Notre Dame's Austin Carr is a distant second with 34.6 points per game (1969–71).

▶ Connie Mack, who owned the Philadelphia Athletics, was a manager for 53 years, including 3 years as player-manager. He managed 20 years longer than the next person, John McGraw, who was a major-league skipper for 33 years.

▶ In January of 1914, speedskater Oscar Mathisen of Norway set a record in the 1,500m (2:17.4 seconds) that stood for 23 years, when it was broken by Michael Staksrud's 2:14.9. Only twice was Mathisen's performance bettered in the 38 years from 1914–52.

▶ New York Yankee Babe Ruth inaugurated the lively-ball era in 1920 with 54 home runs. George Sisler was the runner-up with 19.

In 1927, Ruth's Yankees hit 158 home runs—102 more than the second-best team. That year the Boston Red Sox hit five home runs at Fenway Park; Ruth himself hit eight at Fenway, and teammate Lou Gehrig six.

▶ Cornelius "Dutch" Warmerdam pole-vaulted 15 feet or more 43 times between 1940 and 1944. No one else cleared the height until 1951. When he retired, Warmerdam's best vault was nine inches higher than anyone else's. His world record of 15'7¾", set on May 23, 1942, remained until April 27, 1957, when Bob Gutowski broke it.

▶ In 1962, Los Angeles Dodger Maury Wills led the National League with 104 stolen bases. His teammate, Willie Davis, was next with 32.

▶ Romanian high-jumper Iolanda Balas set 14 world records from 1958–66, the most for any athlete in a single event (at the time), and was the first woman to clear six feet. She had done that in 46 different meets before another woman, Michele Brown of Australia, cleared it.

▶ In 1971, Montreal Expo Rusty Staub was second in the National League in getting hit by pitches, with nine. Ron Hunt, his teammate, led the league with 50.

▶ Wayne Gretzky broke Gordie Howe's NHL career scoring record in his 11th season. Howe played in the NHL for 26 years.

▶ Jim Thorpe's world-record score in the 1912 decathlon, 700 points more than the runner-up, was so high that it would still have won the silver medal in the 1948 Games. (It's important to note that most track & field records set in the early 20th century were regularly and substantially eclipsed so that, by mid-century, they looked deeply unimpressive.)

6 Famous Records and the Records That They Broke

▶ Barry Bonds's 73 home runs in a season (2001) broke Mark McGwire's 70, which, along with Sammy Sosa's 66 that same year of 1998, broke Roger Maris's 61, which broke Babe Ruth's 60, which broke Ruth's 59, which broke Ruth's 54, which broke Ruth's 29, which broke Ned Williamson's 27.

▶ Wilt Chamberlain's 100 points in a game broke his own record of 78, set earlier in the season, December 8, 1961.

▶ Joe DiMaggio's 56-game hitting streak broke Wee Willie Keeler's 44-game streak in 1897.

▶ New Orlean Saint Tom Dempsey's 63-yard field goal in 1970 broke Baltimore Colt Bert Rechichar's 56-yarder in 1953. (Jason Elam of the Denver Broncos tied Dempsey's record in 1998.)

▶ Orel Hershiser's 59-consecutive-innings scoreless streak broke Don Drysdale's 58-innings streak, which broke Walter Johnson's 55⅔-innings streak.

▶ In 1924, Jim Bottomley drove in 12 runs in one game to break Wilbert Robertson's record of 11, set in 1892. Ironically, Robertson was managing the opposing team on that day in 1924 and got to see, in person, his record broken. (In 1993, Mark Whiten of the St. Louis Cardinals tied Bottomley's record.)

And 1 Record That Broke a Famous Record and Should Be More Famous, but Isn't

▶ In 2001, Alan Webb, the best high school miler ever, ran the distance in 3:53.43, easily breaking Jim Ryun's legendary 36-year-old record for high schoolers, 3:55.3. But because of America's nominal interest in track—not to mention high school track—few but real fans of middle-distance running even know the record was broken.

When It Rains, It Pours

Success breeds success. An athlete or team overcomes some psychological or physical barrier and suddenly it's as if the barrier never existed. The best example of this might be that of the four-minute mile. Before Roger Bannister crossed that threshold in 1954, it was widely believed to be physically impossible. By the end of 1957, 16 other runners had broken it. Then again, some things just come in bunches.

▶ At the 1976 Montreal Games, Romanian Nadia Comaneci became the first Olympic gymnast ever to receive a perfect score of 10—and she got *seven* of them.

▶ In his six years with the Baltimore Orioles, Frank Robinson hit only two grand slams—and they came in consecutive at-bats at Washington, on June 26, 1970.

Before 1987, Don Mattingly had never before hit a grand slam. That season, he hit six, a major-league record.

The first grand slam of Chicago Cub slugger Sammy Sosa's career did not occur until July 27, 1998—the 246th homer of his career and the greatest number of homers at the start of a career without a single grand slam. And when did Sammy hit grand slam #2? The next day.

▶ Before the 1986 postseason, no major-league team had ever come back from more than two runs down in the ninth inning to win a playoff or World Series game. In the space of 21 hours, it happened twice during the American League playoffs and once in the National League playoffs.

▶ Golfer David Duval had developed a reputation as a formidable also-ran—but an also-ran nonetheless—as he compiled seven runner-up and four third-place finishes in his first 86 starts. When he finally won his first PGA tour victory in 1997, the dam opened: He won the following tournament. And the one after that, too.

In the following two seasons, Duval won eight more times.

▶ The NFL's Arizona Cardinals didn't play an overtime game for a record 110 games before December 19, 1993. Over the next 67 games, they went to overtime an amazing 14 times.

▶ On May 30, 1927, Chicago Cubs shortstop James Cooney pulled off an unassisted triple play. The next day, Detroit Tigers first baseman John Neun duplicated the feat. In the entire history of baseball, there have been 11 unassisted triple plays.

▶ Before 1997, the American League had not had a pitching Triple Crown winner—leader in wins, ERA, and strikeouts—since 1945, when Hal Newhouser did it. Then, in a three-year span, Roger Clemens of the Toronto Blue Jays did it twice (1997–98) and Pedro Martinez of the Boston Red Sox once (1999).

▶ Because of greater parity in the NBA in the mid-1980s, it had become fashionable to believe that repeating as league champion was highly unlikely; after all, it hadn't happened since 1969, when the Boston Celtics defended their title. However, as soon as the Los Angeles Lakers pulled off a repeat after the 1988 season, it became uncommonly rare *not* to win multiple titles in a row: After the Lakers won two, the Detroit Pistons immediately followed with two consecutive titles, followed by the Chicago Bulls' three, the Houson Rockets' two, three more for the Bulls, a brief respite from multiplicity with the San Antonio Spurs' single title in the strike-shortened 1999 season, then the Lakers brought a return to the new normalcy with three in a row (through 2002).

▶ Fred Dryer, All-Pro defensive end for the Los Angeles Rams, holds the NFL record for most safeties in a game, two, and they are the only ones of his career.

▶ Eddie Collins is the only American Leaguer in the 20th century to steal six bases in a game, and he did it twice in under two weeks in 1912, on September 11 and 22.

▶ Only three batters hit balls during regulation games into the Polo Grounds center-field bleachers—and the second and third, Lou Brock and Hank Aaron, did it on consecutive days in 1962, June 17 and 18.

▶ Through the middle of the 1989 NFL season, Cincinnati Bengals running back James Brooks had not fumbled for 38 consecutive games. In his next seven games, he fumbled seven times.

▶ U. L. Washington hit two homers for the entire 1979 season, both of them on September 21st.

▶ The New York Yankees produced the most famous perfect game in major-league history—Don Larsen's gem in the 1956 World Series—then no more for four-plus decades. In 1998, David Wells pitched one for the Bombers. The following year, Yankee David Cone pitched one, too.

▶ The Tampa Bay Buccaneers lost the first 26 games in their history, the longest losing streak in NFL history. They broke the skein by winning the next-to-last game of the 1977 season. They liked that so much that they won the next week, too.

▶ Not long ago, Randy Johnson of the Arizona Diamondbacks was known as a phenomenal pitcher but one who couldn't perform in the clutch: Indeed, when he lost his first start of the 2001 playoffs, 4-1, to the St. Louis Cardinals, that made seven consecutive postseason losses for The Big Unit. Apparently, that was the last straw: In his next outing, Johnson had a three-hit shutout victory over the Braves in the League Championship Series, followed by the pennant-clincher; in the World Series against the Yankees, Johnson became the first pitcher to win three games since Detroit Tiger Mickey Lolich in 1968, and the first since St. Louis Cardinal Harry Breechen in 1946 to win Game 6 as a starter and Game 7 as a reliever. In shedding his un-clutch image—and shedding it with a vengeance—Johnson became the first pitcher ever to have five wins in one postseason.

▶ In the 14-year period from 1935–48 there were six horse-racing Triple Crown winners, then none until decades later, when Secretariat (1973), Seattle Slew (1977), and Affirmed (1978) each took the Crown in a six-year period. We're in the midst of another drought: Affirmed remains the last Triple Crown winner in 24 years and counting.

▷ Honorable mention: When the New York Rangers won the Stanley Cup in 1994, they broke the hex hanging over them—of being the NHL team that had gone longest without winning the Stanley Cup; 1940 was their previous championship—and happily turned over that unwanted title to the Detroit Red Wings, who hadn't won a Cup since 1955. Within two years, the Red Wings followed suit: In 1997, they broke *their* hex. (Detroit won the Cup again in 1998 and 2002.)

It Happened but Once:
27 of the Most Memorable "Onlys" in Sport

Science tells us that in most cases, if something happens once, it could happen again. If someone actually came along and broke Roger Maris's seemingly untouchable single-season home run record of 61, for example, then we'd have to believe it was possible someone else could break it, too. (And break it. And break it...)

There are other singular achievements, however, that cannot be ravaged by time: Ken Williams of the St. Louis Browns will always be the only non-Yankee to win an American League home run title in the 1920s. Chances are that CCNY will remain the only team to win the NCAA and NIT basketball tournaments in the same year (1950, beating Bradley in both finals) since schools today compete in either one or the other tournament, not both.

What follows is a collection of "onlys" that were true at the time of this writing.

▶ Gallant Fox is the only Triple Crown winner (1930) to sire another Triple Crown winner (Omaha, the 1935 winner).

▶ Eddie Arcaro is the only jockey to ride two Triple Crown winners. He won on Whirlaway in 1941 and Citation in 1948.

▶ Dave Krieg is the only alumnus of Milton College to play in the NFL, and he should remain that way. The school is now defunct.

▶ Brazil is the only nation to qualify for and take part in all 14 World Cups.

▶ England is the only country to participate in every Summer and Winter Olympics since the Games began in the modern era.

▶ Comedian Lenny Bruce claimed that the only baseball game he ever attended was Game 7 of the 1960 World Series (the Bill Mazeroski home run game).

▶ Archie Griffin of Ohio State is the only football collegian to win the Heisman Trophy twice (1974 and 1975).

▶ Jan Stenerud is the only (exclusive) placekicker in the Pro Football Hall of Fame.

(Hall of Famer George Blanda, who also placekicked, is known more for his other skill, quarterbacking, while Lou Groza was a kicker and also an offensive tackle.)

▶ The New York Yankees are the only one of the 30 major-league teams to vote against the 2002 labor agreement (a not surprising vote, since they appeared to have the most to lose, in both money and their ability to dominate).

▶ American Harold Osborn is the only Olympian to win the decathlon and an individual event (the high jump). He accomplished this at the 1924 Paris Games.

▶ The only track and field world record set at the 1984 Los Angeles Olympics was in the men's 4x100m relay (37.83 seconds), by the United States.

▶ Jim Clark of Great Britain is the only race car driver to win the Indianapolis 500 and the World Driving Championship in the same year (1965).

▶ Mel Stottlemyre balked only once in his career. He faced 10,972 batters.

▶ There was only one fan on hand to watch Washington State play a football game against San Jose State, on November 12, 1955.

▶ The U.S. Patent Office issued patent No. 4,911,433 for the Arena Football Game System, making the Arena Football League the only known sports league to play a patented, rival-free game.

▶ Sugar Ray Robinson failed to go the distance only once in 201 pro fights, against Joey Maxim in 1952. Tiring in intense heat, Robinson retired at the end of the 13th round.

▶ The Miami Dolphins are the only Super Bowl team to have gone a whole game without scoring a touchdown—Super Bowl VI, which they lost, 24-3, to the Dallas Cowboys.

▶ Buck Shaw's 1960 Eagles are the only team to beat Vince Lombardi's Green Bay Packers in a playoff game, winning 17-13. Lombardi won the other nine playoff games in which his teams appeared.

▶ Michael Johnson is the only man to win the 200m and 400m race in the same Olympics (the 1996 Atlanta Games).

▶ Mickey Owen is the only man to homer in an All-Star game (1942) who did not hit a home run during the regular season of the same year.

▶ Green Bay Packer Jim Taylor is the only running back to beat Cleveland Brown Jim Brown for the rushing title (in 1962) during Brown's career (1957 to 1965).

▶ Roger Maris won only one home run title, in 1961, though in his case that would seem enough.

▶ Joe Kuharich is the only Notre Dame football coach not to have a winning record. He was 17-23 from 1959 to 1962.

▶ Martina Navratilova's only loss in 87 matches in 1983 was to Kathy Horvath at the French Open, 6-4, 0-6, 6-3.

▶ Hall of Famer George Hainsworth is the only NHL goalie to register a season goals-against average of under 1.00 (0.98 in 1928–29).

▶ The Chicago Cubs are the only National League team not to have posted a winning record against the 1962 Mets.

▶ Pee Wee Reese is the only player to appear in every Brooklyn Dodgers–New York Yankees World Series game.

Babe Ruth Slept Here: A Few Notable Hitting Achievements by Pitchers

▶ Louisville's Guy Hecker is the only major-league pitcher to win a batting title. He hit .342 to lead the American Association in 1886. Hecker started 49 games, going 27-23 (including relief), and also played 22 games at first base and 17 in the outfield.

▶ The oldest man to hit a major-league home run is 46-year-old Jack Quinn, a pitcher for the Philadelphia Athletics, who hit the last of his eight career homers in 1930.

▶ In 1973, Philadelphia Phillies pitcher Ken Brett hit home runs in four consecutive games, on June 9, 13, 18, and 23.

▶ Strangely, before New York Yankee outfielder Marcus Thames hit a home run in his first major-league at-bat in June of 2002, both the last

American Leaguer (Esteban Yan) and the last National Leaguer (Gene Stechschulte) to accomplish the feat were pitchers.

▶ Red Lucas, a National League pitcher in the 1920s and 1930s, is eighth on the all-time pinch-hitting list (through 2001).

▶ Tony Cloninger, a starting pitcher for the Milwaukee Braves, hit two grand slams in one game. He did it against the San Francisco Giants on July 3, 1966. He hit 5 of his 11 career home runs that year.

▶ On April 21, 1898, Philadelphia pitcher Bill Duggleby hit a grand slam in his first major-league at-bat.

Close but No Cigar:
Athletes Who Barely Missed Records and Victories

▶ In less than a year—spanning the 1988–89 seasons—Toronto Blue Jays ace Dave Stieb pitched five one-hitters. In 1988, he twice lost no-hitters with two outs in the ninth. In 1989, he was one out from a perfect game when Roberto Kelly of the New York Yankees doubled. (Happily for Stieb, on September 2, 1990, he finally got his no-hitter, a 3-0 win over the Cleveland Indians.)

▶ Frank Hunter twice came within three games of winning the U.S. Open but lost in five-set finals, first to Henri Cochet in 1928, then to Bill Tilden in 1929.

▶ In recent history, several horses have had the chance to win the Triple Crown but missed—just barely—in the Belmont Stakes, the third leg, after winning the Kentucky Derby and the Preakness Stakes, the first two legs. In 1997, Silver Charm had a chance to achieve horse-racing immortality, but came in second at the Belmont, the sixth horse to place (be runner-up) at Belmont after those two big wins. In 1998, Real Quiet followed Silver Charm's example and also finished in second; the following year, Charismatic became the next Triple Crown near-miss by finishing third.

Bob Baffert trained Silver Charm, Real Quiet, and 2002's War Emblem, who also won the first two legs of the Triple Crown and then, after briefly holding the lead at the Belmont Stakes, faltered and finished a disappointing eighth.

▶ Since the "Curse of the Bambino" fell over the Boston Red Sox following their trade of Babe Ruth after the 1919 season, Boston has won just four American League pennants, and no World Series. What makes it particularly galling and painful to Bosox fans, though, is not just that they haven't won a Series in over 80 years, but that they've come so close to winning one each time they got there. In 1946, 1967, 1975, and 1986, the Red Sox took the Series to a seventh game. Each time, they lost.

▶ The Cleveland Indians were three outs from winning their first World Series in 49 years when they gave up a ninth-inning, Game 7-tying run to the Florida Marlins, who went on to win the game in extra innings.

▶ In the second Indianapolis 500, in 1912, Ralph DePalma, driving a Mercedes, took the lead 10 miles into the race, and led by 10 miles with six laps to go when his connecting rod snapped and the engine blew. Rather than stopping to fix it, DePalma tried to sputter home, slowing to 20 miles per hour—but still leading. Finally, on the home stretch of the 199th lap—still leading—his car died. DePalma and his mechanic tried to push the car to the finish line but couldn't do it. Joe Dawson passed them to win.

▶ On December 10, 1972, St. Louis Cardinals quarterback Jim Hart threw a 98-yard pass completion to Bobby Moore that, astonishingly, did not go for a touchdown.

▶ American Micki King was leading the 1968 Olympics springboard diving competition after 8 of 10 dives. She broke her arm on her penultimate dive, costing her the gold medal. (She took her last dive and finished fourth.)

▶ St. Bonaventure's basketball team was going for its 100th straight home win when Niagara beat them, 87-77, in February of 1961.

▶ Right-hander Charlie Ferguson won 99 games pitching for the National League Philadelphia team from 1884–87. Before he had a chance to win his 100th game, he died of typhoid fever on April 29, 1888, at the start of the new season.

▶ Sam Rice retired with 2,987 hits—the most of anyone not with 3,000 hits.

▶ In 1929, Lefty O'Doul hit .398—the closest anyone has come since 1900 without hitting .400. One more hit would have brought O'Doul to .400. (Harry Heilmann also hit .398 one year but in another year he hit .403.)

▶ Roy Face was 18-1 in 1959.

▶ Basketball star Anne Donovan, the 1983 Naismith College Player of the Year, played in 136 games at Old Dominion and scored 2,719 points, for a career scoring average of 19.9926 points per game. Although that rounds off to 20 points per game, she would have hit it exactly had she scored one more point.

▶ In 1986, Toronto Blue Jays relief pitcher Mark Eichhorn posted a 1.72 ERA but was five innings short of being considered for the ERA title he would have won.

▶ In 1939 and 1940, St. Louis Cardinal Johnny Mize won two of three categories for the hitting Triple Crown.

▶ American Fred Lorz almost got away with victory in the 1904 Olympic marathon. He was standing for a photograph with Alice Roosevelt, Teddy's daughter, and was ready to receive the gold medal when he was found out. Lorz had quit running 9 miles into the race, hitched a car ride for 11 miles, and then began to run again. Lorz was given a lifetime ban by the AAU. (He was re-instated later and won the 1905 Boston Marathon.)

High Heat

The need for speed runs deep in many sports—not only to move one's self faster, but also to send the ball of choice hurtling through space at ever-dizzying velocities. To throw a ball very fast earns one admiration and, particularly in baseball, some compelling, if curious, descriptions. A superior fastball has variously been described as smoke, high heat, high hard one, express, hard cheese, having mustard on it; a pitcher who throws such a ball is airing it out or bringing it.

A list of the top recorded speeds of various balls and other moving bodies, in miles per hour.

▶ A jai alai pelota: 188

▶ A golf ball driven off a tee: 170

▶ A Greg Rusedski tennis serve: 149

▶ A speed skier: 145

▶ A Venus Williams tennis serve: 128

▶ A Shawn Heins slapshot*: 106

▶ A ping pong ball: 105.6

▶ A Nolan Ryan fastball: 100.9

▶ A downhill skiier: 80

▶ A Frisbee (thrown by Alan Bonopane): 74

▶ A cheetah running: 63

▶ A horse running: 43

▶ A greyhound running: 42

▶ A Sugar Ray Robinson punch: 35

▶ Eric Heiden speedskating: 31

▶ Tim Montgomery running (during the fastest 10m interval of his world-record breaking 100m): 27

▶ Ian Thorpe swimming: 5+

And one extremely slow speed:

▶ A rope in tug-of-war, an Olympic sport from 1900 to 1920: 0.00084 (averaged)

*The stick used by the San Jose Shark defenseman to accomplish this is now in Toronto's Hockey Hall of Fame

18 Statistical Quirks, Coincidences, and Intrigues

▶ From 1949 to 1958, the New York Yankees reached 100 victories just once, in 1954—the only season in that stretch that they did *not* win the American League pennant. That year, the Cleveland Indians won an American League record 111 games. In each of the other nine years, the Yankees won the pennant with a victory total numbering in the nineties.

▶ In the 1950 season, Pittsburgh Pirates infielder Pete Castiglione made one error as a first baseman, two as a second baseman, three as a third baseman, and four as a shortstop.

▶ All of the New York Mets runs in a 16-4 win over the Houston Astros on July 27, 1985, were unearned. Houston made five errors in the game.

▶ The record for most career errors committed in baseball, with 1,096, is held by Herman "Germany" Long. The record for the second-most career errors, with 1,007, is held by George "Germany" Smith.

▶ Before 24-year-old quarterback Tom Brady led the New England Patriots to a Super Bowl win in 2002, New York Jet Joe Namath and San Francisco 49er Joe Montana had shared the distinction as the youngest quarterback to lead a team to a Super Bowl title. Each Joe did it when he was 25 years, 227 days old.

▶ Harry Heilmann won the American League batting title every other year from 1921–27.

▶ O. J. Simpson and Marcus Allen each starred as running back at the University of Southern California, each won a Heisman Trophy, and each gained 697 yards in his rookie NFL season.

▶ In the 1962 World Series, the New York Yankees won Games 1, 3, 5, and 7, and the San Francisco Giants took Games 2, 4, and 6.

Checkerboard wins have also marked the 1909 World Series, and the NBA Finals in 1952, 1954, 1960, 1970, and 1974.

▶ In 1953, twins Johnny and Eddie O'Brien each appeared in 89 games for the Pittsburgh Pirates, as rookie infielders.

▶ The fewest yards gained rushing in an NFL or AFL game is minus 53, by the Detroit Lions in 1943. The fewest yards gained passing in a game is minus 53, by the Denver Broncos in 1967.

▶ Eddie Mathews and Hank Aaron, Braves' teammates for over a decade, hit their 500th homers on July 14, one year apart.

▶ The two times that Babe Ruth hit three home runs in a World Series game were in Game 4 of the 1926 Series at Sportsman's Park in St. Louis, and Game 4 of the 1928 Series, at Sportsman's Park.

▶ From 1972–80, the Super Bowl was won by a team whose starting quarterback wore #12.

▶ Billy Herman played in four World Series, in three-year intervals— 1932, 1935, 1938, and 1941.

▶ From 1973–79, the worst regular season record the Washington Bullets compiled was their 44-38 in 1977–78—and that was the year they won their only NBA title.

▶ The all-time record attendance for Chicago's Old Comiskey Park, set on May 20, 1973, for a doubleheader between the White Sox and the Minnesota Twins, was 55,555.

▶ In 1975, the University of California football team gained 2,522 yards rushing and 2,522 yards passing.

▶ During his record 56-game hitting streak in 1941, Joe DiMaggio collected 56 singles and scored 56 runs.

3
CHANGE

●○●○●○●○●○●○●○●

11 Occasions That Were *Not* a Sign of Things to Come

▶ In his first major-league at-bat, New York Giants pitcher Hoyt Wilhelm hit a home run. (He hit no more for the rest of his 21-year career.)

▶ Scotty Bowman, then of the St. Louis Blues, lost the first 12 Stanley Cup Finals games he coached. (Of the next 46 Finals games he coached, he won 36 of them, good for a record nine championships.)

▶ The U.S.A. advanced to the semifinals of the first soccer World Cup, in 1930. (They have not been back to the semifinals since, and after their Cup appearance in 1950, did not qualify again for the competition until 1990.)

▶ On October 7, 1916, the Cumberland College football team's first play of the game was a rush that gained a respectable three yards. (It was their biggest rushing gain of the afternoon and they lost 222-0 to Georgia Tech, the worst rout in major college football history.)

▶ An American was the first to hold the official world ski jumping record, in 1924. (No American has held it since.)

▶ The Chicago Cubs showed promise of a dynasty when they won back-to-back World Series in 1907 and 1908. (They have not won one since.)

▶ The Cubs' American League soulmates, the Boston Red Sox, were also dynasty-bound when they went 4-for-4 in World Series play in a seven-year span during the 1910s. (They have not won another one, and are 0-for-4 in Series play since then.)

▶ Jockey Eddie Arcaro lost his first 250 races. (He went on to win two Triple Crowns, five Kentucky Derbys, six Belmonts, six Preaknesses, and a total of almost 5,000 races.)

▶ On September 17, 1967, the New Orleans Saints scored a touchdown on the opening kickoff of their first regular-season game of their first NFL season. (They went on to lose that game to the Los Angeles Rams, and then have 20 consecutive losing seasons.)

▶ In his first NFL game, Chicago Bear Walter Payton carried the ball eight times for a total of zero yards. (He went on to become the all-time leading rusher in NFL history.)

▶ Mike Parrott of the Seattle Mariners won on Opening Day, 1980. (He finished the season with a record of 1-16.)

There's Good News and There's Bad News: Happy Achievements Deflated by Less Happy Ones

An athlete may win the battle but lose the war; will perform spectacularly but end up with a loss; will achieve success on the field and, off the field, have it taken away.

The good news surrounding the following events was doused by bad news that was at least as, and usually more, profound.

▶ The USFL won its pivotal antitrust suit against the NFL in 1986. The new league had asked for $1,690,000,000 in treble damages; they were awarded $1, tripled to $3. The league disbanded.

▶ On the 1956 day that he pitched his World Series perfect game, New York Yankee Don Larsen was notified that his estranged wife, Vivian, had filed a court action seeking to withhold his Series money. She charged that Larsen was delinquent in his support payments.

▶ Russia's Larissa Lazutina won the 30km classic cross-country skiing gold medal at the 2002 Salt Lake City Games, her record-tying tenth winter Olympics medal. Within hours, she tested positive for darbepoetin, a performance-enhancing drug, and was stripped of the medal.

▶ On July 17, 1990, the Minnesota Twins executed two triple plays in one game—and lost, 1-0, to the Boston Red Sox at Fenway Park. (Oddly, the next night at Fenway, the same two teams combined to turn 10 double plays, a major-league record.)

▶ In June of 1997, six days after helping the Detroit Red Wings to win their first Stanley Cup in 42 years, defensemen Vladimir Konstantinov and Slava Fetisov, along with Red Wings' masseur Sergei Mnatsakanov, hired a limousine to drive them from a team party. The limo driver, who (unknown to the three passengers) had been cited for 11 traffic violations in the past seven years, including speeding and driving under the influence of alcohol, lost control of the car and crashed into a tree. Both Konstantinov and Mnatsakanov suffered life-threatening injuries, and were in comas for weeks; Fetisov suffered a bruised lung and chest contusions. (The driver, Richard Gnida, did not suffer serious injury, thanks to his driver-side airbag.) While both

Konstantinov and Mnatsakanov emerged from their comas, to this day they both suffer great physical and mental trauma.

▶ Ram's Horn finished in the money in the 1905 Kentucky Derby, taking third place. It might have been a distinguished finish except for one fact: In that year's Derby, only three horses ran.

▶ In 1966, American balloonist Nicholas Plantanida set the unofficial altitude record—23.45 miles—but died during the attempt.

▶ On September 15, 1969, St. Louis Cardinals pitcher Steve Carlton set a record for a nine-inning game by striking out 19 New York Mets, including outfielder Ron Swoboda twice. In each of Swoboda's other two at-bats, however, he hit a two-run homer, and the Mets beat Carlton, 4-3.

▶ On August 6, 1926, American Gertrude Ederle became the first woman to swim the English Channel. Her world-record time of 14 hours and 31 minutes was two hours faster than the men's record. Tragically, she became deaf as a result of her Channel swim.

▶ In 1977, Larry Biittner, an outfielder-infielder, once got to pitch an inning for the Chicago Cubs. He struck out the side, but also gave up six runs, for a lifetime ERA of 54.00.

▶ The Gordon Gin Company had a standing offer, until the year 2000, to award $1 million to any athlete who won two U.S. Opens. Unfortunately, the Gordon Gin Company meant tennis's U.S. Open *and* golf's U.S. Open.

▶ The 1960 New York Yankees recorded a team batting average of .338, the highest ever for a World Series, outscored their opponents, the Pittsburgh Pirates, 55-27, and out-hit them 91-60—and lost. (Looked at another way, the 1960 Pirates recorded a team ERA of 7.11—third-worst ever in a World Series—and won.)

▶ The Boston Bruins were 17-0-2 against the Philadelphia Flyers in their previous 19 meetings at Boston Garden and had the home ice advantage for the 1974 Stanley Cup finals—and lost. The 1988 New York Mets were 10-1 against the Los Angeles Dodgers during the regular season, and lost to them in the National League Championship Series.

▶ The longest known tennis point ever played took 51½ minutes, in a match between 11-year-olds Cari Hagey and Collette Kavanaugh at the 1977 Anaheim junior championships. Kavanaugh won the point but lost the match.

▶ On September 23, 2002, the night that St. Louis Rams All-Pro quarterback Kurt Warner attempted his 1,500th pass—the minimum number needed for inclusion in lists of NFL career passing records, many of which Warner immediately owned, or nearly did—he had one of his worst performances ever, throwing four interceptions in a dispiriting loss to the Tampa Bay Buccaneers.

▶ Michael Jordan's 63 points against the Boston Celtics in Game 2 of the first round of the 1986 playoffs set a postseason record, but his Chicago Bulls were still swept in three games.

▶ On April 23, 1964, Ken Johnson of the Houston Colt .45s became the first pitcher in history to throw a nine-inning complete game no-hitter and lose. He was beaten, 1-0, by the Cincinnati Reds.

▶ "Shoeless" Joe Jackson hit a robust .382 in 1920. However, it was his last year in baseball because he was banned for life for allegedly taking part in helping to fix the 1919 World Series.

▶ Johnny Gross won his super middleweight bout over Mike Caminiti in May 1989, but lapsed into a coma an hour later and died on January 28, 1990.

There's Bad News and There's Good News: Not-So-Happy Moments Offset by Somewhat Happier Ones

▶ In 1969, Penny Tweedy lost a coin flip for the right to choose the first foal of Bold Ruler. In compensation, Tweedy was given the first choice the following year. She picked a foal named Secretariat.

▶ In 1903, the Pittsburgh Pirates lost the World Series to the Boston Red Sox but received more money per player ($1,316) than the winners ($1,182) because the Pirates owner gave his share to the team.

▶ On Thanksgiving 1942, Boston College's undefeated football team was heavily favored to beat Holy Cross at Fenway Park. In a stunning upset, Holy Cross crushed BC, 55-12. In no mood to celebrate, the Eagles canceled their post-game party at the Cocoanut Grove nightclub. They ended up missing a massive fire that broke out at the club that night and took the lives of 491 people.

▶ In September of 1996, normally mild-mannered Baltimore Orioles second baseman Roberto Alomar became a national poster child for boorish athletic behavior when, during a game against the Toronto Blue Jays, he spit in the face of Umpire John Hirschbeck during a heated argument over balls and strikes (Alomar claimed that Hirschbeck said something to him that crossed a line). The incident became a flashpoint, and countless newspaper editorials and talk-radio shows dissected issues from the deterioration of respect for authority figures, to athlete-as-role-model, to differences between ethnic groups. Alomar was suspended for five games and would be brutally derided by fans in nearly every city he played in, for being a lout and worse. Alomar didn't help his cause when he surmised that Hirschbeck had been unusually strained because his (Hirschbeck's) son had died of a rare brain disease. In fact, Hirschbeck's other son, Michael, is afflicted with the same thing: adrenoleukodystrophy, or ALD, a degenerative genetic disease that causes brain inflammation. After trying to keep clear of Alomar—going so far as to stand on the shortstop side of second base when umping there for Orioles games—Hirschbeck decided one night to approach Alomar; the ump had been told that—all spitting aside—the second baseman was a good guy. The two men quickly buried the hatchet, and Alomar set to work, devoting time and raising significant money for a foundation the Hirschbecks started to find a cure for ALD.

Today, Hirschbeck and Alomar consider each other friends.

▶ In nine consecutive playoff series, the New York Rangers lost Game 1 —but they won six of the nine series.

▶ The embarrassing record for the fewest field goals made (207) in a seven-game NBA Final is held by Syracuse in the 1955 series against Fort Wayne. Syracuse still won the title.

▶ In 1982, Rickey Henderson was *caught* stealing 42 times—a major-league record. This was overshadowed, however, by his more significant major-league record feat: stealing 130 bases.

▶ Tom Okker lost the men's singles final of the 1968 U.S. Open to Arthur Ashe. However, Ashe was an amateur at the time and thus could receive no prize money, so Okker got the first-place check of $14,000.

▶ New York Yankees pitcher Whitey Ford lost more World Series games than anyone else, but he also won more than anyone else. Overall, he was 10-8 and had a Series ERA of 2.71. Similarly, Nolan Ryan has the record for issuing the most career walks but also the most career strikeouts, and Cy Young holds the record for most career losses (313) but, more significant, the most wins (511).

▶ Jacqueline Pung had the lowest total in the 1957 U.S. Open but signed a scorecard that stated incorrectly that she had made a five at the fourth hole, not a six. While her total score was correct, Pung was disqualified. The sympathetic members of Winged Foot took up a collection for Pung that eventually totaled more than $3,000. The first-prize check for winning the Open was $1,800.

▶ In 1981, the Detroit Pistons lost the coin flip for the #1 pick to the Dallas Mavericks. With the first pick, Dallas chose Mark Aguirre. With the second pick, the Pistons chose Isiah Thomas.

▶ Lars Hall of Sweden won the Olympic modern pentathlon in 1952 when the horse he drew turned up lame and the substitute given to him was the best horse in Finland.

▶ In perhaps the finest example of an athlete losing the battle and winning the war—almost literally: After boxer Eugene Criqui of France was struck in the jaw by a German bullet during World War I, a silver plate was attached to the shattered bone. After the war, the plate actually helped Criqui resist punches and he went on to win the world welterweight title.

Finally, There's Good News and There's Bad News— And Then There's Good News Once Again

▶ When the 1962 AFL title game between the Dallas Texans and the Houston Oilers went into overtime, Dallas won the coin toss. In a moment of paramount stupidity, they proceeded to give up both the ball and the wind.

Dallas still won.

Changing Names

Cassius Clay and Lew Alcindor are the two most prominent American athletes to have changed their names, retitling themselves Muhammad Ali and Kareem Abdul-Jabbar, respectively, when they became Black Muslims. Athletes have changed their names for religious and other reasons—self-promotion, peace of mind, to honor someone else. Many other things in the realm of sport—institutions, prizes, even sports themselves —have changed names.

▶ Boxer Marvin Hagler officially changed his name to Marvelous Marvin Hagler.

▶ Cornelius McGillicuddy was the given name of Philadelphia Athletics owner and manager Connie Mack.

▶ Stanford University's athletic teams, called the Indians since 1930, were renamed the Cardinals in 1972 because of protests by Native Americans.

▶ Los Angeles Laker Michael Thompson had the spelling of his first name legally changed to Mychal.

▶ Lexington, a great thoroughbred racehorse and sire from the late 1800's, was originally named Darley, after the Darley Arabian, one of the three original sires of all modern thoroughbreds. After racing under the name Darley as a three-year-old, the horse was purchased under the condition that his name be changed to Lexington, for Lexington, Kentucky.

▶ Basketball star Walt Hazzard became Mahdi Abdul-Rahman after he graduated from UCLA. He later changed his name back to Walt Hazzard.

▶ Duke All-America basketball guard Jason Williams changed his name to Jay Williams, presumably so he wouldn't be confused with NBA guard Jason Williams (or with Jayson Williams, the former New Jersey Nets forward indicted on reckless manslaughter charges in 2002).

▶ After 1935, the Downtown Athletic Club Trophy was renamed the Heisman Trophy. (Jay Berwanger, the award's first recipient, was the only one to win the Downtown Athletic Club Trophy.)

▶ Andre Rouisimoff and Terry Bollea became, respectively, Andre the Giant and Hulk Hogan, professional wrestlers.

▶ Oakland Athletics owner Charlie O. Finley wanted star pitcher Vida Blue to change his first name to "True." Blue refused and told Finley that if he liked the name so much, he should call himself True O. Finley.

▶ Miami Dolphins wide receiver Mark Duper went to court in 1985 and changed his name to Mark Super Duper.

▶ Tennis player Richard Raskind changed his name to Renee Richards after his sex change operation. In her first women's tournament—the La Jolla Championships—before her previous identity was discovered, she played under the name Renee Clark.

▶ The New York Jets used to be called the New York Titans, the New England Patriots were the Boston Patriots, the Anaheim Angels were the California Angels and before that the Los Angeles Angels, and the New York Yankees were the New York Highlanders.

▶ Philadelphia 76er gunner and playground legend Lloyd Free changed his name to World B. Free.

▶ In 1957, Oklahoma A&M became Oklahoma State. In 1967, Texas Western, whose basketball team won the NCAA finals the year before, became the University of Texas-El Paso (UTEP).

▶ The father of Olympic cross-country skier Bill Koch, exasperated with mispronunciations of his name, had it legally changed to Frederick Coke Is It.

▶ Before it opened in 1965, the Houston Astrodome was called Harris County Domed Stadium. The Astros themselves were called the Colt .45s from 1962–65.

▶ Golfer Phil McGleno changed his name in 1978, combining the nickname of a friend and his mother's maiden name, to arrive at Mac O'Grady.

▶ Tennis used to be known as lawn tennis, and before that, sphairistike.

▶ Heavyweight champion Jack Dempsey, born William Harrison Dempsey, started fighting in 1914 under the name Kid Blackie.

▶ With the addition of Arizona and Arizona State in 1978, the Pacific-8 became the Pacific-10 (Pac-10). (The Big Ten added Penn State in 1990 and, for apparently quaint reason that we applaud, *stayed* the Big Ten. With eleven schools.)

▶ Notre Dame's athletic teams used to be known as the Catholics and later the Ramblers. They officially became the Fighting Irish in 1927.

▶ When José Gonzalez was traded in 1985 from the St. Louis Cardinals to the San Francisco Giants in the Jack Clark deal, Gonzalez decided to use his mother's maiden name and became José Uribe. He has come to be known as the literal "player to be named later."

31 of the Most Dramatic Turnarounds and Comebacks

▶ After retiring from a successful swimming career that included two Olympic gold medals, Dara Torres decided, after many years off, to try coming back. She got herself in shape, became the oldest swimmer, at 33, to break an American swimming record in the modern era, and made the 2000 U.S. Olympic team that went to Sydney, where she won two gold and three bronze medals.

▶ In 1916, the football team from tiny Centre (Danville, Kentucky) College lost 68-0 to the University of Kentucky. In 1917, Centre came back and won, 3-0.

▶ In the 1999 European Cup soccer final, Manchester United was down, 1-0, to Bayern Munich at the end of 90 minutes... and still won, and without going to overtime. The English team scored two goals in stoppage play, the stunning game-winner coming just seconds before the final whistle.

▶ Dave Schultz, the chief Philadelphia Flyer goon of the first half of the 1970s, became the commissioner of the Atlantic Coast Hockey League and tried to rid the league of fighting.

▶ In late 1997, Golden State Warrior swingman and star Latrell Sprewell became a national pariah when, after a tense practice in which he argued with P. J. Carlesimo, who was in his first season coaching the Warriors, Sprewell choked Carlesimo. After team and league suspensions, lawsuits, and much venom on talk radio about the decaying moral fiber of the country, etc., Sprewell was finally unloaded, in 1998, to the New York Knicks. By the end of the 1998–99 NBA season, in which a scrappy Knicks team suprisingly made it to the Finals, Sprewell was not only appreciated for his play, but admired for his calm, reasonable off-court manner.

▶ In April 2001, Annika Sorenstam entered the final day of the Office Depot women's golf tournament 10 strokes back, but won in a playoff (after a major collapse by Pat Hurst), setting an LPGA record. (It also gave Sorenstam her fourth win in a row.)

▶ In 1998, the Ohio State University men's basketball team went 1-15 in the Big Ten. The following season, they made it to the Final Four.

▶ Italy's Paolo Rossi scored three goals in the 1982 World Cup semi-finals, and six goals overall. Only nine weeks earlier, he was still serving a multiple-year suspension by the Italian Football Federation for a 1980 betting scandal (though he'd been found not guilty by the Italian courts).

▶ Down 10-6 against Europe going into the last day of the 1999 Ryder Cup, American golfers stormed back to win 8½ of 12 singles matches to win the competition, 14½-13½, and reclaim the Cup.

▶ On August 5, 2001, in the greatest run-differential comeback in a major-league game in 76 years, the Cleveland Indians beat the Seattle

Mariners, 15-14, in 11 innings, after being down 12-0, and down to their last strike three times.

▶ In 1978–79, the Boston Celtics were 29-53. In June of 1979, they signed Larry Bird. Their next season they were 61-21.

The 1996–97 NBA season—the one that preceded the San Antonio Spurs' drafting of Clemson center Tim Duncan #1 overall—the Spurs were 20-62. In Duncan's rookie season with the Spurs, they were 56-26.

▶ Four years before Brazilian striker Ronaldo was named MVP of the 2002 World Cup—he was the tournament's leading goal scorer and tallied both goals in Brazil's 2-0 victory in the final over Germany—he was widely panned by his countrymates (and soccer fans the world over) for his listless performance in the 1998 World Cup final versus France. His sub-par play in that match was attributed to the aftermath of a fit he'd suffered just hours before the match, the source of which was alleged to have been everything from food poisoning to epilepsy to sheer panic.

▶ Heavyweight Henry Cooper of England lost the first three title fights of his career, for the British, Commonwealth, and European titles. He later won all three.

▶ Although he'd had a legendary career as football coach of Notre Dame, Lou Holtz was thought to have used up the last bit of his magic there when, two years later, he took the head coaching job at the University of South Carolina. And his doubters seemed right when the Gamecocks went 0-11 in Holtz's first year, 1999, extending the school's losing streak to 21 games, the longest in the country. But the following year, USC compiled an 8-4 record, beat Ohio State in the Outback Bowl, and won a place in the final Top 20 national rankings—the biggest turnaround in SEC football history, and the school's best season in their 107 years of playing the game. The following year, the Gamecocks went 9-3 and again beat Ohio State in the Outback Bowl.

▶ Austria's great skier with the idiotic nickname—Herman "The Hermanator" Maier—survived a spectacular fall on the men's downhill event at the 1998 Nagano Olympic Games, then recovered enough to win gold in both the giant slalom and the super G.

▶ Shea Ralph, former All-America basketball player for University of Connecticut and 40th pick in the 2001 WNBA draft, has torn her anterior cruciate ligament (ACL) five times—the left three times, the right twice. She came back after the first four injuries, and, as of this writing, is working her way back to the court following the fifth.

▶ In 1928, the New York Giants were 4-7-2. In 1929, with the University of Michigan's great star, Benny Friedman, at quarterback, the Giants went 13-1-1.

▶ The Atlanta Braves were in a comfortable position after five innings of Game 4 of the 1996 World Series: Already up two games to one, they'd built a 6-0 lead on New York, with the prospect of that year's eventual Cy Young Award winner, John Smoltz, starting the next night at home for a potential Series-clinching win. But the Yankees rallied to tie the game on Jim Leyritz's three-run homer in the eighth inning off of Braves' closer Mark Wohlers, then won it, 8-6, with two runs in the 10th, the tie-breaker coming when pinch hitter Wade Boggs drew a two-out, bases-loaded walk off of Steve Avery, after Boggs had fallen behind on the count, 1-2. The Yankees won the next two games to take their first World Series title of the Joe Torre regime.

▶ Evonne Goolagong lost in the first round of the 1970 Wimbledon. The next year, she won the tournament.

▶ At the other extreme, Manuel Santana won Wimbledon in 1966, but was beaten in the first round the following year by Charlie Pasarell. Santana was the first champion to have been eliminated so unceremoniously.

▶ A few weeks before the U.S. Olympic hockey team upset the Soviets at the 1980 Olympics, the U.S.S.R. beat the Americans by seven goals.

▶ Bobby Lowe of Boston's National League team was 0-for-6 in the first game of a May 30, 1894, doubleheader. In the second game, he hit four home runs.

▶ In 1939, Stanford University's football team lost every conference game. They hired a new head coach, Clark Shaughnessy, who experimented with a T-formation. Stanford responded with an unbeaten season and a Rose Bowl win over Nebraska, and helped to popularize the T-formation.

▶ Between 1930 and 1939, the St. Louis Browns drew an average of 115,000 fans per year. When the franchise moved to Baltimore in 1954, the team's attendance in the first year almost topped the total for that entire decade in St. Louis.

▶ Martin Gison of the Philippines, who finished fourth in the small-bore rifle (prone) competition at the 1936 Olympics, survived the Bataan death march in World War II and competed again in 1948.

▶ The Seattle Mariners, 13 games behind the (then-) California Angels in August of 1995, not only made up the deficit with a tremendous September run—at the end of which the Mariners pummeled the dispirited Angels, 9-1, in a one-game playoff—but in winning over so many late-season fans, may have saved baseball in the Emerald City, since the Mariners were threatening to leave if they didn't get a new stadium. While a September initiative for the funding of a new stadium failed narrowly, the governor called for a special session of the state legislature, which on October 14—while the Mariners were playing the Cleveland Indians in the American League Championship Series—approved an alternate financing plan that resulted in beautiful Safeco Field, which opened in 1999.

▶ Dale Ellis averaged 8.2 points per game in three seasons with the Dallas Mavericks. In 1986, he was traded to the Seattle Supersonics and in his first season there averaged 24.9 points a game.

▶ Al Singer won the lightweight boxing title with a first-round (1:46) knockout of Sammy Mandell on July 17, 1930. Singer lost the lightweight title on November 14, 1930, on a first-round knockout by Tony Canzoneri (1:06).

▶ After clinching the Eastern League pennant in mid-August of 1884, the Wilmington Quicksteps replaced Philadelphia in the Union Association. They proceeded to compile the worst record in the history of the major leagues.

▶ In 1833, Irish heavyweight champion Simon Byrne demolished Sandy McKay, who died from the beating. Three years later, Byrne died as a result of his 98-round beating at the hands of English champion James "Deaf" Burke.

3 Gradual Turnarounds

▶ The Detroit Pistons ushered in the 1980s with a then-NBA record losing streak of 21 games, and saw the decade out with their first NBA championship.

▶ Tennis phenom Jennifer Capriati became the youngest Grand Slam semifinalist ever (at age 14) when she blasted her way through at the 1990 French Open, the following year eliminated Martina Navratilova at Wimbledon, won numerous tournaments, rose to the #6 ranking in the world and, at age 15, was listed 26th in *Forbes* magazine's list of highest-paid athletes, with roughly $500,000 in prize money and an estimated $4.5 million in endorsements. Soon enough, though, she began to lose it—dismissing her coach after arguments about applying herself at practice; injuries or reported injuries; losing in early rounds to lesser players; gaining weight, and / or reacting badly to charges that she was gaining weight; and finally, at age 17, an arrest for shoplifting (though she was never prosecuted). Later, she was arrested on a drug charge (though never formally charged) and entered drug rehabilitation, and began to drop off the tennis map; her career, if not her future in general, was pretty much written off by those who write these things off. After time away, though, Capriati attempted to return to professional tennis, but bad and distracted play and many early-round losses seemed to render the dream just that. In 1999, her results improved, she reached two Grand Slam Rounds of 16 and, at age 23, won multiple Comeback Player of the Year awards. Ups and downs, both on and off the court, continued. Finally, in 2001, Capriati enjoyed her greatest professional success ever, winning the Australian Open, the French Open, earning the #1 rank in the world, and picking up where she'd left off, a decade before.

▶ In their first season, 1962, the New York Mets compiled the worst record in 20th century baseball, 40-120. At decade's end, the Mets won 100 regular season games and the World Series.

1 Excruciatingly Gradual Turnaround

▶ In 1883, the Philadelphia Phillies, in their first season in the National League, were last with a 17-81 record, while Baltimore was last in the American Association at 28-68. One hundred years later, in 1983, Baltimore and the Phillies faced off in the World Series. (Baltimore won.)

Defunct Olympic Events

Ancient Olympic competitions tested not only athletic skills but creative, intellectual, and rhetorical powers, as well. Poetry, music, and eloquence were just three of the "events" contested at the ancient Games.

The modern-day Games are supposedly devoted to testing athletic prowess exclusively, though many surprising events have found their way onto the Olympic docket, primarily in the earliest Games—in Athens in 1896, Paris in 1900, St. Louis in 1904, and Athens again, site of the Interim Olympic Games in 1906. The following events have since been removed from the Olympic program, often after one appearance and usually with good reason.

▶ Live pigeon shooting (1900). This is the only event in Olympic history in which animals were killed intentionally. Leon de Lunden of Belgium won the gold medal, with 21 birds killed, one more than Frenchman Maurice Faure bagged.

▶ A 100m freestyle swim that was open only to members of the Greek navy (1896).

▶ Tug-of-war (1900–20). In 1908, after a humiliating first-round loss to the British, the Americans protested that the British had used illegal spiked boots. When the protest was disallowed, the Americans withdrew.

▶ Croquet (1900).

▶ Dueling pistols (1906).

▶ Plunge for distance (1904).

▶ Underwater swimming (1900).

▶ The standing broad jump (1900–12).

▶ The standing long jump (1900–12).

▶ The standing triple jump (1900 and 1904).

▶ Motor boating (1908).

If You Can't Beat 'Em, Join 'Em

▶ While playing for the St. Louis Cardinals, Jack Clark delivered one of the most infamous home runs in Dodger history, a three-run blast off of reliever Tom Niedenfuer with two outs in the ninth inning of Game 6 in the 1985 National League Championship Series, lifting the Cardinals into the World Series. Clark's homer turned a 5-4 Dodger lead into a 7-5 Cardinal victory. In 2000, the Dodger organization hired Clark—who'd also played for the Dodgers' archrivals, the San Francisco Giants, from 1975–84—as a minor-league hitting coach for Class A San Bernardino, and in 2001 he was made the Dodgers' hitting coach. On Opening Day at Dodger Stadium, he was booed.

▶ Lleyton Hewitt, who was coached for four years by fellow Australian Darren Cahill, seemed finally to have figured out Andre Agassi's number—beating him several times, and soundly—as Hewitt climbed to #1 in the world and won the 2001 U.S. Open. Just months after that Grand Slam victory, Hewitt and Cahill parted ways; just hours after Agassi parted ways with *his* longtime coach, Brad Gilbert, he called Cahill to gauge his interest in coaching him. Cahill agreed and, several months later, watched from his box during the semifinals of the 2002 U.S. Open to see his new pupil, the older player, upset his old pupil, the younger player.

▶ In 1992, Domino's Pizza magnate Tom Monaghan decided to sell the Detroit Tigers, which he'd owned since 1983. The purchaser? His pizza archrival, Mike Ilitch, founder of the competing Little Caesar's chain.

▶ In his first six major-league seasons, Vince Coleman of the St. Louis Cardinals was successful on 57 consecutive steal attempts against the New York Mets before Mets catcher Mackey Sasser finally threw him out twice in 1990. The following off-season, the Mets signed Coleman to a four-year, $11.95 million contract. "On behalf of our catchers, welcome to New York," Mets manager Bud Harrelson told Coleman during a welcoming phone call.

(Coleman, who had averaged 92 steals a season for the Cardinals, stole just 99 bases total in three tumultuous years with the Mets, and was suspended by the team in July of 1993 after detonating a large firecracker near a group of fans outside Dodger Stadium. Owner Fred Wilpon declared that Coleman would never again play for the Mets. After the season, he was traded to the Kansas City Royals.)

▶ In 2002, the name of CMGI Field, home of the New England Patriots, was changed to Gillette Stadium, for their new sponsor, the shaving-products company. From 1988 to 1992, the Patriots were owned by Victor Kiam, who also owned Remington Products Company, the shaving-products company, and one of Gillette's main rivals.

▶ In 1998, the size of the considerable payment that the nearly-bankrupt Pittsburgh Penguins still owed their retired superstar Mario Lemieux became public.

In June of 1999, Lemieux, along with business partners Howard Baldwin and Roger Marino, bought the Penguins.

A year later, Lemieux announced his un-retirement, immediately boosting season ticket sales.

▶ Larry Dierker pitched for the Houston Astros from 1964–76, and was a "color analyst" on Astros broadcasts from 1979 to 1996. When Terry Collins was fired as Houston's manager after the 1996 season, Dierker's job went from analyzing Astros strategy to determining it. Moving from the broadcast booth to become their manager, he led the Astros to four National League Central division titles in four years, but resigned after the 2001 season when the Astros were eliminated in the first round of the playoffs for the fourth time under Dierker, who was no doubt second-guessed by the current Astros broadcasters.

▶ In both 2000 and 2001, Jason Giambi's Oakland Athletics suffered excruciating losses to the New York Yankees in the American League division series, both times extending the Yankees to five games in the best-of-five series. After the 2001 season, Giambi declared free agency and signed with the Yankees for $120 million over seven years. (Unfortunately for Giambi, his first year with the Yankees was the first year since 1997 that they did not go to the World Series.)

▷ Honorable mention #1: In each of the three years that Brett Hull played for the Dallas Stars—from the 1998–99 through 2000–01 seasons—his team went further in the playoffs (including winning the Stanley Cup in 1999, and losing in the Finals in 2000) than their suddenly mortal Western Conference foes, the Detroit Red Wings. In the summer of 2001, the Red Wings signed Hull as a free agent. In the spring, he helped the Red Wings win the Stanley Cup.

▷ Honorable mention #2: For several years running—pun intended—the Sacramento Kings had been one of the NBA's most exciting and uptempo teams, an offensive powerhouse with scant interest in playing defense. In 1997, realizing that they would get no better—and not go far in the postseason, if they could make it—without more defensive effort, Kings management hired as assistant coach Pete Carril, a former basketball coaching legend at Princeton, whose college teams routinely placed in the top ten in the nation in scoring defense. (In Carril's second year there, the Kings posted their first winning record in fifteen years. They also began to play defense.)

Rules and Conventions That Changed

▶ For the first two years of the Indianapolis 500, cars lined up in the order that their entries were received. In 1914, a drawing was held. In 1915, for the first time, cars lined up in order of qualifying speed.

▶ In 19th-century baseball, runners were credited with a stolen base if they went from first to third on a single, and walks were counted as hits when computing batting average.

▶ Until the 1915–16 season, it was against the rules for a basketball player to shoot off the dribble. In 1923–24, the designated foul shooter was eliminated; after that, a fouled player had to shoot his own foul shots.

▶ The Preakness used to be scheduled before the Kentucky Derby.

▶ In 1903, and from 1919 to 1921, the World Series was a best-of-nine games affair.

▶ In the first Rose Bowl in 1902, a touchdown counted for five points, field goals five points, and conversions one point. The game was played on a 110-yard field at Tournament Park.

▶ In 1893, the distance from the mound to home plate was extended from 50 feet to its present distance, 60'6".

▶ In 1920, all "freak" pitches, including the spitball, were outlawed, though pitchers who relied on that pitch and were already in the major leagues—and only they—were allowed to continue throwing the pitch.

▶ Golf's U.S. Open used to conclude with a double round of 36 holes.

▶ Until 1953–54, if an NBA player committed three personal fouls in a quarter, he had to sit out the remainder of the period.

▶ The winner of a running race used to be the first person to cross the line; now, the winner is the first person to reach the finish line. In the 1932 Olympic 100m, American sprinter Ralph Metcalfe finished in a dead heat with teammate Eddie Tolan, but a split second later, pictures showed that Tolan's chest had crossed the line while Metcalfe's had not yet done so. Tolan won the gold medal, Metcalfe the silver. Under the current rules, they would have shared the gold.

▶ There is now an age limit in Olympic gymnastics requiring that competitors be at least 16 years of age during the year of the Games. Had this rule been in effect in 1976, Nadia Comaneci would not have been deemed old enough to compete.

▶ Before baseball adopted the nine-inning-game rule in 1857, the first one to score 21 runs was the winner.

▶ Until 1937, there was a jump ball after every basket in NCAA play. In the 1939–40 season, the National Basketball League did away with the jump ball after every basket.

▶ Wimbledon, the U.S. Championships, and the Davis Cup all used a Challenge Round. The winner of the Challenge Round would face the defending champion to determine the next champion. The America's Cup sailing competition still uses the challenge method.

▶ The PGA tournament used to be match play.

▶ On December 26, 1985, the European Parliament was petitioned to ban the increasingly popular sport of "dwarf throwing."

Alice in Wonderland Meets the Sports World: 16 Mirror Images and Things in Reverse

▶ Ma Chin-shan of Taiwan, who competed in pistol shooting at the 1964 Tokyo Olympics, asked to return to mainland China to live with his parents. He is the only Olympic athlete ever to defect *to* a communist country.

▶ Walter Johnson won Game 7 of the 1924 World Series. In the 1925 World Series, he lost Game 7.

▶ The greatest number of interceptions quarterback Sammy Baugh threw in a single game was four. As a defensive back, Baugh is co-holder of the NFL record for interceptions in a single game, with four.

▶ The heart of Frenchman Joseph Guillemot, the 5,000m champion at the 1920 Olympics, was located on the right side of his chest.

▶ The McKeever twins, Mike and Marlin, were all-conference football players for USC in 1959. Mike wore uniform #68, Marlin #86.

▶ In 1963, at 23 years and two months, Jack Nicklaus became the youngest golfer (at the time) to win the Masters. In 1986, when he was 46, Nicklaus became the oldest player to win the Masters.

▶ St. Louis Cardinals pitcher Bob Gibson lost his first World Series decision, won his next seven, then lost his last decision.

▶ Boxer Nelson Azumah changed his name to Azumah Nelson.

▶ In September 2000, the Indianapolis Motor Speedway hosted its first Formula Once event. It was the first time a race was run there in which cars went clockwise.

▶ When NBC tennis broadcaster Bud Collins was coach of the Brandeis (Massachusetts) University tennis team, one of his players was future radical Yippie leader Abbie Hoffman, whom Collins claimed was one of the most conservative baseliners ever.

▶ In 1998, the Indianapolis Colts were a terrible 3-13. The following season, they were a terrific 13-3.

▶ In 1976, Don Gullett pitched the opening game of the World Series against the New York Yankees. The following year, he pitched the opening game of the Series for the Yankees.

▶ Many trapshooters use alcohol or tranquilizers to slow their heart rates and steady their hands. Paul Cerutti, 65, a trapshooter from Monaco, was disqualified at the 1976 Olympics for taking amphetamines.

▶ In May of 1931, Auguste Piccard of Switzerland, along with a companion, became the first humans to reach the stratosphere when they ballooned to 51,961 feet over Augsburg, Germany. In January of 1960, Piccard's son, Jacques, and a companion, in a bathyscope, reached the record depth of 6.78 miles in the Pacific Ocean, southwest of Guam.

▶ In the 2000–01 college season, Middlebury (Vermont) College won both the women's and men's Division III lacrosse titles; UCLA won both the women's and men's national water polo titles.

▶ "Australian doubles" is what Americans call it when tennis partners, on serve, both stand on the server's half of the court. "American doubles" is what Australians call it when tennis partners, on serve, both stand on the server's half of the court.

11 Commonly Flouted Baseball Rules

Although the game of baseball is structure incarnate, its rulebook a Baedeker that speaks to virtually every on-field occasion, the game conducts itself with a degree of elasticity. Umpires, for instance, routinely allow the "phantom" double play, in which the shortstop makes the relay to first base and avoids colliding with the oncoming runner but never quite touches second base. Third-base coaches who stray from the coaching box to wave a player home or hold him up may literally be breaking Rule 4.05.b.2, but a commentary in the book of *Official Baseball Rules* (published by *The Sporting News*, 2002 Edition) suggests that there is no need to enforce this rule strictly unless the opposing manager complains. And while Rule 2.00 does its best to define the strike zone, God knows that no two umpires call the same one. Ask any pitcher or batter.

Various edicts from the rule book are commonly ignored by players, coaches, and umpires—sometimes with good reason, sometimes with malice aforethought.

▶ From Rule 3.09: "Players of opposing teams shall not fraternize at any time while in uniform."

▶ From Rule 8.04: "When the bases are unoccupied, the pitcher shall deliver the ball to the batter within 20 seconds after he receives the ball. Each time the pitcher delays the game by violating this rule, the umpire shall call 'Ball.'"

▶ From Rule 3.01.e: "After a home run is hit out of the playing grounds, the umpire shall not deliver a new ball to the pitcher or the catcher until the batter hitting the home run has crossed the plate."

▶ Rule 3.02: "No player shall intentionally discolor or damage the ball by rubbing it with soil, rosin, paraffin, licorice, sand-paper, emery-paper, or other foreign substance."

▶ From Rule 3.17: "Players on the disabled list are permitted to participate in pre-game activity and sit on the bench during a game but may not take part in any activity during the game such as... bench-jockeying."

▶ From Rule 1.10.a: "The bat shall be one piece of solid wood."

▶ From Rule 6.02.b: "Umpires may grant a hitter's request for 'Time' once he is in the batter's box, but the umpire should eliminate hitters walking out of the batter's box without reason. If umpires are not lenient, batters will understand that they are in the batter's box and they must remain there until the ball is pitched."

▶ From Rule 9.05 (General Instructions to Umpires): "Umpires, on the field, should not indulge in conversation with players... and do not talk to the coach [in the coaching box] on duty."

▶ From Rule 5.09.e: "When... a foul ball is not caught the umpire shall not put [a new] ball in play until all runners have retouched their bases."

▶ From Rule 9.05 (General Instructions to Umpires): "You no doubt are going to make mistakes, but never attempt to 'even up' after having made one."

▶ From Rule 8.02. d: "To pitch at a batter's head is unsportsmanlike and highly dangerous. It should be—and is—condemned by everybody."

It Makes No Difference to Them: Sports Figures Unflustered by a Change in Circumstance

▶ Ethiopia's Abebe Bikila won the 1960 marathon running barefoot. He defended his title in 1964 running in shoes and socks.

▶ In 1929, Notre Dame's new football stadium was under construction, so the team played no games at home. They went 9-0.

▶ In a three-year period, the Seattle Mariners lost the three best players in their franchise's history and didn't seem to lose a step; indeed, they seemed just to get better. Hall of Fame-bound pitcher Randy Johnson was traded to the Houston Astros late in the 1998 season, and Hall of Fame-bound outfielder Ken Griffey, Jr., was traded to the Cincinnati Reds after the '99 season. In 2000, the Mariners made the playoffs as the American League's wild-card team and advanced to the A.L. Championship Series before losing to the eventual World Series champion Yankees. In 2001, the season following the departure of Hall of Fame-bound shortstop Alex Rodriguez to the Texas Rangers, where he signed the richest contract in baseball history, the Mariners barely regrouped... to win 116 games, tying the record for most victories in a season.

▶ The Mariners' chief rivals, the promising (and low-budget) Oakland As, lost slugging star and team leader Jason Giambi to the New York Yankees in the 2001–02 off-season, after going a robust 102-60. Clearly devastated by Giambi's loss, in 2002 the As ran off an American League-record 20-game winning streak and again made the playoffs.

▶ Boxer Craig Bodzianowski won a 10-round decision over Francis Sargent. Bodzianowski was later involved in a motorcycle accident and lost part of his leg. With an artificial leg, Bodzianowski continued his boxing career. On December 14, 1985, he once again faced Sargent and this time knocked him out in the second round.

▶ College basketball coaches Lefty Driesell, Jim Harrick, and Eddie Sutton have each taken four different schools to the NCAA tournament.

▶ Irina Rodnina of the U.S.S.R. won four skating pairs titles with Aleksei Ulanov, from 1969–72, then six more with her husband, Aleksandr Zaitsev, from 1973–78.

▶ Between 1960 and 1965, Australian tennis star Roy Emerson won six successive French Open doubles titles with five different partners.

Françoise Durr of France was runner-up in six Wimbledon doubles finals with five partners.

▶ Playing in an afternoon game for the New York Mets on August 4, 1982, Joel Youngblood got a single off of Chicago Cubs pitching great

Ferguson Jenkins. During the game, Youngblood was traded to the Montreal Expos. He flew to Philadelphia, and that evening got a single off of Philadelphia Phillies pitching great Steve Carlton.

▶ As a junior at Illinois, Andy Phillips was an All-America basketball player in 1943. Phillips then spent three years in the Marine Corps. He returned for his senior year in 1946–47 and again was an All-America.

▶ Tennis partners Adrian Quist and Frank Bromwich won the Australian men's doubles titles from 1938–40. The tournament was then suspended for five years for World War II. When it resumed, Quist and Bromwich won five more doubles titles.

▶ Moses Malone won the NBA's MVP Award with the Houston Rockets in 1981–82. He was traded to the Philadelphia 76ers the following year and again won the MVP Award.

▶ Despite not having their star first baseman Lou Gehrig in the lineup for the first time in 2,130 consecutive games, the New York Yankee juggernaut went out and crushed the Detroit Tigers, 22-2, on May 2, 1939, and Gehrig's replacement, Babe Dahlgren, hit a home run.

▶ In a 1912 football game against Army, Carlisle's Jim Thorpe scored on a 92-yard run that was called back on a penalty. On the next play, Thorpe scored on a 97-yard run.

▶ In 1974, baseball commissioner Bowie Kuhn banned New York Yankees owner George Steinbrenner from baseball for a year for making illegal contributions to Richard Nixon's presidential campaign. Steinbrenner adapted to his new situation by blistering the team on tape recorder and then making manager Bill Virdon play it for the team.

Athletes Who Helped Lead to Rule Changes

▶ Tommy McCarthy perfected the ploy of letting an infield fly drop with runners on first and second base and fewer than two outs, and then starting a double play. This led to the infield fly rule.

▶ In 1910, Washington Senator Germany Schaefer "stole" first base. With a runner on third, Schaefer, on first, stole second to try to draw a throw. When the catcher did not throw, Schaefer ran back to first. (He would steal second again, this time drawing a throw and allowing the runner to score from third.) A new rule, 7.08.i, was instituted to prevent the stealing of a previously-held base.

▶ In the 1949 British Open, runner-up Harry Bradshaw's drive on the fifth hole of the second round wound up in a broken bottle. He had to play it as it lay, but the incident led to a change in the golf rules.

▶ In college and pro basketball, the dominance of certain big men has inspired several significant new rules. St. John's All-America center Harry Boykoff, George Mikan, Wilt Chamberlain, Bill Russell, and Lew Alcindor, to name a few, each helped to bring about crucial changes, including defensive and offensive goaltending, establishing the three-second rule, widening the lane, and a "no-dunk" rule in college (since revoked).

▶ The ability of Maurice "The Rocket" Richard and the Montreal Canadiens in the 1950s to routinely score several goals during the power play inspired the 1956 rule change in which the power play, on a minor penalty, would not continue if a goal was scored by the team with the man advantage.

▶ Ilie Nastase's on-court behavior helped prod the Association of Tennis Professionals to institute a code of conduct.

▶ After the 2001–02 NBA season, the league approved the use of instant-replay to help referees to determine whether a made shot was taken just before the final buzzer. Although there have been numerous buzzer-beater disputes over the years, the 2002 playoffs featured an inordinate number of crucial ones—three, in particular, that forced the rule change: An end-of-game shot by Baron Davis of the Charlotte Hornets that should have broken a tie with the Orlando Magic but was disallowed (happily, justice prevailed and the Hornets won in overtime); an incredible, end-of-game heave by Reggie Miller of the Indiana Pacers that forced overtime with the New Jersey Nets, and should not have been allowed (happily, justice prevailed and the Nets won in over-time); and an end-of-half heave by Los Angeles Laker Samaki Walker against the Sacramento Kings that should not have been allowed (unhappily, justice did not prevail and the Lakers beat the Kings on another—and perfectly valid—last-second shot by Robert Horrie).

▶ St. Louis Cardinal Conrad Dobler's play led to a rule change stating that an offensive lineman could not reach over his head with his arms. This was designed to prevent, among other things, the "throat block."

▶ The presence of Dummy Hoy, a deaf major leaguer who played in the late 19th century, prompted umpires to begin using hand signals for their calls.

▶ On November 21, 1953, Notre Dame's football team, which became known as the "Fainting Irish," twice faked injuries to stop the clock. Rules were changed to prevent feigned injuries.

▶ The NFL's "taunting rule" prohibiting prolonged, excessive, or pre-meditated celebrations was spurred by the sack dances of New York Jets defensive end Mark Gastineau.

A Rollercoaster Ride

Most durable athletes are known for their ability to look victory and defeat in the eye and to treat them equally (to paraphrase Rudyard Kipling). Some athletes have needed to overdevelop this capacity because they have experienced the highs and lows of sport in particular-ly dramatic fashion. Minor-league left-handed pitcher Steve Dalkowski, for example, was legendary for his blazing fastball, averaging 15 strikeouts per nine innings in his first five seasons in professional baseball. Unfortunately, he was just as legendary for his terrible control and averaged 17 walks per nine innings. Arm problems in 1963 slowed him and he never made it to the major leagues.

Here are some of the more schizophrenic moments and teams and players from the sports world.

▶ In 1972–73, the Philadelphia 76ers registered the worst season record in NBA history, 9-73. Six years before, the team recorded what was at the time the best NBA record ever, 68-13. (The 1971–72 Los Angeles Lakers went 69-13; the 1995–96 Chicago Bulls bested that with a 72-10 record.) Leroy Ellis and John Q. Trapp played on both the then-best (1971–72 Lakers) and worst (1972–73 Philadelphia) teams in NBA history.

▶ In his collegiate debut in 1969, University of Florida quarterback John Reaves threw for five touchdowns, an NCAA record for a first game. Six weeks later, Reaves threw for nine interceptions, a record for most interceptions in a game. His NFL counterpart, Chicago Cardinals quarterback Jim Hardy, threw for a record eight interceptions on September 24, 1950, and the next week passed for six touchdowns, his career high.

▶ One competitor at the 1960 Portland City Amateur golf tournament missed his first tee shot, then hit another one in the lake, and on his third tee shot made a hole-in-one.

▶ In the 1927 singles final of the Cannes championship between French tennis stars Henri Cochet and Jacques Brugnon, Cochet lost the first set badly, 6-1. He won the next two sets easily, 6-1, 6-0. He lost the fourth set badly, 6-1. He won the fifth and final set easily, 6-0.

▶ In 1983, Pat Corrales was fired while managing a first-place team, the Philadelphia Phillies, and rehired to take over a last-place team, the Cleveland Indians.

▶ On September 14, 1986, San Francisco Giant Bob Brenly tied a major-league record by committing four errors in one inning, then hit two home runs, one in the bottom of the ninth inning, to help win the game, 7-6.

▶ Tom Brown played outfield and first base in 61 games for the last-place Washington Senators in 1963, and played safety for the Green Bay Packers in their two Super Bowl victories.

▶ Talk about draining: For fans, the 2001 World Series was already overcharged with emotion because of the recent September 11th terrorist attacks and the raw feelings they inspired. In pure baseball terms, though, it was hard to match this Fall Classic, between the Arizona Diamondbacks and the New York Yankees, for the drama of its ups and downs. All the momentum was with Arizona after Games 1 and 2, which they dominated at home. Back in New York, the Yankees took a close Game 3. But then the momentum seemed to shift right back to Arizona in Game 4 when they had the Yankees down two runs in the bottom of the ninth inning, with a man on base, with two outs...

at which point Yankee first baseman Tino Martinez tied the game with a home run, shifting the momentum back to the Yankees, who won the game in extra innings. The Diamondbacks recovered nicely, though, and apeared to win back momentum in Game 5, when they again had the Yankees down by two runs in the bottom of the ninth inning, with a man on and two outs... at which point Yankee third baseman Scott Brosius hit *another* game-tying home run, unequivocally putting all the momentum behind the Yankees (who won the game in extra innings). In Game 6 in Arizona, though, Randy Johnson and the Diamondback offense dominated the Yankees, and shifted the momentum back to the National Leaguers, especially with ace Curt Schilling going in Game 7. And when Schilling took a 1-0 lead into the late innings, the momentum seemed to be holding... until the Yankees tied the game, then took the lead on an Alfonso Soriano home run in the eighth inning, off of Schilling. When the Yankees automatic-as-they-come closer Mariano Rivera struck out the side in the bottom of the eighth, it appeared as if the momentum would, ultimately, propel the Yankees... until, in an almost-unprecedented occurrence, a less-than-stellar Rivera could not protect the lead, game, or Series, and the Diamondbacks dethroned the three-time defending champion Yankees, in emotional and, undeniably, rollercoaster fashion.

▶ Philadelphia Phillie Mike Schmidt had a club-high .467 batting average in the 1983 National League Championship Series, and a club-low .050 in the World Series.

▶ In 1983, Lamarr Hoyt led the majors in wins with 24. The next year he tied for the major-league lead in losses. Steve Carlton accomplished this feat in the National League, leading in wins in 1972, with 27, and in losses the following year, with 20.

▶ The 1954 Cleveland Indians set an American League record for most wins in the regular season (111), and then got swept by the New York Giants in the World Series.

The 1988–89 Los Angeles Lakers set an NBA record for consecutive playoff wins by sweeping their first three opponents, and then got swept in the finals by the Detroit Pistons.

The St. Louis Blues swept the Philadelphia Flyers and Los Angeles Kings in 1969, then got swept in the Stanley Cup finals by the Montreal Canadiens.

▶ Casey Stengel managed the New York Yankees when they became the only baseball franchise to win five world championships in a row, and won a record 10 pennants with them. He also managed the worst team in modern baseball history, the 1962 Mets, and finished his career with three last-place finishes. He retired in 1965, with the Mets again in last place.

▶ In college football bowl games from 1967–74, the University of Alabama under coach Paul "Bear" Bryant was 0-7-1. In their next—and his last—eight bowl games, they were 7-1.

▶ The Cleveland Indians are the only team in history to have a winning season (1986) between two 100-loss seasons (1985, 1987).

▶ Hall of Famer Red Ruffing spent several years with the second-division Boston Red Sox, where he compiled season records of 9-18, 6-15, 5-13, 10-25, and 9-22, and then with the perennially contending New York Yankees, where he compiled season records of 18-7, 19-11, 20-12, 20-7, 21-7, 21-7, 15-6, 14-7...

▶ Buff Donelli simultaneously coached a football team from the college ranks, Duquesne University, and from the NFL, the Pittsburgh Steelers, for one month in the 1941 season. Under Donelli, Duquesne went undefeated, while the Steelers did not win a game.

▶ Linebacker Larry Ball and defensive lineman Maulty Moore both played for the 1972 Miami Dolphins (17-0) and the 1976 Tampa Bay Buccaneers (0-14).

▶ In the 1972 Olympic Nordic combined event, Japan's Hideki Nakano of Japan finished first in the ski jump and last in the 15km race. (He finished in 13th place overall.)

The 24 Most Intriguing Defunct Leagues

If you lived through the past three decades and never heard of the International Boxing League or Major League Rodeo, it doesn't mean you weren't paying attention. Neither league was a groundbreaking idea; neither is around any more. But they are not alone in the dead-league office. Here are some of the more unusual and / or reasonably successful professional sports leagues that are no longer.

▶ All-American Girls Professional Baseball League, 1943–54
   Notable players: first basewoman Dottie Kamenshek (called a major-league-caliber fielder by New York Yankee Wally Pipp); Sophie Kurys (stole 201 bases in 1946). Jimmie Foxx was the manager of the Fort Wayne Daisies.
   Innovations: Athletes were sent to charm school during spring training; professional chaperones were hired; use of a ball sized between a baseball and a softball.
   Final championship: The Kalamazoo Lassies defeated the Fort Wayne Daisies, September 5, 1954.

▶ International Track Association, 1973–76
   Notable athletes: Jim Ryun, Ben Jipcho, Brian Oldfield, Bob Beamon, Dave Wottle, Kip Keino, Bob Seagren, Wyomia Tyus
   Innovations: Pacer lights on the inside of the track; co-ed 30-yard dashes; athletes wore singlets with corporate sponsors.
   Final championship: None.

▶ XFL, 2001
   A joint venture of Vince McMahon's World Wrestling Federation

Entertainment and NBC, the league closed down after one season. The initial high ratings plummeted after the first week; it seemed that there was no wrestling for wrestling fans, and the football wasn't well-played enough for football fans. Toward the end of the season, the XFL recorded the worst-ever ratings for a prime-time broadcast.

Notable players: "He Hate Me" (Rod Smart), Tommy Maddox (league MVP)

Innovations: No fair catches on punts; 10-minute halftime; cameras located everywhere—including in lockerrooms and on selected helmets and shoes; huddles, sidelines, and lockerrooms were miked; extremely scantily clad cheerleaders; hyper wrestling announcers (including Jesse Ventura and Brian Bosworth) rather than football analysts; more upfront about the obviously violent nature of the game (some team names: Maniax, Hitmen, Enforcers).

Final championship: The Los Angeles Xtreme walloped the San Francisco Demons, 38-6.

▶ Players League, major-league baseball, 1890

Notable players: Monte Ward, Old Hoss Radbourne, Ed Delahanty, Pete Browning, Charles Comiskey, Hugh Duffy

Innovations: Players were part team owners and were to have shared in the profits, had there been any.

Champion: Boston, with an 81-48 record, was five games ahead of Brooklyn.

▶ Federal League, major-league baseball, 1914–15

Notable players: Eddie Plank, Mordecai "Three Finger" Brown, Chief Bender, Joe Tinker, Edd Roush

Innovations: Wrigley Field (known then as Weeghman Field) was built for the Federal League's Chicago Whales.

Final champion: Chicago, with an 86-66 record, finished percentage points ahead of St. Louis, at 87-67.

▶ World Team Tennis, 1974–78

Notable players: Billie Jean King, Ken Rosewall, Chris Evert, Jimmy Connors, Bjorn Borg, Martina Navratilova

Innovations: The term "love" was eliminated; use of a four-point, no-ad scoring system; replacements allowed at any time; crowds were encouraged to be rowdy.

Final championship: The Los Angeles Strings defeated the Boston Lobsters three games to one in a best-of-five series that ended September 21, 1978.

▶ National Bowling League, 1961–62

Notable players: Carmen Salvino, Buzz Fazio, Tony Lindemann, Bud Horn, Bill Bunetta, Steve Nagy, Joe Joseph, Billy Golembiewski

Innovations: There were two ways a player could score: by winning a match, and by earning bonus points for his score (e. g., a score of 210-219 earned one point; 220-229 earned two points, etc.; a 300 earned 10 points). Also, there was a wild-card substitution rule: When a player was faced with a shot he wasn't sure of, the team captain could call in a "specialist" to roll for him—for instance, a lefty for a righty when pins were standing on the right side.

Final championship: The Detroit Thunderbirds defeated the Twin Cities Skippers three games to none in a best-of-five series that ended May 6, 1962, in Allen Park, Michigan.

▶ American Basketball Association, 1967–76

Notable players: Julius Erving, Moses Malone, George Gervin, Dan Issel, Artis Gilmore, Billy Cunningham, Rick Barry

Innovations: A red-white-and-blue ball; the threepoint basket.

Final championship: The New York Nets defeated the Denver Nuggets, 112-106, May 13, 1976, taking the series four games to two. The Nets, Nuggets, Indiana Pacers, and San Antonio Spurs were accepted into the NBA.

▶ All-American Football Conference, 1946–49

Notable players: Lou Groza, Marion Motley, Otto Graham, Frankie Albert

Final championship: The Cleveland Browns defeated the San Francisco 49ers, 21-7, on December 11, 1949, at Cleveland. Cleveland, San Francisco, and the Baltimore Colts were accepted into the NFL for the 1950 season.

▶ International Volleyball Association, 1975–79

Notable players: Mary Jo Peppler (1964 U.S. Olympian), Scott English (former NBA-ABA forward), Eileen Clancy (4'10", 90 pounds), Stan Gosciniak (league MVP)

Innovations: A Mexican franchise (the El Paso-Juarez Sol); men and women playing together (two of six players were required to be women); "designated switchers" (one man and one woman who could change positions on each point).

▶ World Hockey Association, 1972–79

Notable players: Bobby Hull, Gordie Howe, Derek Sanderson, Gerry Cheevers, Bernie Parent, Wayne Gretzky

Innovations: No reserve clause; no option clauses in players' contracts.

Final championship: The Winnipeg Jets defeated the Edmonton Oilers, 7-3, on May 20, 1979, to win the AVCO World Cup. Edmonton, Winnipeg, the Quebec Nordiques, and the Hartford Whalers were admitted into the NHL.

▶ CBA, 1978–2001

The league folded in February, 2001, two years after Hall of Fame NBA guard Isiah Thomas bought the league for $9 million, with half the money up front. When Thomas won the job as Indiana Pacers head coach, the NBA made him divest his interest in the CBA before training camp. The CBA, long used by the NBA as a feeding ground, was also damaged when the NBA announced it would start its own developmental league.

Notable players: Mario Elie, John Starks, Bo Outlaw, Voshon Leonard, Anthony Mason, David Wesley; Phil Jackson coached the Albany Patroons, and George Karl and Flip Saunders also coached in the league.

Final championship: In 2000, the Yakima Sun Kings beat the La Crosse Bobcats, 109-93.

► World Football League, 1974–75

The league disbanded October 22, 1975, 10 weeks into its second season.

Notable players: Larry Csonka, Jim Kiick, Paul Warfield, Danny White, Anthony Davis

Innovations: The "action point": After a touchdown, which was worth seven points, the ball was placed on the 2½-yard line, from where a run or a pass produced the action point (worth one point).

Final championship: The Birmingham Americans defeated the Florida Blazers, 22-21, in the World Bowl in Birmingham, Alabama, on December 5, 1974. Because the Birmingham team was in arrears, their uniforms were confiscated by the sheriff's department after the game.

► American Basketball League, 1996–98

On December 22, 1998, the league filed for bankruptcy, a mess largely precipitated by the NBA's putting its muscle behind the new, competing WNBA, and by increased player defections to the WNBA. While they co-existed with the WNBA, the ABL played a longer season, and during the fall and spring; the WNBA plays during the summer—the NBA off-season. The ABL did not use NBA stadiums, as does the WNBA. The ABL also used a regulation-sized ball, and the three-point line was further away. For many of these reasons, the ABL inspired great fan allegiance, and a sense among devotees that it was the "real" women's league.

Notable players: Kate Starbird, Teresa Edwards, Dawn Staley, Jennifer Azzi; Jim Cleamons coached the Chicago Condors

Final championship: The Columbus Quest beat the Long Beach Stingrays, 3 games to 2, after being down 2-0; Columbus also won the previous title.

► North American Soccer League, 1968–85

The league was formed by the merger of the National Professional Soccer League and the United States Soccer Association. In 1971, three foreign clubs—Portuguesa of Brazil, Lanerossi-Vicenza of Italy, and Apollo of Greece—joined to compete against league members in cup competition, the results of which were included in league standings.

Notable players: Pelé, Giorgio Chinaglia, Franz Beckenbauer, Carlos Alberto, Kyle Rote, Jr., Shep Messing

Innovations: The "shoot-out" tiebreaking procedure; abolition of the 107-year-old FIFA offsides rule—the league changed the demarcation from the midfield line to a line 35 yards from the opponent's goal.

Final championship: The Chicago Sting defeated the Toronto Blizzard, on October 13, 1984.

▶ United States Football League, 1983–86
Notable players: Doug Flutie, Steve Young, Herschel Walker, Jim Kelly, Mike Rozier
Innovations; Spring schedule; instant replay for officiating.
Final championship: The Baltimore Stars defeated the Oakland Invaders, 28-24, on July 14, 1985, at Giants Stadium, in East Rutherford, New Jersey.

▶ Women's Basketball League, 1978–81
The league peaked with 14 teams, and finished with 8. In 1979–80, all 14 teams had male head coaches.
Notable players: Nancy Lieberman, Ann Meyers, Molly "Machine Gun" Bolin, who scored 55 points in one game
Notable coaches: Butch van Breda Kolff, Larry Costello, Dean Meminger
Final championship: The Nebraska Wranglers defeated the Dallas Diamonds, 99-90, on April 20, 1981, at the Omaha Civic Auditorium, to take the best-of-five series.

▶ American Professional Slo-Pitch League, slow-pitch softball, 1977–79
Notable players: Norm Cash, Jim Northup, Joe Pepitone, Benny Holt (who won the league's 1977 Triple Crown with 89 homers, 187 RBIs, and a .690 batting average)
Innovations: A deader ball was used in the final season to curb the offense of the Detroit Caesars, who had won the first two World Series; to lower scores, the base paths were extended to 70 feet, and the distance down the foul lines was made a minimum of 300 feet. Also, the first foul after two strikes meant a strikeout.

▶ American Football League, 1960–69
Notable players: Joe Namath, Lance Alworth, Jim Otto, George Blanda, Fred Williamson, Nick Buoniconti, Billy Cannon, Floyd Little, Jack Kemp
Innovations: Two-point conversions after touchdowns; players names were displayed on the backs of their jerseys; the official time was determined by the scoreboard clock and not, as in the NFL, by an on-field official.
Final championship: The Kansas City Chiefs defeated the Oakland Raiders, 17-7, on January 4, 1970. The Chiefs went on to upset the Minnesota Vikings, 23-7, in Super Bowl IV. All ten AFL teams were merged into the NFL.

▶ National Professional Golf League, 1972
Notable players: Billy Casper, Sam Snead, Dow Finsterwald
Final championship: None was ever played.

▶ Continental Indoor Soccer League, 1993–97
Founded to fill the gap left by the collapse of the Major Indoor Soccer League, the Canadian Soccer League, and the Lone Star Soccer Alliance, the CISL went under, in part, due to differences between team owners and the league commissioner.

Notable players: Paul Dougherty, the shortest player in the CISL at 5'3" and the 1997 league MVP

Innovations: Included a Mexican team; played in the summer.

Final championship: The Seattle SeaDogs defeated the Houston Hotshots, 6-5 and 7-1.

▶ Senior Professional Baseball Association, 1989–1990

The league folded during its second season when the Fort Myers team cancelled its games, and five other clubs voted to follow suit. After the initial hype passed, it became clear that fans—even nostalgic ones in Florida—didn't take to the idea of watching over-the-hill ballplayers remind us of what shadows they'd become.

At one point, the Gold Coast Suns acquired the rights to pitcher Luis Tiant for 500 teddy bears.

▶ International Women's Professional Softball Association, fast-pitch softball, 1976–77

Notable players: Joan Joyce (co-founder, along with Billie Jean King, and star pitcher), Rosie Black (who toured with a team called "The Queen and Her Maids")

Innovations: Pitchers could not appear in consecutive games, a rule adopted mainly because of Joyce's prowess; use of a yellow ball and yellow bases.

▶ Intercontinental Football League, which was announced in June of 1974 by NFL commissioner Pete Rozelle but never came into being. The league was to be made up of six teams and begin play in the spring of 1975. The six designated teams would have been the Istanbul Conquerors; the Rome Gladiators; the Vienna Lippizaners; the Munich Lions; the West Berlin Bears; and the Barcelona Almovogeres.

How Times Have Changed: 8 Formerly Common Things That Have Faded into Memory

▶ *The pre-eminence of the Olympics over war.* When an Olympic Games began in ancient times, wars were suspended for the duration of the competition. Today, the opposite is true: Because of World War I, no Olympics were held in 1916; because of World War II, there were no Games in 1940 or 1944.

▶ *Grass-court tennis tournaments.* There is only one professional grass-court tennis tournament still played in the United States, at Newport Casino in Rhode Island.

▶ *Fights ending in a "no-decision."* In the early 20th century, fighters would routinely record as many as 50 to 100 no-decisions during their career. Middleweight champion Harry Greb, for example, won 112 fights, lost 8, drew 3, and registered 170 no-decisions.

▶ *Rampant basketball violence.* In its early days, the professional game was so reckless that wire cages (hence the name "cagers") were built around courts to protect fans from violence. There was no out-of-bounds, the ball was always in play, players were routinely gashed by wire, and blood on the court was not uncommon. In Pennsylvania coal towns, miners would heat nails with their lamps and throw them at referees and opposing players. Some officials carried guns. The cage was eliminated in 1929.

▶ *Pitchers hurling an entire doubleheader.* The last player to pitch two complete-game wins in one day was Dutch Levsen for the Cleveland Indians, on August 28, 1926.

▶ *Non-astronomical prices paid for the Olympics.* For the broadcast rights to the 1960 Winter Olympics at Squaw Valley, CBS paid a quaint $50,000. For the rights to the 1980 Winter Olympics at Lake Placid, ABC paid a far heftier but still not off-the-charts $15,500,000. For the broadcast rights to the 2002 Winter Olympics at Salt Lake City, NBC paid $545,000,000.

▶ *World Series day games.* Thanks to television viewing habits and the appetite of advertisers, the World Series is always played in prime time —East Coast time—and, at least to them, the later the better. The Series was played exclusively in daytime through 1970; the first night World Series game was Game 4 in 1971, between the Pittsburgh Pirates and the Baltimore Orioles, in Pittsburgh. The last World Series to feature even one measly daytime game was in 1987.

▶ *Greek athletic prowess.* As the birthplace of the ancient Olympics, Greece naturally dominated those Games and even as recently as 1896, when the first modern Olympics were held in Athens, Greece performed admirably, winning 10 golds and 47 total medals. Since 1924, Greeks have won just 34 medals, including 12 golds, at summer Olympics. (Greece has never won a winter Olympics medal.)

Et Plus Ça Change... :
5 Examples That Some Things Never Change

▶ Roman Emperor Theodosius canceled the ancient Olympics in 392 A.D. in part because riots had broken out over charges made by Greek athletes that some of their Roman competitors were professionals.

▶ The Carnegie Report in the late 1920s blasted football administrators for serious abuses. In 1929, a financial scandal involving the University of Iowa's All-America halfback Willis Glasgow led to the Hawkeyes' being suspended by their conference for a year, the first time that had happened.

▶ University of Oklahoma wide receiver Lance Rentzel was declared ineligible for the 1965 Gator Bowl for having signed a professional contract.

▶ Paavo Nurmi, the great Finnish distance runner, was suspended one week before the 1932 Olympic marathon for taking money beyond his expenses on an exhibition tour.

▶ The durability of professional baseball ineptitude in Chicago remains a time-defying marvel. The Cubs have been awful for several generations, with only the briefest pockets of non-awfulness: They celebrated their last world championship in 1908 (the longest drought among non-expansion teams), and haven't won a pennant in 57 years and counting. The White Sox have been consistently bad for about the same span: They haven't won a Series since 1917, and have captured all of one—that's right, one—pennant (1959) since 1919, the year they disgraced themselves and all of baseball in the "Black Sox" scandal. As Jack Brickhouse, the late Cubs' announcer, said of his club—though it could just as easily apply to their cross-town incompetents—"Any team can have a bad century."

4

PLACES

⬤⬤⬤⬤⬤⬤⬤⬤⬤⬤⬤⬤⬤⬤⬤

Home Away from Home

Although home field advantage in sports can rarely be underestimated, some teams have ventured forth, willingly, to use another site as their surrogate home. Other teams have had to move temporarily because of unusual circumstances. And circumstance has also forced events to relocate from their usual site to a home away from home.

▶ A section of the Philadelphia Spectrum blew off in March of 1968. The resident NHL Flyers played their final seven regular season home games at Madison Square Garden in New York City, Maple Leaf Garden in Toronto, and Le Colisée in Quebec. The Spectrum roof was fixed by the time the playoffs began.

▶ Man O' War, perhaps the greatest Kentucky-bred thoroughbred ever, never raced at a track in the state of Kentucky.

▶ During the 1971–72 NBA season, the Houston Rockets played home games at six different sites: 21 at Hofheinz Pavilion, 8 at Astrohall, 6 at the Astrodome, 3 in San Antonio, 2 in Waco, and 1 in El Paso.

▶ Because of fears of a Japanese sneak attack on the West Coast, the 1942 Rose Bowl game—to be played less than a month after the attack on Pearl Harbor—was moved from Pasadena to Durham, North Carolina. Oregon State beat Duke, 20-16.

▶ The AFL All-Star game in 1965 was moved from New Orleans because black players protested widespread discrimination in the city. The game was played the following week in Houston.

▶ In 1957, the Brooklyn Dodgers, who played at Ebbets Field, hosted 15 games in Jersey City's Roosevelt Stadium. Don Drysdale pitched his first career shutout there.

▶ At the last minute, the 1957 British Open was moved from Muirfield to St. Andrews because of a gas shortage caused by the Suez Canal crisis.

▶ At the 1956 Melbourne Olympics, the equestrian events were held separately in Stockholm, Sweden, because of Australian quarantine laws.

▶ Each year from 1975–95, the Boston Celtics played a varying number of "home" games at the Hartford Civic Center in Connecticut.

▶ In 1914, the Boston Braves played their home World Series games at Fenway Park, home of the Red Sox, because the Braves' new park was not ready. The next two years, the Braves let the Red Sox use Braves Field in the World Series because it had a larger capacity than Fenway.

▶ As heavyweight champion, American George Foreman never fought in the United States. His title defenses were made in Kingston, Jamaica; Tokyo, Japan; Caracas, Venezuela; and Kinshasa, Zaire.

▶ When the Houston Oilers agreed to move to Nashville, Tennesse, in 1997, they had to play their first year in Memphis, where, as the Tennessee Oilers, they were an impressive 6-2. The following year, they moved into their new home city of Nashville and played at Dudley Field (Vanderbilt Stadium), where they went a very road-like 3-5. Finally, they changed their name to the Tennessee Titans and moved into Nashville's Coliseum. They won their first 13 games there. Over their next 13 games, however, they were a deeply unintimidating 6-7 (through the 2001 season).

▶ In 1968 and 1969, the Chicago White Sox played 20 home games at Milwaukee's County Stadium.

▶ The New York Yankees used Shea Stadium as their home from 1974–75, while Yankee Stadium was being renovated.

▶ In 1950, the Stanley Cup finalist New York Rangers were bumped from Madison Square Garden by the incoming circus. They played Games 2 and 3 against the Detroit Red Wings in Toronto's Maple Leaf Garden—the first time since 1920, when Ottawa faced Seattle in the finals, that two teams battled for the Stanley Cup without a local team's being involved. Detroit hosted the last four games of the series. The Rangers lost in seven—gamely, it must be said, considering that they played not one of the seven contests at home.

▶ In the 1968 Davis Cup, Rhodesia faced Sweden at a private club in France to stay clear of anti-apartheid demonstrations in Sweden.

▷ Special "Home Away from Home" Honor: Gaston Chevrolet, whose brother Louis founded the car company, won the 1920 Indianapolis 500 driving a Monroe.

The Most Dramatic Examples
of Home-Field Advantage

In 1908, the Spaulding basketball guide said that home court advantage was "easily worth 15 points to the home team." That was quite telling, since the average margin of victory in games then was 15 points.

Playing on familiar ground, with supportive fans—and, on occasion, sympathetic officiating—makes for a serious competitive edge. Teams have even been known to accentuate the advantage, at times unethically. The visitors' locker room at the Boston Garden was notoriously overheated, while the visitors' bench at the Montreal Forum used to be across the ice from the penalty box, thus keeping the enemy team from making player changes (after returning to equal strength) as quickly as the Canadiens could. The Jersey Knights (formerly the New York Raiders and the New York Golden Blades) of the defunct World Hockey Association played in New Jersey's Cherry Hill Arena, which had no showers in the visiting dressing room. Their opponents dressed in a motel two miles away. The following offers a sampling of what "home field" may mean.

▶ Notre Dame did not lose a home football game from 1906–27.

▶ Only 5 times in 17 World Cup competitions has a country from outside the host continent won the Cup—and on two of those occasions, a South American team won in Mexico. Six times, the host country has won it all: Uruguay in 1930; Italy in 1934; England in 1966; West Germany in 1974; Argentina in 1978; and France in 1998. The host country has gone to the Cup semifinals or beyond 11 times.*

▶ At the 1984 Los Angeles Olympics, 37 of the 38 fights that involved U.S. boxers and that went the full three rounds were decided in favor of Americans. Redzep Redzepovski of Yugoslavia, silver medalist in the flyweight division, said, "As long as an American is standing on his feet for three rounds it is hard to get a decision over him."

▶ In its previous 86 home games (through 2001) at Doak Campbell Stadium in Tallahassee, Florida State University's football team was 81-4-1.

▶ The golfers that defeated the American team at Prairie Dunes, Kansas, for the 1986 Curtis Cup, became the first British team to win the Curtis, Walker, or Ryder Cup on American soil.

▶ In December 2001, Butler University became the first school in the 20-year, 40-game history of the Indiana University-hosted Hoosier Classic to beat the Hoosiers.

▶ Japan had won only one Winter Olympics medal before the 1972 Games in Sapporo, Japan, where they swept the 70m ski jump competition.

▶ The University of Kentucky basketball team lost at home on January 2, 1943, and not again until January 8, 1955—a streak of 130 home wins.

*That includes Korea, a co-host in 2002, though co-host Japan did not go as far.

▶ Golfer Larry Mize of Augusta, Georgia, won the Masters in 1987.

▶ In 1955, the Detroit Red Wings beat Montreal four games to three for the Stanley Cup. While the series sounds as if it was competitive, the home team won every game, and no game had a margin of under two goals.

▶ In the 2001 World Series, the Diamondbacks won Games 1, 2, 6, and 7 in Arizona while New York won Games 3, 4, and 5 at Yankee Stadium.

Similarly, in the 1987 World Series, the Minnesota Twins beat the St. Louis Cardinals four games to three, with the home team winning every game.

▶ From 1985–86 through 1986–87, the Boston Celtics were 79-3 in regular season home games.

▶ The Arizona State football team won four of the first five Fiesta Bowls, in 1971, 1972, 1973, and 1975. The site of the Bowl was Sun Devil Stadium, Arizona State's home field.

▶ During the 1981–82 NHL season, the New York Islanders were 33-4-4 at Nassau Coliseum.

▶ Two of the four times that the Winter Olympics have been held in the United States, the American men's hockey team has won the gold medal. Those are the only golds the U.S. men's team has won.

▶ The University of Kansas basketball team won the 1988 NCAA final in Kansas City. North Carolina State won the 1974 title game, played at Greensboro, North Carolina. In 1968 and 1972, the Final Four was held in Los Angeles, and both titles were won by UCLA. In 1950, CCNY won the title game in New York.

▶ "Cobb's Lake" was the area of dirt in front of Tiger Stadium's home plate that was kept wet by groundskeepers to slow down Ty Cobb's bunts and cause infielders to slip while fielding them.

▶ Philadelphia's Connie Mack Stadium sported "Ashburn Ridge" to help speedy Richie Ashburn with his bunts down the third-base line. Similarly, the chalk along the baselines at Dodger Stadium was kept notoriously high to help Maury Wills's bunts stay fair, while the infield at Candlestick Park, home of the Dodgers' rivals, the San Francisco Giants, was kept muddy when the Dodgers were in town to slow Wills on the bases.

▶ Chris Evert, the "touring professional" for Amelia Island, Florida, went almost five years without losing a set in tournament play there, until Carling Bassett beat her in 1983.

▶ The San Francisco 49ers won Super Bowl XIX at Stanford University's football stadium in Palo Alto, 20 miles south of San Francisco.

▶ Some baseball parks are easier to hit home runs in than others, but perhaps no player in the history of the game took greater advantage of the friendly confines of home than Ken Williams of the St. Louis Browns. He hit 142 of his round-trippers at home, most of them at Sportsman's Park, and only 54 on the road. (Elston Howard, on the other hand, hit only 54 home runs at home, mostly at Yankee Stadium, and 113 on the road.)

▶ Amateur Francis Ouimet, 20, stunned the golf world by beating Harry Vardon and Ted Ray in an 18-hole playoff to win the 1913 U.S. Open at the Brookline Country Club in Massachusetts. Ouimet grew up across the street from the club.

▶ Every game of the 1916 New York Giants' major-league record 26-game winning streak was played at the Polo Grounds, their home field.

It Must Be Something in the Water: Places in the World That Grow Athletes

It may be due to the weather or the facilities, the coaching or the tradition, but whatever it is, certain places just have it. Some towns and schools and teams in America and beyond have produced an uncanny number of good athletes, of one kind or another. At various times, Georgetown University has grown basketball centers; the Los Angeles Dodgers, pitchers; Czechoslovakia, tennis players; the University of Florida, U. of Miami, and Brigham Young University, quarterbacks. Why these spots are so fertile is often explainable—for instance, a coach knows how to take good athletes and turn them into great ones; or the appearance of one great athlete makes others want to flock to that school, or to master that specialty; or it's simply the mutual confidence that athletes develop around each other, making everyone better. Or maybe it's none of these, and just coincidence.

Whatever.

▶ San Pedro de Macoris, a city of 100,000 in the Dominican Republic, has produced at least 50 major-league baseball players, including Sammy Sosa, Julio Franco, Jose Offerman, Luis Castillo, Fernando Tatis, Juan Guzman, Mariano Duncan, Joaquin Andujar, George Bell, Pedro Guerrero, Rico Carty (the first from the city to make it), Tony Fernandez, Juan Samuel, Alfredo Griffin, Damaso Garcia, and Rafael Ramirez; and more than 100 minor leaguers.

▶ The men's soccer team of tiny Hartwick College (2002 enrollment: 1,400) has spawned 25 All-Americas and over 40 players who have gone on to play professionally and for the U.S. National and Olympic teams. (They won the national collegiate title in 1977.)

▶ World-class distance runners Kipwambok (Henry) Rono, Kip Keino, and Mike Boit were all members of the Nandi, a subgroup of the Kalenjin tribe in Kenya.

▶ The Miami (Ohio) College football team has included among its coaching and playing ranks the following coaching legends: Ara Parseghian, Red Blaik, Paul Brown, Woody Hayes, Carm Cozza, John Pont, Sid Gillman, and Weeb Ewbank.

▶ In 1976, Guy Drut became the first person from a non-English-speaking country to win the Olympic high hurdles. Drut was born on the same street as Michel Jazy, France's previous track and field medalist.

▶ Eddie Murray, arguably the premier American League first baseman of the 1980s, and Ozzie Smith, arguably the premier National League shortstop of the 1980s, were teammates at Locke High School in Los Angeles, California.

New York Mets outfielders and 1969 world champs Cleon Jones and Tommie Agee were high school teammates at Country Training High School in Mobile, Alabama.

Herb Score and Dick Brown of Lake Worth, Florida, later became batterymates for the Cleveland Indians.

Waxahachie (Texas) High School produced four future major leaguers in one year: Paul Richards, Art Shires, Belv Bean, and Jimmy Adair.

At least four other high schools have each had four future big leaguers on their team at one time: Roosevelt (St. Louis, Missouri) High School and Washington High School of Los Angeles in the 1930s, Beaumont High School in St. Louis in the 1940s, and Compton (California) High School in the 1970s.

Baseball players from Hillsborough High School in Tampa, Florida, include Dwight Gooden, Gary Sheffield (Gooden's nephew), Floyd Youmans (who transferred to Fontana, California in his senior year), Mike Heath, Vance Lovelace, and José Alvarez.

▶ In the 1950s, Australia produced tennis greats Rod Laver, Roy Emerson, Ken Rosewall, Frank Sedgman, Lew Hoad, Rex Hartwig, Mervyn Rose, Mal Anderson, Ashley Cooper, Fred Stolle, John Newcombe, and Tony Roche.

▶ The Los Anglese Dodgers produced the National League Rookie of the Year five years in a row, from 1992 through 1996. (Earlier, they did it four years in a row, from 1979 through 1982).

▶ The Dodgers also produced a more unfortunate cornucopia: Each member of their 1992–93 starting outfield—Eric Davis, Darryl Strawberry, and Brett Butler—was, at some point, stricken with cancer.

▶ Martin's Ferry, Ohio, and its sister villages have produced the following sports stars: Lou and Alex Groza, Bill Mazeroski, John Havlicek, Olympic wrestler Bobby Douglas, NFL linebacker Bill Jobko, and Phil and Joe Niekro.

▶ Basketball players from DeMatha High School in Hyattsville, Maryland, include Adrian Dantley, Dereck Whittenberg, Adrian Branch, Sidney Lowe, Danny Ferry, Kenny Carr, Bennie Bolton, Sid Catlett, Hawkeye Whitney, and CBS announcer James Brown.

▶ Hall of Famers Gabby Hartnett and Nap Lajoie were both born in Woonsocket, Rhode Island.

▶ Tom Landry and Vince Lombardi were assistants together on the New York Giants coaching staff, 1954–58.

▶ Baltimore's New Cathedral Cemetery is the final resting place for three baseball Hall of Famers—John McGraw, Wilbert Robinson, and Joe Kelley.

▶ The University of Indiana basketball team in 1975 produced eight players who went into the NBA—and that does not include Larry Bird, who quit the team and left the school.

▶ The 1937 Newark Bears, perhaps the best minor-league team in baseball history, won the International League championship with a 109-43 record. Of the 17 regular players, 16 eventually made it to the major leagues, including 9 the following year.

▶ Al Arbour and Scotty Bowman each coached the 1970–71 St. Louis Blues. After leaving that post, they would, between them, win nine Stanley Cups in the next 12 years, and 13 overall.

▶ In the 1940s and 1950s, Calumet Farms was likened to the New York Yankees' Murderers Row: Among the horses that came from there were Citation, Armed, Faultless, Wistful, Bewitch, Fervent, Two Lea, Ponder, Coaltown, and Whirlaway. Between 1932 and 1972, Calumet horses won 2,199 races, 456 of those stakes.

▶ Undefeated heavyweight world champion Rocky Marciano and thrice-defeated middleweight world champion Marvin Hagler were both from Brockton, Massachusetts.

▶ Olympic gold medalist skiers Egon Zimmerman, Orthmar Scheider, and Trude Beiser all came from Lech, Austria, a hamlet of fewer than 200 people, which had been converted to a ski resort following World War II.

▶ Although for several years they've been considered a baseball team on the ropes—hardly drawing fans, unable to keep good players because of their tiny budget—the Montreal Expos have consistently produced some of the game's best young players, only to see them go elsewhere and become world-beaters; indeed, the All-Star team you could put together of former, recent-vintage Expos include Pedro Martinez, Randy Johnson, Larry Walker, Moises Alou, John Wetteland, Cliff Floyd, Marquis Grissom, Ugueth Urbina, Rondell White, Jeff Fassero, and Ken Hill.

▷ A special mention goes not to a place but to a year—1982—whose senior class produced the following crop of future NFL quarterbacks: Dan Marino from the University of Pittsburgh, John Elway from Stanford, Jim Kelly from Miami, Ken O'Brien from Cal-Davis, Tony Eason from Illinois, and Todd Blackledge from Penn State.

▷ Another particularly fecund year—1990—also commands our notice for producing a major-league record nine no-hitters.

It *Really* Must Be Something in the Water

In the late 1980s, Minnesota Vikings Tommy Kramer, Rich Gannon, Issiac Holt, Hassan Jones, Tim Newton, Ray Berry, Steve Jordan, and Keith Millard were all charged with Driving While Intoxicated.

11 Athletes Who Should Be from Someplace Else

A baby is about to be named when suddenly, in the next room, a dish drops, the phone rings, perhaps there's a crash of lightning, someone panics, and everything goes a little crazy... and a mistake that cannot be revoked is made: A child is misnamed. A great American woman fencer goes through life as Vincent Bradford, while an NHL defenseman must sign his name as Carol Vadnais—a world turned upside down. Such mistakes even occur years into adulthood. How did the late PR director of Japanese baseball's Pacific League, Kazuo Ito, get the nickname "Pancho"? What is wrong with this picture?

▶ Oskar Schmid, professional basketball player and leading scorer in the 1988 Summer Olympics: Brazil

▶ Vladimir Guerrero, Montreal Expo All-Star: Dominican Republic

▶ Rob de Castella, world-class marathoner and winner of the 1986 Boston Marathon: Australia

▶ Gabriela Sabatini, world-class tennis player: Argentina

▶ Nelli Kim, 1976 and 1980 Olympic gymnast: U.S.S.R.

▶ Socrates, World Cup soccer forward: Brazil

▶ George Bell, Toronto Blue Jay outfielder: Dominican Republic

▶ Greg LeMond, three-time Tour de France winner: U.S.A.

▶ Yolanda Chen, long-jumper: U.S.S.R.

▶ Emerson Fittipaldi, auto racer: Brazil

▶ Pancho Villa, boxer: Philippines

▷ Special recognition is also due the following Davis Cup tennis players: Bob Falkenburg and Tom Koch, both of whom played for Brazil, and Martin Mulligan, who played, naturally, for Italy.

Just When We Thought It Was Safe to Admire the French...

They lovingly preserve their chateaux. They gave us Cousteau, Marceau, Bardot, St. Malo. They taught us that *eau de toilette* can actually be worn on one's person, voluntarily. Without them, there's no Croissanwich.

They know tennis and Formula I; they kick ass in windsurfing and free-climbing. And in 1998, they even won the World Cup.

And then, once again, and over and over, they remind us why we have so much trouble with the whole Jerry Lewis situation.

▶ Although many in France have embraced Lance Armstrong, the American rider who, through 2002, has won their beloved Tour de France four straight years (and counting), a significant segment, including many in the press, have dismissed Armstrong's accomplishment as basically impossible. How (many of them wonder) can a man who has suffered from cancer—which began as testicular, then spread to his lungs and brain—and who then went through the physical depletion of surgery, chemotherapy, and radiation, return not only to the unbelievably conditioned form one needs to be in even to make it to the starting line of the Tour de France, but to win it, and to win it again and again, and to do so in such dominating fashion that he is widely considered both the world's best sprinter (time trialist) *and* the world's best mountain climber? More to the point—goes the logic of Armstrong's detractors—how can he do it without the aid of illegal steroids and other drugs? Given the taint that professional cycling experienced in the last several years—particularly the 1998 Tour, when French customs officials caught a Festina team employee with a stash of EPO (which boosts the production of oxygen-rich red blood cells) and anabolic steroids in his car, and Tour organizers expelled the Festina team after they admitted to systematic drug use—the anti-Armstrong sporting press has presumed there just *has* to be something going on, though nothing has ever been proven. (The syllogism: Armstrong is human; humans can't ride like that; ergo, Armstrong must be doping.)

But Armstrong is well-known—even in a sport where off-the-charts training efforts are the norm—to be the hardest-practicing man on the Tour, and the most driven. He's said repeatedly that he's never taken a banned substance, and has taken no medication since his cancer treatment in late 1996. (Referring to his battle against cancer, Armstrong once told reporters, "Knowing what I've been through, do you think I would be stupid enough to take steroids?") In 1999, *Le Monde* newspaper breathlessly reported that traces of a corticosteroid had been detected in the American's urine, as well as in the urine of several other riders. The International Cycling Union responded to the report by issuing a statement—which normally would violate medical secrecy had Armstrong and his U.S Postal Service team not requested that they issue it—that Armstrong had used a cream, Cemalyt, to treat a skin allergy, resulting in small traces of corticosteroids in his urine; that the ICU had been given a copy of the prescription for the cream; and that its use was permitted. "The UCI declares with the utmost firmness that this was an authorized usage, and does not constitute a case of doping," it said in a statement. (Corticosteroids, anti-inflammatory, and painkilling drugs, though not classed as steroids, are banned unless prescribed by doctors for specific medical conditions.)

Many Armstrong supporters believe that the scrutiny of Armstrong is the result, in part, of other factors: that he's aloof with the press, that he's uncooperative with photographers, that until recently he did not attempt to answer questions in French, that his bodyguard is a kick-boxing champion. It's also pointed out that France's most popular cyclist had been Richard Virenque, who admitted in October of 2000 that he had knowingly taken performance-enhancing drugs.

"An American looks at my story," Armstrong has said, "and says, 'Hell yeah, of course he did it [won the race clean]. He's motivated, he's crazy, he's passionate.' A French guy, he says, 'C'est pas possible'—it's not possible. The stigma there around cancer is what we had probably thirty years ago." In his book, Armstrong wrote, "Doping is an unfortunate fact of life in cycling… some teams and riders feel… they have to do it to stay competitive within the *peloton* [the densely packed group of cyclists riding together]. I never felt that way."

▶ As defending World Cup champions, France hardly made a good account of itself in 2002: They became the first defending Cup champs to be eliminated without scoring a single goal.

▶ In one of the more bizarre stories in Olympic annals—and that's saying something—the Canadian ice pairs team of Jamie Sale and David Pelletier was awarded a second, co-gold medal at the 2002 Salt Lake City Games. It was determined by the International Olympic Committee and International Skating Union that the Canadians, who'd skated nearly without flaw, may have been deprived of a fair evaluation by French judge Marie-Reine Le Gougne, who in an alleged vote-trading scheme with Russian skating officials, would cast her vote for the Russian pairs team of Elena Berezhnaya and Anton Sikharulidze in return for the Russian judge in the ice dancing competition voting for the favored French team (which eventually won the gold). Despite a couple of flubs in their routine, the Russian pairs team won, 5-4, over the Canadians, surprising many, and setting off "Skategate," a weird, ugly exchange of charges and countercharges (among them: Le Gougne allegedly claiming that she'd been pressured to do what she did by French skating federation president Didier Gailhaguet; the French claiming that Canadian and American officials, angered that Sale and Pelletier had lost, browbeat Le Gougne until she felt forced to make up her story). More allegations of coercion and lying were leveled between and among various national factions—in other words, exactly the kind of thing that the Olympics has become so adept in propagating.

… Ah! But We've Found a *New* Reason to Admire the French!

▶ The 1999 British Open at Carnoustie, Scotland, won't be remembered as the major tournament that Scotland's Paul Lawrie came from 10 strokes behind on the final day to win, but rather the one that Frenchman Jean Van de Velde lost. In fact, it may be remembered as the biggest gag in golf history, as Van de Velde took a three-stroke lead into the 72nd and final hole, and somehow managed to blow it with a triple bogey. The "somehow" involved a series of monumentally bad decisions after his tee shot drive (itself a bad decision) went wild right; next came a two-iron at the green, rather than putting it safely back onto the fairway; when that bounced off the grandstand into the rough, Van de Velde, rather than taking another safe shot to the fairway, tried to clear the water hazard—and didn't. At that point he took off his shoes and waded into the stream to contemplate hitting the ball out of the water, but in a wise move (his only one for the hole) he chose not to. "I could see the ball sinking, telling me, 'Hey, you silly man. Not for you today,'" he said afterwards. Van de Velde instead took a drop into the rough—and hit the ball into the bunker. He did eventually sink a six-foot putt to force a four-hole playoff with Lawrie and Justin Leonard, but Van de Velde, who started the day with a five-stroke lead, lost that, too.

How can one not love a man who goes for it like that, and who even stops to consider what his golf ball is saying to him?

Lesser-Known Sports Halls of Fame

"Cooperstown" has become shorthand for the National Baseball Hall of Fame and Museum, situated in Cooperstown, New York, 70 miles west of Albany, and the most widely known and frequently visited sports hall of fame in America. Other popular halls include the Naismith Memorial Basketball Hall of Fame in Springfield, Massachusetts, the Pro Football Hall of Fame in Canton, Ohio, and the International Tennis Hall of Fame and Museum in Newport, Rhode Island.

Dotted about our country and elsewhere, however, are shrines that celebrate lesser sports, athletes from different ethnic groups, and specific competitions. Certain of these institutions, from now and the past, have enshrined some surprising members.

► U.S. Croquet Hall of Fame, in Palm Beach Gardens, Florida
   Notable enshrinees: Harpo Marx, Samuel Goldwyn, George S. Kaufman, Richard Rodgers, Alexander Woollcott, Gig Young, Louis Jordan

► Hall of Fame of the Trotter, in Goshen, New York
   Notable enshrinees: Leland Stanford, founder of Stanford University and a prominent horse breeder; drivers Stanley Dancer, Billy Haughton; horses Dan Patch, Hambletonian

► International Jewish Sports Hall of Fame, in Netanya, Israel
   Notable enshrinees: Sandy Koufax, Mark Spitz, Hank Greenberg, Benny Leonard, Sid Luckman, Mel Allen, Red Auerbach

► American Museum of Fly Fishing, in Manchester, Vermont
   Former board member: Baseball Hall of Famer Ted Williams

► International Swimming Hall of Fame, in Fort Lauderdale, Florida
   Notable enshrinees: Benjamin Franklin, who was an avid swimmer; Julius Caesar, Winston Churchill

▶ National Softball Hall of Fame and Museum, in Oklahoma City, Oklahoma
  Notable enshrinee: Joan Joyce

▶ The Muskegon Area Sports Hall of Fame, in Muskegon, Michigan
  Notable enshrinees: Earl Morrall, Bennie Oosterbaan

▶ Fredonia College Sports Hall of Fame, in Fredonia, New York
  Notable enshrinee: Neil Postman, former basketball star and father of the author

▶ National Italian American Sports Hall of Fame, in Arlington Heights, Illinois
  Notable enshrinees: Joe DiMaggio, Vince Lombardi, Mario Andretti, Rocky Marciano

▶ Mexican Professional Baseball Hall of Fame (Salón de la Fama), in Monterrey, Mexico
  Notable enshrinees: Roy Campanella and Josh Gibson, who played in the Mexican leagues while the color barrier still existed in the major leagues

▶ National Polish American Sports Hall of Fame and Museum, in Detroit, Michigan
  Notable enshrinee: Stan Musial (their first inductee)

▶ Women's Sports Foundation International Hall of Fame, in New York City
  Notable enshrinees: Billie Jean King, Chris Evert, Peggy Fleming, Olga Korbut, Janet Guthrie

You Can Go Home Again

▶ Bill Parcells became a star coach after leading the New York Giants to their first two (and, so far, only) Super Bowl titles. He then swore off coaching. He became a pariah to many New York fans when he returned to the NFL to coach the New England Patriots. He then became a pariah to New England fans when he left there to coach the New York Jets (who, like the Giants, play at the Meadowlands in East Rutherford, New Jersey). When he quickly brought the sad-sack Jets to long-elusive respectability, his coaching once again won him New York's favor.

▶ Cynthia Cooper played professional basketball in Europe. After eleven years, she returned when she was drafted by the Houston Comets of the newly formed Women's National Basketball Association. In her first (and only) four years playing in the WNBA, she led the Comets to the title each time, won three scoring titles, two regular-season MVPs, and the championship MVP each of her four years.

▶ After 15 years with the San Francisco Giants, Willie McCovey left in 1974 and played for the San Diego Padres from 1974–76 and the Oakland Athletics, later in 1976. He returned to the Giants in 1977 for his final four years.

▶ Fran Tarkenton started his career as quarterback with the Minnesota Vikings, was traded to the New York Giants where he played for five years, and then finished his career with the Vikings.

▶ In the last part of his career, Lloyd Waner played for the Boston Braves (1941), Cincinnati Reds (1941), Philadelphia Phillies (1942), Brooklyn Dodgers (1944), and finally the Pittsburgh Pirates (1944–45), the team with which he had played the first 15 years of his career.

▶ Don Bunce, quarterback for Stanford's 1972 Rose Bowl team, became one of Stanford's team physicians.

▶ Although Mark Messier spent his best seasons with the Edmonton Oilers, he became one of the most beloved figures in New York sports history when he helped the Rangers discard their generations-old hex of failure and win the 1994 Stanley Cup, their first in 54 years. After a squabble with Ranger management, he left in 1997 for the Vancouver Canucks, but three years later he was eagerly welcomed back by— and eager to return to—his adopted home.

▶ Maury Wills was traded by the Los Angeles Dodgers to the Pittsburgh Pirates in 1967, went to the Montreal Expos in 1969, and in midseason was traded back to the Dodgers, where he finished his career.

▶ Phil Niekro came back to the Atlanta Braves for one last start in 1987. Niekro played his first 20 years with the Braves before making stops with the New York Yankees (1984–85), the Cleveland Indians (1986–87), and the Toronto Blue Jays (1987).

▶ Lee Mazzilli, Brooklyn-born and a New York City favorite, started his career with the Mets, was traded to the Texas Rangers, then to the Pittsburgh Pirates (with a pit-stop in between to play for New York's other baseball team, the Yankees), then returned to the Mets, and delivered two crucial World Series pinch hits to help win the 1986 title.

He is now a fixture on the Yankee coaching staff.

▶ At Hollywood Park in the 1970s, the great thoroughbred Affirmed once ran off by himself, setting off a frantic search. He was finally discovered back in his stall, which he had found among 2,244 others.

...Or Maybe You Can't Go Home Again

▶ Basketball great Clyde Drexler played for Sterling High School in Houston, grew up near the University of Houston campus, came to national prominence as a star for the UH Cougars' "Phi Slama Jama" team, and helped them to the NCAA title game two years in a row. He then spent most of his NBA career with the Portland Trailblazers, before being traded to the Houston Rockets, where he helped them to win an NBA title. When he retired, Drexler—named one of the NBA's 50 Greatest Players—returned to the University of Houston to coach his alma mater, whose basketball team had fallen on hard times.

After two seasons, he left, with a record of 19-39.

... Or Maybe You Just Stay Where You Are

▶ Pat LaFontaine, the great scoring center whose hockey career was cut short by concussions, played for the New York Islanders, the Buffalo Sabres, and finally the New York Rangers. Despite moving among these three teams, LaFontaine's place of employ was always within New York State, prompting one observer to say, "Boy, that guy really doesn't want to change license plates."

Athletes Without a Home

Some athletes and places were made for each other—Casey Stengel and New York City, for instance. Casey wore the uniforms of all four New York teams in existence during his baseball career—as player for the New York Giants and Brooklyn Dodgers, and as manager of the Yankees and Mets. Pete Rose, a native of Cincinnati, found fame and fortune in his backyard, and Kent Hrbek, from Minneapolis, did not have to move far when he made it to the bigs with the Twins.

Others are not so lucky. They may never find a place that they can call home. Or, they find a home but it's one far from the place where they began.

▶ At the turn of the 20th century, Tacks Latimer had a five-year major-league career, and each year he played with a different team.

▶ The modern-day Tacks Latimer is Mike Morgan, relief pitcher for the Arizona Diamondbacks. In a major-league career that spans 25 years (he missed the 1981, '83, and '84 seasons), he has played with a record 12 teams: Oakland, New York (AL), Toronto, Seattle, Baltimore, Los Angeles, Chicago (NL), St. Louis, Cincinnati, Minnesota, Chicago again, Texas, and Arizona, where he has lasted an amazingly housebound three years. So far.

▶ German Bernard Trautmann, an outstanding soccer player, was taken prisoner of war by the British during World War II. After the war, Trautmann remained in England and became a star goalie for the Manchester City club in the English Soccer League.

▶ Jaroslav Drobny played tennis under four different nationalities. He was born in Prague and first classified as a Czech. After the Nazi invasion of Czechoslovakia, Drobny was listed in 1939 as being from Bohemia-Moravia. From 1946–48, Drobny was Czech again, but in 1949 he became a naturalized Egyptian. In 1960, he was given British citizenship.

▶ Goaltender Gary "Suitcase" Smith was traded or moved 11 times in 15 years in the NHL and WHA.

▶ In 1976, James Gilkes of Guyana, who had won the Pan-Am Games 200m, was kept out of the Olympics by his country's boycott. The International Olympic Committee turned down his appeal to compete under the Olympic flag.

▶ On January 16, 1905, outfielder Frank Huelsman went from the Boston Red Sox to the Washington Senators, the sixth time he was traded or loaned in eight months.

▶ Tennis player Bettina Bunge was born in Switzerland, lived for 14 years in Peru, moved to Florida and then to Monaco.

▶ Major leaguer Glenn Hubbard was born in West Germany and played Little League in Taiwan.

▶ Tom Owens played for the following professional basketball teams: Memphis, Carolina, St. Louis, Memphis again, Kentucky, Indiana, and San Antonio of the ABA; and Houston, Portland, Indiana again, and Detroit of the NBA.

▶ Football coaching legend John Heisman led teams at Oberlin, Akron, Auburn, Clemson, Pennsylvania, Washington and Jefferson, Rice, and Georgia Tech. Georgia Tech was the only one of those schools at which he stayed for as long as six years.

▶ The successful and peripatetic Larry Brown, basketball's John Heisman, has coached the ABA's Carolina (1972–74) and Denver (1974–79) teams; UCLA (1979–81); the New York Nets (1981–83); the University of Kansas (1983–88); the San Antonio Spurs (1988–92); the Los Angeles Clippers (1992–93); the Indiana Pacers (1993–97); and the Philadelphia 76ers (1997–).

▶ Because of liberal college eligibility rules during World War II, football end Barney Poole played for Mississippi in 1942, North Carolina in 1943, Army in 1944–46, and Mississippi again in 1947–48.

Americans Invade Foreign Sports... and Foreigners Invade American Sports

The world keeps getting smaller. The opposing All-Star sides for the suddenly polyglot NHL are no longer the Western and Eastern Conferences, but North America and the World.

The Ryder Cup is no longer a quaint U.S. versus England affair, but U.S. versus Europe; one wonders how long it will be before the former side expands, or the latter expands again.

America's Cup is held by... New Zealand.

The first player taken in the 2002 NBA draft is from... China.

Soccer fans in Italy and Argentina might actually know—and respect—the skills of a player from... New Jersey.

Some examples:

▶ Although he was preceded to the major leagues by Japanese countryman Masanori Murakami, who pitched for the San Francisco Giants in 1964 and 1965, Hideo Nomo started a wave of Asian ballplayers heading west (east?) when he left the Kintetsu Buffalo to sign with the Los Angeles Dodgers in 1995. Unlike Murakami, Nomo went straight from Japanese baseball to the majors, and his every move was chronicled by a horde of Japanese media. Nomo, with his befuddling hesitation delivery and killer forkball, was an immediate sensation, winning Rookie of the Year honors and so endearing himself to Dodger fans that "Nomomania" was born 15 years after Mexican pitcher Fernando Valenzuela spawned "Fernandomania."

Nomo's success—he led the league in strikeouts as a rookie, and pitched a no-hitter against the Colorado Rockies at Coors Field in 1996—paved the way for Japanese pitchers such as Hideki Irabu, Shigetoshi Hasegawa, and Kazuhiro Suzuki to join the major leagues. In 2001, the New York Mets' Tsuyoshi Shinjo and the Seattle Mariners' Ichiro Suzuki—his last name was rarely used—broke another barrier when they became the first Japanese position players to perform in the major leagues. Ichiro, in particular, met with runaway success in Seattle, winning the American League's batting title with his .350 average and being named the American League's Most Valuable Player.

▶ None of the members of the 1998 Los Angeles Dodgers' original rotation was a native-English–speaker: Ramon Martinez (Dominican), Hideo Nomo (Japanese), Chan Ho Park (Korean), Ismael Valdes (Mexican), and Dennis Reyes (Mexican).

▶ It's hard to know who was more shocked by the development—South America, Europe, or America herself—but in August of 2002, for the first time ever, the U.S. men's national soccer team was ranked among the world's top ten—#9, to be precise—by FIFA, soccer's ruling body. The U.S. had just come off an impressive showing at the 2002 World Cup, where they succumbed finally in a spirited quarterfinal loss to Germany, the eventual runner-up.

▶ American men ended a 46-year medal drought in Olympic bobsled competition when the U.S. took both the silver and bronze in the four-man race at the 2002 Salt Lake City Games. Men's bobsled has for decades been dominated by Germany, Italy, Switzerland, and Austria. American men had not won two bobsledding medals since the 1948 Games at St. Moritz.

▶ The NBA is now crawling with foreigners who have shown American fans how good the game has become overseas. (And given, in 2002, America's first-ever medal-free finish at the World Basketball Championships—on home court, in Indianapolis—it still hasn't sunk in for many U.S.-born players just how small the gulf is between them and Europeans, especially.) In the 2001 NBA draft, a record seven foreign-born players were selected, and Spain's Pau Gasol was the highest foreigner ever selected, at #3, by the Memphis Grizzlies. Gasol would win the Rookie of the Year Award, beating out other formidable foreigners like France's Tony Parker and Russia's Andrei Kirilenko. At the 2002 draft, the record for foreigners selected was eviscerated when 17 of them were taken, including six in the first round, including the #1 overall pick, 7'5" Yao Ming of China, who went to the Houston Rockets.

The 28 Most Hallowed Pieces of Sports Real Estate

Without much trouble, most fans could come up with legitimate substitutions—Waveland Avenue behind Wrigley Field, Pauley Pavilion, the streets of Monte Carlo where the Grand Prix is contested, the old Boston Garden, the Cresta Run at St. Moritz, Forest Hills back when it stood for American tennis, the swimming pool in Mission Viejo (California), the Rose Bowl. Some may disagree with our choices, and bother about the holy ground that we ignored, or the sports that we failed even to represent.

So be it. We've chosen the 28 sites or venues (and, where appropriate, the most hallowed part of that site) from today and yesterday—some of which no longer exist—that have taken firmest hold in the collective consciousness of American and world fandom.

▶ Yankee Stadium's home plate, the pitching mound, and the fenced-off shrine behind left-center field

▶ The 16th hole at Cypress Point, in California, called by many the most famous hole in the world, as well as the most beautiful, the most photographed, and the most difficult par-three

▶ Heartbreak Hill, between miles 16 and 18 of the Boston Marathon route

▶ Center ice at the old Montreal Forum

▶ The Carlisle Indian Industrial School fields, where Jim Thorpe played as a collegian

▶ Ebbets Field, where the Brooklyn Dodgers played (and where the Jackie Robinson Apartments stand today)

▶ Centre Court, Wimbledon

▶ The Bonneville Salt Flats, Utah, site of so many world land-speed records

▶ The English Channel, the most famous test for the endurance swimmer

▶ The Green Monster at Fenway Park

▶ The starting line at the Indianapolis Motor Speedway

▶ The Champs Elysées in Paris, the final section of the world's most prestigious bicycle race—the Tour de France

▶ Berlin's Olympic Stadium, site of Jesse Owens's four gold medal-winning performances

▶ Center court, Madison Square Garden, New York City

▶ The Elysian Fields, in Hoboken, New Jersey, where the first baseball game was played

▶ Maracana, in Rio de Janeiro, the biggest soccer stadium in the world and the 1950 site of perhaps the most famous World Cup match of all, the final between Brazil and Uruguay

▶ The home stretch at Churchill Downs, in Louisville, Kentucky

► Olympia, at the northwestern tip of Peloponnesus, site of the original Olympic Games

► The world-class skatepark, including vert ramp, at the Encinitas (San Diego) YMCA, where hometown skateboarding legend Tony Hawk mastered his craft

► The Thames River, where the Henley Regatta is held

► Rome, site of the Circus Maximus and the Colosseum—the ancient meccas, respectively, of chariot racing and gladiator fights

► The Canyon of Heroes in downtown Manhattan, site to so many ticker-tape parades for sports champions over the decades (seemingly a rite of autumn in the last several years, thanks to the New York Yankees)

► The Royal and Ancient Club, St. Andrews (also called the "Old Course" or the "Old Lady"), Kingdom of Fife, Scotland—simply the most famous 18 holes in the world

► The Holmenkollen in Norway, site of the oldest and most prestigious ski jumping event in the world

► The waters off of Newport, Rhode Island, site of so many America's Cup races

► Omaha, Nebraska, home to baseball's College World Series

► YMCAs in Massachusetts—the one in Springfield, where James Naismith invented basketball in 1891, and the one in Holyoke, where William G. Morgan invented volleyball in 1895

► The Bislett track in Oslo, Norway, legendary for great distance performances

5

NAMES

The Most Appropriately Named Figures in Sports

Some athletes spend their careers trying to live down their unfortunate names—reserve NBA center Frank Brickowski, major-league pitcher Bob Walk, pro golfer Bobby Cruickshank come to mind. Others may live up to their names, literally. Stephanie Hightower became a champion American hurdler, Andy Payne triumphed in the 1928 "Bunion Derby," a 3,422-mile coast-to-coast footrace, James Lightbody won the 1904 Olympic 1,500m race. And if the planets line up just so, as they seemed to on January 26, 1960, anything is possible. On that date, a West Virginia high school basketball player scored 135 points in a single game. His name was Danny Heater, his hometown Burnsville.

Here are some athletes and sports figures whose names seem aptly to have anticipated their pursuits, talents, or circumstances.

▶ Largest Agbejemisin, 6'7", 225-pound center for the Wagner College basketball team

▶ Syd Thrift, general manager (at various times) for the Pittsburgh Pirates, New York Yankees, and Baltimore Orioles

▶ Ernie Shavers, bald boxer

▶ Marjorie Gestring, springboard diving gold medalist, 1936 Olympics

▶ Jeff Float, Olympic swimmer

▶ Willie Thrower, NFL quarterback

▶ Jack Crouch, major-league catcher, 1930s

▶ Lake Speed, auto racer

▶ Steve Axman, football coach of the Northern Arizona University Lumberjacks

▶ Mike Quick and Mac Speedie, NFL wide receivers

▶ Johnny High, one of 11 Phoenix Suns players involved in the then-biggest drug bust in professional sports history, in 1987

▶ Anna Smashnova, tennis player

▶ Steve Stonebreaker, NFL linebacker, 1962–68, and his son, Michael, Notre Dame linebacker; Jim Youngblood, linebacker, and Jack Youngblood, defensive end, both NFL

▶ Ban Johnson, American League president, 1901–27, who suspended, among others, John McGraw in 1902 for umpire-baiting, Ty Cobb in 1912 for going into the stands to attack a heckler, Boston Red Sox pitcher Carl Mays in 1919 for leaving his team for two weeks, and Babe Ruth twice in 1922 for umpire-baiting

▶ Johnny Podres, pitcher for the San Diego Padres (in 1969, his final year as a player), and Ken Houston, defensive back for the Houston Oilers, 1967–72

▶ Margaret Court, tennis champion

▶ Brianna Scurry, goalie for the U.S. women's World Cup team

▶ Upset, the horse that beat Man O' War in the 1919 Sanford Memorial Stakes at Saratoga Springs, the only loss of Man O' War's career

▶ John Force, drag racer

▶ Joe Don Looney, 1960s NFL fullback and renowned as one of football's biggest flakes

▷ **Note:** One very notable last name seems simultaneously appropriate *and* inappropriate, depending on how you interpret it: Woods, as in Tiger's last name. (Woods = golf clubs: appropriate. Woods = not in the fairway: inappropriate.)

At Least 14 Other Boxers Named Muhammad or Ali

After heavyweight champion Cassius Clay changed his name in 1964, in accordance with his new faith, many other black athletes followed suit, boxers especially.

▶ Abdullah Muhammad (original name: Lee Holloman; heavyweight; Dallas)

▶ Kato Ali (Tony Curry; junior lightweight; Philadelphia)

▶ Abdul Haleem Muhammad (Edward Riley; middleweight; East Orange, New Jersey)

▶ Ali Salaam (Henry Hank, Jr.; junior middleweight; Gary, Indiana)

▶ Dwight Muhammad Qawi (Dwight Braxton; light heavyweight and cruiserweight; Philadelphia)

▶ Ali Karim Muhammad (Dwayne Thompson; welterweight; Chicago)

▶ Hassan Ali (Herman Ingram; bantamweight; Newark)

▶ Matthew Saad Muhammad (Matt Franklin; light heavyweight; Philadelphia)

▶ Ferra Khan Ali (Ron Merriweather; junior lightweight; Newark)

▶ Asmar Reheem Muhammad (Walter Cowans, Jr.; welterweight; Milwaukee)

▶ Eddie Mustafa Muhammad (Eddie Gregory; light heavyweight; Brooklyn)

▶ Terrance Alli (Terrence Halley; junior lightweight; Guyana and Brooklyn)

▶ Fred Muhammad (Fred Grogan; heavyweight; Denver)

▶ Akbar Ali Muhammed (Charles Buckner; middleweight; Chicago)

Four more that we'd like to mention:

▶ General Ali (middleweight; Philadelphia)

▶ Slim Ali (light heavyweight; Washington, D.C.)

▶ Ali Allen (heavyweight; Patterson, New Jersey)

▶ Ali Jr. (bantamweight; Philippines)

One from Rivington, New Jersey:

▶ Furgan Ali (light heavyweight)

One from his own family:

▶ Laila Ali (daughter)

Honorable mention:

▷ Understanding Allah (William Greenshaw; light heavyweight; Brooklyn)

Mention honorable:

▶ Sugar Brown (Bilal Ali; middleweight; Newark)

Don't ask us:

▶ Abdur Rahim Muhammad (The Great Muhammad; middleweight; Brooklyn)

We have no idea what to do with, but we thought you should be aware of him:

▶ Alhamza "U.F.O." (Maurice Veabro Boykin; welterweight; Chicago)

Are You Sure We Haven't Met Before? Then Why Does Your Name Sound So Familiar?

▶ Craig James, SMU and NFL running back, and Jim Craig, 1980 U.S. Olympic hockey goalie

▶ John Thomas, 1960s high jump world-record holder, and Tommy John, surgery-miracle pitcher

▶ John Salley, NBA center-forward, and Sally John, wife of Tommy John

▶ Samoa Samoa, former Washington State University quarterback, and Samoa Samoa (see previous)

▶ Johnny Jackson, NFL defensive back, and Jack Johnson, first black heavyweight boxing champion

▶ sailboarding, another name for windsurfing, and boardsailing, another name for windsurfing

▶ Kenny Williams, major-league outfielder, and Bill Kenney, NFL quarterback

▶ Jimy Williams, major-league manager, and Bill James, author of countless *Bill James Baseball Abstracts*

Clever NHL Nicknames

Of all the major sports—of all sports, perhaps—hockey has left us the most impoverished legacy of nicknames. This may be confirmed simply by noting the sobriquet of the sport's best player: Gretzky "The Great." On other occasions, he is referred to colorfully as "Gretz."

A small sampling of other evocative hockey nicknames:

▶ Willie "Hubie" Huber

▶ Doug "Hicksy" Hicks

▶ Bob "Boydie" Boyd

▶ Bob "Bournie" Bourne

▶ Jim "Schony" Schoenfeld

▶ Frank "Sully" Sullivan

▶ Jim "Watty" Watson

▶ Paul "Woodsy" Woods

▶ Wally "Hergie" Hergesheimer

▶ Ellard "Obie" O'Brien

▶ Pat "Pricey" Price

▶ Stephen "Wochy" Wojciechowski

▶ Phil "Espo" Esposito

▶ John "Fergie" Ferguson (and Lorne "Fergie" Ferguson)

▶ Craig "Rammer" Ramsay

▶ Dave "Lummer" Lumley

▶ Pete "Stemmer" Stemkowski

▶ Rod "Zainer" Zaine

▶ Pete "Drisk" Driscoll

▶ Rick "Duds" Dudley

▶ Mark "Pav" Pavelich

▶ Jim "Pep" Peplinski

▶ Mark "Mess" Messier

▶ Jerry "Topper" Toppazzini (and Zellio "Topper" Toppazzini)

The Offspring of Unimaginative Parents

Hockey is not alone in its uninspired nicknaming.

From 1929 to 1932, the NFL included one franchise known as the Stapleton Stapes, and in the 1960s, the dominant triumvirate of golfers Arnold Palmer, Jack Nicklaus, and Gary Player was known—brace yourself—as "The Big Three." The award for colorlessness, however, clearly goes to the Canadian Football League. For decades (until 1996), in a league with fewer than ten teams, one of them was named the Ottawa Rough Riders, another the Saskatchewan Roughriders. Apparently, the space makes a difference.

Let's just say that the parents of not a few world-class athletes were simply tired the day that they named their offspring, and leave it there.

- ▶ Billy Williams, Chicago Cubs slugger and outfielder
- ▶ Pete Peeters, NHL goalie
- ▶ John Johnson, NBA forward
- ▶ Bob Robertson, Pittsburgh Pirates first baseman
- ▶ Eddie Edwards, 1988 British Olympic ski jumper and folk hero
- ▶ Tony Anthony, Detroit heavyweight
- ▶ Tommy Thompson, Boston Braves outfielder, 1930s
- ▶ Don O'Donoghue, NHL right wing
- ▶ Willie Wilson, Kansas City Royals outfielder
- ▶ Anthony Toney, Philadelphia Eagles running back
- ▶ University of Illinois Illini (the "Fighting" middle name does not absolve them)
- ▷ Double honor to Hall of Fame pitcher Robin Roberts, who spent most of his career with the Philadelphia Phillies
- ▷ Double-double honor to Edgardo Alfonzo, New York Mets infielder, who has a brother named Edgar
- ▷ Off-the-charts honor to former heavyweight boxing champion George Foreman, whose children include George Foreman, Jr., George III, George IV, George V, George VI, and Georgetta. His non-George-named children will not be named here—yes, he has some—to protect their uniqueness.

9 Inevitable Nicknames

Some athletes are blessed with a name, look, background, or talent that inspires a unique nickname. There's Virgil "Fire" Trucks, for example, and Emil "Hill Billy" Bildilli; lanky George "The Stork" Theodore and home appliance-like William "The Refrigerator" Perry; quarterback Jack "The Throwin' Samoan" Thompson and Swedish world heavyweight champion Ingemar Johannson, whose right hand was known as "Thor's

Hammer"; shotblocking Marvin "The Human Eraser" Webster and sure-handed infielder Bob "Death to Flying Things" Ferguson.

Others are not so lucky. Failing certain obvious distinctions, they quickly become characterized by their most generic feature. A bespectacled player becomes "Spec," a southpaw "Lefty" (there have been over 150 "Leftys" in baseball's first hundred years), a tall player "Stretch," a redhead "Red," a towhead or gray-hair "Whitey," a Fitzsimmons "Fitz." Here are some other names that, given one or two basic circumstances, will almost certainly be applied.

► A boxer—or any athlete, for that matter—with a Ray somewhere in his name will become "Sugar." (See boxers "Sugar" Ray Robinson, "Sugar" Ray Leonard, "Sugar" Ray Seales, basketball player Micheal "Sugar" Ray Richardson, etc.)

► An athlete from the Netherlands or of real or perceived Dutch extraction, regardless of his jumping ability, will be called "The Flying Dutchman." (See tennis player Tom "The Flying Dutchman" Okker, soccer great Johann "The Flying Dutchman" Cruyff, baseball legend Honus "The Flying Dutchman" Wagner, who was actually German but thought to be Dutch, etc.)

► A team executive, especially a general manager, named Jack will be called "Trader," whether he makes many trades or not. (See San Diego Padres GM and sometime manager "Trader" Jack McKeon, Detroit Pistons and Minnesota Timberwolves GM "Trader" Jack McCloskey, etc.)

► A baseball player named Durham will be called "Bull." (See Leon "Bull" Durham, Louis "Bull" Durham, Donald "Bull" Durham, Ed "Bull" Durham, etc.)

► A Native-American will be called Chief. (See major leaguers John "Chief" Meyers, Charles "Chief" Bender, Moses "Chief" Yellowhorse, Allie "Big Chief" or "Superchief" Reynolds, etc.)

► A baseball team located in Milwaukee will adopt a name having to do with beer. (See the 1891 American Association Milwaukee Brewers, the 1901 American League Milwaukee Brewers, the present-day American League Milwaukee Brewers, etc.)

► A Joe who is fast and strong will evoke thoughts of smoke. (See hard-throwing pitcher "Smoky" Joe Wood, Negro League fastballer "Smoky" Joe Williams, hard-punching heavyweight "Smokin'" Joe Frazier, etc.)

► A player named Brown, especially an outside shooter in basketball or a deep threat receiver in football, will be called "Downtown." (See NBA gunner "Downtown" Freddie Brown, speedy NFL wideout "Downtown" Eddie Brown, outfielder "Downtown" Ollie Brown, boxer "Downtown" Leona Brown, etc.)

► An athlete of Italian extraction will at some point be known as "The Italian Stallion." (See running back Franco "The Italian Stallion" Harris, Alabama running back Johnny "The Italian Stallion" Musso, fictional boxer Rocky "The Italian Stallion" Balboa, etc.)

Shared Names I

Both members in each of the following pairs of sports figures answer to the same name. If one chooses to see it, the similarity between them extends beyond that.

▶ Roger Craig, once-San Francisco 49ers running back, and Roger Craig, once-San Francisco Giants manager

▶ Steve Ontiveros, mediocre pitcher in the 1980s, and Steve Ontiveros, mediocre third baseman in the 1970s

▶ Mike Marshall, Los Angeles Dodger in the 1980s, and Mike Marshall, Los Angeles Dodger in the 1970s

▶ Keith Jackson, former burly NFL tight end, and Keith Jackson, burly ABC commentator

▶ Charles Smith, former NBA forward and Big East star, and Charles Smith, former NBA guard and Big East star

▶ Robert T. ("Bobby") Jones, golfing immortal, and Robert T. Jones, golf-course architect immortal

▶ Bobby J. Jones, righthanded pitcher for the New York Mets and San Diego Padres, and Bobby M. Jones, lefthanded pitcher for the New York Mets and San Diego Padres

▶ John Thompson, basketball Hall of Famer from the 1920s, and John Thompson, Georgetown coach and basketball Hall of Famer from the 1970s–90s

▶ Jason (now Jay) Williams, point guard for the rebuilding Chicago Bulls, and Jason Williams, point guard for the rebuilding Memphis Grizzlies

▶ Tim Brown, great Raiders kickoff returner (and receiver), and Tim Brown, great Philadelphia Eagles kickoff returner

▶ Edwin Moses, world-record hurdler, and Ed Moses, world-record breaststroker

▶ Bob Miller, 6'1" lefthanded pitcher for the 1962 New York Mets, and Bob Miller, 6'1" righthanded pitcher for the 1962 New York Mets

Shared Names II

We weren't finished (though these aren't quite so striking).

▶ Mike Tyson, former world heavyweight boxing champion, and Mike Tyson, St. Louis Cardinals reserve infielder in the 1970s

▶ Bill Russell, basketball great, and Bill Russell, baseball so-so

▶ Eddie Murray, home-run belter, and Eddie Murray, field goal booter

▶ Chris Evert, tennis great, and Chris Evert, thoroughbred great named after the tennis great

▶ John Lloyd, Negro League baseball star, and John Lloyd, former Mr. Chris Evert

▶ Joe DiMaggio, baseball immortal, and Joe DiMaggio, *Sports Illustrated* contributing photographer

▶ John Madden, football commentator and former coach, and John Madden, breeder of five Kentucky Derby winners

▶ Pascual Perez, 1950s flyweight champion, and Pascual Perez, 1980s–90s pitcher

▶ John Henry Johnson, journeyman pitcher in the 1970s and 1980s, and John Henry Johnson, Pro Football Hall of Fame fullback (and John Henry, Hall of Fame horse)

▶ Bob Gibson, great pitcher for the St. Louis Cardinals, and Bob Gibson, lousy pitcher for the Milwaukee Brewers

▶ Dick Stockton, tennis player, and Dick Stockton, NBA voice

▶ Kurt Thomas, Olympic gold medal-winning gymnast, and Kurt Thomas, NBA forward

▶ Joe Morgan, Cincinnati Red Hall of Famer, and Joe Morgan, former manager of the Boston Red Sox

▶ Mike Reid, golfer, and Mike Reid, once-defensive tackle for the Cincinnati Bengals

▶ Larry Brown, former Washington Redskins running back, and Larry Brown, Philadelphia 76ers basketball coach, and Larry Brown, former Pittsburgh Steelers tight end

▶ Joe Morris, one-time New York Giants running back, and Joe Morris, second-place horse in the 1910 Kentucky Derby

▶ Jimmy "The Greek" Snyder, betting expert, and Jimmy "Not the Greek" Snyder, former Seattle Mariners manager

▶ Jim Thorpe, all-around superstar, and Jim Thorpe, golfer

▶ Fernando Valenzuela, Los Angeles Dodgers pitcher, and Fernando Valenzuela, jockey

The 34 Best Names in Sports

Everyone who writes about sports, especially baseball, eventually gets around to compiling a list of their favorite sports names. While we're not everyone, this book does purport to be the ultimate collection of sports lists, hence our small contribution. This list contains a curiously large number of major-league pitchers, a fraternity that has contributed a disproportionate number of colorful names to the world. But then we dedicate our list to Van Lingle Mungo, the Brooklyn Dodger and New York Giant pitcher who has graced more lists of this variety—and even inspired the 1970 song by Dave Frishberg, "Van Lingle Mungo," a chronicle of memorable names—than any other athlete living or dead.

▶ Picabo Street, Olympic gold medalist skier

▶ Maurice Archdeacon, 1920s Chicago White Sox outfielder

▶ Tedy Bruschi ("Brewski"), New England Patriots linebacker

▶ André Champagne, NHL left wing, 1962–63

▶ Ugueth ("Oogy") Urbina, Boston Red Sox reliever

▶ Cletus Elwood "Boots" Poffenberger, 1930s pitcher

▶ Ossee Schreckengost, turn-of-the-century catcher

▶ Peerless Price, Buffalo Bills wide receiver

▶ Edward Wineapple, 1920s pitcher

▶ Calvin Coolidge Julius Caesar Tuskahoma "Buster" McLish, pitcher, 1944–64

▶ Thane Gash, Cleveland Browns safety

▶ Earthwind Moreland, cornerback out of Georgia Southern (Yes: He was named after the group Earth, Wind, and Fire).

▶ Pokey Reese, Pittsburgh Pirates second baseman

▶ Y. A. Tittle, NFL quarterback

▶ Fatima Whitbread, British javelin-throwing Olympian

▶ Morris Titanic, NHL left wing, mid-1970s

▶ Apollo Ohno, Olympic gold-medalist short-track speedskater

▶ Razor Shines, brief Montreal Expo, 1980s

▶ Fair Hooker, Cleveland Browns receiver

▶ James Bluejacket, 1910s pitcher

▶ Esteban Yan, Tampa Bay Devil Rays reliever

▶ Climax, Saskatchewan, hometown of 1970s NHL defenseman Gord Kluzak

▶ Vitautris Casimirus Tamulis, pitcher in the 1930s and 1940s

▶ Onix Concepcion, 1980s infielder

▶ Milton Bradley, Cleveland Indians outfielder

▶ Speedy Claxton, San Antonion Spurs point guard

▶ Vida Blue, Oakland Athletics and San Francisco Giants pitcher, 1970s and 1980s

▶ Heinie Manush, Hall of Fame outfielder, 1923–1939

▶ Tim Spooneybarger, Atlanta Braves reliever

▶ Harthorne Wingo, New York Knicks forward, 1972–76

▶ Coco Crisp, minor-league outfielder

▶ Coy Bacon, NFL defensive lineman in the 1960s and 1970s

▶ And, finally, the 1976 Olympic rowing tandem that won the silver medal in the pair-oared shell without coxswain, Calvin Coffey and Michael Staines.

The Briefest Names in Sports

Brevity is the soul of wit, not to mention Mike Witt, the economically named California Angels pitcher. Here are some other athletes best appreciated by fatigued PA announcers and those who sew names on the backs of uniforms.

▶ Willie Pep, world featherweight boxing champion

▶ Henk Vink, Dutch motorcycle champion

▶ J. Torchio (just "J."), University of California football player, 1980–83

▶ Zenon M (just "M"), Cal Poly-Pomona basketball player, 1986–87

▶ Ron Cey, Los Angeles Dodger and Chicago Cub third baseman

▶ Ray Guy, Oakland/Los Angeles Raiders punter

▶ Hap Day, Toronto Maple Leafs defenseman and coach

▶ Ed Ott, Pittsburgh Pirate and California Angel catcher, 1974–81

▶ Hu Na, Chinese tennis player

▶ Pelé, Brazilian soccer immortal

▶ Zev, 1923 Kentucky Derby and Belmont winner

▶ I, Argentina-born colt in 1930

The Most Offbeat and Irreverent Nicknames

▶ Pepe Munoz of Mexico, 200m breaststroke champion at the 1968 Olmpics, was called "Tibio" (lukewarm) because his father was from Aguascalientes (hot waters) and his mother was from Rio Frio (cold river).

▶ A Philadelphia Phillie and Pittsburgh Pirate pitcher in the 1930s and 1940s, Hugh "Losing Pitcher" Mulcahy, had a career won-lost record of 45-89. In his four full seasons, he twice led the National League in losses.

▶ The defunct Southern Hockey League had a team in Georgia called the Macon Whoopees.

▶ Boxer Peter Crawley, who held the bareknuckles prize ring crown for only seven days in 1827, was nicknamed "Young Rump Steak."

▶ John "Superbrat" McEnroe was given the nickname by the British press for his legendary complaining during his Wimbledon matches and elsewhere. In 1981, McEnroe became the only Wimbledon champion to be denied membership to the All-England Club (though he was accepted to the club when he won again in 1983).

▶ In the mixed doubles draw of several tournaments in the 1920s, tennis champion Suzanne Lenglen of France partnered a "Mr. G"—King Gustav V of Sweden.

▶ The end who played opposite Don Hutson, the brilliant Alabama flanker, was known simply as "the other end." Hutson's silent partner would eventually emerge from the shadows to coach football at

Kentucky and Alabama, where Paul "Bear" Bryant grew into his better-remembered nickname.

▶ Heavyweight boxer Andrew Golota, from Poland, is known as "The Foul Pole."

▶ Pearce "What's the Use" Chiles had a brief major-league career at the turn of the century.

▶ Several major leaguers have labored under disparaging, less-than-masculine tags, including Charles "The Old Woman in the Red Cap" Pabor, Grayson "Grandmother" Pearce, William "Mary" Calhoun, and Frank "Flossie" Oberlin.

Spellling Errors

Granted: The editorial precision displayed by most of today's print media would be massively red-pencilled by our grade-school English teacher. But is it really necessary for the following athletes to spell their names the way they do, thus sending us into a further tailspin of confusion over whose mistake it was? Didn't we just get comfortable, after many years, with adding the initial H to Akeem Olajuwon's name, as was once standard, to make it *Hakeem* Olajuwon?

▶ Torii Hunter, Minnesota Twins All-Star outfielder

▶ Deivi Cruz, San Diego Padres (Dominican Republic)

▶ Robb Nen, San Francisco Giants closer

▶ Kelvim Escobar, Toronto Blue Jays reliever (Venezuela)

▶ Jimy Williams, Houston Astros manager

▶ Andruw Jones, Atlanta Braves All-Star outfielder (Curaçao)

▶ Graeme Lloyd, Florida Marlins relief pitcher (Australia)

▶ Micheal Ray Richardson, former NBA guard

▶ Anfernee Hardaway, Phoenix Suns guard

▶ Issiac Holt, NFL cornerback

▶ Isiah Thomas, Basketball Hall of Fame guard

Musical Sports Figures

There's a high correspondence between names in the sports and music world. We've taken note of this because that's the kind of thing we take note of.

▶ Jim Morrison, journeyman infielder/Doors lead singer

▶ Steve Howe drug-troubled Dodger and Yankee pitcher/Yes lead guitarist

▶ Bob Welch, Dodger and As pitcher/Fleetwood Mac member

▶ Joe Jackson, shoeless baseball legend/British singer-songwriter

► Michael Jackson, Georgetown basketball guard/NFL linebacker/wacko half-man, half-child singer

► Darryl Hall, University of Washington defensive back / Hall and Oates co-namesake

► John Oates, journeyman catcher/Hall and Oates co-namesake

► Johnny Ray, All-Star second baseman/1950s rock star

► Muddy Waters, brief Michigan State University football coach/blues legend

► Dave Stewart, All-Star pitcher and pitching coach/Eurythmics co-member

► James Brown, sports anchor/soul singer

► Bob Weir, British hammer-throw Olympian/Grateful Dead guitarist

► Albert King, basketball player/blues legend

► Bobby Brown, Yankees infielder and American League president/pop-rap star

► Dave Clark, journeyman outfielder/Beatles imitator

► Kenny Rogers, Texas Rangers pitcher/pop-country star

Human Typos

Baseball fans thought they'd misheard, in 1981, that the Atlanta Braves had broken in a rookie outfielder named Brett Butler. *Rhett* Butler, we thought; it must have been a takeoff on Rhett Butler, one of Atlanta's favorite sons—Clark Gable in *Gone With the Wind*—and it was not a particularly funny takeoff, at that. Well, Butler—Brett, that is—moved on from the South to other teams, effectively clearing up that confusion*, but the names in each of the following pairs of sports figures look enough alike, without being identical, that if you came across one or the other while reading the sports pages—late at night, after an especially trying day—you might believe you'd encountered a typo. Is this a legitimate basis on which to build a list? Frankly, no. Nonetheless, we soldier on.

*And now a Brent Butler plays second base for the Colorado Rockies. That's just great.

► Robby Thompson, San Francisco Giants player, 1980s, and Bobby Thomson, New York Giants player, 1950s

► Owen Davidson, 1960s tennis star from Australia, and Sven Davidson, 1950s tennis star from Sweden

► Ralph Simpson, ABA star, 1970s, and Ralph Sampson, NBA star, 1980s

► Tom Seelos, great Austrian slalomer, 1930s, and Toni Sailer, great Austrian slalomer, 1950s

► Chris McMullin, who made a record 29 of 29 free throws for Dixie College in the NJCAA national finals in 1982, and Chris Mullin, NBA star and career 87% free-throw shooter

▶ Cot Deal, mediocre pitcher, 1947–54, and Coot Veal, mediocre short-stop, 1958–63

▶ Johnny "Lam" Jones, University of Texas running back / wide receiver, 1976–79, and Johnny "Ham" Jones, University of Texas running back, 1976–78, and A. J. "Jam" Jones, University of Texas running back, 1978–81

▶ Gerry Cooney, great white hope, 1980s, and Gerrie Coetzee, great white hope, 1980s

▶ Jamal Mashburn, University of Kentucky alum and New Orleans Hornets forward, and Jamaal Magloire, University of Kentucky alum and New Orleans Hornets forward

▶ Paul McNamee, former Australian tennis player and doubles part-ner of Peter McNamara, and Peter McNamara, former Australian ten-nis player and doubles partner of Paul McNamee

▶ New York Mets, baseball team, and New York Jets, football team, and New York Nets, relocated basketball team, and New York Sets, defunct World Team Tennis team

▶ Hank Sauer, underappreciated National Leaguer of the 1940s and 1950s, and Hank Bauer, underappreciated American Leaguer of the 1940s and 1950s

▶ Shirley "Cha Cha" Muldowney, drag-racer, and Clarence "Choo Choo" Coleman, former New York Mets catcher, and Juan "Chi Chi" Rodriguez, charismatic golfer

▶ Donald Trump, a driving force behind the United States Football League, and Donald Crump, brief commissioner, Canadian Football League

And Some More Striking Name Tandems

▶ Babe Pinelli, major-league player and umpire, and Babe Parilli, University of Kentucky and NFL quarterback

▶ Francis Ouimet, U.S. Open golf champion, and François Ouimet, NHL defenseman, mid-1970s

▶ Alibi Ike, Ring Lardner's excuse-making baseball player, and Abebe Bikila, two-time Olympic marathon champion from Ethiopia

▶ Kyle Macy, University of Kentucky and NBA guard, and Kyle Mackey, brief NFL backup quarterback

▶ Hal Smith, major-league catcher, 1955–64, and Tal Smith, Houston Astros president, and Al Smith, major-league utility man, 1953–64

▶ Mel Purcell, former pro tennis player and current top tennis coach, and Mel Parnell, Boston Red Sox pitcher, 1947–56

▶ Joan Benoit, 1984 Olympic marathon champion, and Joe Benoit, NHL right wing, 1940s

Q, X, and Z

A brief celebration of athletes whose names begin with any one of our three most neglected letters.

Q

▶ New Zealander Dick Quax, former 5,000m world-record holder

▶ Donald Quarrie, Olympic sprinter from Jamaica

▶ Adrian Karl Quist, Australian tennis player

▶ Anne Quast, U.S. Amateur golf champion in 1958, 1961, and 1963

▶ Dan Quisenberry, All-Star relief pitcher

X

There has yet to be a player in the major leagues whose last name starts with an X, though minor-league infielder Joe Xavier made it to the Triple-A level of the Milwaukee Brewers organization in 1989.

▶ Xu Haifeng, free pistol gold medalist in 1984 and the first Chinese athlete to win an Olympic medal

▶ Thomas Xenakis, second in rope climbing, 1896 Olympics

▶ Dana X. Bible, football coach at the Universities of Nebraska and Texas, 1930s and 1940s

▶ Xavier "The X Man" McDaniel, NBA forward

Z

▶ Tony Zale, middleweight champion, 1940–48

▶ Robert Carl Zuppke, football coach, University of Illinois, 1913–41

▶ Zachary Zorn, once-world-record holder in the 100m freestyle swim, 1968

▶ Zola Budd, world-class distance runner

▶ Golfers Fuzzy Zoeller and Kermit Zarley

▶ Pirmin Zurbriggen, World Cup and Olympic skier

▶ NFL quarterbacks Jim Zorn, Scott Zolak, and Eric Zeier

▶ Zelmo "Big Z" Beaty, NBA and ABA star

▶ Max Zaslofsky, 1950s basketball great

▶ Max, Tony, Joaquin, Luis, and Alan Zendejas, NFL placekickers

▶ Emil Zatopek, four-time gold medalist distance runner from Czechoslovakia

▶ Carlos Zarate, boxer, who knocked out Alfonso Zamora in the fourth round of a 1977 bantamweight bout known as "The Battle of the Z's"

The Most Reverent Nicknames

▶ On the New York City playgrounds, Knicks guard Earl Monroe was known as "Black Jesus."

▶ Hall of Fame goaltender Frankie Brimsek, who had 10 shutouts as a Boston Bruin rookie in 1938–39, was called "Mr. Zero."

▶ For 17 years (1914–30) before the baseball team from Brooklyn was known as the Dodgers, they were called the Robins in honor of their manager, Wilbert Robinson.

▶ While many great athletes have been known by their less-than-common first name—Wilt, for example, or Martina—it's telling that Michael Jordan, arguably the greatest basketball player ever, was known (among other, more forced and marketing-conscious nicknames like "Air" and "His Airness") to every fan by the commonest of first names, Mike.

▶ Finland's Matti Jarvinen, who defined his event by breaking the javelin record 10 times between 1930 and 1936, was called "Mr. Javelin."

▶ First baseman Frank Chance, the final putout in the immortalized Tinker-to-Evers-to-Chance double play combination, became the Chicago Cubs manager in 1905 and led them to three pennants in his first three full years, and a fourth one in 1910. He was called "Peerless Leader" by his troops. This was later shortened to "P. L. Chance."

▶ Steve Zungul, Major Indoor Soccer League star, was tabbed "The Lord of All Indoors."

▶ Louis Sockalexis, a member of the Penobscot Indian tribe, played well for the 1897 Cleveland Spiders until he reportedly fell from a second-story window during a Fourth of July drinking bout and hurt his ankle. Two years after his death in 1913, Cleveland held a contest for a new team name. Fans chose to call the team the "Indians" in Sockalexis's honor.

▶ The Cleveland team that baseball legend Napoleon Lajoie played for and managed in the early 20th century was known as the "Naps."

▶ The Hundred-Guinea Cup, the prize awarded in 1851 to the winner of an international yachting regatta around the Isle of Wight, was won by the schooner, *America*, sent over by the New York Yacht Club. The owners of the victorious *America* deeded the trophy to the NYYC, who renamed it America's Cup. The top prize in yachting has been called that ever since. (In 1983, Australia won, ending perhaps the longest domination in modern sporting history; New Zealand, the current champion, is the only other nation to have won the America's Cup.)

▶ The nickname of umpire Doug Harvey, highly respected National League umpire from the 1960s through 1990s, was "God."

Offensive Nicknames

There have been some unwittingly offensive team names in sports—the Vancouver Canucks in hockey, the New York Yankees in baseball, if you so choose. There have been names that were disparaging—the West German media, for example, called countryman and former swimming champion Michael Gross "The American" because of his disdain for the press—but stopped short of turning truly offensive. And other raw names have been jettisoned to adapt to new times and sensibilities: The Redmen of St. John's (New York) University, for instance, became the Red Storm. (Other teams with Native American-influenced names—most prominently, the Cleveland Indians, Atlanta Braves, and Florida State University Seminoles—have resisted changing. The celebratory mock-tomahawk "chop" gesture made by Braves and Seminoles fans has also come under criticism.)

The following nicknames are offensive.

▶ Sam Langford, a black boxer in the first part of the 20th century, was called the "Boston Tar Baby." Harlond Clift, a white baseball player, was called "Darkie" because Harlond sounded like "Harlem." Babe Ruth, who often barnstormed against Negro League clubs, was sometimes called "Nigger Lips" by major leaguers (all of whom were white).

▶ Boxer Johnny Dundee, born in Italy, was known as "The Scotch Wop."

▶ Abe Attell, featherweight champion in the early 20th century, was called "The Little Hebrew."

▶ In the 1940s, the Southern Association had a team called the Atlanta Crackers.

▶ The Boston Bruin line of Milt Schmidt, Bobby Bauer, and Woody Dumart was known as "The Kraut Line."

▶ Ivan Wilfred Johnson, New York Rangers defenseman in the 1920s and 1930s, was nicknamed "Ching-a-Ling Chinaman."

Cheap homers—ones hit over a short fence—used to be known as "Chinese homers."

Sox

▶ Chicago White Sox, American League

▶ Chicago Black Sox, scandal-ridden 1919 version of the White Sox

▶ Boston Red Sox, American League

▶ Baltimore Black Sox, Negro League

▶ Utica Blue Sox, Class A New York-Penn League

▶ Fort Myers Sun Sox, Senior Professional Baseball Association, 1989

▶ Paterson Silk Sox, semiprofessional, northern New Jersey, early 20th century

▶ Toledo Glass Sox, American Association, 1950s

▶ Reno Silver Sox, Class A California League

▶ Colorado Springs Sky Sox, Class AAA Pacific Coast League

▶ Winter Haven Super Sox, Senior Professional Baseball Association, 1989

▶ Scranton Red Soxx, Atlantic Collegiate League

▷ Honorable mention: Presbyterian (South Carolina) Blue Hose

The Hardest Names to Pronounce or Spell

You say "potayto," I say "potahto." Former Dodger player and itinerant manager Jim Lefebvre says "La-FEE-ver," journeyman outfielder Joe Lefebvre says "La-FAY." Dodger closer Eric Gagne says "GON-yay," Minnesota Twins shortstop Greg Gagne says "GAG-nee." Names that are hard to spell or pronounce are botched so routinely that their owners would be wise to come up with some satisfactory shorthand, like Duke University basketball coach Mike Krzyzewski (pronounced "shuh-SHEF-skee"), known simply as "Coach K," and former New York Jets running back Nu Faaola, a considerable improvement over his given name, Sinatausilinuu Faaola.

▶ Bill Mlkvy (MILK-vee), 1949–52 Temple University basketball player, nicknamed "The Owl without a Vowel"

▶ Dikembe Mutombo Mpolondo Mukamba Jean Jacque Wamutombo, NBA center known best by just his first two names

▶ Bobby Czyz (CHAZ), boxer

▶ Bob Ctvrtlik (stuh-VERT-lick), U.S. Olympic volleyball player

▶ Jackie Ickx, auto race champion, and Eddy Merckx, five-time Tour de France winner, both Belgian

▶ Carl Yastrzemski (yuh-STREM-skee), Boston Red Sox Hall of Famer

▶ Nantclwyd Hall, Wales, the birthplace of tennis

▶ Chris Fuamatu-Ma'afala, Pittsburgh Steelers running back

▶ Slobodan Zivojinovic and Zeljko Franulovic, Yugoslavian tennis players

▶ John and Stan Smrke, brief NHL left wings

▶ Juli Veee (note the third "e"), MISL soccer star

▶ Awaawaanoa Place in Honolulu, once-address of New York Mets pitcher Sid Fernandez

▶ Heikki Riihiranta, Finnish left wing

▶ Nnenna Lynch, Villanova University distance runner

▶ Napoleon Lajoie (lah-ZHWAH), baseball Hall of Famer

▶ Andy Papathanassiou, Stanford University offensive lineman

▶ Alex Wojciechowicz, Hall of Fame football player

▶ Giorgio Chinaglia (kee-NAHL-yuh), soccer star

▶ Jiri Crha, Czech goaltender, NHL

▶ Doug Gwosdz (GOOSH), journeyman catcher, nicknamed "Eyechart"

8 Good Athletes Named for Better Athletes

Ervin Johnson, the middling Milwaukee Bucks center, was *not* named for Earvin "Magic" Johnson, one of the greatest basketball players of all time; if he was, then we'd like very much to speak with Ervin's parents. (While Earvin was no doubt a tremendous talent even when very young, he was still only eight years old when Ervin was born.)

The following athletes had big shoes to fill.

Too big.

▶ Willie Mays Aikens, who played in the major leagues for eight years, was born on October 14, 1954, 12 days after Willie Mays helped the New York Giants sweep the Cleveland Indians in the World Series.

▶ Rogers Hornsby McKee pitched for the Philadelphia Phillies in 1943 and 1944. The year before McKee made it to the big leagues, his namesake was elected to the Baseball Hall of Fame.

▶ Kareema Williams from Southeast High School in Wichita, Kansas, was a basketball Parade All-America in 1986. Kareem Abdul-Jabbar was a Parade All-America, too, in 1964, as well as the NBA's all-time leading scorer.

Sharmon Shah, who changed his name to Karim Abdul-Jabbar while a star running back at UCLA (the NBA great's alma mater, as well) and then went on to a decent NFL career, was sued by Kareem Abdul-Jabbar to stop the football player from using the name on merchandise; the basketball great claimed that it could be confusing for fans who might want to buy merchandise endorsed by one or the other. They settled, and the football player would be known, for commercial purposes, as Karim Abdul.

▶ Charles "Chuck" Klein Stobbs compiled a 107-130 record as a pitcher over 15 major-league seasons. Chuck Klein was a Triple Crown–winning outfielder, whose first five full years in the game are the most awesome and productive of anyone in major-league history.

▶ Jack Dempsey Cassini appeared in eight major-league games and had no at-bats. He weighed 175 pounds, 17 pounds fewer than his namesake, the heavyweight champion of the world from 1919 to 1926.

▶ Larry Doby Johnson was born in Cleveland in 1950, when Larry Doby was a star for the Indians. Johnson debuted as a catcher for the Indians in 1972, played briefly for the Montreal Expos, and then for three games in 1978 with the Chicago White Sox, where his manager was Larry Doby.

▶ Elston Howard Turner, NBA player in the 1980s, was born in 1959, the only year that Turner's namesake, New York Yankees catcher Elston Howard, did not play in the World Series in his first 10 years in the majors.

And 1 Good Athlete Named for a Less Good Athlete

▶ Chuck Connors Person, Auburn University and NBA basketball star and long-range gunner—nicknamed "The Rifleman"—was named for Chuck Connors, who had a brief, unillustrious career with both baseball's Brooklyn Dodgers and Chicago Cubs, and with basketball's Boston Celtics. Connors enjoyed greater success and fame as the star of the television series, "The Rifleman."

30 Legendary Nicknames

Most skilled athletes are christened with a nickname early on, in recognition of their talents or personality. Occasionally, an athlete of such rare stature comes along that several nicknames attach themselves to him or her; Babe Ruth and Muhammad Ali rank at the top of this select group. Besides "Babe," George Herman Ruth was known at times as "Bambino," "The Sultan of Swat," "The Caliph of Clout," "The King of Clout," "Jidge," "Slambino," and "The Wizard of Whack," to name a very few. Not only do we also know Ali by his former name, Cassius Marcellus Clay, Jr., but as "The Greatest," "The Louisville Lip," and "The Mouth," as well. Basketball legend Jerry West was both "Mr. Clutch" and "Zeke from Cabin Creek."

Some nicknames, by themselves, are great—Darryl "Chocolate Thunder" Dawkins, for instance. Others nicknames have greatness thrust upon them: The athlete is brilliant enough and so associated with his or her nickname that it is hard to think of one without the other. For example, as nicknames go, "The Big O" is just all right, but because it belongs to Oscar Robertson, we remember it.

The following is a collection of the most vividly remembered nicknames in sport. If you take umbrage at the omission of certain obvious favorites, you're invited to write your own book of sports lists.

▶ The Georgia Peach—Ty Cobb

▶ Broadway Joe—Joe Namath

▶ The Galloping Ghost—Harold "Red" Grange

▶ The Manassa Mauler—Jack Dempsey

▶ The Rocket—Maurice Richard, Rod Laver

▶ Dr. J—Julius Erving

▶ Tthe Big Train—Walter Johnson

- ▶ Little Mo—Maureen Connolly
- ▶ Sweetness—Walter Payton
- ▶ The Answer—Allen Iverson
- ▶ The Stilt—Wilt Chamberlain
- ▶ The Man—Stan Musial
- ▶ Casey—Charles Dillon Stengel
- ▶ Too Tall—Ed Jones
- ▶ Crazy Legs—Elroy Hirsch
- ▶ Yogi—Lawrence Peter Berra
- ▶ The Big Hurt—Frank Thomas
- ▶ Shoe—Willie Shoemaker
- ▶ Shoeless Joe—Joe Jackson
- ▶ The Golden Jet—Bobby Hull
- ▶ The Golden Bear—Jack Nicklaus
- ▶ The Yankee Clipper—Joe DiMaggio
- ▶ Charlie Hustle—Pete Rose
- ▶ Pistol—Pete Maravich
- ▶ Pee Wee—Harold Reese
- ▶ Catfish—James Augustus Hunter
- ▶ The Flying Finn—Paavo Nurmi
- ▶ Say hey—Willie Mays
- ▶ The Brown Bomber—Joe Louis
- ▶ Magic—Earvin Johnson, Jr.

6

POLITICS

Keep Your Mouth Shut and Nobody Gets Hurt: 8 Examples of How Management Feels About the Rights of Its Employees

▶ One day after speaking out on behalf of the NFL players' union in 1987, All-Pro tackle Brian Holloway was traded from the New England Patriots to the Los Angeles Raiders.

▶ Pauline Betz Addie, Wimbledon champion in 1946, was suspended in 1947 for her public support of a women's professional tennis tour.

▶ In 1986, Jan Kemp, an English professor at the University of Georgia, blew the whistle on academic fraud and preferential treatment to football players at the school, at the cost of her job. (She later sued the school for firing her, and won the case.)

▶ When Toronto Maple Leaf Jimmy Thomson and Detroit Red Wing Ted Lindsay tried to organize an NHL players union in the 1950s, they were traded immediately to the perennially cellar-dwelling Chicago Black Hawks.

▶ In 1993, David Williams, starting right tackle for the Houston Oilers, skipped a road trip to New England to be at his wife's side when she gave birth to their first child, a boy. Mrs. Williams delivered on Saturday night; when Williams would not be coaxed into flying to Boston to make it in time for the early-afternoon Patriots game the next day, opting to stay instead with his family, the Oilers fined him a week's pay of $111,111. (For the eviscerating national criticism the team received for its action, it probably wasn't worth it—especially since the Oilers beat the Pats anyway.)

▶ In February 1989, the National Labor Relations Board ruled that former Seattle Seahawks wide receiver Sam McCullum had been illegally discharged just before the start of the 1982 season because of his activities as the team's player union representative. The Seahawks were ordered to give McCullum back pay with interest, as well as a job "substantially equivalent" to the one that he lost.

144 ● ● ●

▶ In December of 1990, an arbitrator ruled that major-league baseball owners had colluded—that is, had worked together to hold down free-agent player signings and salaries. As a group, the owners were ordered to pay $280 million, to be divvied up among the players deemed to have been affected by the collusion.

▶ Reportedly, when Green Bay Packers All-Pro center Jim Ringo brought an agent with him to see coach Vince Lombardi and help to negotiate Ringo's 1964 contract, Lombardi, who did not have the highest regard for agents, retreated to his office to make a phone call. He re-emerged to tell Ringo that he had just been traded to the Philadelphia Eagles.

Say It Ain't So:
5 Brutal Truths about Athletes and Competition

Mark Twain once said that it was preferable to keep one's mouth shut and give the appearance of being stupid rather than to open it up and remove all doubt.

The sentiment might be paraphrased for athletes who give the appearance of lacking in humanity. Are they or aren't they? Maybe it's better that we not know for sure. After all, for some of them—especially in the more obviously violent sports—the less compassion, the better. That's how they got where they are. NFL coach and defensive whiz Buddy Ryan was often accused of offering his defensive players a "bounty" to put key opponents out of the game. In a more candid moment—if unintentionally so—Kansas City Chiefs cornerback and sometime-wide receiver Dale Carter could be seen laughing on the sideline after he'd injured Denver Broncos cornerback Lionel Washington with a chop block in a 1996 game; Carter was caught by TV cameras as Washington lay writhing on the ground with a sprained medial collateral ligament in his knee.

"Hurting people is my business," boxer Sugar Ray Robinson once said.

▶ Ho-Jun Li of North Korea, Olympic gold medalist in the small-bore rifle competition in 1972, explained his success: "I thought I was shooting at my enemies. Our Prime Minister, Kim-Il Sung, told us prior to our departure to shoot as if we were fighting our enemies. And that's exactly what I did." Li later said he was misquoted.

▶ In 1986, New York Giants linebacker Lawrence Taylor said that he liked to inflict "kill shots" on players—hits that were so hard that "the snot comes from [the victim's] nose and he starts quivering on the ground."

▶ An extensive white-paper report to explore football violence in Europe—produced by the Social Issues Research Centre of Oxford, England, to assess the threat of soccer hooligans, particularly of the English variety—paints a picture disturbingly similar to one we might expect for much more serious criminals: According to the report, the hooligan is generally part of an organized gang that has already caused mayhem in the host country; the hooligan tends to leave a "calling card" on or beside his victim; the hooligan uses any of a range of weapons; the hooligan often possesses incriminating literature.

▶ In *Visions of Eight*, a documentary about the 1972 Munich Olympics —the Games marred by the terrorist killings of 11 Israelis—a British marathoner was asked, "How does the slaughter of the Israelis affect you?"

"It postpones my race for a day," he answered.

▶ Heavyweight Mike Tyson's philosophy of boxing: "I always try to catch [opponents] right on the tip of the nose, because I try to push the bone right into the brain."

Tyson also taunted Lennox Lewis, who would later pummel him, by saying he wanted to rip out Lennox's heart and feed it to him. Furthermore, Tyson said to Lennox, "I want to eat your children." Tyson later claimed that when he said it, he knew that Lewis had no children.

Breaking the Color Barrier

1884: Fleet Walker becomes the first black major-league baseball player.

1904: Charles Follis, with the Shelby (Ohio) Athletic Club, becomes the first black professional football player.

1904: George Poage is one of the first two blacks to compete in the Olympics, in the 400m competition, and also becomes the first black runner to win an Olympic medal, taking third place in the 400m hurdles.

1908: Jack Johnson becomes the first black heavyweight boxing champion.

1908: John Taylor becomes the first black to win an Olympic gold medal, in the 4x400m relay.

1922: Fritz Pollard, player-coach for the Milwaukee Badgers (and later for the Hammond Pros in 1923–25), becomes the NFL's first black head coach, preceding Art Shell by 67 years.

1924: Long-jumper De Hart Hubbard becomes the first black to win an individual Olympic gold medal.

1947: In one of the most significant events in sports, if not American culture, the white walls of baseball begin to crumble when Montreal Royal Jackie Robinson is called up to the parent club, the Brooklyn Dodgers, to become the first black baseball player in the modern era. Later that year, the Dodgers call up Dan Bankhead, the first black pitcher, and the Cleveland Indians call up Larry Doby, the first black American Leaguer.

1948: High-jumper Alice Coachman becomes the first black woman to win an Olympic gold medal.

1949: Jackie Robinson becomes the first black MVP in the major leagues.

1949: George Taliaferro, a University of Indiana backfield star, becomes the first black player drafted by an NFL team when the Chicago Bears pick him in the 13th round.

1950: Chuck Cooper of Duquesne becomes the first black player drafted by the NBA when the Boston Celtics pick him in the second round.

1950: Earl Lloyd of the Washington Capitals becomes the first black player in the NBA, October 31, 1950, in Rochester, against the Royals.

1950: Althea Gibson becomes the first black tennis player accepted to compete in the U.S. Championships at Forest Hills.

1953: Willie Thrower becomes the first black NFL quarterback.

1955: Jim Tucker and Earl Lloyd become the first blacks to play on an NBA championship team, the 1954–55 Syracuse Nationals.

1955: Jockey Isaac Murphy is part of the inaugural group elected to the National Horse Racing Hall of Fame. Murphy, one of the great riders in American history, is the first jockey—black or white—to ride three Derby winners. (At the turn of the century, most jockeys were black, and black jockeys won 15 of the first 28 Derbys. But after Henry King rode in the 1921 Derby, it would be 79 years before another black jockey appeared in the race. In 2000, Marlon St. Julien rode Curule to a seventh-place finish.)

1956: Althea Gibson becomes the first black tennis player to win a major title, the French Open.

1957: Gibson becomes the first black player to win Wimbledon and the U.S. Championships.

1957–58: Willie O'Ree becomes the first black hockey player to play in the NHL, in a two-game stint for the Boston Bruins. He plays for them for most of the 1960–61 season.

1959: Pumpsie Green becomes the first black member of the Boston Red Sox. The Red Sox are the last major-league team to integrate.

1961: John McLendon becomes the first black to coach a professional modern-era team, the Cleveland Pipers of the American Basketball League.

1961: Ernie Davis of Syracuse becomes the first black Heisman Trophy winner.

1963: Arthur Ashe becomes the first black tennis player to compete on the U.S. Davis Cup team.

1963: Elston Howard becomes the American League's first black MVP. (By this time, blacks in the National League have already won 11 MVPs.)

1966: Bill Russell becomes the first black NBA head coach, for the Boston Celtics.

1966: Basketball head coach John McLendon becomes the first black to coach at a predominantly white college, Cleveland State.

1966: Emmett Ashford becomes the first black umpire, for the American League. In 1973, Art Williams will become the National League's first black umpire.

1968: Jim Hines wins the first all-black final in Olympic history, in the 100-meter sprint.

1969: John McLendon becomes the first black head coach in the ABA, for the Denver Nuggets.

1971: Bill White becomes the first black baseball announcer when he joins the New York Yankee broadcast team.

1975: Lee Elder becomes the first black to play in the Masters golf tournament.

1975: Frank Robinson becomes the first black major-league manager, for the Cleveland Indians.

1975: Willie Wood becomes the first black head coach of a modern-era professional football team, the Philadelphia Bell of the World Football League. In 1980, he will become the first black head coach in the Canadian Football League, for the Toronto Argonauts.

1975: Al Attles' Golden State Warriors defeat K. C. Jones' Washington Bullets in the NBA Finals, the first championship matchup of black head coaches in professional sports.

1979: Lee Elder becomes the first black golfer to take part in the Ryder Cup competition.

1984: John Thompson of Georgetown University becomes the first black to coach an NCAA basketball champion.

1986: George Branham III becomes the first black bowler to win a PBA title, the Brunswick Memorial World Open in Glendale Heights, Illinois.

1986: Debi Thomas, becomes the first black U.S. singles figure skating champion, and the first black world women's figure skating champion.

1989: Bill White becomes the first black to head a major professional sports league in America when he is hired as National League president.

1989: Bertram Lee becomes the first black majority owner of a major professional team, the Denver Nuggets.

1992: Cito Gaston becomes the first black manager to win the World Series.

1997–2000: Tiger Woods becomes the first black golfer to win each of the four majors (and, of course, the first to win the career Grand Slam).

2002: Vonetta Flowers, a bobsledder, becomes the first black athlete, man or woman, to win a Winter Olympics gold medal.

2002: Calgary Flames right winger Jarome Iginla becomes the first black to win the NHL goals and scoring titles.

14 Ugly Scenes from Sports History

▶ Near the end of the 1954–55 NHL season, Montreal Canadiens star Maurice Richard was involved in an on-ice altercation that culminated in his hitting a linesman over the head with his stick. When the league suspended Richard for the last week of the regular season and the entire playoffs, protests erupted in Montreal and a riot ensued. There was looting in the city, a fire was set, and damage in the millions of dollars was reported.

▶ In 1972, Boston Marathon officials dragged the first woman entrant, Kathy Switzer, off the course to prevent her from finishing the race.

▶ In the third round of the June 1997 WBA heavyweight championship bout in Las Vegas between challenger Mike Tyson and champ Evander Holyfield, Tyson bit, then bit off, a portion of Holyfield's ear. Referee Mills Lane stopped the fight and declared Holyfield the winner. A plastic surgeon re-attached the one-inch chunk of right ear to Holyfield. Tyson, who was suspended from boxing by the Nevada State Athletic Commission, said that the biting was in response to—in his opinion—Holyfield's repeated head-butting. "This is my career," Tyson said. "I have children to raise. I have to retaliate. He butted me. Look at me. My kids will be scared of me."

▶ In a disappointing 1994 World Cup in which his team was a tournament favorite, Colombian defender Andres Escobar, while trying to clear a crossing pass, accidentally scored an own-goal against the U.S. Shortly after returning home to Colombia in the wake of the unfortunate game, Escobar was murdered outside a restaurant in Medellin. With each of the twelve bullets he shot into Escobar, the killer was reported by police to have shouted "Goal."

▶ In the 1933 Kentucky Derby, the jockey on Head Play, Herb Fisher, twice grabbed for the saddlecloth of Broker's Tip jockey Don Meade. Meade shoved Fisher's hand away. After the finish, Fisher slashed Meade with his whip and they later got into a fistfight. Each jockey was suspended for 30 days, but the penalty did not include stakes races.

▶ South Korean boxer Byun Jong-il's loss by decision in a 119-pound boxing match at the 1988 Seoul Olympics set off a huge brawl in which the referee was attacked and chairs were flung into the ring. Reportedly among the perpetrators were several Korean members of the Olympic security force.

▶ During a changeover between games at a Hamburg, Germany, tennis tournament in the summer of 1993, a crazed, self-professed Steffi Graf fan came up behind Monica Seles and stabbed her in the back. Although the wound was not life-threatening, Seles would not return to the tennis tour, which at the time of the stabbing she'd been dominating, until 1995. The attacker, who pleaded insanity, received a suspended two-year sentence. Seles, disgusted at the insufficiency of the punishment, stated that she would never again play in Germany.

▶ In a basketball game between Minnesota and Ohio State on January 25, 1972, a brawl broke out at Williams Arena in Minneapolis with 36 seconds left and Ohio State leading 50-44. Dave Winfield, a Gopher forward, was in the center of the fight. One source called it "an ugly, cowardly display of violence." After the brawl, Minnesota's Corky Taylor and Ron Behagen were suspended for the rest of the season.

▶ Jimmy Connors was penalized a point, then a game, and then the match, and then fined $20,000 and suspended for 10 weeks, for his protest of a call in the fifth set of a semifinal match with Ivan Lendl at the Lipton Tournament in Boca Raton, Florida, on February 21, 1986. Connors ranted, stormed the umpire's chair, and finally sat down and refused to play.

And in 1991, though the 39-year-old Connors, as a wild-card entry, won the hearts of the U.S. Open crowds as he made a spirited run to the semifinals, he showed his regard for those who might dare to upset the fairy-tale of a tournament he was having. When chair umpire David Littlefield overruled a linesman's call in Connors' match versus Aaron Krickstein—a thrilling 4-hour, 41-minute marathon that Connors would win in a fifth-set tiebreaker—Connors said to Littlefield, "Kiss me before you do that to me... You son of a bitch... Get out of the chair... You're a bum... Get your ass out of the chair... Don't give me that crap... You're an abortion." Crowd darling Connors was neither warned nor penalized and—though the ugly, belittling tirade was audible to live and TV viewers—apparently Connors' ability to put on a good show super-seded all.

▶ A hockey fight between the Minnesota North Stars and the Boston Bruins on February 26, 1981, resulted in 81 penalties totaling over 6½ hours, and 12 ejections.

▶ Cincinnati Red Pete Rose and New York Met Bud Harrelson brawled during Game 3 of the 1973 National League playoffs, a fight set off by Rose's hard slide into second base. When Rose went out to left field in the bottom of the inning, fans threw garbage at him, and Cincinnati manager Sparky Anderson pulled the Reds from the field. They did not return until a Mets contingent headed by manager Yogi Berra and out-fielder Willie Mays went out to left field and pleaded with fans to settle down.

▶ When baseball legend Ted Williams died of a heart attack on July 5, 2002, the mourning quickly turned to morbid fascination, then disgust, over an unseemly family squabble concerning what would become of Williams's body. Mere hours after Williams's death, his son, John Henry, had his father's body shipped to the Alcor Life Extension Foundation in Scottsdale, Arizona. John Henry and his sister, Claudia Williams, claimed that two years earlier, while Williams was in a Gainsville, Florida, hospital, the three of them signed a three-way pact on a scrap of paper declaring their desire to be frozen after death so that they could be reunited. But another of Williams's daughters, Barbara Joyce Williams Ferrell, claimed that The Splendid Splinter wanted his body cremated and his ashes spread in the water off of the Florida Keys. She said that the Williams's signature that they'd produced was actually a practice autograph, and went to court to challenge John Henry's right to freeze their father's remains.

▶ There have been numerous stomach-turning injuries in sports, including those in which bones have been visibly and explicitly bro-ken. The nation watched as Joe Theismann's leg was broken by

Lawrence Taylor in a 1985 *Monday Night Football* game (LT was visibly shaken by the incident), and saw Cincinnati Bengal Tim Krumrie break his leg in Super Bowl XXIII. The ankle of Los Angeles Dodger Tommy Davis was so badly broken in a second-base slide against the San Francisco Giants in 1965 that some of the Giant infielders became physically ill at the sight.

► Monique Ellis and Bobbi Jo Lister—the respective wives of Seattle Supersonics players Dale Ellis and Alton Lister—got into a March 1988 fistfight 10 minutes after Seattle had beaten the Los Angeles Lakers, 114-110, at the Seattle Center Coliseum. The fight, which erupted when a woman claiming to be Monique Ellis's sister kicked and punched Mrs. Lister, interrupted Seattle coach Bernie Bickerstaff's press conference 50 yards away. The two players' wives apparently had been at odds since Alton Lister had signed a four-year, $4.2 million contract in the offseason while Dale Ellis had been unable to renegotiate the final year of a contract that was paying him $325,000 annually.

It's Enough to Make Us Sick:
A Comparison between Yesteryear's Baseball Superstars and Today's Superstars (and Journeymen)

The total payroll for the first all-professional baseball club, the Cincinnati Red Stockings of 1869, was $9,300.

In 1936, 67 years later, the average annual baseball salary was $4,500.

In 1989, 53 years after that, the average salary was nearly $500,000.

In 2002, 13 years later, the average salary is $2.3 million.

This lists the 2002 salaries earned by various current baseball players, and a selected year's salary of various stars of the past.

First Baseman

► Jason Giambi: $8,000,000
► Jose Offerman: $6,750,000
► Andres Galarraga: $500,000
► Bill Terry; 1931: $23,000
► Lou Gehrig, 1927: $8,000

Second Baseman

► Jeff Kent: $6,000,000
► Alfonso Soriano: $630,000
► Jackie Robinson, 1952: $40,000

Third Baseman

► Matt Williams: $9,500,000
► Scott Rolen: $8,600,000
► Pie Traynor, 1932: $14,000

Shortstop

► Alex Rodriguez: $21,000,000
► Rey Ordonez: $6,000,000
► Phil Rizzuto, 1950: $50,000
► Honus Wagner, 1908: $5,000

Outfield

► Barry Bonds: $13,000,000
► Vladimir Guerrero: $8,000,000
► Ichiro Suzuki: $2,000,000
► Gerald Williams: $2,000,000
► Willie Mays, 1965: $105,000
► Mickey Mantle, 1965: $100,000
► Ted Williams, 1951: $100,000
► Joe DiMaggio, 1941: $37,500
► Babe Ruth, 1927: $70,000
► Ty Cobb, 1908: $4,500

Catcher

► Mike Piazza: $10,571,429
► Paul LoDuca: $546,667
► Roy Campanella, 1957: $45,000

Pitcher

► Pedro Martinez: $13,500,000
► Kenny Rogers: $5,250,000
► Graeme Lloyd: $2,000,000
► Rollie Fingers, 1974: $65,000
► Bob Gibson, 1969: $125,000
► Bob Feller, 1940: $27,500
► Cy Young, 1901: $3,000

Money Isn't Everything; It's the Only Thing

► On June 27, 1988, Mike Tyson made approximately $21 million for knocking out Michael Spinks in 91 seconds—roughly a quarter-million dollars per second. Michael Spinks made approximately $13.5 million for being knocked out by Mike Tyson in 91 seconds.

► Prior to the 1999 Ryder Cup—a patriotic challenge between American and European golfers—David Duval told *Golf Digest* that a U.S. golfer might boycott the event unless the PGA of America began paying players.

► In 1994, when the NBA's #1 draft pick out of Purdue, Glenn "Big Dog" Robinson, was selected by the Milwaukee Bucks, he supposedly sought the richest contract in league history; some reports had it at $100 million, which would have been the first time nine figures had been reached in professional basketball. During the re-election campaign of Wisconsin U.S. Senator Herbert Kohl, who was also the Bucks' owner, Kohl commented: "I was thinking of saying to Mr. Robinson: 'I'll tell you what; I'll take your contract and you can have my franchise.'" The contract turned out to be for $68 million over 10 years.

► When former New York Mets pitcher Mike Hampton left the National League champions after the 2000 season to sign with the sub-.500 Colorado Rockies, whose home ballpark, Coors Field, is renowned as a graveyard for pitchers, he said he did it for his family. Specifically, Hampton cited the quality of the school district in the Denver area. The fact that the Rockies paid him $121 million over eight years, the largest contract ever given a pitcher, apparently wasn't a factor.

► During the 1994 baseball players' strike, Detroit Tigers second baseman Lou Whitaker showed up for a union meeting in a chauffeur-driven white stretch limousine, dressed in a blue pinstriped suit and wearing gold-rimmed glasses.

"I'm rich," Whitaker said. "What am I supposed to do, hide it? This is me, just like Tom Selleck."

▶ Bill Johnson, after winning the Olympic downhill gold medal in 1984, was asked what the victory meant to him: "Millions. We're talking millions."

▶ The prize money in professional sports has inflated so dramatically—nowhere more so than in men's golf—that (through September 16, 2002) Jack Nicklaus, the greatest player of all-time (so far), and a man not *that* far removed from the PGA Tour (he played in double-digit numbers of PGA tournaments as recently as 1995), is—are you ready for this?—*76th* on the all-time money list, with $5,722,901. That puts him 31 places behind the immortal Stewart Cink (at #45), and 55 behind living legend Loren Roberts (at #21).

▶ Middle-distance runner Ben Jipcho reflected on his poor times—only one sub-four-minute mile in 27 tries—in his first two years on the pro track circuit: "I am a professional. I run for money, not for times. I realize people like to see Ben Jipcho run sub-four-minute miles, and Ben Jipcho enjoys running sub-four-minute miles more than anything else in the world—except counting money."

▶ "People think we make $3 million and $4 million a year," Texas Rangers outfielder Pete Incaviglia said in 1990. "They don't realize that most of us only make $500,000."

▶ The Pittsburgh Pirates called off Willie Stargell Hall of Fame Day in 1988 because Stargell reportedly wanted more money and gifts than they had offered.

▶ In an apparent attempt to win sympathy for his economic plight during the 1998 NBA lockout, Kenny Anderson of the Boston Celtics allowed the *New York Times* detailed access to his financial dealings. Anderson revealed that he owned eight cars, worth between $50,000 and $120,000 each, and costing him $75,000 a year in insurance. Anderson also paid $12,500 a month for his five-bedroom house in Beverly Hills, $7,200 each month on child support for two daughters, $3,000 a month on mortgage, property taxes, and maintenance for his mother's home on Long Island, and a $10,000-a-month allowance to himself for "hanging out money." (He also spent $250,000 a year on Kenny the Kid Enterprises, his money-losing marketing company.)

"Right now, without my check, I have to start getting tight...I was thinking about selling one of my cars," said Anderson, who was scheduled to make $5.8 million before the lockout. "I don't need all of them. You know, just get rid of the Mercedes."

Not surprisingly, Anderson's plight was met, not with sympathy, but rather with disbelief, outrage, and, especially, ridicule...

▶ ...Patrick Ewing, All-Star center for the New York Knicks and president of the NBA Players Association, also didn't help matters during the lockout by allowing himself to be caught frequently, on camera, speaking in a relaxed manner on his cell phone, while looking incredibly well-dressed. Worse, when Ewing tried to explain (to the Associated Press) what he and the union were fighting for, he chose this plea: "NBA players make a lot of money. But they spend a lot of money, too." In describing the impasse with the owners, Ewing, who at the time made $18 million in salary, also used words like "survival" and phrases like "feeding our families."

▶ The modern Olympic movement has stood for the best in amateur athletics—and for probably the most nonchalant and even systematic in professional money-grubbing. During the tenure of the autocratic International Olympic Committee President Juan Antonio Samaranch (though he certainly wasn't the first Olympic official to encourage such behavior), bribery and conflicts of interest ran rampant between IOC members and bid committees (to name just one sullied relationship). Members of the Salt Lake City Olympic bid committee were accused of spending millions of dollars to influence the votes of 14 IOC members whose task it was to determine which site won the Winter Games in 2002. The monetary favors included cash, medical expenses, travel expenses, *college tuition payments for the children of IOC members* (!), entertainment, and gifts. In the immediate wake of the allegations, six IOC members were let go, three others resigned, and a fourth was given a warning, though the IOC did precious little to ensure that such widespread use of "cash-for-votes" would not occur again. Sites whose bids were unsuccessful for the '96 and '00 Summer Games made numerous substantiated claims that the winning sites played the (illegal) game better, and were not discouraged from doing so: IOC members expected luxurious treatment, and got it. Other gifts bestowed on IOC voters included shopping sprees and plastic surgery.

▶ When the Los Angeles Lakers were seeking their third consecutive NBA title in 1989, their head coach, Pat Riley, was shrewd enough to form a licensing company and copyright the phrase "three-peat" (they wouldn't). By 1993, Riley had moved on to the New York Knicks, who lost in the Eastern Conference playoffs to the eventual champion Chicago Bulls. Riley no doubt was disappointed by the defeat, but it wasn't a total loss. By completing their third straight championship, the Bulls earned Riley an estimated seven-figure royalty fee for use of his "three-peat" on merchandise and licensed goods. The Bulls didn't win the championship the following year, or Riley might have profited even more. Back in '89, just in case, he had also copyrighted the phrase, "Four-ward."

Mike Jones, the St. Louis Rams linebacker who made the Super Bowl XXXIV-preserving tackle—a brilliant open-field grab of Tennessee Titan wide receiver Kevin Dyson on the game's final play, less than a yard from the goal line, to secure the 23-16 Rams win—tried to copyright the phrase "The Tackle," which is what the play was—briefly—known as.

The Age of Enlightenment Continues

Seventeen ambassadors for world harmony share their views:

▶ Los Angeles Dodgers General Manager Al Campanis in April 1987, speaking on an episode of ABC's *Nightline* that commemorated the 40th anniversary of Jackie Robinson's breaking the baseball color barrier: "I truly believe that [blacks] may not have some of the necessities to be, let's say, a field manager or perhaps a general manager . . . . Why are black men or black people not good swimmers? Because they don't have the buoyancy." Soon after making these comments, Campanis lost his job.

▶ Pitcher Bob Knepper, with the Houston Astros in 1988, on the pursuit by minor-league umpire Pam Postema to win a major-league job: "This is not an occupation a woman should be in. In God's society, woman was created in a role of submission to the husband. It's not that woman is inferior but I don't believe women should be in a leadership role." Knepper also said, "N.O.W. [National Organization of Women] is such a blowhard organization. They are a bunch of lesbians."

▶ Then-Atlanta Braves relief pitcher and self-professed redneck John Rocker, in a 1999 interview with *Sports Illustrated's* Jeff Pearlman, shared his disgust over several aspects of American life.

On a Toyota in front of his car that was swerving from one lane to another: "Look at this idiot! I guarantee you she's a Japanese woman." (The woman turned out to be white.)

On the #7 train, which runs from Times Square to polyglot Queens (with a stop at Shea Stadium along the way): "Imagine having to take the 7 train to the ballpark, looking like you're [riding through] Beirut next to some kid with purple hair next to some queer with AIDS right next to some dude who just got out of jail for the fourth time right next to some 20-year-old mom with four kids."

On New York City: "The biggest thing I don't like about New York are the foreigners. I'm not a very big fan of foreigners. You can walk an entire block in Times Square and not hear anybody speaking English. Asians and Koreans and Vietnamese and Indians and Russians and Spanish people and everything up there. How the hell did they get in this country?"

▶ In an address to the Wisconsin State Assembly, Green Bay Packers All-Pro defensive end and ordained minister Reggie White said (among other things): "A lot of us [black people] like to dance, and if you go to black churches, you see people jumping up and down, because they really get into it. White people were blessed with the gift of structure and organization. You guys do a good job of building businesses and things of that nature and you know how to tap into money pretty much better than a lot of people do around the world. Hispanics are gifted in family structure. You can see a Hispanic person and they can put 20 to 30 people in one home... If you go to Japan or any Asian country, they can turn a television into a watch... And you look at the Indians, they have been very gifted in the [sic] spirituality."

▶ Richard Williams, father and coach of the two best women's tennis players in the world, the gracious Serena and Venus, said (among other things), "The only reason we moved to Compton [in the Los Angeles area] was that I felt I could buy more homes there than the Jews. They were buying up the ghetto; I just wanted to give them a little competition...I wanted to give the Weinsteins, the Rubinsteins, the I-forget-the-other-Steins, competition."

▶ In a rant at halftime of the 1966 NCAA title game against Texas Western, which started five black players, Adolph Rupp, legendary basketball coach at the University of Kentucky, was heard to scold his all-white squad, "Are you boys going to lose to a bunch of coons?" (Texas Western won.) Rupp defenders have long claimed that he was not racist—that he detested equally anyone who might cause him to lose a basketball game, and that those who label him a racist are unfairly using the standards of a different time.

▶ Following a loss on December 11, 2001, Denver Nuggets coach Dan Issel was caught on tape telling a heckling fan, "Go drink another beer, you ***** Mexican piece of shit," [**Authors' note:** If you're wondering why we spelled out "shit" but not "*****," it's because we've never seen the first curse corroborated, explicitly.] The Nuggets suspended Issel, without pay, for four games.

▶ Augusta National Golf Club did not admit its first African-American member—Ron Townsend—until September 1990. As of October, 2002, the club had never admitted a female member.

▶ The Indianapolis Motor Speedway did not allow women into the pits or garage area until 1971.

▶ Track athlete Joaquim Cruz, on Florence Griffith Joyner and Jackie Joyner-Kersee at the 1988 Olympics: "Florence, in 1984, you could see an extremely feminine person. But today she looks more like a man than a woman, and Joyner herself, she looks like a gorilla."

▶ John McEnroe, at the 1983 Forest Hills Tournament of Champions, after being hit in the side by a ball struck by his Czech opponent, Tomas Smid: "You'll be sorry the day you hit me, you fucking Communist asshole."

▶ Detroit Piston Dennis Rodman, after his team had been beaten by the Boston Celtics in the seventh game of the 1987 Eastern Conference finals: "Larry Bird is overrated in a lot of areas... way overrated. Why does he get so much publicity? Because he's white. You never hear about a black player being the greatest."

▶ During his five-set match at the 2001 U.S. Open against James Blake, who is black, Australian tennis player (and eventual champion) Lleyton Hewitt, who is white, requested the removal of a black linesman who had called Hewitt for two foot faults. While complaining, Hewitt said, "Look at him. Look at him and you tell me what the similarity is. Just get him off the court." Many thought Hewitt was implying that the linesman's calls were biased because he, like Blake, was black. Hewitt denied the comments had racial undertones, and said he was pointing out that it was the same linesman who continued to call him for foot faults. The match umpire agreed that the remark was not meant to be racially motivated, and the U.S. Open tournament referee agreed, too, concluding that Hewitt did not indicate Blake at any point in his complaint, or obviously mean to suggest racial bias in the officiating.

▶ Cincinnati Reds owner Marge Schott called former Reds outfielders Eric Davis and Dave Parker "million-dollar niggers" and kept a swastika arm band at her home, said former Reds marketing director Cal Levy in a 1992 deposition for a lawsuit by Reds controller Tim Sabo. Sabo claimed he was fired because he opposed a policy of not hiring blacks and because he testified against her in a lawsuit. Sharon Jones, a former Oakland As executive assistant, told the *New York Times* in 1992 that prior to the start of an owners' conference call, Schott said, "I would never hire another nigger. I'd rather have a trained monkey working for me than a nigger."

Schott explained to the *Cincinnati Enquirer* in 1994 why she didn't want her players to wear earrings: "Only fruits wear earrings."

After umpire John McSherry collapsed on the field and died of a heart attack on April 1, 1996, forcing the postponement of the Reds' season opener, Schott said: "I feel cheated. This isn't supposed to happen to us, not in Cincinnati. This is our history, our tradition, our team."

In a May 5, 1996, ESPN interview, Schott commented on Hitler: "Everything you read, when he came in he was good. They built tremendous highways and got all the factories going. He went nuts, he went berserk. I think his own generals tried to kill him, didn't they? Everybody knows he was good at the beginning but he just went too far."

And Schott on Asian-American kids, in the May 14, 1996, *Sports Illustrated*: "I don't like it when they come here, honey, and stay so long and then outdo our kids. That's not right."

▶ On Howard Stern's radio show on September 10, 2002, New York Giants rookie tight end sensation Jeremy Shockey was asked if he thought there were gay players in the NFL. "I don't know," said Shockey. "I don't like to think about that. I hope not." When asked if he'd had gay teammates at the University of Miami, he said, "No. I mean, if I knew there was a gay guy on my college football team, I probably wouldn't, you know, stand for it. You know, I think, you know, they're going to be in the shower with us and stuff, so I don't think that's gonna work." He later apologized for his comments, claiming he was trying to be funny. "It's a show just for comedy," he told the *New York Daily News*. "I guess I do regret saying it. I didn't think anyone was going to make a big deal out of it. I'm not prejudiced against anybody's beliefs or what they do in their off time. I do regret saying something like that. Whatever I did to offend people, I apologize."

▶ Jimmy "The Greek" Snyder, asked on the occasion of Martin Luther King's birthday in 1988 about the progress that blacks had made in

American society: "If they take over coaching like everybody wants them to, there's not going to be anything left for white people. All the players are black. The only thing that the whites control are the coaching jobs." Snyder lost his job as football analyst for CBS Sports.

▶ Washington Redskins running back John Riggins to Supreme Court Justice Sandra Day O'Connor at the Washington Press Club's annual Salute to Congress, in 1985: "Loosen up, baby. You're too tight." Riggins had just asked O'Connor when she would pose for a pin-up poster.

10 Famous Strikes, Boycotts, and Lockouts

▶ In 1977, Chicago Black Hawks star Bobby Hull sat out one game to protest hockey violence.

▶ In 1973, Yugoslav tennis player Nikki Pilic refused to play for his country's Davis Cup team and was banned by the International Lawn Tennis Federation. The players boycotted in support of Pilic, and the Association of Tennis Players (ATP) demanded that Wimbledon accept Pilic. Wimbledon refused, and all but 3 of the 82 ATP players boycotted, including 13 of the 16 seeded players at Wimbledon. The three exceptions were Romanian Ilie Nastase, Englishman Roger Taylor, and Australian Ray Keldie. Czech Jan Kodes won the tournament.

▶ On January 14, 1989, Georgetown University basketball coach John Thompson walked off the court before a game with Boston College to protest Proposition 42, which prevents freshmen who do not meet entrance standards from receiving their scholarships. Thompson claimed the proposition was racially biased.

▶ In 1994, for the first time since professional baseball began in 1871, no end-of-the-year champion was crowned as major-league players struck over the issues of a salary cap and revenue sharing. The regular season was lost from August 12th on, there was no World Series, and the players didn't return until April 1st of the following year.

The next year it was hockey's turn. NHL owners locked out the players for 103 days until the NHL Players Association accepted the owners' proposal, and the league played a stunted 48-game regular season. The Devils won the Stanley Cup in the abbreviated season. Particularly galling to fans (and to hockey itself, had it been able to get out of its own way) was that the lockout occurred following one of the NHL's most rousing seasons ever, capped by one of the league's marquee teams, the New York Rangers, winning their first Stanley Cup in 54 years, in a thrilling seven-game final against the Vancouver Canucks, following a thrilling seven-game semifinal against the New Jersey Devils (with Game 7 going to overtime) that helped bring to the game new fans and great enthusiasm—that is, until all goodwill was extinguished by the lockout.

In the summer of 1998, a 191-day, owners' lockout cost the NBA 32 of its 82 regular-season games and much fan goodwill. The owners essentially clobbered the players, by instituting ceilings on salaries, especially those that may be offered by teams looking to sign free agents from other teams. In the abbreviated season, the San Antonio Spurs won their first NBA championship.

▶ In a 1976 boycott, African nations, led by Tanzania, protested the inclusion in the Olympics of New Zealand, whose rugby team had made a tour of South Africa. Iraq and Guyana also boycotted.

▶ In 1980, President Jimmy Carter led a boycott, which also included West Germany and Japan, of the Moscow Olympics, to protest the Soviet invasion of Afghanistan.

▶ In 1984, the Soviet Union returned the favor and led many communist countries in a boycott of the Los Angeles Olympics.

▶ At the 1912 Olympics, in one of the more petulant boycotts of all time, the Italian Fencing Federation proposed lengthening the épée blade to 94 centimeters. When the proposal was rejected, the Italians refused to participate.

5 Distasteful Episodes in Which Politics Infected Sports

Politics play too large a role in professional sports, as well as supposedly amateur ones, namely the Olympics. To list all the occasions in which nationalism, greed, and generally ugly behavior have affected the outcome of a contest, or who got to play in it, or where it should be played, requires a book in itself. The 1972 Olympic massacre of Israeli athletes, baseball's tacit "whites-only" rule for decades, point-shaving, boxers taking dives, Olympic boycotts, biased judging and officiating—the list of people manipulating sport for political and monetary gains is endless.

Others have used the field of play as a forum for making more egalitarian-minded points, but they have abused sport nonetheless.

We offer just a sampling of invasions—from warfare to television—into the purity of sports.

▶ At the 1956 Olympic Games, Hungary and the Soviet Union faced each other in water polo a month after Soviet troops had invaded Hungary. The "Blood in the Water" match was punctuated by brawls, and was finally stopped by the referee with Hungary leading, 4-0.

▶ The "Futbol War" in 1969 between El Salvador and Honduras was sparked by soccer matches that fueled existing tensions. It was also known as the Soccer War, the One-Hundred Hour War, and the Football War. The two countries met in a World Cup qualifying round in June of 1969. Honduras won the first leg on June 8. El Salvador won the second leg on June 15, necessitating a decisive third game. Both games had set off fierce rioting. In Honduras, Salvadoran residents were attacked, and hundreds of thousands of migrants fled across the border. Reprisals were made against Hondurans in El Salvador. Diplomatic relations were cut off. On June 24, El Salvador declared a state of siege. That day, El Salvador defeated Honduras 3-2 at a neutral Mexico City site. Fighting intensified. On July 3, a Honduran plane was reported to have attacked Salvadoran border troops. On July 14, Salvador forces invaded Honduras. Honduras bombed San Salvador and Acajuta. On July 18, a cease-fire was made.

The death toll was estimated at 2,000.

▶ Emily Davison, a suffragette who was frustrated by the English Parliament's refusal to grant women the right to vote, brought attention to the cause in 1913 by running onto the famed Epsom Downs track during the Derby Stakes, Britain's premier race, and into the path of the leading horse, owned by King George V. To the horror of the crowd, Davison was trampled and killed.

▶ American tennis star Bill Tilden was suspended and ruled ineligible to play in the 1928 Davis Cup, but the French Federation Cup, wanting a full house at their new Roland Garros Stadium, petitioned the president. Eventually the American ambassador in Paris was instructed to usurp the power of the U.S. Davis Cup captain and to reinstate Tilden.

▶ Because of commitments to advertisers, NBC cut away from the November 17, 1968, New York Jets-Oakland Raiders football game with minutes remaining and the Jets leading, 32-29, to begin its presentation of the movie *Heidi*. Oakland scored two touchdowns in the game's thrilling final 42 seconds to win, 43-32, and set off a barrage of complaints from viewers who had been denied the exciting finish. The contest would forever come to be known as "The Heidi Game."

A Happier Marriage of Sports and Politics: 7 Moments in Which Life's Harsher Realities Were Softened by the Spirit of Competition

▶ In 1967, a cease-fire was declared during the Biafran War so that soccer great Pelé could visit both sides of the front.

▶ The father of tennis champion Fred Perry was a Labour member of Parliament and was afraid to leave the House to watch his son at Wimbledon because his party was governing in a minority situation. Arthur Steel-Maitland, leader of the opposition, arranged what is termed "live pairs" for the senior Perry. A member of the opposition who would have been voting against the government in a debate would agree to stay away until the return of his pair—namely, Perry, off watching his son.

▶ Harold Connolly, American hammer thrower, and Olga Fikotová, Czech discus thrower, met during the 1956 Olympics and corresponded by mail after she returned to Prague, and he to Boston. Connolly visited Prague and asked the Czech government for permission to bring her to the United States to marry her. The government refused, but the U.S. State Department intervened and permission was granted. Connolly and Fikotová were married, with Czech marathoner Emil Zatopek as the best man. In 1960, both Mr. and Mrs. Connolly competed for the U.S. team.

► The political and cultural isolation that the U.S.S.R. underwent for 30 years following the October Revolution was broken first in 1946 by the re-affiliation of the country's soccer federation with the Federation Internationale de Football Association.

► In September 2002, North and South Korea played to a 0-0 draw in a soccer "friendly," before 60,000 fans in Seoul, South Korea. Both countries agreed not to fly their national flags or to play their anthems. When the teams entered the field, the flags that were flying depicted a sky-blue image of the undivided Korean peninsula against a white background.

► Despite the threat by the Pakistan Sport Board to kick him out of the country's tennis federation if he didn't drop his doubles partner, Pakistani Aisam-ul-Haq Qureshi, a Muslim, teamed with Israeli Amir Hadad, a Jew, to play men's doubles at the 2002 Wimbledon and U.S. Open tournaments. Hadad, for his part, received almost entirely enthusiastic response to the pairing. "I see it as only a positive that two guys from different nationalities can play together," said the Israeli. "We are good friends and I think we're going to keep playing together in the future."

"Actually, we're not here to change anything," said Qureshi, the #1-ranked Pakistani, whose mother was once ranked #1 in the country, and whose grandfather played at Wimbledon. "Politicians and governments do that. We're just here to play the game and enjoy it." At Wimbledon, the team made the third round; it was the best showing ever for a Pakistani player, and the pair decided to build on that success by also pairing at the U.S. Open.

"It doesn't matter where we come from," said the Israeli. "We are tennis players, improving our ranking. But if something else good can come out of all this, it's even better."

► The first American to visit China after it was reopened to the West in 1971 was table tennis champion Leah "Ping" Neuberger.

And 1 Moment in Which the Predominance of Sports or Politics Is Hard to Determine

► While American light-heavyweight Mike McTigue was winning the world title over Battling Siki in a 20-round victory inside a Dublin arena on St. Patrick's Day, 1923, the Sinn Fein insurrection, in which Irish rebels were battling the British, was going on outside.

18 of the Most Notorious Disqualifications and Suspensions

▶ On June 8, 1920, Cincinnati Reds outfielder Edd Roush was ejected from the game for taking a nap in the outfield during a break in play.

▶ Lee Calhoun was suspended for the 1958 track season for receiving gifts on a TV game show called *Bride and Groom*. (He came back in 1960 to win his second Olympic gold medal in the 110m hurdles, leading a fourth consecutive United States sweep in the event.)

▶ During the second round of the 2002 Scottish PGA Championship, Edinburgh's William Guy ran out of golf balls. By the 7th hole, already at 10-over-par for the tournament, Guy lost his last ball. He couldn't borrow balls from his playing partners because they were playing different compressions and brands.

At golf's French Open, Anders Forsbrand of Sweden once retired because he ran out of balls on the 18th hole. His score had already hit triple digits.

▶ Richard Higham is the only baseball umpire expelled from the game for life, for dishonesty. He had informed gamblers on how to bet on games that he was umping, and was banished from the National League on June 24, 1882.

▶ In 1936, Germany's Toni Merkens won the 1,000m cycling sprint gold medal despite interfering with the second-place cyclist. Instead of being disqualified, Merkens was fined 100 marks.

▶ Heavyweight champion Muhammad Ali was suspended from March 23, 1967, through September 25, 1970, for evading the draft.

▶ In the 1940 U.S. Open at Canterbury, Ohio, two golfing threesomes were disqualified for teeing off 28 minutes early for their final round, in an attempt to beat an impending storm. One of the disqualified golfers, Ed "Porky" Oliver, shot a 71 for a 287 total, the same as champion Lawson Little and Gene Sarazen (whom Little beat in a playoff).

▶ Tennis player Ilie Nastase was banned for a year from representing Romania in Davis Cup play after an outburst in a 1977 match with Britain.

▶ At the 1924 Paris Olympics, a demonstration broke out when French middleweight boxer Roger Brousse was disqualified for biting his opponent in their quarterfinal bout.

▶ In the 1980 Olympic 20,000m walk finals, 7 of the 34 walkers were disqualified for illegal technique.

▶ Golfer Seve Ballesteros was disqualified from the 1980 U.S. Open for being late for his starting tee time on the second day.

▶ Jimmy Connors won three legs of the tennis Grand Slam in 1974—all but the French, from which he had been banned because he had signed a contract with World Team Tennis.

▶ The NCAA levied the "death penalty" on SMU's football team on February 25, 1987, for violating NCAA rules, including making payments to players.

▶ In 1972, swimmer Rick DeMont had his Olympic gold medal for the 400m freestyle taken away because he had taken asthma medication, Marex, that contained ephedrine, a banned drug. DeMont had been taking the medicine since he was four years old, and the American team physicians had neglected to check what was in Marex. DeMont became the first American since Jim Thorpe to be forced to return a gold medal.

▶ At the Mexico City Olympics in October of 1968, Tommie Smith and John Carlos gave the Black Power salute on the 200m victory stand during the playing of the American National Anthem. They were barefoot, wore black gloves, and bowed their heads. They said that the clenched fists represented black strength and unity, the bare feet were reminders of black poverty, and the bowed heads showed that expressions of freedom in the National Anthem did not apply to blacks. The United States Olympic Committee suspended both men and ordered them to leave the Olympic village.

▶ Rocky Graziano had his boxing license revoked because he did not report an attempted bribe to throw a fight with Reuben Shank in 1948. (The fight did not come off because Graziano had injured his back while training. Graziano said that he treated all bribe attempts with disdain and saw no need to report them.)

▶ Lee Trevino was disqualified from the 1981 PGA tournament for not signing his card.

▶ The Parrot, the Pittsburgh Pirate mascot, was suspended for a game for throwing a Nerf ball at umpire Fred Brocklander.

7
TEAMS AND RIVALRIES

With Friends Like That...

To succeed in sports, it's imperative that you be able to distinguish friends from foes, teammates from opponents. Presumably, friends and teammates are the ones that rally and help and support you.

It can be a mistake to presume.

▶ On February 2, 1962, pole vaulter John Uelses cleared a world-record 16′¼″. As track officials moved to verify the height of the bar, fans congratulating Uelses accidentally knocked over the vault supports, thus negating the jump.

▶ Countrymen Kenneth McArthur and Christian Gitsham of South Africa were leading the Olympic marathon in 1912 when they came to a water stand two miles from the stadium. McArthur said that he would wait for Gitsham to take a drink, but he kept on running, opening a lead that Gitsham could not overcome.

▶ The night before Cleveland Indians catcher Ray Fosse was injured badly when he was bowled over at home plate by Cincinnati Red Pete Rose in the 1970 All-Star game in Cincinnati, Fosse was a dinner guest at Rose's home.

▶ In 1999, Hall of Fame guard Isiah Thomas bought the long-standing Continental Basketball Association for $9 million, with half the cash up front. In January 2001 — in part because Thomas, recently named the new Indiana Pacers coach, was forced by the NBA to unload his CBA stake, citing the potential for conflict of interest—the league, in its 55th season, suspended operations.

▶ Johann Muelegg, a German who moved to Spain in 1999 and represented Spain in the 50km classical cross-country race at the 2002 Salt Lake City Olympics, won the gold for his adopted country. Hours later, he brought dishonor to his adopted country when he tested positive for darbepoetin, a performance-enhancing drug, and his medal was stripped from him.

▶ Toronto Blue Jays outfielder George Bell was named the dirtiest player in baseball in a poll in *The Toronto Globe*.

▶ New York Yankees owner George Steinbrenner was suspended from running the team and was placed on the permanently ineligible list by baseball commissioner Fay Vincent after Steinbrenner paid gambler Howard Spira $40,000 in exchange for detrimental information on Yankees outfielder Dave Winfield. Steinbrenner, who ridiculed Winfield's ability to perform in the clutch by calling him "Mr. May," was allowed by Vincent to return on March 1, 1993.

▶ In a legendary bust of a career with the New Jersey Nets that spanned 4 years, 110 games, and 1,002 minutes, center Yinka Dare was hardly what you'd call a team-first player: In his entire tenure with New Jersey, Dare amassed all of... four assists, or an average of one per year.

▶ On May 29, 1993, Texas Rangers manager Kevin Kennedy let outfielder Jose Canseco pitch in a 15-1 loss to the Boston Red Sox. Canseco threw 33 pitches, tore a ligament in his right elbow, was lost for the season, and would never again be the same player.

▶ Jim Pierce, the abusively loud-mouthed, anything-but-calming father of tennis player Mary Pierce, was finally banned from women's tour events in 1993.

▶ Bison Dele (formerly Brian Williams)—the troubled Detroit Piston center who walked away from his pro basketball career, then disappeared, and who may have been murdered—shook up his teammates on the Piston charter when, while the plane was in flight, he tried to open the emergency exit.

▶ At the 1988 Olympics, Americans Calvin Smith and Lee McNeill made an illegal baton exchange on the third leg of the first-round heat of the 4x100m relay. The heavily favored defending champion U.S. team was disqualified, thus denying teammate Carl Lewis a shot at repeating his four-gold-medal-winning performance of 1984, an unprecedented duplication that he had dreamed of achieving.

▶ In 1989, two Buffalo Bill coaches beat each other up after watching a videotape of the previous week's game.

When they were Los Angeles Dodger teammates, Don Sutton and Steve Garvey wrestled—not playfully—in the locker room.

▶ In the 1976 Olympic 200m race, Hasely Crawford suffered a cramp after 50 meters and was listed as not finishing. However, a track fan pointed out that Crawford had never left his lane until he jogged past the finish line, giving him a time of 1:19.60.

▶ In 1977, Texas Rangers second baseman Lenny Randle was suspended for 30 days, lost $13,000 in salary during the suspension, and was fined $10,000 for assaulting Rangers manager Frank Lucchesi and putting him in the hospital for five days.

▶ Byron Nelson's caddie accidentally kicked his golf ball, leading to a penalty stroke that helped cost Nelson the 1946 U.S. Open.

▷ Honorable mention 1: The manager of the 1943 American League All-Stars, New York Yankees skipper Joe McCarthy, did not use any of the six Yankees who were on hand for the game.

▷ Honorable mention 1A: Although referees and officials should not be counted on as either friends or teammates, athletes have a right to count on them at least to pay attention. In the 1932 Olympic Games, France's Jules Noël had apparently made a winning discus throw on his fourth attempt but none of the officials saw where the throw landed because at the time they were all watching the pole vault. Noël was given an extra throw but could not duplicate his effort and did not earn a medal.

Big and Little

Some nicknames are as much a testament to an athlete's affiliation to a better-known teammate or sibling or just contemporary, as they are to the prowess of the athlete him- or herself. The following is a list of athlete pairs who have, for better or worse, forged at least part of their place in history with each other.

▶ Major leaguers Jeff Pfeffer and his brother, Big Jeff Pfeffer

▶ Hall of Famers Paul "Big Poison" Waner and Lloyd "Little Poison" Waner

▶ Hockey Hall of Famers Maurice "The Rocket" Richard and his brother, Henri "The Pocket Rocket" Richard

▶ New York Islanders Duane "Dog" Sutter and his younger brother, Brent "Pup" Sutter

▶ Olympic swimming contemporaries Johnny "Tarzan" Weismuller and Andrew "Boy" Charlton

▶ William "The Refrigerator" Perry, 325-pound Chicago Bear, and Gerald "The Ice Cube" McNeil, 140-pound Cleveland Brown

▶ Cincinnati Reds starting catcher Ernie "The Big Slug" Lombardi and his backup, Willard "The Little Slug" Hershberger

▶ Hall of Fame left wing Frank "Big M" Mahovlich and his brother, center Pete "Little M" Mahovlich

▶ Fierce tennis rivals Helen "Helen the First" Wills and Helen "The Other Helen" Jacobs

▷ Honorable mention: Relatively new Washington Redskins owner Daniel Snyder—intrusive, compulsive, easy to inflame; in short, Steinbrenner-like—is often referred to in the media as "Boy George."

16 Sets of the Most Evenly Matched Competitors

When going head-to-head or simply when compared to each other, the following pairs of teams or individuals were—maybe for one brief moment, maybe for years—exquisitely well-matched.

▶ The football teams of Fordham University and the University of Pittsburgh played to scoreless ties in 1935, 1936, and 1937.

▶ Through 1988, the Boston Celtics' home playoff record was 165-54. Through 1988, the home playoff record of their chief rival, the Los Angeles Lakers, was 164-54.

▶ In the last eight Ryder Cup matches between the U.S. and Europe, from 1987 through 2002, on five occasions the result could have been reversed by simply changing the result of a single match; on the other two occasions, changing two match results would have produced a different winner.

▶ In Game 1 of the opening round of the 1936 Stanley Cup playoffs, the Detroit Red Wings beat the Montreal Maroons, 1-0, in six overtimes, the longest game in Cup history.

▶ Through nine innings on May 2, 1917, the Chicago Cubs' Jim "Hippo" Vaughn and the Cincinnati Reds' Fred Toney pitched the only double no-hitter in major-league history. (Vaughn eventually gave up two hits and a run in the 10th inning.)

▶ After 60 games, through the year 2000, the football rivalry between The Citadel and Virginia Military Institute stood at 29-29-2. (In 2001, The Citadel crushed VMI, 49-7.)

▶ Cary Middlecoff and Lloyd Mangrum played the longest sudden death in history, at the 1949 Motor City Open. After 11 holes, they were declared co-winners by mutual agreement.

▶ In match-play competition at the 1932 PGA, Johnny Golden finally beat Walter Hagen on the 43rd hole.

▶ In the 1975 Surrey Grass Court Championships in Surbiton, England, Anthony Fawcett and Keith Glass played one game of 37 deuces and 80 points. The game lasted 31 minutes.

▶ In a 1969 girls' high school basketball game in Tennessee, Chattanooga East Ridge defeated Ooltewah, 38-37, in 16 overtimes.

▶ The most fumbles in an NFL game is 14. In setting the shoddy record in 1940, the two combatants—the Chicago Bears and the Cleveland Browns—each mishandled the ball seven times.

▶ In a match in Lyons, France, tennis stars Jaroslav Drobny and Budge Patty finally called it a draw at 21-19, 8-10, 21-21.

▶ Leon Cadore of Brooklyn and Joe Oeschger of Boston both pitched all 26 innings—the longest stints ever by a pitcher in a single (modern) game—before their May 1, 1920, game was called for darkness, with the score tied, 1-1.

▶ Jimmy Barry and Casper Leon, bantamweights, fought to a draw twice in world title fights, in May and December of 1898.

Abe Attell and Owen Moran, featherweights, drew in their two world title fights in January and September of 1908.

▶ For a salary arbitration hearing in 1987, the Atlanta Braves and pitcher David Palmer both submitted a figure of $750,000.

And 1 Set of the Most Evenly Matched Compatriots

▶ Ethel Catherwood, 1928 high jump gold medalist, married Harold Osborn, 1924 high jump gold medalist.

I've Got Your Number: Athletes and Teams and Their Favorite Patsies

pat sy (pat'se) *n., pl.* -sies. *Slang.* A person who is cheated, victimized, or made the butt of a joke. [Origin unknown.]

In sports, a patsy is the player or team you most love to face because you have so much success against him or her or them—for a season, a few years, a career. There's just something about them that makes you thrive—you match up well perhaps, or you love their home field, or maybe you just plain have them psyched out. A patsy does not have to be a bad player or team; in fact, your mediocre and lousy opponents might give you a lot of trouble while a very good opponent is your patsy.

In each of the following cases, the patsy was no slouch.

▶ Larry Jaster vs. the Los Angeles Dodgers, 1966: St. Louis Cardinals pitcher Jaster faced the National League champion Dodgers five times, and shut them out each time. He gave up 24 hits, all singles, in 45 innings, and had a 0.00 ERA. Against the rest of the league that year, Jaster was 6-5 with a 4.66 ERA. (His final totals were 11-5, 3.26 ERA.)

▶ Steve Foley vs. Dan Fouts, career: Denver Bronco defensive back Foley made 44 interceptions in his career, 13 off of San Diego Chargers quarterback and All-Pro Fouts.

▶ The Montreal Canadiens vs. the Boston Bruins, the 20th century through 1987: 22 times these two teams met in the Stanley Cup playoffs, and the Bruins lost 20 of those, including 18 straight from 1946–87. (The Bruins finally turned things around after that, winning five of seven playoff series against Montreal through 2002.)

▶ Neale Fraser vs. Alex Olmedo, 1959: That year, Australian tennis star Fraser swept the U.S. Championship singles, doubles, and mixed doubles titles. In all three finals, Olmedo was on the other side of the net.

▶ The Boston Celtics vs. the Los Angeles Lakers, 1960s: The Lakers reached the NBA Finals six times in the decade, each time losing to the Celtics.

▶ Hub Pruett vs. Babe Ruth, 1922–24: During those years, Ruth batted .315, .393, and .378, and hit 35, 41, and 46 home runs, respectively, but he was .190 in 30 at-bats with one home run against the St. Louis Browns lefty reliever Pruett. Pruett, who threw a screwball, struck out Ruth 15 times, including 10 of the first 11 times he faced him. Pruett's lifetime mark was 29-48, with a 4.63 ERA. After Pruett retired, he became a doctor and thanked Ruth for putting him through medical school because, Pruett claimed, his success against Ruth was the main reason he was kept in baseball.

▶ The New York Jets vs. the Miami Dolphins, 1998–2001, and the Dallas Cowboys vs. the Washington Redskins, 1997–2001: For otherwise evenly matched teams—indeed, the Dolphins were probably a little better than the Jets over this span, and the 'Skins were clearly better than the Cowboys during the last several years—it's been no match. Through the beginning of the 2002 season, the Jets had won their previous eight games over the Dolphins, and the Cowboys had won their previous nine against Washington. (The Dolphins finally broke the schneid in September of 2002.)

▶ Billy Williams vs. Steve Blass, September 5, 1969: The Chicago Cubs outfielder had his way with the Pittsburgh Pirates pitcher, collecting two doubles and two home runs. What makes this game remarkable is that while Blass was Williams's patsy on that day, the rest of the Cubs were *Blass's* patsy: He gave up only four hits, all of them by Williams. Blass won the game.

▶ Any bowl opponent vs. a Bo Schembechler-coached team, 1970–90: Schembechler's Michigan Wolverines were 5-12 in bowl games.

▶ University of Michigan vs. John Cooper-coached Ohio State 1988–2000: During his 13-year career at OSU, Cooper's team was a dismal 2-10-1 versus its biggest rival; against everyone else, his team was 109-33-3.

▶ Tony Gwynn vs. Greg Maddux: The four-time Cy Young Award winner had little luck in retiring the eight-time Padres batting champ, who was 39-for-91 (.429) against Maddux. (Oh, yeah: And how did Gwynn do against the other two Atlanta Braves—Tom Glavine and John Smoltz —who, along with Maddux, formed baseball's best pitching trio in the 90s? Against Smoltz, Gwynn hit .462; against Glavine, a paltry .312.)

▶ Rich Gossage vs. Rickey Henderson, career, and Roger Clemens vs. Cory Snyder, start of career: Henderson struck out eight of the first nine times he faced Gossage in the American League, and then again in the 1984 All-Star game. Snyder struck out the first nine times he faced Clemens.

▶ Bob Neyland-coached Tennessee vs. Bear Bryant-coached Kentucky, career; and Notre Dame vs. Bear Bryant-coached Alabama, career: Against the Volunteers, Bryant's Wildcats were 0-5-2; against the Fighting Irish, Bryant's Crimson Tide was 0-4.

▶ The Chicago Cubs vs. Don Sutton, early in his career: The Los Angeles Dodgers pitcher lost the first 13 times he faced the Cubs.

▶ Ned Yost vs. Tommy John, career; and Tommy Hutton vs. Tom Seaver, career: Yost, a .212 career hitter, hit .833 (10-for-12, with two home runs) off of John; Hutton, a .248 hitter, hit .700 against future Hall of Famer Seaver.

▶ Rod Laver vs. Arthur Ashe, 1960–74: Over that span, the American lost 18 straight matches to the Australian.

▶ Harry Coveleski vs. the New York Giants, 1908; and Frank Lary vs. the New York Yankees, 1960s: Philadelphia Phillies pitcher Coveleski earned the nickname of "The Giant Killer" by beating them three times in the final week of the season, to kill the Giants' pennant hopes; Detroit Tigers pitcher Lary was known as "The Yankee Killer."

▶ The New York Yankees vs. the Brooklyn Dodgers, 1940s and 1950s: From 1941 to 1956, the two teams met in seven World Series, several of which are considered classics, but the Dodgers managed only one championship, in 1955.

▶ Lleyton Hewitt vs. American men, May 2001–August '02: Before losing to Andre Agassi in the semifinals of the 2002 U.S. Open, the Australian had won his previous 23 matches versus Americans, including three wins each over Agassi and Pete Sampras.

▶ Among today's baseball stars and teams (through 2002), a number of patsies stand out:

▷ The New York Yankees vs. Aaron Sele: From 1998 through 2001, Sele appeared in four consecutive postseasons, only to watch New York make life miserable for him and his team each time. The Yankees eliminated Sele's Texas Rangers in the first round of the playoffs in 1998 and 1999, before Sele moved to the Seattle Mariners. In 2000 and 2001, the Mariners got by the first round, only to be eliminated both years in the American League Championship Series by the Yankees. In those four years, Sele made five starts against the Yankees, going 0-5 with a 5.00 ERA.

▷ Pedro Martinez vs. the Seattle Mariners: In 10 career starts against Seattle, the Red Sox ace is 10-0 with an 0.94 ERA. In 77 innings, the Mariners managed just 37 hits, with 110 strikeouts. In seven of those starts, Martinez struck out 11 or more Mariners.

▷ Gary Sheffield vs. Pedro Astacio: Sheffield owns a .442 career average off of Astacio in 52 at-bats. The last time Astacio faced Sheffield, in 2002, he hit him with a pitch, earning an ejection and setting off a bench-clearing incident.

▷ Pat Burrell vs. the New York Mets: In 172 career at-bats versus New York, the Phillies slugger has 17 homers and 49 RBI, including several game-winners.

▷ Mo Vaughn vs. David Wells: Vaughn owns Wells, with nine homers in 66 at-bats.

▶ Henry Tillman vs. Mike Tyson, as amateurs: Tillman twice defeated the future heavyweight champion to qualify for the Olympic team in 1984, when he won the heavyweight gold medal.

11 of the Friendliest Rivalries

▶ With Jesse Owens one foul away from being disqualified in the long jump at the 1936 Berlin Olympics, Luz Long, his German competitor and main rival, introduced himself and gave Owens a tip: Make a mark several inches before the takeoff board and jump from there. Owens did that and qualified easily. Owens went on to win (not surpassing Long until his next-to-last jump) and was congratulated first by Long, who won the silver medal, in full view of Adolf Hitler. Owens wrote, "You can melt down all the medals and cups I have, and they wouldn't be a plating on the 24-carat friendship I felt for Luz Long at that moment."

▶ Although Mark McGwire and Sammy Sosa battled all of the 1998 season to break Roger Maris's home-run record, and continued to spar for the home-run title even after McGwire's record-breaking 62nd home run, the two humanized the chase with their evident fondness for each other and mutual respect. McGwire, noticeably uptight as his pursuit gained worldwide attention, credited Sosa with showing him how to relax and enjoy the spectacle. When McGwire hit No. 62 on September 8th at Busch Stadium in St. Louis, it was only fitting that it was against Sosa's Cubs. Sammy trotted in from his right-field position to embrace McGwire after he crossed the plate. McGwire and Sosa each enacted Sosa's ritual of bringing two fingers to his lips and then his heart. It was also fitting that McGwire and Sosa shared the Sportsmen of the Year honor from *Sports Illustrated*.

▶ Australian tennis stars Roy Emerson and Fred Stolle cooked each other breakfast at their Putney flat before playing in Wimbledon finals in 1964 and 1965.

▶ Jackie Fields and Joe Salas, best friends growing up in Los Angeles, fought for the 1924 Olympic featherweight gold. Fields won and then went to his locker room and cried.

▶ In the 1936 Olympic pole vault competition, Japanese Shuhei Nishida and Sueo Oe finished tied for second. They refused to vault off for placing and instead decided by drawing lots that Nishida would be second and Oe third. When they got home, they had their medals cut in half and fused back together so that each had a medal of half silver and half bronze.

▶ After his second run in the 1984 Olympic slalom, Phil Mahre immediately got on the walkie-talkie with advice for Steve, his twin brother and the only person left who could deprive him of his gold medal. Phil won the gold and Steve took the silver.

▶ In 1987, Chris Evert won La Trophée de la Femme at the Pierre Barthes Club in Cap d'Agde. She thought the Cartier-designed silver-and-gold leopard ball that she received was something Martina Navratilova would like, so she gave it to her. It was valued at £20,000.

▶ In 1979, defending U.S. Amateur champion John Cook talked Mark O'Meara into playing in the tournament and put him up at his condominium. O'Meara beat Cook in the finals.

O'Meara became fast friends with another competitor—Tiger Woods, a generation younger, as early Tigermania was setting in. "I just wanted to keep a good eye on the competition," O'Meara said, affectionately. "I consider him a big brother on tour, because I can go to him about anything," said Woods. Neighbor and Ryder Cup partner, O'Meara watched as his younger friend captured his first Grand Slam, the 1997 Masters. Woods then watched as O'Meara—to the surprise of many, since his best golf years appeared to be behind him—won *his* first Slams, the 1998 Masters and British Open. Woods helped his friend slip into the green jacket.

▶ Rafer Johnson and C. K. Yang together attended UCLA and helped each other train for the 1960 decathlon. After the 1,500m, the final event of the competition, the two men fell against each other for support. Johnson edged Yang for the gold.

▶ The 1984 featherweight weightlifting medal ceremony marked the first time a platform was shared by athletes from China (gold medalist Chen Weiqiang) and Taiwan (bronze medalist Wen-Yee Tsai). They shook hands and praised each other.

▶ In 1973, Secretariat beat Riva Ridge, his stablemate at Meadow Stable, in the initial running of the Marlboro Cup. The horses were ridden on different occasions by jockey Ron Turcotte. Riva Ridge won the Kentucky Derby in 1972, and Secretariat won it a year later.

The Most Heated Rivalries

▶ *Jason Kidd and Jimmy Jackson*: A very promising Dallas Mavericks team was torn apart from within, in part because guard/forward Jackson and point guard Kidd were allegedly fighting over the same woman, pop singer Toni Braxton.

▶ *Nancy Kerrigan and Tonya Harding*: It was one of the most bizarre sports stories in many years: In January of 1994, girl-next-door Kerrigan was practicing at a Detroit rink (site of the U.S. Olympic figure skating trials) and preparing for the Winter Olympic skating competition the following month in Lillehammer, Norway, when a bruiser of a guy named

Shane Stant entered the rink, whacked her knee with a collapsible baton, then dashed out of the rink and left in a getaway car. It turned out that the thug was hired by Jeff Gillooly, ex-husband of the blue-collar Harding, Kerrigan's chief American rival, who later claimed (falsely) that she had no knowledge of the planned attack. (Gillooly claimed that he thought that the attack would improve his ex's chance of winning an Olympic medal and thus earning endorsement money; for his part in the crime, Gillooly would later go to jail for racketeering.) Kerrigan's post-attack plea, while clutching her knee, of "Why me?" made the cover of *Time* magazine. She recovered quickly and was able to compete; questions surrounding Harding's possible involvement in the attack remained until the Games, but she was allowed to compete there, too. Tension concerning them was high at the Games, and their every move was chronicled; the cameras—oh, the cameras—were there when they (along with other skaters) were practicing on the Lillehammer rink at the same time. Kerrigan, the more artistic and graceful of the two, skated well enough to take the silver medal, while Harding, the more athletic and better jumper, seemed to wilt from the pressure, finishing eighth. During the free skate portion, Harding caused another stir, one almost as bizarre as the knee-whacking: When her name was called, she failed to appear. With seconds remaining before being disqualified, Harding emerged from behind a curtain, asthma inhaler in hand, played with her skate laces, began her program, missed her first jump, started to cry, skated over to referee Britta Lindgren, put her right foot on the ledge in front of Lindgren, and explained that her lace had broken during her warm-up and she hadn't had time to repair it. After examining the skate, the ref allowed Harding to go again, after the rest of the skaters in her group had performed; on her second try, Harding completed four triple jumps and moved up to eighth place after starting in 10th.

The Kerrigan-Harding "skate-off" (Ukraine's Oksana Baiul took the gold medal) was the sixth most-watched television program in history and, after Super Bowls XVI and XVII, the most-watched sporting event ever.

Harding would plead guilty to conspiring to hinder prosecution of a case, be put on three years probation, be ordered to perform 500 hours of community service, and be fined $100,000.

Kerrigan would go to Disney World.

▶ *Washington Redskins and Dallas Cowboys:* If you want to get perfectly little boy-ish about it (if not politically correct), it's all about Cowboys and Indians. But the passionate rivalry between these long-time NFC East division rivals has been fueled, in part, by the fact that when the 'Skins have been good, so have the Cowboys (generally speaking), and both of them have recent histories of great success. The Cowboys have won five Super Bowls, the Redskins three. The Cowboys are "America's Team" (or were, once); the Redskins have one of the longest, most storied legacies in the league. They play each other twice a year; through the 2001 NFL season, their record against each other was a nearly even 42-39-2 advantage for Dallas; that lead was forged in the last five years, when, for some reason particularly unfathomable (and painful) to Redskin fans, the lately mediocre Cowboys have beaten their hated rivals nine consecutive times. While there are other good NFL rivalries—Denver Broncos-Oakland Raiders, New York Jets-Miami Dolphins, Cleveland Browns-Pittsburgh Steelers, to name three—none compares to this one. Said Washington spokesman Carl Swanson, "Hating the Cowboys is so much a part of the fabric of being a Redskins fan." We're certain his counterpart on the Cowboys would agree, only vice versa.

▶ *New York Knicks and Miami Heat*: For the four seasons from 1996–97 through 1999–2000, the Heat and Knicks met in the playoffs each year, a first in NBA history. On each of those instances, the series went the distance. Because of almost identical systems (Heat coach Pat Riley had previously been the Knick coach), defense-first mentalities, dominating centers from Georgetown (the Heat's Alonzo Mourning and the Knicks' Patrick Ewing), and a palpable loathing of each other (especially by Knick fans for the departed Riley), numerous games were not decided until the last few minutes, or seconds. As much as the evenness of the matchup, it was the incredibly physical play that characterized—at times, marred—the rivalry.

▶ *Detroit Red Wings and Colorado Avalanche*: This is a relatively new rivalry—while the Red Wings are one of the NHL's Original Six teams, the Avalanche were the Quebec Nordiques prior to the 1995–96 season—but what it lacks in duration it makes up for in intensity—or, to be blunt, violence. Over the last several years, these two teams, who have combined for five Stanley Cups since 1996, have battled each other in several Western Conference playoffs that, for their urgency and skill, were the "real" Stanley Cup Finals, in the minds of many serious hockey fans.

A few moments, for background:

▷ It was a humiliating onslaught of Red Wing goals against then-Montreal Canadiens goalie Patrick Roy—he thought he should have been pulled before he'd been allowed to give up a shocking nine scores—that led the great goaltender to tell Montreal he would no longer play for them; he was then traded to... the Avalanche.

▷ In Game 6 of the 1996 Western Conference final, Colorado forward Claude Lemieux hit Red Wing Kris Draper with a blind-side check into the boards, face first, fracturing Draper's jaw, breaking his nose, and causing other injuries. Lemieux was suspended for two games of the Stanley Cup finals for his—these are the NHL's words—"cheap shot"; Colorado won the Stanley Cup anyway.

▷ In Lemeiux's first game in Detroit after the Draper hit, Red Wing Darren McCarty clocked Lemieux, and more fights and bloodiness broke out, including a memorable skirmish between Roy and Detroit goalie Mike Vernon. McCarty won the game on an overtime goal, the Red Wings knocked off Colorado in the playoffs, and won the Stanley Cup.

In 1998, another goalie fight broke out—this time, between Roy and Detroit's Chris Osgood. The Red Wings won the fight, and the game and, later, the Stanley Cup.

In 1999 and 2000, Colorado eliminated the Red Wings from the playoffs.

In 2001, the Red Wings again didn't advance far in the playoffs, and watched their archrivals go on to win the Stanley Cup.

In 2002, *another* goalie fight occurred: Roy took on his third Detroit netminder—this time, Dominik Hasek. In the playoffs, Detroit eliminated Colorado, and went on to win the Stanley Cup.

▶ *Pete Rose and A. Bartlett Giamatti*: Giamatti, the commissioner of baseball, banished Rose from baseball for life on August 24, 1989, ruling that Rose had gambled on baseball games—including games played by the Cincinnati Reds while he was their manager (betting always to win, at least). Despite massive evidence to the contrary, Rose steadfastly has refused to acknowledge that he bet on baseball, and has criticized the investigation and voluminous report by Washington lawyer John Dowd that was the basis of the decision by Giamatti, who died of a heart attack a mere eight days after the judgment. Giamatti's ban, which keeps Rose out of the Hall of Fame, has not been lifted by subsequent commissioners Fay Vincent or Bud Selig, despite allegations by Rose that the report is flawed.

▶ *Pete Rose and Jim Gray*: Interviewing Rose before Game 2 of the 1999 World Series in Atlanta—moments after baseball's all-time hits leader was honored as part of the All-Century team—NBC's Gray acted more like prosecutor than broadcaster, aggressively grilling Rose about his alleged gambling that led to his ban from baseball. Many viewers were outraged at Gray's hardline stance, and Yankee outfielder Chad Curtis snubbed him after his game-winning homer in Game 3.

The Most Dominant Tandems in Sports

After a 1960 game against the New York Knicks in which Elgin Baylor had scored 71 points, his Los Angeles Laker teammate "Hot Rod" Hundley, who scored two, slapped Baylor on the back and exulted, "What a night, buddy! Seventy-three points between the two of us!"

The following pairs of teammates or opponents (individuals, teams, or countries) dominated—in a slightly more equitable fashion—their sports or specialties to an outlandish extent.

▶ Between 1937 and 1973, Australia and the United States won the Davis Cup every year except for 1940–45, when there was no competition. No other country even made it to the finals from 1938 until 1960.

▶ No Ivy League team but the University of Pennsylvania or Princeton University won or shared the league basketball title from 1969 until Brown broke the hold in 1986. In 1987, Penn won again, but then Cornell won in 1988. After that brief hiccup, the domination returned, with either Penn or Princeton winning or sharing the title, until 2002, when a three-way-tie occurred with Yale. (In the mini-tournament to determine who would earn the NCAA berth, Yale eliminated Princeton, but Penn beat Yale.)

▶ A Japanese or Soviet (or former Soviet) gymnast has won the men's all-around title in every Olympics but one since 1952. (1996 is the lone exception.) The U.S. men's team's win in 1984 was the lone time the Soviets (or former Soviets) or Japanese did not win the team competition from 1952 until 1996.

▶ From October 1982 through October 1995, Mark Allen and Dave Scott won 11 of the 14 Ironman Triathlon Championships, in Hawaii. They are also responsible for four runner-up finishes over that span.

▶ But for the scantest exceptions, when it comes to college team wrestling, no states need to exist except for Oklahoma and Iowa. Starting in 1928, when the first national team wrestling champs were named, schools from those two states have won all but seven titles (no champ was named from 1943–45). When the University of Minnesota won the team title in 2001, it was only the second time in one-third of a century that the Oklahoma/Iowa headlock had been broken; when the Gophers repeated in 2002, it was the first time that the two dominant states, as one, had experienced such a drought.

▶ Since 1985, sports broadcasters Bob Costas and Chris Berman have, between them, won 14 National Sportscasters and Sportswriters Association Award, given annually.

▶ The University of Connecticut and University of Tennessee women's basketball teams have won six of the last eight NCAA championships. But a more impressive indication that they are, by far, each other's only equals, is this: Over those eight years, 9 of Tennessee's 32 losses are against UConn; against everyone else, the Lady Vols are 251-23. Over those eight years, 6 of UConn's 17 losses are against Tennessee; against everyone else, the Lady Huskies are 264-11.

▶ Between 1966 and 1979, Larry Mahan or Tom Ferguson was PRCA all-around rodeo world champion every year but 1971–72.

▶ Between them, Jimmy Connors and John McEnroe won all seven U.S. Open men's tennis singles titles from 1978 through 1984.

▶ Philadelphia Eagle Russ Craft had four interceptions and his teammate Joe Sutton three, as they combined for seven interceptions in one September 24, 1950, game against Chicago Cardinals quarterback Jim Hardy.

▶ Either Bill Russell or Wilt Chamberlain led the NBA in rebounding for 16 out of 17 years, from 1957–73.

▶ For every year from 1971 to 1980 but one, either Jack Nicklaus or Tom Watson was the PGA Tour's leading money-winner.

▶ The Los Angeles Lakers and Boston Celtics accounted for 8 of the 10 NBA titles in the 1980s. One of those two teams was runner-up five times.

▶ From 1960 to 1976, only one Australian Championship women's singles final did not include Margaret Court or Evonne Goolagong or both.

▶ In 1961, New York Yankees Roger Maris, with 61, and Mickey Mantle, with 54, combined for 115 home runs.

▶ When the Arizona Diamondbacks engineered a trade with the Philadelphia Phillies in late July of 2000 for Curt Schilling, uniting him on a staff with Randy Johnson, the only other active pitcher to record 300 strikeouts in a season, it created one of the most overpowering one-two punches in baseball history. In 2001, their first full season together, the left-handed Johnson and right-handed Schilling pitched the Diamondbacks to the World Series championship, combining for a 43-13 record with a combined 665 strikeouts, breaking the major-league mark for whiffs by teammates of 624, set by Nolan Ryan and Bill Singer on the 1973 California Angels. Schilling was 13-1 after Arizona losses, Johnson 10-2. Schilling was named the All-Star Game starter but eventually deferred to Johnson. They became the first starting pitchers from the same team since 1956 to finish one-two in the Cy Young Award balloting, with Johnson beating out Schilling. In the Diamondbacks' World Series triumph over the New York Yankees, they were named co-MVPs after accounting for all four of the team's wins. They were also named co-winners of Sports Illustrated's *Sportsman of the Year* award. In 2002, the two again put up dominant—and remarkably similar—numbers, becoming the first teammates ever to exceed 300 strikeouts in the same season. (Johnson once again beat out Schilling for the Cy Young.)

In 1910, Philadelphia Athletics pitchers Jack Coombs (31-9, 1.30 ERA, 35 complete games) and Chief Bender (23-5, 1.58 ERA, 25 complete games) formed another devastating 1-2 starting punch, with a combined record of 54-14. (Just six years later, on the same Philadelphia As team, pitchers Jack Nabors, at 1-20, and Tom Sheehan, 1-16, combined for a 2-36 record between them, an equally devastating 1-2 punch in reverse.)

▶ On February 22, 1981, Quebec Nordique teammates and brothers Peter and Anton Stasny combined for 16 points in a single NHL game. Peter scored four goals and recorded four assists while Anton scored three times and had five assists.

▶ Reggie and Laurie Doherty dominated Wimbledon in the 1890s and early 1900s. Reggie won four singles titles in a row; after a one year break, Laurie won five in a row. Together, they won the doubles title 8 times in 10 years.

7 Three-Headed Monsters

And sometimes there are *three* forces that are head and neck and shoulders above the competition.

▶ From 1941–42 to 1959–60, the Stanley Cup was won by only the Montreal Canadiens (eight times), the Toronto Maple Leafs (six times), and the Detroit Red Wings (five times).

▶ From 1924–52, no competitor from a country other than Norway, Finland, or Sweden finished in the top eight in 15-km Olympic Nordic skiing, and only one outsider finished in the top eight in the 50km. In 1952, those three countries earned the first 17 places in the 15km race.

▶ James Braid, John Henry Taylor, and Harry Vardon, British golfing greats from the 1890s through the 1920s, were born within 13 months of one another and became known as "The Great Triumvirate." For the 21 years from 1894 to 1914, Vardon won the British Open six times, Taylor and Braid five each.

▶ Since 1985, no school but Georgia, Stanford, or USC has won the men's NCAA team tennis title.

▶ From 1981–2000, the Art Ross Trophy—for the NHL's top scorer—was won by only Wayne Gretzky, Mario Lemieux, or Jaromir Jagr.

▶ From 1966–88, the Sportswriter of the Year (voted on by the National Sportscasters and Sportswriters Association and selected national media) was awarded only to the *Associated Press*'s Will Grimsley (four times), *Sports Illustrated*'s Frank DeFord (six times), and *The Los Angeles Times*'s Jim Murray (13 times).

▶ For a quarter-century, the 500cc world motorcycle champion has been dominated by those riding a Suzuki, Honda, or Yamaha.

Take That! 15 Exercises in Sports One-Upsmanship and Revenge

In the first game of a September 21, 1934, doubleheader, St. Louis Cardinals ace Dizzy Dean three-hit the Brooklyn Dodgers. In the second game, Paul Dean, Dizzy's brother, no-hit Brooklyn. Apparently, Dizzy claimed later that had he only known his brother was going to pitch a no-hitter, he would have pitched one, too. For Dizzy the gauntlet had been dropped too late, after his day's work was done. In the following cases, however, a standard was set and then someone else came along to match it, or top it; or a point was made definitively, only to be refuted even more definitively.

▶ On December 19, 1987, Boston Bruin Ken Linseman scored a goal at 19:50 of the 3rd period.

St. Louis Blue Doug Gilmour scored two seconds later, at 19:52, the quickest response in NHL history.

▶ On March 7, 2002, the Atlanta Braves and Los Angeles Dodgers swapped slugging outfielders—the Braves got Gary Sheffield; the Dodgers, Brian Jordan, who was less happy about being dealt than Sheffield was. When the teams met each other in Atlanta, Jordan hit a top-of-the-ninth-inning, two-out homer to give the Dodgers the lead. In the bottom of the inning, Sheffield homered to tie it.

The Dodgers won the game in the 16th inning, on Jordan's second homer of the night.

▶ In 1976, the U.S.S.R., Czechoslovakia, and Hungary angered Federation Cup officials by withdrawing from the tennis competition to protest the Cup's inclusion of South Africa.

The following year, the Federation Cup board banned all three protesting countries from competition for protesting the previous year.

▶ Jim Maloney and Don Wilson pitched back-to-back no-hitters—Maloney for the Cincinnati Reds against the Houston Astros on April 30, 1969, Wilson the following day for the Astros over the Reds. It was only the second time this had happened in major-league history. In 1968, Gaylord Perry pitched a no-hitter on September 17 for the San Francisco Giants over the St. Louis Cardinals, and Cardinals pitcher Ray Washburn returned the favor the next day by no-hitting the Giants.

▶ When Joe Torre, former All-Star catcher and first baseman, turned to managing, he enjoyed only moderate success. In his stints with the New York Mets, Atlanta Braves, and St. Louis Cardinals, Torre was a combined 109 games under .500 in 14 years. His only title came when the Braves won the NL West flag in 1982, but they were swept by the St. Louis Cardinals in the National League Championship Series. When Torre was named by New York Yankees owner George Steinbrenner to replace Buck Showalter as Yankees manager in 1996, the under-whelmed *New York Daily News* headlined its story, "Clueless Joe."

Torre proved to be a brilliant choice. Unusually adept at mollifying the explosive Steinbrenner, Torre won a World Series championship his first year, and after losing in the Division Series to Cleveland in 1997, came back to win four straight American League pennants and three straight World Series titles. Through the 2002 season (during which the Yankees won their fifth straight AL East title), Torre had brought his career record to 131 games over .500.

▶ After his team's repeated failure to advance far in the playoffs, Miami Heat coach Pat Riley traded Jamal Mashburn in a nine-player deal with the Charlotte Hornets, leaving little doubt that he blamed Mashburn for not scoring or leading enough, a criticism Mashburn didn't feel was warranted.

When the Heat faced off against the Hornets in the first round of the 2001 playoffs the following season, Mashburn led his new team to an obliterating sweep over the Heat: They won the three games by an average of 22.3 points, and Masburn averaged 23.6 points in the series, including a playoff-tested 25 for 25 on free throws.

▶ The Minnesota Twins, the intended victim (along with the Montreal Expos) in major-league baseball's push to "contract" the league from 30 to 28 teams, on the notion that they didn't generate enough revenue to compete, got a reprieve prior to the 2002 season when a U.S. district judge ruled that the Twins had to honor their lease at the Metrodome. The Twins then went on to win the Central Division title in the American League, and the new labor agreement reached in late August mandated that no team could be contracted until after the 2006 season.

▶ Only four times in NFL history have consecutive kickoffs been returned for touchdowns. It happened last on September 6, 1998, when Roell Preston of the Green Bay Packers countered Terry Fair's 101-yard return for the Detroit Lions with a 100-yard TD of his own.

▶ About baseball, Yogi Berra once said, "Ninety percent of this game is half-mental." Philadelphia Phillies manager Danny Ozark took him a step further by once saying, in earnest, "Half this game is ninety-percent mental."

▶ In destroying the rest of the field at the 1912 Olympics, Jim Thorpe may have done himself more harm than good: One of the competitors whom Thorpe overwhelmed in the pentathlon and decathlon was Avery Brundage, who finished sixth in the former competition and could not even finish the latter. Brundage later became president of the International Olympic Committee (1952–72) and was empowered to return to Thorpe the two Olympic medals that had been taken from him decades before, following charges that Thorpe had played semi-pro baseball and thus forfeited his amateur standing. A year after Brundage took office, Thorpe died, unredeemed. Not until 1982, a decade after Brundage had left the IOC presidency, was Thorpe's name restored to the record book. In 1983, Thorpe's children were finally presented with his gold medals.

▶ After Roger Clemens went 10-13 for the Boston Red Sox in 1996, he and Red Sox management had an acrimonious breakup that led to his leaving Boston as a free agent and signing with the Toronto Blue Jays. The Red Sox hadn't wanted to give Clemens the four-year contract he desired, pointing out that he'd barely been a .500 pitcher for the past four years. In two seasons with the Blue Jays, Clemens won the Cy Young Award both years after recording pitching "Triple Crowns" both seasons—leading the league in wins, ERA, and strikeouts. Clemens' sweetest moment of revenge came on July 12, 1997, in his return to Fenway Park, when he set a Toronto record by striking out 16 batters in the Jays' 3-1 win. After striking out the side in the eighth—Nomar Garciaparra, John Valentin, and Mo Vaughn—Clemens stared into the Red Sox executive box as he walked off the mound to a standing ovation.

▶ On Mother's Day, 1939, the parents of Cleveland Indian Bob Feller traveled from Iowa to see their son pitch in Chicago against the White Sox. At one point, a foul ball hit by Chicago batter Marv Owen struck Feller's mother, broke her glasses, and opened a cut, for which she later needed stitches. Feller asked for time and went into the stands to check on his mother, then returned to strike out Owen. Feller won the game.

▶ In 1994, New York Yankees manager Buck Showalter criticized Seattle Mariners superstar Ken Griffey, Jr., in a *New York Times Magazine* article for his habit of wearing his baseball cap backwards during pre-game workouts and batting practice, saying that the superstar lacked respect for the game. Before their next game with the Yankees, all Mariner players turned their hats around as they came out for batting practice.

Even the stern and straight-arrow Showalter cracked a smile.

▶ For the 1965–66 season, Philadelphia 76ers center Wilt Chamberlain signed a contract for $100,000. His great rival, Boston Celtics center Bill Russell, then had his own contract negotiated so that he would be paid $100,001.

▶ There have been countless star college athletes who were supposed to fail in the pros—because of insufficient size or speed, say—but went on to prove their critics wrong. One of the most delicious examples of I-told-you-so-ism has to be that of Mark Jackson. A standout point guard for the St. John's (New York) University Redmen, Jackson was deemed too slow to make it in the NBA, and without a good enough outside shot to offset the first deficiency; he was widely acknowledged to be smart and resourceful, sure, but those are generally euphemisms for "too slow" and "not a good outside shooter."

And while it's true that he was never quick of step, and that his outside shot was barely average, it's *also* true that he was named NBA Rookie of the Year in 1988, made the All-Star team, helped to lead his team (the Indiana Pacers) to the NBA Finals, and is breathing down Oscar Robertson's neck for the #3-ranking, all-time, in the history of the NBA, in career assists.

10 Memorable Nicknames of Teams

▶ Bronx Bombers (New York Yankees)

▶ Monsters of the Midway (Chicago Bears)

▶ Big Red Machine (1970s Cincinnati Reds)

▶ Broad Street Bullies (1970s Philadelphia Flyers)

▶ Flying Frenchmen (Montreal Canadiens)

▶ Gashouse Gang (1930s St. Louis Cardinals baseball)

▶ Phi Slama Jamma (1982–84 University of Houston men's basketball)

▶ Four Musketeers (1920s French tennis stars René Lacoste, Henri Cochet, Jean Borotra, and Jacques Brugnon)

▶ Whiz Kids (1950 Philadelphia Phillies; early 1940s University of Illinois men's basketball)

▶ Doctors of Dunk (1980s University of Louisville men's basketball)

... And 10 Parts of Teams

▶ Punch Line (1940s Montreal Canadiens line of Maurice Richard, Toe Blake, and Elmer Lach)

▶ Purple People Eaters (1960s and 1970s Minnesota Vikings front four, including Jim Marshall, Carl Eller, Alan Page, and Gary Larsen, and later, Doug Sutherland)

▶ $100,000 Infield (the 1911 Philadelphia Athletics infield—Stuffy McInnis, 1B; Eddie Collins, 2B; Jack Barry, SS; Home Run Baker, 3B)

▶ $1,000,000 Infield (the 1948 Philadelphia Athletics infield—Ferris Fain, 1B; Pete Suder, 2B; Eddie Joost, SS; Hank Majeski, 3B)

▶ Steel Curtain (1970s Pittsburgh Steelers front four, including "Mean" Joe Greene, Ernie Holmes, L. C. Greenwood, and Dwight White)

▶ Fearsome Foursome (1960s Los Angeles Rams front four, including Deacon Jones, Lamar Lundy, Roosevelt Grier, and Merlin Olsen)

▶ Long Island Power Company (1970s–80s New York Islanders line of Bryan Trottier, Mike Bossy, and Clark Gillies)

▶ Legends 1 and 1A (1970s New York Knicks backcourt of Walt Frazier and Earl Monroe)

▶ Mr. Inside and Mr. Outside (1940s Army backfield of Doc Blanchard and Glenn Davis)

▶ The Nasty Boys (1990 Cincinnati Red relief corps of Randy Myers, Rob Dibble, and Norm Charlton)

...And 10 Fan Clusters

▶ Arnie's Army (Arnold Palmer fans)

▶ Jack's Pack (Jack Nicklaus fans)

▶ Lee's Fleas (Lee Trevino fans)

▶ Cameron Crazies (Duke University basketball fans)

▶ Cheese Heads (Green Bay Packer fans; Milwaukee Brewer fans)

▶ Dawg Pound (Cleveland Brown fans)

▶ K Corner (New York Met Dwight Gooden fans—the original "K Corner")

▶ Coneheads (David Cone fans)

▶ Bleacher Bums (Chicago Cub fans)

▶ The Blair Bunch (Olympic speedskater Bonnie Blair's vocal supporters)

Ladies & Gentlemen, Your New York Yankees: Truly Rotten Things That Members of America's Greatest Team Have Said and Done

▶ After the Yankees signed their first black player, Elston Howard, in 1955—a good eight years after Jackie Robinson had broken the major-league color barrier, and with a deliberateness that sufficiently signaled the organization's long-held reluctance to integrate—manager Casey Stengel lamented his luck in getting the not-particularly-swift Howard (a catcher): "When they finally get me a nigger, I get the only one who can't run." Stengel—the loveable, language-twisting legend who led the Bronx Bombers to 7 world titles and 10 pennants—at first called Howard "Eightball," another derogatory term for African-Americans, and at times referred to black players as "jigs," "jigaboos," and "jungle bunnies."

After Yankee pitcher Allie Reynolds, who was part Creek Indian, struck out Robinson three times in Game 4 of the 1952 World Series, Stengel, who did not like Robinson (who himself hated Stengel and the Yankees, in large part because of their slowness to integrate; Robinson once said "I have felt deep in my heart that the Yankees for years had been giving Negroes the runaround"), must have thought he was offering an evolved judgment when he said, after the game, "Before that black son of a bitch accuses us of being prejudiced, he should learn how to hit an Indian."

▶ According to *Reggie: The Autobiography*, by Reggie Jackson and Mike Lupica, third baseman Graig Nettles called *New York Post* sportswriter Henry Hecht "a back-stabbing Jew cocksucker." Jackson also said that Nettles, manager Billy Martin, catcher Thurman Munson, and pitchers Dick Tidrow and Sparky Lyle told offensive Jewish jokes amongst themselves as they watched teammate Ken Holtzman running laps in the outfield.

▶ According to *Joe DiMaggio: The Hero's Life*, Richard Ben Cramer's extensively researched biography of the Yankee Clipper—unquestionably one of the greatest baseball players of all-time—DiMaggio physically abused wife Marilyn Monroe, and played golf with Mob boss Sam Giancana and was friendly with other organized crime members. Also documented in Cramer's book—though it is hardly the only source of this characterization—are examples of DiMaggio's epic miserliness and his utter lack of graciousness. (Of Ted Williams, perhaps that era's only counterpart to DiMaggio in talent, the Yankee legend said that he "may out-homer me. But I will out-percentage him, I can out-throw him, I can out-run him and out-think him." DiMaggio also said that Williams "throws like a broad.") DiMaggio was estranged from his only child and his two brothers. The hagiographical coverage DiMaggio received during his playing days and after—certainly among the most whitewashed collective accounts ever of an athlete's life—included fictions (to take one example meant to make DiMaggio look friendlier) that he was buddies with fellow outfielder

Tommy Henrich; Henrich would later say that in more than a decade together on the same team, they never once went to dinner.

(On the impossibly heroic press portrayal of DiMaggio, it is Cramer's contention, in part, that no one—not even Joe DiMaggio, the great and graceful champion—could ever have lived up to such a depiction; DiMaggio's efforts to maintain and protect that impossible image in no small part made him the man he became. Indeed, to give a taste of what kind of press coverage DiMaggio received, and then may have felt the painful pressure to live up to, here's a snippet from a 1939 *Life* magazine feature on the great Italian-American player who, for so many, represented the triumph of the American Dream: "Instead of olive oil or smelly bear grease [Joe] keeps his hair slick with water. He never reeks of garlic and prefers chicken chow mein to spaghetti.")

▶ George Weiss, a member of the Yankees organization from 1932-60, architect behind their long-envied farm system, and general manager from 1948-1960, during which he presided over some of the greatest teams in Yankee (or baseball) history, said, "I will never allow a black man to wear a Yankee uniform. Boxholders from Westchester don't want that sort of crowd. They would be offended to have to sit with niggers."

▶ In 1994, Richard Kraft, former Yankee vice president for community relations (and George Steinbrenner's college roommate), complained about the graffitied, beat-up condition of the neighborhood park bordering Yankee Stadium, which is situated in predominantly Latino and black areas: "It's like monkeys… Why do they do this to themselves? These things are for them." After public outcry, Steinbrenner removed his friend.

An Embarrassment of Riches

Some regions or schools or teams or conferences are so superior that they seem almost to be competing among themselves. After New York Giant Willie Mays won the 1954 National League MVP Award over their beloved Duke Snider, Brooklyn Dodger fans said that Mays might be the best centerfielder in the game, but he was only the third best in New York (behind New York Yankee Mickey Mantle, as well).

Internal, comradely competition may help to produce for some team or league a statistical cornucopia.

▶ The 1928 New York Yankees had the top three RBI men in the league: Lou Gehrig and Babe Ruth were tied for the lead, with teammate Bob Meusel third. In 1932, the Philadelphia Phillies repeated the feat in the National League as Don Hurst, Chuck Klein, and Pinky Whitney ran 1-2-3.

▶ In 1985, the Big East basketball conference provided three of the Final Four teams—St. John's, Georgetown, and eventual national champion Villanova.

▶ After the 1972 college bowl games were played, the final national rankings for the 1971 season listed Nebraska first, Oklahoma second, and Colorado third—all Big Eight schools. Nebraska had gone undefeated; Oklahoma had lost, once, to Nebraska; and Colorado had lost twice, to Nebraska and Oklahoma.

▶ The 1965 Michigan State University football team set a record by placing seven men on All-America squads. They placed five more in 1966, for a two-year total of 12, another record.

▶ The state of Oklahoma has an unusual number of fast and run-happy baseball players. At one point in the late 1980s, five of the top six places nationally for most stolen bases in a high school season were held by five different Oklahoma schools.

▶ In 1959, Johnny Unitas's main targets—Ray Berry, Lennie Moore, and Jim Mutschuller—were 1, 2, and 4 among NFL receivers.

▶ In 1986, New York Mets pitchers Bob Ojeda, Dwight Gooden, Sid Fernandez, and Ron Darling were ranked 1, 2, 3, and 4 in National League winning percentage.

▶ The Edmonton Oilers had the first (Wayne Gretzky), second (Jan Kurri), and fourth (Mark Messier) top scorers in the NHL for the 1986-87 season.

Teammates, Forever

▶ Catcher Tim McCarver developed such a close relationship with future Hall of Fame pitcher Steve Carlton, first with the St. Louis Cardinals and later with the Philadelphia Phillies, where he served as Carlton's personal catcher, that McCarver once said, "When Steve and I die, we're going to be buried in the same cemetery, 60 feet 6 inches apart."

▶ There have been numerous other tandems of great pitchers working with preferred catchers who were not the first-string. In 1930, Brooklyn Dodgers backup catcher Hank DeBerry caught 35 games, all when Dazzy Vance pitched. The battery had played together in the minor leagues, came up together to the majors, and DeBerry had caught Vance's 1925 no-hitter.

Detroit Tigers second-stringer Bruce Kimm caught all 29 of Mark Fidrych's starts in 1976.

Eddie Perez, a light-hitting journeyman catcher, might never have made a ripple with the Atlanta Braves except for one little thing: Greg Maddux loved pitching to him. In 1996, Perez started 37 games during the regular season, 17 of them when Maddux was on the mound. The four-time Cy Young Award winner was 10-5 with a 1.88 ERA in 119⅔ innings with Perez behind the plate, compared to 5-6, 3.52 in 125⅔ pitching to the Braves' regular catcher, Javy Perez. That clinched Perez a job as Maddux's personal catcher. He caught 31 of Maddux's 33 starts in 1997, and 32 of 34 in 1998. In 1999, Perez became the Braves' every-day catcher in mid-season after Lopez was injured, and wound up the MVP of the National League Championship Series, in which he hit .500.

▶ No teammates in the NBA have ever been more linked than Karl Malone and John Stockton of the Utah Jazz. Stockton joined the team in 1984, and is (through the 2001–02 season) #1 all-time in assists and steals; Malone joined the Jazz the following year, and is #2 all-time in scoring. Without question, Malone has received more Stockton passes that led to points, and Malone is responsible for more of Stockton's assists, than any NBA duo ever. Their pick-and-roll, in particular, has been run successfully so many times that one wonders how it can still beat opponents, over and over again. "We kind of know what each other is going to do beforehand and then we don't talk about it a lot," Malone once said.

Both men were selected by the league to be included in their elite club of the "50 Greatest Players in NBA History."

▶ Whenever fiery manager Billy Martin got hired for a new job, two things were certain: He would eventually do something to get himself fired, and Art Fowler would be his pitching coach. Martin and Fowler were inseparable drinking buddies, and Fowler worked under Martin in Minnesota, Detroit, Texas, Oakland, and various incarnations with the Yankees. "A billionaire couldn't get him away from me," Martin once said of Fowler.

▶ The friendship between Chicago Bear backfield running mates Brian Piccolo and Gale Sayers was chronicled in the popular 1971 TV movie, *Brian's Song*. In the mid-60s, with the civil-rights movement in full bloom, the teammates became the first white (Piccolo) and black (Sayers) men to room together in the NFL. In the middle of the 1969 sea-son, Piccolo was diagnosed with a lung tumor; after it was removed, doctors determined that it was malignant and that the cancer had spread. When, during a banquet in New York City, Sayers received the George Halas Award as the NFL's most courageous player for that sea-son—in the ninth game the previous year he'd ruptured cartilage and torn two ligaments in his right knee, then worked his way back to win the '69 NFL rushing title—he assured everyone that there was someone who deserved the award much more. "He (Brian) has the heart of a giant and that rare form of courage that allows him to kid himself and his opponent—cancer," Sayers told the audience. "He has the mental attitude that makes me proud to have a friend who spells out the word 'courage' 24 hours a day of his life…I love Brian Piccolo, and I'd like all of you to love him, too. Tonight, when you hit your knees, please ask God to love him."

▶ In the 1928 Olympic 100m hurdles finals, South Africa's Syd Atkinson, who had finished a close second in 1924, drew the inside lane, which had been chewed up by rain. Teammate George Weightman-Smith, who had set a world record in the semifinals, offered to switch lanes with Atkinson, who declined. Weightman-Smith insisted, Atkinson finally accepted, and he ended up winning the gold medal. Weightman-Smith took fifth.

▶ Pam McGee, a basketball All-America from the University of Southern California, made the 1984 Olympic team while her sister, Paula, also a USC All-America, did not. After helping the United States to win, Pam gave her gold medal to Paula.

Just a Few of the Most Frustrated Athletes and Teams of All Time

▶ Hungarian fighter Laszlo Papp won the Olympic middleweight boxing gold medal in 1948 and the light middleweight golds in 1952 and 1956, became the first boxer from a Communist country to turn professional, won the European title... and was prevented by the Hungarian government from fighting for the world title.

He retired undefeated.

▶ There are many tales of undefeated and ultimately untested teams:

The University of Kentucky basketball team finished at 25-0 in 1954 and was ranked #1 in the country but declined an invitation to the NCAA tournament because three stars, all graduate students—Cliff Hagan, Frank Ramsey, and Lou Tsiropolos—would not have been allowed to play in the tournament. The team voted 9-0 to play in the tournament without them but coach Adolph Rupp overruled the team.

In college football, Colgate's 1932 team gained fame for being "unbeaten, untied, unscored upon, and uninvited." The Rose Bowl bypassed the Red Raiders for twice-tied University of Pittsburgh, which lost to the University of Southern California.

▶ Bill Sharman, who would star for the Boston Celtics and later coach the Los Angeles Lakers to an NBA championship, was also a major leaguer, if briefly. He was called up by the Brooklyn Dodgers at the end of the 1951 season and was sitting on the bench during a September 27 game against the Boston Braves when umpire Frank Dascoli ejected the Dodger battery of Preacher Roe and Roy Campanella, as well as the whole Brooklyn bench, after a disputed play at home. Sharman did not get to see any action during the pennant stretch and earned the distinction of having been ejected from a major-league game without ever having played in one.

▶ In 1953, Ben Hogan was prevented from an attempt to win the modern golfing Grand Slam because the PGA tournament was held simultaneously with the British Open. That year, Hogan won the U.S. Open, the Masters, and the British Open.

Homages, from One Sports Figure to Another

► "He plays a game with which I am unfamiliar."

—*Bobby Jones, after watching Jack Nicklaus win the 1965 Masters in then-record-setting fashion, and blowing away the second and third best golfers in the world—Arnold Palmer and Gary Player—by nine strokes*

► "There has been only one manager, and his name is John McGraw."

—*Connie Mack*

► "I'd like to thank... David Thompson for going to the ABA."

—*Alvan Adams, upon being named the 1975–76 NBA Rookie of the Year*

► "I was going to speak from my heart. But, man, he broke my heart so many times, do I have anything left?"

—*Larry Bird on Magic Johnson, who'd selected Bird—his greatest rival through college and the pros, a mutual admirer, and one of his only peers in talent and competitiveness—to present him at Johnson's 2002 induction into the Basketball Hall of Fame*

► "If I were in Jackie Robinson's shoes, I probably never would have made it."

—*Bob Gibson*

► "Lynn Swann was an idol. It would amaze me how he could fly through the air and make those catches. I'll never forget the one versus Dallas. It was the greatest catch I've ever seen."

—*Jerry Rice, arguably the greatest wide receiver—perhaps football player—of all time*

► "He's a better pitcher then I ever hope to be."

—*Dizzy Dean on Satchel Paige*

► "Runners in the western world have a tendency to create psychological barriers for themselves, but [Noureddine] Morceli runs at will, with no inhibitions."

—*Eamonn Coghlan, former indoor mile/outdoor 5,000m world champion*

► "I can see how he won twenty-five games. What I don't understand is how he lost five."

—*Yogi Berra on Sandy Koufax, after the latter's 1963 season*

(Willie Stargell also had a legendary line about Koufax: "Trying to hit him was like trying to drink coffee with a fork.")

► "Win this one for the Gipper."

—*Knute Rockne, legendary Notre Dame football coach, rousing his team with a locker room pep talk by invoking the memory of George Gipp, a Notre Dame fullback who died of a throat infection two weeks before being named an All-America; some question remains as to whether Rockne actually employed the now-famous phrase*

▶ "That god damned Dutchman [Honus Wagner] is the only man in the game I can't scare."
—*Ty Cobb*

▶ "Cobb is a prick. But he sure can hit. God Almighty, that man can hit."
—*Babe Ruth*

▶ "We're playing tennis. He's doing something else."
—*Ilie Nastase on Bjorn Borg, during the latter's dominating run as the world's #1 tennis player, including his incredible 5-plus-year/41-match Wimbledon winning streak from 1976–1981*

▶ "Blind people come to the park just to listen to him pitch."
—*Reggie Jackson on Tom Seaver*

▶ "Cool Papa Bell was so fast he could get out of bed, turn out the lights across the room and be back in bed under the covers before the lights went out."
—*Josh Gibson*

(About Bell, Satchel Paige said: "Once he hit a line drive right past my ear. I turned around and saw the ball hit his ass sliding into second.")

▶ "He just went out and did his job every day."
—*Hall of Famer Bill Dickey on teammate Lou Gehrig*

▶ "You're going to be a great player, kid."
—*Jackie Robinson to Mickey Mantle, after the 1952 World Series*

▶ David Wells's Ruthian physique is not the only way he pays homage to The Babe. Obsessed with Ruth since his childhood in San Diego, when he would write school reports on The Bambino, Wells chose No. 33 when he joined the Yankees—twice Babe's retired No. 3. Wells owns an autographed Ruth ball, and in 1997 he purchased from a collector, for $35,000, a genuine game-worn Ruth hat, dating back to his final season with the Yankees in 1934. Wells wore the hat for one inning in a game against Cleveland on June 28, 1997, before manager Joe Torre made him take it off.

Wells, who'd held the Indians scoreless, promptly gave up four runs the next inning.

16 Of the Most Utterly Dominant Teams and Countries in Sports History

▶ In 1909, Yale's football team not only went undefeated, untied, and unscored upon, but did not allow an opponent inside the 25-yard line. In 1888, Yale outscored their 13 opponents 698-0, a record that still stands. From 1876–1900, Yale football was 231-10-11.

▶ Every male Boston Marathon winner in the 1990s was Kenyan.

▶ The New York Yankees are without question the most renowned organization in baseball history, and probably in all of American sports, mostly because they were and are overwhelmingly good. From 1927–62, the team won 19 World Series in 36 years, including five in a row from 1949–53 and four in a row from 1936–39; they lost in the World Series just four times during that 36-year period. In the 16-year span from 1949 to 1964, the Yankees won 14 pennants. From 1954–63, the American League MVP was a Yankee eight times. The 1939 Yankees (to take just one juggernaut of theirs) outscored their opponents by 411 runs, the largest differential in the modern era, and their team ERA was 1.31 lower than the league average, the biggest differential in modern history.

▶ Canada's hockey team was so dominant that it received one of the ultimate compliments in sport: In the 1928 Olympic competition, Canada was simply advanced straight to the final round—while the other 10 nations were divided into three pools, the winner of each joining Canada in the championship round. On the way to winning their third hockey gold in a row, Canada held the opposition to no goals while averaging 13 a game.

▶ U.S. sailors kept the America's Cup for 132 years, the most sustained domination in any sport, until Australia won it in 1983.

▶ Florida State University's football team finished in the Top 4 for an incredible 13 consecutive years, from 1987–1999. (In 2000, they sank to an embarrassing 5th position.)

▶ From 1969 through 1991, Taiwan won the Little League World Series 15 times in 23 years. They captured the title in 1969, '71, '72, '73, '74, '77, '78, '79, '80, '81, '86, '87, '88, '90, '91.

▶ Various colleges have flexed their muscles in various sports—for example, the University of Maryland women's lacrosse team won seven consecutive national titles from 1995–2001, and the University of Arkansas won the men's indoor track title 16 times in the 17-year period from 1984–2000—but no school has dominated its competition more than the University of North Carolina women's soccer team. From the first NCAA women's soccer championship in 1982 through 2001, the Lady Tar Heels have won every title but four—and on three of those occasions, they were runner-up. In other words, over an entire generation, the 1995 title game in which Notre Dame beat Portland is the lone occasion when UNC women have not been on the field, contesting for college soccer supremacy.

▶ India's men's field hockey team won the Olympic gold from 1928, in its first attempt, until 1960, when Pakistan beat them, 1-0, in the finals at Rome. Before that loss, India won 30 straight matches and outscored its opponents 196-8. In three matches against the United States, India won by a combined 47-1 score. India came back to win the gold in 1964.

▶ The Baltimore Ravens defense was so dominant during the 2000 NFL season, setting a record for fewest points allowed—their 165 points given up over a 16-game season easily undid the previous record of 187, held by the 1986 Chicago Bears; and they also led the league with +23 in takeaways, among other signs of skill, hard hitting, and determination— that it was able, almost singlehandedly, to lead a team with a worse-than-mediocre offense (at one point they went 21 consecutive quarters without scoring a touchdown) all the way to a Super Bowl title.

▶ The Soviet Union women's gymnastics squad won eight consecutive gold medals in team combined exercises from 1952, when that nation, as the Soviet Union, first showed up at the Olympics, until 1984, when they boycotted. They won it again in 1988, and in '92 as the Unified Team.

▶ Since the first modern Olympic Games in 1896, the United States has performed extraordinarily well, particularly in men's track and field (women's track and field has, of course, a much shorter Olympic history). Some of the many track and field events, and a couple of other sports, in which American men have dominated the Olympics: the 4x100m relay, which it has won 15 of 20 times, losing just once by being outrun (in 1996, to Canada; three losses—1912, 1960, and 1988—were due to disqualification, and one, 1980, to boycott); the long jump, which it has won 20 of 24 times; the pole vault, which it won in 16 straight Olympics, from 1896 through 1968 (not including the unofficial 1906 Interim Olympics); sprints, winning 15 of 24 100m golds, and 16 of 23 200m golds; the eight-oared crew race, which it won 8 of the first 10 times it was held, from 1900–56; and swimming, winning (to take just one example) 12 of 13 events in 1976.

▶ The Finns have produced many of the world's greatest distance runners. From 1912 to 1936, only twice would the Olympic 5,000m and 10,000m not be won by a Finn.

▶ In the last 100 years, there have been 46 heavyweight world champions. Of those, 38 have been Americans.

▶ Anchored by Joan Joyce, the greatest woman softball player ever, the Raybestos Brakettes from Stratford, Connecticut, won the national women's major fast-pitch championship 14 times from 1966 to 1983.

▶ Since 1948, no woman from outside of Eastern Europe has held the world shot-put record.

8
SEX AND DEATH

●●●●●●●●●●●●●●●●

Killed in the Line of Duty

Some sports are more obviously dangerous than others—boxing, auto racing, football, to name three—and the number of athletes who have lost their lives competing in these sports is substantial. Since 1884, there have been approximately 500 ring deaths, seven in world title fights. Scores of drivers have been killed during warm-ups, qualifying runs, and actual races; the worst accident in auto-racing history took place at Le Mans in 1955, when driver Pierre Levegh's car spun out of control and careened into the stands, killing himself and 86 others, and seriously injuring 108 people, mostly spectators. President Theodore Roosevelt tried to ban college football, without success, when 18 players died and 73 more were seriously hurt in the year 1905 alone. (At Roosevelt's urging, the "flying wedge" was outlawed, a neutral zone between opposing lines was instituted, and the legalization of the forward pass soon followed, in 1906.)

But along with these three sports, less violent sports, too, have claimed lives. The following is a list of some of those who unwittingly were participating in their final sporting event.

▶ Richard Wertheim, 60, the center service linesman in the 1983 U.S. (tennis) Open boy's final, was killed when, stationed behind the baseline, he was hit in the groin by a ball off the racket of Stefan Edberg. Wertheim toppled backward in his chair and fractured his skull against the ground. His family sued the United States Tennis Association for negligence but lost.

▶ Bill Masterton, 29, a Minnesota North Stars rookie, died on January 15, 1968, from a massive internal brain injury sustained in a game with the Oakland Seals two days earlier. Masterton had fallen over backward after being checked, and hit his head on the ice. His is the only known pro hockey player death in the modern era.

▶ In 1920, Cleveland Indian Ray Chapman became the only baseball player killed during a major-league game. While at bat at the Polo Grounds, Chapman was hit in the head by New York Yankees pitcher Carl Mays. Chapman took two steps toward first, collapsed, and never regained consciousness.

▶ Phil Klusman, 43, a sportswriter for the *Bakersfield Californian*, was killed by an errant hammer throw during a practice round of an NCAA Division II track and field meet at Cal State-Los Angeles, on May 23, 1986.

▶ Soviet diver Sergei Shalibashvili died of a massive cerebral hemorrhage after hitting his head on the edge of the platform while attempting a reverse three-somersault tuck at the World University Games in Edmonton, in July of 1983.

▶ On Sunday, February 18, 2001, probably the darkest day in NASCAR history, 49-year-old Dale Earnhardt—beloved #3, "The Intimidator," perhaps the tour's greatest driver—was killed instantly on Turn 4, on the last lap of the Daytona 500, when, after being grazed by Sterling Marlin's car, Earnhardt slammed into a wall at 180 miles per hour, and was then hit by Ken Schrader's car; it was surmised that Earnhardt died instantly upon hitting the wall. His son, Dale, Jr., took second in the race. Earnhardt, Sr.'s death was the 27th in the history of the Daytona International Speedway in Florida.

Brazilian Ayrton Senna, three-time Formula One champion, was killed in a crash at the San Marino Grand Prix on May 1, 1994, capping a horrific weekend in which Austrian driver Roland Ratzenberger also died.

▶ The first athlete to die in the Olympics was Portuguese marathoner Francisco Lazaro, 21, who collapsed from sunstroke and heart trouble near the end of the 1912 race in Stockholm. He died the next day.

▶ In the 1960 Olympic road race, Danish cyclist Knut Jensen became the second person to die in the Olympics. He collapsed from sunstroke and fractured his skull. It was later discovered that he had taken Ronicol, a blood circulation stimulant, before the race.

▶ Vladimir Smirnov of the Soviet Union, Olympic gold medalist in the foil in 1980, died when the foil of his opponent in the 1982 world championships in Rome, Matthias Behr of West Germany, snapped and pierced Smirnov's mask, penetrated his eyeball, and entered his brain. Smirnov died nine days later.

▶ On April 30, 1981, photographer Michael Zia of the *Tigard Valley (Oregon) Times* was taking pictures of the mechanical rabbit at Multnomah Kennel Club dog-racing track in Fairview, Oregon, and did not see the approaching rabbit's motor, which struck him in the face and severed his arm. He never regained consciousness after the accident. His arm was re-attached and then re-amputated when it became infected. Zia died on May 11 of a massive pulmonary hemorrhage.

▶ In October 2001, skiing champion Regine Cavagnoud of France died of head injuries after she collided with German trainer Markus

Anwander, who crossed her path on the Pitztal glacier in Austria. Communication problems between the French and German teams, who were training for the upcoming World Cup season, were blamed for the accident.

▶ By 1928, 6 of the first 15 Indianapolis 500 winners had died while racing—Dario Resta, Howdy Wilcox, Gaston Chevrolet, Jimmy Murphy, Joe Boyer, and Frank Lockhart. The 1929 winner, Ray Keech, was killed two weeks later on a midwestern dirt track.

▶ When world champion bull rider Lane Frost, 25, was gored and trampled by a bull on July 30, 1989, at the Cheyenne Frontier Days Rodeo, he became the 11th cowboy killed in PRCA rodeos since 1970.

▶ Switzerland's Felix Endrich, 1953 world champion in the two-man bobsled, died less than a week after his victory while running a four-man sled down the same course at Garmisch-Partenkirchen. He crashed into a tree and was killed instantly.

▶ Minnesota Vikings Pro Bowl offensive tackle Korey Stringer died of heat stroke on the second day of practice in the 2001 NFL preseason, a day after he had to be carted off the field because of heat-induced exhaustion. It was the first such death in NFL history. Two days later, Northwestern University free safety Rashidi Wheeler, an asthmatic, died after collapsing during drills.

▶ Kazimierz "Kay" Skrzypeski, British luger, was killed during a trial run on the Olympic course two weeks before the 1964 Innsbruck Games.

▶ Chuck Hughes, Detroit Lions wide receiver, collapsed and died on the field during a game against the Chicago Bears, on October 24, 1971. His heart attack was the result of a blood clot, caused by an injury he sustained during the game.

▶ The thoroughbred Swale collapsed and died of a heart attack after a 10-minute workout at Belmont Park on June 17, 1984. Swale had won the Kentucky Derby in May and the Belmont in June.

▶ At least 130 motorcyclists have been killed in the 80-year history of the Isle of Man Tourist Trophy.

▶ In 1902, in a cavalry endurance race from Brussels to Ostend, 16 of 29 horses died.

▶ Three drivers died in the 22-day, 7,979-mile Paris-to-Dakar rally in 1988, as did three spectators. Three others died in a fire started accidentally by a support team. The rally began in Versailles and crossed the Sahara Desert.

▶ Russell Mockridge, cycling double-gold-medalist in 1952, was hit by a bus and killed while competing in the 1958 Tour of Gippsland race in Melbourne.

▶ Prominent boxers who have killed in the ring include Sugar Ray Robinson, Ezzard Charles, Primo Camera, and Ray "Boom Boom" Mancini. Boxer Frankie Campbell, brother of baseball star Dolf Camilli, was killed by Max Baer in 1930.

Athletes Involved in Murder (and More)

▶ In 1907, Vere Thomas St. Leger Gould, Wimbledon finalist in 1879, was convicted of murdering a Danish widow whose dismembered body he attempted to freight in two luggage trunks from France to England. He died on Devil's Island in 1909.

▶ On January 19, 1900, at a farm near North Brookfield, Massachusetts, Marty Bergen, catcher for Boston's National League team, axed his wife and children to death. He then killed himself.

▶ In certainly the most famous murder case involving an American athlete, former Heisman Trophy-winning, All-Pro running back O. J. Simpson was charged with murdering his wife, Nicole Brown Simpson, and a friend of hers, Ron Goldman. Almost all events surrounding the case—from the investigation to the famous "white Bronco chase" to the murder trial to Simpson's "Dream Team" of lawyers to the outrage (in many circles) over Simpson's acquittal to the civil trial to so many of the distasteful characters involved—captured the attention of the nation, whether it wanted to be captured or not, and provoked discussion on justice, racism, sexism, and favoritism for celebrities, to name a few.

To this day, Simpson, who had beaten his wife, claims he is determined to find the killer.

▶ Auto racer LeeRoy Yarbrough, the top driver on the 1969 stock-car circuit, died December 8, 1984, having spent his last four years in mental institutions because he had tried to strangle his 65-year-old mother in 1980. The judge had ruled then that Yarbrough was not guilty of attempted murder because, at the time of the incident, Yarbrough did not have the capacity to tell right from wrong.

▶ In 1980, six years after retiring from football, former Kansas City Chiefs tackle Jim Tyrer shot his wife to death, and then himself, at their Kansas City home.

▶ British featherweight Owen Swift killed men in two separate bouts, in 1834 and 1838. For the first killing, of Anthony Noon, Swift served six months in prison; for the second killing, of Brighton Bill, Swift was acquitted. He retired from fighting after the acquittal.

▶ On October 15, 1910, on the ranch of middleweight champion Stanley Ketchel, a jealous farmhand named Walter A. Dipley interrupted Ketchel's breakfast and killed him in an argument over Ketchel's girlfriend.

▶ Brian Spencer, an NHL player from 1969 to 1979, was indicted on December 12, 1987, for murder and kidnapping. He stood trial in the fall of 1987 in Palm Beach County, Florida, and was eventually acquitted. In June of 1988, Spencer was himself murdered in Riviera Beach, Florida, when a man walked up to the truck in which Spencer was a passenger and demanded money. The man then shot Spencer, 39, in the chest.

▶ Carolina Panthers wide receiver Rae Carruth was sentenced to a minimum of just under 19 years in prison after he was convicted of conspiracy to commit murder, and two other offenses. Prosecutors said that Carruth had set up a drive-by shooting of his girlfriend, eight months pregnant at the time, so that Carruth would not have to pay child support; his white Ford Explorer, it was argued, was used to block her car, so another man could shoot her. The woman died; the baby was delivered prematurely by Caesarean section. The dead woman's mother testified that her grandson was born with cerebral palsy because of the premature birth and the fact that the baby's mother had lost so much blood in the shooting.

▶ In June 1929, Dr. James H. Snook, a gold medalist for the 1920 U.S. Olympic military revolver team, was arrested for first-degree murder in the killing of Theora Hix, his 25-year-old mistress. Snook confessed that he had used a hammer to beat Hix after violent sex. Snook died in the electric chair.

▶ Months before he was named MVP in Super Bowl XXXV for leading the Baltimore Ravens to a convincing win over the New York Giants, linebacker Ray Lewis was in court, defending himself on a murder charge for his part in a fatal stabbing after a post-Super Bowl party in Atlanta the previous year. During the trial, the murder charge was dropped; Lewis pleaded guilty to misdemeanor obstruction of justice and testified against two former companions. He was also fined $250,000 by the NFL.

▶ Jayson Williams, former All-Star power forward for the New Jersey Nets and charismatic TV commentator, was charged with reckless manslaughter in the fatal shooting of limo driver Costas Christofi at Williams' New Jersey mansion, and of then trying to tamper with evidence. He is set to go on trial in February, 2003.

Women Competing With, and Against, Men

▶ In 1988, Winning Colors became the third filly to win the Kentucky Derby. Genuine Risk won it in 1980, Regret in 1915.

▶ Jackie Mitchell struck out Babe Ruth and Lou Gehrig in an exhibition baseball game in 1931. Babe Didrickson toured briefly as the only female member of the House of David baseball team, and pitched an inning against the Philadelphia Athletics in an exhibition game.

▶ Driver Janet Guthrie was the first woman to qualify for and compete in the Indianapolis 500. In May of 1976, she competed in the qualifying round but failed to win a place in the actual race when she had to withdraw her car with mechanical problems. In 1977, she competed but had to quit after 27 laps because her car again failed. She finished the race in 1978, completing 190 laps and finishing ninth.

In 1992, Lyn St. James, the second woman to qualify for the race, started in 27th place and finished 11th. In 2000, for the first time, there were two women drivers in the race—St. James and 19-year-old Sarah Fisher.

▶ Jimmy Connors is the only great male tennis player coached by a woman—his mother, Gloria.

Billie Jean King was the first woman to coach a co-ed sports team, the Philadelphia Freedom of World Team Tennis, in 1974.

▶ The majority of the fastest English Channel swims have been accomplished by women.

▶ Lynnette Woodard became the first female member of the Harlem Globetrotters, in October 1985. Nancy Lieberman competed for the Springfield Fame of the United States Basketball League on June 10, 1986, the first woman in a men's pro league.

▶ Edna Jameson, director of the Cleveland Indians ticket office in 1948, became the first woman to receive a World Series share.

▶ In 1954, Marguerite Norris, president of the NHL Detroit Red Wings, was presented with the Stanley Cup. She became the first woman to have her name engraved on the Cup. Sonie Scurfield, co-owner of the Calgary Flames, became the second, in 1989.

▶ Before the 1993 season, Sherry Davis beat out more than 500 entrants in an open-mike tryout at Candlestick Park and was hired by the San Francisco Giants as the first full-time female public-address announcer in major-league history. Davis, a legal secretary, held the job for seven seasons before she was fired by the Giants after the 1999 season and replaced by another woman, Renel Brooks-Moon.

▶ Georgia Frontiere of the St. Louis Rams and Denise DeBartolo York of the San Francisco 49ers are the NFL's only female owners.

▶ Women compete head-to-head with men in all equestrian competitions and classes. In 1972, Lisolett Linsenhoff of West Germany became the first female individual equestrian gold medalist. Women and men also began to compete with each other in Olympic shooting competitions in 1968, though some of the events are segregated by sex. In 1976, American Margaret Murdock won a silver medal in the small-bore rifle, three positions competition, becoming the first woman to win an Olympic shooting medal.

▶ LPGA pro Cathy Sherk, winner of the women's U.S., Canadian, and world amateur championships, qualified in the summer of 1989 for the men's $100,000 Times-BIC Ontario Open. The only women to have appeared in a PGA-sanctioned event before that were Kathy Whitworth and Mickey Wright, who teamed to play in the 1985 Legends Classics on the PGA Seniors Tour.

▶ Eleanor Engel signed to play minor-league baseball with the Harrisburg (Pennsylvania) Senators of the Inter-State League in June

1952. National Association president George Trautman, backed by major-league commissioner Ford Frick, voided the signing. Engle appeared in uniform but never played.

▶ Dee Kantner and Violet Palmer became NBA referees in 1997, the first time in major U.S. pro sports that women officiated regular-season games in an all-male league. (Kantner was fired in the summer of 2002, as was a male ref; the NBA's VP of basketball operations claimed that the dismissal was for performance reasons.)

▶ Diana Crump was the first female jockey to ride against males, at Hialeah on February 7, 1969, and later became the first woman jockey to ride in the Kentucky Derby. Barbara Jo Rubin was the first woman jockey in the United States to win a parimutuel race, on February 22, 1969, at the Charles Town (West Virginia) racetrack.

▶ Julie Krone is considered the greatest woman jockey in history. She is the first ever to win five races in one day at a New York track, first to win a riding title at a major track, first to ride in the Breeder's Cup (finishing fourth in 1988), and the first to win a Triple Crown race (the 1993 Belmont, aboard Colonial Affair). When she retired in 1999, she had ridden to to more than 3,500 victories in her 18-year career, for over $80 million in purses.

▶ Amanda Clement was the first woman umpire in organized baseball. Starting in 1903, she umped six years in the Dakotas, Nebraska, Iowa, and Minnesota.

▶ Eva Shain became the first woman judge for a heavyweight title fight on September 29, 1977, for a bout between Muhammad Ali and Earnie Shavers.

▶ From 1985–88, Carol White coached the Georgia Tech football team's placekickers.

▶ Libby Riddles won the Iditarod dogsled race in 1984. Susan Butcher won it in 1986, 1987, 1988, and in 1990, when she set a then-course record.

The Most Notable Suicides in Sports

▶ Shingo Furuya, managing director of Japan's Hanshin Tigers, jumped from his eighth-floor hotel window and killed himself because he was despondent over negotiations with one of the team's star players—American Randy Bass—and because Hanshin was in sixth place in a six-team league. After learning of Furuya's suicide, Hanshin decided to go ahead with its game against the Yomiuri Giants, and interim manager Minoru Murayama announced that in memory of Furuya, Hanshin wanted to win at any cost. Hanshin lost, 1-0.

▶ Catcher Willard Hershberger is the only major-league player since the start of the 20th century to commit suicide during the season. In 1940, he was Ernie Lombardi's backup on the Cincinnati Reds, who would go on to win the pennant that year. On August 3, the day after Hershberger, 29, played poorly in the second game of a doubleheader in Boston—he went hitless in five at-bats—he cut his throat over the bathtub in his hotel room.

▶ Peter Gregg, the all-time leading winner of the International Motor Sports Association GT Championship, committed suicide in December 1980, at age 40. Earlier that year, on June 10, while Gregg was trying to qualify for the 24 hours of Le Mans, he suffered a concussion and double vision, and was forced to miss half of the 14 IMSA GT events on the 1980 schedule. A friend of Gregg's said that the driver had been despondent over not being able to race.

▶ Colonel M. Lewis Clark, the man who founded the Kentucky Derby and built Churchill Downs, committed suicide on April 22, 1899. He shot himself in the head with a pistol, primarily because of his failing health.

▶ Larry Bethea, Dallas Cowboys defensive lineman, killed himself in 1987 after suffering drug and financial problems. The suicide occurred hours after Bethea was named as a suspect in two armed robberies.

▶ In 1971, Bruce Gardner, a former pitching phenom for the powerhouse University of Southern California baseball team, killed himself on the mound at USC.

▶ In the summer of 1989, after a solid rookie season in which he'd averaged 11 points and 3 rebounds a game, 24-year-old guard Ricky Berry of the Sacramento Kings was found dead of apparent suicide in his Fair Oaks, California, home by shotgun.

▶ National League President Harry Pulliam shot himself during the 1909 season. During the previous season, he had let stand umpire Hank O'Day's ruling on Fred Merkle's notorious boner (which helped cost the New York Giants the pennant), a decision for which Pulliam was much abused.

▶ Takeichi Nishi, 1932 Olympic gold medal winner for equestrian jumping, died in a mass Japanese suicide in World War II.

▶ Jake Powell, one of the outfielders with whom the New York Yankees tried to replace Babe Ruth in the 1930s, shot himself in the head at a Washington, D.C., police station in November of 1948 after being picked up for writing bad checks. Powell had been suspended from baseball for 10 days in 1938 when he said in a radio interview that he was a "cop" who liked "beating up niggers and then throwing them in jail."

▶ Kokichi Tsuburaya, who became a national hero in Japan after finishing third in the 1964 Olympic marathon in Tokyo, was ordered to begin training immediately for the 1968 Olympics. In 1967, he suffered two injuries and spent three months in the hospital. When he started running again, he realized that he would never approach his prior form. On January 9, 1968, Tsuburaya killed himself by using a razor blade to cut his right carotid artery. He left a note that said simply, "Cannot run anymore."

▶ Richard Johnson, basketball star for Long Beach State, shot himself with a .38-caliber revolver in June 1978, shortly after being passed up in the NBA draft. In his suicide note he admitted to a drug problem.

▶ Win Mercer, a turn-of-the-century pitcher and infielder, died in a San Francisco hotel room in 1903. According to a newspaper account, "Mercer... had attached a hose to a gas jet, gone to bed with the end of the hose in his mouth and the bed clothing pulled over his head." Mercer had been hired to manage the American League Detroit team the following year. He had become depressed when treatment failed to cure a pulmonary ailment.

▶ Of the 70 known major leaguers who have committed suicide, none was a left-handed pitcher.

10 Individual Sports Figures Killed in Air Crashes

▶ March 31, 1931: Notre Dame football coach Knute Rockne, age 43, in Kansas.

▶ October 27, 1949: Marcel Cerdan, age 33, former world middleweight champion, en route to fight Jake LaMotta for the title.

▶ February 13, 1964: Ken Hubbs, Chicago Cubs second baseman, in a crash in Utah. He had been named the National League Rookie of the Year in 1962.

▶ July 24, 1966: Golfer Tony Lema, shortly after winning the British Open. He was 32.

▶ August 31, 1969: Rocky Marciano, who retired as unbeaten heavyweight champion, in a private plane near Des Moines. He was 46.

▶ December 31, 1972: Roberto Clemente, future baseball Hall of Famer, en route to Managua, Nicaragua, to aid earthquake victims.

▶ March 3, 1974: John Cooper, 1964 silver medalist in the 400m hurdles, age 33. He was one of 346 people killed in a Turkish Airlines crash over France.

▶ June 24, 1975: New York Nets forward Wendell Ladner, age 26. The identity of his burned body was partially confirmed by the 1974 ABA championship ring on his finger.

▶ August 2, 1979: Thurman Munson, New York Yankees catcher, in Canton, Ohio. He was 32.

▶ October 25, 1999: Payne Stewart, golfer and recent winner of the U.S. Open, in South Dakota, along with five others, in a Learjet that lost cabin pressure. He was 42.

10 Teams Killed in Air Crashes

▶ May 4, 1949: Torino, the Italian soccer champion, returning home after a game in Lisbon. The plane crashed into the Superga Basilica near Turin. The entire team, including reserves, coaches, and trainers, was killed.

▶ February 6, 1958: English soccer champion Manchester United, returning home from a European Cup match in Belgrade. The plane crashed at Munich airport, killing eight players, the manager, trainer, a secretary, and eight journalists.

▶ October 29, 1960: The Cal Poly-San Luis Obispo football team, near Toledo, Ohio. Sixteen team members were killed

▶ February 15, 1961: The U.S. figure skating team, near Berg, Belgium. Eighteen team members were killed.

▶ April 3, 1961: Green Cross, a first-division Chilean soccer team, returning to Santiago from a game in Osorno. The plane crashed into the side of Las Lastimas Mountains, killing all passengers.

▶ September 26, 1969: The Bolivian soccer team, called "The Strongest," returning home to La Paz from an out-of-town game. The plane crashed in the Andes. The entire team of 19 players and all club officials died.

▶ November 14, 1970: The Marshall University football team, when their chartered plane crashed in Kenova, West Virginia. Forty-three players and coaches died.

▶ December 13, 1977: The University of Evansville (Indiana) basketball team, soon after taking off in dense fog. Twelve team members and head coach Bobby Watson perished.

▶ March 14, 1980: The U.S. amateur boxing team, near Warsaw. Twenty-two team members were killed.

▶ January 27, 2001: Eight people associated with the Oklahoma State University men's basketball team—two players, and six broadcasters and staffers—along with the two pilots died when their plane crashed in a snowstorm east of Denver, while returning from a game in Colorado.

Homosexuality in Sports

It's hard to tell how extensive a role homosexuality plays in professional athletics because to this day discussion of its presence, especially in men's sports, remains taboo. A man who succeeds on the field is viewed as having greater sexual—heterosexual—powers and confidence. Statements to the contrary are unwelcome among the jock fraternity.

▶ Dave Kopay, NFL running back from 1964–72 for the San Francisco 49ers, Detroit Lions, Washington Redskins, New Orleans Saints, and Green Bay Packers, was the first American professional athlete to admit his homosexuality openly. He discussed it in his book, *The David Kopay Story.*

▶ Jerry Smith, tight end for the Washington Redskins from 1965–77, talked anonymously about his homosexuality in a *Washington Star* article in the early 1970s, and had a brief affair with Dave Kopay when they were teammates. Smith died of an AIDS-related disease on October 15, 1986, possibly the first professional athlete in America to do so.

▶ Glenn Burke, a .237 lifetime hitter for the Los Angeles Dodgers and Oakland Athletics from 1976-79, is one of only two major leaguers known to admit publicly to his homosexuality.

▶ Billy Bean, an outfielder who played parts of six major-league seasons for the Detroit Tigers, Los Angeles Dodgers, and San Diego Padres from 1987–95, became the first baseball player to extensively discuss his homosexuality, in 1999. Bean (not to be confused with a contemporary of his, outfielder and eventual Oakland Athletics general manager Billy Beane) came out in an interview with the *Miami Herald*. He said he quit baseball in 1996 after meeting his partner, Miami restaurateur Efrain Veiga, while in town to play the Florida Marlins.

▶ Baron von Cramm, the great and gentlemanly German tennis player who opposed the Nazi regime, was summoned home from Davis Cup play in 1937 and imprisoned by the Gestapo for alleged homosexual offenses.

▶ Martina Navratilova, one of the greatest tennis players of all time, was the first woman tennis player to voluntarily go public about being gay, in 1981. (That same year, tennis great Billie Jean King was outed when ex-lover Marilyn Barnett sued King for "galimony.") It's impossible to know how much fan support and endorsement money was withheld Navratilova because of her candor. A noted advocate of animal rights and the environment, she became outspoken for gay rights when controversial Amendment 2, which sought to make the rights of gays "special rights," was passed in her home state of Colorado. (The amendment was eventually ruled unconstitutional by the U.S. Supreme Court.) "I came to live in a country I love; some people label me a 'defector,'" Navratilova once said. "I have loved men and women in my life; I've been labeled 'the bisexual defector.' Want to know another secret? I'm even ambidextrous. I don't like labels. Just call me Martina."

Like King, Navratilova was involved in a high-profile palimony case, in which a former lover sought post-breakup compensation.

▶ Amelie Mauresmo, a top French tennis player, is only the second woman on the tennis tour (after Navratilova) to talk openly about being a lesbian. Before the 1999 Australian Open final, in which Mauresmo was to meet Martina Hingis, Hingis was asked to compare Mauresmo then to when they'd played each other in the Federation Cup a year earlier. "She's here with her girlfriend. She's half a man," Hingis reportedly said, to much criticism later. Mauresmo's relaxed way in public with her girlfriend, Sylvie Bourdon, prompted former player and tennis commentator Pam Shriver to say, "Martina Navratilova and Billie Jean King would probably have liked to have been so open. Times have moved on since Martina, and it's a pretty liberal world right now, although there are still some conservative people around."

▶ Greg Louganis, the greatest diver of his generation and four-time Olympic gold medalist, announced in February of 1995 that he had AIDS and that he had been HIV-positive when he competed in the 1988 Seoul Games. In his post-athletic life, he has, among other things, acted, written a memoir (*Breaking the Surface*), and lectured about living with the secrets of being gay and HIV-positive. On one frightening dive at the Seoul Games, on his way to his second pair of golds, Louganis hit his head on the board, opening a bad cut; later, he would be much criticized for not having revealed his HIV status while competing.

▶ American tennis great Bill Tilden, a homosexual, was jailed twice on indecency charges.

▶ Dave Pallone, the former National League umpire (1979–88)—best remembered for being bumped in an argument by Cincinnati Reds manager Pete Rose, which led to a controversial month-long suspension for Rose—felt that he was fired because he was gay. He said, "leading a double life for a decade was not easy. Obviously, I could never be myself. I'd be introduced in a gay bar, for instance, and the inevitable question was, 'What do you do for a living?' For years, I would lie."

▶ After Pam Parsons resigned in 1981 as women's basketball coach at the University of South Carolina for what she said were personal reasons, a local newspaper reported that Parsons had been driven from her job by an allegation by the mother of one of the players that Parsons had had a lesbian relationship with a player and had made sexual advances toward another. *Sports Illustrated* printed similar accusations. Parsons sued *SI* for libel and lost. Federal charges were in turn filed against her and Tina Buck, one of Parsons' former players, for lying at the trial when they said that they had not patronized a lesbian bar in Salt Lake City. Parsons and Buck both pleaded guilty.

24 of the Strangest Ailments, Freakiest Injuries, and Weirdest Deaths

▶ St. Louis Cardinal Vince Coleman was knocked out of the remainder of postseason play in 1985 when the tarpaulin-spreading device at Busch Stadium ran over his left leg during a workout before Game 4 of the National League playoffs.

▶ Eddie Machen, once a top heavyweight contender, fell to his death while sleepwalking in his San Francisco apartment.

▶ James Mitchel, a top American competitor in the now-defunct stone throw competition, was forced out of his event in the 1906 Interim

Olympics in Athens because he had dislocated his shoulder when the ship he took to Europe hit a wave.

▶ On January 1, 1977, former major-league pitcher Danny Frisella was killed near Phoenix in a dune-buggy accident.

▶ Orlando Brown, offensive tackle for the Cleveland Browns, lost much vision in one eye, and consequently his football career when, during a game in 1999, referee Jeff Triplette tossed his BBs-weighted penalty flag in Brown's direction and, freakishly, the flag got behind the facemask, hitting Brown in the eye. Brown staggered to the sideline, came back on to the field to shove the ref to the ground, and was suspended indefinitely by the NFL for the push. The league lifted the suspension after the season; Brown's vision was blurred enough that he was unable to play again, and at the start of the 2000 season, Cleveland released him.

▶ Six weeks before the 1956 Olympics, Czech Emil Zatopek suffered a hernia while training with his wife on his shoulders. He still finished sixth in the marathon.

▶ Spectacular Bid lost the 1979 Belmont—and the Triple Crown—because he stepped on a safety pin that he had picked off of his leg bandage. It penetrated his front left hoof.

▶ Michelle Akers, forward for the 1999 U.S. World Cup soccer champions and the national team's all-time leading scorer, suffers from Chronic Fatigue Syndrome (CFS).

▶ Lyle Kurtenbach, a 41-year-old spectator, was killed by a flying tire at the 1987 Indianapolis 500.

▶ Detroit Tigers second baseman Lou Whitaker hurt his knee while dancing at a wedding.

▶ After missing the cut at the 1998 British Open, Australian golfer Stuart Appleby was in London with his wife Renay when she was crushed to death by a car while unloading luggage at a train station.

▶ Christine Truman was out of tennis for most of 1962 after she put her foot through a rotten floorboard on a tennis court in Jamaica.

▶ In 1983, Jack Newton, a 33-year-old Australian golfer, lost his right arm when he accidentally walked into the spinning propeller of a small airplane.

▶ Before a game with the Detroit Tigers on April 12, 1978, Texas Rangers relief pitcher Rogelio Moret stood trance-like for at least 45 minutes in the locker room, holding a shower shoe in his extended hand. After he was given five sedative injections, he was taken to a local neuropsychiatric hospital. The team physician called it "a definite catatonic state."

▶ San Francisco Giant Dave Dravecky broke his arm while delivering a pitch in a 1989 game. His arm had already been weakened by surgery to remove a malignant tumor, and would lated be amputated.

▶ In July 1883, Matthew Webb, the first person to swim the English Channel, died attempting to swim the violent Whirlpool Rapids below Niagara Falls.

▶ New York Mets pitcher Bob Ojeda was lost for the 1988 National League playoffs when he almost sliced off his left middle finger while gardening with an electric hedge clipper.

▶ On July 17, 1914, New York Giants outfielder Red Murray was struck by lightning while running the bases. He was not seriously injured.

▶ A bird dropping hit Boyd Gittins in the eye and dislodged his contact lens before he reached the first hurdle at the 1968 Olympic semi trials, forcing him to pull out of the race. (He later won a runoff to qualify for the trials, where he earned a spot on the Olympic team.)

▶ A year after his best season, Pittsburgh Pirates pitcher Steve Blass inexplicably lost his control. In 1972, when he was 19-8, he walked 84 batters in 249⅔ innings. In 1973, he walked 84 in 88⅔ innings. By 1974, Blass was out of baseball.

Chuck Knoblauch was a Gold Glove second baseman for the Minnesota Twins in 1997, and with the Yankees he helped save perfect games by David Cone and David Wells with great fielding plays—and clean throws—at second base. But midway through the 1998 season, Knoblauch began having problems making routine throws to first from second base, and despite seeing a sports psychologist and spending countless hours fielding grounders and working on throws, he never could shake it. His error total increased from 13 in 1998, his first year with the Yankees, to 26 in 1999, and 15 in just 82 games at second base in 2000. In June of 2000, after making three throwing errors in a game at Yankee Stadium, Knoblauch asked manager Joe Torre to pull him. In the postseason, Torre replaced Knoblauch at second base with Luis Sojo and Jose Vizcaino. The following spring, Knoblauch was shifted to left field, where he has played since.

One of the players Knoblauch consulted was Steve Sax, a former second baseman who had a strangely similar throwing problem in 1983 with the Los Angeles Dodgers. In an April game against the Expos, Sax threw wildly home on a relay play, and from that point on he struggled to make the throw to first base. Sax had 24 errors by the All-Star break. Fans began to display taunting signs, and in Philadelphia, Phillies players pretended to dive in the dugout when he threw to first. A newspaper headline read, "Sax's Throws Are Second to No One." But Sax eventually conquered his problem, going on to play another 10 seasons and, in one year, to lead the American League in fielding.

Rick Ankiel was considered one of the top young pitching prospects in baseball in 2000, and his rookie season with the St. Louis Cardinals only enhanced his reputation. Ankiel, 20 years old when the season started, went 11-7 with a 3.50 ERA, striking out 194 in 175 innings and walking 90. But in the playoffs that year, the lefthander developed the worst case of wildness since Steve Blass. Earning the start in the opening game of the division series against the Atlanta Braves, Ankiel became the first major-league pitcher in 110 years to throw five wild pitches in an inning. He drew another start in the National League Championship Series against the New York Mets and lasted just two-thirds of an inning. Five of his first 20 pitches went to the backstop. Ankiel's woes continued the following season, and though he began the year in the Cardinals' rotation, he had a 7.13 ERA in six starts, with 25 walks in 24 innings, before the Cardinals sent him to the minors. Ankiel ended the year pitching in Class A Johnson City, the lowest rung of the minor leagues, where he finally found his control (18 walks and 158 strikeouts in 87⅔ innings). But in spring training of 2002, Ankiel hurt his elbow after pitching just two innings against major-league competition, and missed the entire season.

▶ At the 1984 Los Angeles Olympics, several American cyclists, including Steve Hegg, gold medalist in the 4,000m individual pursuit, "blood boosted"—a technique in which some of one's blood is extracted, frozen, and then re-injected just before competition to increase hemoglobin level and endurance. However, some cyclists did not have time to freeze their own blood and instead injected themselves with other people's blood. Two of the racers became ill.

Sexism in Sports

▶ The International Olympic Committee refused to add the women's 3,000m run for the 1980 Moscow Olympics because the distance was "deemed a little too strenuous for women." In the 1928 Olympic 800-yard run, several women collapsed, inciting IOC president Compte de Baillet-Latour to try and rid the Games of all women's track competition. Women's running events of longer than 200 meters were eliminated until 1960, when the 800m was reinstated. In 1972, the 1,500m was added; in 1984, the 3,000m and marathon; in 1988, the 10,000m.

▶ In August 1890, W. S. Franklin announced the formation of a women's professional baseball league. He required that players be under 21 years old, good-looking, and have a good figure.

▶ In the 1920 Olympics, American figure skater Theresa Weld was cautioned by the judges for making jumps considered unsuitable for a lady. Previously, it had been considered "unfeminine behavior" to jump altogether.

▶ Women were not allowed on center court for the Italian championship tennis finals until the late 1960s.

▶ In early bobsled races, two of the five riders had to be women, but could not drive or work the brakes.

▶ In 1936, Avery Brundage, while president of the U.S. Olympic Committee, said, "I am fed up to the ears with women as track and field competitors... her charms sink to something less than zero. As swimmers and divers, girls are [as] beautiful and adroit as they are ineffective and unpleasing on the track." In 1952, Brundage became president of the International Olympic Committee.

▶ Before 1916, women were not allowed to attend boxing matches.

▶ The Women's AAA in Britain did not allow women to compete in long-distance road races until 1975.

▶ The 1900 Paris Olympic field was made up of 1,308 men competitors and 11 women.

▶ In 776 B.C., ancient Greeks banned women as competitors and spectators from the Olympic Games. Any married woman caught near the stadium was hurled from a cliff.

In Cars

Race car drivers know that what they do is dangerous. We, too, know that cars and drivers can be dangerous.

▶ Sadly, car accidents that have claimed the lives of athletes are not uncommon enough. Some who have lost their lives in this manner:

▷ Kansas City Chiefs All-Pro linebacker Derrick Thomas, while driving on an icy road on the way to the airport (neither he nor a second passenger who died was wearing a seatbelt; a third man, wearing a seatbelt, sustained only minor injuries);

▷ Eight members of the University of Wyoming men's cross-country team, on September 16, 2001, when the station wagon in which they were driving was hit, head-on at almost 75 miles per hour, by a pickup truck driven by another Wyoming student, a member of the school's rodeo team who was legally drunk (and who survived);

▷ Malik Sealy, Minnesota Timberwolves guard, whose car was crashed into by a drunk driver;

▷ Drazen Petrovic, a top Croatian national player who became a 20+-point-a-game scorer for the New Jersey Nets, while driving in Germany (he was posthumously inducted into the Basketball Hall of Fame, in 2002);

▷ and a member of the Kenyon (Ohio) College swimming team (eight teammates were injured; the woman who died was not wearing a seatbelt), in January of 2000.

▶ In an act of supreme and tragic stupidity, Charlotte Hornet teammates Bobby Phills and David Wesley drag-raced their cars after a January, 2000, practice. As their speeds exceeded 75mph in a 45mph zone, Phills's 1997 Porsche 993 Cabriolet skidded into oncoming traffic, and collided head-on with another car, killing Phills instantly. Two others were injured.

▶ On May 21, 1992, the California Angels team bus crashed en route from Yankee Stadium to Baltimore, about 20 miles from Philadelphia, on the New Jersey Turnpike. Manager Buck Rodgers seriously injured his elbow, rib, and knee, putting him out for several months; player Alvin Davis bruised his kidney; and ten others were also injured.

▶ At the 2002 Salt Lake City Olympics, American Jim Shea, Jr., won the gold medal in the skeleton competition, but the victory was bittersweet: Just a month before, Shea's grandfather, Jack—a two-time speed-skating gold medalist at the 1932 Lake Placid Games and America's oldest living Olympian—was killed when hit by a drunk driver. The younger Shea had hoped that the occasion of the Salt Lake City Games would serve as a reason for two celebrations: first, his being a third-generation Olympian (his father, Jim, Sr., had competed in cross-country skiing at the 1964 Games); and second, the return to the Olympics of an event, the skeleton, that had previously only been contested in the Olympics in 1928 and 1948, both times in St. Moritz, Switzerland, in which competitors ride a heavy sled headfirst and steer by shifting their weight and dragging their feet.

Instead, Jim, Jr., won the race with a heavy heart. For inspiration, he wore his grandfather's funeral card inside his helmet.

▶ During spring training in 2002, San Francisco Giants star second baseman Jeff Kent informed team officials that he had fractured his wrist when he slipped while he was washing his truck. But several eyewitnesses reported that Kent had actually suffered the injury when he fell off his motorcycle while driving recklessly on a road near the Giants' minor-league training facility. Riding a motorcycle is prohibited in Kent's contract, so the Giants could have tried to void his $6 million contract or fined him. They chose not to dock his pay.

▶ American diver Bruce Kimball was known as "The Comeback Kid" because he almost died as a result of a 1981 automobile accident with a drunk driver, but he recovered to win the 1984 Olympic silver medal in platform diving. In 1988, Kimball killed two teenagers in Florida while driving drunk. He was sentenced to 17 years in prison.

13 Athletes Who Died from War

War is a fact of life. In a move that inspired many Americans, especially so soon after the September 11th terrorist attacks, Arizona Cardinals safety Pat Tillman displayed rare selflessness when he decided, in the spring of 2002, to give up his football career to enlist in the Army. He wanted to join the elite Rangers (of the U.S. Army, that is; not the Texas baseball team or the New York hockey team), along with his brother Kevin, a minor-league infielder for the Cleveland Indians. For Tillman, 25, the matter was made more urgent by military age restrictions on entry in special forces units, but his allegiance to country is unquestionable—especially when you consider that he announced his decision to his coach and owner two days after returning from his honeymoon.

The following athletes, unfortunately, knew too much of war.

▶ Germany's Alfred Flatow, Olympic gold medalist in the parallel bars in 1896, was exterminated in a German concentration camp in 1945.

▶ A year after winning the 400m at the 1920 Olympics, Great Britain's Eric Liddell (of *Chariots of Fire* fame) joined his father in China to do missionary work. He died of a brain tumor in a Japanese internment camp in China during World War II.

▶ Freddie Tait, the British Amateur golf champion in 1896 and 1898, died in the Boer War.

▶ German Luz Long, 1936 Olympic silver medalist and great friend to American track star Jesse Owens, was killed in the Battle of St. Pietro, July 14, 1943.

▶ Ron Zinn, sixth in the Olympic 20,000m walk in 1964, was killed in Vietnam less than nine months later, at age 26.

▶ Laurie Doherty, Wimbledon champion from 1902–06, died serving for the Air Ministry during World War I.

▶ Norwegian-born American ski jumper Torger Tokle, who broke 24 records in his career, was killed while fighting with the U.S. Army in Italy in 1945.

▶ Endre Kabos, Hungarian Olympic gold medalist in the saber in 1936, was killed when the Budapest Margaret Bridge blew up in World War II.

▶ Hall of Fame pitcher Christy Mathewson died of tuberculosis in 1925, presumably from poison gassing that he had suffered in France in World War I.

▶ Jean Bouin of France and George Hutson of Great Britain, the silver and bronze medalists, respectively, in the 1912 Olympic 5,000m race, were both killed in action in 1914.

▶ Anthony Wilding, four-time Wimbledon winner (1910–13) from New Zealand, was killed in action at Neuve Chapelle, France, in 1915, at age 31.

▶ Attila Petschauer, Hungarian gold medalist in the Olympic team saber competitions in 1928 and 1932, was tortured to death in 1943 while fighting in Ukraine.

9

OFF THE FIELD, AND EXTRACURRICULAR ACTIVITY

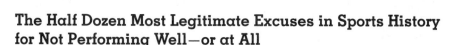

The Half Dozen Most Legitimate Excuses in Sports History for Not Performing Well—or at All

▶ Susan Butcher, four-time winner of the Iditarod dogsled race, did not finish in 1985. She and her dog team were trampled by moose.

▶ Gladiators were being prepared to fight in 79 A.D., in Pompeii, but never participated. Mt. Vesuvius erupted and lava buried the city and everyone in it. Four gladiators were found shackled in chains in one room; in another room were 17 more who had tried to take refuge from the volcano.

▶ The Wichita State University football team went 0-9 in 1960. Soon after the season started, a plane crash killed 14 players, the coach, and the athletic director. The team was reinforced with freshmen for the remainder of the season.

▶ The NHL's New York Americans suspended operations in 1942 and eventually disbanded in 1945 because they had lost most of their players to World War II.

▶ Pelle Lindbergh, Philadelphia Flyer goalie, was voted to the NHL All-Star team in 1986 but did not play because he was killed in an auto accident in November 1985. He became the first dead man voted to an all-star team.

▶ New York Yankees first baseman Lou Gehrig hit just .143 in limited action in 1939. At the time, he was suffering from amyotrophic lateral sclerosis, the disease that would soon kill him (and later bear his name).

The Half Dozen Worst Excuses in Sports History for Not Performing Well—or at All

▶ Outfielder Claudell Washington, after being traded in 1978 from the Texas Rangers to the Chicago White Sox, failed to report for four days. "I overslept," he explained.

▶ Ted Tinling designed a special dress for Betty Hilton, a top British player, in 1948. She wore the dress and lost badly to American Louise Brough in a Wightman Cup match. Hilton's defeat was blamed on her self-consciousness over the color of her dress.

▶ In the 1987 U.S. Open, John McEnroe blamed his boorish on-court behavior on temporary insanity, brought about by the tension of his wife expecting their second child.

▶ The same excuse was used after a Japanese baseball game in September 1982 between the Taiyo Whales and the Hanshin Tigers in Yokohama, in which two Tiger coaches brutally beat up an umpire on national television. The coaches pleaded temporary insanity and were suspended for the rest of the season.

▶ Fullerton State football coach Gene Murphy said that one of his players claimed that he was late because he had "pulled his wrist while running."

▶ After he missed a basketball practice, New York Net Sly Williams called the team's office and attempted to pass himself off as his brother. "Sly has some personal problems," Williams said. "There's been a slight death in the family."

The Worst Excuse for Not Allowing Someone to Perform

▶ John Kelly (father of Princess Grace of Monaco), who would go on to win three Olympic rowing gold medals, was refused entry to the 1920 Diamond Sculls at Henley, England, because it was said that, as a bricklayer, he had had an unfair advantage in developing bigger muscles than his gentlemen competitors.

No Excuse, Period

▶ On July 21, 1970, San Diego Padres manager Preston Gomez removed pitcher Clay Kirby in the ninth inning of a game against the New York Mets, even though Kirby was pitching a no-hitter. The relief pitcher not only lost the no-hitter but the game, as well.

Los Angeles Dodgers in 1960s TV Sit-Coms

One reason so many professional athletes include southern California on their wish list of trade or free-agent or draft destinations is the weather. Another is the generally comfortable lifestyle. Another, the beach. The main reason, of course, is that with Hollywood nearby, you greatly increase your chance of making a cameo appearance in a movie or TV show.

Immortality may be achieved in many ways. For Dodger righthander Don Drysdale, that may mean pitching a record 58 consecutive scoreless innings, as he did in 1968. With television syndication, however—not to mention the fact that another Dodger, Orel Hershiser, would eventually break Drysdale's seemingly untouchable record—it's more likely that Drysdale will achieve immortality because of his guest appearance the following year on *The Flying Nun*.

▶ Jim Lefebvre, infielder, on *Batman*, 1966, ABC. "Batman's Anniversary: A Riddling Controversy": A two-episode show to celebrate Batman's anniversary with the Gotham Police Department. The Riddler wants to legalize crime; Lefebvre plays a henchman.

▶ Sandy Koufax, pitcher, on *Dennis the Menace*, 1962, CBS. "Dennis and the Dodger": Mr. Quigley offers to coach the boys' baseball team to keep the kids and their families as customers.

▶ Lefebvre and Al Ferrara, outfielder, on *Gilligan's Island*, 1966, CBS. "High Man on the Totem Pole": Gilligan, the "headhunter," finds a head on a totem pole with a striking resemblance to himself. Lefebvre and Ferrara play savages.

▶ Maury Wills, shortstop, on *Get Smart*, 1969, NBC. "The Apes of Rath": K.A.O.S. transforms an ape into a human being so that he can act as their agent, but when a bell rings, he reverts back to ape form and wreaks havoc.

▶ Larry Sherry and Stan Williams, pitchers, on *The Tom Ewell Show*, 1961, CBS. "Out of Left Field": A real estate deal grows out of an accidental meeting between Tom and the two Dodgers.

▶ Vin Scully, announcer, on *Karen*, 1964, NBC. "Beethoven or Baseball": Confusion reigns when Karen makes three dates for Saturday night.

▶ Scully and Don Drysdale, pitcher, on *The Joey Bishop Show*, 1964, CBS. "Joey and the Dodgers": Joey is stranded without guests when the Dodger game goes into extra innings.

▶ Willie Davis, outfielder, and Drysdale on *The Flying Nun*, 1969, ABC. "The Big Game": Sister Bertrille (Sally Field) enjoys a moral victory in spite of her baseball team's loss by a score of 43-1.

▶ Drysdale on *Leave It To Beaver*, 1962, ABC. "The Long Distance Call": Beaver and his friends make a long distance call to Drysdale.

▶ Drysdale on *Our Man Higgins*, 1963, ABC. "Who's on First?": Higgins invites Drysdale to make an appearance at the Little League season opener.

▶ Drysdale on *The Donna Reed Show*, 1962, ABC. "The Man in the Mask": Jeff is chosen to umpire a girl's baseball game and gets tips from Drysdale.

▶ Drysdale on *The Donna Reed Show* again in 1962. "All Those Dreams": Jeff and his family take a trip to Chicago and he decides to interview Drysdale.

Anna Kournikova, Athlete *Non-Pareil*

▶ She has won exactly zero professional singles titles.

▶ After Kournikova lost in the first round of Wimbledon in 2002—and looked out-of-playing-shape doing so—tennis great Chris Evert wondered aloud if Kournikova might benefit by playing lower-tier tournaments to rediscover her tennis form. When, during a BBC interview following the loss, Evert's suggestion was relayed to Kournikova, she stood up, flustered, and demanded that the interview be re-started.

▶ In 2002, the Hoboken, New Jersey-based pop/rock band Binge released the CD *Anna Kournikova*, featuring the single "Anna Kournikova," a musical rumination about wanting to be Anna's ball boy. (The band, obviously expecting the song to be a hit, included on the album four different versions of it—rock, acoustic, Euro dance, and Sports Instrumental.)

▶ For 2000 and 2001, she was the most "searched" athlete on the search engine Lycos. For the week ending September 28, 2002, she was the 26th overall term on Lycos (down from #12 the week before), just ahead of "The Simpsons" and just behind "Avril Lavigne." It was Kournikova's 51st week in their Top 50.

She has also had a computer virus named after her.

▶ As of the fall of 2002, she had won 16 doubles tournaments, including two majors (the Australian Open, both with Martina Hingis). In 1999, she achieved the rank of #1 doubles player in the world.

▶ She earns an estimated $10–15 million yearly pitching tennis shoes and racquets, sports bras, and other merchandise. Adidas, one of her many endorsees, has dubbed her one of their eight "brand symbols"— which means (in their minds) endorsers whose products sell beyond the sport category in which they play. (Other brand symbols include Kobe Bryant, Martina Hingis, and Sergio Garcia.)

▶ Citing Kournikova's made-in-heaven agreeability to push product, Alex Briggs, spokesperson for Adidas's tennis division, said, "When she sits down after a match and has a jacket on, she makes sure that there is nothing covering her sponsor logos." Adidas even got a surprise bonus: In a new workout video, Kournikova wore Adidas gear, which she was not contractually bound to do.

▶ Apparently believing that referring to her appearance just once was insufficient, Kournikova once said, "I'm beautiful, famous, and gorgeous."

7 Things with Wings or Tails That Made an Impact

▶ A dog named Pickles found the World Cup soccer trophy that had been stolen in England in 1966 prior to the competition. Pickles found the cup wrapped in a newspaper, buried in a garden.

▶ Golfer Lloyd Mangrum's chances of winning the 1950 U.S. Open disappeared when he was penalized two strokes for lifting his ball to brush off a bug during an 18-hole playoff with Ben Hogan and George Fazio. Mangrum, who trailed Hogan by a stroke at the time of the incident on the 16th green, lost by four strokes.

▶ With the score tied 14-14 in the 1985 Orange Bowl, the University of Oklahoma was penalized 15 yards for unsportsmanlike conduct when its horse-drawn wagon, the "Sooner Schooner," rode onto the field to celebrate an apparent 22-yard field goal during the third quarter. In fact, the field goal had been nullified by an illegal-procedure call. The two penalties moved the ball back 20 yards, where a 42-yard field goal attempt was blocked. Oklahoma went on to lose 28-17 to the University of Washington, costing them a shot at the national title.

▶ Just before an Oakland Athletics-Kansas City Royals game in June 1986, As' slugger Dave Kingman, who neither liked, nor was liked by, the press, had a live rat delivered to the press box to sportswriter Susan Fornoff of *The Sacramento Bee*.

▶ At Toronto's Exhibition Stadium on August 4, 1983, New York Yankees outfielder Dave Winfield accidently killed a seagull with a between-innings throw toward the bullpen. Winfield was met by several plain-clothes policemen after the game and taken to a Toronto station house, where he was charged with cruelty to animals. He posted the $500 bond, and a day later the charges were dropped.

In a related story... in an exhibition game on March 25, 2001, against the San Francisco Giants, Arizona Diamondbacks ace Randy Johnson threw a pitch just as a dove with historically bad timing flew into the ball's path, halfway between mound and home plate. The bird was killed instantly, feathers scattered like confetti, and the video clip has become a perverse staple of sports highlight and blooper reels.

▶ A Sudanese soccer match between Betuan and Al Kubra in the early 1970s was interrupted in the 62nd minute by lions on the field.

A Dozen Golf Tournaments
Named for Show Business People

It is no longer the rage to name golf tournaments after celebrities, as it once was. Of the following tournaments, only the first two are still named for the given "star" (a moniker, Jamie Farr, that we use with great ambivalence).

▶ Bob Hope Chrysler Classic (PGA Tour)

▶ Jamie Farr Kroger Classic (LPGA Tour)

▶ Gatlin Brothers Southwest Classic (Seniors Tour)

▶ Nabisco Dinah Shore Tournament (LPGA)

▶ Ed McMahon Quad Cities Open (PGA)

▶ Andy Williams San Diego Open (PGA)

▶ Sammy Davis, Jr., Greater Hartford Open (PGA)

▶ Glen Campbell Los Angeles Open (PGA)

▶ Bing Crosby National Pro-Am (PGA)

▶ Jackie Gleason Inverarry Classic (PGA)

▶ Dean Martin Tucson Open (PGA)

▶ Danny Thomas Memphis Classic (PGA)

3 Very Stupid Questions...

▶ To Raiders quarterback Jim Plunkett, at the Super Bowl: "Jim, is it your father that's blind and your mother that's dead, or your mother that's blind and your father that's dead?"

▶ To New York Yankees pitcher Don Larsen, after his perfect game in the 1956 World Series: "Is it the best game you've ever pitched?"

▶ To Washington Redskin Doug Williams, at the Super Bowl: "How long have you been a black quarterback?"

...And 6 Very Snappy Answers

▶ Boxer Bruce Woodcock, after being knocked out by Tami Mauriello, was asked which punch bothered him the most: "The last one."

▶ Washington Redskins running back Duane Thomas, asked how it felt to play in the Super Bowl, the "ultimate" football game: "If it's the ultimate game, how come they're playing it again next year?"

▶ On the 18th hole, in the second round of the 1961 Los Angeles Open, Arnold Palmer's game fell apart. He was asked how he could have shot a 12: "I missed my putt for an 11."

▶ *New York Daily News* sportswriter Jenny Kellner was confronted in the New York Jets' locker room in 1981 by an unclothed Mark Gastineau, who asked her, "What do you think of this?"
"It looks like a penis, only smaller," she answered.

▶ Babe Ruth, when told that President Herbert Hoover earned less than the $80,000 that Ruth was demanding in 1930: "I had a better year than he did."

▶ Washington Redskins quarterback Sammy Baugh, when asked if the 73-0 rout that his team had just suffered in the 1940 NFL title game against the Chicago Bears would have turned out differently had Redskin Charlie Malone not dropped a wide-open pass in the end zone in the first quarter: "Yeah, it would have been 73-7."

The World's Most Famous Lineup

The comedy team of Bud Abbott and Lou Costello first performed their signature routine, "Who's on First?," on the *Kate Smith Show* on radio in the early 1940s, then later in the 1945 movie, *The Naughty Nineties*, and many times in between and after.

Here's the lineup from the routine, around the horn:

▶ Pitcher—Tomorrow

▶ Catcher—Today

▶ First Baseman—Who

▶ Second Baseman—What

▶ Third Baseman—I Don't Know

▶ Shortstop—I Don't Give a Darn (or sometimes "I Don't Care")

▶ Leftfielder—Why

▶ Centerfielder—Because

The name of the right fielder is not referred to in the routine.

The Most Memorable Trades in Sports

▶ In 1948, the Brooklyn Dodgers wanted Ernie Harwell, announcer for the Atlanta Crackers of the Southern Association, to be their broadcaster. Earl Mann, owner of the Crackers, needed a catcher. The Dodgers sent Cliff Dapper, who was catching for their Triple-A Montreal Royals team, to Atlanta for Harwell.

▶ In 1972, New York Yankee pitchers Mike Kekich and Fritz Peterson traded wives and families—or, viewed another way, Susanne Kekich and Marilyn Peterson traded husbands and families. Mrs. Kekich moved in with Fritz, but Marilyn Peterson eventually decided not to live with Mike.

▶ On September 2, 1988, Mel Turpin of the Utah Jazz became the first NBA player traded to another country when he was sent to Zaragoza of Spain for José Ortiz.

▶ In 1986, in the Trade of the Kevins, the New York Mets traded Kevin Mitchell, Kevin Armstrong, Kevin Brown, Shawn Abner, and Stan Jefferson to the San Diego Padres for Kevin McReynolds, Gene Walter, and Adam Ging.

▶ On July 14, 1972, NFL owner Carroll Rosenbloom traded his Baltimore Colts to Robert Irsay for the Los Angeles Rams.

▶ In 1978, Irv Levin, owner of the Boston Celtics, gave his NBA franchise to Buffalo Braves owner Hank Iba, and in return received the Braves franchise, which he then moved to San Diego, where they became the Clippers.

▶ In January of 1983, Tom Martin of the Western Hockey League's Seattle Breakers was traded to Victoria for a team bus. "I didn't think that much about it at the time," said Martin. "But it was a real nice bus."

▶ In the middle of the 1960 season, the fourth-place Cleveland Indians traded their manager, Joe Gordon, to the sixth-place Detroit Tigers for *their* manager, Jimmy Dykes.

▶ Quarterback Jacky Lee was leased by the Denver Broncos from the Houston Oilers during the 1964 and 1965 seasons. The Broncos needed help after a 2-11-1 season in 1963, and made a deal in which they sent Bud McFadin, a first-round draft choice, and cash to the Oilers for Lee for two seasons. In 1966, the lease expired and Lee was returned to Houston.

▶ On March 15, 1978, the San Francisco Giants traded seven players and $390,000 for Oakland Athletics pitcher Vida Blue.

In 1959, Los Angeles Rams General Manager Pete Rozelle sent seven players and two draft choices to the Chicago Cardinals for star running back Ollie Matson. In 1952, the Rams dealt 11 players for Les Richter.

On October 12, 1989, the Dallas Cowboys helped set the foundation for their championship teams of the 90s by pulling off a blockbuster: They traded running back Herschel Walker to the Minnesota Vikings for up to 12 players: Vikings Jesse Solomon, David Howard, Ike Holt, Darrin Nelson, and Alex Stewart; a 1992 #1 draft choice; and six conditional draft choices spread over three years.

▶ In another one of the biggest trades in NFL history, New Orleans Saints coach Mike Ditka gave the Washington Redskins all six of his draft selections in the 1999 draft, and two more in the 2000 draft, in exchange for their #5 position in the '99 draft, where they chose Heisman Trophy-winning running back Ricky Williams. (Three years later, the Saints traded Williams to the Miami Dolphins for two draft picks.)

▶ Dale Holman was playing for Syracuse against Richmond on June 30, 1986, when the game was suspended. Before the game was resumed, Holman was released, and signed with the Braves organization. Holman was called up to the Richmond club and played in the continuation of the Syracuse game, this time for Richmond. He had a single and double for Richmond to go with the double and two RBIs he'd had for Syracuse.

▶ On November 5, 1976, the Pittsburgh Pirates traded catcher Manny Sanguillen and $100,000 for Oakland Athletics manager Chuck Tanner.

On June 18, 1987, the New York Rangers General Manager Phil Esposito traded their 1988 first-round draft choice and $100,000 to the Quebec Nordiques for Quebec coach Michel Bergeron.

While it was not technically a trade, when Dick Vermeil, a consultant with the St. Louis Rams (and their recently retired Super Bowl-winning head coach) signed to coach the Kansas City Chiefs, the NFL ruled that the Chiefs had to compensate the Rams with a second- and third-round draft pick, and that Vermeil had to return to the Rams his $500,000 salary (which loss was more than offset by the 3-year, $10 million deal he would be getting from Kansas City). Similarly, when New England Patriots coach Bill Parcells left to join the New York Jets, the NFL ordered the Jets to remunerate the Pats with a first-, second-, third-, and fourth-round draft choice, spread over three years.

▶ Rocky Colavito, the 1959 American League home run co-champion, was traded for Harvey Kuenn, the 1959 American League batting champion, after the 1959 season.

▶ In February of 1921, the Cincinnati Reds traded outfielder Ed "Greasy" Neale and Jimmy Ring to the Philadelphia Phillies for Eppa Rixey. Neale later coached in the NFL and was elected to the Pro Football Hall of Fame, while Rixey was later elected to the Baseball Hall of Fame. Ring was also thrown into a 1926 trade of Hall of Famers Frank Frisch for Rogers Hornsby.

▶ Dickie Noles was traded from the Chicago Cubs to the Detroit Tigers late in the 1987 season for a player to be named later. At the end of the season, Noles was designated as the player to be named later.

▶ Max Flack and Cliff Heathcote played against each other in the first game of a May 30, 1922, doubleheader between the St. Louis Cardinals and the Chicago Cubs, then were traded for each other and played on the other side in the second game.

▶ Between March 1955 and June 1961, the New York Yankees and Kansas City Athletics made 17 trades involving 64 players.

▶ Wayne Nordhagen and Dick Davis were traded for each other twice in the same week. On June 15, 1982, the Toronto Blue Jays traded

Nordhagen to the Philadelphia Phillies for Davis. That same day, Philadelphia traded Nordhagen to the Pittsburgh Pirates for Bill Robinson. Days later, the Pirates traded Nordhagen to Toronto for Davis.

Cocky and Good: The Most Famous Boasts

God knows there's too much ego, arrogance, selfishness, all-about-me-ness—you name it—in the modern sports world. But every now and then, you've just got to admire the self-confidence: After all, that's just one reason they're there doing it, while we're at home rooting. "The only reason I don't like playing in the World Series," Reggie Jackson once said, "is I can't watch myself play."

Nice.

▶ In one of the most renowned displays of confidence in sports, quarterback Joe Namath, in a speech to the Miami Touchdown Club three days before the 1969 Super Bowl, predicted that his New York Jets would upset the Baltimore Colts, who were favored to win by 17 points. "I guarantee it," he said. The final score was Jets 16, Colts 7.

▶ In 1932, on the Monday after Stanford's varsity lost to USC for the first time ever, Stanford's freshman football team vowed never to lose to USC during their playing days. They became known as "The Vow Boys" and lived up to their promise, beating the Trojans in 1933, 1934, and 1935.

▶ Before the 1984 Olympic men's downhill competition in Sarajevo, American skier Bill Johnson said, "I don't even know why everyone else is here. They should hand [the gold medal] to me... this course was designed for me, and everyone else can fight for second place." Johnson won the gold.

▶ It was just before his 1964 fight with Sonny Liston that Cassius Clay first said "I am the greatest," using a line that he borrowed from wrestler Gorgeous George. Liston did not come out for the seventh round, and for more than a decade, Clay—later Muhammad Ali—lived up to his self-titled superlative.

▶ Before teeing off, golfing great Walter Hagen would often ask, "Well, who's going to be second?"

▶ Lloyd Honeyghan bet $5,000 on himself at 5-1 odds in his welterweight title fight with Donald Curry in September of 1986. Honeyghan won the fight.

▶ Bobby Riggs bet on himself to sweep the men's singles, doubles, and mixed doubles at Wimbledon in 1939, and did just that.

▶ In a Nike ad, the great Algerian middle-distance runner Nourredine Morceli was seen musing while running: "When I race, my mind is full of doubts... Who will finish second? Who will finish third?"

▶ On the night the Los Angeles Lakers won the NBA title in 1987, coach Pat Riley said that his team would become the first to repeat as champions since the Boston Celtics had accomplished the feat 20 years earlier. "I'm going to guarantee everyone we're going to repeat," Riley said. The Lakers repeated.

A Baker's Dozen of Examples of Language Abuse by People Not Named Casey Stengel or Yogi Berra

New York favorite sons Casey Stengel and Yogi Berra both gained as much affection and popularity for the way they expressed themselves— at once comically confounding and bracingly clear—as they did for the way they played, coached, and managed the game of baseball. Their malapropisms have been well documented elsewhere, but there is room in the sports world for others to rise to the verbal heights that Casey and Yogi did routinely.

▶ While announcing the "Game of the Week," broadcaster and former St. Louis Cardinals pitching great Dizzy Dean referred to courage as "testicle fortitude."

▶ Chicago Cubs announcer Jack Brickhouse once said an unaccompanied singer had performed the national anthem, "Acapulco."

▶ Phil Heck, University of California linebacker in the mid-1970s, once said of Golden Bears quarterback Joe Roth, "I'd give my right arm to be in his shoes."

▶ Heck's teammate, University of California linebacker Pete Citta, speaking of a knee injury suffered by Heck, said, "You could tell his knees were in the back of his mind."

▶ Following a road trip during which the Chicago Cubs had gone 4-4, Don Zimmer assessed his team's play by saying, "It just as easily could have gone the other way."

▶ Of an unflattering newspaper photograph of himself, New York Mets pitcher Jeff Innis said, "That picture was taken out of context."

▶ After getting hit by a pitch, infielder Tito Fuentes remarked that "they shouldn't throw at me. I'm the father of five or six kids."

▶ San Francisco Giants broadcaster and former major leaguer Ron Fairly once said, "Last night, I neglected to mention something that bears repeating."

▶ Before going up against New York Mets ace Dwight Gooden in a 1989 preseason game, New York Yankees first baseman Don Mattingly said, "His reputation preceded him before he got here."

▶ New York Mets announcer Ralph Kiner once segued into a commercial by saying, "We'll be back after this word from Manufacturers Hangover."

▶ San Diego Padre announcer Jerry Coleman, renowned for his unintentionally twisted imagery, said that on a wild pitch, baserunner Keith Hernandez had taken off "with the crack of the ball."

▶ During the 1989 NFL season, San Francisco 49ers offensive tackle Bubba Paris asserted that the defending champions would not get complacent by "resting on our morals."

▶ In 1982, Texas Rangers outfielder Mickey Rivers said, "Ain't no sense in worrying about things you got control over, 'cause if you got control over them, ain't no sense in worrying. And there ain't no sense worrying about things you got no control over, 'cause if you got no control over them, ain't no sense worrying."

How Teeth and Dentistry Have Impacted the Sports World

▶ In 1895, in the first professional football game, John Brailler, a future dentist from Latrobe, Pennsylvania, was paid $10 to play quarterback for Latrobe against rival Jeannette (Pennsylvania) and helped his team to win, 12-0.

▶ When ex-heavyweight boxing champion Leon Spinks was mugged on January 16, 1982, they not only took his money and the jewelry he was wearing, but also removed his two gold front teeth.

▶ On July 14, 1925, world flyweight champion Pancho Villa, age 23, died of blood poisoning, the result of an infected tooth.

▶ At the turn of the century, Coburn Haskell, a Cleveland dentist, invented a dimpled ball that was made of elastic thread and wound under tension around a rubber core. It would be the precursor of the modern golf ball.

▶ Mark Spitz had planned on becoming a dentist after retiring from competitive swimming. He won seven gold medals at the 1972 Olympic Games and never got around to dental school.

▶ Edward Flynn, Olympic welterweight gold medalist in 1932, became a dentist in New Orleans.

Peter George, who won the Olympic middleweight weightlifting gold medal in 1952, became a dentist in the U.S. Army.

▶ LSU football star Billy Cannon, winner of the 1959 Heisman Trophy, became a Baton Rouge orthodontist. He was later sentenced to five years in prison and fined $10,000 for counterfeiting.

▶ When heavyweight champion Jack Johnson returned to his dressing room on October 16, 1909, after pummeling Stanley Ketchel in a 12th-round knockout to retain the heavyweight title, he found two of Ketchel's teeth lodged in his glove.

You, the Fan

Fans—i.e., you. Us.

Some of the time—most of the time—we deserve more (and ought to pay less). Some of the time, we act like knuckleheads. Some of the times we cheer when we shouldn't (see Philadelphia Eagle fans reveling in the sight of a prone Michael Irvin of the Dallas Cowboys). Some of the time we think we're being clever with our chants, and some of the time we actually are clever with our chants (see the Cameron Crazies of Duke University). Some of the time we think our team should win every single year or something's constitutionally wrong (see New York Yankee fans). Sometimes we're passionate but polite (see St. Louis Cardinal fans). Sometimes we're passionate but profane (see Boston Red Sox fans, among many, many others). Sometimes, the first seven innings are enough, no matter what the score (see Los Angeles Dodger fans).

▶ In the "White Flag" trade of 1997, Chicago White Sox ownership, supposedly looking to rebuild, essentially flipped the bird to its fans and surrendered the American League Central title to the Cleveland Indians, whom they trailed by a mere 3½ games with a full two months to play, when they traded the heart of their pitching staff— Wilson Alvarez, Roberto Hernandez, and Danny Darwin—to the San Francisco Giants. The Indians had lost 10 of their previous 14 games before the trade.

▶ A 59-foot-high stack of logs, being assembled for a bonfire accompanying the annual pep rally at Texas A&M University prior to its football game against arch-rival University of Texas, collapsed and killed 12 A&M students on November 18, 1999. The log stack, weighing more than two jumbo jets, collapsed because of flawed construction techniques and a lack of adequate supervision of the students assembling it, according to a five-member commission funded by the university.

▶ When the slapshot of Columbus Blue Jackets center Epsen Knutsen deflected off the stick of a Calgary Flames player, it ricocheted into the stands and hit Brittanie Cecil, 13, in the head. She died two days later, on March 18, 2002, becoming the first spectator to die at an NHL game from being hit by a puck.

Fourteen-year-old baseball fan Alan Fish died of a head injury four days after being struck by a foul ball hit off the bat of Manny Mota at Dodger Stadium, May 16, 1970. The boy's parents sued the Dodgers for negligence but the jury absolved the team of blame.

▶ On November 29, 1900, 13 fans died while watching the California-Stanford football game when the Pacific Glass Works factory roof they were viewing from collapsed and they fell into vats of molten glass.

▶ With the shattering of home run records in recent years has come an unseemly byproduct: The wild, sometimes vicious scramble in the stands for what many fans view as their ticket to wealth and fame. Especially wealth. Mark McGwire's 70th home run from the 1998 season was purchased from Philip Ozersky, a 26-year-old research scientist who grabbed the ball at Busch Stadium in St. Louis, for $3 million by Todd McFarlane, the creator of *Spawn*. McFarlane also acquired six other McGwire balls from that year—Nos. 1, 63, 64, 67, 68, and 69—and three Sammy Sosa home-run balls—Nos. 33, 61, and 66. An exhibit of the 10 balls toured the country to raise money for the fight against Lou Gehrig's disease. That was a happy result of home-run-ball mania; there have been others. Deni Allen, who caught McGwire's 60th homer in '98, exchanged it for a ball, a couple of bats, and the opportunity to take batting practice with the Cardinals. And Tim Forneris, recipient of McGwire's record-breaking 62nd homer, gave it up for no compensation. More typical, however, is the long court battle over Barry Bonds's 73rd home run ball: Patrick Hayashi came away with it at San Francisco's Pacific Bell Park, but had to relinquish it when he was sued by another fan, who claims he caught it first before he was mobbed and the ball popped free. Perhaps even more alarming was the free-for-all that ensued at Pac Bell Park for Bonds' 600th home run ball. Jay Arsenault came away with the ball but was sued by his buddy, Tim Fisher, and two other men who accused Arsenault of violating a verbal contract to split any proceeds from the sale of the ball.

New York Yankees fan Sal Durante retrieved Roger Maris's 61st home run ball and traded it in for $5,000 and two trips to the West Coast.

▶ The unwritten code of conduct at Wrigley Field in Chicago dictates that any home run ball hit by a Cubs' opponent must be thrown back onto the field with disdain, a tradition believed to have originated in the 1960s by Wrigley's famed Bleacher Bums.

▶ In 1978, Texas Rangers pitcher George "Doc" Medich administered CPR to a 61-year-old fan who had suffered a heart attack. Medich was involved in a similar incident as a Pittsburgh Pirate in 1976.

▶ Many games have been forfeited because of rowdy fans, including the final game ever played in Washington, in 1971, before the Senators left for Texas, as fans stormed the field for souvenirs. The Rangers were the recipients of a forfeit win from the Indians in 1974 on the evening of Cleveland's promotional disaster, "Ten Cent Beer Night."

▶ The first baseball team to draw one million fans in a year was the Chicago Cubs, in 1927.

▶ The NFL's Seattle Seahawks retired #12 to honor "The Twelfth Man," their fans. The NBA's Sacramento Kings retired #6 for their fans, "The Sixth Man."

▶ In the 1989 season, Portland State held a contest asking their fans to send in plays for the football team. When the team was about to run the play that won the contest, the coach waved a white towel to let the fans know. The winning playcaller received $10 for every yard that the play gained, $20 per yard if the play went for a touchdown.

Examples of Religion's Place in Sports

Many athletes have declined to compete on certain days for religious reasons. One of the most celebrated instances was of Los Angeles Dodgers pitcher Sandy Koufax, who would have started Game 1 of the 1965 World Series but did not because it took place on Yom Kippur.

Eric Liddell, whose life was chronicled in the movie, *Chariots of Fire*, withdrew from the 100m and the 4x100m relay at the 1924 Olympics because the heats or final were run on Sunday. He spent the Sunday of the 100m heats delivering a sermon at a Scottish church in Paris. (He finished third in the 200m and won the gold in the 400m.)

At the 1900 Olympics, several Americans refused to participate in their events because they were held on Sunday: William Remington and Walter Carroll (high jump final), John Cregan and Alex Grant (1500m), and Dixon Boardman, Harry Lee, and William Moloney (400m final).

Tennis player Dorothy Round also refused to play on Sunday in the U.S. and French championships.

▶ Pittsburgh became the last major-league city to allow Sunday baseball, on April 29, 1934.

▶ At the 1900 Olympics, Meyer Prinstein was prohibited by his coach from taking part in the long jump final on Sunday—even though Prinstein was Jewish. He won the silver medal on the strength of his jump from the qualifying round.

▶ In 1996, Denver Nuggets guard and practicing Muslim Mahmoud Abdul-Rauf (formerly Chris Jackson) would not stand during the pre-game playing of the American or Canadian national anthems; for the first three-quarters of the NBA season, he would either remain in the locker room or be on or near the bench, stretching, sitting, or facing away from the flag. He said he did so because his beliefs precluded him from participating in any "nationalistic ritualism"; he said, too, that he meant no disrespect but saw the flag and anthem as symbols "of tyranny, of oppression...You can't be for God and for oppression." When Nuggets fans began to take notice of Abdul-Rauf's during-anthem ritual, they complained to talk radio shows, and the issue gripped the national media, as people tussled with the notion of freedom of expression versus patriotism and respect for the flag. The NBA suspended him without pay, citing a league rule requiring "players to line up in a dignified posture for the anthem." After one game, Abdul-Rauf agreed to stand, during which time he would silently "offer a prayer."

▶ Although his father was a non-practicing Jew and his mother wasn't Jewish, boxer Max Baer wore a Star of David on his trunks. Before each at-bat, perennial batting champion Wade Boggs, who also is not Jewish, drew a "חי" (the Hebrew word "chai," which means life) in the dirt with his bat.

▶ In 1980, at the age of 27, Dave Meyers quit the NBA's Milwaukee Bucks to spend more time at his activities as a Jehovah's Witness.

▶ Dust Commander was blessed by Archbishop Emanuel Milingo of Zambia at Keeneland before the running of the Blue Grass Stakes, which Dust Commander won. He later won the 1970 Kentucky Derby in an upset.

▶ Whatever it may mean, the talented point guard God Shamgod elected to make his college of choice... Providence.

▶ Orel Hershiser knelt on the mound to say a prayer after winning the 1988 World Series. To relax while pitching, he would sometimes sing hymns to himself.

▶ Elzbieta Krzesinska read the New Testament between jumps at the 1956 Melbourne Olympics. She won the long jump gold medal.

▶ El Sayed Nosseir, an Egyptian Olympic gold medalist weightlifter in 1928, would raise his arms and face to the sky before each lift and call out for Allah's assistance.

▶ In September 1974, the New York Stars WFL game against the Detroit Wheels at Downing Stadium on Randall's Island, New York, was moved from a Wednesday to a Tuesday because of Yom Kippur.

▶ Willie Davis, Los Angeles Dodgers outfielder in the 1960s, was a practicing Buddhist.

The Bronx Zoo

The late New York Yankee player and manager Billy Martin was known not just for his pinstriped heart but for his fury on the field, in the dugout, even far away from the field or the dugout. The controversies that followed him were well-chronicled by the New York press during his five stints as Yankee skipper.

Billy Martin's lawyer must have had nice houses.

▶ Chicago Cubs pitcher Jim Brewer sued Martin in 1960 after Martin broke Brewer's jaw in a brawl. Brewer was awarded $10,000 by a circuit court jury in Chicago.

▶ In 1983, Umpire Dale Ford sued Martin in Federal Court in Philadelphia. Martin had called Ford a "stone liar" after Ford ejected him from a game in Chicago.

▶ In 1957, Martin and Yankee teammates Mickey Mantle, Yogi Berra, Hank Bauer, and Johnny Kucks brawled at New York's Copacabana club. Martin was fined $1,000 and soon after was traded to the Kansas City Athletics.

▶ Umpire Terry Cooney went to a Toronto court in 1981 to formally charge Martin, then the Oakland Athletics manager, with common assault, after a game in which Cooney had ejected Martin for questioning strike and ball calls, to which Martin had responded by bumping Cooney, kicking dirt on his shoes, and throwing dirt at his back.

Cooney dropped the charges after Martin dropped an appeal of his one-week suspension and $1,000 fine, and also apologized.

▶ In addition to innumerable brawls on the baseball field, Martin was involved in several extracurricular altercations. In 1978, he fought a Nevada sportswriter; in 1979, a Minnesota marshmallow salesman; and in 1983, 1985, and 1988, hotel bar patrons in California, Baltimore, and Arlington (Texas), respectively.

In 1982, after breaking a finger when he hit a piece of furniture in anger over the way his Oakland As team had played, he said, "I'm getting smarter. I finally punched something that couldn't sue me."

▶ One day after Martin died, the Internal Revenue Service filed three liens against his estate to collect $86,137 in back taxes.

14 Prominent Ex-Cheerleaders

▶ Dwight Eisenhower
▶ Patty Hearst
▶ Joyce Brothers
▶ Donna Rice
▶ James Stewart
▶ Ann-Margret
▶ Lily Tomlin

▶ Carly Simon
▶ Jane Pauley
▶ Raquel Welch
▶ Dinah Shore
▶ Cybill Shepherd
▶ Dyan Cannon
▶ Gerald Ford

Athletes Who Made an Impact on the World Outside of Sports

▶ Byron "Whizzer" White, who led the NCAA and later the NFL in rushing, became a United States Supreme Court Justice.

▶ Olympic 400m hurdler Edward H. White became Astronaut Lieutenant Colonel White and a member of the Gemini 4 crew.

▶ Gino Marchetti, Hall of Fame defensive end for the Baltimore Colts in the 1950s and 1960s, helped to start Gino's, the national fast-food chain. (The chain was eventually sold to the Marriott Corporation, which converted many of the restaurants into Roy Rogers outlets.)

▶ Thomas Sopwith, who challenged unsuccessfully for the America's Cup in 1934 and 1937 with his yachts *Endeavour* and *Endeavour II*, started an aviation firm that produced World War I military aircraft such as the Triplane and the famous Sopwith Camel, which downed 1,294 enemy aircraft.

▶ In his post-NBA life, Magic Johnson continues to establish himself as an immensely successful businessman, helping to develop numerous movie theaters and shopping complexes, often named for him, in urban areas nationwide.

▶ 1932 Olympic swimming gold medalist Clarence "Buster" Crabbe gained great recognition playing Tarzan, Flash Gordon, and Buck Rogers in the movies. Three other Olympic medalists also played Tarzan—swimmer Johnny Weissmuller, the most renowned portrayer; shotputter Bruce Bennett (whose real name was Herman Brix); and marathoner Glenn Morris.

▶ Billy Sunday played major-league baseball for eight years (1883–90) and was the first outfielder to execute an unassisted double play before he went on to become America's most famous evangelist in the early 20th centuiy.

▶ Alfred Gilbert, gold medalist in the pole vault in 1908, invented the Erector Set.

▶ Major-league catcher Moe Berg became a spy and helped to discover the whereabouts of German nuclear physicist Werner Heisenberg during World War II.

▶ Many athletes have acted in movies, usually forgettable roles in forgettable films. A few, however, have appeared in film classics: Adhemar Ferreira da Silva, the Brazilian triple jump world-record holder in the 1950s, appeared in *Black Orpheus* in 1958; Giuseppe Gentile of Italy, the 1968 Olympic triple-jump bronze medalist, acted opposite Maria Callas in *Medea*; and boxer Eddie Mustafa Muhammad played a boxer in Martin Scorcese's 1980 film, *Raging Bull*. Victor McLaglen, the opponent in 1909 for heavyweight champion Jack Johnson's first title defense, would later win an Academy Award for his performance in *The Informer*.

▶ In 1917, Rutgers end Paul Robeson became the second black All-America in football (Fritz Pollard was the first), then went on to a renowned concert career as a bass-baritone and became a political activist, as well.

▶ Philip Baker, 1920 Olympic silver medalist in the 1,500m who later changed his name to Philip Noel-Baker, was a member of the British Parliament for 36 years. He won the 1959 Nobel Peace Prize for his work toward disarmament.

▶ Bobby Avila, the Cleveland Indian who won the 1954 American League batting title, later became mayor of Vera Cruz, Mexico.

In 1996, Romanian former tennis great Ilie Nastase ran for mayor of Bucharest, the nation's capital. He did not win.

▶ Benjamin Spock, a member of Yale's Olympic gold medal eight-oared crew in 1924, wrote one of the world's all-time best-selling books, *Baby and Child Care*, and ran for president in 1972 as a People's Party candidate.

5 Unusual Crimes for Which Athletes Have Been Convicted

Athletes have served time in prison for crimes such as drug dealing (Miami Dolphins running back Mercury Morris), tax evasion (baseball hits champ Pete Rose), armed robbery (boxer Rubin "Hurricane" Carter), and racketeering (Denny McLain, baseball's last 30-game winner). Others have been on the wrong side of the law, and some have served time, for more unusual transgressions.

▶ Jack Johnson, the first black heavyweight boxing champion, was convicted in 1912 of violating the Mann Act (White Slave Act). He was charged with "transporting" a white woman for "immoral" purposes. He fled to Europe to avoid imprisonment.

▶ In 1973, Jerry Priddy, American League infielder from 1941–53, was found guilty of attempted extortion. He threatened to blow up the steamship *Island Princess* if he did not get $250,000.

▶ Dino Ciccarelli of the Minnesota North Stars was sentenced to one day in jail and fined $1,000 for his on-ice attack of Toronto Maple Leafs defenseman Luke Richardson, on August 24, 1988. Ciccarelli was the first NHL player to go to jail for attacking another player.

Boston Bruins defenseman Marty McSorley was convicted of assault with a weapon for using his stick to hit the head of an unsuspecting Donald Brashear of the Vancouver Canucks, on February 21, 2000. The court gave McSorley a conditional discharge but the NHL suspended him for a year.

▶ Armin Hary of Germany, gold medalist in the 1960 Olympic 100m, was convicted in 1981 of diverting Roman Catholic Church funds for personal investment.

▶ Latu Vaeno, a New Zealand rugby player, was jailed for six months for biting off the ear of an opponent on December 5, 1985.

10
EXTREMES

●●●●●●●●●●●●●●●

The Shortest-Lived Glory

As thrilling as it is for an athlete to achieve a great victory or personal goal, it's made sweeter by being able to bask in it, share it with family and friends and fans. For some athletes, unfortunately, that pleasure is not long-lived. And others may not realize that the first or second time that they get to experience such a joyous athletic moment is also the last.

▶ In the 1980 Olympic pentathlon, Soviet Olga Rukavishnikova finished second in the final event, the 800m, to set a world record—for four-tenths of a second. When her countrymate, Nadezhda Tkachenko, who had been leading the competition after four events, finished in third place, right behind Rukavishnikova, she established a new pentathlon world record.

▶ In the 1972 season finale against the Kansas City Chiefs, Atlanta Falcons running back Dave Hampton reached the 1,000-yard mark for the season. The game was stopped briefly to award him the ball. A few plays later, Hampton was thrown for a six-yard loss. He carried the ball one final time, for a one-yard gain, and finished the season with 995 yards.

▶ Two hours after what was, to then, probably the biggest win of his tennis career—a semifinal victory over Frenchman Yannick Noah at the 1989 Lipton International Players Championships at Key Biscayne, Florida—Austrian Thomas Muster was hit by a car and suffered knee ligament damage while heading for a restaurant in downtown Miami.

▶ On the second play of the 2002 NFL season, in which the Tennessee Titans were picked by many to contend for the Super Bowl, All-Pro defensive end Jevon "The Freak" Kearse broke his foot, requiring surgery that would keep him out for almost half the season.

In 1999, in the first inning of his first regular-season game after signing a giant free-agent contract with the Anaheim Angels, first baseman Mo Vaughn fell into the home dugout while catching a foul pop. He badly twisted his ankle and spent several weeks on the disabled list.

▶ In what would be his only major-league game, 21-year-old Ray Jansen went 4-5 for the 1910 St. Louis Browns, giving him a lifetime .800 average. More than 20 brief major leaguers have a lifetime average of 1.000. While most had one hit in their one at-bat, John Paciorek went 3-for-3, drew a pair of walks, and scored four times for the Houston Colts in the final game of the 1963 season. The next season, Paciorek started in the minor leagues, then had a back operation, and never got to play again in the big leagues.

▶ Bill Barilko scored the winning overtime goal in the fifth and final game of the 1951 Stanley Cup finals to help the Toronto Maple Leafs beat the Montreal Canadiens, then died that summer in a plane crash.

▶ The only run batted in of Philadelphia Phillie Howie Bedell's 1968 season broke the record 58-consecutive-innings scoreless streak of Los Angeles Dodgers pitcher Don Drysdale. It was also the third and last RBI that Bedell had in his career.

▶ Richard Sanders, bantamweight wrestling silver medalist in 1972, died at 23 in a car accident seven weeks after the Olympics.

Odon Tersztyanszky of Hungary, gold medalist in the saber in 1928, died in a car accident outside Budapest 10 months later.

Ivo van Damme, silver medalist in the 800m in 1976, died in a car crash on December 29 of that year, at age 22.

▶ Tony Canzoneri held the light-welterweight title for 33 days (May 21–June 23, 1933), the shortest reign of any boxing champion.

▶ On March 12, 1956, in an NBA game against the St. Louis Hawks, Syracuse National Dick Farley fouled out after playing only five minutes.

▶ New York Yankees infielder Brian Doyle, with only 52 previous major-league at-bats, hit .438 (7-for-16) in the 1978 World Series. He would have only 147 more at-bats in his major-league career.

▶ Jack Givens scored 41 points to lead Kentucky over Duke for the 1978 NCAA basketball title. He played two seasons in the NBA, and averaged 6.7 points a game for his career.

▶ Detroit Tigers pitcher Floyd Giebell's third major-league victory beat the Cleveland Indians and future Hall of Famer Bob Feller, 2-0, and helped the 1940 Tigers clinch the pennant. Giebell would not win another major-league game.

In his pitching debut on April 14, 1967, at Yankee Stadium, Billy Rohr of the Boston Red Sox came within an out of a no-hitter. He lost that but still won the game, beating Whitey Ford, 3-0. Rohr won just two more games in his major-league career.

▶ In the first significant tournament Lee Mackey, Jr., ever competed in, he shocked the golf world by shooting a first round 33-31-64 at the 1950 U.S. Open to break by one stroke Jimmy McHale's 1947 record for a round at the Open, and took the lead by three strokes. The next day, with a flock of fans in tow, Mackey bogeyed the second hole, double-bogeyed the fourth, bogeyed the fifth, and shot a second-round 81, good enough for a 22nd-place tie. He shot 75-77 over the last 36 holes and won $100 for tying for 25th place.

Short-Lived Ignominy

▶ In 1969, their first season, the Seattle Pilots baseball team went 64-98 and finished in last place. It was also their last season because the franchise moved to Milwaukee.

25 Bad Things About Sports (With No Naming of Names)

1. All labor disputes—that means all strikes, all lockouts, and everything in between

2. Athletes not running hard to first base, or putting their hands up on defense, all the time, and other unfathomable displays of laziness or lack of interest

3. Starting World Series games at almost 9:00 P.M. Eastern

4. Players pointing to God as they round first after hitting a single or score a touchdown

5. In fact, any public inclusion of higher beings as it relates to winning a game

6. Announcers using the word "courage" when referring to a player returning to the court with a twisted ankle, or a golfer going for the flag rather than laying up

7. Putting the score on the corner of the TV screen (see "25 Good Things About Sports")... in unreadable typeface

8. Rioting after your team loses a championship final

9. Rioting after your team wins a championship final

10. Singers who perform the national anthem as if it's a career move

11. Golfing fans yelling "You da man!" as soon as the clubface makes contact with the ball, and independent of where the shot may end up

12. Witless banners using the initials of the network covering the game

13. Most team mascots

14. Dancing in the end zone

15. Styling after hitting a home run

16. The Wave

17. Egregiously biased voting in subjective sports, especially figure skating

18. Unretiring

19. Baseball players charging money for autographs

20. Relentless corporate sponsorship of bowl games, "Plays of the Week" segments, scoreboard updates, home runs, hits, errors, strikes, balls, balks, etc.

21. Super Bowl halftime extravaganzas

22. Tennis players who feel obligated to climb into the stands to hug loved ones immediately—immediately!—after winning the last point of a tournament, barely showing respect to their vanquished opponent who remains courtside

23. Basketball promos that show only dunks, football promos that show only vicious hits, baseball promos that show only home runs...

24. Penalty-kick shootouts to decide tied soccer games

25. TV timeouts

And 25 More Bad Things About Sports (With Some Naming of Names)

1. Los Angeles fans leaving in the seventh inning of Dodger games, and the middle of the fourth quarter of Laker games

2. Endless TV shots of Jack Nicholson and Dyan Cannon cheering for the Lakers, and Spike Lee cheering for the Knicks

3. Sports media going on and on about how the lack of a championship ring makes a superior athlete on a team sport a somehow lesser performer. (Does anyone seriously believe that, say, Trent Dilfer—the quite average and very fortunate quarterback of the 2001 Super Bowl–winning Baltimore Ravens—has that "special something" that, say, Reggie Miller—one of pro basketball's clutchest-ever performers, though ring-less—lacks?)

4. John 3:16

5. The media coverage given the eBay auction of Arizona Diamondback Luis Gonzalez's discarded 2002 pre-season gum

6. Credit being given to the wrong hero, blame being heaped on the wrong goat. (The meltdown in the 10th inning of Game 6 of the 1986 World Series is more attributable to pitchers Bob Stanley, Calvin Schiraldi, catcher Rich Gedman, and / or manager John McNamara, *not* to first baseman Bill Buckner.)

7. The hype for, and very existence of, the fight between Laila Ali, Muhammad's daughter, and Jackie Frazier, Joe's daughter. (Like anyone asked for this?)

8. The smug, snotty, seen-everything delivery of every sports anchor, especially those under 35. (You listening, ESPN?)

9. The severely slicked-back and gelled look of every basketball-coaching Pat-Riley-wannabe. (Are you listening, Billy Donovan? How about you, Steve Lavin?)

10. Boston Garden giving way to the Fleet Center

11. The Montreal Forum giving way to the Molson Center

12. Continually giving coaching jobs to mediocre practitioners just because they've been in the game a long time. (Are you listening, Jeff Torborg?)

13. The NFL Pro Bowl

14. Any and all boxing commissions

15. North-South and East-West all-star college football games—or, at least, the televising of them

16. The following sports using professionals in the Olympics, or even being represented in the Olympics, when they're more than well-represented already, and just take attention away from athletes in other sports that don't have another such showcase: tennis, men's basketball and, soon, golf

17. Networks lying to us about when the first pitch is

18. Overstating the importance of coaches

19. Endless shots of coaches

20. Overmanaging

21. Scamdicapping

22. The vicious fights for, and subsequent marketing of, significant home run balls hit into the bleachers

23. Endless World Series shots of stars of TV shows that will be premiering or starting up a new season on that very network as soon as the Series is over

24. The NBA All-Star slam dunk contest

25. Players not showing up for their league's all-star game

Boys Among Men, Girls Among Women: The Most Precocious Athletes of All Time

▶ Montreal Canadiens goalie Ken Dryden won the Conn Smythe Trophy as the 1971 Stanley Cup playoff MVP. The next season, he won the Calder Trophy for Rookie of the Year. Dryden had played in few enough regular season games the previous year to still be considered a rookie in 1971–72.

▶ At the 1998 Nagano Games, figure skater Tara Lipinski, 15, became the youngest female to win gold at a Winter Games.

▶ When Mats Wilander won the French Open in 1982 at age 17, becoming at the time the youngest winner ever of a Grand Slam men's singles title, he achieved a rare distinction: He had won the French boy's and men's titles in consecutive years.

▶ When swimmer Alex Baumann was having trouble producing a urine sample after his 400m individual medley victory in the 1984 Olympics, officials gave him a beer. In the middle of his third beer, they found out that he was underaged and gave him a soft drink instead.

   In 1980, after scoring 42 points playing center against the Philadelphia 76ers and becoming, at age 20, the youngest player to win the NBA playoff MVP Award, Magic Johnson celebrated with his Los Angeles Laker teammates in the winning locker room, but was still legally too young to drink the champagne.

▶ Tiger Woods has been ridiculously precocious at every age. To mention just a very few instances: At 3, he shot 48 for nine holes on his hometown golf course in Cypress, California. At 5, he was featured in *Golf Digest* magazine. At 18, he became the youngest player to win the U.S. Amateur. At 24, he became the youngest player to win the career Grand Slam.

▶ On July 1, 1952, 12-year-old Joe Reliford, the batboy for Fitzgerald in the Georgia State League, appeared in a minor-league game. Reliford was used as a pinch hitter with Fitzgerald losing 13-0 and the crowd chanting, "Put in the batboy." He grounded out sharply to third. He stayed in the game to play centerfield and made a putout.

▶ The youngest major leaguer ever was Joe Nuxhall. In 1944, at age 15, he pitched two-thirds of an inning for the Cincinnati Reds, allowing two hits, five walks, and five runs.

▶ Kathy Horvath is the only player to win all four junior tennis age groups (the U.S. Girls Clay Courts) in consecutive years.

▶ In 2000, Santino Quaranto, 16, of Major League Soccer's D.C. United team, became the youngest professional athlete in an American team sport. He was named an all-star and also scored five goals in one game.

▶ In the 1964–65 season, Dave DeBusschere became the youngest player-coach in the NBA when, at 24, he both coached and played power forward for the Detroit Pistons.

▶ In 1924, Bucky Harris, 27, took over as manager for the Washington Senators and led them to two pennants and a World Series title in his first two years. Lou Boudreau, at 24, became the Cleveland Indians manager after the 1941 season. Roger Peckinpaugh managed the 1914 New York Yankees for 17 games at the age of 23.

▶ Mike Tyson became the youngest heavyweight champion ever when, at 20, he knocked out Trevor Berbick in November of 1986. Floyd Patterson was 21 when he beat Archie Moore for the title in 1956.

   Wilfred Benitez, then 17, became the youngest boxer to win a world title, defeating Antonio Cervantes in a 15-round decision for the junior welterweight title, on March 6, 1976.

▶ Seve Ballesteros won the 1980 Masters at 23. Gene Sarazen won the 1922 PGA at 20. Tom Morris, Jr., won the 1868 British Open at 17.

▶ In a 1963 game, the Houston Colts used an all-rookie lineup and lost 10-3 to the New York Mets.

▶ Gertrude Ederle of the United States is the youngest world-record holder. She was 12 when she set the record for the women's 880-yard freestyle swim (13 minutes, 19 seconds) on August 17, 1919.

▶ At age 19, Dwight Gooden became the youngest major leaguer to appear in an All-Star Game. Al Kaline (20) was the youngest to win a batting title, and Vida Blue (22) the youngest to win an MVP Award.

▶ The youngest person to participate in a world title event was an anonymous French boy, who was coxswain for the Netherlands' gold medal-winning rowing pair at the 1900 Olympics. It is known that he was not more than 10 and perhaps as young as 7. He replaced the regular coxswain, who was deemed too heavy.

▶ With the formidable weight of the host country weighing on his formidable shoulders, Australian swimming phenom Ian Thorpe, 17, won four Olympic golds and one silver at the 2000 Sydney Games.

▶ Bob Mathias, at 17, was the youngest male track and field Olympic gold medalist ever when he won the 1948 decathlon.

▶ For a long time, before it became commonplace for high schoolers to join the NBA, three high schoolers—and three only—made the jump to the big time: Bill Willoughby was the youngest NBA player ever, debuting in 1975 at age 18 for the Atlanta Hawks. Darryl Dawkins also began at 18, while Moses Malone began his pro career at age 19, with Utah of the ABA.

In the last decade, numerous teenagers—notably, Kobe Bryant of the Los Angeles Lakers and Kevin Garnett of the Minnesota Timberwolves—have bypassed college for the pros, and thrived. In the 2001 NBA draft, high schoolers went as the #1, #2, #4, and #8 overall picks. With the top pick, the Washington Wizards selected Kwame Brown, a senior at Glynn Academy in Brunswick, Georgia, and the state's player of the year—the first time a high schooler was picked first.

▶ Twenty-two-year-old Gary Kasparov became the youngest world champion in chess history when he defeated 34-year-old Anatoly Karpov for the title in 1985. ·

▶ At the age of eight, Joy Foster represented Jamaica in the 1958 West Indian Championships in table tennis.

▶ In 1988, 11-year-old Thomas Gregory of England swam the English Channel.

▶ American Marjorie Gestring became the youngest individual Olympic gold medalist ever when she won the springboard diving title at the 1936 Berlin Games at age 13.

▶ In 1975, Houston McTear, 18 years old and a high school junior, equaled the world record in the 100-yard dash (9.0 seconds).

Men Among Boys, Women Among Girls: The Most Experienced Athletes of All Time

▶ When Florida State quarterback Chris Weinke won the Heisman Trophy in 2000, he was 28 years old.

▶ Hoyt Wilhelm was the first player still active in the major leagues while eligible for a pension.

▶ Because many foreign baseball players did not—at least until recently —have the chance to play in the major leagues at the start of their careers, when they do get the chance now, they're often fully bloomed talents. In 2001, Ichiro Suzuki joined the Seattle Mariners as a 27-year-old and an established star in Japan. Ichiro (who's popularly known by his first name) proceeded to win the American League Rookie of the Year Award. (He also won the MVP, becoming only the second major leaguer, along with Fred Lynn, to win both in their first year.) The year before Ichiro won it, the AL rookie award went to his Seattle teammate and fellow countryman, reliever Kazuhiro Sasaki, who was then 32.

▶ Gerhard Weidner of West Germany is the oldest world-record breaker. He was 41 when he set a 20-mile walk record on May 25, 1974.

▶ The oldest jockey to win the Kentucky Derby is Willie Shoemaker. He was 54 when he rode Ferdinand, who was trained by 73-year-old Charlie Whittingham, to the 1986 Derby win.

▶ Amos Alonzo Stagg coached the College of the Pacific football team at age 84, then assisted Amos Alonzo Stagg, Jr., his son, at Susquehanna University until he was 90. He retired from coaching at 98.

▶ Archie Moore, at 48, was the oldest boxer to hold a world title, the light-heavyweight crown. When George Foreman knocked out 26-year-old Michael Moorer on November 5, 1994, Foreman became the oldest heavyweight champion ever, at 45. He held onto the title until he was 48, joining Moore as the oldest-ever boxing world champ.

▶ The oldest Olympic gold medalist is Oscar C. Swahn, who, at 64, was part of the 1912 Olympic team running deer shooting competition. He won a silver medal in shooting at the 1920 Games, at age 72.

▶ In 1967, the Toronto Maple Leafs, with an average age of 31, became the oldest lineup ever to win the Stanley Cup. The 2002 Detroit Red Wings sported an average age of 30.6.

▶ In 1976, Minnie Minoso played in three major-league games for the Chicago White Sox at age 53, and became the oldest player to get a hit. He pinch-hit twice in 1980, at age 57, going 0-for-2.

It is surmised that Satchel Paige was 59 when he pitched in a 1965 game. He hurled three scoreless innings for the Kansas City Athletics, giving up one hit and striking out one.

▶ Hale Irwin is the oldest golfer to win the U.S. Open, doing so at age 45, in 1990.

▶ Nolan Ryan (44) is the oldest to throw a no-hitter, Warren Spahn (42) to win 20 games, and Ted Williams (40) to win a batting title.

▶ Gardner Mulloy is the oldest man to win a Wimbledon final. At age 43, he won the 1957 men's doubles title with Budge Patty. The oldest woman to win at Wimbledon is Margaret Osborne du Pont, who was 44 when she and Neale Fraser captured the 1962 mixed doubles crown.

▶ Masao Takemoto, a member of Japan's Olympic team in 1960 at age 40, became the oldest gymnastics gold medalist in history.

▶ In 1980, Hub Kittle became, at 63, the oldest man to appear in an organized baseball game when he started for Springfield, the AAA farm team for the St. Louis Cardinals, against Iowa in an American Association game. Kittle retired the side in order in the first inning and threw one pitch in the second inning before leaving the game.

▶ Sam Snead is the oldest winner of a PGA (non-Senior) tourney—the 1965 Greater Greensboro Open—at 52 years, 10 months, and became, in 1974, the oldest to make the cut at the Masters, at 61. He tied for third in the PGA championship in 1974 at age 62.

▶ Gordie Howe played 25 years in the NHL, six more in the WHA, then returned to the NHL in 1979–80 for one more year. As a 51-year-old grandfather, he made the all-star team.

▶ Clifford Batt of Australia, 68, swam the English Channel in 1987.

▶ Luke Appling, at age 75, hit a home run off of Warren Spahn in the 1981 Cracker Jack's Old-Timer's Game at RFK Stadium, in Washington, D.C. Dubbed "Home Run" Appling, he was suddenly in hot demand on the banquet circuit.

▶ In 1984, the horse John Henry, nine years old, won the Turf Classic at Belmont and the Arlington Million.

▶ Former Yale All-America guard William "Pudge" Heffelfinger played in an organized football game at age 66.

▶ Joe Sweeney, 71, was a member of the Salem (Massachusetts) State College tennis varsity.

25 Good Things About Sports

1. The penalty shot in hockey
2. The "love of the game" clause that Michael Jordan once had in his contract
3. Sudden-death
4. Nike ads
5. Sports talk-radio
6. Super slow-mo
7. Tailgate parties

8. Doubleheaders that aren't makeup doubleheaders

9. Plays of the Month

10. Plays of the Year

11. The Negro League Hall of Fame in Kansas City, Missouri, and its overseer, Buck O'Neil, who at age 89 remains an enthusiastic advocate and historian of the sport

12. Showing us the score in the corner of the screen all the time

13. Hockey's four-on-four-in-overtime rule

14. The projected yellow first-down marker

15. The expanded box score

16. Cleveland getting to keep the name and colors of its NFL team

17. The Brooklyn Cyclones—minor-league baseball in the shadow of Coney Island

18. The Gonzaga University men's basketball team

19. Spirals

20. Fantasy leagues

21. Sprawling hockey saves

22. Wrigley Field on a sunny day, with a full house, fans watching from the rooftops, and Lake Michigan shimmering in the background

23. The arc of the ball

24. The swish of the net

25. The crack of the bat

It Can All Change in an Instant

▶ On Sunday, February 18, 2001, the day NASCAR legend Dale Earnhardt was killed at the Daytona 500, the crash occurred on the final lap.

▶ In 1945, Snuffy Stirnweiss of the New York Yankees never led in the race for the American League batting title... until the very last day. He won it by .3085443 to .3084557 over Tony Cuccinello of the Chicago White Sox.

▶ The sudden death of a robustly healthy athlete is always jarring, but one particularly shattering example is that of Darryl Kile, 33-year-old pitcher and team leader for the St. Louis Cardinals, who had never been on the disabled list during nearly 12 years in the major leagues. With no warning, on June 22, 2002, he died of a heart attack from blockage of his coronary artery.

▶ Very soon after a pipe bomb exploded at the 1996 Atlanta Summer Olympic Games, killing one (a second person would die after rushing to the scene) and injuring 111, Richard Jewell, a security guard working at Olympic Park, would go from an unknown to hero (instantly) to villain (almost as instantly) to wronged man (not nearly so instantly, and with nowhere near the media coverage). Jewell was lauded for alerting police to a suspicious knapsack and helping to evacuate people moments before the bomb exploded... then was demonized after he became a suspect in the blast... then, later, had his name cleared by federal officials of any involvement. Jewell would claim that his name had been ruined forever.

▶ In one instant, he was a goat.

In a second instant (the following night), he was a goat for the ages. In a third instant (albeit a few days later), he was a very happy young man.

Byung-Hyun Kim, closer for the Arizona Diamondbacks, was victimized in two of the most crushing postseason losses imaginable, at Yankee Stadium during the 2001 World Series. One out from victory in Game 4 that would have put the Diamondbacks ahead three games to one, Kim gave up a stunning game-tying home run to Tino Martinez. In the 10th inning, he yielded a homer to Derek Jeter that lifted the Yankees to a 4-3 win. The next night, Kim was once again an out from victory in the ninth, protecting a 2-0 lead, before giving up a two-run homer to Scott Brosius that left the pitcher crouching in disbelief on the mound as teammates attempted to prop him up. Kim was removed from the game (eventually won by the Yankees, 3-2, in 12 innings) and didn't pitch again in the Series.

Two instants that might define Kim's life—certainly his baseball career—forever.

Kim was smiling and celebrating along with his teammates when Arizona, improbably, scored two runs in the ninth inning off of New York Yankees closer Mariano Rivera and won the clinching Game 7, 3-2. Kim, more than any other Diamondback—not to mention any other Earthling —could savor not only the series victory, but also the sudden change in fortune that earned him a reprieve from eternal baseball goat-hood.

Enough Already: Comments, Contests, and Ideas That Show Serious Signs of Getting Carried Away

Englishman Henry Higgins, a toreador in Spain, once said, "I would rather be gored in the Madrid ring than fail."

To paraphrase Alexander Woollcott: Not on our carpet, Hank.

Some more examples of excess:

▶ The seventh hole at the Sano Course at the Satsuki Golf Club in Japan is the longest in the world. It is par seven, 909 yards long.

▶ On December 29, 1989, at the funeral Mass for New York Yankee player and manager Billy Martin, Bishop Edwin Broderick said, "We gather here this morning not to celebrate Billy's way of life, but to pray that his is a safe slide into home plate. We pray as he negotiates his lifelong contract with St. Peter, that Billy would agree to play it out on the bench, in the bullpen, even in the locker room until the divine umpire, the inventor of instant replay, decides that Billy really is in shape for the eternal World Series..."

▶ Roger Clemens, king of the strikeout—known as "Ks" for short—has four sons: Koby, Kory, Kacy, and Kody. "The boys kept coming and the Ks kept coming," said Clemens.

▶ There have been four different AFLs (American Football League) in professional football history, the first one in 1926.

The name "New York Yankees" was used for four pro football teams in five leagues from 1926–49. If that wasn't enough, there was also a New York Yanks in the NFL in the 1950–51 seasons.

▶ After Australia won the America's Cup sailing competition for the first time ever in 1983, Australian broadcaster Rob Mundel called it "the race... of the millennium."

▶ In the 1912 Olympic middleweight Greco-Roman semifinal, Russia's Martin Klein and Finland's Alfred Asikainen wrestled outdoors for 11 hours, stopping every half hour for a refreshment break. Klein won by a pin but was too tired to compete in the final.

▶ To make sure their marriage "vows are kept sacred," Sacramento Kings guard Doug Christie and his wife Jackie abide by certain rules: Because she's uncomfortable that women working for the team enter the locker room to distribute statistics after the game, he dresses in another room; female reporters are not allowed to interview Christie unless his wife is present; and, with few exceptions, he avoids talking to, and even making eye contact with, other women.

▶ There have been six major-league players named William Moore.

▶ After he died, the heart of Pierre de Coubertin, the founder of the modern Olympics, was removed and placed in a monument in a sacred grove in Olympia, Greece.

▶ Following the 2000 baseball season, Texas Rangers owner Tom Hicks signed free-agent All-Star shortstop Alex Rodriguez to a $252 million, 10-year contract, far and away the largest deal in the history of professional baseball. While Rodriguez may well be the best player in the game, and put up sensational numbers in his first two seasons with the Rangers, it is widely agreed that Hicks—given the state of the market when he signed Rodriguez, and a very limited number of competing suitors (the New York Mets, for one, dropped out of the running almost immediately)—paid at least $50 million more than was necessary to land Rodriguez.

▶ Cleveland Municipal Stadium used to be 435 feet down each foul line. The distance from home plate to dead centerfield in New York's old Polo Grounds was 483 feet.

▶ The 2002 World Cup-winning Brazilian soccer team featured a Ronaldo, a Rivaldo, a Ronaldinho, and a Rogerio.

▶ The Miami Dolphins and the Oakland Raiders are the only NFL teams to have helmets painted on their helmets.

▶ French tennis great Suzanne Lenglen often entered the court wearing a fur coat, no matter how warm the weather.

▶ Canadian Diana Gordon-Lennox, downhill and slalom skier at the 1936 Olympics, wore a monocle while competing.

▶ English cyclist Tommy Simpson, who collapsed from fatigue and drugs in the 1967 Tour de France, said "Put me back on my bike" just before he died.

▶ The longest professional baseball game—a 1981 International League contest in which the Pawtucket Red Sox beat the Rochester Red Wings, 3-2, in 33 innings—took eight hours and 25 minutes of actual playing time but 66 days from start to finish, because the game was suspended before completion.

Davids Among Goliaths

▶ Robert James Fitzsimmons is the lightest heavyweight champion, 167 pounds, in history. He defeated James Corbett, March 17, 1897. The shortest heavyweight champ was Tommy Burn, at 5'7". He beat Marvin Hart on February 23, 1906.

▶ Houston Astros closer Billy Wagner, who may throw the fastest fastball in the major leagues at 100 mph (not infrequently, and not on inflated speed guns), is listed at 5'11".

▶ At 6'5", Charles Barkley is the shortest rebound champion in NBA history.

▶ Walter Payton, 5'10", held the NFL records for most number of carries, 3,692, and rushing yards, 16,193 (before Emmitt Smith broke them).

▶ Kenyan Tegla Loroupe, women's former marathon world-record holder and two-time winner of the New York City Marathon, stands 4'11" and weighs under 90 pounds.

▶ Barney Sedran, 5'4", starred at CCNY from 1909–11, and played on 10 pro basketball championship teams in 15 years.

▶ Wee Willie Keeler was 5'4½" and Hack Wilson 5'6". Both are in the Baseball Hall of Fame. Harry Chappas, 5'3", played shortstop for the Chicago White Sox from 1978–80.

▶ Although bareknuckles champion Tom Johnson was six inches shorter and 70 pounds lighter than Isaac Perrins, his opponent and challenger, he beat Perrins in one hour and 15 minutes, on October 22, 1789.

▶ Tyrone Bogues is the shortest NBA player ever, at 5'3½". Spud Webb, 5'7", won the NBA All-Star Slam Dunk competition in 1986.

▶ Scott Hamilton was 5'2½" and 108 pounds when he won the men's figure skating gold at the 1984 Winter Olympics.

▶ In an Olympic judo match in 1976, 5'6½", 259-pound Sumio Endo of Japan beat 7', 350-pound Jong-Gil Pak of North Korea

▶ Five-foot eight-inch, 135-pound Michael Chang won the 1989 French Open.

▶ Golfer Fred McLeod, winner of the 1908 U.S. Open, weighed 108 pounds.

▶ Young Zulu Kid, an American flyweight fighter, was 4'11". Jimmy Wilde, a flyweight world champion, weighed 96 pounds.

▶ St. Louis Brown Eddie Gaedel, who walked in his only major-league at-bat, stood 3'7" and weighed 65 pounds.

▶ In 1980, Liechtenstein's Hanni Wenzel won the slalom and giant slalom gold medals and the downhill silver, and her brother, Andreas, won the giant slalom silver. The Wenzels' four medals converted to one medal for every 6,250 people in the tiny country.

▷ Special honor to diminutive former New York Knicks head coach Jeff Van Gundy who, in trying to break up a fight between 6'7", 235-pound forward Larry Johnson of the Knicks and 6'10", 260-pound center Alonzo Mourning of the hated Miami Heat during a 1998 playoff game, found himself hanging onto Mourning's leg, much to onlookers' amazement and Mourning's irritation. Indeed, Mourning did not at first seem to notice that an entire human being was hanging, seemingly for his life, onto his leg, and had to shake him off as one does a bug.

Hypocrites, Liars & Cheaters

Lest we paint with too broad a brush, we break this into two sub-lists: Hypocrites, and Liars & Cheaters. They've been around as long as sports have (and before, we're sure); we document here some morsels from the last several years.

Hypocrites:

▶ On the eve of the first-ever Super Bowl in the history of the Atlanta Falcons franchise, veteran safety and team leader Eugene Robinson was arrested for soliciting oral sex from an undercover Miami police officer. Hours before, the Christian group Athletes in Action had presented to Robinson, married with children, the Bart Starr Award, given to the NFL player who best displays "high moral character." (The next day, the Falcons seemed distracted and flat in the Super Bowl; Robinson was burned on one of the game's key plays, an 80-yard touchdown reception by Denver Broncos receiver Rod Smith, which gave the Broncos a 17-3 lead late in the first half.)

▶ Arizona Diamondbacks manager Bob Brenly prides himself on being an "old school" baseball man—so how does he defend his outrage over the eighth-inning bunt single by Ben Davis of the San Diego Padres, which broke up Curt Schilling's perfect game on May 26, 2001? Brenly fumed that Davis had broken baseball's unwritten code that says you don't bunt to break up a perfect game or no-hitter.

"The way I was raised in this game, the guys who taught me how to play the game when I was coming up taught me there's a certain respect for the game, respect for the opponents, especially when they're doing something exceptional," Brenly said. "And there's no question that's what Curt was doing."

But the Padres were only trailing 2-0 at the time, and Davis's hit brought the tying run to the plate. Doesn't the "old school" approach dictate, first and foremost, that teams should respect the game by using all the means at their disposal to win it?

▶ We won't comment on specific actions taken by Baseball Commissioner Bud Selig, whose job is to act in the "best interest of the game" … nor are we questioning his integrity. We *would* like to ask, though, how Selig—owner of the Milwaukee Brewers who placed his share of the team in a trust when he became commissioner in 1998, and whose daughter, Wendy Selig-Prieb, was team president until the fall of 2002 (when she became board chairperson)—can act impartially (as much as it's reasonable to ask someone to do)? Anyone? Could the reasoning behind our question perhaps be at the core of why baseball seems, sadly, to be descending into antiquatedness and, ultimately, irrelevancy?

▶ Following the Green Bay Packers Super Bowl victory in 1997, All-Pro tight end Mark Chmura skipped the trip to the White House because he said he didn't want to shake the hand of President Bill Clinton, for whom he had little respect after the Monica Lewinsky scandal.

Four years later, Chmura, then 31, was acquitted of sexually assaulting his children's 17-year-old babysitter but agreed to pay a fine for contributing to underage drinking at the same party where the alleged assault occurred. "He took active participation as an adult," by playing a drinking game with several teens, District Attorney Paul Bucher contended. Waukesha County (Wisconsin) Circuit Judge Mark Gempeler agreed, saying that, "It's difficult for me to come to any other conclusion" than that Chmura was guilty (of contributing to underage drinking).

▶ Not so much hypocrisy as it is a case of "Do as I say, not as I do": Tennis great John McEnroe, perhaps the most ill-behaved, put-upon tennis player of all-time, has forged a reputation as perhaps the finest tennis commentator on television. When players rant against officials or seem to be distracted by possibly mistaken line calls, McEnroe is not hesitant to admonish them, from afar, that they'd be much better off forgetting about it, and just playing the game.

▶ And not so much hypocrisy as a case of "It sure *sounds* like hypocrisy but maybe it's not, if I'd only just look at it really carefully for a long time...but I did that, and you know what? It really *is* hypocrisy": When Tiger Woods—who, through his brilliant ability and competitiveness, has broken numerous barriers in the generally white world of professional golf—was asked what he thought about Augusta National, site of the Masters, not having any women members, or that Muirfield, the Scottish course that served as the site of the 2002 British Open, does not allow women even in the clubhouse, he said: "It's one of those things where everyone has... they're entitled to set up their own rules the way they want them. It would be nice to see everyone have an equal chance to participate if they wanted to, but there's nothing you can do about it." Woods, who years ago would not have been able to play in certain Grand Slam tournaments because of his color, claimed that his answer would be the same if the golf club involved admitted no blacks or Asians. "It's unfortunate," he said. "But it's just the way it is."

Liars & Cheaters:

▶ As a first-year manager with the Toronto Blue Jays in 1998, Tim Johnson led the Blue Jays to their first winning season since 1993. But during the year, the team discovered that Johnson had been lying about his claims of serving in Vietnam. He would often try to inspire players with stories about his combat duty, including a false story about shooting a young girl. Johnson, a former Marine, taught mortar training to recruits going to Vietnam, but didn't serve there. Johnson made a public apology and announced plans to seek counseling, but when the issue continued to dog him the following spring, the Blue Jays fired Johnson during spring training of 1999 and replaced him with Jim Fregosi.

▶ Danny Almonte became a national celebrity in the summer of 2001, first for his staggering pitching during the Little League World Series, then for the scandal that followed. The lefthander, representing the Rolando Paulino team from the Bronx in New York City, struck out 46 in three starts, including a 16-strikeout perfect game, the first in 44 years at the Series, as the Bronx team finished third. Almonte was compared to Randy Johnson, who even called to offer his congratulations.

It was later discovered, however, that Almonte was not 12, the maximum age for Little Leaguers, but actually 14. All of the team's victories, as well as Almonte's perfect game, were expunged from the record. Paulino, founder of the Bronx team, was banned for life from any association with Little League baseball, and Almonte's father, Felipe, briefly faced charges in the Dominican Republic for falsifying his son's birth records.

▶ Irish swimmer Michelle Smith, the surprise star of the 1996 Olympics in Atlanta when she won three gold medals, was subjected to immediate suspicion that she had used performance-enhancing drugs. The rumors were vehemently—and indignantly—denied by Smith and the Irish delegation, who accused the Americans of poor sportsmanship.

"I just have to laugh at [the accusations]," Smith said. "Every time I'm tested it's always negative. For every one time a person on the U.S. national team is tested, I'm tested five times."

"They (the Americans) are jealous that a little country like Ireland took a gold medal off them," said Pat Hickey, president of the Irish Olympic Committee. "The Americans are doing all they can to get Michelle Smith thrown out... It's scandalous."

In January of 1998, Smith was banned by the international swimming federation (FINA) after finding that she had contaminated a urine sample with alcohol during an out-of-competition test. The alcohol could mask the presence of banned drugs. Although Smith claimed that a third party manipulated the samples, an arbitration panel upheld the ban, which made her ineligible for the 2000 Sydney Olympics and effectively ended her career.

▶ In December of 2000, former Georgia Tech football coach George O'Leary landed his dream job: head coach at the University of Notre Dame. But he lasted less than a week. When it was revealed that O'Leary had lied on his résumé, falsely claiming for nearly 20 years that he had a master's degree in education from New York University, and had earned three letters in football at the University of New Hampshire, he stepped down as Notre Dame coach. Actually, O'Leary had attended UNH for just two years and didn't play in any games.

With scrutiny increased after the O'Leary incident, other examples of résumé fraud soon surfaced. Rick Smith, the defensive coordinator hired at Georgia Tech by O'Leary's replacement, resigned after it was found that he had twice provided false information in his bio while at Georgia Tech in the late 1970s and early 1980s. He claimed to have played football and baseball at Florida State University, when he did neither. In May of 2002, U.S. Olympic Committee president Sandra Baldwin resigned after admitting she'd lied about her academic credentials. In June of 2002, Charles Harris stepped down as Dartmouth's athletic director hours before the press conference to introduce him in the job. Dartmouth's dean said questions arose about Harris's representation of his educational record to a previous employer. Harris had included a master's degree in journalism from Michigan that he didn't earn, though he was enrolled in the program. The next day, Blair Hrovat resigned as football coach at Allegheny College after admitting that his resume incorrectly listed a bachelor's degree from Edinboro University. Hrovat had held the job since 1998.

▶ In 1984, Puerto Rico pulled out of the 4x400m relay finals when it learned that Margaret de Jesus, who was not a team member, had substituted for her twin sister, Madeline de Jesus, in the qualifying heat. Madeline had injured herself in the long jump.

The Greatest Debuts and Starts

On April 25, 1933, New York Yankees rookie Russ Van Atta, in his first start, hurled a five-hit shutout over the pennant-bound Washington Senators in Griffith Stadium, went 4-for-4 at the plate, scored three runs, knocked in one, and the Yanks won, 16-0.

Here are the best examples of athletes and teams who started things —their careers, a season, a game—in spectacular fashion.

▶ On October 30, 1943, Toronto Maple Leaf Gus Bodnar scored a goal against the New York Rangers 15 seconds into the first period of his first NHL game.

▶ Bennie Oosterbaan, assistant football coach at the University of Michigan, became the head coach in 1948, won all nine games and the national title, the first and only man to do that in his first year as head coach.

Forty-one years later, Steve Fisher replaced Bill Frieder as head coach of Michigan's basketball team as the NCAA tournament started, and led them to their first-ever national championship. He is the only coach known to have won a national title before he had won a regular-season game.

▶ Jockey Steve Cauthen won the Kentucky Derby in his first attempt, riding Affirmed in 1978.

▶ In Nancy Lopez's first full season on the LPGA tour, she won nine tournaments, including a record five in a row.

▶ Minnesota Vikings quarterback Fran Tarkenton threw four touchdown passes in his first NFL game, a 1961 victory over the Chicago Bears.

▶ On May 6, 1953, St. Louis Brown Alva Lee "Bobo" Holloman became the only major leaguer in the modern era to throw a no-hitter in his first start (he had pitched in relief four times before that).

▶ Pittsburgh Steelers running back Franco Harris's famous "Immaculate Reception" in 1972 was made in the first playoff game of his career.

▶ On September 14, 1951, Bob Nieman of the St. Louis Browns became the only player to homer in his first two major-league at-bats.

Gary Gaetti, Bert Campaneris, and Chuck Tanner, among others, all hit the first major-league pitch they ever saw for home runs.

With his first big league swing, San Francisco Giants first baseman Will Clark hit a homer off of all-time strikeout king Nolan Ryan.

In June of 2002, on the first pitch he saw in the major leagues, New York Yankee Marcus Thames hit a home run off of future Hall of Famer Randy Johnson.

▶ In the first game of the 1951 season, Los Angeles Rams quarterback Norm Van Brocklin threw for an NFL-record 554 yards against the New York Yankees football team at the Los Angeles Coliseum.

▶ At age 16, Aaron Krickstein won the first tournament he entered as a professional, the Israel Tennis Center Classic.

▶ Dick "Night Train" Lane set the NFL record for most interceptions in a season, 14, when he was a rookie.

▶ Marvell Wynne, Tony Gwynn, and Jack Clark hit back-to-back-to-back home runs on Opening Day, 1989, for the San Diego Padres. It was the first time that feat was achieved on the first day of the season.

▶ Wilt Chamberlain, in 1959–60, and Wes Unseld, in 1968–69, are the only two players to be named NBA MVPs in their rookie years.

▶ Boston Red Sox outfielder Fred Lynn and Seattle Mariner outfielder Ichiro Suzuki are the only two baseball players to win the major-league MVP Award in their rookie years (when—here's a shocker—they each won the Rookie of the Year Award, too).

▶ In his first start for the California Angels after signing as a free agent, Mark Langston combined with Mike Witt to pitch a 10-inning no-hitter, on April 11, 1990. Langston worked the first seven innings.

▶ The Atlanta Braves won their first 13 games in 1982. The Milwaukee Brewers won their first 13 games of the 1987 season.

▶ In his first college game, LSU wide receiver Carlos Carson caught five passes, all for touchdowns.

▶ On May 21, 1952, the Brooklyn Dodgers scored 15 runs in the first inning against the Cincinnati Reds.

▶ Toe Blake coached the Montreal Canadiens to the Stanley Cup in his first five years as coach, from 1955–56 to 1959–60.

▶ In 2001, Jason Jennings of the Colorado Rockies became the first major-league pitcher to throw a shutout and hit a home run in his first major-league game.

▶ In 1940, Cleveland Indians pitcher Bob Feller became the only pitcher to throw an Opening Day no-hitter.

▶ Cecil Travis got five hits in his first major-league game.

▶ In 1977, Ted Cox got six hits in his first six official at-bats for the Boston Red Sox.

▶ Walter Johnson pitched seven Opening Day shutouts.

▶ The Dallas Cowboys had an Opening Day win streak of 17 years, from 1965 to 1981.

▶ In his first NHL game on February 14, 1977, Philadelphia Flyer Al Hill scored five points.

▶ On April 12, 1962, Pete Richert struck out the first six major-league batters he ever faced.

▶ Dave "Boo" Ferris began his pitching career with 22 consecutive scoreless innings.

▶ Tony Lema won the British Open on his first try, in 1964.

▶ In 1961–62, New York Yankees manager Ralph Houk became the first man to lead his team to World Series victories in his first two years at the helm. In 1963, he again won the pennant.

▶ In his first five full seasons in the majors, Chuck Klein won four home run titles.

▶ In his rookie year in the NHL, Wayne Gretzky led the league in scoring and assists, won the Hart Trophy as league MVP, and the Lady Byng Trophy for gentlemanly play and effectiveness.

▶ Baltimore Colts kicker Jim O'Brien was a rookie when he made a field goal with five seconds left to beat the Dallas Cowboys in Super Bowl V.

▶ Si Re Pak and Juli Inkster are the only golfers to have won two majors in their rookie year on the LPGA tour. Pak, the youngest winner of the U.S. Open, won eight times in her first two years on the tour.

▶ Jack Nicklaus won the U.S. Open in his first year on the tour, and added the Masters and PGA after less than two years as a pro.

▶ In his freshman year, University of Louisville center Pervis Ellison won the 1988 Final Four MVP Award.

▶ New York Giants pitcher Rube Marquard won his first 19 decisions in the 1912 season.

▶ Hank Aaron hit his 714th home run, tying him with Babe Ruth, with his first swing of the 1974 season.

▶ From 1937 to 1949, the New York Yankees did not lose a World Series Game 1. They won nine in a row during that stretch.

▶ In 1934, Chicago Bear Beattie Feathers became the first NFL back ever to gain over 1,000 yards, and he did it in his rookie year.

▶ Joe Jackson hit .408 in his first full season, with the 1911 Cleveland Indians.

▶ In 1973, Ben Crenshaw won his first tournament as a member of the PGA. Robert Gamez repeated that feat to win the Tucson Open in January of 1990.

▶ Michigan State placekicker Rolf Mojsiejenko's first field-goal attempt in college, against Illinois in 1982, was a successful 61-yarder.

8 Openings Not to Write Home About

▶ In his NHL debut on January 10, 1980, Boston Bruins goalie Jim Stewart gave up three goals in the first four minutes, and two more goals before the first period ended. He was yanked with the score 5-2, sent to the minors, and never played in the NHL again.

▶ Kevin Cogan, starting from the front row at the 1982 Indianapolis 500, initiated a pile-up during the 80mph pace lap that knocked Mario Andretti, Roger Mears, Dale Whittington, and himself out of the race before it had even begun.

▶ Brazil's Maria de Amorin served 17 double faults in a row at the start of her first match at Wimbledon in 1957. She lost to Mrs. L. Thung of Holland, 3-6, 6-4, 1-6.

▶ On July 11, 1974, when the Jacksonville Sharks and the New York Stars met in the World Football League's first nationally televised game, the lights at the Gator Bowl went out at halftime, delaying the start of the second half for 10 minutes.

▶ In his major-league debut on May 18, 1912, Aloysius J. Travers gave up 14 runs and 26 hits. It was his only game.

▶ The Baltimore Orioles began the 1988 season by losing 21 games in a row, a major-league record for the start of a season.

▶ In 29 seasons under head coach Tom Landry, the Dallas Cowboys were shut out twice. In Jimmy Johnson's first season as Dallas head coach, they were shut out three times.

▶ On February 4, 1987, the Sacramento Kings went 9:06 before scoring a point against the Los Angeles Lakers at the Forum. At the time, the score was 29-0. In the quarter, the Kings were outscored 40-4 and went 0-18 from the field. They did not make a field goal until the second quarter, on their 22nd attempt.

Impressive Examples of Versatility

The following athletes have shown a rare ability to perform a variety of skills, or a singular skill in different ways, or in different places.

Point is: They're versatile.

▶ Al Oerter won four consecutive Olympic discus gold medals, each on a different continent.

▶ As a quarterback, Washington Redskin Sammy Baugh holds the NFL record for highest average gain per pass in a game (24 passes for 446 yards, average gain per pass of 18.58 yards, on October 31, 1948, against Boston). As a punter, Baugh holds the NFL record for highest yard-per-punt average in a season (35 punts for 1,799 yards, a 51.4 yard-per-punt average, in 1940). As a defensive back, he co-holds the record for most interceptions in a game, four, against Detroit, November 14, 1943.

▶ Dave Kingman played for four teams in 1977, one in each of the (then-) four divisions: the New York Mets (NL East), the San Diego Padres (NL West), the New York Yankees (AL East), and the California Angels (AL West).

▶ John Wooden was elected to the Basketball Hall of Fame as a player in 1960, and then re-honored as a coach in 1972. Lenny Wilkens is the only other person honored as both player and coach.

▶ Bob Fitzsimmons held the heavyweight, light-heavyweight, and middleweight boxing titles at different times during his career. Georges Carpentier fought in every weight division from featherweight to heavyweight. Ted "Kid" Lewis of England fought successfully in all divisions from bantamweight to heavyweight.

▶ Veikko Hakulinen of Finland won three gold medals, each in a different event (50km Nordic skiing, 30km race, and 4x10km relay), each in a different Olympics (1952, 1956, 1960).

▶ Baseball history had never seen a "40-40" player—someone strong enough to hit 40 home runs and fleet enough to steal 40 bases in the same season—until Jose Canseco did it in 1988. Barry Bonds and Alex Rodriguez were next to join the exclusive club.

In 2002, Alfonso Soriano and Vladimir Guerrero just missed joining the club, and had to settle for being the charter members of a still-impressive, only marginally dubious, and likely to be even more exclusive club: those with 40 or more stolen bases and exactly 39 home runs.

▶ Ex-New York Jet Joe Klecko made the Pro Bowl at three different positions. Denver Bronco Karl Mecklenburg has played seven different positions.

▶ Rusty Staub is the only man to play at least 500 games with four different teams (the Houston Astros, the Montreal Expos, the New York Mets, and the Detroit Tigers).

▶ When he was at the University of Minnesota in the late 1920s, Bronko Nagurski was named All-America as both fullback and defensive tackle in the same season.

▶ Wilt Chamberlain is the only person to lead the NBA, at various times, in scoring, rebounding, and assists in a season.

▶ In 1978, Cleveland Indian Andre Thornton hit for the cycle (single, double, triple, home run), with each hit coming off of a different pitcher.

▶ Andre Agassi has won tennis titles with long hair, with short hair, and bald.

▶ In 1999, St. Louis Rams running back Marshall Faulk became the second player, along with former San Francisco 49er Roger Craig (who did it in 1985), to gain more than 1,000 yards each rushing and receiving in a single season.

▶ Rick Barry won scoring titles in the NCAA, the ABA, and the NBA.

▶ Switch-hitters Garry Templeton and Willie Wilson are the only two players to get 100 or more hits from both sides of the plate in a season.

On April 30, 1979, Gary Pellant of the Carolina League Alexandria Mariners became the first professional baseball player to hit a home run from opposite sides of the plate in the same inning.

▶ Bert Campaneris and Cesar Tovar were the first two major leaguers to play every position (except DH) on the field in a single game.

▶ Hank Greenberg, Stan Musial, and Robin Yount are the only major leaguers to win MVP Awards at different positions.

▶ Jimmy Connors won the U.S. Open tennis title on three different surfaces. He won on grass in 1974, on clay in 1976, and on hardcourt in

1978, 1982, and 1983. Billie Jean King is the only woman to win U.S. singles titles on all four surfaces: grass, clay, carpet, and hard.

▶ Carl Westergren won three Greco-Roman Olympic golds, each in a different division.

▶ The 1965 Los Angeles Dodgers had an all-switch-hitting infield of Wes Parker, Jim Lefebvre, Maury Wills, and Jim Gilliam.

▶ In 1993, Charlie Ward won the Heisman Trophy as quarterback of the national champion Florida State Seminoles. The following spring, he was drafted by the New York Knicks and, through the 2001–02 season, had played in the NBA for eight years.

▶ In one 1989 game against the New Jersey Devils, Pittsburgh Penguin Mario Lemieux scored five goals: one shorthanded, one on a penalty shot, one on a power play, one at even strength, and one into an empty net.

8 *Really* Impressive Examples of Versatility

▶ Transsexual Renée Richards is the only tennis player to compete in both the men's and women's draw in the U.S. Championships: As Richard Raskin in 1960, she lost 6-0, 6-1, 6-1 in the first round to Neale Fraser; as Richards in 1977, she lost 6-1, 6-4 in the first round to Virginia Wade.

▶ Karoly Takacs, a member in 1938 of Hungary's world championship pistol shooting team, had his right hand—his shooting hand—severely damaged by a grenade. Takacs switched to his left hand and won the gold medal 10 years later, in 1948.

▶ Lamar Johnson, first baseman/designated hitter for the Chicago White Sox, sang the National Anthem before a 1977 game, then hit two home runs and a double—Chicago's only hits—in a 2-1 victory.

▶ Martina Navratilova played on winning Federation Cup teams for two different nations—Czechoslovakia in 1975, and the United States in 1982 and 1986.

▶ Stan Kasten is president of the Atlanta (baseball) Braves, the Atlanta (basketball) Hawks, and the Atlanta (hockey) Thrashers.

▶ Hank Gowdy is the only major leaguer to have served both in World Wars I and II.

▶ In the 1940s, the Bluegrass All-Stars barnstormed throughout the Southeast, performing their music at the ballpark and then taking on the local baseball team.

▶ Dora Ratjen, fourth in the 1936 Olympic high jump, was discovered to be a hermaphrodite and banned from competition in 1938.

11 Streaks to Forget

▶ An Englishman has not won his "home" tennis singles title—Wimbledon—since Fred Perry did it in 1936.

▶ In the 2001 World Series, New York Yankees outfielder David Justice struck out in eight consecutive at-bats, a Series record.

▶ No Frenchman has won his country's—and the world's—most prestigious bike race, the Tour de France, since 1985, when the great Bernard Hinault won his fifth title. It's the longest drought for the home country since the race's inception in 1903.

▶ In 2002, the New York Mets went 0-for-August: They tied a National League record for home ineptitude by losing every single game—14 straight—that they played that month at Shea Stadium. In their first home date in September—the initial game of a doubleheader—they also lost, giving them the new record of 15 straight home losses. (Mercifully, that was as far as it went, as the Mets took the nightcap, winning at Shea for the first time since July 31st.)

▶ In 1997, Las Vegas-based professional handicapper Tony Diamond, respected among peers for his solid game-picking ability, went on an unenviable tear when he bet on the wrong NBA team (against the spread) 27 times in a row. A math professor at the University of Nevada at Las Vegas calculated the odds of such a streak at roughly 4.5 million-to-1.

▶ For just shy of a full decade—from November 1989 through September 1998—Prairie View A&M (Texas) University, a Division I-AA school, lost 80 consecutive football games, a national record.

  From 1983–88, Columbia University lost 44 straight games.

▶ As of September 2002, Zippy Chippy, an 11-year-old gelding, was 0-for-96 in horse races, many of those at Finger Lakes Race Track. The encouraging news is that Northampton (Massachusetts) track where Zippy Chippy now races is the bottom rung on the thoroughbred racing circuit. The discouraging news is that Northampton is the bottom rung on the thoroughbred racing circuit... and Zippy Chippy is 0-for-96. And counting.

▶ In pro football, the Tampa Bay Buccaneers went 26 straight games, over nearly two full seasons—1976–77, which were, not surprisingly, their *first* two seasons—knowing only losing.

▶ Through the fall of 2002, Winston Cup driver Mike Skinner had entered 194 races, and won exactly... none. Not only doesn't he win, but he almost always (20 of 27 races in 2002) finishes in lower position than where he started. His average start was 20.8; his average finish was 28.5. To give one example, Skinner qualified fifth for the New Hampshire 300, in September of 2002. The engine on his No. 4 Kodak Film Chevy surrendered on the 41st lap, and Skinner finished in 43rd place, out of 43 participants.

▶ For two months in 1980, the NHL's Winnipeg Jets went 30 games without a win.

9 of the Most Memorable Days in Sports History

When Atlanta Braves slugger Bob Horner hit four home runs in a 1986 game against the Chicago Cubs, becoming only the 11th major leaguer to do so, he said after the game, "I had a good week today." It's a line that's often dusted off when an athlete (or team) has that rare kind of day when everything is so well-synched that he or she performs better than ever, maybe even seeming to exceed his or her capabilities, a day when records fall, often by the bushel, a day when heroic pictures are burned into the mind's eye... in short, the kind of day that, years later, at least 500,000 people claim to have attended, live.

▶ *July 23, 1952*: Brazil's Adhemar Ferreira da Silva breaks his own triple-jump world record four times in six attempts in the Olympic finals.

▶ *May 25, 1935*: At the Big Ten championships at Ann Arbor, Michigan, Jesse Owens breaks five world records and equals a sixth in 45 minutes. At 3:15 P.M., he wins the 100-yard dash in 9.4 seconds to tie the world record; at 3:25, he long-jumps—his only attempt of the day—26'8¼" for a world record that will stand for 25 years; at 3:45, he runs the 220-yard dash in 20.3 seconds for a world record, and is also credited with the world record in the 200m; at 4:00 P.M., he runs the 220-yard low hurdles in 22.6 seconds, the first time anyone breaks 23 seconds. He is also given credit for the world record in the 200m hurdles.

▶ *October 25, 1974*: John Bunch of Elkins (Arizona) High School rushes for 608 yards against Winslow High School.

▶ *April 26, 1905*: It's not hard to choose the defensive star of the game as Chicago Cubs centerfielder Jack McCarthy starts three double plays, a feat no other outfielder has ever accomplished, and each runner he shoots down represents the tying run. The Cubs beat the Pittsburgh Pirates, 2-1.

▶ *November 8, 1980*: Across America, passing records fall like autumn leaves. Portland State's Neil Lomax throws for eight touchdowns, including a record seven in the first quarter, in a 105-0 win over Delaware State. Illinois' Dave Wilson throws for a Big Ten-record 621 yards and six TDs against Ohio State; Purdue's Mark Herrmann also surpasses the old record with 439 yards against Iowa; Duke's Ben Bennett passes for an Atlantic Coast Conference record 469 yards against Wake Forest; and Washington's Tom Flick sets an NCAA record by completing 16 of 17 passes (94.1 percent) against Arizona. (BYU's Jim McMahon manages only 464 yards that day against North Texas State.)

▶ *October 16, 1976*: In College Station, Texas, Texas A&M placekicker Tony Franklin makes three field goals against Baylor, by no means an extraordinary day for a kicker, but one is a 64-yarder, another a 65-yarder. That's not all, though: 300 miles away, in a game against East Texas State, Ove Johannson of Abilene Christian University kicks a 69-yard field goal, the longest in the history of football.

▶ *June 29, 1990*: Oakland As pitcher Dave Stewart throws a no-hitter against the Toronto Blue Jays, and Los Angeles Dodger Fernando Valenzuela does the same against the St. Louis Cardinals. It's the first time in the 20th century that two pitchers throw complete-game no-hitters on the same day.

▶ *July 4, 1932*: Babe Didrickson enters the women's AAU championships (which also serves as the Olympic trials) as a one-woman team. She takes part in 8 of the 10 events and wins 6 of them, setting world records in the 80m hurdles, the javelin, and the high jump. She also wins the shot put, long jump, and baseball throw, and is fourth in the discus. She wins the team title with 30 points, earning 8 points more than the 22-woman group from the University of Illinois.

▶ *April 20, 1912*: The Boston Red Sox play the first game ever at Fenway Park, and the Detroit Tigers play the first game ever at Tiger Stadium. (Both home teams win.)

▷ Honorable mention: to the *weekend* of August 6–8, 1999: On Friday, Mark McGwire hits his 500th home run; on Saturday, Tony Gwynn gets his 3,000th hit; on Sunday, Wade Boggs gets *his* 3,000th hit.

11

THE GAME AND
THE PLAYERS

●●●●●●●●●●●●●●

Clutch

▶ In the 1993 NCAA women's basketball championship final, Sheryl Swoopes scored an *is-that-a-typo?* 47 points—an NCAA record for a title game—to lead Texas Tech to an 84-82 squeaker over Ohio State.

▶ On September 20, 1999, now-Cleveland Indians outfielder Milton Bradley lived out *the* baseball dream, though at the minor-league level: In the bottom of the 9th inning… of the deciding fifth game… of the Eastern League championship series… with two outs…bases loaded …his Harrisburg Senators down by three runs to the Norwich Navigators… and, yes, with a 3-2 count… Bradley hit a grand slam to lift his team to a 12-11 win and the title.

▶ In 1993, the Montreal Canadiens won the Stanley Cup in thrilling, utterly clutch fashion: They won two overtime games in the first round of the playoffs, three in the second round, two in the third, and three in the finals against the Los Angeles Kings. Their incredible 10 overtime playoff victories in one postseason is far and away the record.

▶ Reggie Jackson was forever branded as "Mr. October" in Game 6 of the 1977 World Series, when he hit three homers on three consecutive swings for the Yankees to lead them over the Dodgers, 8-4, in the title-clinching game. Babe Ruth is the only other player to hit three homers in a World Series game. In 21 seasons, Jackson played on 11 division champions, six pennant winners, and five World Series winners. He hit .357 with 10 homers and 24 RBI in 27 Series games.

▶ Pete Sampras's record in Grand Slam tennis singles finals is 14-4.

▶ Whatever team outfielder David Justice has been on has reached the postseason every year since 1991 (except for 1994, when there was no postseason).

▶ Over the past decade, pitcher Randy Johnson's record in the critical month of September is 28 wins and... 1 loss.

▶ Much to the dismay of University of Kentucky basketball fans, Christian Laettner of Duke University nailed one of the most difficult, ice-water-in-the-veins shots in NCAA tournament history. In an epic 1992 overtime battle in Philadelphia, the #2-ranked Kentucky Wildcats seemed finally to have taken control of their Elite Eight match-up with the top-ranked Blue Devils when Kentucky guard Sean Woods hit a running one-hander with 2.5 seconds left, giving UK a 103-102 edge. After a Duke timeout with 2.1 seconds, Grant Hill threw a pass three-quarters of the length of the court. Laettner, his back to the basket, caught the ball, turned in the key, and hit a jumper with two Kentucky defenders in his face. Laettner hit for 31 points in the game, shooting an incredible 20-for-20: He made all ten of his field goal attempts, and all ten of his free throw attempts. Duke would win the national title that year, and the shot has been replayed on television many, many, many times—not enough "many"s if you're from Durham, at least three too many if you're from Lexington.

And if it all seemed familiar? It was: In the Elite Eight match-up two years before, Laettner hit a buzzer-beating 15-footer, in overtime, to deny the top-ranked University of Connecticut Huskies. third-ranked Duke would make it to the 1990 title game.

▶ After the Minnesota Twins rallied to win Game 6 of the 1991 World Series against the Atlanta Braves on Kirby Puckett's 11th-inning home run, their announced starter for Game 7, Jack Morris, told reporters, "In the immortal words of the late, great Marvin Gaye, 'let's get it on.'" The 36-year-old Morris then went out and turned in one of the great clutch performances in World Series history, blanking the Braves for 10 innings before the Twins finally pushed across the Series-clinching run in the bottom of the 10th on Gene Larkin's one-out, bases-loaded single. Twins manager Tom Kelly intended to pull Morris after nine innings, but he told Kelly, "I have a lot left."

▶ In his first ten games against Top 10 opponents as football coach at the University of Oklahoma, Bob Stoops lost only once.

▶ Throughout the 1990s, John Smoltz was the pitcher the Atlanta Braves most wanted to start in games they had to win. Before the New York Yankees beat him in Game 4 of the 1999 World Series to complete a sweep, Smoltz had been 3-0 with two no-decisions in five postseason starts when Atlanta faced elimination. One of the no-decisions was his brilliant seven-inning shutout effort against the Minnesota Twins in Game 7 of the 1991 World Series (see previous page), a game in which Jack Morris worked 10 shutout innings and the Twins won it, 1-0, in the 10th inning. Now Smoltz is the pitcher the Braves most want to *finish* games they have to win. In 2002, his first full season as a closer, Smoltz set a National League record with 55 saves.

▶ Through September 2002, Tiger Woods had been in seven playoffs in PGA events, and had won six of them, including the 2000 PGA Championship.

▶ Although veteran third baseman Robin Ventura has long been a very good player, he's not among the league's elite—except when it comes to coming through with bases loaded. Ventura is the major league's active leader in grand slams with 16, tied with Babe Ruth, Hank Aaron, and Dave Kingman for sixth-best all-time. In 162 at-bats with the bases loaded (through July 28, 2002, when he hit his 16th slam against the Tampa Bay Devil Rays), Ventura was 58-for-162 (.358) with a beefy 193 RBI.

▶ No one in the NBA is more renowned for his ability to hit clutch shots, especially in the playoffs, especially in the Finals, than Robert Horry. A member of five championship teams—twice with the Houston Rockets, three times with the Los Angeles Lakers—his contributions are made even more impressive when one considers that he's not a star but just an above-average—not much above-average—player during the regular season, and even for parts of the postseason—those parts that aren't in the fourth quarter, or when the game hangs in the balance. What makes Horry's reputation more impressive *still* is that the 6'10" forward does almost all of his clutch work from behind the three-point arc. Although one could put together a lengthy catalogue of all of his clutch three-pointers, Horry's most recent memorable one—a top-of-the-arc trey, with one second left to beat the Sacramento Kings, 100-99, in Game 4 of the 2002 Western Conference finals, knotting the series at two games—may well have been the difference in the Lakers "three-peating" or not.

▶ Although a middling player who drifted through four organizations, Craig Counsell played a significant role in two World Series championships (so far). As a member of the 1997 Florida Marlins (after starting the year in the minor leagues in the Colorado Rockies' organization), Counsell hit .421 (8-for-19) in the first two rounds of the playoffs, then delivered a sacrifice fly in the bottom of the 9th inning of Game 7 of the World Series, pulling the Marlins into a 2-2 tie with Cleveland. In the 11th inning, Counsell scored the deciding run on Edgar Renteria's bases-loaded single. In the 2002 postseason with the Arizona Diamondbacks, Counsell delivered a three-run home run that provided the winning margin in a victory over the St. Louis Cardinals in the division series; was named the MVP of the National League Championship Series after hitting .381 with 5 runs, 3 doubles, and 4 RBI against the Atlanta Braves; and scored Arizona's first run in the World Series with a

Game 1 homer off the Yankees' Mike Mussina, tied a record in Game 4 with three sacrifice bunts in his first three plate appearances, and was hit by a Mariano Rivera pitch to load the bases just ahead of Luis Gonzalez's series-winning hit in the ninth inning of Game 7.

The Most Notable Delays, Postponements, and Cancellations

▶ The first Wimbledon final in 1877 was delayed a day so that fans could watch the Eton vs. Harrow cricket match, which always took place on the second Saturday in July.

▶ On September 15, 1946, the second game of a Chicago Cubs–Brooklyn Dodgers doubleheader was postponed when gnats descended on Ebbets Field in the sixth inning. The sun was shining and fans waved white scorecards to shoo the insects, creating a hazard to the players' vision. The Dodgers 2-0 lead was good enough for a win, since five innings had been completed.

▶ The WHA's Philadelphia Blazers, who played in a refurbished convention hall, could not play their first game because no one knew how to make ice. It cracked whenever skated upon.

The two games of the 1927 Stanley Cup finals that went into overtime were both eventually called because of rough ice.

▶ From 1917–18, the Indianapolis 500 was suspended for the war. The Speedway's brick track became a landing strip and the garages were used as hangars for army planes.

▶ The September 11th terrorist attacks precipitated unprecedented cancellations of sporting events. Major-league baseball wiped out its schedule until Monday, September 17th. The NFL cancelled its roster of games for Sunday, September 16th.

Because of the damage to downtown New York, the Downtown Athletic Club, four blocks from the site of the World Trade Center and the annual host for the presentation of the Heisman Trophy to college football's top player, was shut down. While the building (and the original trophy) was undamaged, the elevator system was declared unsafe. The DAC could have fixed it by the time of the 2001 presentation, but opted instead to hold the event at the Marriott Marquis.

▶ On Sunday, November 24, 1963, two days after the assassination of President John F. Kennedy, the NFL did *not* cancel its games, provoking severe criticism. Pete Rozelle later said that the decision to play the games was his biggest regret as football commissioner.

▶ The premier Six Nations (rugby) Tournament was postponed for several months in 2001 because of the onset of foot-and-mouth disease in Ireland.

▶ A 1963 Minnesota Twins-Washington Senators game in Washington, D.C., was called off because of a civil rights march.

▶ The University of California had its entire 1889 football schedule rained out.

▶ The U.S. Amateur golf championship was postponed a week in 1901 because of the death of President McKinley.

▶ On June 15, 1976, a baseball game at the Houston Astrodome was rained out when the city was flooded with up to 10 inches of water. The Astros and Pittsburgh Pirates made it to the Dome but fans, umpires, and stadium personnel did not.

▶ A flu epidemic caused the cancellation of the remainder of the 1919 Stanley Cup series between the Seattle Metropolitans and the Montreal Canadiens, with the series tied 2-2-1.

▶ The Billy Conn-Bob Pastor heavyweight fight, scheduled for May 11, 1942, was postponed when Conn broke his left hand in a fight with his father-in-law, Jimmy Smith, at an Irish post-christening party.

▶ On May 20, 1960, a Chicago Cubs-Milwaukee Braves game was called because of fog at Milwaukee County Stadium. Umpire Frank Dascoli took three crew members into the outfield and had Frank Thomas of the Cubs hit a fungo. When none of the umpires nor any of the three Cubs outfielders could see the ball, Dascoli wiped out the game, which was tied 0-0 in the fifth inning.

▶ On January 28, 1961, a basketball game between West Hazelton (Pennsylvania) High School and McAdoo was rained out with West Hazelton leading, 31-29, because an open window caused condensation on the floor of the heated gym.

▶ In November 1989, officials at Northeastern University canceled their final football game of the season at James Madison in Virginia after blood tests showed that 21 of their players had not developed antibodies to the measles virus.

▶ The 1989 World Series between the Oakland Athletics and the San Francisco Giants was delayed for 10 days because of the Bay Area's worst earthquake since 1906.

12 Sports Figures Who Earned Their Paychecks

On June 25, 1976, Texas Rangers shortstop Toby Harrah established a standard for inactivity. He played an entire doubleheader without handling a single chance, a major-league record. Most likely, Harrah would have preferred to have some balls hit his way, get into the flow, enjoy himself.

The following athletes and teams did not have this problem.

▶ On May 27, 1984, Manuela Maleeva beat Virginia Ruzici in the Italian Open quarterfinals—a match that took three days to complete because of rain—then beat Carling Bassett in the semifinals and Chris Evert in the finals.

▶ Oakland Athletics relief pitcher Darold Knowles appeared in all seven games of the 1973 World Series.

▶ On November 1, 1924, Forest Peters, a freshman for Montana State's football team, kicked 17 field goals in 22 attempts.

▶ To beat the Penguins, 2-1, in Pittsburgh, in Game 4 of the 2000 Eastern Conference semifinals, the Philadelphia Flyers needed only five overtimes, or a total (including regulation) of 152 minutes and 1 second, the third-longest playoff game ever.

▶ Jim Galvin, pitcher for the 1878 Buffalo Bisons of the International Association, gave the most impressive display of pitching stamina in a season in baseball history. Of 116 league and non-league games, he pitched in 101, of which 96 were complete games. His record was 72-25-3, with 17 shutouts. He started and finished the first 23 games that the team played and pitched at least 895 innings.

▶ Boxer Johnny Greb had 44 fights in 1914.

▶ In the 1968–69 season, Walt Bellamy played in 88 regular-season NBA games, six more than the scheduled 82. Bellamy was traded from the New York Knicks to the Detroit Pistons in mid-season.

▶ When running back Red Grange first signed with the Chicago Bears in 1925, they tried to capitalize immediately on his fame by playing 16 games in a little over a month.

▶ Los Angeles Dodger Mike Marshall is the only pitcher in baseball's modern era to appear in 100 games in a season—106 games in 1974.

▶ Welterweight champion Henry Armstrong accepted five welterweight title defenses between October 9 and 30, 1939. He won them all.

▶ In a 1925 victory over the University of California, Stanford's All-America running back Ernie Nevers ran the ball on all but three of his team's offensive plays.

▶ In June 1989, announcer Vin Scully called 45 innings of baseball in 29 hours: a 10-inning NBC daytime "Game of the Week" in St. Louis on June 3, the Los Angeles Dodgers 22-inning marathon that night in Houston, and a 13-inning Dodgers-Astros game the next day.

Worth the Price of Admission:
The Most Fun and Exciting Teams and Events

The styles of some teams and athletes are methodical, deliberate, yawn-inspiring. Then there are others that, win or lose, are styled somehow to perpetually engage us. A team may be naturally thrilling (in which case, you can be sure, they'll come to be called "The Cardiac Kids"), or spectacularly inept, or too strange or brilliant or comical for us to know what it is. Athletes and teams that most of us would like to have seen, or see—at least once, anyway—might include the laughably terrible 1962 New York Mets; "Air Coryell," the San Diego Chargers under pass-happy coach Don Coryell in the late 1970s and '80s, and today's new, improved version of that offense, the lightning-fast St. Louis Rams; the brilliant and explosive John McEnroe; colorful golfers Lee Trevino and Chi Chi Rodriguez; dynamic soccer star Mia Hamm; and the fluid, Wayne Gretzky-led Edmonton Oilers of the mid-80s, to name a few.

Some games or matches are like that, too. They may or may not pit the best against the best but they are intensely competitive, or they somehow feel big...historic.

Whatever qualities they possess, dull isn't one of them.

▶ The first official American ski race was conducted in 1854 in Sierra County, California. The race was a straight downhill, with no turns, on 15-foot skis.

▶ In early September 2001, in a three-game series in Fenway Park that was undeniably thrilling—if not for Boston Red Sox fans, then for baseball fans, and certainly for New York Yankee fans—the Yankees swept the Red Sox in unprecedentedly tense fashion: In each nail-biter, the deciding run was scored in the eighth inning or later. If that wasn't enough, in the series finale, Yankee pitcher Mike Mussina came within a strike of pitching the first perfect game in the 89-year history of Fenway Park. He lost the perfect game, and the no-hitter, when pinch hitter Carl Everett singled, but Mussina won the game over a nearly-as-good David Cone, the last person to throw a perfect game; Cone gave up a measly six hits and an unearned run in the ninth inning and may have pitched his finest game in the previous three years, and against his former team.

▶ Since 1982, 15 of the previous 21 NCAA men's basketball championship games have been decided by single-digit points. Ten have been decided by 4 points or less and/or went to overtime.

▶ In probably the most exciting Super Bowl ever—XXXIV, in January 2000—the St. Louis Rams beat the Tennessee Titans, 23-16, with back-and-forth drama that featured what is certainly the most thrilling final play in Super Bowl history: With six seconds left and the Titans at the Ram 10-yard line, Tennessee quarterback Steve McNair hit receiver Kevin Dyson on a slant and Dyson headed for the goal-line. Rams linebacker Mike Jones caught Dyson's legs with his left hand, making a tremendous open-field tackle (since dubbed, merely, "The Tackle") that stopped Dyson—a reaching, lunging, desperate man—less than a yard from game-tying paydirt.

▶ The 1930 Philadelphia Phillies had eight .300 hitters; an astonishing team batting average of .315; a team ERA of 6.70, a major-league record for ineptitude; and a defense that made 239 errors. They were also a last-place team, 40 games out of first.

▶ The 1957 University of North Carolina Tar Heels won the NCAA title by winning two consecutive triple-overtime games—74-70 over Michigan State, then 54-53 over the Wilt Chamberlain-led Kansas Jayhawks.

▶ In the 1964 Stanley Cup finals between the Toronto Maple Leafs and the Detroit Red Wings, the winning goal in each of the first three games was scored in the final minute of play, and five of the first six games were decided by one goal.

▶ Teresa Witherspoon of the New York Liberty made the shot every kid dreams of—a last-second, almost full-court, desperation fling that not only goes in, but wins the game—and not only wins the game, but wins the *playoff* game. Witherspoon made her miraculous heave in Game 2 of the best-of-three 1999 WNBA Finals against the Houston Comets, whose fans were already showering the court with confetti. The shot sent the series to a deciding Game 3 (which Houston won, allowing its fans to shower the court with confetti). Witherspoon's famous shot stands above Jerry West's famous end-of-game fling against the New York Knicks in Game 3 of the 1970 NBA Finals because that shot only tied the game (though, because it pre-dated the three-point shot, it counted then for only two points), and the Knicks still won in overtime.

Another player who once called Madison Square Garden home, Knicks forward Larry Johnson, made a miraculous four-point play with seconds to go, and the Knicks down by three, against the Indiana Pacers, in Game 3 of the 1999 NBA Eastern Conference Finals. Johnson was fouled by Antonio Davis while shooting a three-pointer that went in (though Larry Bird, the Pacers coach who watched the play unfold from just feet away, would later express great incredulousness that the play was a "continuation," contending that either the shot should not have counted or the foul should not have been whistled). Madison Square Garden erupted as one when the three-pointer went in. Johnson then made the free throw and the Knicks won the game, 92-91, and eventually the series, to reach the NBA Finals.

▶ The men's 1973 Wimbledon doubles and 1975 U.S. Open doubles crowns were won by perhaps the most volatile pairing in tennis history: Ilie Nastase and Jimmy Connors.

▶ For adrenalin pump, what participants feel at the X Games—ESPN's Extreme Games—takes a back seat (presumably without seat belt) to no one, though it's not clear that the thrill always translates to the spectators. Events include bicycle stunts, big-air snowboarding, bungee jumping, street luge, skysurfing, snow mountain bike racing, and, for just one year (1998), super-modified shovel racing.

▶ The scores of the Holiday Bowl in 1979, 1980, and 1981 were, respectively, 38-37, 46-45, and 38-36. BYU was involved in all three games.

▶ In 1934, in one of the most famous moments in All-Star history, New York Giants pitcher Carl Hubbell struck out the following five future Hall of Famers in a row: Babe Ruth, Lou Gehrig, Jimmie Foxx, Al Simmons, and Joe Cronin.

▶ Each of the five games in the 1951 Stanley Cup finals was tied at the end of regulation. The Toronto Maple Leafs defeated the Montreal Canadiens, four sudden-death victories to one.

▶ The two greatest underdogs and fan favorites at the 1988 Calgary Olympics were the Jamaican bobsled team and English ski jumper Eddie "The Eagle" Edwards. Edwards finished dead last in his competition, while the Jamaicans crashed on their third heat and skipped the fourth and final heat.

▶ In the closest finish in Grand Prix racing, Brazilian Ayrton Senna beat Englishman Nigel Mansell in the 1986 Spanish Grand Prix by 0.014 seconds: 1:48:47.735 to 1:48:47.749.

▶ At the 1979 U.S. Open, John Lloyd beat Paul McNamee 5-7, 6-7, 7-5, 7-6, 7-6.

▶ One of the rules of luge, a dangerous sport to begin with, requires that one of four runs must be negotiated at night.

▶ Despite the sneers or indifference of many big-city football fans who have local NFL teams to root for, the Arena Football League—whose fast-paced games are played indoors on converted-hockey-rink–type fields, and which increasingly supplies the NFL with players (most notably, All-Pro St. Louis Rams quarterback Kurt Warner)—continues to grow in popularity in mid-sized and even bigger American cities like Grand Rapids, Dallas, Chicago, and Buffalo, to name a few.

▶ The 1981–82 Denver Nuggets are the only NBA team ever to go an entire season scoring 100 points or more in every game. They are also the only team to go an entire season allowing 100 points or more in every game.

Exercises in Futility

▶ Los Angeles Lakers center Shaquille O'Neal holds the record for the most free throws attempted in one game, 11, without making one, accomplished against the Seattle Supersonics on December 8, 2000. Perhaps the only NBA player in history strong enough to have been able to handle Shaq—Wilt Chamberlain—held the previous record for free-throw futility in a single game, with an 0-for-10; Wilt also had a game of 0-for-9 from the free-throw line, which is also called—almost mockingly, to such brick-laying big men—the "charity stripe."

▶ On two occasions, NBA player Howie Dallmar took 15 shots from the field and made none. In one 1978 NBA Finals Game against the Washington Bullets, Seattle Supersonic Dennis Johnson went 0-for-14 from the field.

▶ Through the end of 2002, five managers had lost every World Series game they had ever managed: Donie Bush with the 1927 Pittsburgh Pirates, Gabby Hartnett with the 1938 Chicago Cubs, Eddie Sawyer with the 1950 Philadelphia Phillies, Roger Craig with the 1989 San Francisco Giants, and Bruce Bochy with the 1998 San Diego Padres.

▶ Bobby Wallace spent the most years as an active major leaguer, 25, without playing on a pennant winner. Buddy Bell retired after playing

2,405 games and never appearing in postseason play. In more than a quarter-century of managing, Gene Mauch never won a pennant.

▶ In 1961, Puerto Rican jockey Juan Vinales retired at age 28, after making 360 career mounts and winning no races.

▶ In the 1968 World Series, St. Louis Cardinals shortstop Dal Maxvill went 0-for-22.

▶ The 1953–54 NBA Baltimore Bullets had a road record of 0-20.

▶ Terry Felton, who pitched for the Minnesota Twins from 1979–82, finished his career with a record of 0-16.

▶ New York Mets pitcher Randy Tate was 0-for-41 at the plate in 1975, his only season. Chicago Cubs pitcher Bob Buhl went 0-for-70 for the 1962 season.

▶ Fred Merkle went to the World Series five times in eight years with three teams, and lost each time.

▶ Philadelphia Eagles owner Bert Bell founded the NFL draft in 1936 but could not sign any of the nine picks his club made that first year.

▶ In a doubleheader on July 2, 1933, the St. Louis Cardinals were shut out 1-0 in 18 innings in the first game, and 1-0 in regulation in the second game.

You'll Be Sorry If You Shut It Off...: 7 Games, 2 Matches, 1 Fight, 1 Series, 1 Season, and 1 Career You Might Have Walked Out On, and Probably Shouldn't Have

Some games are dull from beginning to end, some exciting from beginning to end, some start off with a rush and dissipate from there.

Variations on each of these aside, the fourth and last possibility is the kind of game most dreaded by the restless fan who invariably walks out in the seventh inning, if not before: a contest that one side dominates at the outset, but that eventually turns into a thriller, or goes to overtime, or in the end yields a record-setting performance. It's almost as if one or more of the players had not shown up at the beginning and then, almost inexplicably, bounces to life.

This list is dedicated to all of those Los Angeles Dodger fans who, to beat the traffic, left before the end of Game 1 of the 1988 World Series. If they timed it right, they made it home just as the late news was showing the replay of Kirk Gibson hitting the game-winning home run, one of the most famous World Series shots of all time.

▶ On October 23, 2000, entering the fourth quarter of an ABC *Monday Night Football* game, the New York Jets were getting hammered, 30-7, by their division rivals, the Miami Dolphins, prompting not a few of the disgusted in attendance at the Meadowlands to give up... but the Jets put on the greatest fourth-quarter offensive display in their history, outscoring Miami 30-7—including an almost unfathomable 20 first downs and four touchdown catches, capped by a last-minute tying TD grab by tackle Jumbo Elliott. A 40-yard field goal in overtime sent the Jets, and those who remained faithful to them, home happy with a 40-37 win, in the longest-ever (4 hours, 10 minutes) *MNF* game.

▶ On April 17, 1976, the Philadelphia Phillies were being humiliated 13-2 by the Chicago Cubs on a windy day at Wrigley Field... when the Phillies came back to win 18-16 in 10 innings, largely on the strength of four Mike Schmidt home runs.

▶ France's Laurent Dauthuille was ahead on the scorecards of all three judges in the last round of his world middleweight title fight with Jake LaMotta on September 13, 1950... until 13 seconds remained in the fight, when LaMotta knocked Dauthuille out.

▶ On November 18, 1972, the Milwaukee Bucks were leading the New York Knicks comfortably, 86-68, at Madison Square Garden with 5½ minutes to play... but the Bucks did not score another point in the game, while the Knicks scored 19, to win 87-86.

▶ In the second quarter of a 1974 game, Notre Dame was romping over the University of Southern California at the Rose Bowl, 24-0... but Trojan running back Anthony Davis woke up and scored four touchdowns, USC totaled 55 points in the next 17 minutes, and the *Trojans* romped, 55-24.

▶ John McEnroe beat Bjorn Borg handily in the first set of the 1980 Wimbledon final, 6-1... but those who shut it off there to play Sunday-morning doubles at the club missed a Borg victory that eventually went five sets and included a fourth-set tiebreaker, won 18-16 by McEnroe, that is widely considered the most exciting game in tennis history.

▶ The Chicago Bears were beating the punchless New York Giants 13-3 entering the fourth quarter of their 1934 NFL title game... but behind 27 fourth-quarter points, the Giants won going away, 30-13.

▶ The Houston Oilers were clobbering the Buffalo Bills in the 1992 AFC wildcard playoff game, 35-3, early in the third quarter... when Buffalo backup quarterback Frank Reich, subbing for the injured Jim Kelly, and the Bills seemed finally to remember where they were playing—in Buffalo's highly charged Rich Stadium—and redeemed their fans' belief in them with the greatest comeback (biggest deficit overcome) in NFL history, winning 41-38 in overtime.

▶ In the 1987 Federation Cup finals, Chris Evert and Pam Shriver were on their way to a slaughter over Steffi Graf and Claudia Kohde, 6-1, 4-0... until the German team awoke. Graf and Kohde went on to win 1-6, 7-5, 6-4.

▶ On November 10, 1984, the University of Miami, at home in the Orange Bowl, was battering Maryland, 31-0, at the half and imagining the avalanche of scoring that might occur... and it did, as Maryland scored six second-half touchdowns to squeak out a thrilling road upset, 42-40.

► In the 1942 Stanley Cup finals, the Toronto Maple Leafs were down three games to zero to the Detroit Red Wings, who were probably starting to think about their victory parade… until Toronto proceeded to win the last four games of the series and become the only major professional team to have accomplished such a comeback in a championship final.

► The 1914 Boston Braves were in last place on July 19… and gained 21½ games on the New York Giants to win the National League pennant. Dubbed the "Miracle Braves," the charmed team went on to sweep the World Series—the first sweep in Series history—over a heavily favored Philadelphia Athletics team that featured five future Hall of Famers.

► Sandy Koufax was mediocre for the first half of his career.

Contests We're Glad We Missed or Wish We Had: The Most Unexciting Occasions, Teams, and Athletes

Why are we fans? Because we enjoy the fun and excitement of a competition that pits talented athletes against one another, or an athlete showing mastery against some objective standard. Not every competition, however, is engaging. Perhaps the opponents are too well-matched, or mismatched, or simply intent on slowing down the flow of a contest to a virtual standstill to gain an edge. Must we be subjected to this? Exactly who—besides beer companies, that is—determined that it's perfectly fine for a nine-inning baseball game to last three-and-a-half hours? Yogi Berra suggested that it was Velcro that was killing baseball. That's right: Hitters in the batter's box now spend such ridiculous amounts of time putting on and re-adjusting their Velcroed gloves and other accoutrements, that an already slow-paced game often borders on the catatonia-inducing.

And if a sporting event is truly unengaging, then even the participants can get bored. The impending retirement of four-time Grand Slam tennis champion Jim Courier was anticipated when he was observed reading novels during court change-overs.

It's games and competitions like the ones listed below that made remote control imperative.

► In the 1964 Olympics, sprint cyclists Giovanni Pettenella of Italy and Pierre Trentin of France, each waiting for the other one to start first so that he could follow and "draft"—force the lead cyclist into fighting the wind for the trail cyclist—stood still on their bicycles for 21 minutes, 57 seconds.

► In an 1881 football contest between Yale and Princeton that came to be known as "The Block Game," Princeton held the football for the entire first half without trying to score, and Yale did the same thing in the second half. The 60 minutes of inactivity inspired a rule change that required the offensive team to try moving the ball at least five yards in three tries ("downs") or relinquish the ball.

► Although one of the most charismatic and talented players on the

PGA Tour, Sergio Garcia has made himself almost unwatchable—to fans, broadcasters, and fellow players—because of a nervous, pre-shot ritual in which he grips and re-grips the club approximately twenty to thirty times before finally taking his shot. His routine has irked so many that golfing legend Jack Nicklaus, a notoriously methodical player but never *that* slow or maddening, sought Garcia out and give him a friendly pep talk. It is not known how many times Nicklaus squeezed Garcia's shoulder.

▶ From 1995 through 1998, the Stanley Cup Finals featured four consecutive sweeps.

▶ First baseman Mike Hargrove was nicknamed "The Human Rain Delay" because it took him so long to get set in the batter's box. His soulmate in basketball, Milwaukee Buck Ricky Pierce, had one of his free throws voided by referee Jack Madden for delay of game, on April 5, 1988. Madden claimed that Pierce, a notoriously slow foul shooter, had violated the 10-second rule before taking his second shot.

▶ In a boy's basketball game on March 7, 1941, Las Animas (Colorado) High School defeated La Junta, 2-0, in overtime.

▶ In the Olympic free pistol competition, shooters are allotted 2½ hours to fire 60 shots.

▶ Dean Smith's maddening, if successful, use of the four-corner stall with his University of North Carolina Tar Heels in the 1970s helped lead to the institution of the shot clock in college basketball.

▶ For the 12-year span from 1984 through 1995, only two Super Bowls were competitive: XXIII, a four-point thriller in which the San Francisco 49ers beat the Cincinnati Bengals, and XXV, in which the Buffalo Bills barely missed edging the New York Giants on a last-second field goal attempt. For the other 10 Super Bowls, the average margin of victory was 27 points.

▶ In their first heavyweight bout in 1871, neither Joe Coburn nor Jem Mace landed a punch.

▶ For most fans, the Los Angeles Rams of the 1970s meant a deliberate —that is, boring—style of play: very little passing, and not very much in the way of sweeps, either. They were so boring, in fact, that coach Chuck Knox resigned under pressure despite winning five divisional titles in five years. "I'd rather have a team with an even record with exciting games than one that goes to the playoff and then loses," said Rams owner Carroll Rosenbloom in 1978.

What They Play for: 10 Trophies and Artifacts Fought Over in College Football Rivalries

▶ Minnesota—Michigan: The Little Brown Jug

▶ California—Stanford: The Axe

▶ Texas—Oklahoma: The Cowboy Hat

▶ Notre Dame—Michigan State: The Megaphone

▶ Florida—Miami (Florida):   The Seminole War Canoe

▶ Clemson—South Carolina: The Tea Cup

▶ Princeton—Rutgers: The Rusty Old Cannon

▶ Wichita—Wichita State: The Dog Collar

▶ Idaho—Montana: The Wooden Beer Stein

▶ Susquehanna—Lycoming: Amos Alonzo Stagg's Bronze Felt Halt

All-Time Chokes

▶ In the 1990s, the University of Kansas men's basketball team made it almost a rite of spring to underperform in the NCAA tournament, and render the seeding system pointless when it came to them. In 1990, the #2 seed Jayhawks lost in the 2nd round to #7 UCLA. In 1992, the #1 Jayhawks lost in the 2nd round to #9 University of Texas-El Paso. In 1995, the #1 Jayhawks lost in the 3rd round to #4 Virginia. In 1996, the #2 Jayhawks lost in the 4th round to #4 Syracuse. In 1997, the #1 Jayhawks lost in the 3rd round to #4 Arizona. In 1998, the #1 Jayhawks lost in the 2nd round to #8 Rhode Island.

▶ In one of the painful chokes to witness, Jana Novotna of Czechoslovakia was one good serve away from taking a 5-1 lead in the third and deciding set over Steffi Graf in the 1993 Wimbledon final when she fell apart. Novotna double-faulted, lost that game, lost the ensuing four games, and lost the match, 7-6, 1-6, 6-4. "I didn't expect Jana to choke like that," 1977 Wimbledon champ and BBC commentator Virginia Wade told the TV audience. "Jana's the biggest choker I've ever seen!" remarked Gigi Fernandez, Wade's boothmate and Novotna's former doubles partner.

What made the choke particularly memorable, though, was Novotna's reaction after the match. During the presentation ceremony, the Duchess of Kent said a few consoling words to Novotna, then smiled at her—at which point Novotna began to weep uncontrollably on the Duchess's shoulder.

Two years later, Novotna reinforced her choker's label when, in the third round of the French Open, she held three match points at 6-7, 6-4, 5-0, 40-love against unseeded teenager Chanda Rubin... and did not close it out, blew three more match points in that game, blew three more at 5-4, then lost the final set, 8-6. Novotna didn't help matters when she later said, "I didn't really feel I had the match under control."

Finally, while playing against 16-year-old Martina Hingis at the 1997 Wimbledon, Novotna was a point from a 3-0 lead in the final set when Hingis reversed fortunes, swept the remaining games, and took the title that now seemed destined to elude Novotna.

This story has a happy ending: Jana Novotna can always say that she, and she alone, is the 1998 Wimbledon women's champion.

▶ In football bowl games (through the beginning of the 2002 college season), Texas Tech is an almost head-scratchingly, *it's-actually-difficult-for-a-bowl-bound-team-to-lose-that-much* 5-20-1. In bowl games under coach Bo Schembechler, the University of Michigan Wolverines were 5-12.

▶ The Houston Astros, established in 1962, have never made it to the World Series. In fact, they've never won a postseason series, losing in the National League playoffs in 1980 (to the Philadelphia Phillies), in 1981 (to the Los Angeles Dodgers), in 1986 (to the New York Mets), in 1997 (to the Atlanta Braves), in 1998 (to the San Diego Padres), in 1999 (to the Braves again), and in 2001 (to the Braves one more time).

▶ Armando Benitez has sparkling numbers as a short reliever, first for the Baltimore Orioles and then for the New York Mets. But he may not be the one you want on the mound when you need to finish off a crucial victory—not a particularly good recommendation for a closer. In nine career playoff opportunities, Benitez has blown six saves, some in spectacularly deflating fashion for his team, including the decisive Game 6 of the 1999 National League Championship Series against the Atlanta Braves, Game 1 of the 2000 World Series against the New York Yankees, and, with Baltimore, Game 2 of the 1997 American League Championship Series against the Cleveland Indians. In his first 28 innings of postseason pitching, Benitez gave up a record seven homers. In 2001, when the Mets were trying to catch Atlanta in September, Benitez twice in six days failed to hold big leads against the Braves, severely harming their comeback hopes.

▶ Cliff Robinson, the talented forward for the Portland Trailblazers, Phoenix Suns, and Detroit Pistons, has been plagued throughout his career by the label of postseason underachiever. Through the 2001–02 NBA season, Robinson's regular-season points-per-game average was 16.1; his playoff ppg was 11.4.

▶ Phil Mickelson, with 21 tour victories, more than $20 million in earnings, and the #2 world ranking behind Tiger Woods, has the dreaded title of "greatest golfer never to win a major championship." Through the 2002 season, Mickelson was 0-for-42 in majors—the U.S. Open, Masters, British Open, and PGA Championship." On seven occasions, Mickelson has been within two strokes of the lead entering the final round.

▶ Among the top 25 winningest coaches in NFL history, Jim Mora is the only one without a postseason victory. He is 0-6 as a playoff coach.

▶ Although a graceful figure skater and a gracious competitor, American Todd Eldridge has had trouble rising to his Olympic occasions. He was #1 in America and #3 in the world in 1991; at the 1992 Olympics, he finished 10th (though, to be fair, he was enduring back problems at the time). In 1997–98, he was #1 in America, #2 in the world; in the 1998 Olympics he finished 4th. In 2001, he was #3 in the world, and in 2002 #1 in America; at the 2002 Olympics, he finished 6th.

(He didn't compete in the 1994 Olympics because he was ill at the nationals and was left off the team.)

▶ Through October 12, 2002, promising University of Texas Longhorns quarterback Chris Simms was 0-4 in games he started against Top Ten teams; in those four contests, he threw fourteen interceptions and zero touchdown passes.

▶ In May of 2002, the lowly Tampa Devil Rays took a lead into the ninth inning for three consecutive games... and lost each one. The unfortunate feat had not been accomplished since the Chicago White Sox did it 82 years before.

The Most Memorable Ties

Victory brings joy; defeat, despair. A tie? A tie, it's said, is like kissing your sister. Yet, while many ties may be psychologically indigestible, the following deadlocks had at least something noteworthy to recommend them.

▶ Yevgeny Grishin of the U.S.S.R. tied for the 1,500m speedskating gold in 1956. In 1960, he skated in the same event and again tied for the gold.

▶ In the inaugural London Marathon in 1981, American Dick Beardsley and Norwegian Inge Simonsen held hands to cross the finish line in a tie.

▶ In the 1944 Carter Handicap at Aqueduct, thoroughbreds Bossuet, Brownie, and Wait a Bit crossed the finish line together, in a triple dead heat.

▶ Baseball commissioner Bud Selig had long anticipated having the All-Star Game in his hometown of Milwaukee at Miller Park, the two-year-old stadium for which he'd spent years arranging financing while he was the Brewers owner. But the 2002 showcase, already marred by the focus on labor unrest, turned ridiculous when the game went into extra innings and both managers, the New York Yankees' Joe Torre of the American League and the Arizona Diamondbacks' Bob Brenly of the National League, ran out of pitchers. When it was announced with one out in the bottom of the 11th inning that the game would end if the National League didn't score, fans booed, threw bottles, and chanted, "Refund!" and "Let them play!" The NL went scoreless in the 11th, and the game ended at 7-7.

▶ In the 100m freestyle at the 1984 Olympics, Americans Nancy Hogshead and Carrie Steinseifer finished in a dead heat, earning the first double gold medals in Olympic swimming history.

▶ Unbeaten Michigan State and unbeaten Notre Dame played to a 10-10 tie in 1966. The game's finish has become one of the most famous in college football history as the Irish ran out the clock to preserve the tie and their top ranking. Notre Dame is criticized to this day for making little, if any, attempt to win the game.

▶ The National Football League has not seen a scoreless tie since a 0-0 contest on November 7, 1943, between the New York Giants and the Detroit Lions.

▶ Martin Sheridan and Ralph Rose of the United States finished in a dead heat in the 1904 Olympic discus competition, each of them throwing exactly 128'10½ ". In the "throw-off," they were each awarded three throws. Sheridan won by over seven feet.

▶ Five times in the National League and three times in the American League have two teams tied for first place at the end of the regular season. Remarkably, the Dodgers—first in Brooklyn, then in Los Angeles —have been involved in all five National League ties, losing four and winning one. The Boston Red Sox have been involved in two of the three American League playoffs, and have lost both.

▷ In 1995, the Seattle Mariners and California Angels finished at 78-66 in the American League West. Seattle won a one-game playoff at the Kingdome.

▷ In 1980, the Houston Astros and Los Angeles finished at 92-70 atop the National League West. Houston won a one-game playoff.

▷ In 1978, the New York Yankees and Red Sox finished at 99-63 in the American League East. The Yankees won a one-game playoff at Fenway Park.

▷ In 1962, Los Angeles and the San Francisco Giants finished at 101-61. The Giants won the National League pennant by taking the best-of-three playoff, two games to one.

▷ In 1959, Los Angeles and the Milwaukee Braves finished at 86-68. The Dodgers won the National League pennant by sweeping the playoff, two games to none.

▷ In 1951, the New York Giants and Brooklyn Dodgers finished at 96-58. The Giants won the playoff, two games to one, and took the National League pennant.

▷ In 1948, the Cleveland Indians and Red Sox were tied at 96-58 atop the American League. Cleveland won a one-game playoff at Fenway Park.

▷ In 1946, the St. Louis Cardinals and Brooklyn finished tied at 96-58. St. Louis won the best-of-three game playoff, two games to none, for the National League pennant.

▶ Of their 76 regular season games in the 1969–70 season, the Philadelphia Flyers played in an NHL-record 24 ties.

▶ In the 11th game of the 1960 AFL season, the Buffalo Bills were beating the Denver Broncos 38-7 late in the third quarter and managed to settle for a tie.

▶ The Brooklyn Dodgers and the Cincinnati Reds played in the longest scoreless tie in baseball, 19 innings at Ebbets Field, on September 11, 1946.

Bridesmaids

Some of the more habitual second-place finishers and runners-up:

▶ Ernie Els finished in second place five times during the 2000 PGA season—four of those to Tiger Woods.

▶ Stirling Moss never won the world driving championship, coming in second from 1955–58 and third from 1959–61.

▶ The Buffalo Bills lost four consecutive Super Bowls, from 1991 through '94 (though, in fairness, no team has ever *made* it to four consecutive Super Bowls, the more enduring fact).

▶ In 1998, the state of Utah was basketball runner-up in both the NBA (the Jazz) and the men's NCAA tournament (the University of Utah).

▶ The St. Louis Blues made the Stanley Cup finals in 1968, 1969, and 1970, and got swept each year.

▶ The New York Liberty has gone to the finals in four of the six years of the WNBA's existence, and has lost each time.

▶ The Minnesota Vikings lost in each of their four Super Bowl appearances.

▶ Philadelphia Warriors great Hal Greer made the All-NBA second team seven times. He never made the first team.

▶ Gottfried von Cramm was Wimbledon runner-up three years in a row, from 1935–37.

▶ Ken Rosewall was 0-for-4 in Wimbledon singles finals.

▶ American swimmer Shirley Babashoff won six Olympic silver medals (plus two golds, both in relays).

▶ Brian Orser won the Olympic men's figure skating silver medal in 1984 and again in 1988.

▶ Guy Lewis made five trips to the Final Four and never won an NCAA crown. He lost in 1967, 1968, 1982, 1983, and 1984, each time to the eventual national champion.

▶ American Jack Davis was credited with the same time as the champion in the 110m hurdles in both 1952 and 1956—on each occasion setting an Olympic record—but was edged out for the gold both times. (Before 1972, times were measured in tenths of seconds and so a runner-up who was anywhere from one hundredth to nine hundredths of a second behind the winner might show an identical clocking.)

▶ Alydar came in second to Affirmed in each of the three Triple Crown races in 1978.

▶ For four years in a row, 1969–72, American figure skater Julie Holmes took second place to Janet Lynn at the U.S. championships.

▶ In 1984, golfer Greg Norman tied with Fuzzy Zoeller at the U.S. Open. In an 18-hole playoff, Norman lost by eight strokes. In the 1986 Masters, Norman bogeyed the final hole and finished one stroke behind Jack Nicklaus. At the 1986 U.S. Open, Norman led going into the final round but fell all the way to twelfth (Ray Floyd won). At the 1986 PGA, Norman finished second to Bob Tway, after leading by four strokes with nine holes to play. At the 1987 Masters, Norman finished in a four-way tie in regulation and lost to Larry Mize in the playoff. At the 1989 Masters, Norman bogeyed the final hole to miss the playoff. At the 1989 British Open, Norman lost in a three-way playoff with Wayne Grady and eventual winner Mark Calcavecchia.

The Dandiest Streaks in Sports

Included among the most famous streaks in sports would have to be Joe DiMaggio's 56-game hitting streak in 1941; UCLA's string of 88 wins and seven NCAA basketball titles; in tennis, Martina Navratilova's 74 consecutive singles wins in 1984, and Bjorn Borg's five Wimbledons, from 1976 to 1980; Edwin Moses's 107-race unbeaten streak in the 400m hurdles that spanned 11 years and 22 countries; the Boston Celtics eight consecutive NBA titles (1959–66); and the run of five straight championships accomplished by the New York Yankees in baseball (1949–53), and the Montreal Canadiens in hockey (1956–60).

Some of the other memorable streaks by teams and individuals:

▶ In the 1922 season, the Pittsburgh Pirates enjoyed a five-game stretch in which every hitter in the lineup, including pitchers, pinch hitters, and other replacement players, got at least one hit.

▶ Scott Palmer made a hole-in-one in each of four consecutive rounds from October 9–12, 1983, at Balboa Park, San Diego.

▶ Boxer Lamar Clark holds the record for most consecutive knockouts, 44, from 1958–60. The most consecutive first-round knockouts is 18, by One-Round Hogan, in 1910.

▶ Chick Hearn broadcast 3,338 consecutive Los Angeles Lakers games, from November 21, 1965, through December 16, 2001.

▶ Relief pitcher Paul Linblad went from 1966 to 1974—385 games—without making an error.

▶ Green Bay Packers quarterback Bart Starr threw 294 consecutive passes without an interception during the 1964 and 1965 seasons.

▶ Starting with Game 3 of the 1996 World Series through Game 2 of the 2000 Series, the New York Yankees won 14 consecutive World Series games, including two sweeps (they did not appear in the 1997 Series).

▶ The Louisiana State University women's track team won the NCAA outdoor title 11 years in a row, from 1987–97.

▶ From 1992 through 2001, the National League batting title was won by either a San Diego Padre or a Colorado Rockie.

▶ For six years—from August 1973 to May 1979—Chris Evert did not lose a singles match on clay. She had won 125 consecutive matches when Tracy Austin finally ended the streak by beating her in the 1979 Italian Open semifinals.

▶ The University of Oklahoma won 47 straight football games from 1953–57, and from 1946–59 had a 74-game win streak in the Big Eight.
    The longest unbeaten streak in college football is 63 games, by the University of Washington, from 1907–17 (they won 59 and tied 4).

▶ Through the 2002 season, the Atlanta Braves have won 11 divisional titles in a row (and counting).

▶ Pitcher Jim Barr of the San Francisco Giants retired a record 41 consecutive batters in 1972.

▶ University of Illinois defensive back Al Brosky intercepted at least one pass in 15 consecutive games in the early 1950s.

▶ In the 1945 Stanley Cup finals, Toronto Maple Leafs goalie Frank McCool had three consecutive shutouts and went 192 minutes without allowing a goal.

▶ In 1957, Ted Williams reached base a record 16 consecutive times: He had four homers, two singles, nine walks, and was hit by a pitch.

▶ On January 5, 1971, the Harlem Globetrotters lost to the New Jersey Reds, 100-99, breaking their consecutive-games winning streak at 2,495.

▶ The Buffalo Germans, a barnstorming basketball team at the turn of the 20th century, won 111 straight games.

▶ The Philadelphia Flyers once went an NHL record 35 games without a loss, from October 14, 1979, through January 6, 1980. During that period, they won 25 games and tied 10.

▶ In 1982, the New York Islanders won a record 15 consecutive games.

▶ Annemarie Moser-Proll won 11 consecutive World Cup downhill races from December 1972 to January 1974.

▶ In 1967, Wilt Chamberlain made a record 35 field goals in a row.

▶ During the 1980–81 season, Calvin Murphy sank a record 78 free throws in a row.

▶ In the 1940s, Byron Nelson was "in the money" in 113 consecutive tournaments. In 1945, he played 19 consecutive rounds under 70.

▶ The U.S. women's tennis team won the Wightman Cup 21 times in a row from 1931 to 1957. (There was a six-year break for World War II.)

▶ Between 1948 and 1954, Emil Zatopek won 38 consecutive races at 10,000m.

► East German backstroker Roland Matthes was undefeated for seven years until American John Naber beat him in 1974.

► Roberto Clemente hit safely in all 14 World Series games in which he played—7 games in 1960, and 7 more in 1971.

► Woody Stephens was the trainer for five consecutive Belmont winners, 1982–86.

► From 1947 to 1949, the Toronto Maple Leafs won nine straight games in the Stanley Cup finals.

► In 1974, Los Angeles Dodgers pitcher Mike Marshall appeared in 13 consecutive games. In 1986, Texas Rangers pitcher Dale Mohorcic also appeared in 13 games in a row.

► In the 1971–72 season, the Los Angeles Lakers won a record 33 games in a row.

► New York Giants pitcher Carl Hubbell won 24 games in a row in 1936–37.

► Walter Alston signed 23 consecutive one-year contracts to manage the Brooklyn, and then Los Angeles, Dodgers before he retired in 1976.

► From 1979 to 1983, Dave Jennings punted 623 times without having one blocked.

► When right-handed Ivan Lendl won the U.S. Open in 1985, he broke a streak of lefty men's singles winners at the Open that began in 1974 with Jimmy Connors. (Oddly, Martina Navratilova was the first lefty to win the women's U.S. draw since Bertha L. Townsend did it back in 1888 and 1889.)

► In 1925, Brooklyn Robin Milt Stock got four hits in each of four consecutive games.

► The Cleveland Browns went 21 seasons, 1950–71, without being shut out.

► From 1981 through 1994, every Super Bowl featured at least one starting quarterback whose first name started with a "J": Jim Plunkett (1981), Joe Montana (1982), Joe Theismann (1983), Joe Theismann and Jim Plunkett (1984), Joe Montana (1985), Jim McMahon (1986), John Elway (1987), John Elway (1988), Joe Montana (1989), Joe Montana and John Elway (1990); Jeff Hostetler and Jim Kelly (1991); and Jim Kelley (1992, 1993, 1994). Not until 1995, when Steve Young and Stan Humphries squared off, did the streak end.

► Chris Evert won at least one Grand Slam singles title a year for 13 years, from 1974 to 1986.

► Jack Nicklaus and Arnold Palmer each won at least one tournament for a record 17 consecutive years.

► Johnny Unitas threw for at least one touchdown in 47 consecutive games, from 1956–60.

The Purest Rules in Baseball

Purity may be found in every sport, with the obvious exceptions—professional wrestling, tractor pulls, dwarf throwing, a few others. Generally, there are the players and the field, perhaps there's a ball, maybe a stick of sorts, always an objective. Simple. Some games and their practitioners succeed more than others in remaining true to the ideal; among America's popular sports, golf has probably comported itself the most admirably. But there's purity elsewhere. There is purity in Wimbledon, where there are still no stadium lights, and the tournament always begins at 2 P.M. There is purity in fall Saturdays in the Ivy League, where football games are still played primarily for the fun they engender, not the revenue they produce. There is purity in the Cleveland Browns' uniforms, which eschew fancy color schemes, and in their simple helmets, the only ones in the NFL without emblems.

No sport, though, is more conscious of its tradition than baseball. We come close to being overwhelmed by the skyrocketing salaries, the labor disputes, the Multiplex Domes, the exploding scoreboards, yes; but then we still have Cracker Jack and seventh-inning stretches, Topps baseball cards and the sign behind home plate that says NO PEPPER GAMES, and there are still 108 double stitches in a regulation baseball. And, most important, there is still the game itself, infinitely varied but infinitely simple, too. Home, first, second, third, home again. In a hundred years, the playing field has changed little, and why not? Sportswriter Red Smith said, "Ninety feet between bases is perhaps as close as man has ever gotten to perfection."

From the book of *Official Baseball Rules* (2002), some other elegances:

▶ Rule 1.01: "Baseball is a game between two teams of nine players each..."

▶ Rule 1.10a: "The bat shall be a smooth *round* stick..."

▶ Rule 4.02: "The players of the home team shall take their defensive positions, the first batter of the visiting team shall take his position in the batter's box, the umpire shall call 'Play' and the game shall start."

▶ Rule 5.03: "The pitcher shall deliver the pitch to the batter who may elect to strike the ball, or who may not offer at it, as he chooses."

▶ From Rule 9.05 (General Instructions to Umpires): "It is better to consult the rules and hold up the game ten minutes to decide a knotty problem than to have a game thrown out on protest and replayed."

▶ Rule 10.05.b: "A base hit shall be scored... when a batter reaches first base safely on a fair ball hit with such force, or so slowly, that any fielder attempting to make a play with it has no opportunity to do so."

▶ And these definitions from Rule 2.00:

▷ "A DOUBLE PLAY is a play by the defense in which two offensive players are put out as a result of continuous action, providing there is no error between putouts."

▷ "The BATTERY is the pitcher and catcher."

▷ "A FLY BALL is a batted ball that goes high in the air in flight… A LINE DRIVE is a batted ball that goes sharp and direct from the bat to a fielder without touching the ground… A GROUND BALL is a batted ball that rolls or bounces close to the ground."

▷ "A DOUBLE-HEADER is two regularly scheduled… games, played in immediate succession." [**Author's note:** Thus, the newly concocted, revenue-mindful "day-night" doubleheader is not, according to the rules, a doubleheader.]

▷ "The BATTER'S BOX is the area within which the batter shall stand during his time at bat."

▷ "An OUTFIELDER is a fielder who occupies a position in… the area of the playing field most distant from home base."

▷ "A THROW is the act of propelling the ball with the hand and arm to a given objective… "

▷ "A WILD PITCH is one so high, so low, or so wide of the plate that it cannot be handled with ordinary effort by the catcher."

▷ "'SAFE' is a declaration by the umpire that a runner is entitled to the base for which he was trying."

6th Men, Pinch Hitters, and Role Players: The Most Notable Substitutes

▶ Red Auerbach believed that the Boston Celtics could demoralize their opponents if their first substitution *strengthened* rather than weakened the team on the floor. Building on this philosophy, the Celtics developed some of the best "bench players" in all of sports, including the NBA's first great sixth man, Frank Ramsey. Other Celtics who made a great impact but often did not start included John Havlicek, Don Nelson, Paul Silas, and, early in his career, Kevin McHale, who twice won the NBA's Sixth Man Award. Among the league's other teams, notable sixth men have included Cazzie Russell, Irv Torgoff, Michael Cooper, Roy Tarpley, Dennis Rodman, and Detlef Schrempf.

▶ Jesse Owens replaced Marty Glickman on the U.S. 4x100m relay team at the 1936 Berlin Olympics, and Ralph Metcalfe replaced Sam Stoller. Glickman and Stoller were the only two Jews on the U.S. track team and the only two members who did not compete.

▶ In the bottom of the sixth inning of Game 6 of the 1947 World Series, Brooklyn Dodger Al Gionfriddo replaced Eddie Miksis defensively in the outfield. With two outs in the inning, Gionfriddo made one of the most famous catches in World Series history, robbing New York Yankee Joe DiMaggio of a three-run home run that would have tied the game.

▶ In the 1922 Walker Cup competition, Bernard Darwin, covering the match for *The London Times*, was called to replace Robert Harris, the British team captain, who had become ill. Darwin, twice a semifinalist in the British Amateur (and the grandson of Charles Darwin), won his single.

▶ Minnesota Viking Bob Berry made it to three Super Bowls—as back-up quarterback to Fran Tarkenton—and did not get to play in any of them.

▶ On September 28, 1960, in one of the most memorable replacements in baseball history, Boston Red Sock Carroll Hardy took over in Fenway Park's left field for Ted Williams in the ninth inning of Williams's last game. In the eighth inning, Williams had hit a home run in the final at-bat of his career.

▶ New York Giant Dusty Rhodes is remembered as one of baseball's great pinch hitters, thanks to one remarkable year—1954—and several clutch performances, including key pinch hits in the first three games of that year's World Series. His career pinch-hitting average is .212.

▶ The Texas A&M "12th Man" kickoff team is made up of regular students at the school who try out during the first week in August.

▶ San Diego Chargers running back Hank Bauer played almost exclusively in goal-line situations during the 1979 season. He carried the ball 22 times all year and scored eight touchdowns.

▶ From the middle of the 1939 season through 1942, Chicago White Sox great Ted Lyons, in the twilight of his career, pitched almost exclusively on Sundays.

.500

One of the worst things you can say about a professional sports team is, "They're a .500 club." (Theoretically, "They're a .400 club" is a worse thing to say but no one ever says it.) Considering that every game results in one win and one loss (or two ties); that at each season's end, the cumulative winning percentage of all teams in any league is .500; and that there should be roughly, and often exactly, as many teams worse than a .500 club as there are teams that are better, the comment should not be treated as the condemnation that it is. Someone's got to be at .500, and it's a lot better than being a cellar-dweller.

None of that matters. Pointing out anyone's .500-ness is still not a nice thing to do.

Some of the more exquisite examples:

▶ During the 1979–80 season, San Antonio Spurs coach Doug Moe was replaced with the basketball team's record at 33-33. Bob Bass took over and the team went 8-8 the rest of the way.

▶ The 1967 Pittsburgh Pirates were 42-42 under manager Harry Walker and 39-39 under Danny Murtaugh.

▶ As Brooklyn Dodger manager, Walter Alston was 7-7 in two World Series. The team then moved west. Alston's record managing the Los Angeles Dodgers in World Series games was 13-13.

► Rube Marquard pitched for 18 seasons. Of those, eight were winning seasons, eight were losing, and two were exactly .500.

► In 1907, Detroit Tigers pitcher George Mullin won exactly 20 games—but he lost exactly 20 games, too.

► In 2000, for the first time in major-league history, no team finished over .600 or below .400.

► In 1985, the Cleveland Browns won the AFC Central title with an 8-8 record. They were the only team in the division to reach .500.

► The Minnesota Twins of 1972–73, the San Diego Padres of 1982–83, and the Montreal Expos of 1988–89 are the only major-league teams to play .500 ball in consecutive seasons.

A Dozen and One Things in Professional Sports That You Could Probably Do Without Embarrassing Yourself

1. Coach first base

2. Shoot free throws as well as former NBA player Chris Dudley (a 46% career foul shooter)

3. Sink a two-foot putt (with no break)

4. Intentionally walk a batter

5. Hold for a point-after attempt

6. Roll a frame in a pro bowler's tournament

7. Umpire the left-field or right-field line at the All-Star Game

8. Sit out a two-minute penalty

9. Make a soccer throw-in

10. Sweep in a curling match

11. Drive in the back row on the pace lap

12. Make the proper club selection

13. Net-judge in tennis

Tanking: 15 Noted Examples of Not Giving It Your All

"Tanking"—willfully putting out a half-hearted effort—is a delicate subject in sports. It suggests athletes who don't care, coaches and general managers conniving for a higher draft pick, the 1919 Black Sox. Nonetheless, tanking has been known, admittedly or not, to happen.

► In a 1971 game, with the University of Florida leading Miami 45-8, the entire Gator defense fell to the ground—in what would later be known as the "Florida Flop"—letting Miami quarterback John Hornibrook run in uncontested for a touchdown so that Florida quarterback John Reaves could have another shot at breaking Jim Plunkett's career passing record. Florida got the ball back with 1:06 to go and Reaves set the record. Miami coach Fran Curci called it "the worst thing I have ever seen in football."

▶ Speaking before a Senate subcommittee on June 14, 1960, middleweight Jake LaMotta confessed to throwing a fight against Billy Fox in 1947.

▶ The 41-year-old Pancho Gonzalez, who'd lost 24-22 in the first set of his first-round Wimbledon match in 1969 with 26-year-old Charlie Pasarell, was booed when he seemed to give up in the second set and lose it, 6-1, because he was disgusted that the match was not being suspended for failing light. When the match continued the next day, however, Gonzalez took the next three sets, 16-14, 6-3, and 11-9, saving seven match points in the deciding set of what became the longest match ever played at Wimbledon.

▶ As the last game of the 2001 NFL season wound down, it appeared that New York Giants All-Pro defensive end Michael Strahan would not get the opportunity to make one more sack, and thus set a new single-season mark of 22½—especially since the Giants' opponents, the Green Bay Packers, were up by nine with under three minutes to go and had every reason (because it was both the competitive *and* the sportsmanlike thing to do) simply to run the ball. But Packers quarterback Brett Favre, a buddy of Strahan's, called an audible, took the snap, and, oddly, ran a naked bootleg toward Strahan's side of the field; almost immediately, as Strahan was gaining on him, Favre fell to the ground, allowing Strahan to touch him harmlessly and get credit for the sack and the record—one long held by the widely disliked former New York Jet, Mark Gastineau. However, in falling down, Favre did both his friend and himself a disservice: Strahan, because his record would now always be tainted; and the normally fiery Favre himself, because most observers were quite certain he'd taken a dive.

▶ On the final day of the 1976 baseball regular season, Kansas City Royal George Brett, who was virtually tied for the lead in the American League batting title race with teammate Hal McRae, hit what seemed to be a routine fly ball. However, Minnesota Twins outfielder Steve Brye suddenly stopped and the ball bounced over his head for an inside-the-park home run. McRae, the next batter, grounded out and ended up at .3321, with Brett at .3333. McRae, who is black, accused Twins manager Gene Mauch, who is white, of ordering Brye, who is white, to let the ball hit by Brett, who is white, fall safely. Mauch denied the charge. "I would protect the integrity of the game at all costs," Mauch said.

▶ In late 2001, All-Pro wide receiver Randy Moss of the Minnesota Vikings confessed that he only "plays" when he feels like it.

▶ On the night in 1982 that the Oakland Athletics' Rickey Henderson was trying to break Lou Brock's single-season steal record, manager Billy Martin ordered Fred Stanley to get picked off of second base to open a steal opportunity for Henderson.

▶ In a 1960 Greco-Roman lightweight wrestling competition, Russian Avtandil Koridze needed a fall to qualify for the gold medal match with a Yugoslavian wrestler. In his bout with Bulgarian Dimitro Stoyanov, Koridze said something to Stoyanov with one minute left in the bout, then threw him to the ground and pinned him. Yugoslavia protested, and Stoyanov was disqualified. Koridze was not punished and went on to win the gold.

▶ Ingemar Johansson of Sweden was disqualified in the super heavyweight final at the 1952 Olympics for not making sufficient effort against American H. Edwards Sanders: Johansson did not throw a single punch. He was denied his silver medal because of the disqualification. (It was finally awarded to him in 1982.)

▶ Detroit Piston coach Doug Collins grew livid in an imminent blowout loss to the Orlando Magic in March of 1996 when, with just 3 seconds left, Magic forward Anthony Bowie called a timeout so that a play could be set up for him to record his tenth assist of the game which, along with his 20 points and 10 rebounds, would give him an impressive "triple double," the first (and only) of his career. Disgusted that a player would call the otherwise meaningless timeout just so he could benefit personally, Collins called his Pistons players off the court, simply letting Bowie pass to a teammate and achieve his milestone.

▶ Rickey Henderson and Bobby Bonilla, both of whom had feuded during the season with New York Mets manager Bobby Valentine, spent the final three innings of the Mets' thrilling and decisive loss to the Atlanta Braves in Game 6 of the 1999 National League Championship Series playing cards in the clubhouse. According to published reports, neither player was paying attention to the game as the Mets lost, 10-9, in 11 innings when Kenny Rogers walked Andruw Jones with the bases loaded to force in the winning run.

▶ On November 30, 1983, with the Portland Trail Blazers nearing a club scoring record of 150 points, Denver Nuggets coach Doug Moe, fed up with his team's defense, called timeout with 1:12 left in the game and told his players, "Let them have it. You understand what I'm saying, don't you?" The Nuggets let the Blazers score five uncontested layups in the closing minute for a 156-116 win. Moe was fined $5,000 and suspended for two games.

▶ Heavyweight champion Jack Johnson was believed by some to have taken a fall in his outdoor title fight against Jess Willard in Havana, Cuba, on April 5, 1915. In one of the most famous photographs in boxing history, Johnson is seen on the canvas, shielding his eyes from the sun as the referee counts the champion out in the 26th round.

▶ After being knocked down and cut early in his October 21, 2000, bout with Mike Tyson, Polish heavyweight Andrew Golota would not come out to fight for the third round.

▶ On April 2, 1987, in a close game between the Houston Rockets and the Phoenix Suns, starting forward Ralph Sampson did not play the fourth quarter, center (then-) Akeem Olajuwon sat out the final 8:31, and forward Rod McCray played only 4:43 of the period. Even when Houston got within 96-94 with 6:42 to play, coach Bill Fitch did not substitute. Sampson, Olajuwon, and McCray were seen laughing on the bench. Dallas Mavericks coach Dick Motta, who was watching the game, suggested that the Rockets were "messing around" in order to set up a favorable playoff schedule, which meant avoiding the Los Angeles Lakers as long as possible. Motta was suspended for one game and his team was fined $5,000 for his comments.

Ironmen

During the 1995–96 NHL season, goalie Grant Fuhr started an amazing 76 games for the St. Louis Blues, a record, and played in 79.

Wuss.

Note to Grant: It's an 80-game season! You want a vacation, become a cruise director!

The athletes below took no games off, for a long, long time. Some of the most durable men in sports, and their consecutive-games streaks:

Baseball

▶ 2,632—Cal Ripken, Baltimore Orioles (May 30, 1982–September 19, 1998, which includes an 8,243-consecutive-innings streak, also the longest in major-league history, that started on June 5, 1982, and ended September 14, 1987)

▶ 2,130—Lou Gehrig, New York Yankees (June 1, 1925–April 30, 1939; the last game of the streak was the last game of his career)

Japanese Baseball

▶ 2,215—Sachio Kinugasa, Hiroshima Toyo Carp (October 19, 1970–October 22, 1987)

Football

▶ 282—Jim Marshall, Cleveland Browns (1960), Minnesota Vikings (1961–79)

Basketball

▶ 906—Randy Smith, NBA: Buffalo Braves, San Diego Clippers, Cleveland Cavaliers, New York Knicks, San Diego Clippers, Atlanta Hawks (February 18, 1972–March 13, 1983; the streak ended when he was given his release)

▶ 1,041—Ron Boone, ABA-NBA

Hockey

▶ 962—Doug Jarvis, Montreal Canadiens, Washington Capitals, Hartford Whalers (October 8, 1975–April 5, 1987; includes every game for the first twelve years of his career)

And some of the most durable and loyal men in sports—a sample of athletes and coaches who've had incredibly long, continuous reigns with one team (in years):

Baseball

Playing:

▶ 23—Brooks Robinson, Baltimore Orioles, 1955–77

▶ 23—Carl Yastrzemski, Boston Red Sox, 1961–83

▶ 22—Cap Anson, Chicago Cubs, 1876–97

▶ 22—Stan Musial, St. Louis Cardinals, 1941–63 (except '45, when he was in military service)

▶ 22—Mel Ott, New York Giants, 1926–47

▶ 22—Al Kaline, Detroit Tigers, 1953–74

Managing:

▶ 50—Connie Mack, Philadelphia Athletics, 1901–50

Football

Coaching:

▶ 29—Tom Landry, Dallas Cowboys, 1960–88

▶ 29—Curly Lambeau, Green Bay Packers, 1921–49

▶ 23—Steve Owen, New York Giants, 1931–53

Basketball

Coaching (college):

▶ 42—Ed Diddle, Western Kentucky, 1923–64

▶ 42—Ray Meyer, DePaul, 1943–84

▶ 41—Adolph Rupp, Kentucky, 1931–72 (the team was on probation for one year)

Flops

▶ On July 25, 1990, "Working Women's Night" at San Diego's Jack Murphy Stadium, the Padres, to their everlasting regret, invited actress-comedienne Roseanne Barr to sing the national anthem. Barr, holding her fingers in her ears, delivered a tortured, off-key rendition— but that wasn't the end of it. As the crowd of 25,000-plus booed, Barr topped off her performance by grabbing her crotch and spitting. When the video clip of her act was shown repeatedly on television, more than 1,000 protest calls flooded the Padres' switchboard, President George Bush (Sr.) called her performance "disgraceful," the Padres issued an apology, and finally Barr held a press conference to ask forgiveness.

▶ Left-handed pitcher Brien Taylor looked to have a limitless future when the New York Yankees made the high school senior from Beaufort, North Carolina, the #1 overall pick in the 1991 amateur baseball draft. With a fastball clocked at 100 mph, Taylor was given a then-record $1.55 million signing bonus, and was expected to become a future Yankee ace. But Taylor never got out of the minor leagues. His career was derailed by an injury he suffered in a 1993 fight, during the winter after his second minor-league season. When Brien's younger brother, Brenden Taylor, was attacked by a man said by police to be jealous of the Taylors' new wealth, Brien went to the man's trailer and confronted him. A fistfight ensued with a friend of the man, and Taylor fell, tearing the labrum and capsule in his left shoulder. He was never the same after surgery, eventually getting released by the Yankees and two other teams without ever pitching in the major leagues.

▶ It's hard to believe in retrospect, but some respected NFL people hotly debated who was the better pro prospect coming out of college in the 1998 draft: Tennessee's Peyton Manning or Washington State's Ryan Leaf. The San Diego Chargers engineered a trade with Arizona to get the #2 overall pick and used it (after the Indianapolis Colts selected Manning at #1) to draft Leaf, whom they then gave an $11.25 million signing bonus. Leaf was the personification of a draft disaster as he clashed with coaches, teammates, and media, and performed abominably when given the starting job. The Chargers suspended him for four weeks in 1999 after he berated general manager Bobby Bethard in front of the team. The Chargers eventually released Leaf, as did the Tampa Bay Buccaneers and the Dallas Cowboys. Leaf signed with the Seattle Seahawks in 2002 but retired before training camp, finishing his career with a 4-17 record as a starter, with 36 interceptions and 14 touchdown passes.

▶ Notre Dame football coach Bob Davie was a flop from his first year, 1997, when the Fighting Irish went a very modest 7-6. His five-year record of 35-25, for a .583 winning percentage, is not awful—unless, of course, you're the coach at Notre Dame. Of the 28 total men who've had the similar privilege (including Ty Willingham, who began as coach in the 2002 season), Davie's winning percentage is 5th-worst all-time. After denying repeatedly that he wouldn't be coaching the team following the 2001 season—an embarrassing 5-6 campaign—Davie was gone (mercifully, in the minds of many Notre Dame boosters), and Willingham eventually got the job.

Through November 3, 2002, Willingham was 8-1 in his first year as Notre Dame football coach.

▶ Heading into the 1992 Olympics, Dan O'Brien was heavily favored to be officially crowned "the world's greatest athlete," the title traditionally bestowed upon the decathlon champion. But after being featured, along with American decathlon teammate Dave Johnson in Reebok's high-profile, $25 million "Dan or Dave" advertising campaign, O'Brien shockingly failed to make the Olympic team when he didn't clear his opening height in the pole vault at the Olympic Trials, after passing on the first four heights; going into the pole vault, the eighth of 10 events in the decathlon, O'Brien had been leading the event at a world-record pace. The Reebok ad campaign continued through the Olympics, though it had to be adjusted from a competition between Johnson and O'Brien to them poking fun at each other. Johnson went on to take the bronze medal in Barcelona, and O'Brien would win the decathlon gold at Atlanta in 1996, but he was so devastated by his failure to qualify in '92 that he sought counseling from a sports psychologist.

▶ IBM spent $80 million-plus for the privilege of being the technology coordinator for the 1996 Atlanta Olympic Games, thus allowing it a global showcase for its state-of-the-art Internet capability, which promised "bullet-proof reliability."

Bullet-ridden is more like it.

Some of IBM's systems and networks produced outdated or otherwise inaccurate information to the media, or to others using the Internet, and did it slowly; on numerous occasions, reporters couldn't get scores or accurate statistics to their news organizations on time. To give one example: The system—seemingly unprepared for basketball games to go to overtime—listed the final score of the Australia-Brazil game as 82-82 (which was the score at the end of regulation), rather than the 109-101, double-overtime Australian victory it turned out to be. On other occasions, the system would not recognize the names of prominent athletes who were competing at the Games.

"We're obviously very upset about it," Rick Thoman, IBM's chief financial officer, said at the time. The European Union sought reimbursement from the International Olympic Committee for money it had spent on computer terminals that failed to deliver timely results consistently.

"If self-parody were an Olympic sport," hissed *Fortune* magazine, "IBM would have medalled." Others called it "The Glitch Games."

▶ Numerous Heisman Trophy winners have flopped in the pros, among them Pat Sullivan, the 1971 winner from Auburn, whose NFL career consists of 5 touchdowns and 16 interceptions; John Huarte, the 1964 winner from Notre Dame, who played on taxi squads for parts of seven NFL seasons (in winning the Heisman, he beat out, among others, Gale Sayers and Dick Butkus); Andre Ware, the 1989 winner from the University of Houston, who amassed a total of 83 NFL completions; and Gino Torretta, the 1992 winner from the University of Miami, whose most impressive pro football stat may be that he was waived eight times, including four by one team (the San Francisco 49ers).

▶ Rick Pitino, and Boston Celtic fans, had every reason to be optimistic when Pitino took over as coach of the once-great, now-floundering franchise in 1997. After all, Pitino had been successful every place he'd been head coach, in the college ranks and in the pros. In 1978, at 25 years old, Pitino became head coach at Boston University. In five years, his teams were 91-51, the most successful run in their history; in his last season there, the Terriers gained their first NCAA Tournament appearance in 24 years. He was twice named New England Coach of the Year (1979, 1983).

In his two years at Providence College, his teams went 42-23 record, and the Friars went to the NCAA Tournament both years, including a charmed run to the Final Four in 1987.

In his first year as head coach of the New York Knicks, the team improved by 14 wins and made the playoffs for the first time in four seasons. The next year, Pitino's final one with the Knicks, New York won 52 games and swept the Philadelphia 76ers in the first round.

As head coach at the University of Kentucky, Pitino guided the Wildcats to three Final Four appearances in his last five years, won the whole thing in 1996, and was runner-up in 1997. In eight seasons there, he compiled a 219-50 record (.814).

Then came the Celtics.

Pitino, serving as head coach and team president, made a positive impact in his first year—Boston went from a franchise-worst 15-67 record the season before he arrived to an impressive 36-46—but his coaching never quite took, and all sides viewed it as a disappointment. In the strike-shortened season of 1998–99, the team went 19-31; the following year, 35-47. While Pitino continually put great demands on himself, he finally resigned on January 8, 2001, after 3½ years, with the team at 12-22. His overall record while there was a very un-Pitino-like 102-146 record. (In the first full season after Pitino left, Coach Jim O'Brien helped guide the team to the Eastern Conference finals.)

Pitino departed for the University of Louisville, where in his first year the team went 19-13 (they'd finished the previous year at 12-19), and made it to the second round of the postseason NIT Tournament.

6 Weird Hybrid Sporting Events

▶ *Boxing and Wrestling*: Heavyweight champion Muhammad Ali fought Japanese wrestler Antonio Inoki in Tokyo, in 1976. The 15-rounder—in which Inoki spent most of the time lying on the mat, kicking up at Ali—was called a draw.

▶ *(Basketball,) Track, and Horse Racing*: In 1986, New York Knick Kenny Walker defeated a pacer named Pugwash by a nose in a ¹⁄₁₆-mile match race at Monticello Raceway. Walker's time was 10.4 seconds, a world record for a human versus a horse.

▶ *(Football,) Track, and Horse Racing*: The record that Walker broke had been set by former New York Giants defensive back Beasley Reece, who had defeated a horse named Super Chris.

▶ *Tennis and Ice Skating*: In 1953, tennis stars Gardner Mulloy and Bobby Riggs played a charity exhibition on skates.

▶ *Roller Derby, Tag, Motocross, Team Handball, and Criminal Assault*: The 1975 James Caan movie *Rollerball* featured a futuristic and violent international sport in which roller-skating players, propelled around a track by motorcycles, would attempt to throw a metal ball into a goal that was defended by large men wearing metal-studded gloves. Jonathan E., Caan's character, was the top scorer for the Houston team.

▶ *Basketball and Tennis*: University of Florida's 7'2" center Dwayne Schintzius was suspended for the first four games of the 1989–90 season for hitting Florida student Paul Sullivan over the head with a tennis racket.

▷ Honorable mention: The New Zealand syndicate that challenged the San Diego Yacht Club to race for America's Cup in 1988 believed that the Americans engaged unfairly in "hybrid yachting" when New Zealand's 133-foot mono-hull was routed by the SDYC's 60-foot catamaran.

The Most Notable Falls in Sports

▶ American runner Mary Decker has been involved in several falls:
In 1974, at a U.S.A.-U.S.S.R. meet in Moscow, Decker was shoved off the track by Sarmite Shtula in the 4x800m relay. Decker threw her relay baton at Shtula, picked it up, finished the race, and again threw her baton at Shtula.

At the 1983 Millrose Games in New York, Decker shoved Puerto Rican runner Angelita Lind to the ground when she failed to move aside and let Decker pass.

In her most famous fall, in the 1984 Olympic 1,500m race, Decker tripped, fell, and screamed at South African Zola Budd, who also fell. Budd was initially disqualified for the incident, but after watching videotapes, a jury voted unanimously to reinstate her.

▶ American speedskater Dan Jansen fell going around the first turn of the 1988 Winter Olympic 500m race, just a few hours after learning of the death of his sister, Jane. Four days later, in the 1,000m, Jansen was on a gold-medal pace when he fell on a straightaway two-thirds through the race.

▶ In the men's Olympic slalom in 1952, skier Antoin Miliordos of Greece fell 18 times and was so disgusted that he sat down and crossed the finish line backward.

▶ In the fourth and clinching game of the 1970 Stanley Cup finals, Boston Bruins star defenseman Bobby Orr flew through the air, lunged, and fell as he scored the overtime goal against the St. Louis Blues, to give the Bruins their first Stanley Cup in 29 years. The image of Orr sprawled on the ice has become one of the most enduring in hockey history.

▶ At the 1972 Munich Olympics, American miler Jim Ryun tried to squeeze between two runners in the opening heat of the 1,500m when he tripped and fell. He got to his feet but did not qualify. It turned out to be his last amateur race.

▶ Cuban sprinter Silvio Leonard seriously injured his leg at the 1975 Pan-Am games in Mexico City when he pulled a muscle as he crossed the finish line, was unable to stop, and fell into a 10-foot moat that surrounded the track.

▶ As the bell rang to indicate the last lap in the 1996 Olympic 1,500m race, Moroccan Hicham El Guerrouj and Algeria's Noureddine Morceli, two of the greatest middle-distance runners of all-time, collided. El Guerrouj fell to the track and finished last; Morceli won the gold.

▶ Finn Lasse Viren fell during the 12th lap of the Olympic 10,000m in 1972, got up, and still won—and set a world record in the process.

And 1 Notable Fall That Never Happened

▶ On November 19, 1978, the John McVay-coached New York Giants led the Philadelphia Eagles, 17-12, with 31 seconds to go and possession of the ball. Instead of falling down, Giants quarterback Joe Pisarcik attempted to hand off to fullback Larry Csonka, but the ball bounced off of Pisarcik's hands and Eagles defensive back Herm Edwards picked up the loose ball and ran for the winning touchdown, thus setting off perhaps the darkest moment in the history of the Giants franchise.

20 Heralded Upsets

If games were played on paper, there would be no upsets. The deeper, more talented team would win and that would be that. But since games are usually played on grass and turf and clay and ice and hardwood, the outcome occasionally differs from the expected.

Any list of notable upsets should probably include the New York Mets' win over the Baltimore Orioles in the 1969 World Series; the American hockey team's semifinal victory over the Soviets at the 1980 Olympics; another Olympic hockey team—Czechoslovakia, led by Dominic Hasek and Jaromir Jagr—beating the U.S., Canada, and Russia for the gold at the 1998 Games; that same year, Harvard women's basketball team knocking off Stanford in the national tournament to become the first #16 seed in NCAA tournament history to knock off a #1 seed; and Truman over Dewey, 1948. We include here some of the other most heralded upsets of all time.

▶ In one of the greatest upsets in international competition, American wrestler Rulon Gardner, farmboy from Wyoming, won the 130-kg Greco-Roman gold medal when, at the 2000 Sydney Olympics, he beat the three-time Olympic champion, Russia's Alexandre Karelin, who'd never before lost an international match, and barely ever been challenged; indeed, Karelin had been so dominant for so long that he'd attained near-mythical status in his home country and among wrestlers. In the remaining seconds of the bout, which Gardner won, 1-0, Karelin slumped, as if to say he knew he was finally beaten.

▶ In 1899, Sewanee (Tennessee) College won 12 straight football games, including five games in six days. Among their opponents were teams from much larger Tennessee, Georgia, Georgia Tech, Texas, Tulane, Louisiana State, Mississippi, and Auburn. Of the 12 schools, only Auburn even scored on the tiny college.

▶ Arthur Ashe beat Jimmy Connors in the 1975 Wimbledon finals by playing a tactical match designed to slow down the pace of the game and upset Connors' rhythm. The year before, Connors had won the Wimbledon and U.S. Open finals, losing a total of just eight games in six sets.

▶ The Oakland As were being proclaimed as baseball's newest dynasty in 1990 when they wrapped up their third straight American League pennant behind the vaunted "Bash Brothers," Mark McGwire and Jose Canseco, and eventual MVP Rickey Henderson. But the Reds, led by the "Nasty Boys" relieving corps of Randy Myers, Rob Dibble, and Norm Charlton, none of whom was scored upon in a combined $8\frac{2}{3}$ innings, swept Oakland in the World Series. Cincinnati outscored the As' 22-8 and limited them to a .207 batting average.

▶ The 2002 World Cup was overloaded with upsets: Senegal shutting out defending champion France in the opening match; the U.S. beating Portugal and Mexico; Korea beating Italy; and Argentina not even making it out of the first round.

In Brazil in 1950, in what has been called "the greatest upset in the history of international competition," the United States defeated England, 1-0, in World Cup play. The American goal was scored by a Haitian immigrant from New York named Joe Gaetjens, who was carried around the field on the shoulders of Brazilian fans.

▶ James L. Corbett beat John L. Sullivan in the first heavyweight fight under Marquis of Queensberry rules, September 7, 1892. Corbett, outweighed by 34 pounds—178 to 212—knocked out Sullivan in the 21st round.

▶ In Tokyo on February 10, 1990, James "Buster" Douglas shocked pretty much all sports fans and won the world heavyweight belt when he became the first man to knock out Mike Tyson. Odds for the fight, considered by most to be a Tyson tune-up for his bout with #1-ranked challenger Evander Holyfield, were not even posted by many Las

Vegas bookmakers. It is widely considered the biggest upset in boxing history.

▶ Native Dancer's only loss was to Dark Star in the 1953 Kentucky Derby, in one of horse-racing's biggest upsets ever.

Dragon Blood, ridden by Lester Piggot, started at 10,000-to-1 odds in the Primio Naviglio at Milan on June 1, 1967, and won.

▶ The Kirkland (Washington) Little League team shocked Taiwan, the perennial champions, in 1982.

▶ Unknown American Billy Mills won the 10,000m Olympic gold medal in 1964. Mills, who was 7/16 Sioux Indian, ran 46 seconds faster than his previous best.

▶ In 1921, the Centre (Kentucky) College Prayin' Colonels football team beat Harvard 6-0 at Cambridge, and used only five substitutes (plus the starters) to do it. The loss was the Crimson's first intersectional defeat in 40 years.

▶ Sarava, at 70-1, became the longest-shot winner in Belmont history, in 2002. War Emblem, who would have won the Triple Crown with the victory, stumbled out of the gate, briefly took the lead mid-race, then fell back and was not a factor.

▶ #14 seed and unknown Weber State (in Utah) beat the #3 seed powerhouse University of North Carolina in the first round of the 1999 men's NCAA men's basketball tournament.

▶ In 1938, the Chicago Black Hawks, with eight Americans on their squad, surprised the Toronto Maple Leafs and won the Stanley Cup.

▶ In 1984, 17-year-old Australian Jon Sieben pulled off one of the biggest upsets in Olympic swimming history when he out-touched West German star Michael Gross in the 200m butterfly, Gross's best event. Sieben set a world record (1:57.04) and bettered his previous personal best by more than four seconds.

▶ French tennis rejoiced when the home country beat the heavily-favored U.S.A. in the 1991 Davis Cup finals, in Lyon, to win their first Cup in 59 years.

▶ The Denver Nuggets beat the Seattle Supersonics in Round 1 of the 1994 NBA playoffs, the first time a #8 seed beat a #1 seed. The Nuggets swept the last three games, and won the deciding game on Seattle's floor, which Nuggets center Dikembe Mutombo, after the final buzzer, joyously collapsed on, while hugging the ball.

▶ On December 23, 1982, Ralph Sampson and his #1-ranked, undefeated Virginia Cavaliers were beaten 77-72 by Chaminade, an NAIA school in Hawaii that had a student body of 850 and a basketball program that was just seven years old.

Running Away With It:
A Few of the Most Memorable Routs of All Time

▶ On April 22, 1939, skier Toni Matt finished the Inferno, a course that begins atop New England's highest mountain, in 6 minutes, 21.4 seconds. He finished one minute ahead of Dick Durrance, the runner-up. It is the largest winning margin in the history of modern American skiing.

At the 1956 Cortina Winter Olympics, Toni Sailer, the first skier to sweep the Alpine events, won the giant slalom competition by a whopping six seconds-plus, and the downhill by 3.5 seconds.

▶ The worst Super Bowl drubbing ever was the San Francisco 49ers' 55-10 pasting of the Denver Broncos in 1990. The worst rout in NFL history is the Chicago Bears' 73-0 dissection of the Washington Redskins for the 1940 championship.

Other notable, and recent, NFL postseason routs include the New York Giants blow-out of the Minnesota Vikings, 41-0, in the 2001 NFC Championship game (though the game seemed to be over before the 20-minute mark, with the Giants already up 24-0); the Jacksonville Jaguars' destruction of their cross-state rivals, the Miami Dolphins, by a score of 62-7, in the first round of the 1999 playoffs; and the Buffalo Bills' pitiless head-handing of the Raiders, 51-3, in the 1990 AFC Championship Game.

▶ In a 1909 race at Madison Square Garden, Italian Dorando Pietri, who was beaten famously by American Johnny Hayes in the 1908 Olympic marathon, lapped Hayes five times.

▶ The Kansas City Royals beat the St. Louis Cardinals 11-0 in Game 7 of the 1985 World Series.

▶ The New York Rangers lost to the Detroit Red Wings 15-0, the most lopsided score in NHL history, on January 23, 1944.

▶ Bobby Locke won the 1948 Chicago Victory National Championship by 16 strokes, the largest winning margin in PGA Tour history.

In the U.S. Open, Bobby Jones won the 36-hole playoff with Al Espinosa by 23 strokes, 141 to 164.

Tiger Woods eviscerated the field at the 1997 Masters, beating runner-up Tom Kite by 12 shots. If that wasn't enough, at the 2000 U.S. Open, no one could get better than 15 shots from Tiger.

▶ The largest margin of victory in an NBA game is 63 points: In 1972, the Los Angeles Lakers beat the Golden State Warriors, 162-99.

▶ Secretariat won the 1973 Belmont on June 9 by 31 lengths.

On the same track on September 4, 1920, Man O' War won the Lawrence Realizations Stakes by 100 lengths, or more than a quarter of a mile, over the only other entrant, Hoodwink.

▶ On its way to the 1980 Olympic women's basketball gold, the Soviet Union won their games by an average of 45 points. (The United States did not compete because of the boycott.)

► A number of long-standing intra-state college football rivalries would require the habitual vanquisher to not show up for several decades before the habitual vanquishee could make at least a relatively even series of it. Through the end of the 2001 season, Kansas was 61-33-5 vs. Kansas State, LSU was 65-22-7 vs. Tulane, Michigan was 61-28-5 vs. Michigan State, Tennessee was 64-26-5 vs. Vanderbilt, and Oklahoma was 74-15-7 vs. Oklahoma State.

► In the 1953 Wimbledon doubles semifinals, Shirley Fry and Doris Hart won by a 6-0, 6-0 score. In the final, they again won 6-0, 6-0.

► In the first Rose Bowl in 1902, Michigan beat Stanford, 49-0.

12
FAMILY

Lesser-Known Siblings

All of these "lesser" brothers and sisters were at least competent athletes. Some rose to the top of their sport, hung around for the cup of coffee, then moved on to another profession; others were quite talented and forged respectable sports careers. But their athletic accomplishments in each case were overshadowed publicly by those of their more famous siblings. That's how you get to be lesser-known.

► Sam Wright played in the major leagues for three years and hit .109. His two brothers, Harry and George, are in the Baseball Hall of Fame.

► Jeanne Evert, Chris's sister, played on the women's tennis tour briefly in the late 1970s.

► Mack Robinson, Jackie's older brother, was second to Jesse Owens in the 1936 Olympic 200m.

► Adeline Gehrig, sister of Lou, competed in the 1924 Olympics as a fencer. She was American women's foil champion from 1920 to 1923.

► Henry Mathewson appeared in the major leagues in two seasons, compiling a record of 0-1. His brother, Christy, won 373 games, which ties him for the third-highest total in major-league history.

► Eddie Payton, brother of Walter, was a running back and kick returner for four NFL teams in five years.

► Yo-Yo Davalillo, brother of 16-year veteran Vic, played in 19 games for the 1953 Washington Senators.

► Nelson Munsey, older brother of star running back Chuck Muncie, was a defensive back for the Baltimore Colts from 1972–77, and for the Minnesota Vikings in 1978. Chuck not only outshined Nelson on the field but changed the spelling of the family name.

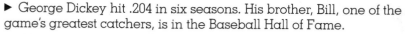

▶ George Dickey hit .204 in six seasons. His brother, Bill, one of the game's greatest catchers, is in the Baseball Hall of Fame.

▶ Carol Lewis, sister of Carl, was an Olympian in the long jump in 1984 but did not win a medal.

▶ Joey LaMotta, brother of middleweight champion Jake, was also a professional boxer.

▶ Joe and Johnny Evers combined to play in 1,784 major-league games —1 for Joe and 1,783 for Johnny. Tommie and Hank Aaron hold the record for home runs by brothers with 768—13 for Tommie and 755 for Hank. The stolen base record for brothers is held by the Wagner boys: 4 for Albert "Butts" Wagner, 723 for Honus.

▶ Marlene Floyd, sister of Raymond Floyd, was a member of the LPGA tour. Janet LePera, sister of Donna Caponi, has played on the LPGA tour. Bobby Wadkins, Lanny's brother, played on the PGA tour.

▶ Former San Francisco Giants reliever Randy Moffitt is the brother of tennis great Billie Jean King.

▶ Bubba Wyche, Sam's brother, was a quarterback for the WFL Detroit Wheels in 1974, the same year that Sam was quarterback for Detroit's other professional football team, the NFL Lions.

▶ Faye Throneberry, brother of Marv, had an eight-year major-league career and a lifetime average of .236, one point lower than Marv's.

▶ Darren Flutie, Doug's brother, was a wide receiver for Boston College.

▶ Ozzie Canseco, José's twin brother, got to bat 65 times in the majors. Gordon Hershiser, Orel's brother, was a pitcher in the Los Angeles Dodgers minor leagues.

▶ Phil and Orrin Olsen, brothers of Hall of Famer Merlin, both played in the NFL. Phil was a defensive lineman for the Los Angeles Rams from 1971–74, teaming with Merlin. Orrin was a center for the Kansas City Chiefs in 1976.

▶ Buddy Baer, younger brother of heavyweight champion Max, twice lost to Joe Louis in heavyweight title fights.

▶ Dave Dryden, Ken's brother, was also a professional goaltender and both lost 57 NHL games in their career. Dave, however, won just 48 NHL games while Ken won 258.

Winning Is Thicker Than Blood or Marriage

There are many instances of athletic family members and spouses help-ing and sharing: hockey-playing brothers on the same line looking to feed each other the puck; fathers and sons working together to win Olympic gold in yachting; countless tennis phenoms being coached by parents (Richard Williams, Stefano Capriati, Melanie Molitor—Martina Hingis's mom—come to mind); Bob Kersee rooting for and coaching his wife, Olympian track and field star Jackie Joyner-Kersee. The emotions stirred up by family loyalty push some past sensible behavior, as was the case when Minna Wilson climbed into a boxing ring in Southampton, England, in the summer of 1989, and with one of her shoes began to batter the head of boxer Steve McCarthy, who himself had been administering a third-round battering to Wilson's son, former British light-heavyweight champion Tony Wilson. We may condemn Mrs. Wilson for her methods but not her show of fealty.

Fealty is not something that those in the following list will ever be accused of.

▶ In 1987, Pittsburgh Steeler President Dan Rooney fired his brother, Art Rooney, Jr., vice president of player personnel, who had been with the organization for 26 years.

▶ In the early 1970s, Clark Graebner, the World Team Tennis player-coach of the Cleveland Nets and recently separated from his wife, Carole, also a member of the Nets, traded her to the Pittsburgh Triangles.

▶ In December of 1968, Los Angeles Dodgers General Manager Al Campanis traded his son, Jim, to the Kansas City Athletics for two minor leaguers.

▶ John Laupheimer, a senior USGA administrator, assessed British Curtis Cup member Mary Everard a penalty stroke because her caddie had cleaned off a ball—an infringement of Rule 23.2—that Everard had marked and lifted at the request of her playing companion. Laupheimer and Everard had been married earlier that year.

▶ Paul Brown, so revered that his team, the Cleveland Browns, was named for him, was fired as head coach and general manager on January 9, 1963, by owner Art Modell.

▶ Washington Senators owner Clark Griffith sold his nephew, Sherry Robertson, to the Philadelphia Athletics in May 1952 for an undisclosed sum of money. Robertson was the brother of Calvin Griffith, the Senators' vice president and Clark's adopted son.

▶ On June 28, 1989, San Diego Padres General Manager Jack McKeon traded his son-in-law, Greg Booker, to the Minnesota Twins for Freddie Toliver.

It's My Ball, So I Make the Rules:
6 Examples of Favoritism and Nepotism in Sports

On the other hand, there have been occasions in sports where competitive judgment is sacrificed to help out a friend or relative, or to give privileged treatment to someone who perhaps didn't earn it by athletic prowess.

A few examples:

▶ Haiti's Olympic track teams in 1972 and 1976 consistently finished last with awful times. The country's despot, "Baby Doc" Duvalier, peopled the teams with friends and trusted soldiers, regardless of their athletic abilities.

▶ Earle Mack played five games spread out over three seasons for the Philadelphia Athletics, managed and owned by his father, Connie. Earle's career statistics were two hits in 16 at-bats for a .125 average.

▶ William Marcy "Boss" Tweed, kingpin of Tammany Hall, placed almost all of the members of the New York Mutuals, a semipro baseball team from 1860–71, on the New York City payroll as clerks and street sweepers. Tweed was also president of the Mutuals.

▶ In 60 A.D., the Roman Emperor Nero instituted an Olympic Games in his honor and entered a musical event specially created for him, which he won.

▶ The Duke of York, who was the second son of King George V and Queen Mary and who later became King George VI, played in the men's doubles draw at Wimbledon in 1926. He and Sir Louis Grieg, later the chairman of the All-England Club (which runs Wimbledon), were beaten in the first round.

▶ The California Angel players retired #26 in honor of the contributions made to the team by Gene Autry. It should be mentioned that Gene Autry was the owner of the California Angels.

▷ **Respectful but necessary note:** There is no doubt that San Francisco 49ers quarterback Steve Young earned his place in the NFL on merit—tremendous merit—after a spectacular career at Brigham Young University. However, while his acceptance to BYU was certainly of great benefit to the school (and Young's professional career), it cannot have been a surprise to him since his great-great-great-grandfather is Brigham Young.

Athletic Mothers and Mothers-to-Be

▶ In a 1969 race six days before she gave birth, jockey Mary Bacon rode a mount that was a mare in foal. "The four of us finished last," Bacon said after the race.

▶ Fanny Blankers-Koen, the great Dutch track and field star and mother of two, practiced with her baby carriage next to the track. At the 1948 London Olympics, she won all four women's track events—the 100m, 200m, 80m hurdles, and the 4x100m relay. (She did not enter the long jump, though she held the world record.) She was called "The Flying Housewife."

▶ Motherhood did not appear to have a negative effect on Sheryl Swoopes's basketball career. After giving birth to her son, Jordan, she led the Houston Comets to their fourth consecutive WNBA title, in 2000, and won the league MVP Award.

▶ When Evonne Goolagong beat Chris Evert in 1980 to win Wimbledon, she became the first mother to win the singles title since Dorothea Lambert Chambers in 1914.

▶ At the world shooting championships in 1970, Margaret Murdock won the standing small-bore rifle event while four months pregnant. In 1952, Juno Irwin was 3½ months pregnant with her second child when she won the Olympic bronze in platform diving.

▶ Of the 20 Russian women medal winners at the 1956 Olympics, 10 of them were pregnant.

▶ The U.S.S.R.'s Tatyana Kazankina had her first child in 1978, two years after winning the Olympic 1,500m race. In 1980, she defended her title. In 1982, she had another child, and in 1984, she set world records in the 2,000m and 3,000m.

American sprinter Evelyn Ashford had a daughter in May, 1985, and the following year was ranked #1 in the world in the 100m.

Ingrid Kristiansen ran the fastest marathon of her career five months after having a son.

▶ Nancy Lopez had a daughter in 1983 and two years later won LPGA Player of the Year honors. She had another daughter in 1986 and two years later was again named Player of the Year.

Giving Birth to Sports

Historians like to determine the lineage of things: George Washington was the Father of his Country, Necessity is the Mother of Invention. The need to determine who, in spirit, gave birth to what is apparently rampant among historians of sport, too.

▶ Senda Berenson Abbot, a coach who helped popularize her sport and was later inducted into its Hall of Fame, has been called "The Mother of Women's Basketball."

▶ Dr. James Dwight, a former player, referee, and president of the USTA, has been called "The Father of American Tennis"; Mary Ewing Outerbridge, who, while vacationing in Bermuda, saw British officers playing a racket game and had equipment sent to her Staten Island home, is "The Mother of American Tennis"; and Hazel H. Wightman, a top American player in the first half of the 20th century and the donator of the Wightman Cup, is "The Queen Mother of Tennis."

▶ Duke Kahanamoku, who played a major role in introducing his sport to the world, is "The Father of Modern Surfing."

▶ Baron Pierre de Coubertin, who helped rekindle an idea dead for 1,500 years, is known as "The Father of the Modern Olympics."

▶ Jack Broughton, who, among his other achievements, helped to devise "mufflers" (gloves) to minimize the risk of facial damage, is known as "The Father of British Boxing" or simply "The Father of Boxing," while Jacob Hyer, who fought in the first American championship bout, was called "The Father of the American Ring."

▶ Hugo Meisl, a coach and innovator, is known as "The Father of Austrian soccer."

▶ Fred C. Waghorne, who popularized the technique of tossing the hockey puck between opposing players, has been called "The Father of the Face-Off."

▶ Dr. Elisha Warfield, an early-nineteenth-century horse breeder, was called "The Father of the Kentucky Turf."

▶ Harry Wright, who organized the Cincinnati Red Stockings, baseball's first professional team, was often called "The Father of the Game."

▶ Konnie Savickus is known as "The Father of Lithuanian Basketball."

▶ Friedrich Ludwig Jahn (1778–1852) is called "The Father of German Gymnastics."

▶ Dr. Kenneth Cooper is called "The Father of Aerobics."

The Best Sports Pedigrees

What happens when parents want their kids to go into the family business, and the family business happens to be big-time sports? It's a lot easier for the kids to disappoint, for one: So few succeed at that level, and your last name doesn't count for much when you're trying to hit a 95mph fastball.

On the other hand, the offspring of great athletes do have the benefit of good genes. Here are some notable sports lineages:

▶ Ramanathan Krishnan was India's #1 men's tennis player in the 1960s. His son, Ramesh, was their #1 player in the 1980s.

▶ Auto racing is famous for its familial heritages. There have been four generations of Pettys—Lee, Richard, Kyle, and Adam—and the father-son teams of Al Unsers (Sr. and Jr.), Mario and Michael Andretti, Bobby and Davey Allison, and Dale Earnhardt Sr. and Jr.

▶ Ron Retton, the father of Olympic gold medal gymnast Mary Lou Retton, was co-captain with Jerry West of the University of West Virginia basketball team that lost in the1959 NCAA finals. Retton was also a shortstop in the New York Yankees farm system until 1963.

▶ There are three three-generation major-league families: the Bells— (from youngest to oldest)—David, Buddy, and Gus; the Boones—brothers Bret and Aaron, Bob, and Ray; and the Hairstons—Jerry, Jr., Jerry, and Sam. Two of the kids, David Bell and Bret Boone, were teammates on the 2001 Seattle Mariners.

▶ Golfer Catherine Lacoste, daughter of tennis legend René, won the U.S. Women's Open in 1967, becoming the only amateur to do so. Catherine also won the U.S. and British amateur titles. Lacoste's mother, Thion de la Chaume, won the French women's golf title six times and the British title once, the first Frenchwoman to do so.

▶ All thoroughbred horses in the world today are descended from at least one of three stallions: Darley Arabian, Byerly Turk, and Godolphin Barb.

Fifty-two of the first 61 Kentucky Derby winners carried the blood of Lexington, who was regarded as the most successful stallion ever. In 20 years of stud duty at Woodburn Farm, Lexington topped the sire list 16 times, including 14 years in a row. Lexington sired more than 600 colts and fillies, 260 of them winners.

▶ Golfer Clay Heafner played for the American Ryder Cup team in 1949 and 1951. His son, Vance, played for the 1977 American Walker Cup team. Both were unbeaten.

▶ Jack Nicklaus, Jr., won the 1985 North and South Amateur and played in the 1986 British Amateur before turning professional. His brother, Gary, has also played professionally.

▶ Leo Nicholson and his son, Dean, were the only men's basketball coaches at Central Washington University, in Ellensburg, Washington, from before FDR was president through the Bush (Sr.) Adminstration. Leo coached from 1929–64; Dean took over and coached the next 26 years.

▶ Hungarian Imre Nemeth, Olympic gold medalist in the hammer throw in 1948, fathered Miklos Nemeth, gold medalist in the javelin in 1976.

▶ Norway's Peder Lunde won an Olympic yachting gold medal in 1960. His father and mother, Peder and Vibeke, had won silvers in 1952; his grandfather, Eugen, a gold in 1924.

▶ Peter Press Maravich—"Pistol Pete"—played basketball at LSU for his father, Press.

▶ Samantha Stevenson, who in 1999 became the first female qualifier in Wimbledon history to reach the semifinals, is the daughter of basketball legend Julius Erving.

▶ Einer Ulrich was a Danish Davis Cup star for 15 years, from 1924–38. His sons, Torben and Jorgen, were mainstays of the Danish Davis Cup team for 25 years, Torben from 1948, Jorgen from 1958.

▶ Peyton Manning, star quarterback of the Indianapolis Colts, is son of Archie Manning, former star quarterback of the New Orleans Saints.

▶ Tom Hyer, America's first heavyweight champ, was the son of Jacob Hyer, the first American to fight professionally in public.

▶ Erna Bogen, the daughter of 1912 Olympic team saber silver medalist Albert Bogen, was bronze medalist in the 1932 women's foil. Erna married seven-time fencing gold medalist Aladar Gerevich. Their son, Pal, won two bronze medals in the team saber in 1972 and 1980.

▶ Skip Caray, the voice of the Atlanta Braves, is son of Chicago Cubs broadcasting legend Harry Caray; Skip's son, Chip, trying to fill the hole left by his grandfather, is a broadcaster for the Cubs.

9 Happy Families

To make the moment special, an athlete wants to share his or her individual achievement with family and turn it into a group achievement. For certain families, that's literally what it is.

▶ The Ken Griffeys—Senior and Junior—hit back-to-back homers for the Seattle Mariners against the California Angels, on September 14, 1990. Two weeks before, the dad, age 40, and the son, age 20, became the first father and son to play together in the majors. Each had a first-inning single against the Kansas City Royals.

▶ Baseball great Tim Raines, at the end of an illustrious career (and having missed the 2000 season with lupus), stuck it out long enough so that he and his son, Tim, Jr., could realize the Griffey dream, too. In the final days of the 2001 season, the Baltimore Orioles called Tim (the son) up from the minors; less than two days later, Tim (the father) learned that he had been traded by the Montreal Expos to the Orioles. Tim (the father) flew to Baltimore, though it's likely he didn't even require a plane.

▶ Before each free throw he attempts, NBA All-Star guard Jason Kidd blows a little kiss—to his wife, Joumana. Former NBA sharpshooter Jeff Hornacek would slide his hand across the side of his face before each free throw, a greeting to his three kids watching at home.

▶ On August 21, 1975, Paul and Rick Reuschel of the Chicago Cubs became the first brothers to combine for a major-league shutout.

▶ In 1979, sisters Arta, Sherri, Denean, and Mattina Howard set a national high school record in the mile relay (3:44.89) while running for San Gorgonio High School in San Bernardino, California.

▶ At the 1981 Indianapolis 500, Bill Mears, working in the pits for his son, saved Rick's life by putting out a fire on his suit.

▶ In 1943, left wing Doug Bentley set an NHL record with five points in a single period. His brother, Max, helped him, recording four assists.

▶ The Swedish Olympic team that won the cycling team time trial silver medal in 1968 was made up of four brothers: Erik, Gosta, Sture, and Tomas Pettersson. All four later changed their last name to Faglum, which was the name of their home village.

▶ Larry Yount, who pitched one game for the Houston Astros in 1971, was the agent for his brother, eventual Hall of Famer Robin Yount.

Oedipal Triumphs and Families That Compete Against Each Other

▶ The only home run of Joe Niekro's batting career came on May 29, 1976, off his brother, Phil.

▶ In 1906, Alex Smith defeated his brother Willie for the U.S. Open golf title. In 1910, Alex again won the title, this time in a playoff over his brother Macdonald.

▶ Bobby Allison,50, held off son Davey to win the 1988 Daytona 500.

Al Unser, Sr., edged his son, Al, Jr., 151 points to 150, to win the CART-PPG championships in 1985.

▶ In 1973, Madame and Mademoiselle Becquet—mother and daughter—ran against each other in the French 800m national championships.

▶ In a classic transfer of power from one generation to the next, "Young" Tom Morris succeeded his father, "Old" Tom Morris, as British Open champion in 1868. In 1869, Young and Old Tom finished 1-2.

In the 1903 British Open, Tom Vardon finished second to his brother, Harry.

▶ In his major-league debut on May 31, 1979, Detroit Tiger Pat Underwood pitched 8+ innings of three-hit ball and beat his brother, Toronto Blue Jays pitcher Tom Underwood, 1-0.

▶ German sporting-goods giant Adidas was started by Horst Dassler. Their major rival, Puma, was started by Rudolf Dassler, his brother.

▶ During the 1999 football season, in the first such father-son showdown in NCAA history, man taught boy as Bobby Bowden's Florida State Seminoles beat his son Tommy's Clemson Tigers—but barely, 17-14.

▶ Twins Sylviane and Patricia Puntous of Montreal finished 1-2 in the 1983 and 1984 Ironman women's triathlons.

▶ Matty and Felipe Alou are the only brothers to finish 1-2 in a batting title race, in the National League in 1966.

▶ In 1906, the Honorable Denys Scott defeated the Honorable Osmund Scott, his brother, in the final of the Italian Open Amateur golf championship.

▶ With four games remaining in the 1985 season, Wade Phillips took over coaching the New Orleans Saints after his father, Bum, resigned.

▶ In the middle of the 1989–90 NHL season, Washington Capitals coach Bryan Murray was fired and replaced by his brother, Terry.

▶ The Williams sisters, Venus and Serena, have made a habit of competing against each other on tennis's biggest stages. "Venus, can I win a game?" a 9-year-old Serena is said to have asked her 10-year-old sister before they met in the final of a junior tournament in California. (Charitable Venus only beat her kid sister 6-1, 6-1.) In professional encounters, Venus won five of their first six meetings, but in 2002, Serena beat her big sister in three consecutive Grand Slam finals—the French Open, Wimbledon, and the U.S. Open. As of Fall 2002, Serena was ranked #1 in the world, Venus #2.

In 1884, in the first Wimbledon women's final, Maud Watson beat her sister Lillian in three sets.

William Renshaw beat his brother Ernest in the 1882, 1883, and 1889 Wimbledon finals.

▶ Oedipal Jam: For one of his dunks in the 1986 Slam Dunk competition, New York Knicks guard Gerald Wilkins planned to play out his own genteel variation on the Oedipal myth by soaring over his mother, seated in a chair in the three-second lane. (Ultimately, Wilkins decided against elements of the jam and merely leapt over an empty chair—perhaps an even more compelling metaphor.)

▶ Surrogate Oedipal success: In 1921, Harry Heilmann won the batting title, outhitting his manager, Ty Cobb, by five points.

▷ Honorable mention: On April 29, 1931, catcher Rick Ferrell of the St. Louis Browns almost broke up a no-hitter being pitched by his brother, Cleveland Indian Wes Ferrell. On a ball that Rick hit into the hole, the Cleveland shortstop made a tough play but his throw pulled the first baseman off the bag. It was ruled an error, a call that would later be questioned.

19 Famous Athletic Marriages

World-class athletes are so used to being in the public eye that they often feel most comfortable with other high-profile people. Such commingling has produced celebrated marriages: baseball's Leo Durocher and actress Laraine Day, tennis player Gottfried von Cramm and Woolworth heiress Barbara Hutton, jockey Robyn Smith and Fred Astaire, John McEnroe and actress Tatum O'Neal, and perhaps most famous of all, Joe DiMaggio and Marilyn Monroe. In a famous exchange, Monroe, after spending part of her honeymoon performing for troops in Korea, said to her new husband, "Joe, Joe, you never heard such applause."

"Yes, I did," DiMaggio said simply.

But just sharing fame does not guarantee an understanding of the particular demands the athlete faces. Perhaps the best partner for an athlete can only be another athlete. When Jackie Jensen, All-America football player and also the 1958 American League Most Valuable Player, married Zoe Ann Olsen, 1948 Olympic springboard diving silver medalist, they became known as "the sports world's most famous sweethearts." Leslie Godfree and Kathleen "Kitty" McKane Godfree were compatible enough to become, in 1926, the only married couple ever to win the Wimbledon mixed doubles championship.

The following is a list of a few of the most famous unions of athletes:

▶ Steffi Graf, winner of 22 Grand Slam singles tennis titles / Andre Agassi, winner of 7 Grand Slam singles tennis titles

▶ East German swimmer Roland Matthes, winner of eight Olympic and four gold medals / East German swimmer Kornelia Ender, winner of eight Olympic and four gold medals

▶ Gabrielle Reece, professional volleyball stud / Laird Jones, surfing-speedsailing stud

▶ Nancy Lopez, LPGA star / Ray Knight, 1986 World Series MVP

▶ Soviet Valery Borzov, once the "fastest man in the world" (gold medalist in the Olympic 100m and 200m in 1972) / Lyudmila Tourischeva, winner of eight Olympic and four gold medals in gymnastics

▶ Amy Van Dyken, Olympic gold medalist swimmer / Tom Rouen, Denver Broncos punter

▶ Chris Evert, tennis great / John Lloyd, tennis okay (later divorced)

▶ Chris Evert, tennis great / Andy Mill, skiing okay
(Chris Evert, tennis great, was also once engaged to Jimmy Connors, tennis great.)

▶ Mary Decker, track great / Ben Tabb, marathon good (divorced)

▶ Mary Decker, track great / Richard Slaney, discus okay

▶ Marion Jones, Olympic track and field gold medalist / C. J. Hunter, world shotput champion (divorced)

▶ Don Drysdale, Hall of Fame pitcher / Ann Meyers, UCLA All-America and 1976 Olympic basketball player

▶ Florence Griffith Joyner, 1988 Olympic sprints gold medalist / Al Joyner, 1984 Olympic triple-jump gold medalist

▶ Jackie Joyner-Kersee, Olympic heptathlon and long-jump champion / Bob Kersee, coach of Jackie Joyner-Kersee

▶ Emil Zatopek, Czech distance star and winner of four Olympic distance gold medals / Dana Zatopkova, 1952 Czech Olympic javelin gold medalist

▶ Carol Heiss, 1960 women's figure skating Olympic gold medalist / Hayes Jenkins, 1956 men's figure skating Olympic gold medalist

▶ Carling Bassett, once-highly ranked singles player / Robert Seguso, once-highly ranked doubles player

▶ Sandra Farmer, 1989 World Cup champion in the 400m hurdles / David Patrick, 1989 World Cup champion in the 400m hurdles

▶ Ekaterina Gordeeva, two-time Olympic skating pairs champion / Sergei Grinkov, two-time Olympic pairs champion and her skating partner (Shockingly, Grinkov died in 1995, at 28, of a heart attack.)

*On the same day that Zatopkova won the javelin title with an Olympic record throw, Zatopek won the 5,000m, on the way to an unprecedented sweep of the 5,000m, 10,000m, and the marathon. The two Czechs were also born on the same day, September 9, 1922.

More Athletic Siblings

▶ The greatest number of brothers to play in the major leagues is five, the Delahanty boys, who played from 1888 to 1915: Ed, the best of them, an outfielder; Frank, an outfielder; Jim, an infielder; Joe, an outfielder; and Tom, an infielder.

Four O'Neill brothers—Steve, Jim, Jack, and Mike—played in the majors, from 1901–28.

▶ John and Tracy Austin won the 1980 Wimbledon mixed doubles, the first brother-sister combination to do so.

▶ Tony Granato, a top NHL right wing, played for the 1988 U.S. Olympic men's hockey team. His sister, Cammi, was captain of the Olympic gold medal-winning women's hockey team one decade years later.

▶ In his relatively short time in the major leagues, New York Yankees pitcher Orlando "El Duque" Hernandez has produced some of the gaudiest postseason numbers and a reputation as a clutch performer. Obviously, it runs in the family: His half-brother, Livan Hernandez, won the 1997 National League Championship Series and World Series MVP as a rookie, going 4-0 that postseason and helping the Florida Marlins to win a world championship.

▶ Placekicker Mike Duvic is the University of Dayton's all-time leading scorer in football. His brother John, also a kicker, was Northwestern's all-time leading scorer (until running back Darnell Autry broke his record).

▶ Boog Powell and Carl Taylor, his stepbrother who played in the majors for six years with Pittsburgh and St. Louis, both had career averages of .266.

▶ From September 22-26, 1975, brothers Gaylord and Jim Perry had identical major-league won-lost totals—215-174.

▶ Bunny Austin was the first male player to appear at Wimbledon in tennis shorts. His sister, Joan Lycett, was the first woman to play on Centre Court without stockings.

▶ William Dod won an archery gold medal in 1908 and his sister Lottie, a tennis star, won an archery silver medal in the national round competition at the same Games. They are the first brother-sister Olympic medalists.

▶ Scott Cornwell of Parkton Hereford won the Maryland state high school cross-country title in 1970. His brother Greg won it in 1971. Their brother David won it in 1972, 1973, and 1974. And their brother John won it in 1977.

▶ All three major-league Alou brothers—Felipe, Matty, and Jesus—played together in the same outfield for the San Francisco Giants, in a game on September 15, 1963.

▶ Lucious, Lee Roy, and Dewey Selmon were each All-America football players at the University of Oklahoma.

▶ Former Dallas Cowboys All-Pro wide receiver Michael Irvin is one of 17 children.

Sacramento Monarchs All-Star guard Ruthie Bolton is one of 20 children.

▶ Brothers Joey, Keith, Ross, and Jim Browner all played in the NFL.

▶ Six Turnesa brothers played pro golf. Among them, Jim won the 1952 PGA; Willie won the U.S. Amateur in 1938 and 1948; and Joe was runner-up to Walter Hagen at the 1927 PGA.

▶ During the 1980s, six Sutter brothers played in the NHL.

▶ There were five boxing brothers known as "The Fighting Zivics," the best of whom, Fritzie Zivic, was a world welterweight titleholder in 1944–45.

▶ Brothers Paul and Lloyd Waner are both in the Baseball Hall of Fame.

▶ Cheryl Miller, former USC basketball star and ex-coach of the WNBA Phoenix Mercury, is sister of Reggie Miller, future Hall of Fame guard for the Indiana Pacers, and of Darrell, former utilityman for the California Angels.

▶ Soviet wrestlers Sergei and Anatoly Beloglazov, twin brothers, won gold medals in the bantamweight and flyweight divisions, respectively, at the 1980 Olympics.

▶ Twins Ed and Lou Banach were both wrestling gold medalists in 1984.

▶ Hayes Jenkins won the men's figure skating gold in 1956, and younger brother David won it in 1960.

▶ Lionel Hebert won the PGA in 1957, and his brother Jay won the title in 1960.

▶ Joe Corbett, younger brother of heavyweight champion James J. Corbett, was 24-8 in 1897 for Baltimore of the National League.

▶ Tiki Barber, star halfback for the New York Giants, and Ronde Barber, All-Pro cornerback for the Tampa Bay Buccaneers, are identical twins.

▶ Brothers Vijay, Anand, and Ashok Amritraj of India all played on the professional men's tennis tour.

▶ Clete and Ken Boyer are the only brothers to hit home runs in the same World Series, and they did it in the same game. In Game 7 of the 1964 Series, Ken hit one for the St. Louis Cardinals and Clete hit one for the New York Yankees.

▶ Brothers Mike and Jerry Quarry both lost on the same card on one June 1972 night in Las Vegas.

▶ The Mullen boys—Joey, the first U.S.-born player to score 500 NHL goals, and Brian, who scored over 200 goals in an 11-year NHL career—grew up playing roller hockey in New York City's Hell's Kitchen.

▶ Nancy and Cliff Richey were both highly ranked tennis players in the 1960s.

▶ Frank McGuire coached the 1957 University of North Carolina Tar Heels to the NCAA title. His brother, Al, won the 1977 title with Marquette.

▶ Dixie and Harry Walker both won major-league batting titles.

▶ Bob and Ken Forsch are the only brothers to pitch no-hitters.

▶ Don and Bruce Curry are the only brothers to hold boxing world titles simultaneously, reigning together from May 20, 1983, to January 29, 1984. Don was welterweight champion and Bruce light-welter-weight champion.

▶ Leon and Michael Spinks held the heavyweight world title at different times.

Extended Family

We're *not* dedicating this list to Great Britain's 1980 Olympic figure skating gold medalist Robin Cousins. That would just be too punny and cutesy and silly, and that's not what we're about.

This list is dedicated to Robin Cousins' cousins.

▶ Basketball superstars and sensational dunkers Vince "Vin-Sanity" Carter of the Toronto Raptors and Tracy "T-Mac" McGrady of the Orlando Magic are cousins. They used to be teammates on Toronto.

▶ The baseball-slugging Vaughns—Mo and Greg—are cousins.

▶ Speedy Preston Wilson of the Florida Marlins is nephew *and* stepson (you do the math) to the once-speedy Mookie Wilson, coach and former player of the New York Mets and a hero of the 1986 World Series. Preston made his major-league debut with the Mets.

▶ Oft-traveled hitting stud Gary Sheffield is the nephew of Dwight Gooden, former New York Met (and Yankee) pitching great.

▶ The next player that Barry Bonds is set to pass on the all-time home run list—at #3, with 660 career home runs—is Willie Mays, his godfather.

▶ Bobby Valentine, the New York Mets manager who once traveled around the world to manage (in Japan), is the son-in-law of Ralph Branca, the Brooklyn Dodger pitcher who delivered perhaps the most famous home run ball ever, the "shot heard 'round the world" by New York Giant Bobby Thomson, that clinched the 1951 National League pennant.

▶ Former Los Angeles Dodgers manager Tommy Lasorda is godfather to perennial All-Star catcher Mike Piazza, now of the New York Mets, formerly with L.A. Lasorda is said to have largely been doing a favor for a friend—Piazza's father—when he drafted Piazza in the 62nd round of baseball's amateur draft. The gamble obviously paid off, as Piazza blossomed into the game's greatest-hitting catcher.

▶ American cyclist Greg LeMond, 1986 Tour de France winner, was accidentally shot and nearly killed by his brother-in-law while they were turkey hunting in April of 1987. LeMond returned to win the Tour de France in 1989 and 1990.

▶ Golfers Jerry Pate and Bruce Lietzke are brothers-in-law.

▶ Pancho Gonzalez, the passionate and fiery tennis star, was once married to Rita Agassi, sister of Andre Agassi, the passionate and cool tennis star.

▶ "Sweet Lou" Pinella is cousins with sweet-swinging Dave Magadan.

▶ The brother-in-law of University of Arizona basketball player Miles Simon, named Most Outstanding Player of the 1997 NCAA Tournament, is Darryl Strawberry.

13

HISTORY

Déjà Vu: 20 of the Most Haunting Cases

So many athletes play so many games so many days of the year that it should not seem unusual for circumstances to repeat themselves. Some repetitions, however, are particularly powerful in the way they recall previous events.

► In 1936, Jesse Owens was one foul away from elimination in the Olympic long jump when competitor Luz Long offered him a helpful tip: Play it safe by making a mark several inches before the take-off board. Owens made a successful jump and would go on to win the gold medal, with Long taking the silver. In 1968, Bob Beamon was one foul away from elimination when competitor Ralph Boston offered the same tip to Beamon that Long had offered Owens. Beamon would go on to win the gold medal, with Boston taking the bronze.

► In Week 7 of the 2001 NFL season, Chicago Bears safety Mike Brown returned an interception for a touchdown for an overtime victory over the San Francisco 49ers. In Week 8, Brown returned an interception for a touchdown for an overtime victory over the Cleveland Browns.

► In the 1973 National League playoffs between the New York Mets and Cincinnati Reds, Bud Harrelson and Pete Rose got into a bench-clearing fight at second base. Several years later, Harrelson's son, Buddy Jr., and Rose's son, Pete Jr., got into a fight near the Phillies batting cage in Philadelphia, where their fathers were teammates.

► University of Mississippi defensive back Chucky Mullins suffered a paralyzing injury against Vanderbilt on October 28, 1989. He died on May 6, 1990. University of Washington defensive back Curtis Williams suffered a paralyzing injury against Stanford on October 28, 2001. He died on May 6, 2002.

▶ After a 1925 game, Philadelphia Athletics infielder Jimmy Dykes was asked why he hadn't slid into second base. "I couldn't," he said. "I carry my cigars in my back pocket and I was afraid I'd break them." In 1982, Montreal Expo Tim Raines avoided feet-first slides because he kept his cocaine vial in his back pocket and was afraid he would break it.

▶ Harry Agganis, Boston University quarterback star from 1949–52, signed with the Boston Red Sox and played first base for them in 1954. In 1955, he died of a massive pulmonary embolism. Tony Gastall, a Boston University quarterback star (1953–54) after Agganis, signed with the Baltimore Orioles in 1955. In 1956, he died when the plane he was piloting crashed into Chesapeake Bay.

▶ Movie star Paul Newman was kicked off of the Kenyon College JV football team for brawling. His co-star in *Butch Cassidy and the Sundance Kid* and *The Sting*, Robert Redford, was kicked off of the University of Colorado baseball team for drinking and missing practice.

▶ In the 1960 Wimbledon quarterfinals, Earl Buchholz held match point five times against Neale Fraser but eventually retired because of muscle cramps. In the U.S. Championship semifinals later that year, Buchholz had match point three times against Rod Laver and again had to default eventually because of cramps.

▶ In 1936, Jersey Joe Walcott knocked out Phil Johnson in three rounds in Philadelphia. Fourteen years later, Walcott knocked out Harold Johnson, Phil's son, in three rounds in Philadelphia.

▶ In 1960, in front of a partisan American crowd in Squaw Valley, California, Bill Christian and his teammates upset the Soviet Union in the semifinals and went on to win America's first Olympic hockey gold medal. In 1980, in front of a partisan American crowd in Lake Placid, New York, Dave Christian, Bill's son, and his teammates upset the Soviet Union in the semifinals and went on to win America's second Olympic hockey gold medal.

▶ In 1907, Detroit Tiger Charlie "Boss" Schmidt popped up to make the last out of the World Series against the Cubs. The next year, Schmidt grounded into the last out of the 1908 Series, also against the Cubs.

▶ In 1981, the New York Islanders eliminated the New York Rangers from the Stanley Cup playoffs and made it to the finals. In 1982, the Islanders eliminated the Rangers and eventually made the finals. In 1983, the Islanders eliminated the Rangers and eventually made the finals. In 1984, the Islanders eliminated the Rangers and eventually made the finals.

▶ Los Angeles Dodgers pitcher Don Drysdale's record scoreless-innings streak in 1968 continued at one point only after an umpire invoked an infrequently used rule to decree that an opposing batter had not tried to get out of the way of a pitch by Drysdale that had hit the batter with the bases loaded. Twenty years later, in 1988, Dodgers pitcher Orel Hershiser's scoreless innings streak, which broke Drysdale's, continued at one point only after an umpire invoked an infrequently used rule to call a double play rather than a force out, stating that an opposing runner going from first to second had slid outside the basepath. The call ended the inning and negated the run that had crossed the plate. Both calls were made against the San Francisco Giants.

▶ In 1920, world heavyweight champion Jack Dempsey and his manager, Jack Kearns, were indicted on charges of conspiracy to avoid the draft during World War I. They were found not guilty. In 1967, heavyweight champion Muhammad Ali was sentenced to five years in jail for refusal to join the army during the Vietnam War. The sentence was overturned in 1970.

▶ Michelle Kwan, the #1-ranked American figure skater in 1998 (and second at the worlds) went into the 1998 Nagano Olympics as one of the gold-medal favorites. In Japan, she skated well but not great, and the gold medal was won by the younger Tara Lipinski, an American who skated the performance of her life. Four years later, Kwan, now the #1-ranked skater in the world went into the 2002 Salt Lake City Olympics as the clear gold-medal favorite. Again, she skated well but not great, and again the gold was won by a younger skater, Sara Hughes, an American who performed the routine of her life.

▶ On August 23, 1952, Bob Elliott of the New York Giants was ejected by umpire Augie Donatelli for complaining and kicking dirt over a called strike two. Bobby Hofman finished the at-bat by being called out on strikes and was also ejected by Donatelli.

▶ Korean Olympic boxer Dong-Kih Choh, disqualified in his 1964 semifinal for holding his head too low, sat in the middle of the ring and refused to leave for 51 minutes. South Korean boxer Byun Jong-il, loser of a disputed decision in a 119-pound bout at the 1988 Olympics, sat in a corner of the ring and refused to leave for 67 minutes.

▶ In 1923, Detroit Tigers pitcher Herman Pillette went 14-19 to lead the American League in losses. Twenty-eight years later, in 1951, St. Louis Browns pitcher Duane Pilette, Herman's son, went 6-14 to lead the American League in losses.

▶ In a game against the Houston Astros on July 21, 1975, New York Met Felix Milan had four singles. After each hit, Joe Torre, the next batter, hit into a double play, wiping Milan out.

▶ On January 29, 1989, Chris Dudley of the Cleveland Cavaliers went to the foul line to shoot two free throws. He missed the first shot. He missed the next shot, but Washington Bullet Darrell Walker was called for a lane violation. Dudley missed again, but Dave Feitl of the Bullets committed a lane violation. Dudley missed again, but Feitl again committed a lane violation. Dudley then missed for the fifth straight time.

What If... ?

History—sports and world—and its various cherished records might be a little different but for a wrinkle here or there.
What if...

▶ ... Cuban dictator Fidel Castro, who had had a tryout with the old Washington Senators on September 27, 1947, had been called back?

▶ ... World War II had not interrupted Chicago Cubs owner Phil Wrigley from installing lights at Wrigley Field in 1942? (For the war effort, he donated to the lights he'd bought to a shipyard.)

▶ ... the 1994 baseball players' strike had not stopped San Francisco Giant Matt Williams from becoming the player to break Roger Maris's home run record (his 43 homers after 115 games was on pace for just under 61 home runs), or San Diego Padre Tony Gwynn from becoming the first man in more than a half-century to bat .400 (when the players struck in mid-August, he was hitting .394)?

▶ ... Monica Seles had not been stabbed by a crazed fan of Steffi Graf's in Hamburg, Germany, in 1993? Given that Seles had won 7 of the previous 8 Grand Slams she'd played in before the horrible event, and would win only one in the almost-decade following, isn't it likely that Seles would have made a formidable run at the title of greatest woman tennis player of all time rather than Graf, who in the ensuing years would win eight singles titles at three Grand Slam tournaments—the Australian, French, and U.S. Opens—where Seles had been multiple-defending champ at the time of the stabbing?

▶ ... Pearl Harbor had not interfered with the vote on whether the St. Louis Browns could move to Los Angeles in 1941?

▶ ... Nick Anderson of the Orlando Magic had not missed all four free throws he attempted in the final seconds of Game 1 of the 1995 NBA Finals against the Houston Rockets, any one of which would have iced the game, which Houston then won by hitting a game-tying three-pointer with 1.6 seconds left and outscoring the Magic in overtime, then sweeping the series over a young, dispirited Orlando team? (Would Shaquille O'Neal have left Orlando a few years later for the Los Angeles Lakers if he'd brought the Magic at least one title and had felt more accepted in Florida?)

▶ ... Eulace Peacock, who'd beaten Jesse Owens in the 100m and the long jump at the 1935 AAU championships, had not been kept out of the 1936 Olympics by a hamstring injury?

▶ ... school custodian Pop Stebbins had found "two boxes about 18 inches square"—precisely what James Naismith had asked him to bring for the new game he was inventing—rather than some old peach baskets? (Presumably, the NBA would today stand for National Boxball Association.)

▶ ... football legend Red Grange had remained discouraged by the stiff competition at the University of Illinois, which made him walk off the team as a freshman? And what if basketball superstar Michael Jordan had become discouraged when he didn't make his high school varsity as a sophomore?

▶ ... Mickey Mantle had not been turned down for military service because of a knee injury? And what if Ted Williams, Bob Feller, Joe DiMaggio, and Stan Musial *had* been turned down for military service?

▶ ... New York Yankees owner George Steinbrenner, when an assistant football coach at Northwestern and Purdue, had loved and been good at it?

▶ ... the 1999 NBA lockout had not severely shortened the season and allowed the San Antonio Spurs to hit their stride at just the right time and win the title? (Given the inevitable ups and downs of every NBA season, isn't it likely that, had the season been regulation length, another contender would have hit *their* stride at the right time and won the title?) And what if the '95 NHL lockout had not severely shortened the season and allowed the New Jersey Devils to hit their stride at just the right time and win the Stanley Cup—who might have won it then?

▶ ... Detroit Lions running back Barry Sanders hadn't retired? Just how many yards would he have amassed by now?

▶ ... Jack Crawford had won just one more set in the 1933 U.S. Championship final, and thus the Grand Slam, to become the first player to do it? (Who but real tennis aficionados knows his name now?)

▶ ... CBS/ABC sportscaster Brent Musburger had flourished in his 1959 job as a Midwest League umpire?

▶ ... the two most abundantly talented players for the New York Mets in the 1980s—Dwight Gooden and Darryl Strawberry—had not lost years of their prime baseball career because of drug and alcohol addiction? Would Strawberry—who by age 29 had hit 280 home runs, or 21 more than Barry Bonds had by that age—have been the first one on pace to break the career home run record? Would Gooden—whose record his first eight years in the majors was 132-53, a .714 winning percentage that put him at #1 all-time—now be considered one of the five greatest pitchers of all time?

▶ ... Cuban Teofilo Stevenson, who won the super-heavyweight gold medal at the 1972, 1976, and 1980 Olympics and was considered to be in Muhammad Ali's class, had turned professional?

▶ ... Jeremy Giambi of the Oakland As had slid into, rather than run to, home plate in Game 3 of the first round of the 2001 American League playoffs, thereby avoiding New York Yankee catcher Jorge Posada's tag, after a miraculous flipped relay by shortstop Derek Jeter, a slide that would have tied the game in the late innings, which the As might well have won, thus winning the series? And if they'd won the series, vanquishing the hated Yankees, might that have been enough to convince Jeremy's brother Jason, the As' best player and spiritual leader, to not leave and *join* the Yankees?

▶ ...the coin flip between the 12th Earl of Derby—who conceived of a one-mile run for three-year-olds at Epsom Downs in England and who would become the namesake of the most famous American horse race—and Sir Charles Bunbury over whether to call the Epsom race the Derby Stakes or the Bunbury Stakes, had gone the other way? (Then perhaps the major event on the American horseracing calendar today would be known as the Kentucky Bunbury.)

The Most Famous Quotations in Sports History

The sounds we associate with sports are varied: the static of a crackly but trusted radio, the knock of wood against ball or the bounce of rubber on parquet, the music of the game, the noise of the fans, the often-annoying organist, the catch phrases we associate with different sports— "Play ball!" ... "Gentlemen, start your engines" ... "On your mark" ... "Let the games begin." Our ears prick up at the occasional offering from the public address announcer: "That was goaltending"; "Ladies and gentlemen, now pitching for the Baltimore Orioles..."—and it all makes a sort of symphony.

The avid fan remembers, too, the words of (often unintentional) poets about the game, lines that resonate for their simplicity and passion ("*The Giants win the pennant! The Giants win the pennant!*") or their already-carved-in-stone sense of history ("*Do you believe in miracles?*"). It doesn't matter that most of us never actually heard these words spoken; the words have appeared in print or been quoted often enough that we hear them in the mind's ear.

▶ "Float like a butterfly, sting like a bee."
   —Cassius Clay's strategy for his 1964 fight with Sonny Liston; the line was probably coined by Clay's corner man, Drew "Bundini" Brown

▶ "When the one Great Scorer comes to write against your name—He marks—not that you won or lost—but how you played the game."
   —Grantland Rice

▶ "It ain't over till the fat lady sings."
   —Washington Bullets coach Dick Motta's rallying cry with his team down two games to one to the Seattle Supersonics in the 1978 NBA Finals, and he was right: The Bullets won the series in seven games

▶ "Let's play two."
   —Ernie Banks

▶ "No más."
   —Roberto Duran to Sugar Ray Leonard in the eighth round of their second welterweight title fight, 1980

▶ "You are the pits of the world!"
   —John McEnroe to Wimbledon chair umpire Edward James, in McEnroe's first-round match in 1981 against Tom Gullikson

▶ "We wuz robbed."
—Manager Joe Jacobs after his fighter, Max Schmeling, lost his heavyweight championship to Jack Sharkey in a 15-round decision in New York, June 1932

▶ "I shoulda stood in bed."
—Again, fight manager Jacobs, after leaving his sick bed to attend a 1934 World Series game and betting on the wrong team

▶ "Win one for the Gipper."
—Knute Rockne's admonition to the Notre Dame team at halftime of a scoreless Army-Notre Dame game in 1928; according to legend, Notre Dame quarterback George Gipp, dying of a viral throat infection, had told Rockne to save the inspirational ploy for just the right moment (dispute lingers about whether the deathbed scene ever really took place)

▶ "There goes Ted Williams, the greatest hitter who ever lived."
—What Ted Williams—according to his autobiography, My Turn at Bat—wanted people to say about him when he walked by

▶ "Four-four-four."
—Moses Malone, predicting three consecutive NBA playoff series sweeps for the Philadelphia 76ers in 1983; they missed a triple sweep by one game, losing the fourth game of the Eastern Conference finals to the Milwaukee Bucks

▶ "He can run but he can't hide."
—Joe Louis's warning before beating Billy Conn in their heavyweight title fight

▶ "Today, I consider myself the luckiest man on the face of the earth."
—Lou Gehrig, giving a farewell speech to the fans at Yankee Stadium on July 4, 1939, Lou Gehrig Day; at the time, he was dying of amyotrophic lateral sclerosis, the disease that a year later would kill him, and become better known as "Lou Gehrig's Disease"

▶ "Nice guys finish last."
—Brooklyn Dodgers manager Leo Durocher, talking to some writers before a game with the last-place New York Giants, gestured toward the Giants and said, "Take a look at them. All nice guys. They'll finish last. Nice guys. Finish last."

▶ "Gentlemen, you are about to play football for Yale against Harvard. Never in your lives will you ever do anything so important."
—Yale's football coach Tad Jones to his players before "The Game"

▶ HARVARD BEATS YALE, 29-29
—Headline in The Harvard Crimson the day after undefeated and previously untied Harvard scored 16 points in the last minute of their 1968 game to deadlock the undefeated and previously untied Bulldogs

▶ "Whoever wants to know the heart and mind of America had better learn baseball."
—*Jacques Barzun, God's Country and Mine, 1954*

▶ "Don't look back. Something might be gaining on you."
—*The sixth and final of "Satchel Paige's Rules for Staying Young," first published in* Collier's *magazine*

▶ "Hit 'em where they ain't."
—*Wee Willie Keeler's advice for hitting success; Keeler was a lifetime .345 hitter*

▶ "The bigger they are, the harder they fall."
—*Heavyweight Bob Fitzsimmons about Jim Jeffries, who outweighed him by 53 pounds, before their 1899 title fight; Jeffries knocked out Fitzsimmons in the 11th round*

▶ "Good field, no hit."
—*Report filed by scout Mike Gonzalez about a minor-league prospect*

▶ "I'm the straw that stirs the drink."
—*Reggie Jackson, shortly after being signed as a free agent by the New York Yankees*

▶ "Thanks, King."
—*Jim Thorpe to Sweden's King Gustav V, who presented a bust of himself to Thorpe for winning the 1912 Stockholm Olympic pentathlon*

▶ "I lost it in the sun."
—*Brooklyn Dodgers pitcher Billy Loes, on missing a ground ball in the 1952 World Series*

▶ "I ain't got no quarrel with them Viet Cong."
—*Muhammad Ali's explanation for his decision not to report for the draft in 1966*

▶ THIS IS NEXT YEAR
—*Headline in the* New York Daily News, *after the Dodgers won their only world championship in Brooklyn, in 1955*

▶ "Just win, baby."
—*Oakland Raiders owner and general manager Al Davis; the directive has become the team's motto*

▶ "These are the saddest of possible words: 'Tinker-to-Evers-to-Chance."
—*From "Baseball's Sad Lexicon," by newspaperman and poet Franklin P. Adams, about the Chicago Cubs' legendary double-play trio; the poem was first published in the* New York Evening Mail, *July 1910*

▶ "How the hell did they get in this country?"

—*John Rocker, pondering the abundance of "foreigners" in New York City, in a* Sports Illustrated *interview whose sentiments would inflame the country, including many of his Atlanta Braves teammates, and may have helped to unravel the pitcher's career*

▶ "It breaks your heart. It is designed to break your heart."

—*A. Bartlett Giammatti, former baseball commissioner, in his elegiac essay about his favorite game. (It continues: "The game begins in the spring when everything else begins again, and it blossoms in the summer, filling the afternoons and evenings, and then as soon as the chill rains come, it stops and leaves you to face the fall alone.")*

▶ "Yes! And it counts!"

—*Marv Albert's memorable and animated call of a basketball player, especially a New York Knick, making the shot and getting fouled in the process*

▶ "Say it ain't so, Joe."

—*A small boy to "Shoeless" Joe Jackson, as Jackson emerged from the courtroom after testifying in the grand jury investigation of the 1919 Chicago Black Sox; Jackson denied to his death that such a plea was ever made*

10 Non-Immortals Who Had a Nose for Historical Occasions

Some athletes who are not great have a knack for being on hand for more than their share of great moments. Bert Campaneris has appeared in 11 no-hitters, the most in major-league history. Perhaps it is fate, perhaps it is their only way of getting into the record books, perhaps it is something to make a list of.

▶ Bobby Thomson, who hit possibly the most famous home run in baseball history, was replaced by a young outfielder named Willie Mays on the New York Giants. Thomson was traded to the Milwaukee Braves, where he was replaced by a young outfielder named Hank Aaron.

▶ John Mohardt blocked for George Gipp (of "Win one for the Gipper" fame) when he was a running back at Notre Dame, blocked for Red Grange when he was with the NFL Chicago Bears, and pinch-ran for Ty Cobb when he was with the Detroit Tigers.

▶ One more Ty-in: Jack Coffey was a teammate of both Cobb (Detroit Tigers) and Babe Ruth (Boston Red Sox) in the same season (1918).

▶ When he was with the Oakland Raiders in 1976, placekicker Fred Steinfort replaced George Blanda, the NFL's all-time leading scorer.

When Steinfort was traded to Denver in 1980, he replaced Jim Turner, the NFL's then-second all-time leading scorer.

▶ Cesar Tovar has broken up the most no-hitters in history—having the only hit in the game—doing it five times between 1967 and 1975. In 1969, Baltimore Orioles teammates Dave McNally and Mike Cuellar each took a no-hitter into the ninth inning, only to have Tovar break it up with a single.

▶ Major-league second baseman Davey Johnson is a trivia buff's dream: He batted behind both Hank Aaron, the all-time home run king in America, and Sadaharu Oh, the all-time home run king in Japan; he is the last man to get a hit off of Sandy Koufax; and he made the final out of the 1969 World Series against the underdog New York Mets (whom he would later manage).

▶ Harvey Kuenn was the final batter in two of Sandy Koufax's four career no-hitters, in 1963 and 1965.

▶ On May 6, 1925, Paul "Pee Wee" Wanninger replaced shortstop Everett Scott to break Scott's then-record 1,307 consecutive-games playing streak. Almost four weeks later, Wanninger would give way to pinch hitter Lou Gehrig in the first game of the consecutive-games streak that would break Scott's record.

▶ Cesar Geronimo was the 3,000th strikeout victim of both Bob Gibson and Nolan Ryan.

▶ Tracy Stallard was a pivotal victim in two of the most famous baseball moments of the 1960s. He gave up Roger Maris's 61st home run on the last day of the 1961 season, and he was the losing pitcher in Jim Bunning's perfect game on Father's Day, 1964.

And 1 Immortal Who Had a Nose for Historical Occasions

▶ Washington Senators pitching great Walter Johnson yielded his first hit ever, in his losing debut on August 2, 1907, to Ty Cobb. Johnson's final appearance in baseball—as a pinch hitter, in 1927—was somewhat obscured because it was the same game in which Babe Ruth hit his 60th home run.

7+ Almost Incomprehensibly Great Years

▶ Barry Bonds, San Francisco Giants/MLB, 2001: The slugging left fielder most famously set the major-league record for home runs in a season —73—breaking Mark McGwire's short-lived 1998 record of 70. But Bonds also broke Babe Ruth's record for walks (Bonds had 177) and slugging percentage (.863), and had the highest on-base percentage in the National League since 1899 (.515).

In 2002, Bonds's home run total dropped significantly—but not because he slumped: In fact, this season was, in certain ways, even sillier than 2001. With 198 walks, Bonds shattered the record for walks he'd set the previous year; he blew away Willie McCovey's all-time record for intentional walks, with 68; he broke Ted Williams's major-league record for on-base percentage, with .582; and in hitting for a .370 average, he won his first batting title, at age 38. And he *still* hit 46 home runs.

To put in perspective how good Bonds was, and how infrequently he got pitches to swing at: If he'd not had a single, solitary base hit in his 403 official at-bats, his on-base percentage—counting his 198 walks and the 9 times he was hit by a pitch—would still make for a very respectable .339 on-base percentage.

▶ Steffi Graf, women's tennis tour, 1988: The West German star became only the fifth player, and third woman, to win the Grand Slam (Wimbledon, the U.S. Open, the French Open, and the Australian Open) in a calendar year, and the first to accomplish the feat in nearly two decades. That was impressive enough. But what made Graf's achievement *uniquely* special was that she made it an unprecedented "Golden Slam" when she beat Gabriela Sabatini in a final in Seoul, Korea, to win that year's Olympic tennis gold medal.

▶ Wilt Chamberlain, Philadelphia Warriors/NBA, 1961–62: Even within an almost incomprehensibly great career, this campaign stood out, as The Big Dipper averaged for the season 50.4 points (and 25.7 rebounds) per game, easily the highest season ppg ever recorded. (The second-best season ppg average belongs to Chamberlain at 44.8; third is Chamberlain at 38.4; fourth is Chamberlain at 37.6; and fifth is Michael Jordan at 37.1.) It was also the season in which Chamberlain set the all-time scoring record for a single game—100 points, against the New York Knicks.

▶ Oscar Robertson, Cincinnati Royals/NBA, 1961–62: In that very same season that Chamberlain made fans shake their heads in disbelief, "The Big O" averaged a triple-double—an achievement which, if you just do it in *one* game, is usually enough to earn you top billing on that night's sports wrap-up. The season-long feat has not been accomplished before or since.

▶ John Clarkson, Boston Beaneaters/MLB, 1889: Forget just winning the pitching "Triple Crown" (wins, ERA, strikeouts)... Clarkson led the National League in wins, ERA, strikeouts, shutouts, complete games, innings pitched, games, and winning percentage.

▶ Tiger Woods, PGA Tour, May 28, 2000–June 3, 2001: Starting with his win in the 2000 Memorial Tournament, his final tournament before that year's Masters, and concluding with his victory in the Memorial the following year, Woods won 10 PGA tournaments, including all four majors, so that he was at one point defending champion in each (though quibblers would insist he hadn't *technically* achieved the Grand Slam of golf—winning the Masters, U.S. Open, British Open, and

PGA Championship in the same calendar year; whatever). Showing his tremendous and consistent ability to rise to the occasion, Woods's final scores in the four majors he nabbed over that year-long period are 12, 19, 18, and 16 shots, respectively, under par.

▶ Sandy Koufax, Los Angeles Dodgers/MLB, 1965: Not only did Koufax go 26-9 to lead the major leagues in victories, but he established the major-league strikeout record of 382 (later surpassed by one by the California Angels' Nolan Ryan in 1973), fired eight shutouts, completed 27 games, led the National League in innings pitched (335) and ERA (2.04), and limited opponents to a .179 batting average.

Furthermore, Koufax endeared himself to many Jews when he skipped the World Series opening game assignment against the Minnesota Twins to observe the Jewish holiday of Yom Kippur. He returned for Game 2, losing 5-1, but Koufax shut out the Twins on four hits in Game 5, then came back on two day's rest to blank Minnesota, 2-0, on three hits in the decisive seventh game. He struck out 10 in each victory.

"The Game of the Century"

In any century, presumably, there can be only one "Game of the Century" —*if* one—in any sport. However, those who would most likely apply the label—sports promoters—are not known as a judicious bunch, and they've trotted out the phrase a tad more than once every hundred years. Boxing promoters are especially notorious for their overzealous billing of virtually every fight as one for the ages.

From all of those games and matches and fights deemed to be the sporting event of the century, a few stand out. Some were billed "The Game of the Century" beforehand and failed to live up to the title; others made no pretense to the title and in retrospect, because of the fierceness of the competition and the exciting finish, have come to be regarded as such.

▶ The first Muhammad Ali-Joe Frazier bout in 1971 was dubbed "The Fight of the Century." Frazier won a 15-round decision in New York.

▶ The 1958 sudden-death NFL title game between the Baltimore Colts and the New York Giants has been called pro football's "Game of the Century." The Colts won, 23-17.

▶ The 1935 matchup between unbeatens Notre Dame and Ohio State has been called "The Game of the Century." Notre Dame won 18-13 on a last-seconds touchdown pass from Bill Shakespeare to Wayne Miller.

▶ Notre Dame was involved in at least one other monumental game with a Big Ten opponent. The 10-10 tie between Notre Dame and Michigan State in 1966, which determined the national championship, has been called college football's "Game of the Century"

▶ When Lew Alcindor's UCLA Bruins took on Elvin Hayes's Houston Cougars at the Astrodome on January 20, 1968, it was called college basketball's "Game of the Century." Houston won by two points, 71-69, as Hayes outscored Alcindor, 39-15. (Alcindor was recovering from an eye injury suffered the previous week.)

▶ In 1926, in the only meeting of their careers, tennis great Suzanne Lenglen defeated Helen Wills in what was proclaimed "The Match of the Century."

The Billie Jean King-Bobby Riggs showdown in 1973 was billed as "The Tennis Match of the Century."

▶ The three contests in the 1940s between Tony Zale and Rocky Graziano have been called the "greatest series of fights in boxing history."

▶ The 1937 Davis Cup match between American Don Budge and German Gottfried von Cramm was voted "The Greatest Match Ever." Budge won in five sets, after being down 2-5 in the final set.

▶ The 1921 fight between Jack Dempsey and European champion Georges Carpentier was proclaimed "The Battle of the Century." Dempsey won in a fourth-round knockout.

▶ "The Mile of the Century" was contested in 1935 at Princeton, where New Zealand's Jack Lovelock defeated Glenn Cunningham.

The next supposed "Mile of the Century" took place in 1954 in Vancouver, British Columbia, where England's Roger Bannister ran 3:58.8 to beat world-record holder John Landy of Australia, who ran 3:59.6.

20 Who Followed in the Steps of Legends

▶ Kevin Harvick: Harvick was picked to drive the famous No. 3 GM Goodwrench Chevrolet, the car driven by Dale Earnhardt, the NASCAR legend who was killed on the final lap of the 2001 Daytona 500. Team owner Richard Childress changed 3 to 29, and Earnhardt's trademark black became white, but it was quite apparent what an honor had been bestowed upon Harvick. "I'd like to say one thing," Harvick said, graciously. "Dale Earnhardt is probably the best race car driver that ever came through NASCAR. I hope you guys don't expect me to replace him because no one ever will." Harvick enjoyed almost immediate success, winning in his third Winston Cup start (Atlanta), and won the 2001 Busch series title.

▶ Steve Patterson: After Lew Alcindor graduated from UCLA, Patterson took over at center and, in his junior and senior years, averaged 12.5 and 12.9 points, respectively, and helped the Bruins to win national championships in 1970 and 1971.

▶ Ryan Minor: Eleven days after getting called up to the major leagues from Double-A Bowie, Minor got his first start at third base for the Orioles, on September 20, 1998. He was just another rookie getting a look in September—except that Minor was starting in place of Cal Ripken, Jr., who'd decided to end his streak of 2,632 consecutive games played. Minor, who was eight years old when Ripken's streak began, went 1-for-4 with three assists in the field. Minor wound up playing just 87 games for the Orioles, batting .185, before they traded him to the Montreal Expos after the 2000 season.

▶ Heartley "Hunk" Anderson: After Knute Rockne was killed in a plane crash, Anderson succeeded him as football coach at Notre Dame, compiling a 16-9-2 record from 1931–33.

▶ Garry Maddox: In 1972, Maddox hit .266 as the San Francisco Giant centerfielder after Willie Mays was traded to the New York Mets. Maddox hit .319 and .284 in the next two years before he was traded in 1975 to the Philadelphia Phillies.

▶ Leroy Kelly: Three times a 1,000-yards-in-a-season rusher, Kelly was Jim Brown's successor as running back for the Cleveland Browns.

▶ Manny Sanguillen/Richie Zisk: Sanguillen, a catcher, started in right field for the Pittsburgh Pirates on Opening Day in 1973, the first game after Roberto Clemente's death, but that year the position was patrolled mostly by Zisk, who batted .324 with 10 home runs and 54 RBIs.

▶ Frank Solich: University of Nebraska coaching legend Tom Osborne left on a high note, winning three national championships* and losing just 2 of 51 games in his last four years, and going 255-49-3 overall in his 25-year career. Solich, who'd been a player, freshman coach, and assistant coach for the Cornhuskers, took over in 1998. He didn't enjoy quite the success of Osborne (who himself had had to replace coaching legend Bob Devaney), going 9-4 in his debut year, for an altogether un-Nebraska-like #19 national ranking.

*including a split 1997 title with Michigan

▶ Carlos Guillen: Guillen came to the Seattle Mariners from the Houston Astros in 1998 as part of the trade for future Hall of Famer Randy Johnson, and wound up replacing another Seattle legend three years later. When Alex Rodriguez signed with the Texas Rangers after the 2000 season, Guillen became the Mariners' regular shortstop in 2001. While Rodriguez was hitting .318 with 52 homers and 135 runs batted in for Texas, Guillen batted .259 with five homers and 53 RBI. It was revealed in September that Guillen had contracted tuberculosis during the season.

▶ Phil Bengston: As Vince Lombardi's replacement as coach of the Green Bay Packers, Bengston compiled a 20-21-1 record from 1968–70.

▶ Gene Bartow: In the first two years after John Wooden retired, Bartow compiled a 52-9 record as the UCLA basketball coach, from 1975–76.

▶ Doug DeCinces: Taking over the hot corner from Brooks Robinson, the Baltimore Orioles new first-string third baseman hit .234 in 1976 and had a .941 fielding percentage, the lowest of any full season in his 15-year career. He finished with a .958 career fielding percentage, compared to .971 for Robinson. Robinson won 16 Gold Gloves, DeCinces none.

▶ Bill Terry: The great New York Giant first baseman replaced the man who had managed the Giants for 31 years, John McGraw. Terry led the team to three pennants and one world championship in 10 years.

▶ Ray Perkins: A former player under Alabama coach Paul "Bear" Bryant, Perkins succeeded the outgoing coach after the 1982 season; Bryant died 37 days after retiring. Perkins went 8-4 the first year, then 5-6, 9-2-1, and 10-3. He lasted four years.

▶ Mike Cameron: Replacing Ken Griffey, Jr., in centerfield seemed like a losing proposition for Mike Cameron—for anyone, really. Cameron was obtained by the Seattle Mariners in the February 2000 trade that sent Griffey, chosen to the All-Century team, to the Cincinnati Reds. But while Griffey was stymied by injuries and stuck on a poor team in Cincinnati, Cameron became one of the most popular and productive players on the Mariners, who made the playoffs his first two years in Seattle, including a 2001 team that won a record-tying 116 games. When the All-Star Game was played in Seattle in 2001, Mike Cameron was playing in the game, while Griffey, sidelined by a hamstring injury, wasn't chosen.

▶ Joe B. Hall: Successor to Adolph Rupp as basketball coach at the University of Kentucky, Hall compiled a 297-100 record from 1973–85 and won the national championship in 1978.

▶ Jim Gilliam: The Brooklyn Dodger pushed Jackie Robinson out of his second-base job in 1953, hitting .278 and leading the league in triples.

▶ Joe Nolan: In 1981, Nolan replaced Johnny Bench as the Cincinnati Reds' regular catcher and hit .309.

▶ Bill Guthridge: A trusted, veteran assistant to Dean Smith at the University of North Carolina, Guthridge had to coach the Tar Heels men's basketball team not only in the metaphorical shadow cast by Smith, who'd won an all-time record 879 games and two national championships over 36 years at Chapel Hill, but he had to play his home games in the Dean E. Smith Center—known to all as "The Dean Dome." The 60-year-old Guthridge, who'd been friends with Smith for 44 years, was seen as an interim replacement—indeed, he'd repeatedly said that when Smith would retire, he would, too—but in 1997–98, his first season as head coach, Guthridge led the Tar Heels to the Final Four, and he did so again in his third and final year.

▶ Terry Miller: When O. J. Simpson was traded in 1978, Miller replaced him in the Buffalo Bills backfield and rushed for 1,060 yards that season. He gained only 523 total yards in the three seasons after that.

13 Immortalized Athletes

Many athletes have been turned into legends not so much because of their talents and accomplishments—though those are obvious components with great athletes—but because of the lore surrounding their lives. Perhaps the most mythologized athlete of the 20th century was Joseph Jefferson "Shoeless Joe" Jackson, who has helped to inspire an astonishing outpouring of creativity: songs ("Shoeless Joe from Hannibal, Mo." from the musical *Damn Yankees*), books (W. P. Kinsella's *Shoeless Joe*; Eliot Asinof's *Eight Men Out*), and much more. Jackson was a brilliantly talented baseball player and, as a member of the 1919 Black Sox, a tragic figure—an immortal-in-waiting if there ever was one.

The following athletes—some great, some downright obscure—have become part of our mythology in a way that far exceeds what they ever or never did on the field of play.

▶ Either Dan Casey or his brother Dennis, major leaguers in the 1880s, are the reputed models for Ernest Lawrence Thayer's poem, "Casey at the Bat."

▶ Yugoslav ski jumper Vinko Bogataj was immortalized by the famous opening TV segment of ABC's "Wide World of Sports." His vicious wipeout off a ski jump at the 1970 World Ski Flying Championships in Oberstdorf, West Germany, came to embody the "agony of defeat."

▶ Ed Smith, a New York University football player who played briefly in the NFL, posed for the Downtown Athletic Club Trophy—later renamed the Heisman Trophy—that was sculpted by Frank Eliscu.

▶ Eddie Waitkus, a career .285 hitter and one of the 1950 Philadelphia Phillie "Whiz Kids," was partially the model for Roy Hobbs in Bernard Malamud's novel *The Natural*. Waitkus was mysteriously shot by Ruth Steinhagen, an obsessed fan, who told him, "For two years you have been bothering me and now you are going to die." Waitkus did not die but healed enough to be named Comeback Player of the Year and lead the Phillies to the pennant. In the novel, Hobbs is mysteriously shot by an obsessed fan but returns to lead the fictional New York Knights into pennant contention.

▶ Chuck Wepner, a New Jersey club fighter nicknamed "The Bayonne Bleeder," was Sylvester Stallone's inspiration for *Rocky*. Wepner got his big chance when he fought heavyweight champion Muhammad Ali on March 24, 1975, in Cleveland. As Rocky would, Wepner, 32-9-2 at the time, earned a moral victory by going the distance—or all but—with the champ: Wepner was knocked out with 19 seconds left in the 15th round of the fight that Ali called the toughest of his career.

▶ Harold Sakata, the 1948 Olympic silver medalist in light-heavyweight weightlifting, earned cult status by portraying "Oddjob" in the James Bond movie *Goldfinger*.

▶ Terry Schroeder, a U.S. Olympic water polo player, modeled for the nude Olympic statue in front of the Los Angeles Coliseum.

▶ Brian Dowling, quarterback for Yale in the late 1960s (and later in the NFL), is the inspiration for the football-helmeted "B. D." in Garry Trudeau's comic strip "Doonesbury." As a starting quarterback, Dowling, whose career at Yale overlapped Trudeau's, compiled a 16-1-1 record in his junior and senior years.

▶ The model for the graceful silhouetted player that appears on the NBA official logo—emblazoned on every NBA uniform—is Hall of Fame guard Jerry West.

The model for the leaping, on-his-way-to-a-dunk silhouetted figure on so much Nike apparel is Michael Jordan.

▶ The life of Annie Oakley (1860–1926), one of the greatest shooters of all time (she consistently scored 100-for-100 in trapshooting), was the basis for the popular Irving Berlin musical *Annie Get Your Gun.*

▶ René Lacoste, one of the "Four Musketeers"—the four great Frenchmen who, along with Bill Tilden, dominated tennis in the 1920s and early 1930s—gained much greater fame when he founded a clothing company and chose as its logo an alligator, which symbolized his own tenacious determination as a player to hang on and devour opponents. His shirts would come to be known, simply, as "Lacostes."

▶ Mario Mendoza, a journeyman infielder with Seattle, Pittsburgh, and Texas from 1974–82, was a lifetime .215 hitter and finished five seasons batting under .200. To hit below the "Mendoza Line" has come to mean having a sub-.200 batting average.

Debunking 11 Sports Myths

Stories about athletes, who are so often viewed in heroic terms, themselves achieve a grandeur, a mythic quality, without much nudging. Sometimes the stories are actually true; other times they just make for good stories. Every now and then, it's important to clean out the locker and set the record straight. What follows is a list of myths, and the truths behind them.

▶ *There was an asterisk affixed to Roger Maris's home run record*: For eight years, there were, in fact, separate records kept for 154- and 162-game seasons. In 1969, however, the Special Baseball Rules Committee determined that baseball would have one set of records and that "no asterisk or official sign shall be used to indicate the number of games scheduled." (Obviously, the implications of the asterisk were rendered largely irrelevant once Mark McGwire and Sammy Sosa, in 1998, shattered the Maris record—or, more to the point, once they shattered *Babe Ruth's record* of 60 home runs, which was accomplished in the shorter season, thus fueling the argument of Ruth defenders/Maris detractors for decades. Barry Bonds's 73 home runs in 2001 was just piling on.)

▶ *Tinker-to-Evers-to-Chance formed one of baseball's great double-play combinations*: These three Chicago Cubs were immortalized by the Franklin P. Adams poem, "Baseball's Sad Lexicon," but during their time together from 1906 to 1909, they actually completed only 54 double plays—fewer than 14 DPs, on average, a year.

▶ *Wilt Chamberlain was routinely outplayed throughout his career by Bill Russell:* While Russell's Boston Celtics won 85 games and lost only 57 against Wilt's teams, in those 142 contests Chamberlain averaged 28.7 points and an identical 28.7 rebounds to Russell's 14.5 points and 23.7 rebounds.

▶ *"The Four Horsemen" of Notre Dame, 1922–24, were swift, strong, and big:* While the Four Horsemen—Harry Stuhldreher, Jim Crowley, Don Miller, and Elmer Layden—were swift and strong, the four backs averaged just 165 pounds.

▶ *Having sex too soon before a competition will harm one's athletic performance:* Bob Beamon claimed that the only time he had sex right before a long jump competition was on the eve of his world-record-shattering jump at the 1968 Olympics.

To enhance training, Eastern European nations have secluded male athletes with their wives the night before an important competition, in the belief that sexual activity dissipates nervous tension. Sexual activity *after* a competition is considered potentially harmful, because the athlete is depleted.

▶ *A jury found several members of the 1919 Chicago White Sox guilty for their actions during the World Series:* The eight White Sox players who were tried for conspiracy to defraud the public were found *not* guilty by a jury, acquitted for lack of evidence. It was baseball commissioner Judge Kenesaw Mountain Landis who decided to ban the accused players for life.

▶ *Harold Abrahams, the sprinter whose athletic and collegiate exploits were portrayed in the film* Chariots of Fire, *raced around the courtyard of Trinity College in Cambridge, and his victory in the 100m was redemption for his failure in the 200m:* Lord Burghley ran around the courtyard, and the 100m preceded the 200m.

▶ *Don Zimmer has a steel plate in his head:* Contrary to baseball lore, Zimmer, the round-faced baseball lifer and now the right-hand man/bench coach for New York Yankees skipper Joe Torre, does *not* have a steel plate in his head. Instead, there are four buttons, made from a rare metal called tantalum, that doctors installed to fill the holes they drilled in his skull to relieve pressure on his brain when he was beaned in 1953. A minor-leaguer in St. Paul, Minnesota, at the time, Zimmer wasn't wearing a helmet and was semi-comatose for 13 days.

▶ *Enos "Country" Slaughter scored all the way from first on a single in Game 7 of the 1946 World Series:* Slaughter did score from first base on the hit, but the batter, Harry Walker, was credited with a double on the play.

▶ *"The Seven Blocks of Granite" was the name inspired by Vince Lombardi and his six defensive linemates on the Fordham football powerhouse of the late 1930s*: They were indeed called that—but the name was a retread, having been applied to the Fordham defensive line in 1930, six years before Lombardi starred for them.

▶ *Vince Lombardi originally said, "Winning isn't everything, it's the only thing"*: The line was first uttered by Henry B. "Red" Sanders, head coach at Vanderbilt and UCLA, in 1940. John Wayne repeated it in the 1953 movie *Trouble Along the Way*. On April 8, 1962, in a speech in Milwaukee, Lombardi said, "Winning isn't everything; trying to win is."

The Coolest Firsts in Sports

Records, they say too frequently, were made to be you-know-what, and most great athletes who do something better than anyone has ever done it before usually get to see someone else come along and do it a little better. But those who were first to do something: *Ah*. They can live in peace that their place in history, however small, is untouchable.

We've compiled a few of the coolest "firsts" in sports.

▶ The first person to circumnavigate the world alone in a balloon: Steve Fossett, 2002, on his sixth try

▶ The first NCAA school to have a women's athletic team placed on probation for recruiting violations: Northeast Louisiana University (basketball), 1986

▶ The first winning Super Bowl coach to wear headphones on the sidelines: Bill Walsh, San Francisco 49ers, Super Bowl XVI, 1982

▶ The first Little Leaguer to play in the major leagues: Joey Jay, 1961

▶ The first *Sports Illustrated* cover subject: Eddie Mathews, Milwaukee Braves, 1954

▶ The first to score a Super Bowl touchdown: Max McGee of the Green Bay Packers, 1967

▶ The first American woman to dunk a basketball in official competition: Georgeann Wells of West Virginia University, December 21, 1983, in a game against the University of Charleston

▶ The first American woman to dunk professionally: Lisa Leslie (6'5") of the Los Angeles Sparks, July 30, 2002

▶ The first to swim 100 meters in under a minute: Johnny Weissmuller, July 9, 1922

▶ The first sprinter to break 10 seconds in the 100m: Jim Hines, 9.9 seconds, at the 1968 AAU Championships

▶ The first woman to run the marathon in under three hours: Adrienne Beames of Australia, August 31, 1971 (2:46.30)

▶ The first marathoner to average under five minutes per mile: Derek Clayton of Australia, December 3, 1967 (2:09:36.4)

▶ The first lunar athlete: Alan Shepard, Jr., February 6, 1971; as Apollo 14 commander, he hit a six-iron shot on the moon

▶ The first high school student to break the four-minute mile: Jim Ryun, 3:58.3, in 1965, for Wichita East High School

▶ The first ex-athlete to become a broadcaster: Jack Graney, former leftfielder for the Cleveland Indians, in 1932

▶ The first President to throw out the first ball of the season: William Howard Taft, April 14, 1910, in Washington, for a game against Philadelphia

▶ The first All-America football team selected by Walter Camp: January 7, 1899, published in *Collier's Weekly*

▶ The first year the New York Yankees won a World Series: 1923

▶ The first to climb the "Nose" route of Yosemite's El Capitan "free"— using no gear: Lynn Hill, 1994

▶ The first NBA player to reach 20,000 career points: Bob Pettit, 1964

▶ The first major-league game played at night: May 24, 1935, at Crosley Field in Cincinnati

▶ The first time the result of an Olympic final was changed after viewing film of the event: 1932, the 110-yard hurdles; Donald Finley was originally listed as fourth but moved to third, ahead of Jack Keller, and awarded the bronze medal

▶ The first to win the tennis Grand Slam: Don Budge, 1938

▶ The first woman to win the tennis Grand Slam: Maureen "Mo" Connolly, 1953

▶ The first major leaguer to hit a home run: Ross Barnes, 1876

▶ The first lefty to win a golf major: Bob Charles, the 1963 British Open

▶ The first black player elected to Cooperstown: Jackie Robinson, 1962

▶ The first Latin player elected to Cooperstown: Roberto Clemente, 1973

▶ The first thoroughbred to reach $1 million in career earnings: Citation

▶ The first golfer to reach $1 million in career earnings: Jack Nicklaus, 1970, after taking second place in the Bing Crosby Pro-Am

▶ The first woman golfer to reach $1 million in career earnings: Kathy Whitworth, 1981, after taking third place in the U.S. Women's Open

▶ The first track and field Olympian disqualified for taking drugs: Danuta Rosani, discus thrower from Poland, 1976, for steroids

▶ The first designated hitter: Ron Blomberg, New York Yankees, April 6, 1973

▶ The first race of the modern Olympics: Opening heat of the 100m dash, 1896 (won by Francis Lane of Princeton in 12.2 seconds)

► The first college team to have two 200-yard rushers in the same game: Tulsa, on November 2, 1985, with Gordon Brown (214 yards) and Steve Gage (206 yards) in a 42-26 win over Wichita State

► The first Jewish major leaguer: Lipman Pike, 1876

► The first soccer-style kicker in pro football: Cornell's Pete Gogolak, who signed a contract with the Buffalo Bills in 1964

► The first pitcher to throw a curveball: Candy Cummings, 1867

► The first baseball player to reach 3,000 career hits: Cap Anson, 1897

► The first Indianapolis 500 winner to average more than 100 miles per hour: Peter DePaolo, 101.27 mph in 1925, in a Duesenberg Special

► The first million-dollar gate for a fight: 1921, Georges Carpentier vs. Jack Dempsey

► The first paid football coach with faculty status: Amos Alonzo Stagg, at the University of Chicago, 1892

► The first woman play-by-play announcer for a network NFL game: Gayle Sierens, December 27, 1987, for NBC, the Seattle Seahawks at the Kansas City Chiefs

► The first woman to be named Athlete of the Year by *Sports Illustrated*: Billie Jean King, 1972

... And Just a Few of the Coolest Lasts

It's a much more fleeting endeavor to say who did something last than who did something first, since with many records it's obviously just a matter of time before someone else comes along to become the new last person to do something. As of this writing, for example, we know that Shawn Green of the Los Angeles Dodgers is the last to hit four home runs in one game (on May 23, 2002), and Affirmed the last horse to win the Triple Crown (in 1978). Either or both of these distinctions could be outdated within a year.

So we will just offer a very few lasts, some of which may change soon, some of which won't.

► The last active Brooklyn Dodger to play in the majors: Bob Aspromonte, 1971, New York Mets

► The last bareknuckles heavyweight title fight: July 8, 1889; John L. Sullivan knocked out Jake Kilrain in the seventh round

► The last legal spitball pitcher: Burleigh Grimes, 1934

► The last player who did not wear a glove on the field: Jerry Denny, Louisville, 1894

► The last baseball team to start the season with a scheduled double-header: The Chicago White Sox against the Oakland Athletics, 1971 (Oakland had already played a game)

► The last ABA champions: New York Nets, 1976

▶ The last National Leaguer to hit .400: Bill Terry, .401 in 1930

▶ The last National Leaguer to win baseball's Triple Crown: Joe Medwick, 1937

▶ The last golfer to win a calendar Grand Slam: Bobby Jones, 1930 (back then, the Slam was the Open and Amateur championships in the United States and Britain)

▶ The last to start both ends of a doubleheader: Wilbur Wood, on July 20, 1973

"I Won't See *That* in My Lifetime..."

▶ *... Roger Maris's single-season home run record broken (or broken more than once, or broken resoundingly...)* One of baseball's most hallowed records, Maris's mark of 61 home runs (in 1961) seemed able, for the longest time, to withstand any assault. It lasted through the rest of the 1960s, all of the '70s and '80s, and even through most of the homer-happy 1990s. Finally, in 1998, Mark McGwire of the St .Louis Cardinals not only shattered Maris's record by hitting 70 home runs but, amazingly, that year's runner-up, Sammy Sosa of the Chicago Cubs, also shot by Maris, with 66 homers. Suddenly, 61 homers hardly seemed like such an overwhelming accomplishment, as McGwire and Sosa beat it *again* the next year: McGwire hit 65, Sosa 63. In 2001, Sosa went past Maris for a *third* time with 64 homers, only to again finish a distant second, this time to Barry Bonds of the San Francisco Giants, whose staggering 73 home runs suddenly made Maris's once-untouchable 61 seem downright quaint.

▶ *... an American dominating the Tour de France.* The Tour was first contested in 1903, and it was an American-free sporting event until 1981, when Jonathan Boyer became the first U.S. rider to compete—fairly amazing when one considers the number and variety of world-class athletes that America had produced to that point. (Boyer finished an impressive 12th.) In 1986, an American—Greg LeMond—shocked Europe when he won professional cycling's most famous race, then won it twice more. But competitive Americans have not been the rule: Only three U.S.-based teams have competed in the Tour—7-Eleven, Motorola, and the U.S. Postal Service—and only five American riders have ever won stages: LeMond, Davis Phinney, Jeff Pierce, Andy Hampsten, and Lance Armstrong. Top American riders have never been supported in their home country as they have in Europe, where the sport is much more popular.

In the 2002 race, more than a dozen American cyclists competed—"a credit," said Bobby Julich of Philadelphia, who finished third in the 1998 race—"to everyone that has been a part of cycling in the U.S. in the last 15 years." Now, thanks to Armstrong (with help from his USPS team), an American is far and away the class of the Tour. Through the 2002 race, Armstrong had won four straight years, and counting.

▶ ... *Blacks doing well in professional hockey.* It wasn't until the 1957–58 season that the NHL had a black player—Willie O'Ree, who played two games for the Boston Bruins; later, he would play most of the 1960–61 season with them. But from then until recently, there was rarely more than one or two (or no) African-American or African-Canadian players in the game at any time. Grant Fuhr, goalie for the Edmonton Oiler dynasty of the mid- to late 1980s, was talented and successful enough (a five-time Stanley Cup champion) that he could overcome being identified merely as a black hockey player (though many probably remember him for that, foremost). Eventually, though, black players have begun to make NHL rosters: In 2002, there were 13 black players (American and Canadian) across eight teams. Among the most prominent players, past and present, are Anson Carter, Fred Brathwaite, Donald Brashear, Tony McKegney (a 320-goal career scorer), and the best so far (along with Fuhr), Jarome Iginla, who led the NHL in scoring in 2002, and who scored two goals for Canada in the 2002 Olympic gold- medal game against the U.S. "Iginla may be the best forward in the NHL," said Wayne Gretzky.

▶ ... *An abundance of black quarterbacks in the NFL.* Al Campanis was speaking of baseball when he said, infamously, that blacks lacked "the necessities" for leadership positions, but for much of the 20th century, that opinion seemed also to prevail among the football geniuses who considered who got to man their sport's top leadership position, quarterback. There were a sprinkling of black quarterbacks in the NFL, starting with Willie Thrower, who replaced George Blanda for the Chicago Bears in a 1953 game, and then players like Marlin Briscoe of the Denver Broncos, Joe Gilliam of the Pittsburgh Steelers, and James Harris of the Los Angeles Rams. But they were eye-catching aberrations. The barriers began to break when Warren Moon excelled first in the Canadian Football League and then in the NFL, and Doug Williams, out of Grambling, became not only a #1 draft pick by the Tampa Bay Buccaneers but also a Super Bowl winner (and Most Valuable Player) with the Washington Redskins. Now, black quarterbacks are proliferating in the NFL, their presence as a starter no longer causing even a second thought. In the 1999 draft, three were taken in the first round—Syracuse's Donovan McNabb, Oregon's Akili Smith, and Central Florida's Daunte Culpepper, as Andre Ware and Steve McNair had been before them, and Michael Vick after. McNair guided the Tennessee Titans to the Super Bowl, McNabb signed the richest contract in NFL history, and "America's Team"—the Dallas Cowboys—are guided by a black quarterback, Quincy Carter.

▶ ... *American men holding their own in international soccer.* Because of the incredible soccer tradition that permeates the cultures of so many countries in South America, Europe, Central America, and other regions —where in many ways the sport is more central to the collective consciousness than baseball is to the American consciousness—U.S. soccer skill (at least men's) has always been a significant rung down from much of the rest of the world.

In the 2000 Sydney Games, however, America made it past the first round of the men's Olympic soccer competition for the first time since 1924. In another first, the Los Angeles Galaxy of Major League Soccer qualified for the World Club Championship, by defeating Olimpia of Honduras in the CONCACAF Champions Cup.

More significant, the 2002 World Cup signaled a genuine emergence that America has become a force for reckoning. After typical struggles during Cup qualifying and tune-ups for the tournament, the U.S. men enjoyed the most significant soccer success in their history when they upset Portugal, the world's 5th-ranked team; Mexico, the 7th-ranked team; then lost in the quarterfinals in a tight match to eventual Cup runner-up, Germany. Following the tournament, the FIFA world rankings put the U.S. at #9, the first time American men had ever cracked the Top Ten. It is no longer uncommon for American men to be good enough to play in top leagues in other great soccer nations, like England (John Harkes, Brad Friedel, Cobi Jones), Germany (Jeff Agoos, Eric Wynalda), Spain (Kasey Keller), Scotland (Claudio Reyna), and others.

It's Appropriate

The history of sport is filled with stories of the unforeseeable. A great man fails miserably in the clutch. A lesser man accomplishes something spectacular. Who would have guessed, for example, that Don Larsen, the pitcher with one of the worst season winning percentages ever for anyone with more than 20 decisions (3-21, in 1954) would become, two years later, the only man in history to pitch a perfect World Series game?

But sometimes things that *should* happen, do. If you didn't know the following facts, you might well have guessed them. It's appropriate, for instance…

▶ …that the first home run in Yankee Stadium should be hit by Babe Ruth. He did it on April 18, 1923, in the first game ever played in "The House That Ruth Built." Ruth hit a three-run homer in the third inning and the Yankees won, 4-1, over (appropriately) the Boston Red Sox.

▶ …that the player to receive the first official warning in Wimbledon history should be John McEnroe. He got it in the 1980 semifinals against Jimmy Connors (a contest in which McEnroe saved seven match points to win).

▶ …that the first NFL game played in a Scandinavian country should include the Minnesota Vikings. They hosted the Chicago Bears in Gothenburg, Sweden, in a 1988 preseason game.

▶ …that the date on which New Orleans should officially be named the site of a new NFL franchise was All Saints Day, November 1, 1966.

▶ …that the first official car speed record—91.370 mph, set in January of 1904—should be recorded by Henry Ford.

▶ ...that the 2002 earned run average for John Rocker, the Texas Rangers relief pitcher who carved an unfortunate reputation as a bigot and who brought negative attention to each team he was on—in short, who became a kind of baseball Anti-Christ—was 6.66.

▶ ...that the Los Angeles Lakers' NBA record 33-game winning streak in 1971–72 should be stopped, on January 9, 1972, by the Milwaukee Bucks and Lew Alcindor—later to become Kareem Abdul-Jabbar, the centerpiece of the Laker dynasty of the 1980s.

▶ ...that the first career NFL reception by Don Hutson, once the league's all-time leader in touchdown receptions (until Steve Largent broke the record in 1989), should go for a touchdown (of 83 yards).

▶ ...that the first notable title won by Bjorn Borg, who captured dozens of championships but who is best remembered for winning five consecutive Wimbledons, should be the boys' singles at Wimbledon (in 1972).

9 Possibly Overlooked Moments That Signaled a Major Change in Sports

Certain moments in the history of sport prefigured a change that might well have been anticipated. In 1947, for instance, when Jackie Robinson became the first black in the major leagues' modern era, it was clear that the character of the game would forever be altered. In 1972, President Richard Nixon signed Title IX, part of the Higher Education Act —legislation that barred sex bias in athletics and other activities at colleges receiving federal assistance—which led to a considerable expansion in women's athletics.

Other moments have caused changes that were equally or almost as significant, but the profoundness of the moment was not necessarily gauged at the time.

▶ To raise money in 1877 for a "pony-roller" for croquet, a club in England held a tennis tournament, which proved a success. The All-England Croquet Club would hold the competition again and the Wimbledon tournament grew into the most famous and prestigious tennis competition in the world.

▶ Due to snow, the 1932 NFL title game was played indoors at Chicago Stadium. Because of the 80-yard field, the game rules were modified and were so successful that they would lead to permanent rule changes concerning hashmark positioning, having goalposts at the goal line, and permitting passes from anywhere behind the line of scrimmage.

▶ No soccer competition was included at the 1932 Los Angeles Olympics, an absence that helped to stifle the progress of the game in America. The popularity of amateur soccer in the United States had been growing during that era and the showcasing of world-class soccer on American soil, at the L.A. Games, would likely have given the sport needed credibility.

► In the 1966 NCAA finals, Texas Western, with five black starters, beat Adolph Rupp's University of Kentucky team, with five white starters, an event called "'Brown vs. the Board of Education' of college basketball." The notion of black "quotas" ended and helped to change the complexion—figuratively and literally—of the game.

► In September of 1972, the U.S.S.R. surprised the world by compiling a more-than-respectable 3-4-1 record in their series with Canada, after everyone had expected Canada to sweep. Not long after the series, NHL scouts began to scour Europe for players, and the league adapted to the more wide-open, passing-intensive European style of play. In 2001–02, more than one-third of all NHL players were European-born, with the Czech Republic contributing the most, then Russia, Sweden, Finland, and Slovakia. The percentage of Canadian-born players reached its lowest level, at just over 50%.

► The 24-second clock—an innovation meant to increase scoring and especially to prevent stalling—was used for the first time in an NBA game on October 30, 1954, when the Rochester Royals defeated the Boston Celtics, 98-95. The clock radically transformed pro basketball into the fast-paced, high-scoring game that it has become. "The adoption of the clock was the most important event in the NBA," said Maurice Podoloff, the NBA's first president.

► On October 27, 1906, the first forward pass in a professional football game was completed. George "Peggy" Parratt of Massillon, Ohio, threw it, and Dan "Bullet" Riley caught it, in a victory over the combined Benwood-Moundsville team. Football's connection to rugby would grow increasingly remote as the forward pass was exploited as an offensive weapon.

► In 1970, Billie Jean King, along with Rosie Casals, led a boycott of the Pacific South West Championships, where the men's prize money was 10 times greater than the women's. Helped by *World Tennis* magazine publisher Gladys Heldman, they formed the Women's Pro Tour, sponsored by Virginia Slims, which would grow to its current immense success.

► East German swimmers wore skintight, semi-see-through Lycra suits at the 1973 swimming world championships, in Belgrade, Yugoslavia, an occasion that coincided with the beginning of East Germany's domination of women's swimming. They had not won a single event at the 1972 Olympics; in 1976, they took 11 of 13 gold medals. "Belgrade suits" soon became standard.

The Most Moving Moments in Sports History

▶ For one memorably spontaneous and beautiful minute—for athlete and fan—22-year-old Eric Moussambani of Equatorial Guinea, not a world-class athlete, found himself at the center of the sporting world.

Correction: Make that nearly two beautiful minutes.

At the 2000 Summer Olympic Games in Sydney, Moussambani swam alone in the first qualifying heat of the 100m freestyle; the two other swimmers for that heat (from Nigeria and Tajikistan) had been disqualified. But it's not that Moussambani swam alone that put him front and center.

It's that he'd started swimming competitively all of eight months before; that he'd only had a 20-meter pool in which to practice, in his tiny West African country; that, before that heat, he'd never swum a full 100 meters *without stopping for breath*; that before arriving in Sydney, he'd never seen an Olympic-size 50-meter pool. So why was Moussambani even there, in what would clearly be, for him, an impossible struggle? He had been allowed to compete at the Games because of a plan by FINA, swimming's governing body, to promote swimming in countries that were not already competing in the Olympics. The Equitorial Guinea Swimming Federation was formed just six months before Moussambani's swim, and so far had attracted seven members. Moussambini was given the honor of carrying his country's flag at the Games' opening ceremony.

Then came the "race."

Moussambani went out for the first of his two laps in remarkably slow time—swimming about half the speed of those who'd be in the pool moments later—and his form was terribly labored and anything but world-class. At the wall, he made an awkward (to be charitable) tumble-turn, then set out for the second and final lap. Struggling mightily, dog-paddling more than swimming, he looked as if he might simply sink—until the crowd, understanding that they were witnessing effort every bit as profound as that exerted by champions like their countryman Ian Thorpe and others, rose to cheer him on. During the final strokes of the race (Moussambani would later say), as the crowd roared at deafening pitch, the lone swimmer from Equitorial Guinea, who appeared as if he was poised between finishing and drowning, believed that the booming cheer signaled that he had set a record.

Moussambani's second lap took 1:11.75, for a total 1:52.72—a time that would turn out to be nearly 50 seconds slower than the next-to-last, and 70th, of all the swimmers trying to qualify for the next round of the 100m freestyle.

A delighted Moussambani announced after the race that he was eager to practice his swimming and wished to compete at the 2004 Athens Olympics. "I want to send hugs and kisses to the crowd because it was their cheering that kept me going," he said.

▶ Marc Buoniconti—son of the great, undersized Miami Dolphins linebacker Nick Buoniconti, who captained the Dolphins famed "No-Name

Defense," helped Miami to record the NFL's only undefeated season, and also to win two Super Bowls, in 1973 and '74—was paralyzed from the neck down while playing high school football in 1985. Since that moment, the Buoniconti family became leaders in helping to find and fund a cure for spinal cord injuries, starting the Buoniconti Fund and the Miami Project to Cure Paralysis, which has raised, on average, about $10 million each year for a decade and a half.

When Buoniconti, the elder, was finally inducted into the Pro Football Hall of Fame in Canton, Ohio, in the summer of 2001, he chose Marc to present him.

"… [W]hen they started using labels for me and telling you all the medical clichés that I'd never be able to walk again," said the wheel-chair-bound Marc, in his presenter's speech, "that I needed a machine to breathe for me, that paralysis can't be cured—once again you didn't listen. Dad, you never believed the labels and limitations that others ascribed to you. You faced each challenge head-on and made believ-ers out of them. So in closing, I've got a label for you that I've never mentioned.

"Dad, as I look at all the things they say you just couldn't do, it seems to me that you're just not a very good listener."

After the crowd laughed, Marc concluded by introducing his father: "My hero, my friend, my dad, Nick Buoniconti."

His father, crying—along with pretty much everyone else—bent over and kissed his son.

▶ On the night of December 3, 1987, in a ceremony honoring Phil Esposito, Boston Bruin captain and All-Star defenseman Ray Bourque surprised Esposito and the Boston crowd by pulling off his own jersey—the #7 he'd worn for eight years—so that Esposito's old #7 could be retired by the Bruins. Underneath Bourque's old jersey was another one that displayed his new number, 77.

▶ Throughout his career, Pete Sampras has been known as a mechan-ical, emotionless tennis player, but no one who watched his quarterfi-nal match with Jim Courier at the 1995 Australian Open would ever again question the depth of his emotions. Sampras had recently learned that his coach and close friend, Tim Gullikson, had tumors in his brain, and a day earlier Gullikson, after collapsing and being hos-pitalized during the tournament, had flown back to the United States for tests. Sampras would say afterward that during the match, "I had this mental picture of Tim crying in his hospital bed. I broke down." Sampras began sobbing into his towel during the changeover after winning the first game of the final set. Although he composed himself, throwing ice water on his face to hide the tears, he cried throughout the remainder of the match, often bending over between points to sob. After beating Courier 6-7 (4-7), 6-7 (3-7), 6-3, 6-4, 6-3, Sampras broke down again in the press room. Sampras called Gullikson after the match, who told him, "Pete, you gotta win in straight sets because I don't want to see you cry anymore." Gullikson died of brain cancer five months later.

▶ After repeated heartbreak and humiliating falls in races at the '88 Calgary and '92 Albertville Winter Olympics—including a wipeout in the 500m in Calgary just hours after learning that his sister Jane had died of leukemia—world speedskating sprint champion Dan Jansen entered the '94 Lillehammer Games for a final shot at gold and Olympic glory. But during his first event—the 500m, his specialty—he stumbled and finished eighth. In his final Olympic race, the 1,000 meters, Jansen finally skated to his ability... and won the gold medal in a world-record 1:12.43. During his joyous, years-belated victory lap, Jansen—in front of 10,000 cheering Norwegian fans and fellow Olympians, and millions of misty-eyed Americans and viewers the world over—carried in his arms Jane, his baby daughter named for his sister.

▶ An unexpectedly poignant twist was put on Chris Evert's farewell to major tournament tennis when she hugged and consoled Zina Garrison, who had just conquered Evert in the 1989 U.S. Open quarter-finals and could not contain her tears over what she'd just done.

▶ In a moment that was poignant and cathartic for an entire country, Cathy Freeman, Australia's first Aborigine to win an individual Olympic event—the 400m—was the last of a seven-woman chain to carry the Olympic torch during the opening ceremonies at the 2000 Sydney Games. She climbed the final steps and lit the flame.

Aborigines—Australia's indigenous people—number just under 400,000 and are mostly poor, and they and the country's white majority had (and have) been moving toward "reconciliation," including a formal apology by the government for the wrongs—and crimes—committed against the Aborigines. (Before Freeman, tennis great Evonne Goolagong-Cawley was Australia's most celebrated Aboriginal athlete.)

▶ Cal Ripken, Jr., was summoned for five curtain calls in the fifth inning on September 6, 1995, after his 2,131st consecutive game, break-ing Lou Gehrig's cherished record for durability, became official. On the last of the curtain calls—Ripken was pushed out of the dugout by Oriole teammates Rafael Palmeiro and Bobby Bonilla—the Baltimore legend embarked on an emotional, impromptu lap around Camden Yard. Ripken high-fived fans, greeted police officers and grounds crew members, slapped palms with Orioles relievers in the bullpen, embraced longtime bullpen coach Elrod Hendrick, and finally finished up by shaking hands, one by one, with members of the Orioles' oppo-nents, the Anaheim Angels, in front of their dugout. In the stands, besides Ripken's family, were President Bill Clinton, Vice President Al Gore, and Joe DiMaggio, a teammate of Gehrig's.

▶ Dennis Byrd, once a star defensive player for the New York Jets, was temporarily paralyzed after an awkward 1992 collision with teammate Scott Mersereau, while trying to sack the quarterback. Byrd underwent surgery for a fractured vertebra, and vowed he would again walk and hold his children.

Three months later, aided by crutches, Byrd walked into a room packed with news media. Later, he would be able to walk unaided.

► Captured in a lasting television image right after the United States beat Finland to clinch the 1980 Olympic hockey gold medal, American goalie Jim Craig was seen skating around the Lake Placid rink and beyond the bedlam of his celebrating teammates to search out his father.

► Great mystery surrounded the identity of the person who would light the Olympic flame to officially start the 1996 Atlanta Games. Speculation centered on Edwin Moses or Evander Holyfield, maybe Michael Jordan. But many in the crowd of 80,000 gasped when swimmer Janet Evans handed the torch to Muhammad Ali, who had almost magically appeared under the Olympic cauldron. His left arm shaking from the Parkinson's Disease that had long stricken him, his body trembling, Ali lit the wire that would illuminate the flame, as chants of "Ali! … Ali!" filled the stadium.

► In 1952, four women were allowed to participate in the equestrian dressage competition for the first time in Olympic history. One of them, Lis Hartel of Denmark, had to be helped on and off of her horse because she had been paralyzed below the knees from polio. She won the silver medal, and in a poignant scene, gold medalist Henri Saint Cyr of Sweden helped her up onto the victory platform. (Hartel won the silver again in 1956.)

► Following a seven-year battle with liver disease, Chris Klug received a liver transplant. Eighteen months after that, the American snowboarder won the bronze medal in the men's parallel giant slalom at the 2002 Winter Olympics in Salt Lake City. Post-surgery, Klug was still required to take two drugs three times a day to ensure that his body didn't reject the donated liver. "With the drugs you can't be one hundred percent," said Fred Steinbaum, an oncologist working with Klug; Steinbaum added that he considered what Klug had done to be the greatest athletic achievement of all-time. Said Carlon Colker, Klug's personal physician, "The bottom line is, eighteen months ago, [Chris] was lying on a hospital bed, filleted open, jaundiced and circling the drain… Today he's on the podium."

► In a moment that pretty much left no conscious viewer dry-eyed, Dick Hoyt, age 59, competed in the 1999 Ironman Triathlon along with his 37-year-old son, Richard, a spastic paraplegic who suffers from multiple sclerosis. Father pulled son on a rubber raft during the swim; rode with him on a bike specially outfitted with another seat; then pushed him in a wheelchair for the marathon portion. The two competitors finished in just over 16 hours—45 minutes before the midnight cutoff time.

► John Daly, the supremely talented golfer who has probably become known more for his personal struggles, especially with alcohol, than for his booming drives and two Grand Slam victories, experienced "the shakes"—from alcohol withdrawal—in front of the golf crowd and a TV audience, on the 15th green of the 1998 Greater Vancouver Open. Despite temperatures in the mid-80s, Daly, trying to quit booze again, put on two sweaters to offset the chills. (At the 1997 U.S. Open, Daly had quit after playing nine holes of the second round because he'd felt the shakes coming on.)

7 Very Good Athletes We'll Remember Primarily for Their Misfortunes

▶ Brooklyn Dodgers pitcher Ralph Branca, for the home run he gave up to New York Giant Bobby Thomson in 1951, "the shot heard 'round the world"; Branca pitched for 12 seasons and had a .564 winning percentage

▶ Brian Piccolo, the subject of the movie *Brian's Song*, for dying young of cancer; Piccolo won the NCAA rushing title in 1964 for Wake Forest and played for four years with the Chicago Bears

▶ New York Yankee Wally Pipp, for giving way one summer day to a rookie first baseman named Lou Gehrig, who proceeded not to miss a game for the next 13 years; Pipp was a 15-year veteran who twice won the American League home run title

▶ Los Angeles Laker Kermit Washington, for delivering a December 1978 punch to Houston Rocket Rudy Tomjanovich that caused massive facial injuries requiring several operations; Washington was not only a top NBA power forward for nine years but, ironically, considered around the league as one of the kindest men in the game

▶ California center Roy "Wrong Way" Riegels, for running the wrong way with a fumble that set up the decisive score for Georgia Tech in the 1929 Rose Bowl; Riegels was an All-America and a team co-captain the following year

▶ Brooklyn Dodgers catcher Mickey Owen, for the third strike that he dropped against the New York Yankees in Game 4 of the World Series in 1941; earlier that season, Owen had set a National League record for most consecutive errorless chances in a season by a catcher.

▶ Boston Red Sox first baseman Bill Buckner, for the two-out, 10th-inning ground ball hit by New York Met Mookie Wilson that scooted through Buckner's legs, allowing Ray Knight to score the winning run as the Mets beat the Red Sox, 6-5, in Game 6 of the 1986 World Series; Buckner, one of the most maligned men in the history of New England sports, was a terrific player: He won a batting title with the Chicago Cubs in 1980, hit over .300 eight times, accumulated 2,715 career hits, made the All-Star team, and received 10 votes for the Hall of Fame in 1996, his first year of eligibility; although Buckner is said to be haunted by the error, he has shown up at Mets' reunions to sign his autograph, for a fee

14

GREATS

If You Think They're Good, Check Out the *Third*-String: The Greatest Plan Bs in Sports

▶ In 1960, the U.S. reserve swim team set the world record in a 400m freestyle relay qualifying round.

▶ In the 1984 Olympics, West German swimmer Thomas Fahrner set an Olympic record in the 400m freestyle in the consolation race.

▶ In 1996, John Wetteland became just the second relief pitcher to win the World Series MVP Award, saving all four victories for the New York Yankees. A free agent after the season, he signed with the Texas Rangers and left the Yankee closer job to the young set-up reliever, Mariano Rivera. As good as Wetteland was—saving 74 games over two seasons with the Yankees—Rivera turned into the greatest postseason closer of all-time, with a 0.32 ERA in 18 division series games, a 0.76 ERA in 16 championship series games, and a 1.33 ERA in 18 World Series games.

▶ In 1928, New York Rangers coach Lester Patrick, age 44, was pressed into duty as goalie because of an injury to Lorne Chabot. Patrick won a 2-1 overtime game in the Stanley Cup finals, which the Rangers won, three games to two.

▶ Norwegian Birger Ruud went to the 1948 Olympics as ski jumping coach but decided to compete in place of a less experienced team member. Ruud won the silver medal.

Models of Perfection

Perfection outside of nature is rare. But some examples in sports do come to mind: the 1972 Miami Dolphins, who recorded the only perfect—unbeaten and untied—season in NFL history; Rocky Marciano, the only heavyweight champion to go through his whole professional career without a loss, recording a spotless 49-0 record; Nadia Comaneci, the first gymnast to earn a perfect 10 at the Olympics, in 1976; Don Larsen's perfect game in 1956, the only one in World Series history; in golf, the hole-in-one.

Here are some other examples of individual contests (or parts of them), seasons, and, in that most uncommon instance, careers that were devoid of blemish.

▶ Arguably the most outrageous (single-sport) career in the history of college athletics was capped in March of 2002 by wrestler Cael Sanderson, who went 159-0 over his four years at Iowa State and won the national championship each year (the first three at 184 pounds, his senior year at 197).

▶ The Chicago Bulls are a perfect 6-for-6 in NBA finals, and Michael Jordan won the Finals MVP all six times.

▶ Jayne Torvill and Christopher Dean of Great Britain were awarded the maximum number of points possible when they received perfect 6's from all nine judges for artistic presentation in the World Ice Dance Championships at Helsinki, on March 12, 1983, and again at Ottawa, in March of 1984. They hold the record for receiving the most 6's in a career, and the most in one competition.

▶ In the 1924 Olympic rapid-fire pistol competition, 8 of the 55 competitors had perfect scores, and all eight were again perfect in the second-round shoot-off. After five rounds, American Henry Bailey and Swede Wilhelf Carlberg were left, each having hit 48 targets in a row. They were perfect in the sixth shoot-off, as well, and Bailey was perfect in the seventh despite a stuck cartridge. Carlberg then missed two, and Bailey won the gold.

▶ The 1957 NCAA men's basketball champions, the University of North Carolina, were 32-0. The 1976 Indiana University basketball team won the national title and also sported a 32-0 record. The seemingly perennial champion John Wooden-coached UCLA Bruins finished undefeated in 1964, 1968, 1972, and 1973.

Both the 1995 and 2002 University of Connecticut champion women's basketball team went undefeated, as did the 1998 University of Tennessee Lady Volunteers.

▶ The only known "golden set"—in which one player wins every point in the set—in tennis's open era was recorded by Bill Scanlon in a first-round win over Marcos Hocevar, at the WCT Gold Coast Cup at Delray Beach, Florida.

▶ In the second half of Super Bowl XXI, New York Giants quarterback Phil Simms threw 10 passes and completed all 10 (for 166 yards).

▶ Wrestler Robin Reed, gold medalist at the 1924 Olympics, retired undefeated.

▶ Mark Spitz was perfect at the 1972 Summer Olympics: He entered seven swimming events (four individuals, three relays), won seven gold medals, and set seven world records. Eric Heiden entered five speedskating races in the 1980 Winter Games, became the first person in Olympic history to win five individual gold medals in one Games, and set an Olympic record in each event.

▶ In 2001, University of Arizona softball pitcher Jennie Finch was 32-0, and shut out UCLA in the title game.

▶ At the U.S. Olympic trials in Chicago in 1972, diver Michael Finneran was awarded perfect 10's by all seven judges for a backward 1½ somersault, 2½ twist (free) from the 10-meter platform. Greg Louganis matched this feat in 1982. They became the only two divers in international competition to receive straight 10's from all the judges.

▶ The only major professional football team besides the 1972 Miami Dolphins to record an unbeaten, untied season was the 1948 Cleveland Browns, who were 15-0 in winning the All-America Football Conference title.

▶ In international competition, Japanese wrestler Osamu Watanabe won the 1964 Olympic freestyle featherweight championship without giving up a point in his six matches.

▶ In the Olympic equestrian jumping competition, a perfect score—for a run with no faults—has been awarded twice: to Frantisek Ventura of Czechoslovakia riding Eliot in 1928, and by Alwin Schockemohle of West Germany riding Warwick Rex in 1976.

▶ Aleksandr Dityatin of the U.S.S.R., the first person to win eight medals in one Olympics, was also the first male gymnast to receive a perfect 10 for the vault, in 1980.

▶ American weightlifter John Davis was never defeated in Olympic competition in the press, snatch, or jerk.

▶ In 1998, kicker Gary Anderson of the Minnesota Vikings set the NFL record for most points-after-touchdown (PATs) made in a season, 59, without a miss. (During the regular season, he also went 35-for-35 on field-goal attempts.)

▶ Pitching for the 1946 Peekskill (New York) Highlanders of the Class D, North Atlantic League, Tony Napoles was 18-0 in the regular season and 4-0 in the playoffs.

▶ Laurie Doherty of Great Britain is the only man in tennis history never to lose in a challenge round in Davis Cup. He was 7-0 in singles and 5-0 in doubles.

▶ Dan Patch, a great turn-of-the-20th-century pacer, never lost a final heat.

▶ Pitcher Michele Broussard of the Vanderbilt (Louisiana) Catholic High School girl's softball team was 88-0 for her career (including 32-0 as a sophomore, 27-0 as a junior, and 27-0 as a senior) and helped to lead Vanderbilt to four consecutive state titles.

▶ Sybil Bauer held the world record in every backstroke event when she captured the 100m Olympic backstroke gold medal in 1924. She was undefeated when she died of intestinal cancer on January 31, 1927, at age 23.

▶ In 1926, his rookie year for the Philadelphia Athletics, relief pitcher Joe Pate won all nine of his decisions.

▶ Major-league pitcher J. R. Richard had an 0.00 ERA in his senior season at Ruston Lincoln (Louisiana) High School in 1969.

▶ National Leaguer Steve Garvey was 10-0 in All-Star games.

▶ Maureen Connolly was never beaten in a Grand Slam singles event. She won three U.S. titles, three Wimbledons, two French, and one Australian.

11 of the Most Utterly Dominating Individuals in Sports History

▶ Squash player Heather McKay lost only two games, and no matches, from 1961–80.

▶ In the 1910s, Fanny Durack of Australia once held every world record in women's swimming from 50 yards to one mile.

▶ Chiquito de Cambo was rated as the world's best jai alai player from the beginning of the 20th century through 1938.

▶ In women's figure skating, no one was greater than Sonja Henie. She won the Norwegian figure skating championships at age 10, first competed in the Olympics at 11, captured 10 consecutive world championships from 1927 to 1936, and the Olympic gold medals in 1928, 1932, and 1936. Her reported earnings at the time of her death were $45 million.

▶ With the lone exception of 1993, horse trainer D. Wayne Lukas was the top money-winner every year during the 15-year span from 1983–97.

▶ From 1986–96, Paula Newby-Fraser won the Ironman Triathlon Championship eight times.

▶ Gary Kasparov was world chess champion for 15 years, from 1985–2000.

▶ Mariano Rivera, arguably the greatest relief pitcher of all-time—inarguably the greatest in postseason history—was just the third reliever to win the World Series MVP (1999), was on the mound when the

Yankees won their titles in 1998, 1999, and 2000, and his astonishing sub-1.00 ERA, after 79 innings, is actually the result of having been touched up a bit in 2000 and 2001: before that, he hovered in the 0.35 range. He converted 23 straight postseason saves before finally, in blowing the save in Game 7 of the 2001 World Series, showing any vulnerability.

▶ The most famous ancient Olympian was Milo of Croton, who won the boys' wrestling event in 540 B.C., six successive senior Olympiads, and more than two dozen crowns in other Pan-hellenic festivals.

▶ Kelso was named Horse of the Year five times, from 1960 through 1964.

▶ Between 1972 and 1980, Soviet Vassily Alexeyev broke 80 official world weightlifting records. He won two Olympic golds, eight world titles, and nine European championships.

It Should Have Been Enough: Great Performances Overshadowed by Even Better Performances

On March 2, 1962, New York Knick Cleveland Buckner, a career 6.4 points-per-game scorer, had a career night, scoring 33 points against the Philadelphia Warriors. Reporters should have surrounded him after the game. It didn't matter that teammate Richie Guerin also scored over 30 points; he was one of the NBA's top scorers, so that kind of performance was expected. It didn't matter that teammate Willie Naulls also scored over 30 points; he, too, was a top scorer.

It *did* matter, however, that on that night Wilt Chamberlain, of the opposing Warriors, scored 100 points, the all-time NBA record.

A collection of fine performances that would have received more recognition, had someone else not outshined them.

▶ Ken Griffey's 56 home runs in 1998 were enough to win the major-league home run title—and easily—in all but five previous years since the century began, but that year didn't even earn him runner-up status (Mark McGwire and Sammy Sosa fought it out for the title, with 70 and 66 homers, respectively).

In 2001, Sosa's phenomenal 64 home runs were barely enough to keep him within double-digits of that year's home run king, Barry Bonds, who clocked 73, the single-season record.

▶ In the 1960 Olympic speedskating 10,000m race, Viktor Kosichkin of the U.S.S.R. broke the world record by more than 43 seconds...and earned the silver medal. His time was more than two seconds slower than that of Knut Johannesen of Norway.

▶ Jack Nicklaus had the second-lowest total score in British Open history, 269, in 1977. Unfortunately for Nicklaus, that was the same year that Tom Watson shot a 268, the *lowest* British Open score ever, to beat Nicklaus by a stroke.

▶ In 1993, the San Francisco Giants won a sterling 103 games—and didn't make the playoffs. The Atlanta Braves won the National League West with one more win than they.

The 1942 Brooklyn Dodgers won 104 games but finished 2 games behind the St. Louis Cardinals.

The 1909 Chicago Cubs won 104 games and finished 6½ games behind the Pittsburgh Pirates.

▶ Sprinter Charlie Borah equaled the then-Olympic 200m record (21.6 seconds) in the 1928 quarterfinal heat but was still eliminated.

▶ Lou Gehrig's season slugging percentage of .765 in 1927 is the fifth-best all-time, but only the second best on the team that year, behind Babe Ruth's .772, fourth-best all-time.

▶ Rickey Henderson's 939th stolen base—breaking Lou Brock's career record—should have been quite enough to make him the lead baseball story on May 1, 1991, but the 44-year-old Nolan Ryan decided to use the same date to throw his seventh (and final) no-hitter, while striking out 16, against Toronto.

▶ In 1971, Oakland Athletic Vida Blue became the first pitcher in the modern era to strike out 300 or more batters in a season and *not* lead the league in strikeouts. His total of 301 lost to the 308 of Detroit Tiger Mickey Lolich.

▶ USC's 1971–72 basketball team had only two losses (24-2), but they did not go to the NCAA tournament because of the (then) one-school-per-conference rule. Their two defeats were both to conference-mate UCLA, the eventual national champion.

▶ Ty Cobb and Joe Jackson are the only two players with a .400 season average in baseball's modern era not to win the batting title.

▶ In the Olympic 800m finals in 1976, Anita Weiss of East Germany broke the world record but did not even win a medal, as three other runners broke the record more resoundingly.

▶ Pittsburgh Pirate Omar Moreno stole a dazzling 96 bases in 1980 but finished second in the league to Montreal Expo Ron LeFlore, who stole 97.

▶ In 1930, Chuck Klein had 250 hits, tied for seventh-best ever, and 170 RBIs, tied for eighth-best ever... and won neither a hits nor an RBI title. Bill Terry had a National League record-tying 254 hits that year and Hack Wilson set the all-time record for RBIs with 191.

The Homages That Ruth Built

Babe Ruth was known as much for the larger-than-life way in which he did things as for the things themselves. A home run of "Ruthian" proportions is one that will long be remembered, and to be nicknamed "Babe" is often a testament to both an athlete's charisma and great skill. More than two dozen major leaguers have been nicknamed "Babe" (though several preceded Ruth: Jay Towne and Charles Adams, both of whom began playing in 1906, are the earliest-known "Babes") but none approached Ruth's reputation.

To be compared to Babe Ruth is the ultimate compliment to a baseball player—to any athlete, for that matter.

▶ John Beckman, captain of the Original Celtics and his sport's first great gate attraction, was called "the Babe Ruth of Basketball."

▶ Billy Gonsalves, member of the United States World Cup teams in 1930 and 1934, was called "the Babe Ruth of Soccer." He is considered the greatest American player ever.

▶ Moses Solomon, a slugger who played at the end of the 1923 season for the New York Giants, was known as "the Jewish Babe Ruth." Before being called up to the majors, he hit 49 home runs for Hutchinson of the Southwestern (Class C) League. He was also called "The Rabbi of Swat."

▶ Howie Morenz, the swift and great scorer for the Montreal Canadiens in the 1920s and 1930s, was called "hockey's answer to Babe Ruth."

▶ Joe Bauman, who hit 72 home runs for the 1954 Roswell (New Mexico) Rockets in the Class C Longhorn League, a professional baseball record for one season, was known as "the Babe Ruth of the Minors." He later became manager of a beer distributorship in Albuquerque, where he was known as "the Sultan of Schlitz."

▶ Josh Gibson, who hit 89 home runs in one Negro League season and 75 in another, was called "the black Babe Ruth."

▶ Sadaharu Oh, the great Japanese player who launched 868 home runs in 22 years, was called "the Babe Ruth of Japan."

▶ Enrico Rastelli is considered "the Babe Ruth of Juggling."

▶ Billy Haughton, winner of 4,910 races in his career, was considered "the Babe Ruth of Harness Racing."

▶ While at Columbia University, Lou Gehrig, Ruth's future New York Yankee teammate, was called "the College Babe Ruth."

▶ Outfielder Sammy Byrd, the New York Yankees' defensive replacement from 1929–34, was known as "Babe Ruth's Legs."

Just a Small Sampling of Tiger Woods's Sick Golf Records & Accomplishments

▶ He's the youngest ever, at 24, to win the career Grand Slam (Masters, U.S. Open, British Open, PGA Championship).

▶ He's only the second man to win three majors in a calendar year (Ben Hogan did it in 1953).

▶ During his run of winning four consecutive majors, he carded a total of 53 under par for those four tournaments; the next best performance was by Ernie Els, who was a distant 18 under par.

▶ His nine Tour victories in 2000 were the most since Sam Snead won 11 in 1950.

▶ From late 1999 to early 2000, he won six consecutive tournaments (in which he appeared), matching Hogan's feat of 1948.

▶ With seven holes to play at the 2000 AT&T Pebble Beach National Pro-Am, he trailed Mark Gogel by seven shots, but finished eagle-birdie-par-birdie and won by two strokes over Gogel and Vijay Singh.

▶ He won the 2000 U.S. Open by the largest margin ever in a major tournament—15 strokes.

▶ He holds the record for the lowest U.S. Open score (in relation to par), and tied for the lowest U.S. Open score (in number).

▶ He's the first player in over 60 years to successfully defend the PGA Championship.

▶ At the 2000 WGC-NEC World Series of Golf, he set the PGA Tour record for the lowest two-day opening score—125 (rounds of 64 and 61).

▶ He's the only player, along with Lee Trevino in 1971, to win the U.S., British, and Canadian Opens in the same year.

▶ In 1997, he set the record for the Masters, with a 270.

▶ In 1996, he became the youngest athlete to be named *Sports Illustrated* "Sportsman of the Year" since Mary Lou Retton won the honor in 1984.

▶ In 1994, he became the youngest-ever winner, at 18, of the U.S. Amateur Championship.

▶ In 1996, he became the first ever to win three consecutive U.S. Amateurs.

▶ He owns the U.S. Amateur records for consecutive match-play wins (18) and winning percentage (.909).

▶ He won the 1996 NCAA golf championship.

▶ His 2000 scoring average of 68.17 beat Sam Snead's half-century-old record of 69.23.

▶ He's the only athlete to win the Associated Press Male Athlete of the Year Award three times (and counting).

▶ He's the second golfer ever to appear on the cover of *Time* magazine (Arnold Palmer was first, in 1960).

▶ In 2000, he set or tied 27 PGA Tour records.

▶ He has been ranked #1 in the world, without break, longer than anyone before him.

The Best Innovators and Pioneers in Sports

▶ The origin for the "high-five" is claimed by Derek Smith of the 1980 NCAA champion University of Louisville basketball team. Smith was quoted in the *New York Times, The Sporting News*, and other publications as saying that he and teammates Wiley Brown and Daryle Cleveland wanted something "a little odd." The high-five was created and fine-tuned during pre-season practice and introduced to the nation on TV in 1979.

▶ Elston Howard invented the warm-up donut.

▶ In the 1930s, U.S. swimmers in the breaststroke began bringing their arms back above the surface of the water. In 1952, this stroke was officially recognized as the butterfly and added to the Olympics as a separate event.

▶ Arch Ward, sports editor for the *Chicago Tribune*, came up with the idea of a baseball All-Star Game in 1933.

▶ Montreal Canadien Jacques Plante introduced the goalie mask on November 1, 1959.

▶ Stanford's Hank Luisetti helped to revolutionize the game of basketball when he pioneered the one-handed jump shot on the run, at a time when players scored only with layups or two-handed set shots. Luisetti, along with Seton Hall's Bob Davies, also helped to popularize the behind-the-back dribble in the early 1940s.

▶ In 1948, Los Angeles Rams halfback Fred Gehrke painted blue Rams logos on 70 of the team's plain leather football helmets, leading to colorful insignias on helmets for the league's other teams.

▶ Pitcher Jim Brosnan's book, *The Long Season*, published in 1960, paved the way for sports "tell-all" biographies, including Jim Bouton's controversial account, *Ball Four*.

▶ Arnold Lunn organized the first downhill ski race in Switzerland in 1911, and invented the modern slalom in 1922.

▶ René Lacoste had the first tennis ball-throwing machine constructed to his design. He also analyzed his own game by using slow-motion photography, and developed the round-headed, open-throated racket.

▶ The baseball warning track was inspired by Brooklyn Dodger Pete Reiser, who was seriously injured in 1947 crashing into the outfield wall at Ebbets Field.

▶ Harry Miller designed the front-wheel-drive car in 1925.

▶ Arthur Howie Ross, namesake of the Ross Trophy (given to the NHL's leading scorer), designed the modern hockey puck and nets.

▶ Joe Pepitone was the first player to use a blow-dryer in the locker room.

▶ Dick Young was the first sportswriter to get post-game locker-room quotes for his story.

▶ Charlie Waitt wore the first baseball glove in 1875.

▶ Kid Gavilan, who gave the world the bolo punch—half-hook, half-uppercut—claimed that it was developed after years of using a machete to cut sugar cane in his native Cuba. Others have credited Ceferino Garcia with inventing the punch.

▶ In the 1890s, American jockey Todhunter "Tod" Sloan popularized the technique of crouching forward while riding, rather than sitting upright, for better weight distribution. He also helped to popularize the use of stirrups and short reins.

▶ German figure skaters Ernst Baier and Maxi Herber pioneered "shadow skating," in which partners perform the same moves without touching.

▶ The valve-free, hidden-lace basketball was developed by Walter Meanwell, coach at Wisconsin and Missouri.

▶ Tommy McCarthy and Hugh Duffy developed the hit-and-run play.

▶ Fred Perry introduced the short-sleeved, knitted white tennis shirt.

▶ James Van Alen was the originator of the tie-break scoring system in tennis.

▶ Alvin Kraenzlein of the United States, gold medalist in the 120-yard hurdles in 1900, introduced the leg-extended style of hurdling.

▶ Marie Provaznikova of the 1948 Czech gymnastics team refused to return to her native country, becoming the first Olympic athlete to defect.

▶ Cincinnati Reds shortstop Dave Concepcion was the first to bounce a throw, intentionally, on Astroturf from deep in the hole.

▶ Florence Griffith Joyner unveiled her wildly colored, one-legged body suit at the Olympic trials at Indianapolis in 1988. Evelyn Ashford is acknowledged to have first popularized the full-body suit.

▶ R. C. Owens, San Francisco 49er receiver, is credited with originating the "Alley Oop" play while he was a rookie in 1957. He would outjump defenders for passes lofted by quarterback Y. A. Tittle.

Innovations Named for Their Innovators

▶ Sweden's Ulrich Salchow, men's world figure skating champion from 1901–05 and 1907–11, originated the figure skating jump now called a "salchow," in which a skater takes off from the back inside edge of one skate, makes a complete turn in the air, and lands on the back outside edge of the opposite skate. Norwegian figure skater Axel Paulsen gave his name to the "axel," Alois Lutz his name to the "lutz," and American Dorothy Hamill her name to the "Hamill camel."

▶ Along with figure skating, no sport so honors its own the way gymnastics does. American gymnast Bart Conner developed the "Conner spin" on the parallel bars, and Kurt Thomas the "Thomas flair" on the pommel horse. Japanese gymnast Mitsuo Tsukahara first performed the "Suk" vault—a backward 1½ somersault—in the 1972 Olympics. Haruhiro Yamashita executed the first handspring in a piked position off the vault in the 1964 Olympics, for which he received a perfect 10 from the Swiss judge. The move became known as a "yamashita."

▶ Dick Fosbury introduced the "Fosbury Flop" high jump internationally at the 1968 Olympics, where he won the gold medal. His technique —jumping headfirst, and back to the ground—would become favored by most high jumpers in the world.

▶ Pole vaulter Dave Volz was the first to steady the bar with his hand as he went over, a technique now known as "volzing."

▶ Heavyweight champion Muhammad Ali developed the "Ali shuffle," copied by a generation of quick-footed boxers.

Cinderellas: They Came Seemingly Out of Nowhere

▶ Kurt Warner's rise to Most Valuable Player of Super Bowl XXXIV with the St. Louis Rams, and two-time MVP of the National Football League, strains credibility. Undrafted out of Northern Iowa University, where he didn't start until his senior year, Warner tried out with the Green Bay Packers but was cut, after which he returned to Iowa and worked as a grocery clerk for minimum wage. Warner eventually tried out for the Iowa Barnstormers of the Arena League, leading them to two championships. His performance caught the eye of a coach with NFL Europe, who began calling NFL teams on Warner's behalf, because players must be affiliated with the NFL to play in Europe. Only the Rams were interested, and they signed Warner, assigning him to the Amsterdam Admirals. After a year in Europe, where he led the league in passing and took the Admirals to the title game, he became the third-string quarterback of the Rams in 1998. In 1999, Warner ascended to the starting job after an injury to starter Trent Green and had one of the greatest offensive seasons in NFL history, leading the league in touchdowns, quarterback rating, and passing efficiency while guiding the Rams to a 23-16 win over the Tennessee Titans in the Super Bowl. He passed for a Super Bowl-record 414 yards in the victory. Warner is now one of the premier quarterbacks in the league, leading St. Louis to Super Bowl XXXVI (they lost to the New England Patriots) in 2002 while earning his second MVP award and passing for 4,830 yards, second-most in NFL history.

▶ Looking more like a Harry Potter stand-in than a world-class athlete, Swiss winter Olympian Simon Amman, age 20, shocked the ski-jumping world by winning not one but two gold medals—the 90m and 120m jumps—at the 2002 Salt Lake City Games. He became just the second competitor, after the legendary Finn, Matti Nykanen, to achieve that Olympic ski-jumping "double." (Not only did Amman look green, but the bespectacled kid from the tiny hamlet of Unterwasser had amassed exactly zero wins in 33 World Cup events dating back five years, and, not long before the Olympics, had been out of action for almost two weeks after a horrific crash on a practice jump.)

▶ Before the 1991 PGA Championship began, John Daly was the ninth alternate. At 5:30, Wednesday evening—less than 24 hours before the tourney would begin—Daly got a call to say he'd moved up to first alternate. When Daly, who drove through the night, got to Carmel, Indiana, he discovered that Nick Price had dropped out to attend the birth of his son, and Daly was in. Having no time to practice on the Crooked Stick Golf Club course, Daly simply went on to card a 12-under 276 for the tournament, and beat Bruce Lietzke by three shots. In a PGA-conducted survey in 1999, golf fans would select Daly's story and triumph as the #1 "Special Moment in PGA Championship" history.

▶ Actress/model/Internet icon Pamela Anderson, born in a small town in British Columbia, was wearing a tight Labatt's Blue T-shirt while attending a Canadian Football League game (the B.C. Lions were playing) when a cameraman pointed his camera at her. Anderson's image appeared on the stadium Jumbotron, inspiring crowd frenzy. Labatt's signed her to be the company's "Blue Zone" girl.

▶ Golf's U.S. Open has seen several middle-of-the-pack golfers suddenly flourish, if only for that moment. Janet Alex Anderson's only career win was the 1982 U.S. Open. The next year, she shot 82 and missed the cut. Unknown Jack Fleck beat Ben Hogan in a playoff in the 1955 tournament, preventing Hogan from winning his fifth Open. Fleck, a municipal-course pro from Iowa, made two birdies on the final two regulation holes to tie Hogan. And although Orville Moody was a familiar figure on the PGA Tour, the only win of his career before joining the Seniors circuit was the 1969 U.S. Open.

▶ Boxer Buster Mathis injured his hand and could not compete in the 1964 Olympics. The man he beat at the Olympic trials, Joe Frazier, took his place and won the super-heavyweight gold medal.

▶ When All-Pro quarterback Drew Bledsoe of the New England Patriots went down with an injury in Game 2 of the 2001 season, his backup, Tom Brady, stepped in and led the Pats to their first-ever Super Bowl title. (After the season, Bledsoe was traded to the Buffalo Bills.)

▶ Ten days before the 1918 Kentucky Derby, Exterminator was purchased as a workhorse to extend Sun Briar in workouts. When Sun Briar did not train well, Exterminator started in his place and won the Derby against 30-1 odds.

Iron Liege replaced the 1957 Derby favorite General Duke, who had become lame, and won.

▶ Soviet gymnast Olga Korbut, the darling of the 1972 Olympics, qualified for the Games only as an alternate but got to compete after a teammate was injured.

▶ Francisco Fernandez Ochoa of Spain won the Olympic slalom gold medal in 1972, despite never before finishing higher than sixth in an international meet.

Austria's Leonhard Stock won the 1980 Olympic downhill gold. He was an alternate and had never won a World Cup downhill race.

The Greatest Multi-Sport Talents

Bo Jackson starred as a slugger and outfielder for baseball's Kansas City Royals and as a Heisman Trophy-winning running back for football's Raiders. Deion Sanders is another famously multi-talented athlete: He and the great Jim Thorpe are the only two people ever to have scored an NFL touchdown and hit a major-league home run in the same week (Deion did it in September 1989; Thorpe did it twice, in 1917 and 1919). Even more recently, Marion Jones, five-time track and field medalist (three gold) at the 2000 Sydney Olympics, was co-captain and starter on the University of North Carolina women's basketball team that won the 1994 NCAA title.

Others have also been great at two, and even more, sports.

▶ Mildred "Babe" Didrickson Zaharias may have been the most talented athlete ever. She was an All-America basketball player, took the silver medal in the high jump and gold medals in the javelin throw and 80m hurdles in the 1932 Olympics (in track and field, she held or tied world records in the javelin, the 80m hurdles, the high jump, and the long jump), won 31 golf championships, including 10 majors, and held the women's world record for the longest throw of a baseball (296 feet). She got her nickname for hitting five home runs in a baseball game. She was also a superior diver, roller skater, boxer, bowler, and tennis player.

▶ Amos Alonzo Stagg is the only man in both the Pro Football and Basketball Halls of Fame. Besides his many contributions to football, he played in the first public basketball game on March 11, 1892, organized the University of Chicago National Interscholastic Basketball Tournament in 1917, and established basketball at the University of Chicago.

▶ Cal Hubbard is the only man in both the Baseball and Pro Football Halls of Fame. He was a star NFL lineman (1927–33, 1935–36) and an American League umpire (1936–51).

▶ Jim Thorpe starred in pro football, played major-league baseball, and won the decathlon and pentathlon gold medals at the 1912 Olympics. If that wasn't enough, he won the 1912 intercollegiate ballroom dancing championship.

▶ Washington Redskins coach Joe Gibbs took three years before winning his first Super Bowl (he would win two more, and appear in four altogether). As owner of Joe Gibbs Racing team, he took nine years to win a championship, the NASCAR Winston Cup Series.

▶ Bowler Walter Ray Williams, Jr., is four-time PBA Player of the Year and six-time world horseshoe pitching champion.

▶ Althea Gibson, #1 in the world in tennis in 1957–58, later played on the women's golf tour. Ellsworth Vines became one of the top 15 golfers in America after leaving the tennis tour in 1939.

▶ Vic Janowicz, 1950 Heisman Trophy winner, played major-league baseball, as did 1953 Heisman runner-up Paul Giel.

▶ Lottie Dod, five-time Wimbledon singles champion, represented England in field hockey in 1899, won the British Ladies Golf Championship in 1904, and won an Olympic silver medal for archery in 1908.

▶ In 1976, Sheila Young held world titles simultaneously in two sports: She won the Olympic 500m speedskating gold medal (as well as a speedskating silver and bronze) and a world title in cycling.

▶ Three years after winning the U.S. Amateur golf title in 1909, Robert Gardner broke the world pole-vault record, becoming the first man to clear 13 feet.

▶ Golfing great Jack Nicklaus, fishing off of the Australian coast in the early 1980s, caught what was then the fourth-largest blue marlin ever taken, weighing 1,358 pounds.

Ted Williams, maybe baseball's greatest hitter ever, was inducted into the National Fresh Water Fishing Hall of Fame in 1995, and into the Fishing Hall of Fame in 2000, at the age of 81. He caught and recorded more than 1,000 tarpon, as well as over 1,000 bonefish and over 1,000 Atlantic salmon, all on a fly. He's also credited with catching a 1,235-pound black marlin in Peru that Williams believed to be the eighth-biggest fish ever caught on rod and reel, and a 500-pound thresher shark in New Zealand.

▶ Michael Carter, All-Pro nose guard for the San Francisco 49ers, won the silver medal in the 1984 Olympic shot put.

▶ Edward Eagan won the light-heavyweight boxing gold medal in 1920, and the four-man bobsled gold in 1932. He is the only person to win gold medals in both the Summer and Winter Olympics.

▶ Earl Quigley coached his teams to 18 consecutive boys' state high school track titles in Arkansas. His football teams were 134-61-12 and won seven state titles. His basketball teams won 306, lost 95, and won six state titles. His baseball teams were 207-37 and won nine state titles. He won 40 state titles overall.

▶ Seven Pro Football Hall of Famers played in the major leagues, including Ernie Nevers and George Halas.

▶ Tennis star Jaroslav Drobny won a silver medal as a member of Czechoslovakia's 1948 Olympic hockey team.

▶ Oregon State's Terry Baker, 1962 Heisman Trophy winner and #1 pick in the 1963 NFL draft, played starting guard in the NCAA basketball Final Four in 1963.

▶ Major-league outfielder Phil Bradley was the Big Eight passing leader for three years, 1978 through 1980, while quarterback at the University of Missouri.

▶ Olympic heptathlete and long-jumper Jackie Joyner-Kersee was a starter on UCLA's basketball team. Olympic swimmer Matt Biondi was co-captain of the University of California's water polo team.

▶ Major-league pitchers Bob Gibson and Ferguson Jenkins both played for the Harlem Globetrotters.

▶ NFL tight end Russ Francis's high school javelin record (254'11") lasted from 1971 to 1988.

▶ Golfer Hale Irwin was an All-Big Eight defensive back in football for Colorado in 1965 and 1966.

▶ On November 8, 1968, Don Gullett, future major-league pitcher, scored 72 points in a football game for South Shore (McKell, Kentucky) High School—at the time the seventh best scoring performance nationally in high school history.

▶ Former major-league player and manager Alvin Dark led LSU in passing and rushing in 1942. His play pushed Steve Van Buren, a future star running back in the NFL, into the role of blocking back.

▶ As a youngster, major leaguer Lee Mazzilli won eight national speedskating championships.

▶ Dallas Cowboys defensive lineman Ed "Too Tall" Jones was 6-0 as a professional boxer in 1979.

▶ Football legend Jim Brown is considered one of the greatest lacrosse players of all time.

Staying Power

Some examples of extraordinary stamina and conditioning in sports:

▶ For the 1961–62 season, Wilt Chamberlain averaged 48.5 minutes per game—*more* than a full regulation game per game. In 79 games (including overtime games) that year, he didn't miss a minute. For his career, Chamberlain averaged 45.8 minutes per game.

▶ For each of the seven seasons from 1955–56 through 1961–62, goalie Glenn Hall played 4,200 minutes—every minute of every game.

▶ Jack Taylor of the Chicago Cubs and St. Louis Cardinals threw 188 consecutive complete games from 1901–06. He also made 15 relief appearances during the streak, finishing each game; thus, he went 203 consecutive appearances without being replaced. The Brooklyn Dodgers finally knocked him out in the third inning of a game on August 12, 1906.

▶ Pitcher George Zabel of the 1915 Chicago Cubs finished one game with 18⅓ innings of relief.

For the half-decade span of 1997-2001, Cincinnati Reds relief pitcher Scott Sullivan worked 522⅔ innings. He exceeded 100 innings for four straight years (it would have been five but he fell 2⅔ innings short in 1997). He's the first reliever to lead the major leagues in relief innings four times in a row.

▶ Chief Bender completed all but one of his 10 World Series starts.

▶ The New York Rens, an all-black basketball team that was formed in 1922 and that was renowned for their stamina, never called a timeout.

▶ In a 1909 fight in Paris, heavyweight Joe Jeannette was knocked down 27 times but still beat Sam McVey in the 49th round.

Staying Power II: Sports Figures Who Excelled When Young and Not So Young

▶ In 1972, 16-year-old Ulrike Meyfarth of West Germany won the Olympic high jump to become the youngest individual track gold medal winner ever. Twelve years later, in 1984, she won the gold again to become the oldest Olympic high jump winner ever.

▶ In 1990, at age 19, Pete Sampras was a suprise winner of the U.S. Open, and the youngest man to do so. In 2002, at 31, he was a surprise winner at the U.S. Open, and one of the the oldest men to do so.

▶ Ty Cobb and Rusty Staub both hit homers as teenagers and in their forties.

▶ Gene Upshaw played in Super Bowls in three decades—II, in 1968; XI, in 1977; and XV in 1981.

▶ Al Unser, Sr., first won the Indianapolis 500 in 1970 and last in 1987 (with two others in between).

▶ Bucky Harris managed World Series winners 23 years apart.

▶ Willie Mays has the longest stretch between MVP seasons, 11 years, winning the award in 1954 and 1965.

When George Brett won the 1990 A.L. batting title, he became the first player to win titles in three decades (14 years separated his first and last).

▶ Ken Rosewall won his two U.S. championship singles titles 14 years apart, and his first and last Australian Championships 19 years apart.

▶ Gary Player won golf tournaments in the 1950s, 1960s, 1970s, 1980s, and 1990s.

▶ Texas lineman K. L. Berry lettered in 1912, 1914, and 1915. He left school for military service, then returned to win All-SWC honors in 1924, at age 31.

▶ Betty Richey was a U.S. Women's Lacrosse Association All-America for 22 straight years, from 1933 to 1954.

▶ C. Alphonso Smith won the U.S. National Boys tennis title in Chicago on August 14, 1924. Fifty-five years later, in August of 1979, he won the National 70-and-over title, in Santa Barbara, California.

▶ Although he was a formidable pitcher for almost all of his lengthy career, pitcher David Cone won 20 games only twice—once, in 1988, at age 25, and then not again until he was 35.

▶ Dick Weber is the first professional bowler to win major championships in four decades.

▶ Pete Sheehy was the New York Yankees clubhouse man for 60 years, from Babe Ruth through Don Mattingly.

That Missing Something:
29 Greats and the Milestones They Never Achieved That You'd Think They Would Have

▶ Maurice Richard never led the NHL in scoring.

▶ Pelé was never the leading goal scorer in a given World Cup.

▶ Dwight Gooden never won (i.e., was never credited with the win in) a postseason game.

▶ Jack Nicklaus never won the Vardon Trophy (for the year's lowest adjusted scoring average).

▶ Neither Don Sutton, with 3,574 career strikeouts, nor Gaylord Perry, with 3,534 strikeouts, ever won a season strikeout title.

▶ Kathy Whitworth, the winningest golfer on the LPGA or PGA Tour, never won the U.S. Open.

▶ Ken Rosewall never won Wimbledon, and neither did Pancho Gonzales.

▶ Jim Ryun, nine-time holder of the world record in the mile, never won an Olympic gold medal. Mary Decker never won an Olympic medal.

▶ Man O' War never ran in the Kentucky Derby.

▶ Joe Morgan, with 689 stolen bases, never won a stolen base title.

▶ Hall of Famers Nap Lajoie, Ernie Banks, Luke Appling, Harry Heilmann, George Sisler, Ralph Kiner, Jim Bunning, Ferguson Jenkins, Rod Carew, and Phil Niekro never played in a World Series game.

▶ Tom Watson and Arnold Palmer never won the PGA.

▶ Sam Snead never won the U.S. Open.

▶ Nolan Ryan never won a Cy Young Award.

▶ Neither Bjorn Borg nor Evonne Goolagong ever won the U.S. Open, losing four finals each.

▶ Joe Namath was never an All-America.

Living Legends

The following athletes have been honored in ways usually reserved for athletes who have passed away, or at least were very ill.

▶ Tennis player Billie Jean King has a mountain in the Catskills named for her.

▶ Former Negro League legend James "Cool Papa" Bell lived on James Cool Papa Bell Avenue in St. Louis, Missouri.

▶ The name of the tournament played on Sam Snead's home course in White Sulphur Springs, West Virginia, was eventually changed from the Greenbrier Open to the Sam Snead Festival.

▶ After Pelé's great debut at age 17 in the 1958 World Cup, in which he scored two goals against Sweden in the finals to help his country to victory, European clubs offered the Brazilian star huge sums to play for them. However, the Congress of Brazil stepped in and declared Pelé an official national treasure, and his sale or trade was forbidden.

▶ Boston Celtic and native Hoosier Larry Bird has not one but two streets named for him in Indiana: Larry Bird Avenue in Terre Haute, and Larry Bird Boulevard in French Lick, his hometown.

▶ When Joan Joyce, the greatest softball pitcher ever, played in the International Women's Professional Softball Association, a rule was adopted, mostly because of Joyce's prowess, that a pitcher could not appear in consecutive games.

▶ Brian Boitano, 1988 Olympic men's figure skating gold medalist, has been elevated to pop icon status thanks to the irreverent Comedy Central TV hit, *South Park*, and the movie it spawned, *Bigger, Longer, and Uncut*, in which characters Stan, Kyle, and Cartman sing the song —and ponder the philosphical question—"What Would Brian Boitano Do?"

▷ Special "living legend" commendation to a dead person: Athletic superstar Jim Thorpe was buried in a Pennsylvania town, Mauch Chunk, that agreed to change its name to Jim Thorpe in exchange for his body.

Beyond 60 + 714: Some Lesser-Known Facts About and Records Held by Babe Ruth

▶ He is the only starting pitcher in World Series history to bat anywhere but ninth in the order.

▶ On May 6, 1915, he hit his first major-league home run. On May 7, 1915, a German submarine sank the *Lusitania*.

▶ Until 1931, or for the first 17 years of his career, a ball that bounced over the fence—what would today be a ground-rule double—counted as a home run. Although none of his record 60 home runs in 1927 is believed to have bounced over the fence, there is no way of telling how many of his career total were of this variety. To his credit, however, until 1920, sluggers of his era were disadvantaged by a now-defunct rule that stated that any ball that cleared the fence fair but landed in the stands in foul ground was considered foul. Today, such a hit would be ruled a home run.

► He pitched the longest complete game, 14 innings, in World Series history, in 1916.

► Despite popular belief, he was not an orphan. His parents felt he needed guidance and discipline, and in 1902 enrolled him in St. Mary's Industrial School for Boys, a reform school.

► Along with fellow Yankee Bob Meusel, he was fined his World Series share of $3,500 and suspended in the fall of 1921 by baseball commissioner Kenesaw Landis for barnstorming after the World Series over Landis's objections. The two players were reinstated on May 20, 1922.

► He was the first major athlete to endorse Jockey, famed for Jim Palmer's underwear ads many decades later.

► He won his last nine decisions as a pitcher, spread out over 15 years. His last pitching appearance was a 1933 complete-game victory over the Boston Red Sox.

► The "Baby Ruth" candy bar, which made its appearance in 1917, was named not after him but after Ruth Cleveland, the daughter of President Grover Cleveland.

► On September 5, 1914, he hit his first and only minor-league home run, for Providence of the International League.

► In 1923, he stole 17 bases but was caught stealing 21 times.

► In 1918, he hit all 11 of his home runs on the road.

► He co-holds the record for shutouts in a season by an American League left-hander with nine, in 1916.

► He pitched in 10 seasons, and had a winning record in every one of them.

► The last man to pinch-hit for him was Ben Paschal in the 1927 season opener. Babe had been 0-for-3 that day, with two strikeouts. Paschal singled.

► In his final major-league at-bat, he grounded out to Philadelphia Phillies first baseman Dolf Camilli. The pitcher was Jim Bivin, the date May 30, 1935, the place Baker Bowl.

► Of all pitchers in history with 15 or more wins over the New York Yankees, the one with the best won-lost percentage against them, with a sparkling 17 victories and just 5 defeats, is, of course, Babe Ruth.

Chronic Winners:
Ridiculously Successful Sports Figures

Professional and Olympic athletes are, by definition, winners; they got where they are by beating out many others for the privilege. But some athletes, to paraphrase Orwell, are more victorious than others.

This list includes those who are addicted to winning wherever they go, and often.

▶ Chris Drury pitched his Trumbull, Connecticut, team to the Little League World Series championship. At Boston University, he won the Hobey Baker Award, hockey's Heisman Trophy, and was a star of their NCAA championship team. He then became a key player on the Colorado Avalanche's Stanley Cup-winning team in 2001.

▶ Phil Jackson won two NBA titles as a player, with the New York Knicks. He coached the Albany Patroons of the Continental Basketball Association to a title. As coach of the NBA's Chicago Bulls, he won six world championships. He left immediately after the last one (as did, not insignificantly, Michael Jordan), then returned to the league to coach the Los Angeles Lakers. In his first three years with them, they won three world titles (and counting, through 2002). His NBA teams have won 24 straight playoff series (and counting).

▶ In college, Doug Flutie won the Heisman Trophy and became the NCAA's all-time passing leader. In the Canadian Football League, he was named league MVP six times. In 1998, he brought out a cereal called "Flutie Flakes," with portions of each sale going to the Doug Flutie, Jr. Foundation for Autism, which supports research into the disorder, which plagues Flutie's son. Flutie Flakes became a top-selling cereal in New England.

▶ At Christ the King High School in Queens, New York, Chamique Holdsclaw won four consecutive state basketball titles. In her first three years at the University of Tennessee, the Lady Volunteers won the national title.

▶ Ken Morrow went straight from the 1980 U.S. Olympic gold medal-winning hockey team to four straight Stanley Cup titles with the New York Islanders, from 1980 to 1983.

▶ Bill Bradley was a Rhodes Scholar, College Player of the Year, Final Four MVP, first-round draft pick, two-time NBA world champion, best-selling author, and three-time U.S. senator.

▶ Otto Graham was the first player chosen by the new AAFC pro football league, played on all four championship Cleveland Brown teams during the league's four-year tenure, then joined the NFL, where he led his team to the title game six out of their first six years, winning it all in his first year (and in two later years), and was elected to the Pro Football Hall of Fame. He was also a basketball All-America and played in the NBL (precursor to the NBA).

▶ Lew Alcindor, later Kareem Abdul-Jabbar, led his Power Memorial (New York) High School team to a 79-2 record, his UCLA freshman team to a 21-0 record, the UCLA varsity to three consecutive NCAA titles, the Milwaukee Bucks to their first and only NBA championship, and the Los Angeles Lakers to five more NBA titles. He was the most sought-after player out of high school, twice College Player of the Year, the #1 overall draft choice out of college, and won six NBA MVP Awards and two NBA playoff MVP Awards.

▶ Anyone associated with the New York Yankees in their glory years was bound to find himself on at least one winner. Some of the timelier Yankees include Yogi Berra, who played on a record 10 championship teams; Casey Stengel, who managed 10 pennant-winning teams, also a record; Billy Martin, whose first six years with the team led to the American League pennant; and Joe DiMaggio, each of whose first four years with the Yankees resulted in a World Series ring.

▶ Bill Russell played on two national championship teams at the University of San Francisco, where he led a 55-game winning streak, played on the U.S. Olympic gold medal basketball team, and won 11 titles in 13 years with the Boston Celtics, including eight straight from 1959–66.

▶ Magic Johnson, Billy Thompson, and Henry Bibby all went straight from NCAA title teams to NBA championships.

▶ The three biggest gold medal winners in Olympic history, for events still contested, are Russian gymnast Larissa Latynina, with nine (plus five silvers and four bronzes, for 18 total medals, also the most in history); Finnish runner Paavo Nurmi, also with nine (and three silvers, between 1920–28); and American swimmer Mark Spitz, also with nine (and a silver and a bronze).

▶ Wide receiver Lynn Swann played in the Rose Bowl with USC in 1973 and 1974, then in the Super Bowl with the Pittsburgh Steelers in 1975 and 1976 (as well as in 1979 and 1980).

▶ Henri Richard played on 11 Stanley Cup champions with the Montreal Canadiens. Jean Beliveau played on 10.

▶ Gene Conley played for the 1957 World Series champion Milwaukee Braves and the 1959, 1960, and 1961 NBA champion Boston Celtics.

Overshadowed: The 24 Most Prominent— or Is It Neglected?—Second Bananas of All Time

This list is dedicated to the second most-watched basketball team in history, the Washington Generals. With that kind of exposure, they should be household names, but they have the honor of having played—and lost—thousands of games all over the world and almost anonymously against the *most* watched and entertaining basketball team in history, the Harlem Globetrotters.

▶ Notre Dame of Louisiana

▶ Wrigley Field in Los Angeles, torn down in 1966

▶ Harry Steinfeldt, the third baseman in the Chicago Cubs' Tinker-to-Evers-to-Chance infield

▶ The London Prize Ring Rules, the principles that guided boxing before they were replaced by the Marquis of Queensberry Rules in 1865

▶ Joe Dimaggio's streak... of playing every inning of every All-Star game from 1936 through 1942.

▶ Indiana University, of Pennsylvania, located in Indiana, Pennsylvania

▶ Klaus Beer's 26'10½" Olympic silver medal-winning long jump in 1968

▶ Dallas Smith, the main Boston Bruin defensive mate of Bobby Orr

▶ Chicago Cub Bob Hendley's beautiful one-hitter on September 9, 1965, which was just enough to barely lose to the perfect game of Los Angeles Dodgers pitcher Sandy Koufax

▶ Parry O'Brien's May 1954 track and field world record (becoming the first to break 60 feet in the shot put), which was overshadowed by Roger Bannister's slightly more prominent May 1954 track and field world record two days earlier (becoming the first to break the four-minute mile)

▶ The travel article that's always included in the *Sports Illustrated* swimsuit issue

▶ The four at-bats that Cleveland Indian Vic Wertz had in Game 1 of the 1954 World Series—two singles, a double, and a triple—which were overshadowed by his other at-bat, a long fly ball that New York Giants centerfielder Willie Mays turned into a spectacular, over-the-shoulder out

▶ 1970s Montreal Canadien goalie Bunny Larocque, co-Vezina Trophy winner, and backup to Ken Dryden, co-Vezina Trophy winner and the starting Canadien goalie

▶ Roger Maris's national high school record for most touchdowns scored on kickoff returns in a game (four, for Shanley High School in Fargo, North Dakota, in 1951), a record somewhat overshadowed by the single-season home run record he set with the New York Yankees

▶ The 1959 NFL title game between the Baltimore Colts and the New York Giants, a rematch of their 1958 NFL title clash, the sudden-death contest that has been called "the most exciting football game ever played"

▶ The RBI single that New York Yankee Thurman Munson had nullified because there was pine tar too far up his bat handle, which is overshadowed by the home run that Kansas City Royal George Brett did—and then did *not*—have taken away, also for pine tar reasons, eight years later

▶ The 1981 Cincinnati Reds, who won more games than anyone in the National League that year but did not go to the playoffs because of the strike-format system for the postseason

▶ The two home runs, including the game-winner, hit by New York Yankee Lou Gehrig in a 1932 World Series game against the Chicago Cubs, forgotten in the wake of another home run hit that day, team-mate Babe Ruth's "called shot"

▶ Chicago Black Hawk Gus Bodnar's record for the fastest three assists in NHL history (21 seconds) at 6:09, 6:20, and 6:30 of the third period, March 23, 1952, against the New York Rangers—overshadowed because with those three assists, Bodnar helped linemate Bill Mosienko to set a more prominent record: the fastest hat trick in NHL history

▶ The steroid-related disqualification and nullified world record of one Ben—American discus thrower Plucknett, who was banned indefinitely by the International Amateur Athletic Federation on July 13, 1981, when traces of anabolic steroids were found in his system—which was dwarfed by those of another Ben—Canadian sprinter Johnson, whose 100m world record at the 1988 Olympics was nullified when he tested positive for Stanozolol, a steroid

▶ Larry Doby, the second black player in baseball's modern era after Jackie Robinson, and who was the second black manager after Frank Robinson

▶ Bernie Carbo's three-run, score-tying home run in Game 6 of the 1975 World Series, that enabled his Boston Red Sox teammate Carlton Fisk to hit his more famous extra-inning home run

▶ Catfish Metkovich, major-league infielder, 1943–54

▶ UCLA's Brad Holland, the Los Angeles Lakers' other first-round pick in 1979

10 Great Coaches and Mentors

▶ Angelo Dundee trained nine world boxing champions: Carmen Basilio (welterweight), Willie Pastrano (light heavyweight), Ralph Dupas (light middleweight), Luis Rodriguez (welterweight), Sugar Ramos (featherweight), Muhammad Ali (heavyweight), Jimmy Ellis (heavyweight), José Napoles (welterweight), and Sugar Ray Leonard (welterweight).

▶ At one time, Paul "Tony" Hinkle, a 49-year man at Indiana's Butler University as basketball coach and athletic director, had 55 protégés coaching basketball in the state.

▶ Harry Hopman was the non-playing captain of the Australia Davis Cup team that won 16 Cups between 1939–67. (The Cup was not contested from 1940–45.)

▶ Romanian gymnastics coach Bela Karolyi coached Nadia Comaneci to seven perfect 10s and a gold medal-winning performance at the 1976 Olympics. Karolyi later defected to the United States and fashioned another gold medal-winning performer out of Mary Lou Retton, at the 1984 Olympics. Later, he coached the American women to the team gold at the 1996 Games. Aside from Comaneci and Retton, his most famous pupils, Karolyi also coached Phoebe Mills, Kim Zmeskal, Kerri Strug, and Dominique Moceanu.

▶ Charlie Lau, a marginal major leaguer with a lifetime .255 batting average, was the hitting guru for George Brett.

Walt Hriniak, who played for just two years in the majors, was instrumental in the success of perennial American League batting champion Wade Boggs.

▶ Italian Carlo Fassi coached Olympic gold medalist figure skaters Peggy Fleming, Dorothy Hamill, John Curry, and Robin Cousins, as well as world champions Jill Trenary and Todd Eldredge.

▶ The IMG Bollettieri Tennis Academy in Florida, founded by Nick Bollettieri, has been the training ground for (among others) Andre Agassi, Monica Seles, Jim Courier, Venus Williams, Serena Williams, Aaron Krickstein, Mary Pierce, Marcelo Rios, Carling Bassett, Jimmy Arias, and Anna Kournikova.

▶ In 27 years as UCLA's basketball coach, John Wooden compiled a 620-147 record and won 10 national titles, including seven in a row from 1967–73. He coached 24 first-team All-Americas and presided over UCLA's NCAA record 88-game winning streak. In Wooden's last 12 years, the Bruins were 335-22.

▶ Horse trainer Michael Dickson saddled the first five finishers in the 1985 Cheltenham Gold Cup.

▷ And two great coaching chains: Curly Lambeau, who later bought the Green Bay Packers, was the high school football coach of Jim Crowley, who became one of the "Four Horsemen" at Notre Dame under Knute Rockne. Later, as the football coach at Fordham, Crowley would coach "The Seven Blocks of Granite," including Vince Lombardi, who would in turn go on to become a coaching legend at Green Bay.

In the autumn of 1890 in Springfield, Massachusetts, James Naismith, the founder of basketball, played center on the first organized football team under Amos Alonzo Stagg, the founder of football.

15

CURIOSITIES

●●●●●●●●●●●●●

One Dozen of the Stupidest Ideas in Sports

▶ *Color-coordinated uniforms.* In 1882, the color of a baseball player's cap and shirt signified his position: pitchers wore blue, catchers scarlet, shortstops maroon, leftfielders white, rightfielders gray, and the other positions a combination of two colors. A team could only be told apart by its socks. The idea fizzled when someone pointed out that you could tell a player's position by where he stood on the field.

▶ *Reverse psychology.* Already behind 28-0 to Georgia Tech in a 1916 game, Cumberland College opted to kick off instead of receive in the hope that its defense could pin Tech deep in its own territory. Tech returned the ensuing kickoff 70 yards to the Cumberland 10, scored yet again, and continued on its way to registering the worst rout in the history of college football, 222-0.

▶ *Messing with tradition.* The NBA tried a 12-foot basket in a March 7, 1954, game between Minneapolis and Milwaukee, and just as soon abandoned that for the traditional 10-foot basket. This desire to change the scope of the game had precedent. For the first Olympic basketball competition, in 1936, the International Basketball Federation passed a rule banning all players taller than 6'3". The United States objected and the rule was withdrawn.

▶ *Stealing—especially from the meal ticket.* While trying out for the New York Yankees in spring training of 2002, itinerant outfielder Ruben Rivera stole the glove and bat of perennial All-Star shortstop Derek Jeter, then sold them for $2,500 to a memorabilia dealer. When the thievery was discovered, the Yankees let Rivera go, potentially costing him way more money than a couple thousand dollars. John Croce, brother of Pat Croce, then-president of the Philadelphia 76ers, was allegedly caught stealing money in the locker room from the pants of superstar guard Allen Iverson. John Croce was relieved of his duties as trainer.

▶ *Eyeglasses for horses.* Legendary horse owner Colonel Edward Riley Bradley tried to fit eyeglass blinkers on a nearsighted racehorse. When the blinkers were fitted over the horse's head, the horse panicked, tossed the rider, and ran off.

▶ *Overdoing a good thing.* From 1959–62, baseball held two All-Star games a year.

▶ *Overzealousness.* In 1923, the town of Shelby, Montana, guaranteed to put up $300,000 to stage a fight between heavyweight Jack Dempsey and Tommy Gibbons. The fight attracted only 7,202 paying customers and the town went bankrupt.

▶ *Strange baseballs.* Because of the rubber shortage during World War II, the major leagues experimented in 1943 with Balata, a rubber substitute around the core of the baseball (the same material that covers most golf balls). Balata substantially reduced the ball's resiliency: By April 29, the entire American League had hit just two home runs. By May 9, Balata balls were no longer shipped. The major leagues also tried yellow baseballs for one game, an August 2, 1938, contest between the Brooklyn Dodgers and the St. Louis Cardinals, and that was that.

▶ *Overextending yourself at something that's not even your specialty.* Dave Rowe, an outfielder in the 1870s and 1880s, tried pitching a game in 1882. He went the distance, giving up 29 hits and 35 runs.

▶ *Coaching by committee.* In 1961 and 1962, the Chicago Cubs' experimental "Council of Coaches," which had several coaches rotating as manager, produced zero geniuses. In 1961, the winningest coach had a percentage of .442. In 1962, coach Lou Klein, who managed wins in 40% of his games, was the most successful.

▶ *Consolation prizes.* From 1960 to 1970, the losers of the NFL conference finals played in the NFL Playoff Bowl—known colloquially as the "Third Place Bowl." The consolation game to determine third place at the NCAA basketball Final Four was abolished in 1981.

▶ *Marine life as fashion statement.* Former Pittsburgh Steelers running back John "Frenchy" Fuqua, a noted clotheshorse, once wore platform shoes with see-through heels. The heels were filled with water and goldfish.

The Most Notable Draft Oddities

▶ The Boston Celtics drafted former University of Indiana star Landon Turner in the 10th round of the 1982 NBA draft. Turner had been paralyzed in a car accident eight months before but had expressed a lifelong dream to be drafted by the Celtics.

▶ In 1983, the Philadelphia 76ers used their 10th-round pick to select Norman Horvitz, a 50-ish doctor who worked for 76ers owner Harold Katz's Nutri-Systems, Inc.

▶ At the player draft for the short-lived National Bowling League in July 1960, New York Yankees Mickey Mantle and Yogi Berra were selected.

▶ In 1986, Bo Jackson was the #1 pick of the NFL Tampa Bay Buccaneers, the fourth-round pick of baseball's Kansas City Royals, and the fifth-round pick of the Continental Basketball Association's Savannah Spirits.

▶ In 1977, Lucille Harris of Delta State was drafted in the seventh round by the New Orleans Jazz, the only woman ever drafted in NBA history.

▶ In 1984, the Chicago Bulls drafted track star Carl Lewis in the 10th round.

In 1977, the NBA's Kansas City Kings drafted Olympic marathon champion Bruce Jenner in the seventh round.

▶ In 1987, the Atlanta Hawks drafted Song Tao of China in the third round; Theo Christodoulou of Greece in the fourth round; Jose-Antonio Montero of Spain in the fifth round; Ricardo Morandoti of Italy in the sixth round; and Franjo Arapovic of Yugoslavia in the seventh round. The Hawks did not sign any of them.

▶ The Pittsburgh Steeler team that won the NFL championship in 1980 is the only Super Bowl squad made up entirely of players who had never played for another team: Thirty-nine of the players had been Steeler draft picks, and six others had been free agents right out of school.

▶ In 1955, the Los Angeles Rams drafted K. C. Jones of the University of San Francisco in the 30th round. Jones was also drafted by the Boston Celtics and opted for a basketball career. In 1983, Jones became coach of the Celtics. His counterpart on the opposing sidelines for several NBA Finals, Los Angeles Laker coach Pat Riley, had also opted for a career playing and coaching basketball, not football. Riley had been drafted out of the University of Kentucky by the Dallas Cowboys in the 11th round in 1967.

▶ The 1966 Michigan State University football team produced four of the first eight picks in the 1967 NFL-AFL draft. Five players from the University of Southern California were taken in the first round of the 1968 NFL-AFL draft. In 1984, 17 University of Texas players were chosen in the NFL draft.

▶ In 1981, Vic Sison was drafted by the New Jersey Nets in the 10th round. He was the head student-manager at UCLA when Nets coach Larry Brown was there.

18 Examples of Bad Timing,
Rotten Luck, and Generally Bad Karma

▶ Harriet Quimby was the first woman to fly across the English Channel but she received virtually no publicity for the achievement. She took off on April 16, 1912, at 5:00 A.M. Soon after, the details of another event—the April 14 sinking of the Titanic—reached the world, obscuring Quimby's accomplishment.

▶ In 1981, the New York Yankees won their fourth pennant, and made their fifth postseason, in the previous six seasons. In 1982, first baseman Don Mattingly, their future captain and league MVP, played his first year with the team. For the next thirteen years—from '82 through '94—the Yankees would not make the postseason. In 1995, Mattingly's last season before he retired with recurring back trouble, the Yankee great got a taste of the playoffs—and flourished—as New York lost in the first round to the Seattle Mariners. The following year, with Mattingly newly retired, the Yankees won the World Series, and would also make it to the postseason the next six years (and counting), including four more World Series appearances and three more championships (through Fall '02).

▶ Javelin thrower Bruce Kennedy was kept out of the 1972 and 1976 Olympics when his country, Rhodesia—now Zimbabwe—was banned. In 1977, Kennedy became a U.S. citizen, qualified for the 1980 Olympic team, and was kept out for a third time by the U.S. Olympic boycott. In 1980, Zimbabwe was allowed to compete.

▶ Because of a sore arm, Philadelphia Phillies starting pitcher Wayne LaMaster left his May 5, 1938, game against the Chicago Cubs after making just three pitches; he had a 2-1 count on Stan Hacker, the lead-off batter. Relief pitcher Tommy Reis walked Hacker, the walk was charged to LaMaster, as was the run that he scored, as was the loss, a 21-2 wipeout by the Cubs.

▶ The year after star quarterback Peyton Manning left the University of Tennessee, having broken virtually all the passing records there, become a UT legend, and being chosen the # 1 overall pick in the NFL draft by the Indianapolis Colts, the Volunteers won their first national football championship in almost half a century.

▶ Bill Bevens, Al Gionfriddo, and Cookie Lavagetto—three of the pivotal performers in the 1947 World Series between the New York Yankees and the Brooklyn Dodgers—never played in a major-league game after that Series.

▶ Three members of the U.S. gold medal-winning four-man bobsled team in 1932 died within a one-year period starting in 1940.

▶ Here is what has happened to just a few members of the 1969 "Miracle" New York Mets: First baseman Donn Clendenon pleaded guilty to a charge of cocaine possession, catcher Jerry Grote served time in jail for cattle-sale fraud, outfielder Cleon Jones received a suspended sentence for forging checks, and reliever Jack DiLauro joined a California commune in 1970 and has not been heard from since.

▶ In 1985, Johnnie LeMaster played for three last-place teams—the San Francisco Giants, the Pittsburgh Pirates, and the Cleveland Indians.

▶ Jim Perry was the losing pitcher in three of the four no-hitters pitched in the American League from the 1970 All-Star Game through the 1973 All-Star Game.

▶ In 1978, California Angel outfielder Lyman Bostock was accidentally shot to death in Gary, Indiana, while riding in a car with, among others, a childhood friend. The friend's estranged husband had been shooting at her. (The shooter was later found not responsible by reason of insanity.)

▶ Ron Hansen is the only man to play in the last game in the history of both the original and the second Washington Senator franchises, in 1960 and 1971. (In both cases, Hansen played against the Senators.)

▶ Gary Davidson was involved in the formation of the WFL, the ABA, and the WHA—all defunct leagues.

▶ Jim Weaver pitched for the 1931 New York Yankees and was then demoted to the minors. In 1932, the Yankees won the pennant. In 1934, Weaver pitched for the Chicago Cubs. After the season, he was traded to the Pirates; in 1935, the Cubs won the pennant. In 1939, Weaver pitched early in the year for the Cincinnati Reds before being let go. That season, the Reds won the pennant.

▶ Heavyweight Jack Johnson, financially strained, finally landed a profitable fight to defend his title, against Frank Moran in Paris. Johnson triumphed in the June 27, 1914, bout. The following day, news of the assassination of Austrian archduke Francis Ferdinand—the spark that ignited World War I—reached Paris. In the ensuing chaos, Johnson never collected his purse.

▶ The St. Louis Cardinals spent the 2002 season in an almost constant state of mourning. In spring training, the team's long-time vice president, Jim Toomey, died of brain cancer at age 84. In June, beloved broadcaster Jack Buck died, followed four days later by the shocking death of 31-year-old pitcher Darryl Kile, who suffered a massive coronary. In August, former St. Louis catcher Darrell Porter, the Most Valuable Player of the 1982 National League Championship Series and World Series for the Cardinals, died at age 50 from what the autopsy report revealed as "the toxic effects of cocaine." Less than two weeks later, Cardinal Hall of Fame outfielder Enos "Country" Slaughter died at age 86.

▶ The New York Yankees, like the St. Louis Cardinals, endured a not dissimilar streak of unfortunate occurrences, though spread out over a longer period. While Joe Torre's regime as Yankees manager has been marked by immense on-field success—through 2002, the club had won five American League pennants and four World Series titles—the organization also suffered the following: Torre fought prostate cancer in 1999 (successfully); pitching coach, Mel Stottlemyre overcame multiple myeloma, a cancer of the bone marrow, in 2000; Torre's brother, former major-leaguer Frank Torre, underwent a heart transplant in October of 1996 (while Joe was in the process of leading the Yankees to his first World Series triumph); and the sister of star shortstop Derek Jeter completed successful treatment for Hodgkin's Disease in 2000. In 1999, besides Torre's cancer, the team had to deal with the emotional trauma from the death of the fathers of Scott Brosius (in September), Luis Sojo (in October) and Paul O'Neill (before Game 4 of the World Series). The father of All-Star outfielder Bernie Williams died in May of 2001. Williams had left the Yankees for nearly two weeks in April to be with his ailing father in Puerto Rico.

▶ Although Rich "Goose" Gossage enjoyed a long, very successful major-league career, he is also the only player whose tenure bridged the three player strikes that caused games to be cancelled—1972, 1981, and 1994.

Right Place, Right Time

A day before baseball players went on strike in August of 1994, Houston Astros slugger Jeff Bagwell was hit by a pitch, breaking a bone in his left hand. Bagwell, one of several National League players having outstanding seasons, would have been sidelined about a month, most likely allowing others to surpass him statistically. But because the strike wiped out the rest of the season, Bagwell's numbers—a .368 average, 39 homers, 116 runs batted in—held up, and he was the unanimous winner of the National League's Most Valuable Player award.

▶ In 1997, basketball forward Kevin Garnett signed a $126 million contract with the Minnesota Timberwolves—at the time the richest total contract in professional sports. The deal motivated many players to seek similar money (largely without luck), while NBA team owners felt that Garnett's contract was outrageously overpriced, even for one of the finest young talents in the game. The following year, the NBA locked out the players, and an ugly impasse ensued, wiping out more than a third of the season. Finally, an agreement was reached in which various caps were put on future salaries. While a player of sufficient tenure in the league could still re-sign with his own team for gigantic money (as, say, Shaquille O'Neal would do, later, with the Los Angeles Lakers), the new agreement effectively halted salary escalation, and players who'd been in the league the same number of years as Garnett had been at the time of his historic contract were now "capped" by the league from getting "KG" money—from other teams or their own.

▶ For a hole-in-one he made at a 1987 tournament, Dan Pooley received $1 million—more than he'd earned during his whole PGA career, and 10 times more than what the winner of the tournament earned.

▶ A number of players and coaches, especially veterans, have been fortunate enough to be picked up by powerhouse teams or defending champions looking for a little injury insurance or role-playing or just staying of the course; sometimes the team will wait until late in the season to do it. For the player, it's a great deal: It's almost as if the team is saying, "Come here, do what you usually do, and you'll get your ring."

Clyde Drexler was obviously a talent—he was voted one of the "NBA's 50 Greatest Players"—when he left the Portland Trailblazers to join the Houston Rockets late in his career. The 1994 defending champion Rockets, looking to keep themselves bolstered, re-united Drexler with All-World center Hakeem Olajuwon, his former teammate at the University of Houston. The Rockets easily repeated; Drexler got his ring.

Ray Bourque was given a gift when the already dominating Colorado Avalanche picked him up for the 1999–2000 stretch run. While the 21-year Boston Bruin defenseman didn't win his long-cherished Stanley Cup that year, he got it in 2001.

Bill Walton was lucky enough to get tabbed by the Larry Bird-led, almost-perennial Eastern Conference champion Boston Celtics; as sixth man for Boston, Walton earned his second NBA championship following the 1985–86 season.

Brett Hull *twice* found himself on great teams that just needed someone like him to put them over the top—first the Dallas Stars, then the Detroit Red Wings.

Barry Switzer was able to win an NFL title just by not screwing up the system that had been developed by departed coach of the Dallas Cowboys, Jimmy Johnson; ditto George Seifert for the post-Bill Walsh San Francisco 49ers.

9 Sports Superstitions and Jinxes, Real or Imagined

▶ Starting on April 15, 1952, when a Detroit hockey fan flung an octopus onto the ice and the Red Wings went on to win the Stanley Cup, an octopus has been tossed onto the ice during every Detroit Red Wings playoff series.

▶ For every game for three years, a man named Charles "Victory" Faust warmed up for the New York Giants baseball team because manager John McGraw thought Faust brought luck.

▶ A prevailing theory states that when one of the original NFL teams wins the Super Bowl, the stock market will be up for the year, and when a team from the old AFL wins, the stock market will be down. This theory held true for 23 years in a row.

▶ Another stock market theory held that, on a daily basis, when the New York Mets win, the stock market falls; when they lose, it goes up.

▶ After Canada's men beat the host Americans for the Olympic hockey gold at the 2002 Salt Lake City Olympics, thus satisfying the incredible expectations of an entire nation, it was revealed that Trent Evans, an Edmontonian and one of those recruited to make the ice at the Olympic rink, had imbedded a "loonie"—a Canadian bronze-plated dollar coin—under center ice for good luck. The coin was dug out after the men's win—the Canadian women also beat the Americans for *their* hockey gold—and given to Wayne Gretzky, executive director of the men's team. He in turn gave the loonie to the Hockey Hall of Fame.

▶ A baseball superstition says that whichever World Series team has the most ex-Chicago Cubs on its roster will lose the Series.

▶ Although a player of only average ability, utility infielder Luis Sojo was continually put on the New York Yankees' postseason roster in part because manager Joe Torre and others considered Sojo something of a good luck charm. His best-remembered contribution is the ninth-inning, tie-breaking, seeing-eye groundball single he hit in the clinching game of the 2000 Subway Series against the New York Mets, sealing the Yankees' third straight championship.

When he was with the Seattle Mariners earlier in his career, Sojo had another crucial hit—a bases-clearing double that was the decisive blast in Seattle's victory over the California Angels in their one-game playoff for the 1995 AL West title. When Sojo came to bat in the 7th inning, the Mariners were holding on to a slim 1-0 lead.

▶ Under Connie Mack, the 1911–14 Philadelphia Athletic mascot was a good-luck hunchback named Louis Van Zelst.

▶ Perhaps the most renowned superstition in sports is the "*Sports Illustrated* cover jinx," which suggests that to appear on the cover of the magazine is to be doomed to failure—or worse. While it is true that no one makes note of the numerous cases in which a cover boy or girl does not run into bad luck, it is also true that, to cite just a few cases, skier Jill Kinmont, the January 31, 1955, cover girl, broke her back and was paralyzed in an accident that week in the Snow Cup Giant Slalom race in Alta, Utah; that the Chicago Cubs began perhaps their most famous collapse after third baseman Ron Santo appeared on the June 30, 1969, cover; and that after Magic Johnson appeared on the June 4, 1984, cover, the Los Angeles Lakers not only lost in the NBA Finals to the Boston Celtics in seven games, but did so after they had a one game to none lead, and the lead and the ball with only 15 seconds left in Game 2 (which they lost); and a five-point lead with 56 seconds left in Game 4 (which they lost). Even the series MVP, Larry Bird, was surprised by the turn of events. "To be honest, they should have swept," he said.

Huh?: One Dozen Sports Things
We Simply Don't Understand

Certain profound mysteries in sports baffle us—why, for example, pitchers who have runners on first and third base fake a throw to third, then wheel around to try to catch the runner on first napping. We have never seen this ploy work in hundreds—nay, *thousands*—of attempts. If you have, don't tell us.

Why do sportswriters think they should tell us who in football to bet on—and who to BEST BET on—when their record against the spread is almost always under .500?

Why do so many major-league hitters check their swing on a 3-0 count?

Why do defensive linemen taunt quarterbacks whom they have just sacked, when the lineman's team is losing 45-7 with three minutes to go?

What kind of a doctor is Jerry Buss, anyway?

Why does any football announcer ever talk about "quarterback ratings" when no one—not even John Madden, not even the ghost of Amos Alonzo Stagg—has any idea how to calculate it or what it really signifies?

What follows is a collection of sports questions that mystify us. We don't understand, for example:

▶ Why, on August 6, 1941, Al Benton became the only player ever to sacrifice-bunt twice in one inning—an inning in which the Detroit Tigers scored 11 runs.

▶ Why the fittingly christened boxer, John Badman, lightweight fighter in the 1840s, changed his given name to Johnny Walker.

▶ How Cincinnati Red and Brooklyn Dodger catcher Bill Bergen, a .170 lifetime hitter, had an 11-year career.

▶ Why the 1980 Olympic women's pair-oared shell (without coxswain) competition had two elimination heats and a repechage (a second-chance round) to trim the original field of six crews to five for the finals.

▶ Why golfer Tommy Armour, who had just shot—or so everyone thought—a 22 on one hole at the 1927 Shawnee Open, claimed that it was really a 23.

▶ Why infielder Larry Gardner of the Cleveland Indians continued to try to steal bases during the 1920 season, during which he was successful three times and was thrown out 20 times.

▶ Why Harvey Johnson, who had coached the Buffalo Bills to a 1-10-1 record as interim coach in 1968, was rehired as interim coach in 1971. (This time he went 1-13.)

▶ How *Sports Illustrated* could have tabbed San Diego Padres relief pitcher Trevor Hoffman (postseason stats: 1-2, 3 saves, 2 blown saves, 4.09 ERA) as the best closer ever, when his career has run simultaneously with that of New York Yankees closer Mariano Rivera (postseason stats: 6-1, 24 saves, 2 blown saves, 0.91 ERA).

▶ How the University of Michigan football team beat Ohio State, 9-3, in 1950 without making a first down.

▶ Why pitcher Bill Gray of the Washington Senators was left in long enough to walk eight batters in one inning in a 1909 game.

▶ Why the national high school record for the longest field goal is 68 yards (by Dirk Borgognone, Reno, Nevada, 1985), and the NFL record is only 63 yards (by Tom Dempsey, New Orleans Saints, 1970, and Jason Elam, Denver Broncos, 1998).

▶ Why certain people in 1954 felt it necessary to additionally honor basketball star Bobby McDermott—who nine years earlier had been voted "the greatest pro basketball player of all time"—with the accolade of "the greatest Fort Wayne Zollner Piston player of all time."

Just Plain Weird Stuff About the Home Run

▶ On April 12, 1985, Marty Burke of Huffman (Alabama) High School had the kind of day you'd feel silly even *dreaming* about. Against Woodlawn High School, he hit three grand slams.

Three.

▶ Eddie Murray hit 504 career home runs, but never more than 33 in a season.

▶ Bob Meusel was the only Yankee to hit more home runs during a given season in the 1920s than Babe Ruth. In 1925, Meusel out-homered Ruth 33-25.

▶ Of Hank Aaron's four home run titles, three were won with a figure of 44, which was also his uniform number.

▶ In May of 1938, Bob Seeds of the International League's Newark Bears hit a home run in four successive innings.

▶ Jimmie Foxx hit 30 or more home runs for 12 consecutive years. Hank Aaron hit 20 or more homers for 20 consecutive years.

▶ Milwaukee Brewers pitcher Rafael Roque put his stamp on the historic home run derby of 1998 by giving up home run #64 to Mark McGwire, then giving up home run #64 to Sammy Sosa.

▶ In 2002, four players—Mike Cameron, Shawn Green, Andruw Jones, and Troy Glaus—each homered in four consecutive at-bats. In the decade of the '80s, it happened all of once, by Larry Herndon. The last season in which it happened twice was 1971.

▶ Willie Mays twice hit 50 homers in a season, ten years apart.

▶ Dave Winfield was born on the day in 1951 that Bobby Thomson hit his legendary "shot heard 'round the world" home run.

▶ On May 27, 1968, something slugger was in the air: Eddie Mathews hit his final home run (#512), and both Jeff Bagwell and Frank Thomas were born.

▶ St. Louis Cardinals infielder Fernando Tatis enjoyed the greatest individual hitting inning in the history of major-league baseball when, in the third inning of an April 23, 1999, game against the Los Angeles Dodgers, he hit two grand slams off of pitcher Chan Ho Park. (His eight RBIs in an inning are also a record.)

10 Great Sports Ironies

Isn't it ironic...

...that George S. Patton, the future U.S. Army general who placed fifth in the 1912 Olympic modern pentathlon, might have won had he not finished 21st out of 32 in the shooting competition?

...that Al Campanis, the shortstop for the Brooklyn Dodgers' AAA Montreal farm team in 1946, the same year that Jackie Robinson made his professional debut as the Montreal second baseman (and the year before Robinson joined the big club), and who was one of Robinson's leading supporters and best friends on the team, should lose his job over racist remarks he made in 1987 on ABC's *Nightline*?

...that Jim Thorpe, probably the greatest American athlete of the 20th century, should be stripped of his Olympic 1912 decathlon and pentathlon gold medals for having played professionally the one sport at which he was truly mediocre—baseball? Thorpe, who played baseball off and on from 1913–19, apparently could not hit the curveball and had a lifetime average of .252.

...that Ted Williams served for nearly two years and 39 flying missions in the Korean War without getting seriously injured, and then, on the first day of spring training after he came back, he broke his collarbone?

...that Hank Aaron, first in career home runs—perhaps the most cherished of all individual baseball records—is the first player alphabetically in major-league history? And isn't it ironic, too, that Kareem Abdul-Jabbar, first in career points—perhaps the most cherished of all individual basketball records—is third alphabetically (behind Alaa Abdelnaby and Zaid Abdul-Aziz) in NBA history? (As Lew Alcindor, he would have been listed 23rd).

...that the 1972 Munich Olympic marathon champion, American Frank Shorter, was born in Munich? (His father had been a U.S. Army doctor there.)

...that American Helen Stephens, who beat Stella Walsh in the 1936 Olympic 100m, was accused by a Polish journalist—falsely—of being a man, while Walsh, upon her death, was discovered to be a man?

...that Mahmoud Abdul-Raud (formerly Chris Jackson), who holds the NBA record for the second highest single-season free throw percentage (.956), suffered from Tourette's Syndrome? (Some might say it's decidedly unironic.)

...that Dickie Kerr, one of the clean Chicago White Sox players during the tainted World Series of 1919, should be suspended for three years (1923–25) for pitching against an outlaw team during a contract dispute?

…that running author and guru James Fixx, whose books helped fuel the jogging craze, died in Vermont on July 21, 1984, of a heart attack —while jogging?

19 Facts You Might Easily Have Forgotten or Never Knew

► The country that has won the most gold medals, and most total medals, in all winter Olympics combined, is Norway. (The U.S. is third in both categories.)

► Roger Bannister did not break the four-minute mile in an actual race. On May 6, 1954, he ran 3:59.4 while being carefully paced by rabbits Chris Brasher and Chris Chataway.

► Soviet gymnast Olga Korbut only finished seventh in the all-around competition at the 1972 Olympics, where she became a fan darling.

► Except for the 1925 Rose Bowl, Notre Dame did not play in bowl games until the 1969 Cotton Bowl.

► Roger Maris was the American League MVP in 1960, the year *before* he hit his record 61 home runs (when he again won the MVP).

► Pete Rozelle, the powerful former NFL commissioner who found tremendous popularity among the owners and greatly helped to engineer the league's growth, was not elected to that post until the 23rd ballot on January 26, 1960. At that time, Rozelle, 33 years old and the general manager of the Los Angeles Rams, emerged as the compromise candidate when owners became deadlocked between choosing acting commissioner Austin Gunsel or attorney Marshall Leahy.

► At the 1992 Albertville Olympics, the U.S. won five gold medals—all by women.

► Jackie Robinson's first position with the Brooklyn Dodgers was first base. He played all of his 151 games there in 1947. The next year he moved to second base.

► Keith Jackson was in the booth for ABC *Monday Night Football's* first season, before Frank Gifford replaced him the next year.

► Lew Alcindor passed up the 1968 Olympics in support of the threatened black boycott of the Games.

► O. J. Simpson started his collegiate career at City College of San Francisco, a two-year college, before transferring to the University of Southern California.

► Joe Theismann spent the first three seasons of his professional football career in the Canadian Football League, with the Toronto Argonauts.

► Mark Spitz was once considered an Olympic disappointment because he was projected to win several gold medals in the 1968 Olympics and won only two, both in relays.

▶ For more than half of the Miami Dolphins' perfect 1972 season, quarterback Bob Griese was on the bench with a broken leg, and backup QB Earl Morrall led the team.

▶ The Celtics basketball team was founded not in Boston but in New York, in 1914. When the team was reorganized after World War I, they continued to be based in New York but called themselves the Original Celtics.

▶ Wayne Gretzky began his professional hockey career in 1978 with the Indianapolis Racers of the WHA.

▶ Tom Watson, the Los Angeles Lakers, and Ivan Lendl were all once as well-known for their inability to win in the clutch as they were for their talent. Each would shed their "choke" label and soon came to be known as much for their *ability* to win in the clutch as for their talent: Watson by capturing eight majors, several with magnificent charges on the final holes; the Lakers by dominating the 1980s with five NBA titles, including victories the last two times they faced their perennial rivals, the Boston Celtics; and Lendl by winning two Australian Opens, three French Opens, and three U.S. Opens.

▶ The current New York Mets are the second major-league incarnation of that club. The New York Metropolitans, or Mets, of the American Association played their first game in the original Polo Grounds and appeared in what was an early version of the World Series, in 1884.

▶ The jockey who owned the longest losing streak—110 straight defeats —in the history of American horse racing is Steve Cauthen.

Surreal

Some moments in life are simply indescribable. You can't believe your eyes, your ears. It may be tragic—9/11 comes immediately to mind; it may be magic—childbirth comes immediately to mind. Either way, it's something that simply does not compute—not at first, anway. Logic, past experience... might as well shelve them for the time being.

Sports has those moments, too.

▶ Perhaps the surrealest sports story of the last generation—one of the surrealest news stories, in fact—was the famous "low-speed chase" of a white Ford Bronco, in which O.J. Simpson, days after the brutal murder of his ex-wife Nicole Brown Simpson and her friend Ronald Goldman, and soon after charges were filed against Simpson for the killings, floated along Los Angeles freeways that had essentially been shut down, heading apparently toward Mexico, while Simpson and his friend Al Cowlings (who drove) were tailed by dozens of Los Angeles police cruisers, as almost 100 million Americans watched on a Friday night in June of 1994. So many elements of the story were unexpected: its very public, real-time unfolding (many sports fans were home watching the Houston

Rockets play the New York Knicks in the NBA Finals; coverage would toggle between the chase and the game); the suggestion of a *de facto* confession (Simpson's attempted escape seemed, at least at the time, a rather poor strategy for fighting murder charges); the utter breakdown of a formerly celebrated and generally well-liked personality; and the fact that cars on the side of the road had stopped, people had emerged from their vehicles to cheer mindlessly, and no one knew when, or how, the "chase" would end—with a crash? A suicide? Was it all a ploy for sympathy? The only thing anyone could say, for sure, was that it was surreal.

Simpson was arrested in front of his home, and then became the TV star of the most-followed trial in American history.

▶ It's not an uncommon occurrence at major-league baseball games for fans to jump out of the bleachers and run onto the field, usually resulting in a drunken romp around the bases while security officials chase them down. But when two shirtless, heavily tattooed fans ran onto the field at Chicago's Comiskey Park with two outs in the ninth inning on September 19, 2002, what resulted was one of the most bizarre and frightening scenes in baseball history. The two—a father and son, no less—ran to the first-base coaching box, and to the horror of all watching, began pummeling Tom Gamboa, first-base coach of the Kansas City Royals. Royals players raced out of the dugout to protect Gamboa and began pummeling the attackers, until security personnel restored order. A closed pocket knife was found near the coaching box. Gamboa was bloodied but not seriously injured, though he did suffer hearing loss. The assailants claimed that Gamboa provoked them with an obscene gesture, which he vehemently denied. William Ligue, Jr., the father, was charged with aggravated battery, a felony. His 15-year-old son was charged with two juvenile counts of aggravated battery.

▶ In Game 4 of the 2001 World Series, the New York Yankees were down to their last out in the bottom of the ninth inning, down two runs, with a man on base, against Arizona Diamondbacks closer Byung Hyun-Kim. Yankees first baseman Tino Martinez hit a game-tying home run, and the Yankees won the game in extra innings. Improbable as that was, it could not begin to compare to the improbability of the same thing happening two nights in a row—which, of course, it did. In Game 5, the exact same situation occurred: Yanks down by two, two outs in the bottom of the ninth, a man on base, closer Kim on the mound. This time, it was Yankees third baseman Scott Brosius who hit the game-tying home run, which not only delighted Yankee fans, but utterly amazed all baseball fans, actuaries, and oddsmakers, to the point of a weird tingling at the back of the neck. As they'd done the night before, the Yankees won the game in extra innings.

▶ It was a tragic twist that, had it been in a novel, would have made any reader discard the book for its juvenile disconnection with reality. But on October 20, 1995, it happened, absurd as it seems: Eleven seconds after college freshman Travis Roy realized his lifelong dream of playing hockey for Boston University, he crashed into the boards, cracked his fourth vertebra, and was paralyzed from the neck down. Almost no one who saw it happen or heard about it later could at first grasp that it had really occurred, a cosmic prank beyond reasoning.

As of seven years later, Roy remains confined to a wheelchair, though he has regained some movement in his right arm. His accounts of his life, the accident, and his rehabilitation are the basis for the book *Eleven Seconds: A Story of Tragedy, Courage & Triumph.*

▶ Magic Johnson, All-World point guard of the Los Angeles Lakers, shocked America with his announcement on November 7, 1991, that he had tested positive for the AIDS virus, and was retiring. Although other celebrated figures had contracted the virus, none quite matched Johnson's profile: extremely famous; at the height of his physical powers; loved and respected across many segments of society; heterosexual.

When the shock wave of the news passed, Johnson's announcement would be viewed as one of several watershed moments to facilitate a more open discussion of AIDS in the media.

11 Things in Sport You Rarely, If Ever, See

▶ *A false start in a marathon.*

▶ *An intentional walk with the bases loaded.* This ultimate sign of respect has happened all of four times in major-league history, the last instance on May 28, 1998. The San Francisco Giants were losing to the Arizona Diamondbacks, 8-6, in the ninth inning, with two outs, bases loaded, and Barry Bonds at the plate. Arizona manager Buck Showalter was willing to walk Bonds and bring the Giants within one run, and his strategy panned out: The next batter, Brent Mayne, lined out to right field to end the game. Before that night, the last intentional walk with bases loaded was issued to Swish Nicholson on July 23, 1944.

▶ *A white heavyweight boxing champion.* There has been only one (widely accepted) white champion in the last 40-plus years: Gerrie Coetzee, who held the WBA title from September 1983 through December 1984. Before that, Ingemar Johansson was the last white heavyweight champ, from 1959-60.

▶ *A triple steal.* The last triple steal in the major leagues occurred on October 1, 1987, when Atlanta Braves Gerald Perry, Jeff Blauser, and Ken Oberkfell accomplished it. The last triple steal in the American League happened on May 3, 1980, when Oakland Athletics Dwayne Murphy, Mitchell Page, and Wayne Gross pulled it off. There have been only six triple steals in the last 40 years.

▶ *A southpaw catcher.* Since 1906 the major leagues have seen just three—the Chicago Cubs' Dale Long in 1958, the Chicago White Sox' Mike Squires in 1980, and the Pittsburgh Pirates' Benny Distefano in 1989.

(Don Mattingly played five innings of a game at third base for the New York Yankees in 1986. He is believed to be the 11th southpaw to play third since 1900; Squires did it in 1983.)

▶ *A goaltender score a goal.* Only nine times in NHL history has a goalie been credited with a goal: Billy Smith of the New York Islanders had the first, in 1979; Ron Hextall of the Philadelphia Flyers the next two, one in 1987 and one in 1989, during the playoffs; Chris Osgood of the Detroit Red Wings scored a goal in 1996; Martin Brodeur of the New Jersey Devils scored two—one in 1997, also in the playoffs, and one in 2000—the first-ever game-winner; Damian Rhodes of the Ottawa Senators scored a goal in 1999; Jose Theodore of the Montreal Canadiens scored one, in 2001; and Evgeni Nabokov of the San Jose Sharks scored one, in 2002.

▶ *A left-throwing, right-hitting baseball player.* Since 1876, approximately 40 such non-pitchers, including Rickey Henderson, have played in the major leagues.

▶ *A golfer miss a tournament because of a groin injury.*

▶ *An American League pitcher hit a grand slam.* The last to do so was Steve Dunning of the Cleveland Indians in 1971.

▶ *A defenseman win the NHL All-Star MVP Award.* In the last 30 years of these laughably pinball-like affairs, only Ray Bourque, in 1996, has copped the prize, after a disturbingly low-scoring 5-4 East win.

▶ *An NBA Player win the Most Improved Player Award*—twice.

20 of the Most Unusual College Mascots

The most common team mascot in America is the Tiger. Next on the list are Bulldogs and Wildcats.

It is unlikely that the popularity of those mascots will be challenged any time soon by those favored by the following colleges and universities.

▶ Santa Cruz (California) Banana Slugs
▶ Trinity Christian (Illinois) Trolls (and the Lady Trolls)
▶ Evergreen State (Washington) College Geoducks
▶ Alaska Southeast Humpback Whales (and the Lady Whales)
▶ Southern Illinois Salukis
▶ Washburn (Kansas) Ichabods
▶ Simon Fraser (Burnaby, B.C., Canada) Clansmen
▶ Pittsburgh State (Kansas) Gorillas (and the Gussies)
▶ Coastal (South) Carolina Chanticleers
▶ South Dakota Tech Hardrockers
▶ Hawaii-Loa Mongoose

▶ Pomona Pitzer (California) Sagehens

▶ Elon (North Carolina) Fightin' Christians (and the Lady Fightin' Christians)

▶ Southeastern Oklahoma Savages (and the Savagettes)

▶ Albany State (New York) Great Danes

▶ Irvine (California) Anteaters

▶ Southern Arkansas Muleriders (and the Riderettes)

▶ Arkansas-Monticello Boll Weevils (and the Cotton Blossoms)

▶ University of Tennessee-Chattanooga Moccasins

▶ Oglethorpe (Georgia) Stormy Petrels

Get a New Agent: Bad Career Moves

▶ Upset at having to compete for the Pittsburgh Pirates' starting right-field job with Armando Rios and Craig Wilson in spring training of 2002, Derek Bell—who had hit .173 the previous season after signing a two-year, $9.75 million contract with the Pirates—told a reporter: "I ain't going out there and hurting myself in spring training battling for a job. If there is competition, I'm going into 'Operation Shutdown' and let them two battle for it. I'll kick back and relax." Pirates fans (and management) were outraged, and Bell, who hurt his groin in a baserunning drill the day the comments were published, never played for them again. The Pirates gave him his outright release at the end of spring training.

▶ After the 1993 season, infielder Jody Reed turned down a three-year, $7.8 million contract offer from the Los Angeles Dodgers, thinking he could do better on the open market.

He eventually signed with the Milwaukee Brewers for $350,000.

▶ Mike "Fluff" Cowan, who caddied for Tiger Woods for 3½ years—a tenure that coincided with Woods's early success on the PGA Tour—was fired by Woods for (among other things) reportedly revealing too much to the press about their financial arrangement.

▶ After the 1999 season, baseball superstar Ken Griffey, Jr., told the Seattle Mariners that he wouldn't sign with them when he became a free agent the following year, and furthermore he would only accept a trade to the Cincinnati Reds. The Mariners obliged Griffey, trading him to the Reds on February 10, 2000. Although Griffey's first year in Cincinnati was decent enough—he hit 40 homers and drove in 118 runs —the Reds did not make the playoffs while the Mariners did. In 2001, while Griffey was suffering through an injury-plagued year and the Reds were losing 96 games, the Mariners tied a major-league record with 116 victories. In 2002, Griffey was again hurt much of the year (he played in just 70 games and hit a mere eight homers), and the Reds again finished under .500.

► On August 15, 1991, New York Yankees manager Stump Merrill benched Don Mattingly, who'd been named Yankee captain in spring training, for refusing to get a haircut. Mattingly was fined $250, then $100 a day until he got the haircut.

Merrill was fired at year's end.

► Chuck Knoblauch of the New York Yankees needed all the media friends he could get while he suffered through a bizarre, psychologically-inspired throwing problem that led to frequent wild flings from second base. In a game in June of 2000, one of his errant throws whizzed past first baseman Tino Martinez, skipped off the Yankee dugout and into the stands, where it hit a fan in the face, breaking her glasses—none other than the mother of Fox TV broadcaster, Keith Olbermann.

▷ Honorable mention: On the eve of the 2001 NBA playoffs, born-again-Christian Charlie Ward, Knicks point guard who plays in a city with nearly two million Jews, not a few of them Knick fans, was quoted in an article in the April 20th issue of the *New York Times Magazine* story: "Jews are stubborn. Tell me, why did they persecute Jesus unless he knew something they didn't want to accept? They had his blood on their hands." The article states that Allan Houston, the Knicks' shooting guard, pulled out a Palm Pilot in which he'd indexed a Bible passage. "Matthew 26, Verse 67. Then they spit in Jesus's face and hit his with their fists," he read. According to the article, Ward also said: "There are Christians getting persecuted by Jews every day. There's been books written about this—people who are raised Jewish and find Christ, and then their parents stop talking to them."

While many called for the Knicks to release Ward (especially) and Houston, the latter was treated to a different reception: Three months later, the Knicks signed him to a six-year, $100.4 million contract.

The Most Ingrained Misnomers in Sports

The following names are unsuitable to the things named—not that our pointing this out will stop anyone from continuing to call them that.

► *Foul pole*. A ball that hits the foul pole is fair.

► *Boxing ring*. The traditional boxing stage is square, and experiments on this standard have been infrequent and unsuccessful. A circular ring was used in England in 1912 and in San Francisco in 1944 but did not catch on.

► *Los Angeles Lakers*. There are no natural lakes in the city of Los Angeles. The franchise name was appropriate when the team, originally the Minneapolis Lakers, was based in Minnesota, "Land of 10,000 Lakes."

► *Madison Square Garden*. The latest and fourth version of the New York City sports mecca is a good half-mile from Madison Square.

MSG I was built at Madison Square—26th Street and Madison Avenue —but was demolished in 1889. The current Garden is on Seventh Avenue, between 31st and 33rd Streets.

▶ *Charley Winner.* Winner, a football coach, was 9-14 in one-plus seasons as the New York Jets head coach in 1974–75, and 35-30-5 in five seasons as coach of the St. Louis Cardinals in 1966–70. His total was 44-44-5.

▶ *The All-England championships.* The official name for Wimbledon belies not only the tournament's international field but also the infrequency of an English champion. An Englishman has not won the men's singles draw since Fred Perry did it in 1936, and only three Englishwomen have won the Wimbledon singles crown in the last sixty years.

▶ *Polo Grounds.* Polo was never played in the defunct stadium that opened in July of 1889 and became home to baseball and football's New York Giants and, for various and brief periods, the early New York Yankees and the New York Mets. Polo had been played at the original Polo Grounds at 110th Street and Sixth Avenue, which served as home park for the old New York Metropolitans and Giants from 1880–88.

▶ *Utah Jazz.* Again, as with the Lakers, the name once fit—when the franchise was based in New Orleans, home of Dixie, incubator of jazz. The name was preserved even after the team relocated before the 1979–80 season to one of the most conservative states in the Union.

▶ *Yankee Sullivan.* The bareknuckles heavyweight in the 1850s was actually a British fighter who toured America.

▶ *The Bagel Twins.* The nickname for the pair of diminutive, highly ranked American tennis players in the 1970s—Harold Solomon and Eddie Dibbs—was only half-wrong. Solomon is Jewish but Dibbs is of Lebanese descent. (They also "bagelled"—won 6-0 sets—against numerous opponents.)

▶ *The NBA lifetime ban for drug abusers.* "Lifetime" means two years; after that, a multiple drug offender may apply for reinstatement.

Notable League Commissioners and Assorted Executives

▶ Henry Kissinger became Chairman of the Board of the North American Soccer League (NASL) after the 1978 season.

▶ In 1987, Hamilton Jordan, White House Chief of Staff under Jimmy Carter, was elected executive director for the Association of Tennis Professionals (ATP).

▶ In 1951, General Douglas MacArthur was nominated to be commissioner of baseball but declined the candidacy.

▶ It is not unusual to select former stars to head new leagues. Jim Thorpe was the first president of pro football's first league, the

American Professional Football Association. (The APFA eventually became the NFL.)

▶ Former Minneapolis Laker great George Mikan was the first commissioner of the American Basketball Association (ABA).

▶ The president of the Argentine World Cup organizing committee, retired general Omar Actis, was assassinated by left-wing guerrillas on August 19, 1976.

▶ Former basketball star Wilt Chamberlain was the commissioner of the International Volleyball Association in the late 1970s.

▶ Former Los Angeles Rams quarterback Roman Gabriel was general manager of the Charlotte Knights in baseball's AA Southern League, from 1987–92.

▶ Former University of Michigan athletic director and football coach Bo Schembechler was president of baseball's Detroit Tigers.

▶ Richard Nixon was chosen in October of 1985 to arbitrate a dispute between the Major League Umpires Association and the owners. Nixon ultimately decided to award umpires a 40% pay increase.

▶ The NFL Los Angeles Rams advisory board included Bob Hope, Henry Mancini, Maureen Reagan, and Danny Thomas.

Intriguing Team Owners

▶ President George W. Bush became managing partner of the Texas Rangers in 1989, when he fronted a group that bought the team for $75 million. Bush's share was $606,302, one-third of his net worth. In 1998, four years after The Ballpark in Arlington opened, Bush's group sold the team to businessman Tom Hicks for $250 million. Bush not only came away with $14.9 million, but gained visibility that helped lead to his election as Texas governor in 1994. According to former baseball commissioner Fay Vincent, Bush at one time expressed interest in becoming commissioner.

▶ Bing Crosby was a Pittsburgh Pirates minority owner from 1946 until his death in 1977.

▶ Danny Kaye was one of a group of six that purchased the Seattle Mariners in 1976, and was involved with the team until 1981.

▶ David Letterman became a Seattle Mariners minority owner in 1989.

▶ In 2000, three former Microsoft executives—Chris Peters, Rob Glaser, and Mike Slade—bought the financially troubled Professional Bowlers Association (PBA), aiming to restructure its operation, including increasing prize money and bringing coverage of the sport online (Glaser is founder/CEO of RealNetworks).

▶ Soccer player Giorgio Chinaglia, once a New York Cosmo, took controlling interest in the Cosmos by purchasing 60% of the team in July 1984, and held it until the team suspended operations in June 1985.

▶ The irrepressible and often-fined Mark Cuban, co-founder of Broadcast.com and MicroSolutions, bought the NBA's Dallas Mavericks in January 2000. On the one hand, confoundingly egocentric—his rooting often devolves into a string of look-at-me gesticulations—on the other, an undeniably enthusiastic and shrewd leader, Cuban quickly increased attendance by turning the Mavericks from a perennial loser into one of the league's best, most exciting, and most international teams, with players from Germany, Canada, China, Yugoslavia, and Mexico (and the U.S.).

▶ Pete Rose was part owner of the Major Indoor Soccer League's Cincinnati Kids. On December 22, 1978, he kicked out the first ball in the team's history.

▶ Bob Hope, a Cleveland Indians minority owner, sold his interest in December of 1986. He was also part owner of the Los Angeles Rams in the 1950s and early 1960s before Dan Reeves purchased full interest in 1962.

▶ In 1975, Elton John became a part-owner of the Los Angeles Aztecs of the North American Soccer League. He was also part-owner of the Philadelphia Freedom of World Team Tennis.

Serious Trivia: 40 Things Worth Knowing, Late at Night, in a Bar

▶ The first Super Bowl was covered by CBS and NBC. They fought over who should cover it—CBS had rights to the NFL, NBC to the AFL—and finally resolved that they would both do it.

▶ At one point, in rhythmic gymnastics, exposure of bra straps was an automatic deduction.

▶ Blacks played in the NFL from 1920–33, then not at all from 1934–45.

▶ A false start in the 1904 Olympics resulted in a two-yard penalty.

▶ Until 1938, records were not counted in hurdle events if any hurdles were knocked over.

▶ In early auto races, including the Indianapolis 500, two people rode in the car: a driver and a mechanic. Also, relief drivers were routine at Indy.

▶ Winners at the first modern Olympics in 1896 were presented with olive branches and silver medals, while runners-up received laurel boughs and bronze medals. Gold medals for winners were first awarded in 1900.

▶ In the 1908 Olympic marathon in London, the route was the 26 miles from Windsor Castle to the Olympic Stadium, concluding with 385 yards around the stadium track so that the finish would be directly in front of the royal box of Queen Alexandra. The distance of 26 miles and 385 yards became standard for the marathon.

▶ The first modern Olympic swimming competition was held outdoors in open water, in 1896, in the Bay of Zea, Greece.

▶ Since 1986, the best single-season field goal percentage registered by any NBA player is Golden State Warrior Chris Gatling's .633 in 1995.

▶ There were no written rules forbidding blacks from playing professional baseball. In the last two decades of the 19th century, approximately 30 blacks played organized ball. In the 20th century, the first one is Jimmy Claxton, who pitched briefly in 1916 for the Oakland Oaks in the Pacific Coast League.

▶ Foul balls were not counted as strikes until 1901 in the National League and 1903 in the American League, except for foul bunts and foul tips.

▶ Figure skating was part of the Summer Olympics until 1924, when the first Winter Olympics were staged.

▶ During the Los Angeles Olympics in 1932, when the U.S. was in the midst of Prohibition, French team members were given special permission to drink wine because they argued that it was an essential part of their diet.

▶ In the Calgary Flames' 13-1 trouncing of the San Jose Sharks on February 10, 1993, Flames goaltender Jeff Reese had 3 assists (not suprisingly, it's the NHL record for a goaltender).

▶ Former Minnesota Vikings coach Bud Grant, who led his team to four Super Bowls without winning, played on the NBA championship 1949–50 Minneapolis Lakers.

▶ The Houston Astrodome had natural grass during its first season in 1965. In 1966, an Astroturf infield was put in, and later that year the outfield surface was changed.

▶ Roger Maris received no intentional walks in 1961, the year that he hit a then-record 61 home runs. Batting behind him was Mickey Mantle, who hit 54 home runs that season.

▶ In tennis doubles, if the server hits either opponent with a serve on the fly, the serving team gets the point.

▶ There is a World Elephant Polo Association (in Chitwan, Nepal).

▶ In 1948, singer-entertainer Bing Crosby got a hole-in-one at the 16th at Cypress Point, an achievement duplicated just once since then. The hole is 180 yards across the Pacific Ocean.

▶ In 1890, two legs of horse-racing's Triple Crown—the Belmont and the Preakness—were run on the same track, New York's Morris Park, on the same day, June 10.

▶ The distance from home plate to second base is 127 feet 3⅜ inches.

▶ The Tour de France bicycle race used to include several legs of night riding.

▶ The official baseball rulebook requires that a major-league stadium built after June 1, 1958, must be a minimum distance of 325 feet from home to the nearest fence and a minimum of 400 feet from home to the center-field fence.

▶ There was an Olympics in 1906, in between the 1904 and 1908 Games, called the Intercalated or Interim Games.

▶ In 1952, all three medalists in the Olympic individual foil competition were left-handed.

▶ If a greyhound catches the mechanical rabbit (because of mechanical failure), it's considered a "no race."

▶ The maximum number of clubs you're allowed to carry during a golf match is 14.

▶ Jack Nicklaus played for Upper Arlington High School, whose nickname is the Golden Bears.

▶ Boston Red Sox slugger Jim Rice once broke his bat in two on a checked swing.

▶ In 1995, as a collegian at Texas Christian University, Kurt Thomas, the workmanlike power forward for the New York Knicks, led the country in both scoring and rebounding.

▶ On September 4, 1916, Mordecai Brown and Christy Mathewson, both future Hall of Famers, pitched against each other in what was the final major-league game for each.

▶ The first televised sporting event was of a college baseball game, in Japan in 1931.

▶ In 1975, Houston Astros first baseman Bob Watson scored the one millionth run in major-league history.

▶ The winner of the second Boston Marathon, in 1898, was named Ronald McDonald.

▶ The wind reading for Bob Beamon's world-record long jump at the 1968 Olympics was 2.0 miles per second, the exact legal maximum.

▶ David Thompson's 73 points in a 1978 game are the most scored in one NBA game by anyone not named Wilt Chamberlain.

▶ The original suggested name for basketball was Naismith Ball.

▶ In Auckland, New Zealand, on April 16, 1983, Kenya's Mike Boit ran the fastest mile ever—3:28.36, about 15 seconds faster than the current world record. His time was not official because the course was downhill all the way.

16

THE ENDS

●●●●●●●●●●●●●●

Memorable Victory Celebrations

Victories—especially pennant-clinching, gold medal-winning, title belt-capturing victories—are followed by celebrations that have become familiar to all fans. Some of these images remain vivid and particular, others gather to form a tableau in the mind's eye. (Who do we think we are, with the highfalutin language?) We've seen catchers jumping into pitchers' arms (Yogi Berra and Don Larsen after the latter's perfect game in the 1956 World Series); pitchers jumping into catchers' arms (Jerry Koosman and Jerry Grote after the New York Mets captured the 1969 World Series); countless football coaches lifted onto players' shoulders, or having their heads drenched by bucketsful of icy Gatorade; North Carolina State coach Jim Valvano running wildly around the basketball court in search of someone to hug, after his team's gigantic upset of the University of Houston in the 1983 NCAA title game; Bjorn Borg dropping to his knees after winning Wimbledon; the young Muhammad Ali in half-snarl, standing over Sonny Liston after conquering him for the second time; the train of players snaking around the hockey rink with the Stanley Cup aloft; and an ocean of champagne, flowing in locker rooms of all kinds.

A collection of the most memorable celebrations of sporting triumphs:

▶ Jeff Float, an American swimmer who contracted viral meningitis at 13 months and lost 80% of the hearing in his right ear and 60% in his left ear, signed "I love you" on the victory stand at the 1984 Los Angeles Olympics after winning the gold medal for the 4x200m freestyle relay. During the relay final, the roar of the crowd was so great that he heard it for the first time in his life.

▶ When defender Brandi Chastain converted the clinching shot during the penalty-kick shootout of the 1999 World Cup final against China, giving the U.S. the soccer championship in front of a Rose Bowl crowd and huge television audience, she fell to her knees and stripped off her shirt, revealing a black sports bra (and incredible abs), and raised her arms just before being mobbed by teammates. Inevitably, many who witnessed the moment of exultation thought it staged or tasteless; others thought it appropriate—and pointed out that it would have received hardly any negative attention had a man done the same thing.

▶ New York City has staged many ticker-tape parades for victorious athletes. The only parade ever given for a golfer honored Bobby Jones on his return from England after winning the 1930 British Open. New York also gave a ticker-tape parade in 1926 for 19-year-old Gertrude Ederle, the first woman to swim the English Channel.

▶ After winning the Tournament Players Championship in 1982, golfer Jerry Pate took a dive into the lake at the 18th hole, after first pushing in PGA commissioner Deane Beaman and course architect Pete Dye.

▶ After Luciano Giovannetti of Italy won the 1980 trapshooting gold, he tossed his cap into the air and shot a hole through it.

▶ Fathers and sons have been involved in many memorable celebrations. Captured in photographs that made newspapers all over the world, Australian tennis player Pat Cash ran into the crowd to hug his father after beating Ivan Lendl to win Wimbledon in 1987. (While Cash's gesture seemed utterly spontaneous and touching, it set off an unfortunate—that is, far more staged—barrage of freshly crowned Grand Slam winners rushing into the stands to hug loved ones.)

When Jean Boiteux of France won the 400m freestyle at the 1952 Olympics, his dad leaped fully clothed into the water to embrace him.

And after winning a gold medal at the 1984 Olympics, American cyclist Mark Gorski took his 13-month-old son, Alexander, on a victory lap.

▶ Gabriella Dorio received a bath in wine from her husband after winning the Olympic 1,500m race in 1984.

▶ After each New York Giant win in the 1986 season, including their culminating Super Bowl XXI victory over the Denver Broncos, several members of the Giants, led by linebacker Harry Carson, poured a bucket of Gatorade over head coach Bill Parcells. The ritual has been copied countless times by countless teams.

▶ After knocking out Benny Paret, welterweight Emile Griffith did a headstand. Valerio Arri did three cartwheels after crossing the finish line to take third place in the 1920 Olympic marathon. Don Bragg let out a Tarzan yell after winning the 1960 pole vault.

▶ Boxer Evander Holyfield was disqualified in the 1984 Olympics for throwing a late punch that knocked out his opponent. At the awards ceremony, gold-medal winner Anton Josipovic of Yugoslavia pulled Holyfield up onto the top platform with him.

The Most Notable and Unusual Retired Numbers

One of the highest honors bestowed upon an athlete, outside of election to his or her sport's hall of fame, is the retiring of one's number. Retiring numbers is an art more than a science, and unusual honorees and circumstances have marked these occasions.

▶ The minor-league Williamsport Bills retired the #59 that was worn by catcher Dave Bresnahan in 1988 to commemorate his most famous act as a player—firing a previously concealed potato past third base to trick a runner into coming home. "He's probably the only .149 hitter in baseball to ever have his jersey retired," said a team spokesman.

▶ To honor Jackie Robinson's breaking of the color barrier in major-league baseball—and to honor, too, the man's rare courage, ability, and grace—then-acting baseball commissioner Bud Selig announced at Shea Stadium, on April 15, 1997, that Robinson's number with the Brooklyn Dodgers—42—would be retired for the entire major leagues, the first number so commemorated; it would no longer be issued. However, those who were wearing it at the time of the announcement (Met Mo Vaughn and Yankee Mariano Rivera among them) would be allowed to continue wearing #42 until they left the league.

▶ In April of 1999, in a ceremony in New York City's Madison Square Garden preceding his final game in the NHL, Wayne Gretzky, hockey's greatest player, listened as league commissioner Gary Bettman told him (and everyone listening) that "when you take off that sweater, your jersey, after today's game, you will be the last player in the NHL to ever wear 99."

▶ The Boston Celtics have retired the most numbers in basketball, 20. The New York Yankees have retired more numbers, 14, than any major-league team, including every single-digit number except for #2 (now worn by shortstop Derek Jeter) and #6 (manager Joe Torre)—those may go yet—and several two-digit numbers. The Chicago Bears lead the NFL with 13 numbers, including #7 for late founder and owner George Halas, and the Boston Bruins have retired 8 numbers to lead the NHL. The Montreal Canadiens have nine players with retired numbers, but only 7 retired numbers: Jean Beliveau and Aurel Joliat both had their #4 retired, and Henri Richard and Elmer Lach both had their #16 retired.

▶ Henri and Maurice Richard of the Montreal Canadiens are the only brothers in pro sports to have their numbers retired.

The University of Michigan retired jersey #11, which was worn by brothers Francis, Albert, and Alvin Wistert, All-America tackles—Francis in 1933, Albert in '42, Alvin in '48 and '49.

▶ Running back Floyd Little had his jersey retired... four times. He wore #33 for Hillhouse High School in New Haven, Connecticut; they retired it. He wore #77 for the Bordentown (New Jersey) Military Institute, a prep school; retired it. He wore #44 at Syracuse University; ditto, sort of. (see next item.) He again wore #44 for the NFL's Denver Broncos; you guessed it.

▶ Little (see previous) starred for Syracuse after Jim Brown and Ernie Davis had also starred there. Each was an All-America who wore #44. The number—44—thus became the most esteemed in the school's sports history. Rather than retire it, though, Syracuse gives the number to a player only if he's special enough to epitomize what Brown, Davis, and Little epitomized. The number 44 is so special to the Orangemen, in fact, that the school's ZIP code was changed from 13210 to 13244, and the first three numbers of the school's telephone numbers were changed from 423 to 443.

▶ Syracuse is on to something—or at least Morgan Wootten, the legendary basketball coach at DeMatha, an all-boys Catholic high school in Hyattsville, Maryland, near Washington, D.C., might agree with their policy. He didn't retire jerseys or numbers. Instead, Wootten—who has seen more than a dozen players go on to the NBA—believed in giving a former great player's number to a new, promising player, as inspiration. "We certainly don't lack candidates," Wootten once said. "But my attitude is, more than one player of mine has brought honor to each particular number. Why not perpetuate that number? I think it's more fun to say to a player, 'You're wearing Joseph Forte's number,' or Adrian Dantley's number, or Danny Ferry's number."

(The only number—#13—retired in DeMatha history belonged to football player Tim Strachan. The quarterback was being recruited by Penn State and Maryland when a swimming accident in the summer of 1993 left him paralyzed.)

▶ The Cincinnati Reds retired #5 for star catcher Johnny Bench in August of 1984. The Reds had also retired #5 when their backup catcher, Willard Hershberger, committed suicide in 1940. Apparently, it was not a permanent honor.

▶ The Cleveland Browns retired #45, the number that 1961 Heisman Trophy winner and #1 draft choice Ernie Davis was supposed to wear for them but never did. He died of leukemia in 1963.

▶ Several athletes have had their numbers retired by two teams:

▷ Casey Stengel's #37 by the New York Yankees and Mets

▷ Hank Aaron's #44 by the Atlanta Braves and the Milwaukee Brewers

▷ Rod Carew's #29 by the Minnesota Twins and the California Angels

▷ Julius Erving's #32 by the New Jersey Nets, and his #6 by the Philadelphia 76ers

▷ Oscar Robertson's #14 by the Cincinnati Royals, and his #1 by the Milwaukee Bucks

▷ Nate Thurmond's #42 by the Golden State Warriors and the Cleveland Cavaliers

▷ Gordie Howe's #9 by the Detroit Red Wings and the Hartford Whalers

▷ Bobby Hull's #9 by the Chicago Black Hawks and the Winnipeg Jets

▶ No NFL player has had his number retired by more than one team.

▶ The New York Yankees retired #8, honoring at once Yogi Berra and Bill Dickey, their two greatest catchers.

▶ In 1939, the #4 worn by Lou Gehrig became the first number in the major leagues ever retired when the New York Yankees accorded him the honor.

▶ The Boston Celtics have retired #2 for mastermind and former coach Red Auerbach, #1 for Celtics founder Walter Brown, and the name "Loscy" for former player Jim Loscutoff.

▶ Baseball's San Francisco Giants retired the jerseys of pitcher Christy Mathewson and manager John McGraw, both of whom were major leaguers before numbers were worn.

▶ The NBA's Philadelphia 76ers retired the microphone of announcer Dave Zinkoff.

Ending with a Flourish, Closing with a Rush: The Greatest Finales

The best examples of athletes and teams who ended their careers, or the season, or a game, in a way they and their fans would cherish:

▶ In his last regular-season college game, Syracuse running back Jim Brown totaled 43 points, a record for most points scored in a major college game.

▶ Gary Cowan won the 1971 U.S. Amateur tournament with an eagle two on the 18th hole.

▶ Future Hall of Famer Ted Williams could have sat out the last day of the 1941 season and been credited with a .400 average—he was hitting .39955 at the time—but he chose to play the first game of a doubleheader. He went 4-for-5. He could have sat out the second game to make sure he protected his average (now .4039), but he played that one, too, went 2-for-3, and finished at .406 (.4057).

Williams also finished his career dramatically in 1960, by homering in his final at-bat, at Fenway Park.

▶ American cyclist Greg LeMond won the 1989 Tour de France on the final day of the race by overcoming what was considered an impossible margin, 50 seconds, with the fastest time trial in Tour history.

▶ Goran Ivanisevic, a perennial Top 10 player who'd always underperformed in big tournaments—often melting down in finals—was watching his career fading due to age and injury when he received a wild-card entry into the 2001 Wimbledon draw; he intimated that he would not play past that season. In a fortnight that shocked both Ivanisevic and tennis fans who'd watched him for years, the fiery Croat beat Australia's Patrick Rafter in five sets to take the world's most prestigious tennis title, and finally live up to years of unmet expectations.

▶ After a tremendous career in which he proved himself one of pro football's greatest and clutchest quarterbacks ever, Denver Bronco John Elway was still saddled with a reputation that he couldn't get his team the final prize. In his 15th and 16th seasons, he led the Broncos to Super Bowl victories, then retired.

▶ In arguably the most exciting finish ever in a major college championship game, the University of North Carolina women's basketball team, down 59-57 to Louisiana Tech, inbounded the ball with seven-tenths of a second left, and Charlotte Smith hit a buzzer-beating three-point bomb to win the 1994 NCAA title game.

▶ The most consecutive games won at the end of an NBA season is 15, by the 1950 Rochester Royals.

▶ In the 2001 All-Star Game, the final one of his illustrious career, Baltimore Oriole infielder Cal Ripken hit a home run in his first at-bat, which would earn him the All-Star MVP award.

▶ In a frozen instant as painful to University of Michigan fans as it is thrilling to Colorado University fans, Buffalo quarterback Kordell Stewart threw a last-second, 64-yard Hail Mary pass that wide receiver Michael Westbrook caught for a touchdown, giving Colorado a stunning 27-26 victory on September 24, 1994, and silencing most of the 106,427 fans at the Big House in Ann Arbor.

▶ California Angel Mike Witt pitched a perfect game on the last day of the 1984 season.

▶ Phil Niekro won his 300th major-league victory on the last day of the 1985 baseball season.

▶ Johnny Miller shot a final round 63 to win the 1973 U.S. Open.

▶ On January 22, 1983, the Portland Trail Blazers outscored the Houston Rockets 17-0 in overtime to win 113-96.

▶ New York Yankee Roger Maris hit his record 61st home run on the final day of the 1961 season.

▶ The Chicago Cubs captured the 1935 National League pennant with one of the greatest stretch runs ever, winning 21 consecutive games from September 4 to September 27.

▶ In the last game of the 1985 NFL season, Kansas City Chiefs wide receiver Stephone Paige caught passes totaling 309 yards, breaking a 40-year-old record for receiving yardage.

▶ Just past the halfway mark of the 90s, the Atlanta Braves appeared to have a lock on the title of "Team of the Decade"—informally bestowed, but worth its weight in bragging rights. By 1996, they'd captured their fifth straight divisional title, their fourth pennant in the same span, and were heavily favored to take their second consecutive World Series title, especially as they prepared for Game 3 of the '96 Series, up two games to none against the New York Yankees. The Yankees, whose winning ways had only returned after a decade-and-a-half drought, had been outscored by the Braves 16-1 in New York. Back in Atlanta, however, the Yankees swept Games 3, 4, and 5, clinched in New York for the '96 title, then won back-to-back championships in 1998 and 1999, the latter against the Braves, again, and emphatically claimed *their* stake as "Team of the Decade."

▶ In his last start of the 1973 season, California Angel Nolan Ryan struck out 16 batters (in 11 innings), giving him 383 for the year, to beat Sandy Koufax's single-season record of 382.

▶ In the 1957 World Series, Milwaukee Braves pitcher Lew Burdette was unscored upon in his final 24 innings.

▶ In 1951, New York Yankee pitcher Allie Reynolds pitched a no-hitter to beat the Boston Red Sox, 8-0, and clinch a tie for the American League pennant.

▶ The last game Babe Pinelli umpired behind the plate before retiring was Don Larsen's perfect game in the 1956 World Series.

Going Out with a Thud: The Sorriest Finishes in Sport

▶ On September 30, 1962, in his last major-league at-bat, New York Mets catcher Joe Pignatano hit into a triple play.

▶ In December of 1965, in his last regular-season game in football, Cleveland Browns running back Jim Brown was ejected for fighting with St. Louis Cardinal Joe Robb just before halftime, the only time in Brown's career that he was thrown out of a game.

▶ In the twilight of his playing career, Maradona—star of the 1986 World Cup, pride of Argentina and the Napoli soccer club, and one of soccer's all-time great performers—failed a drug test at the 1994 World Cup and was banished from the tournament. In the years following, he was dogged by charges of more drug use, petulant behavior, and other scandals.

▶ In a charmed regular season, the 2001 Seattle Mariners tied the modern-day record for wins, with 116... then watched the good feeling generated by their tremendous accomplishment get dwarfed by derision for their failure even to make it to the World Series, as they were easily knocked out by the New York Yankees, four games to one, in the American League Championship Series.

▶ In the final game of his college career—the 1986 Rose Bowl against UCLA—University of Iowa running back Ron Harmon fumbled four times in the first half and dropped a touchdown pass. Before that day, he had fumbled once all season.

▶ In 1899, baseball's Cleveland Spiders, managed by an Australian undertaker, lost 40 of their final 41 games.

▶ The Los Angeles Dodgers were shut out in the final three games of the 1966 World Series.

▸ On October 10, 1904, the last day of the regular season, the New York Highlanders (later the Yankees) sent their ace, Jack Chesbro, to the mound to help win the pennant over the Boston Red Sox. Chesbro was 41-11, a major-league record for wins, and had an ERA under 2.00, but he threw a wild pitch in the ninth inning, allowing the Red Sox to score the winning run and clinch the pennant.

▸ The final-season average for Harmon Killebrew was .199 (in 1975); for Babe Ruth, .181 (1935); for Brooks Robinson, .149 (1977); for Ernie Banks, .193 (1971); and for Bill Mazeroski, .188 (1972). Willie Mays hit .211 in his last year and fell down in the outfield in the 1973 World Series. He said, "Growing old is just a helpless hurt."

▸ In the last regular-season game of his career, Wilt Chamberlain scored one point on a free throw. (In his next-to-last game, he did not even attempt a shot from the field.)

▸ As a three-year-old in 1948, Citation won 19 of 20 races, including the Triple Crown, and earned $865,150. His owner wanted him to be the first million-dollar winner and kept him racing despite the fact that Citation was suffering from an osselet, a bony growth on the ankle which put the horse out for a year. Citation lost races to horses vastly inferior. He finally surpassed the million-dollar mark in 1951 and retired.

▸ On October 6, 1911, in the last game of his career, future Hall of Famer Cy Young, pitching for the Boston Braves against the Brooklyn Dodgers, went 6⅓ innings, gave up 11 hits and 11 runs, and lost, 13-3.

▸ In 1925, Roger Peckinpaugh, the Washington Senator shortstop and American League MVP, led his team to the pennant. In the seven-game World Series against Pittsburgh, Peckinpaugh committed eight errors, a Series record.

If At First... :
Athletes Whose Perseverance Happily Paid Off

▸ In 1953, Jockey Gordon Richards, aboard Pinza, won the Epsom Derby on his 28th and last attempt.

▸ After crashing at 270 mph while attempting to set a new motorcycle world speed record at the Bonneville Salt Flats in September of 1975, Don Vesco tried again and became the first man to exceed 300mph.

▸ After almost 16 years in the game, relief pitcher John Franco owned the dubious distinction of being one of the longest-tenured players to never appear in a postseason game. Finally, in 1999, after 878 appearances, Franco made the playoffs with the New York Mets. He performed admirably, apearing in 6 games, going 1-0, and giving up just one earned run in 6⅓ innings. The following year, Franco made it to his first World Series, and again pitched well throughout the playoffs, giving up two earned runs in nine games, and recorded the Mets' lone victory in their five-game Series loss to the Yankees.

Pitcher Joe Niekro appeared in his first World Series game in his 21st major-league season.

▶ In 1993, after 43 years of failure, Charlie Brown of *Peanuts* fame finally hit a home run to win a game. "I think it's a mistake to be unfaithful to your readers, always to be letting them down," said *Peanuts* creator Charles Schultz.

▶ In his eighth and final playoff year, Montreal Canadiens defenseman Jack Portland scored the only playoff goal of his career, in his last series.

▶ Satchel Paige was allegedly the oldest rookie in baseball history at 42. Diomedes Olivo broke into the major leagues at 41.

▶ In 1993, Genuine Risk gave birth to her first foal after 16 years of trying.

▶ Tom Gullikson won his first professional singles tennis title, the 1985 Volvo Hall of Fame at Newport, Rhode Island, when he was 35.

▶ As a freshman running back at the University of Georgia, Herschel Walker was third in the Heisman Trophy voting. As a sophomore, he was second. As a junior, he won the Trophy.

▶ For decades, the city of Houston had been host to several major pro teams (the Astros, Oilers, and Rockets) without winning a championship. Finally, in 1994, the NBA Houston Rockets won the title, and defended it successfully the following year. The city so enjoyed the taste of winning that in the late 90s, the Houston Comets, the city's WNBA entry, won the championship its first four years in the league.

▶ Boxer Archie Moore won his first title at either 36 or 39—depending on whether you believe the birthdate he gave or the one his mother gave—in a 1952 decision over Joey Maxim.

▶ Brooklyn Dodger Pee Wee Reese played on five World Series losers before winning one.

▶ Casey Stengel did not lead a pennant winner until his 10th year as manager. (Perhaps we should also mention that his 10th year was also his first year managing the New York Yankees.)

▶ Coach Dick Vermeil took the Philadelphia Eagles to their only Super Bowl trip (through the 2001 season) in 1981, where they lost to the Oakland Raiders, 27-10. Unable to reach the ultimate prize, Vermeil said he was "burned out," and left coaching. Fifteen years later, he returned to coach the St. Louis Rams, leading them to a 23-16 win over the Tennessee Titans in the 2000 Super Bowl, and finally achieving his goal.

▶ Simone Mathieu lost the French singles finals six times, then won it twice.

▶ In 1964, owner Charlie Finley's proposal to move his Athletics from Kansas City to Louisville was rejected by the other American League owners. Four years later, Finley tried to move the team to Oakland, and succeeded.

1 Athlete Whose Perseverance Unhappily Paid Off

▶ While trying to set a land speed record at Daytona Beach in February 1928, driver Frank Lockhart crashed on the sand, flipped into the sea, and almost drowned. Two months later, he went back to Daytona, crashed again and, this time, died.

1 Athlete Who Simply Waited Long Enough

▶ In the 1924 Olympic 90m hill ski jumping competition, Thorleif Haug won the bronze medal. In 1974, a scoring error was discovered that demoted Haug, dead for 48 years, to fourth. Norwegian-born American Anders Haugen, now 83, was moved up to third and awarded the bronze medal in a special ceremony in Oslo. Fifty years after the competition, Haugen officially became the first—and, so far, only—American ever to win an Olympic ski jumping medal.

I Shoulda Stood in Bed:
More Than Enough Lessons on Why to Stay Retired

▶ Tight end Jackie Smith came out of retirement in 1978 to play one more season with the Dallas Cowboys. During the 1979 Super Bowl, Smith was wide open in the end zone when he dropped a touchdown pass that cost the Cowboys a chance to tie at the end of the third quarter. The Cowboys lost, 35-31, to the Pittsburgh Steelers, and the dropped pass would become probably Smith's most renowned moment as a pro.

▶ Heavyweight Joe Louis retired as an unbeaten champion in 1949, then came back and lost to Ezzard Charles and Rocky Marciano. Muhammad Ali came out of retirement to fight—and lose to—Larry Holmes (1980) and Trevor Berbick (1981). In 1981, Joe Frazier tried a comeback after a five-year retirement and could only fight to a draw with a journeyman named Jumbo Cummings. Larry Holmes unretired to try and outshine Marciano's unblemished record, and lost to Michael Spinks and Mike Tyson.

Sugar Ray Leonard retired from his brilliant boxing career, then unretired, then retired, then...as with so many fighters, he came back one time too many. He lost in a 5th-round TKO to Hector Camacho, in March 1997. It was the first time in Leonard's career that he'd been stopped.

▶ Bud Wilkinson, the University of Oklahoma coaching legend who led the Sooners to a 47-game winning streak in the 1950s, came out of retirement to coach the NFL's St. Louis Cardinals in 1978 and was fired in 1979 after compiling a 9-20 record.

Coaching legends Bill Walsh, Johnny Majors, and John Robinson all returned to schools where they'd coached earlier in their careers, with enormous success—Stanford, Pitt, and USC, respectively—and all of them experienced far more humbling results.

▶ Hall of Fame pitcher Jim Palmer attempted a comeback in 1991. During spring training he tore his hamstring, and quit.

▶ The 1987 exhibition matches scheduled between former tennis stars Bjorn Borg and Vitas Gerulaitis were canceled because of low ticket sales.

▶ Jim Thorpe, who had starred for the 1916 Canton Bulldogs, considered one of the greatest teams in the history of pro football, came back to play for a new version of the team in 1926. This time they went 1-12.

The Most Memorable Farewells

Whether they like it or not, great athletes are often seen as gods, and the super-mortal acts they perform are what we remember best. Then the day comes when they are finished performing and we bid them farewell. Sometimes we remember these moments, too.

▶ On July 4, 1939, Lou Gehrig Day at Yankee Stadium, the great first baseman gave his farewell speech and uttered one of the most famous lines in sports history: "Today, I consider myself the luckiest man on the face of the earth." At the time, Gehrig was in the advanced stages of amyotrophic lateral sclerosis, the disease that a year later would kill him (and later bear his name).

▶ When Man O' War, age 30, died on November 1, 1947, he became the first thoroughbred to be embalmed in preparation for his funeral. Two thousand people turned out for the ceremony, which was broadcast nationwide on radio. He was extolled by nine speakers, and many who filed by his open casket reached down to touch his flesh. Local merchants draped their storefronts in black.

(When the horse retired in 1920, the Lexington, Kentucky, Chamber of Commerce announced that school children would throw flowers in his path during a parade through town. Owner Samuel Riddle rejected the idea. "He's only a horse," he said via telegraph.)

▶ After the Los Angeles Lakers lost the fourth and final game of the 1989 NBA Finals to the Detroit Pistons, which also marked the final game in the career of Laker center and basketball legend Kareem Abdul-Jabbar, Laker coach Pat Riley took Abdul-Jabbar's sweaty jersey home with him as a memento. Magic Johnson took Abdul-Jabbar's warm-up jacket, Byron Scott his shoes, and PR director Josh Rosenfeld his shorts.

▶ In 1974, in Brazilian soccer immortal Pelé's supposed final game after 18 years with Santos, he trotted around the stadium with tears streaming down his face, before leaving the field at halftime as the fans chanted, "Stay! Stay! Stay!" A year later, he signed with the NASL's New York Cosmos.

During a pre-game ceremony before his final professional game on October 1, 1977, Pelé led the crowd of 75,646 at the Meadowlands in a chant of "Love! Love! Love!" He played the first half with the Cosmos and at halftime removed his #10 Cosmos jersey and gave it to his father. Pelé then donned his old #10 for Santos, the Cosmos' opponent, and played the second half with them. After the game, he gave his Santos jersey to his first coach and took a lap around the field. Cosmo goalies Shep Messing and Erol Yasin then carried him off on their shoulders.

▶ Three days after distance runner Steve Prefontaine's death at age 24 in a May 1975 car accident, a hearse carrying his body took a lap around the Marshfield High School track in his hometown of Coos Bay, Oregon. A crowd of 2,500 attended.

▶ On "Yaz Day" in 1983, the day before his final game with the Boston Red Sox, outfielder Carl Yastrzemski grounded into the last out of the game. After reaching first base, he ran to the stands, then circled the field counterclockwise, shaking hands with fans and saluting the crowd.

▶ After Wayne Gretzky's final game in the NHL, in April 1999, he skated several times around the rink of Madison Square Garden while his New York Ranger teammates and the opponent Pittsburgh Penguins banged their sticks in appreciation and thanks, and The Great One waved to adoring fans—#99 gliding in the spotlight, while everyone else sat or stood in the dark, savoring their last moments of Gretzky, the player, on the ice.

▶ On May 7, 1959, a major-league record of 93,103 fans turned out at the Los Angeles Coliseum for an exhibition game between the Dodgers and the New York Yankees to honor Roy Campanella. At the end of the fifth inning, Campanella, the former Dodger All-Star catcher who had been paralyzed in an automobile accident in January of 1958, was wheeled to the center of the infield. The stadium lights were turned out, and for a full minute fans stood, each holding a lighted match or cigarette lighter.

It Ain't Over...It Ain't Over...

Yogi warned us that "It ain't over till it's over." He was right—he usually is—but, amazingly, people still forget. A few examples of finishes and done deals that turned out not to be:

▶ With the bases empty of New York Mets, who were down by two runs with Boston up three games to two, and with two outs in the bottom of the 10th inning of Game 6 of the 1986 World Series, New York's Shea Stadium scoreboard flashed the message, "Congratulations, Red Sox."

▶ In a United States-Africa meet in North Carolina in 1971, Miruts Yifter sprinted to an apparent win over Steve Prefontaine in the 5,000m but he had miscounted and quit running one lap too soon.

▶ Down by a score of 39-37, with the ball on their own 47-yard line and mere seconds on the clock, Kansas City Chiefs quarterback Trent Green scrambled desperately, searching to make something of nothing. When Cleveland Browns linebacker Dwayne Rudd tackled Green, he thought he'd sacked him and the game was over, so he pulled off his helmet and threw it in celebration. In fact, he *hadn't* tackled Green before the resourceful KC quarterback had flipped the ball to offensive tackle John Tait, who ran 28 yards to the Cleveland 25 as time expired —a play that would have ended the game had Rudd not tossed his headgear. Because a game cannot end on a defensive penalty, Rudd was called for unsportsmanlike conduct, the Browns were penalized half the distance to the goal, and, with no time on the clock, Morten Anderson kicked a 30-yard field goal to beat the Browns, 40-39.

▶ 1960 pole vault Olympian Ron Morris failed to clear the height necessary to qualify for the finals. But because only 10 vaulters had cleared the height, and rules stated that 12 had to compete in the finals, the three next-best vaulters, one of whom was Morris, were advanced. Morris won the silver medal.

▶ On September 22, 1927, in the famous "Long Count" fight, Jack Dempsey knocked down Gene Tunney in the seventh round. The referee did not start the count right away because Dempsey was standing over Tunney and did not at first heed the ref's warning to go to a neutral corner. Tunney, up at the count of nine, actually had at least 14 seconds of rest, and went on to win in a 10-round decision.

▶ In the sixth inning of a scoreless Game 1 of the 2000 "Subway" World Series, speedy New York Met Timo Perez, standing on first base with two outs and Todd Zeile at the plate, watched as Zeile lined a ball to deep right-field. Sure the ball would clear the wall, Perez began jogging around the bases and making the (umpire's) home-run gesture. In fact, the ball hit the very, *very* top of the wall and bounced back in play, where New York Yankee rightfielder David Justice retrieved it and relayed it to shortstop Derek Jeter, who threw it to catcher Jorge Posada, who tagged out Perez, who'd only begun running hard about halfway around the bases, after realizing that the ball *wasn't* a home run.

The Mets would lose the game in extra innings, and the momentum was irretrievably seized by the Yankees, who won the Series in five games.

▶ In the 1984 Olympics, Daley Thompson apparently finished a point away from equaling the decathlon world record. Two years later, the IAAF announced that his time in the 100m hurdles was actually 14.33 seconds and not 14.34, and a point was added, allowing him to tie the world record.

▶ In the 1957 Kentucky Derby, jockey Willie Shoemaker, leading on Gallant Man, mistakenly pulled up 110 yards before the finish line, and was passed by Iron Liege.

▶ On June 15, 1976, Oakland Athletics owner Charlie Finley sold Vida Blue to the New York Yankees for $1.5 million, and Joe Rudi and Rollie Fingers to the Boston Red Sox for $1 million each. On the night of the sale, the Red Sox were in Oakland, and Rudi and Fingers changed clubhouses and donned their new Red Sox uniforms, though neither player was used in the game. The next day, baseball commissioner Bowie Kuhn ordered the Red Sox and the Yankees to refrain from using any of the three players while he investigated the deal. On June 18, Kuhn voided the trades, saying they were not in the best interests of baseball.

▶ Jockey Ralph Neves was declared dead by doctors after he fell at Bay Meadows Racetrack on May 8, 1936. They were wrong. Neves came back to race.

▶ On October 8, 1981, Bobby Unser was finally declared the winner of the Indianapolis 500, held 4½ months earlier on May 24. Unser had crossed the finish line first but a protest was filed claiming that he had violated the no-pass rule under a yellow caution. The next day, the protest was upheld and Mario Andretti was declared the winner. A USAC appeals panel eventually restored Unser's victory.

▶ In a steeplechase race on December 29, 1945, Never Mind II balked at the fourth hurdle, and horse and rider eventually returned to the paddock without completing the course. The jockey was then informed that all of the other horses had fallen. He and Never Mind II returned to the course and won the race in a time of over 11 minutes, almost three times the expected clocking.

It's Over! It's Over!

For those who've been too often burned by not heeding Yogi's dictum, here are five examples of competitions that went on even after they were over.

▶ In an August 8, 1903, Eastern League (now International League) game, Rochester and Providence went into extra innings before someone discovered that Providence had already won the game, 1-0. No one on the visiting Providence bench had kept score, and the scoreboard boy had forgotten to tally their run in the fifth inning. In the bottom of the 10th inning, someone finally showed an official scorecard to the umpire, and he awarded the game to Providence, 1-0 winners in nine innings.

▶ On May 25, 1965, in his second loss to Muhammad Ali, Sonny Liston went down at 1:42 of the first round. The knockdown timekeeper had counted all the way to 22 when Liston finally got to his feet. He and Ali began to throw punches but referee Jersey Joe Walcott, responding to shouts that Liston had not stood in time, separated the men and declared Ali the winner at 2:12.

▶ In the 1932 Olympic steeplechase, the runners took an extra lap because the lap checker forgot to change the lap count after their first circuit. During the extra lap, Thomas Evenson passed Joseph McCluskey for second.

▶ In 1973, Australian Steve Holland, in his first international race, beat Rick DeMont and Brad Cooper in the 1,500m freestyle in world-record time, and kept on swimming even after the distance was covered. The more experienced DeMont and Cooper, skeptical that their lap count was wrong, followed anyway for 100 more meters. Holland made the turn for his third extra lap before officials could stop him.

▶ With Dartmouth leading Cornell, 3-0, late in the fourth quarter of their November 18, 1940, football game, Cornell drove to the six-yard line, where they had first down. The Big Red ran three rushing plays to the one-yard line, then were moved back five yards after a penalty was called. They then threw an incomplete pass on what should have been fourth down. But Red Friesell, an official, miscalculated and on fifth down Cornell threw for a touchdown and won, 7-3. When the mistake was later discovered, Cornell relinquished the victory. Ivy League commissioner Asa Bushnell sent Friesell a telegram that read, "Don't let it get you down, down, down, down, down."

It's Almost Over But Certaintly It Ain't *Totally...* Ouch. Yeah, It's Over

▶ Chris Webber, fabbest of the University of Michigan's Fab Five, brought the ball upcourt for the final possession of the 1993 NCAA title game, with his Wolverines down by two to the University of North Carolina. Cornered by multiple Tar Heels, a desperate Webber called a timeout with 11 seconds to go—only the Wolverines had none left to call. The Tar Heels shot the two free throws for the technical foul, essentially closing out the game. (Despite Webber's All-World NBA career, many basketball fans remember this moment too well, and continue to ridicule Webber for it—excessively and even unfairly, it should be noted, given the heat of the moment and the very real possibility that Michigan's coaching staff hadn't made it clear that the team was out of timeouts.)

Let's Pretend It Never Happened: 23 Greats Who Finished Their Careers on Unholy Ground

Few athletes (or people) have the integrity that Jackie Robinson showed in 1956. When the lifelong Brooklyn Dodger was traded, at age 37, to the New York Giants, he retired rather than play for the hated crosstown rivals. But he's the exception. Too often, athletes cannot bring themselves to retire even though their skills are fast deteriorating—and, sadly, this is more true of great athletes, since their careers usually last longer than those of lesser competitors. The team on which the fading star flourished no longer wants him, so he takes his act elsewhere. Sometimes we'll forgive the athlete, who may be trying to cap a career with some monumental achievement that's clearly within grasp: For example, while Wade Boggs will be remembered as a Boston Red Sock first, a New York Yankee second, it was as a Tampa Bay Devil Ray that he collected his 3000th major-league hit, in August of 1999; Gaylord Perry didn't last even two seasons with the Seattle Mariners, the seventh of eight teams for whom he pitched in his Hall of Fame career, but he did record his 300th career victory there, in May of 1982.

But to see a great descend into mediocrity—and worse, and quickly, too—is an experience as jarring for fans as it is for the player. We try to hold fast to the memory of pitcher Steve Carlton's brilliant 21-plus seasons with the St. Louis Cardinals and the Philadelphia Phillies, all the while looking askance at his pathetic showings, in his last year-and-a-half, with the San Francisco Giants (1986), the Chicago White Sox (1986), the Cleveland Indians (1987), and finally, briefly—mercifully—the Minnesota Twins (1987).

The following is a list of great athletes and the teams with which they finished their careers—not the one (or two) with which they will forever be associated.

We'll just pretend none of it ever happened.

► Hank Aaron as a Milwaukee Brewer (1975–76)

► Yogi Berra as a New York Met (1965)

► Bob Cousy as a Cincinnati Royal (1969–70)

► Dave Cowens as a Milwaukee Buck (1982–83)

► Patrick Ewing as a Seattle Supersonic (2000–01) and an Orlando Magician (2001–02)

► Dizzy and Paul Dean as St. Louis Browns (1947 and 1943, respectively)

► Jimmie Foxx as a Chicago Cub (1942, 1944) and a Philadelphia Phillie (1945)

► Walt Frazier as a Cleveland Cavalier (1977–79)

► Franco Harris as a Seattle Seahawk (1984)

► Harmon Killebrew as a Kansas City Royal (1975)

► Ralph Kiner as a Chicago Cub (1953–54) and a Cleveland Indian (1955)

▶ Vince Lombardi as coach of the Washington Redskins (1969)

▶ Christy Mathewson as a Cincinnati Red (1916—for one game)

▶ Willie Mays as a New York Met (1972–73)

▶ Hakeem Olajuwon as a Toronto Raptor (2001-02)

▶ Joe Namath as a Los Angeles Ram (1977)

▶ Bobby Orr as a Chicago Blackhawk (1976–77, 1978–79)

▶ Babe Ruth as a Boston Brave (1935)

▶ O. J. Simpson as a San Francisco 49er (1978–79)

▶ Duke Snider as a New York Met (1963) and a San Francisco Giant (1964)

▶ Warren Spahn as a New York Met (1965) and a San Francisco Giant (1965)

▶ Johnny Unitas as a San Diego Charger (1973)

▶ Paul Waner as a Brooklyn Dodger (1941), a Boston Brave (1941–42), a Brooklyn Dodger again (1943–44), and a New York Yankee (1944–45)

Athletic Careers Cut Short

▶ After six years in which he drove in more runs than anyone in the American League, including Mickey Mantle, outfielder Jackie Jensen of the Boston Red Sox quit baseball in his prime, mainly because of his fear of flying. He retired after the 1959 season, in which he hit 28 home runs and drove in 112. Hypnotism failed to cure him. He came back to play in 1961, then retired again.

▶ Toronto Maple Leaf Ace Bailey was checked from behind by Boston's Eddie Shore in 1933 and his head struck the ice. Bailey was carried off with a cerebral concussion and teetered on the brink of death for several days. He recovered but never played hockey again.

▶ New England Patriots wide receiver Darryl Stingley was paralyzed and confined to a wheelchair after a notorious hit that he received from Oakland Raider Jack Tatum in a 1978 preseason game.

▶ While horseback riding at age 19, Maureen "Mo" Connolly, the youngest woman to win the tennis Grand Slam, broke her leg when a truck hit her. She never played competitive tennis again. She died of cancer in 1969, at age 34.

▶ In 2001, Alex Zinardi, two-time CART driving champion, lost both legs above the knee after a horrific accident at the German 500 (renamed the American Memorial 500 because it was run the weekend following the September 11th attacks). Zinardi, who was leading the race when he entered the pits, seemed to accelerate too early as he came out of them, lost control, swerved sideways, and was hit broadside by a competitor going 200 mph.

▶ Bo Jackson was well on his way to becoming a two-sport superstar in 1989, rushing for 950 yards for the Los Angeles Raiders after hitting 32 home runs and driving in 105 runs for the Kansas City Royals. But in the 1991 NFL playoffs against the Cincinnati Bengals, after a 34-yard-run in the third quarter, Jackson badly hurt his hip on the tackle. Diagnosed with avascular necrosis, a degenerative disease that restricts the blood flow to the hip socket, he never played football again. Released by the Royals in March of 1991, Jackson signed with the Chicago White Sox and had 71 at-bats in September, batting .225 with three homers. With·his hip condition worsening, Jackson underwent hip replacement surgery on April 4, 1992. After undergoing extensive rehabilitation, Jackson returned to the major leagues in 1993, playing two more seasons with the White Sox and California Angels.

▶ In March of 1958, 24-year-old Cincinnati Royal Maurice Stokes, a three-time NBA All-Star, hit his head on the floor while scrambling for a loose ball, and was knocked unconscious. Stokes revived and continued to play, but three days later he collapsed while on a plane and went into a six-month coma, apparently caused by swelling on the brain from his collision. He suffered permanent paralysis and died in 1970, at 36.

▶ Brett Lindros, first-round draft pick of the New York Islanders and brother of oft-concussed superstar Eric, retired from the league in 1996 after only 51 games and parts of two seasons, following his third NHL concussion, which followed the several previous concussions he'd endured in junior hockey.

▶ Denver Bronco Terrell Davis, one of the most talented running backs in NFL history and the MVP of Super Bowl XXXII, retired at the start of the 2002 season because of degenerative arthritis in his left knee. Davis suited up for a Monday night exhibition game against the San Francisco 49ers so that he could salute the fans once more—and they him—before he was placed on the injured reserve list the next day, ending his season and, unofficially, his career.

▶ In spring training of 1993, Cleveland Indians pitchers Steve Olin and Tim Crews were killed, and pitcher Bobby Ojeda was seriously injured, in a boating accident on Little Lake Nellie in Florida, 30 miles south of the Indians' training camp in Winter Haven. The three were riding at twilight when the speeding boat hit the dock. Olin, 27, was killed instantly, while Crews, 31, died 10 hours after the accident. Ojeda, 35, suffered severe lacerations to the head and later was diagnosed with post-traumatic stress disorder, but he came back to pitch in the major leagues with the Indians later that season.

▶ Bill Carr, Olympic 400m champion in 1932, broke both his ankles and fractured his pelvis in a car accident on March 17, 1933, ending his career.

▶ Talented Detroit Tiger righthander Mark "The Bird" Fidrych went 19-9 his rookie year, then "blew" his arm and won only 10 more games in the majors.

▶ Brazil's Joao Carlos de Oliveira, triple-jump world-record holder and third at both the 1976 and 1980 Olympics, had to have his right leg amputated below the knee after a car accident in January of 1982.

▶ The career of tennis player Tracy Austin was substantially shortened by various injuries including sciatic nerve damage, a stress fracture in her back, and a shoulder injury.

▶ Reggie Lewis, Boston Celtics star, collapsed and died while practicing in the gym on July 27, 1993. The autopsy stated that his heart was enlarged and scarred from a viral infection that made him susceptible to an abnormal heart rhythm. (Other doctors suggested the scarring could have resulted from cocaine use—suggestions that were never proven and that would plague his family.)

▶ The repeated punishment that NFL running backs absorb each week has hastened the end of several brilliant careers, notably Chicago Bears halfback Gale Sayers, who retired from the league with knee injuries after only seven years (1965–71), though he was great enough in those years to become the youngest inductee into the Pro Football Hall of Fame; and Detroit Lions running back Billy Sims, who also retired with knee injuries, after just five seasons (1980–84), rushing for over a thousand yards in three of them.

▶ The athletic careers of Australian James Carlton, world-record holder in the 200m and the favorite for an Olympic gold medal in 1932, and of American John Mostyn, a world-class sprinter, were abbreviated when each, still in his twenties, became a monk.

And One Race That Was Cut Short

▶ The 1916 Indianapolis 500 was actually the Indianapolis 300. The race was shortened because World War I had limited European entries and curtailed American car-making. Carl Fisher, the Indy president, did not think that older cars would survive 500 miles.

Perfection Undone

▶ On November 21, 1982, University of Washington placekicker Chuck Nelson was a perfect 30-for-30 in field goals for the season. Late in the fourth quarter of the final regular-season game of the year, Nelson missed a field goal from 30 yards that would have given Washington the lead. Washington State went on to win, 24-20. A Washington victory would have put the Huskies in the Rose Bowl.

▶ In his sophomore, junior, and senior years playing for St. John's (New York) University, Chris Mullin scored in double figures in every game but his last, the 1985 Final Four semifinal against Georgetown. Mullin had eight points in the game.

▶ On September 2, 1972, Chicago Cubs pitcher Milt Pappas had a perfect game going for 8⅔ innings. He went to a 3-2 count on the 27th batter before walking him.

In 2001, New York Yankees pitcher Mike Mussina worked 8⅔ perfect innings against the Boston Red Sox and had two strikes on pinch hitter Carl Everett before losing the perfect game and no-hitter.

On April 20, 1990, the Seattle Mariners Brian Holman pitched 8⅔ perfect innings against the Oakland As before pinch hitter Ken Phelps hit a home run to spoil almost everything. (Holman did win the complete game, 6-1.)

▶ The Duke Blue Devils were unbeaten, untied, and unscored upon going into the 1939 Rose Bowl. They led the University of Southern California 3-0 in the last quarter when fourth-string Trojan quarterback Doyle Nave threw a touchdown pass to second-string receiver Al Krueger with 41 seconds left in the game to win 7-3 and destroy Duke's visions of perfection.

▶ Majestic Prince's only defeat was in his last race, the 1969 Belmont. His trainer did not want to run him because the horse was tired, but he relented to pressure by racing officials and the press. Majestic Prince finished second to Arts and Letters, developed leg trouble, and never raced again.

▶ The Chicago Bears finished with perfect regular-season records twice, in 1934 and again in 1942, but in both years lost in the championship game.

▶ In 1964, Ara Parseghian's first year as head coach, Notre Dame was unbeaten in nine games and ranked #1. In their final game, they were leading USC 17-0 at halftime but lost the game, 20-17, and their top ranking.

▶ Cleveland Indians pitcher Johnny Allen lost his last start of 1937, making his season's final record 15-1.

▶ Olympic wrestling champion Dan Gable was 64-0 at West High School in Waterloo, Iowa, and won his first 117 matches in college at Iowa State, then lost his final college match to Larry Owings of Washington in the NCAA finals, 13-11.

▶ Mickey Wright won three legs of the women's golf Grand Slam in 1961—the LPGA, the U.S. Open, and the Titleholders tournament—but finished second to Mary Lena Faulk in the final leg, the Western Open.

▶ Chic Harley, Ohio State's All-America halfback, played on two undefeated teams in 1916–17, then left for military service. He returned in 1919, and Ohio State again went undefeated up to the final game against Illinois. Harley had never played on a losing side in college, and Ohio State led 7-6 late in the fourth quarter. In the last 10 seconds of the game, Illinois' Bob Fletcher kicked a field goal for a 9-7 win.

▶ Lew Hoad won the first three legs of the tennis Grand Slam in 1956. In the last leg, the U.S. championships, he lost in the final to Ken Rosewall.

▶ Minnesota Viking Gary Anderson was having a dream year: He'd made his first 44 field goal attempts of the 1998–99 NFL season, and he and his team were just 127 seconds from going to the Super Bowl. Anderson could ice the NFC Championship game, which the Vikings were leading, 27-20, over the Atlanta Falcons, but for the first time all year he missed—less than a foot wide left, on a 38-yarder. The Falcons, given new life, scored a tying touchdown, then won the game, and the right to go to the Super Bowl, on their own 38-yeard field goal attempt, by their own Andersen—Morton.

▶ For the three-year span from 1948–50, the University of California went 29-0-1 during the regular season. After each of those three undefeated seasons, the Golden Bears lost in the Rose Bowl.

▶ The Oakland Raiders lost the first 13 games of the 1962 AFL season but ruined their spotless record by winning the final game of the year.

Going Out on Top: Sports Figures Who Got Out Before the Cheers Turned to Boos

▶ Philadelphia Eagles quarterback Norm Van Brocklin led a fourth-quarter drive that culminated in the winning touchdown in the 1960 NFL title game, to beat the Green Bay Packers and give Vince Lombardi his only title game loss as coach. Van Brocklin quit football after the season.

▶ In his last five years in the big leagues, Los Angeles Dodgers pitcher Sandy Koufax led the National League in ERA every season. In his final season, 1966, he was 27-9, with a 1.73 ERA and 317 strikeouts. Only 30 years old, Koufax retired because of arm trouble.

▶ Bruce Jenner did not even take his vaulting poles with him after winning the 1976 Olympic decathlon because he knew he would not compete again.

▶ Despite injuring his right front ankle during the Belmont race, Count Fleet won the Triple Crown in 1943 and then retired to stud.

▶ Cleveland Browns running back Jim Brown retired in 1965 at age 29, at the peak of his career, to make movies. He was the NFL's rushing champion for eight of his nine years, including his last three.

▶ San Francisco 49ers coach Bill Walsh retired from coaching in the NFL after winning his third Super Bowl.

▶ East German Katarina Witt won her fourth figure skating world championship and then retired.

▶ Although he was just 28 years old, Bobby Jones retired after winning the golfing Grand Slam in 1930.

▶ Aleksandr Tikhonov won his fourth straight Olympic team biathlon gold medal in 1980, then announced his retirement.

▶ Frank Hadow won the second Wimbledon tournament in 1878 and then never played in it again.

▶ Ray Harroun, the winner of the first Indianapolis 500, retired from driving after the race. (His car, a single-seater, was banned from future races.)

▶ Middleweight champion Carlos Monzon retired in 1977, going undefeated in his last 13 years.

The 11 Most Unfulfilling Celebrations

To the victor go the spoils—and on each of the following occasions, the victor's celebration was indeed spoiled.

▶ Abebe Bikila of Ethiopia won his second Olympic marathon gold medal at the 1964 Tokyo Games. At the awards ceremony, no one in the band knew the Ethiopian national anthem, so they played the Japanese anthem instead.

▶ On the day that the Detroit Pistons were to visit the White House to be honored for their 1989 NBA championship, starting forward Rick Mahorn, left unprotected in the expansion draft, was chosen by the Minnesota Timberwolves.

▶ During the medal ceremony for the 200m backstroke in 1984, American gold-medal winner Rick Carey hung his head in disappointment because he had not broken the world record.

▶ At the 1972 Munich Games, Americans Vincent Matthews and Wayne Collett finished 1-2 in the 400m run. While the National Anthem played, Matthews and Collett talked and fidgeted. The West German crowd booed them and the International Olympic Committee banned the runners from further competition.

▶ After the Philadelphia Phillies won the World Series in 1980, the team's first Series victory ever, star pitcher Steve Carlton, known for his aversion to the media, hid in the Phillies training room rather than celebrate with the team. He drank from his own bottle of champagne while teammates sprayed each other with theirs.

▶ In the 5,000m final at the 1932 Los Angeles Olympic Games, American Ralph Hill tried to pass Lauri Lehtinen of Finland. Lehtinen swerved twice to block Hill and crossed the finish line first by three inches. The crowd booed until public-address announcer Bill Henry uttered what would become a renowned admonition: "Please remember, folks, that these people are our guests." Lehtinen tried to lift Hill onto the first-place platform, but Hill refused.

▶ After being drafted as the #1 pick by the Boston Celtics on June 17, 1986, and then spending time in New York and Boston for media coverage, basketball star Len Bias returned to his University of Maryland dormitory to celebrate with friends. He collapsed into convulsions on Thursday morning, June 19, and died of intoxication from cocaine.

▶ In 1976, the victory lap by the three Olympic medalists in the 200m was delayed 10 minutes for the awards ceremony in the javelin.

▶ Fairfield University basketball coach Mitch Buonaguro, certain that his team had wrapped up a 1988 Metro Atlantic Athletic Conference tournament win over St. Peter's, bolted joyously across the court with two seconds left to hug Harold Brantley, whose layup had just given Fairfield a 60-59 lead. Buonaguro was assessed a two-shot technical foul for leaving the coaching box. St. Peter's made both shots, as well as two more after a foul on the ensuing inbounds pass, to win, 63-60.

▶ Czech Vera Caslavska won the all-around Olympic gymnastics gold in 1968, two months after her country was occupied by Russian troops. In the floor exercise, she tied for first with Russian Larissa Petrik, requiring that both stand on the top platform during the ceremony. Caslavska bowed her head and turned away during the Soviet anthem.

▶ In 490 B.C., a Greek courier, a man perhaps named Pheidippides and the unwitting father of the marathon race, ran from the Plain of Marathon to Athens, to announce the Greek victory over the larger Persian army. The story has it that upon covering the great distance and parting with his news—"Rejoice! We have won." (*"Nenikekamen"*) —the courier died of exhaustion.

A List of 15 Empty Lists

▶ Major leaguers who hit grand slams off of Baltimore Orioles pitcher Jim Palmer

▶ NBA games—regular season, All-Star, or playoff—in which Wilt Chamberlain fouled out

▶ Punters in the Pro Football Hall of Fame

▶ Times that heavyweight boxer George Chuvalo was knocked down in his career

▶ Fair catches made by the Dallas Cowboys during the 1982 NFL season

▶ Times the 1932 Yankees and 2000 Cincinnati Reds got shut out

▶ Postseason series the Houston Astros have won in their history

▶ Home runs Mark McGwire hit in All-Star games

▶ Major-league managers who were fired in the year 2000 or 1942

▶ Triples hit by Sammy Sosa in his MVP year of 1998, when he collected 198 hits

▶ NBA playoff series that Grant Hill has won

▶ Pitchers who threw no-hitters in the 61-year history of Pittsburgh's Forbes Field

▶ Non-English–speaking men who have won golf's U.S. Open

▶ Boston Celtics who have led the NBA in scoring

▶ Lists that follow this one

INDEX